Daniel Defoe
SELECTIONS

VOLUME III

OF CAPTAIN MISSON

●

DICKORY CRONKE

●

THE TRUE-BORN ENGLISHMAN

●

THE MILITARY MEMOIRS OF CAPT. GEORGE CARLETON

●

THE MEMOIRS OF MAJR. ALEXANDER RAMKINS,

●

VINDICATION OF THE PRESS

●

SECOND THOUGHTS ARE BEST

●

AN APPEAL TO HONOUR AND JUSTICE

●

ATALANTIS MAJOR.

●

AUGUSTA TRIUMPHANS

●

AN HUMBLE PROPOSAL TO THE PEOPLE OF ENGLAND

●

THE FORTUNES & MISFORTUNES
OF THE FAMOUS MOLL FLANDERS &C.

OF CAPTAIN MISSON

THE HISTORY OF THE PYRATES.
VOL. II.

We can be somewhat particular in the Life of this Gentleman, because, by very great Accident, we have got into our Hands a *French* Manuscript, in which he himself gives a Detail of his Actions. He was born in *Provence*, of an ancient Family; his Father, whose true Name he conceals, was Master of a plentiful Fortune; but having a great Number of Children, our Rover had but little Hopes of other Fortune than what he could carve out for himself with his Sword. His Parents took Care to give him an Education equal to his Birth. After he had passed his Humanity and Logick, and was a tolerable Mathematician, at the Age of Fifteen he was sent to *Angiers*, where he was a Year learning His Exercises. His Father, at his Return home, would have put him into the Musketeers; but as he was of a roving Temper, and much affected with the Accounts he had read in Books of Travels, he chose the Sea as a Life which abounds with more Variety, and would afford him an Opportunity to gratify his Curiosity, by the Change of Countries Having made this Choice, his Father, with Letters of Recommendation, and every Thing fitting for him, sent him Voluntier on board the *Victoire*, commanded by Monsieur *Fourbin*, his Relation. He was received on Board with all possible Regard by the Captain, whose Ship was at *Marseilles*, and was order'd to cruise soon after *Misson's* Arrival. Nothing could be more agreeable to the Inclinations of our Voluntier than this Cruize, which made him acquainted with the most noted Ports of the *Mediterranean*, and gave him a great Insight into the practical Part of Navigation. He grew fond of this Life, and was resolved to be a compleat Sailor, which made him always one of the first on a Yard Arm, either to Hand or Reef, and very inquisitive in the different Methods of working a Ship: His Discourse was turn'd on no other Subject, and he would often get the Boatswain and Carpenter to teach him in their Cabbins the constituent Parts of a Ship's Hull, and how to rigg her, which he generously paid 'em for; and tho' he spent a great Part of his Time with these two Officers, yet he behaved himself with such Prudence that they never attempted at a Familiarity, and always paid the Respect due to his Family. The Ship being at *Naples*, he obtained Leave of his Captain to go to *Rome*, which he had a great Desire to visit. Hence we may date his Misfortunes; for, remarking the licentious Lives of the Clergy (so different from the Regularity observ'd among the *French* Ecclesiasticks,) the Luxury of the Papal Court, and that nothing but Hulls of Religion was to be found in the Metropolis of the Christian Church, he began to figure to himself that all Religion was no more than a Curb upon the Minds of the Weaker, which the wiser Sort yielded to, in Appearance only. These Sentiments, so disadvantageous to Religion and himself, were strongly riveted by accidentally becoming acquainted with a lewd Priest, who was, at his Arrival (by meer Chance) his Confessor, and after that his Procurer and Companion, for he kept him Company to his Death. One Day, having an Opportunity, he told *Misson*, a Religious was a very good Life, where a Man had a subtle enterprising Genius, and some Friends; for such a one wou'd, in a short Time, rise to such Dignities in the Church, the Hopes of which was the Motive of all the wiser Sort, who voluntarily took upon them the sacerdotal Habit. That the ecclesiastical State was govern'd with the same Policy as were secular Principalities and Kingdoms; that what was beneficial, not what was meritorious and virtuous, would be alone regarded. That there were no more Hopes for a Man of Piety and Learning in the Patrimony of St. *Peter*, than in any other Monarchy, nay, rather less; for this being known to be real, that Man's rejected as a Visionary, no way fit for Employment; as one whose Scruples might prove prejudicial; for its a Maxim, that Religion and Politicks can never set up in one House. As to our Statesmen, don't imagine that the Purple makes 'em less Courtiers than are those of other Nations; they know and pursue the *Reggione del Stato* (a Term of Art which means Self-Interest) with as much Cunning and as little Conscience as any Secular; and are as artful where Art is required, and as barefaced and impudent when their Power is great enough to support 'em, in the oppressing the People, and aggrandizing their Families. What their Morals are, you may read in the Practice of their Lives, and their Sentiments of Religion from this Saying of a certain Cardinal, *Quantum Lucrum ex ista fabula Christi!* which many of 'em may say, tho' they are not so foolish. For my Part, I am quite tir'd of the Farce, and will lay hold on the first Opportunity to throw off this masquerading Habit; for, by Reason of my Age, I must act an under

Part many Years; and before I can rise to share the Spoils of the People, I shall, I fear, be too old to enjoy the Sweets of Luxury; and, as I am an Enemy to Restraint, I am apprehensive I shall never act up to my Character, and carry thro' the Hypocrite with Art enough to rise to any considerable Post in the Church. My Parents did not consult my Genius, or they would have given me a Sword instead of a Pair of Beads.

Misson advised him to go with him Voluntier, and offer'd him Money to cloath him; the Priest leap'd at the Proposal, and a Letter coming to *Misson* from his Captain, that he was going to *Leghorn*, and left to him either to come to *Naples*, or go by Land; he chose the latter, and the *Dominican*, whom he furnish'd with Money, clothing himself very Cavalierly, threw off his Habit, and preceeded him two Days, staying at *Pisa* for *Misson*; from whence they went together to *Leghorn*, where they found the *Victoire*, and Signor *Caraccioli*, recommended by his Friend, was received on Board. Two Days after they weigh'd from hence, and after a Week's Cruize fell in with two *Sally* Men, the one of twenty, the other of twenty four Guns; the *Victoire* had but thirty mounted, though she had Ports for forty. The Engagement was long and bloody, for the *Sally* Man hop'd to carry the *Victoire*; and, on the contrary, Captain *Fourbin*, so far from having any Thoughts of being taken, he was resolutely bent to make Prize of his Enemies, or sink his Ship. One of the *Sally* Men was commanded by a *Spanish* Renegade, (though he had only the Title of a Lieutenant) for the Captain was a young Man who knew little of Marine Affairs.

This Ship was called the *Lyon*; and he attempted, more than once, to board the *Victoire*, but by a Shot betwixt Wind and Water, he was obliged to sheer off, and running his Guns, &c. on one Side, bring her on the careen to stop his Leak; this being done with too much Precipitation, she overset, and every Soul was lost: His Comrade seeing this Disaster, threw out all his small sails, and endeavour'd to get off, but the *Victoire* wrong'd her, and oblig'd her to renew the Fight, which she did with great Obstinacy, and made Monsieur *Fourbin* despair of carrying her if he did not board; he made Preparations accordingly. Signior *Caraccioli* and *Misson* were the two first on board when the Command was given; but they and their Followers were beat back by the Despair of the *Sally* Men; the former received a Shot in his Thigh, and was carried down to the Surgeon. The *Victoire* laid her on board the second time, and the *Sally* Men defended their Decks with such Resolution, that they were cover'd with their own, and the dead Bodies of their Enemies. *Misson* seeing one of 'em jump down the Main-Hatch with a lighted Match, suspecting his Design, resolutely leap'd after him, and reaching him with his Sabre, laid him dead the Moment he going to set Fire to the Powder. The *Victoire* pouring in more Men, the *Mahometans* quitted the Decks, finding Resistance vain, and fled for Shelter to the Cook Room, Steerage and Cabbins, and some run between Decks. The *French* gave 'em Quarters, and put the Prisoners on board the *Victoire*, the Prize yielding nothing worth mention, except Liberty to about fifteen Christian Slaves; she was carried into and sold with the Prisoners at *[text unreadable]*. The Turks lost a great many Men, the *French* not less than 35 in boarding, for they lost very few by the great Shot, the *Sally* Men firing mostly at the Masts and Rigging, hoping by disabling to carry her. The limited Time of their Cruize being out, the *Victoire* returned to *Marseilles*, from whence *Misson*, taking his Companion, went to visit his Parents, to whom the Captain sent a very advantageous Character, both of his Courage and Conduct. He was about a Month at home when his Captain wrote to him, that his Ship was ordered to *Rochelle*, from whence he was to sail for the *West-Indies* with some Merchant Men. This was very agreeable to *Misson* and Signior *Caraccioli*, who immediately set out for *Marseilles*. This Town is well fortified, has four Parish Churches, and the Number of Inhabitants is computed to be about 120,0000; the Harbour is esteemed the safest in the *Mediterranean*, and is the common Station for the *French* Gallies.

Leaving this Place, they steer'd for *Rochelle*, where the *Victoire* was dock'd, the Merchant Ships not being near ready. *Misson*, who did not Care to pass so long a Time in Idleness, proposed to his Comrade the taking a Cruize on board the *Triumph*, who was going into the *English Channel*; the *Italian* readily contented to it.

Between the Isle of *Guernsey* and the *Start Point* they met with the *Mayflower*, Captain *Balladine* Commanded, a Merchant Ship of 18 Guns, richly laden, and coming from *Jamaica*. The Captain of the *English* made a gallant resistance, and fought his Ship so long, that the *French* could not carry her into Harbour, wherefore they took the Money, and what was most valuable, out of her; and finding she made more Water than the Pumps could free, quitted, and saw her go down in less than four Hours after. Monsieur *le Blanc*, the *French* Captain, received Captain *Balladine* very civilly, and would not suffer either him or his Men to be stripp'd, saying, *None but Cowards ought be treated after that Manner; that brave Men ought to treat such, though their*

Enemies, as Brothers; and that to use a gallant Man (who does his Duty) ill, speaks a Revenge which cannot proceed but from a Coward Soul. He order'd that the Prisoners should leave their Chests; and when some of his Men seem'd to mutter, he bid 'em remember the Grandeur of the Monarch they serv'd; that they were neither Pyrates nor Privateers; and, as brave Men, they ought to shew their Enemies an Example they would willingly have follow'd, and use their Prisoners as they wish'd to be us'd.

They running up the *English* Channel as high as *Beachy Head*, and, in returning, fell in with three fifty Gun Ships, which gave Chace to the *Triumph*; but as she was an excellent Sailor, she run 'em out of Sight in seven Glasses, and made the best of her Way for the *Lands-End* they here cruized eight Days, then doubling Cape *Cornwall*, ran up the *Bristol* Channel, near as far as *Nash Point*, and intercepted a small Ship from *Barbadoes*, and stretching away to the Northward, gave Chase to a Ship they saw in the Evening, but lost her in the Night. The *Triumph* stood then towards *Milford* and spying a Sail, endeavour'd to cut her off the Land, but found it impossible; for she got into the Haven, though they came up with her very fast, and she had surely been taken, had the Chase had been any thing longer.

Captain *Balladine*, who took the Glass, said it was the *Port Royal*, a *Bristol* Ship which left *Jamaica* in Company with him and the *Charles*. They now return'd to their own Coast, and sold their Prize at *Brest*, where, at his Desire, they left Captain *Balladine*, and Monsieur *le Blanc* made him a Present of Purse with 40 *Louis's* for his Support; his Crew were also left here.

At the Entrance into this Harbour the *Triumph* struck upon a Rock, but receiv'd no Damage: This Entrance, called *Genlet*, is very dangerous on Account of the Number of Rocks which lie on each Side under Water, though the Harbour is certainly the best in *France*. The Mouth of the Harbour is defended by a strong Castle; the Town is well fortified, and has a Citadel for its farther Defence, which is of considerable Strength. In 1694 the *English* attempted a Descent, but did not find their Market, for they were beat off with the Loss of their General, and a great many Men. From hence the *Triumph* return'd to *Rochel*, and in a Month after our Voluntiers, who went on board the *Victoire*, took their Departure for *Martineco* and *Guadalupe*; they met with nothing in their Voyage thither worth noting.

I shall only observe, that Signior *Caraccioli*, who was as ambitious as he was irreligious, had, by this Time, made a perfect Deist of *Misson*, and thereby convinc'd him, that all Religion was no other than human Policy, and shew'd him that the Law of *Moses* was no more than what were necessary, as well for the Preservation as the Governing of the People; for Instance, said he, the *African* Negroes never heard of the Institution of Circumcision, which is said to be the Sign of the Covenant made between God and this People, and yet they circumcise their Children; doubtless for the same Reason the *Jews* and other Nations do, who inhabit the Southern Climes, the Prepuce consolidating the perspired Matter, which is of a fatal Consequence. In short, he ran through all the Ceremonies of the *Jewish*, Christian and *Mahometan* Religion, and convinced him these were, as might be observed by the Absurdity of many, far from being Indications of Men inspired; and that *Moses*, in his Account of the Creation, was guilty of known Blunders; and the Miracles, both in the New and Old Testament, inconsistent with Reason. That God had given us this Blessing, to make Use of for our present and future Happiness, and whatever was contrary to it, notwithstanding their School Distinctions of *contrary* and *above* Reason, must be false. This Reason teaches us, that there is a first Cause of all Things, an *Ens Entium*, which we call God, and our Reason will also suggest, that he must be eternal, and, as the Author of every Thing perfect, he must be infinitely perfect.

If so, he can be subject to no Passions, and neither loves nor hates; he must be ever the fame, and cannot rashly do to Day what he shall repent to Morrow. He must be perfectly happy, consequently nothing can add to an eternal State of Tranquillity, and though it becomes us to adore him, yet can our Adorations neither augment, nor our Sins take from this Happiness.

But his Arguments on this Head are too long, and too dangerous to translate; and as they are work'd up with great Subtlety, they may be pernicious to weak Men, who cannot discover their Fallacy; or, who finding 'em agreeable to their Inclinations, and would be glad to shake off the Yoke of the Christian Religion, which galls and curbs their Passions, would not give themselves the Trouble to examine them to the Bottom, but give into what pleases, glad of finding some Excuse to their Consciences. Though as his Opinion of a future State has nothing in it which impugns the Christian Religion, I shall set it down in few Words.

That reasoning Faculty, says he, which we perceive within us, we call the Soul, but what that Soul is, is unknown to us. It may die with the Body, or it may survive. I am of Opinion its immortal; but to say that this Opinion is the Dictate of Reason, or only the Prejudice of Education, would, I own, puzzle me. If it is immortal, it must be an Emanation from the Divine Being, and consequently at its being separated from the Body, will return to its first Principle, if not contaminated. Now, my Reason tells me, if it is estranged from its first Principle, which is the Deity, all the Hells of Man's Invention can never yield Tortures adequate to such a Banishment.

As he had privately held these Discourses among the Crew, he had gained a Number of Proselytes, who look'd upon him as a new Prophet risen up to reform the Abuses in Religion; and a great Number being *Rochellers*, and, as yet, tainted with *Calvinism*, his Doctrine was the more readily embrac'd. When he had experienced the Effects of his religious Arguments, he fell upon Government, and shew'd, that every Man was born free, and had as much Right to what would support him, as to the Air he respired. A contrary Way of arguing would be accusing the Deity with Cruelty and Injustice, for he brought into the World no Man to pass a Life of Penury, and to miserably want a necessary Support; that the vast Difference between Man and Man, the one wallowing in Luxury, and the other in the most pinching Necessity, was owing only to Avarice and Ambition on the one Hand, and a pusillanimous Subjection on the other; that at first no other than a Natural was known, a paternal Government, every Father was the Head, the Prince and Monarch of his Family, and Obedience to such was both just and easy, for a Father had a compassionate Tenderness for his Children; but Ambition creeping in by Degrees, the stronger Family set upon and enslaved the Weaker; and this additional Strength over-run a third, by every Conquest gathering Force to make others, and this was the first Foundation of Monarchy. Pride encreasing with Power, Man usurped the Prerogative of God, over his Creatures, that of depriving them of Life, which was a Privilege no one had over his own; for as he did not come into the World by his own Election, he ought to stay the determined Time of his Creator: That indeed, Death given in War, was by the Law of Nature allowable, because it is for the Preservation of our own Lives; but no Crime ought to be thus punished, nor indeed any War undertaken, but in Defence of our natural Right, which is such a Share of Earth as is necessary for our Support.

These Topicks he often declaimed on, and very often advised with *Misson* about the setting up for themselves; he was as ambitious as the other, and as resolute. *Caraccioli* and *Misson* were by this expert Mariners, and very capable of managing a Ship: *Caraccioli* had founded a great many of the Men on this Subject, and found them very inclineable to listen to him. An Accident happen'd which gave *Caraccioli* a fair Opportunity to put his Designs in Execution, and he laid Hold of it; they went off *Martinico* on a Cruize, and met with the *Winchelsea*, an *English* Man of War of 40 Guns, commanded by Captain *Jones*; they made for each other, and a very smart Engagement followed, the first Broadside killed the Captain, second Captain, and the three Lieutenants, on Board the *Victoire* and left only the Master, who would have struck, but Misson took up the Sword, order'd *Caraccioli* to act as Lieutenant, and encouraging the Men fought the Ship six Glasses, when by some Accident, the *Winchelsea* blew up, and not a Man was saved but Lieutenant *Franklin*, whom the *French* Boats took up, and he died in two Days. None ever knew before this Manuscript fell into my Hands how the *Winchelsea* was lost; for her Head being driven ashore at *Antegoa*, and a great Storm having happend a few Days before her Head was found, it was concluded, that she founder'd in that Storm. After this Engagement, *Caraccioli* came to Misson and saluted him Captain, and desired to know if he would chuse a momentary or a lasting Command, that he must now determine, for at his Return to *Martinico* it would be too late; and he might depend upon the Ship he fought and saved being given to another, and they would think him well rewarded if made a Lieutenant, which Piece of Justice he doubted: That he had his Fortune in his Hands, which he might either keep or let go; if he made Choice of the latter, he must never again expect she would court him to accept her Favours: That he ought to let before his Eyes his Circumstances, as a younger Brother of a good Family, but nothing to support his Character; and the many Years he must serve at the Expence of his Blood before he could make any Figure in the World; and consider the wide Difference between the commanding and being commanded: That he might with the Ship he had under Foot, and the brave Fellows under Command, bid Defiance to the Power of *Europe*, enjoy every Thing he wish'd, reign Sovereign of the Southern Seas, and lawfully make War on all the World, since it would deprive him of that Liberty to which he had a Right by the Laws of Nature: That he might in Time, become as great as *Alexander* was to the *Persians*; and by encreasing his Forces by his Captures, he would every Day strengthen the Justice of his Cause, for who has Power is always in the Right. That *Harry* the Fourth and *Harry* the Seventh, attempted and succeeded in their Enterprizes on the Crown of *England*, yet their Forces did not equal his. *Mahomet* with a few Camel Drivers, founded the *Ottoman*

Empire and *Darius*, with no more than six or seven Companions got Possession on of that of *Persia*.

In a Word he said so much that *Misson* resolved to follow his Advice, and calling up all Hands, he told them, 'That a great Number of them had resolved with him upon a Life of Liberty, and had done him the Honour to create him Chief: That he designed to force no Man, and be guilty of that Injustice he blamed in others; therefore, if any were averse to the following his Fortune, which he promised should be the same to all, he desired they would declare themselves, and he would set them ashore, whence they might return with Conveniency;' having made an End, they one and all cryed, *Vive le Capitain* Misson *et son Lieutenant le Seavant* Caraccioli, God bless Capt. *Misson* and his learned Lieutenant *Caraccioli. Misson* thanked them for the Honour they conferr'd upon him, and promised he would use the Power they gave for the publick Good only, and hoped, as they had the Bravery to assert their Liberty, they would be as unanimous in the preserving it, and stand by him in what should be found expedient for the Good of all; that he was their Friend and Companion, and should never exert his Power, or think himself other than their Comrade, but when the Necessity of Affairs should oblige him.

They shouted a second Time, *vive le Capitain*; he, after this, desired they would chuse their subaltern Officers, and give them Power to consult and conclude upon what might be for the common Interest, and bind themselves down by an Oath to agree to what such Officers and he should determine: This they readily gave into. The School-Master they chose for second Lieutenant, *Jean Besace* they nominated for third, and the Boatswain, and a Quarter-Master, named *Matthieu le Tondu*, with the Gunner, they desired might be their Representatives in Council.

The Choice was approved, and that every Thing might pass methodically, and with general Approbation, they were called into the great Cabbin, and the Question put, what Course they should steer? The Captain proposed the *Spanish* Coast as the most probable to afford them rich Prizes: This was agreed upon by all. The Boatswain then asked what Colours they should fight under, and advised Black as most terrifying; but *Caraccioli* objected, that they were no Pyrates, but Men who were resolved to assert that Liberty which God and Nature gave them, and own no Subjection to any, farther than was for the common Good of all: That indeed, Obedience to Governors was necessary, when they knew and acted up to the Duty of their Function;

were vigilant Guardians of the Peoples Rights and Liberties; saw that Justice was equally distributed; were Barriers against the Rich and Powerful, when they attempted to oppress the Weaker; when they suffered none of the one Hand to grow immensely rich, either by his own or his Ancestors Encroachments; nor on the other, any to be wretchedly miserable, either by falling into the Hands of Villains, unmerciful Creditors, or other Misfortunes. While he had Eyes impartial, and allowed nothing but Merit to distinguish between Man and Man; and instead of being a Burthen to the People by his luxurious life, he was by his Care for, and Protection of them, a real Father, and in every Thing acted with the equal and impartial Justice of a Parent: But when a Governor, who is the Minister of the People, thinks himself rais'd to this Dignity, that he may spend his Days in Pomp and Luxury, looking upon his Subjects as so many Slaves, created for his Use and Pleasure, and therefore leaves them and their Affairs to the immeasurable Avarice and Tyranny of some one whom he has chosen for his Favourite, when nothing but Oppression, Poverty, and all the Miseries of Life flow from such an Administration; that he lavishes away the Lives and Fortunes of the People, either to gratify his Ambition, or to support the Cause of some neighbouring Prince, that he may in Return, strengthen his Hands should his People exert themselves in Defence of their native Rights; or should he run into unnecessary Wars, by the rash and thoughtless Councils of his Favourite, and not able to make Head against the Enemy he has rashly or wantonly brought upon his Hands, and buy a Peace (which is the present Case of *France*, as every one knows, by supporting King *James*, and afterwards proclaiming his Son) and drain the Subject; should the Peoples Trade be wilfully neglected, for private Interests, and while their Ships of War lie idle in their Harbours, suffer their Vessels to be taken; and the Enemy not only intercepts all Commerce, but insults their Coasts: It speaks a generous and great Soul to shake off the Yoak; and if we cannot redress our Wrongs, withdraw from sharing the Miseries which meaner Spirits submit to, and scorn to yield to the Tyranny. Such Men are we, and, if the World, as Experience may convince us it will, makes War upon us, the Law of Nature empowers us not only to be on the defensive, but also on the offensive Part. As we then do not proceed upon the same Ground with Pyrates, who are Men of dissolute Lives and no Principles, let us scorn to take their Colours: Ours is a brave, a just, an innocent, and a noble Cause; the Cause of Liberty. I therefore advise a white Ensign, with Liberty painted in the

Fly, and if you like the Motto, *a Deo a Libertate*, for God and Liberty, as an Emblem of our Uprightness and Resolution.

The Cabbin Door was left open, and the Bulk Head which was of Canvas rowled up, the Steerage being full of Men, who lent an attentive Ear, they cried, *Liberty, Liberty; we are free Men.* Vive *the brave Captain* Misson *and the noble Lieutenant* Caraccioli. This short Council breaking up, every Thing belonging to the deceased Captain, and the other Officers, and Men lost in the Engagement, was brought upon Deck and over-hawled; the Money ordered to be put into a Chest, and the Carpenter to clap on a Padlock for, and give a Key to, every one of the Council: Misson telling them, all should be in common, and the particular Avarice of no one should defraud the Publick.

When the Plate Monsieur *Fourbin* had, was going to the Chest, the Men unanimously cried out avast, keep that out for the Captain's Use, as a Present from his Officers and Fore-mast Men. *Misson* thanked them, the Plate was returned to the great Cabbin, and the Chest secured according to Orders: Misson then ordered his Lieutenants and other Officers to examine who among the Men, were in most Want of Cloaths, and to distribute those of the dead Men impartially, which was done with a general Content and Applause of the whole Crew: All but the wounded being upon Deck. *Misson* from the Baracade, spoke to the following Purpose, 'That since they had unanimously resolved to seize upon and defend their Liberty, which ambitious Men had usurped, and that this could not be esteemed by impartial Judges other than a just and brave Resolution, he was under an Obligation to recommend to them a brotherly Love to each other; the Banishment of all private Piques and Grudges, and a swift Agreement and Harmony among themselves: That in throwing off the Yoak of Tyranny of which the Action spoke an Abhorrence, he hoped none would follow the Example of Tyrants, and turn his Back upon Justice; for when Equity was trodden under Foot, Misery, Confusion, and mutual Distrust naturally followed.'—He also advised them to remember there was a Supream; the Adoration of which, Reason and Gratitude prompted us, and our own Interests would engage us (as it is best to be of the surest Side, and after-Life was allowed possible) to conciliate. —That he was satisfied Men who were born and bred in Slavery, by which their Spirits were broke, and were incapable of so generous a Way of thinking, who, ignorant of their Birth-Right, and the Sweets of Liberty, dance to the Musick of their Chains, which was, indeed, the greater Part of the Inhabitants of the Globe, would brand this generous Crew with the insidious Name of Pyrates, and think it meritorious, to be instrumental in their Destruction.—Self-Preservation therefore, and not a cruel Disposition, obliged him to declare War against all such as should refuse him the Entry of their Ports, and against all, who should not immediately surrender and give up what their Necessities required; but in a more particular Manner against all *European* Ships and Vessels, as concluded implacable Enemies. *And I do now,* said he, *declare such War, and, at the same time, recommend to you my Comrades a humane and generous Behaviour towards your Prisoners; which will appear by so much more the Effects of a noble Soul, as we are satisfied we should not meet the same Treatment should our ill Fortune, or more properly our Disunion, or want of Courage, give us up to their Mercy.*

After this, he required a Muster should be made, and there were able Hands two Hundred, and thirty five sick and wounded; as they were muster'd they were sworn. After Affairs were thus settled, they shaped their Course the *Spanish West-Indies,* but resolved, in the Way, to take a Week or ten Days Cruize in the Windward Passage from *Jamaica,* because most Merchant Men, which were good Sailors and did not slay for Convoy, took this as the shorter Cut for *England.*

Off St. *Christophers* they took an *English* Sloop becalmed, with their Boats; they took out of her a couple of Puncheons of Rum, and half a dozen Hogsheads of Sugar (she was a *New England* Sloop, bound for *Boston*) and without offering the least Violence to the Men, or stripping them, they let her go. The Master of the Sloop was *Thomas Butler,* who owned, he never met with so candid an Enemy as the *French* Man of War, which took him the Day he left St. *Christophers;* they met with no other Booty in their Way, till they came upon their Station, when after three Days, they saw a Sloop which had the Impudence to give them Chace; Captain *Misson* asked what could be the Meaning that the Sloop stood for them? One of the Men, who was acquainted with the *West-Indies,* told him, it was a *Jamaica* Privateer, and he should not wonder, if he clapp'd him aboard. I am, said he, no Stranger to their Way of working, and this despicable Fellow, as those who don't know a *Jamaica* Privateer may think him, it is ten to one will give you some Trouble. It now grows towards Evening, and you'll find as soon as he has discovered your Force, he'll keep out of the Reach of your Guns till the 12 a-Clock Watch is changed at Night, and he'll then attempt to clap you aboard, with Hopes to carry you in the Hurry: Wherefore Captain, if you will give me Leave to advise you, let every Man have his small Arms; and at twelve, let the Bell ring as usual; and rather more Noise than ordinary be made, as if the one Watch was turning in, and the other out, in a Confusion and Hurry, and I'll engage he will venture to enter his Men. The Fellow's Advice was approved and resolved upon, and the Sloop work'd, as he said she would, for upon coming near enough to make distinctly the Force of the *Victoire*, on her throwing out *French* Colours, she, the Sloop, clapp'd upon a Wind, the *Victoire* gave Chace, but without Hopes of gaining upon her; she went so well to Windward, that she cou'd spare the Ship some Points in her Sheet, and yet wrong her: At Dusk of the Even, the *French* had lost Sight of her, but about Eleven at Night, they saw her hankering up their Windward Bow, which confirmed the Sailors Opinion, that she would attempt to board them, as she did at the pretended Change of the Watch; there being little or no Wind, she lashed to the Bow-Sprit of the *Victoire* and enter'd her Men, who were very quietly taken, as they enter'd and tumbled down the Forehatch, where they were received by others, and bound without Noise, not one of the Privateers killed, few hurt, and only one *Frenchman* wounded. The *Victoire* the better Part of the Sloop's Men secured, they boarded in their Turn, when the Privateer's suspecting some Stratagem, were endeavouring to cut their Lashing and get off:

Thus the Englishman caught a Tartar. The Prisoners being all secured, the Captain charged his Men not to discover, thro' a Desire of augmenting their Number, the Account they were upon.

The next Morning Monsieur *Misson* called for the Captain of the Privateer, he told him, he could not but allow him a brave Fellow, to venture upon a Ship of his Countenance, and for that Reason he should meet Treatment which Men of his Profession seldom afforded the Prisoners they made. He asked him how long he had been out, what was his Name, and what he had on Board? He answered he was but just come out, that he was the first Sail he had met with, and should have thought himself altogether as lucky not to have spoke with him' that his Name was *Harry Ramsey*, and what he had on Board were Rags, Powder, Ball, and some few half Anchors of Rum. *Ramsey* was ordered into the Gun-Room, and a Council being held in the publick Manner aforesaid, the Bulk Head of the great Cabbin rowled up. On their Conclusion, the Captain of the Privateer was called in again, when Captain *Misson* told him, he would return him his Sloop, and restore him and his Men to their Liberty, without stripping or plundering of any Thing, but what Prudence obliged him to, their Ammunition and Small-Arms, if he would give him his Word and Honour, and his Men to take an Oath, not to go out on the Privateer Account in six Months after they left him: That he did not design to continue that Station above a Week longer, at the Expiration of which Time he would let them go.

Ramsey, who had a new Sloop, did not expect this Favour, which he thanked him for, and promised punctually to comply with the Injunction, which his Men as readily swore to, tho' they had no Design to keep the Oath. The Time being expired, he and his Men were put on Board their own Sloop. At going over the Ship's Side *Ramsey* begg'd Monsieur *Misson* would allow him Powder for a salute, by way of Thanks; but he answered him, the Ceremony was needless, and he expected no other Return than that of keeping his Word, which indeed *Ramsey* did. Some of his Men had found it more to their Advantage to have been as religious.

At parting Ramsey gave the Ship three Chears, and *Misson* had the Complaisance to return one, which *Ramsey* answering with three more, made the best of his Way for *Jamaica*, and at the East End of the Island met with the *Diana*, who, upon Advice, turn'd back.

The *Victoire* steer'd for *Carthagene*, off which Port they cruised some Days, but meeting with nothing in the Seas, they made for *Porto Bello*; in their Way they met with two *Dutch* Traders, who had Letters of Mart, and were just come upon the Coast, the one had 20, the other 24 Guns; *Misson* engaged them, and they defended themselves with a great Deal of Resolution and Gallantry; and as they were mann'd a Peak, he darst not venture to board either of them, for fear of being at the same Time boarded by the other. His Weight of Mettal gave him a great Advantage over the *Dutch*, though they were two to one; besides, their Business, as they had Cargoes, was to get off, if possible, wherefore they made a running Fight, though they took Care to stick close to one another.

They maintained the Fight for above six Hours, when *Misson*, enraged at this Obstinacy, and fearing, if by Accident they should bring a Mast, or Top-Mast, by the board, they would get from him. He was resolved to sink the larger Ship of the two, and accordingly ordered his Men to bring all their Guns to bear a Midship, then running close along Side of him, to raise their Mettal; his Orders being punctually obey'd, he pour'd in a Broad Side, which open'd such a Gap in the *Dutch* Ship, that she went directly to the Bottom, and every Man perish'd.

He then mann'd his Bowsprit, brought his Sprit-sail Yard fore and aft, and resolved to board the other, which the *Dutch* perceiving, and terrified with the unhappy Fate of their Comrade, thought a farther Resistance vain, and immediately struck. *Misson* gave them good Quarters, though he was enraged at the Loss of 13 Men killed outright, beside 9 wounded, of which 6 died. They found on board a great Quantity of Gold and Silver Lace, brocade Silks, Silk Stockings, Bails of Broad- Cloath, bazes of all Colours, and *Osnabrughs*.

A Consultation being held, it was resolved Captain *Misson* should take the Name of *Fourbin*, and returning to *Carthagene*, dispose of his Prize, and set his Prisoners ashoar. Accordingly they ply'd to the Eastward, and came to an Anchor between *Boca Chieca* Fort, and the Town, for they did not think it expedient to enter the Harbour. The Barge was manned, and *Caraccioli*, with the Name of *D'Aubigny*, the first lieutenant, who was killed in the Engagement with the *Winchelsea*, and his Commission in his Pocket, went ashore with a Letter to the Governor, sign'd *Fourbin*, whose Character, for fear of the worst, was exactly counterfeited. The Purport of his Letter was, that having discretionary Orders to cruize for three Months, and hearing the *English* infested his Coast, he was come in search of 'em, and had met two *Dutch* Men, one of which he had sunk, the other he made Prize of. That his limited Time being near expired, he should be obliged to his Excellency, if he would send on board him such Merchants as were willing to take the Ship and Cargoe off his Hands, of which he had lent the *Dutch* Invoice. Don *Joseph de la Zerda*, the then Governor, received the Lieutenant (who sent back the Barge at landing) very civilly, and agreed to take the Prisoners ashoar, and do every Thing was required of him; and ordering fresh Provisions and Sallading to be got ready as a Present for the Captain, he sent for some Merchants who were very ready to go on board, and agree for the Ship and Goods; which they did, for two and fifty thousand Pieces of Eight. The next Day the Prisoners were set ashoar; a rich Piece of Brocade which was reserv'd, sent to the Governor for a Present, a Quantity of fresh Provision bought and brought on board, the Money paid by the Merchants, the Ship and Goods deliver'd, and the *Victoire*, at the Dawn of the following Day, got under Sail. It may be wonder'd how such Dispatch could be made, but the Reader must take Notice, these Goods were sold by the *Dutch* Invoice, which the Merchant of the Prize affirmed was genuine. I shall observe, by the by, that the *Victoire* was the *French* Man of War which Admiral *Wager* sent the *Kingston* in search of, and being afterwards falsly inform'd, that she was join'd by another of seventy Guns; and that they cruiz'd together between the Capes, order'd the *Severn* up to Windward, to assist the *Kingston*, which had like to have prov'd very fatal; for these two *English* Men of War, commanded by Captain *Trevor* and Captain *Padnor*, meeting in the Night, had prepared to engage, each taking the other for the Enemy. The *Kingston's* Men not having a good Look-out, which must be attributed to the Negligence of the Officer of the Watch, did not see the *Severn* till she was just upon them; but, by good Luck, to Leeward, and plying up, with all the Sail she could crowd, and a clear Ship. This put the *Kingston* in such Confusion, that when the *Severn* hal'd, no answer was retun'd, for none heard her. She was got under the *Kingston's* Stern, and Captain *Padnor* ordered to hale for the third and last Time, and if no answer was return'd, to give her a Broadside. The Noise onboard the *Kingston* was now a little ceas'd, and Captain Trevor, who was on the poop with a speaking Trumpet to hale the *Severn*, by good Luck heard her hale him, answering the *Kingston*, and asking the Name of the other ship, prevented the Damage.

They cruised together some time, and meeting nothing which answer'd their Information, return'd to *Jamaica*, as I shall to my Subject, begging Pardon for this, as I thought, necessary Digression.

Don *Juan de la Zevda* told the Captain in a Letter, that the St. *Joseph*, a Gallion of seventy Guns, was then lying at *Port a Bello*, and should be glad he could keep her Company till she was off the Coast. That she would sail in eight or ten Days for the *Havana*; and that, if his Time would permit him, he would send an Advice-Boat. That she had on board the Value of 800,000 Pieces of Eight in Silver and Bar Gold. *Misson* return'd Answer, that he believ'd he should be excus'd if he stretched his Orders, for a few Days; and that he would cruize off the Isle of *Pearls*, and Cape *Gratias a Dios*, and give for Signal to the Gallion, his spreading a white Ensign in his Fore-Top-Mast Shrouds, the cluing up his Fore-sail, and the firing one Gun to Windward, and two to Leeward, which he should answer by letting run and hoisting his Fore- Top-Sail three times, and the firing as many Guns to Leeward. Don *Joseph*, extreamly pleased with this Complaisance, sent a Boat express to advise the St. *Joseph*, but she was already sailed two Days, contrary to the Governor of *Carthagene's* Expectation, and, this Advice Captain *Misson* had from the Boat, which returning with an Answer, saw the *Victoire* in the Offin, and spoke to her. It was then resolved to follow the *St. Joseph*, and accordingly they steer'd for the *Havanna*, but by what Accident they did not overtake her is unknown.

I forgot to tell my Reader, on Board the *Dutch* Ship were fourteen *French* Hugonots, whom *Misson* thought fit to detain, when they were at Sea. *Misson* called 'em up, and proposed to 'em their taking on; telling them at the same Time, he left it to their Choice, for he would have no forc'd Men; and that if they all, or any of them, disapproved the Proposal, he would either give 'em the first Vessel he met that was fit for 'em, or set 'em ashoar on some inhabited Coast; and therefore bid 'em take two Days for Consideration before they returned an Answer; and, to encourage 'em, he called all Hands up, and declar'd, that if any Man repented him of the Course of Life he had chosen, his just Dividend should be counted to him, and he would set him on Shoar, either near the *Havanna*, or some other convenient Place; but not one accepted the Offer, and the fourteen Prisoners unanimously resolved to join in with 'em; to which Resolution, no doubt, the Hopes of a good Booty from the *St. Joseph*, and this Offer of Liberty greatly contributed.

At the Entrance of the Gulph they spied and came with a large Merchant Ship bound for *London* from *Jamaica*; she had 20 Guns, but no more than 32 Hands, that its not to be wonder'd at she made no Resistance, besides, she was deep laden with Sugars. Monsieur *Misson* took out of her what Ammunition she had, about four thousand Pieces of Eight, some Puncheons of Rum, and ten Hogsheads of Sugar; and, without doing her any further Damage, let her proceed her Voyage. What he valued most in this Prize was the Men he got, for she was carrying to *Europe* twelve *French* Prisoners, two of which were necessary Hands, being a Carpenter and his Mate. They were of *Bourdeaux*, from whence they came with the *Pomechatraine*, which was taken by the *Maremaid* off *Petit Guavers*, after an obstinate Resistance, in which they lost forty Men; but they were of Opinion the *Maremaid* could not have taken 'em, having but four Guns less than she had, which was made amends for, by their having about thirty Hands. On the contrary, had not the *Guernsey* come up, they thought of boarding and carrying the *Maremaid*. These Men very willingly came into Captain *Misson's* Measures.

These Men, who had been stripp'd to the Skin, begg'd Leave to make Reprisals, but the Captain would not suffer them, though he told the Master of the Prize, as he protected him and his Men, he thought it reasonable these *French* should be cloathed: Upon this the Master contributed of his own, and every Man bringing up his Chest, thought themselves very well off in sharing with them one half.

Though *Misson's* Ship pass'd for a *French* Man of War, yet his Generosity in letting the Prize go, gave the *English* Grounds to suspect the Truth, neither the Ship nor Cargoe being of Use to such as were upon the grand Account.

When they had lost all Hopes of the St. *Joseph*, they coasted along the North-Side of *Cuba*, and the *Victoire* growing now foul, they ran into a Landlock'd Bay on the East North-East Point, where they hove her down by Boats and Guns, though they could not pretend to heave her Keel out; however, they scraped and tallowed as far as they could go; they, for this Reason, many of them repented they had let the last Prize go, by which they might have careened.

When they had righted the Ship, and put every Thing on Board, they consulted upon the Course they should steer. Upon this the Council divided. The Captain and *Caraccioli* were for stretching over to the *African*, and the others for the *New-England* Coast, alledging, that the Ship had a foul Bottom, and was not fit for the Voyage; and that if they met with contrary Winds, and bad Weather, their Stock of Provision might fall short; and that as they were not far from the *English* Settlement of *Carolina*, they might either on that or the Coast of *Virginia, Maryland, Pensylvania, New-York,* or *New-England,* intercept ships which traded to the Islands with Provisions, and by that Means provide themselves with Bread, Flower, and other Necessaries. An Account of the Provisions were taken, and finding they had Provisions for four Months. Captain *Misson* called all Hands upon Deck, and told them, as the Council differed in the Course they should steer, he thought it reasonable to have it put to the Vote of the whole Company. That for his Part, he was for going to the Coast of *Guiney*, where they might reasonably expect to meet with valuable Prizes; but should they fail in their Expectation one Way, they would be sure of having it answered another; for they could then throw themselves in that of the *East-India* Ships, and he need not tell them, that the outward bound dreined *Europe* of what Money they drew from America. He then gave the Sentiments of those who were against him, and their Reasons, and begg'd that every one would give his Opinion and Vote according as he thought most conducive to the Good of all. That he should be far from taking it ill if they should reject what he had proposed, since he had no private Views to serve. The Majority of Votes fell on the Captain's Side, and they accordingly shaped their

Course for the Coast of Guiney, in which Voyage nothing remarkable happened. On their Arrival on the Gold-Coast, they fell in with the *Nieuwstadt* of *Amsterdam*, a Ship of 18 Guns, commanded by Capt. *Blacs*, who made a running Fight of five Glasses: This Ship they kept with them, putting on Board 40 Hands, and bringing all the Prisoners on Board the *Victoire*, they were Forty three in Number, they left *Amsterdam* with Fifty six, seven were killed in the Engagement, and they had lost six by Sickness and Accidents, one falling overboard, and one being taken by a Shark going overboard in a Calm.

The *Nieuwstadt* had some Gold-Dust on Board, to the Value of about 2000 l. Sterling, and a few Slaves to the Number of Seventeen, for she had but begun to Trade; the Slaves were a strengthening of their Hands, for the Captain order'd them to be cloathed out of Dutch Mariners Chests, and told his Men, 'That the Trading for those of our own Species, cou'd never be agreeable to the Eyes of divine Justice: That no Man had Power or the Liberty of another; and while those who profess'd a more enlightened Knowledge of the Deity, sold Men like Beasts; they prov'd that their Religion was no more than Grimace, and that they differ'd from the *Barbarians* in Name only, since their Practice was in nothing more humane: For his Part, and he hop'd, he spoke the Sentiments of all his brave Companions, he had not exempted his Neck from the galling Yoak of Slavery, and asserted his own Liberty, to enslave others. That however, these Men were distinguish'd from the *Europeans* by their Colour, Customs, or religious Rites, they were the Work of the same omnipotent Being, and endued with equal Reason: Wherefore, he desired they might be treated like Freemen (for he wou'd banish even the Name of Slavery from among them)' and divided into Messes among them, to the End they might the sooner learn their Language, be sensible of the Obligation they had to them, and more capable and zealous to defend that Liberty they owed to their Justice and Humanity.

This Speech of *Misson*'s was received with general Applause, and the Ship rang with *vive le Capitain* Misson. Long live Capt. *Misson.*— The Negroes were divided among the *French*, one to a Mess, who, by their Gesticulations, shew'd they were gratefully sensible of their being delivered from their Chains. Their Ship growing very foul, and going heavily through the Water, they run into the River of *Lagoa*, where they hove her down, taking out such Planks as had suffer'd most by the Worms, and substituting new in their Room.

After this they careened the Prize, and so put out to Sea, steering to the Southward, and keeping along the Coast, but met with Nothing. All this while, the greatest Decorum and Regularity was observed on Board the *Victoire*; but the *Dutch* Prisoners Example began to lead 'em into Swearing and Drunkenness, which the Captain remarking, thought it was best to nip these Vices in the Bud; and calling both the *French* and *Dutch* upon Deck, he address'd himself to the former, desiring their Captain, who spoke French excellently well, to interpret what he said to those who did not understand him. He told them, 'before he had the Misfortune of having them on Board, his Ears were never grated with hearing the Name of the great Creator prophaned, tho' he, to his Sorrow, had often since heard his own Men guilty of that Sin, which administer'd neither Profit nor Pleasure, and might draw upon them a severe Punishment: That if they had a just Idea of that great Being, they wou'd never mention him, but they wou'd immediately reflect on his Purity and their own Vileness. That we so easily took Impression from our Company, that the *Spanish* Proverb says, *let a Hermit and a Thief live together, the Thief wou'd become Hermit, or the Hermit Thief.* That he saw this verified in his Ship, for he cou'd attribute the Oaths and Curses he had heard among his brave Companions, to nothing but the odious Example of the *Dutch*. That this was not the only Vice they had introduced, for before they were on Board, his Men were Men, but he found by their beastly Pattern they were degenerated into Brutes, by drowning that only Faculty, which distinguishes between Man and Beast, *Reason*. That as he had the Honour to command them, he could not see them run into these odious Vices without, a sincere Concern, as he had a paternal Affection for them; and he should reproach himself as neglectful of the common Good, if he did not admonish them; and as by the Post which they had honour'd him, he was obliged to have a watchful Eye over their general Interest; he was obliged to tell them his Sentiments were, that the *Dutch* allured them to a dissolute Way of Life, that they might take some Advantage over them: Wherefore, as his brave Companions, he was assured, wou'd be guided by Reason, he gave the *Dutch* Notice, that the first whom he catch'd either with an Oath in his Mouth or Liquor in his Head, should be brought to the Geers, whipped and pickled, for an Example to the rest of his Nation: As to his Friends, his Companions, his Children, those gallant, those generous, noble, and heroick Souls he had the Honour to command, he entreated them to allow a small Time for Reflection, and to consider how little Pleasure sure, and how much Danger, might flow from imitating the Vices of their Enemies; and that they would among themselves, make a Law for the Suppression of what would otherwise estrange them from the Source of Life, and consequently leave them destitute of his Protection.'

It is not to be imagined what Efficacy this Speech had on both Nations: The *Dutch* grew continent in Fear of Punishment, and the *French* in Fear of being reproach'd by their good Captain, for they never mentioned him without this Epithet. Upon the Coast of *Angola*, they met with a second Dutch Ship, the Cargo of which consisted of Silk and Woolen Stuffs, Cloath, Lace, Wine, Brandy, Oyl, Spice, and hard Ware; the Prize gave Chase and engaged her, but upon the coming up of the *Victoire* she struck. This Ship opportunely came in their Way, and gave full Employ to the Taylors, who were on Board, for the whole Crew began to be out at Elbows: They plundered her of what was of Use to their own Ship, and then sunk her.

The Captain having about ninety Prisoners on Board, proposed the giving them the Prize, with what was necessary for their Voyage, and sending them away; which being agreed to, they shifted her Ammunition on Board the *Victoire*, and giving them Provision to carry them to the Settlements the Dutch have on the Coast, *Misson* called them up, told them what was his Design, and ask'd if any of them was willing to share his Fortune: Eleven *Dutch* came into him, two of which were Sail- makers, one an Armourer, and one a Carpenter, necessary Hands; the rest he let go, not a little surprised at the Regularity, Tranquillity, and Humanity, which they found among these new fashioned Pyrates.

They had now run the Length of *Soldinia* Bay about ten Leagues to the Northward of *Table* Bay. As here is good Water, safe Riding, plenty of Fish and fresh Provision, to be got of the Natives for the Merchandize they had on Board, it was resolved to stay here some little Time for Refreshments. When they had the Bay open, they spied a tall Ship, which instantly got under sail, and hove out *English* Colours. The *Victoire* made a clear Ship, and hove out her *French* Ensign, and a smart Engagement began. *The English* was a new Ship built for 40 Guns, though she had but 32 mounted, and 90 Hands. *Misson* gave Orders for boarding, and his Number of fresh Men he constantly poured in, after an obstinate Dispute obliged the *English* to fly the Decks, and leave the *French* Masters of their Ship, who promised, and gave them, good Quarters, and stripp'd not a Man.

They found on Board the Prize some Bales of *English* Broad-Cloath, and about 60000 l. in *English* Crown Pieces, and *Spanish* Pieces of Eight. The *English* Captain was killed in the Engagement, and 14 of his Men: The *French* lost 12, which was no small Mortification, but did not, however provoke them to use their Prisoners harshly. Captain *Misson* was sorry for the Death of the Commander, whom he buried on the Shoar, and one of his Men being a Stone-Cutter, he raised a Stone over his Grave with these Words, *Icy gist un brave Anglois*, Here lies a gallant *English* Man; when he was buried he made a tripple Discharge of 50 small Arms, and fired Minute Guns.

The *English*, knowing whose Hands they were fallen into, charm'd with *Misson*'s Humanity, 30 of them, in 3 Days Space, desired to take on with him. He accepted 'em, but at the same Time gave 'em to understand, that in taking on with him they were not to expect they should be indulged in a dissolute and immoral Life. He now divided his Company between the two Ships, and made *Caraccioli* Captain of the Prize, giving him Officers chosen by the publick Suffrage. The 17 Negroes began to understand a little *French*, and to be useful Hands, and in less than a Month all the *English* Prisoners came over to him, except their Officers.

He had two Ships well mann'd with resolute Fellows; they now doubled the Cape, and made the South End of *Madagascar*, and one of the *English* Men telling Captain *Misson*, that the *European* Ships bound for *Surat* commonly touch'd at the Island of *Johanna*, he sent for Captain *Caracciola* on Board, and it was agreed to cruise off that Island. They accordingly sailed on the West-Side of *Madagascar* and off the Bay *de Diego*. About half Seas over between that Bay and the Island of *Johanna*, they came up with an *English East-India* Man, which made Signals of Distress as soon as she spy'd *Misson* and his Prize; they found her sinking by an unexpected Leak, and took all her Men on Board, though they could get little out of her before she went down. The *English*, who were thus miraculously saved from perishing, desired to be set on Shoar at *Johanna*, where they hop'd to meet with either a *Dutch* or *English* Ship in a little Time, and the mean while they were sure of Relief.

They arrived at Johanna, and were kindly received by the Queen-Regent and her Brother, on account of the *English* on the one Hand, and of their Strength on the other, which the Queen's Brother, who had the Administration of Affairs, was not able to make Head against, and hoped they might assist him against the King of *Mohila*, who threaten'd him with a Visit.

This is an Island which is contiguous, in a manner, to *Johanna*, and lies about N. W. and by N. from it. *Caraccioli* told *Misson* he might make his Advantage in widening the Breach between these two little Monarchies, and, by offering his Assistance to that of *Johanna*, in a manner rule both, For these would count him as their Protector, and those come to any Terms to buy his Friendship, by which Means he would hold the Ballance of Power between them. He followed this Advice, and offered his Friendship and Assistance to the Queen, who very readily embraced it.

I must advise the Reader, that many of this Island speak *English*, and that the *English* Men who were of *Misson's* Crew, and his Interpreters, told them, their Captain, though not an *Englishman*, was their Friend and Ally, and a Friend and Brother to the *Johanna* Men, for they esteem the *English* beyond all other Nations.

They were supplied by the Queen with all Necessaries of Life, and *Misson* married her Sister, as *Caraccioli* did the Daughter of her Brother, whose Armory, which consisted before of no more than two rusty Fire-Locks, and three Pistols, he furnish'd with thirty Fuzils, as many Pair of Pistols, and gave him two Barrels of Powder, and four of Ball.

Several of his Men took Wives, and some requited their Share of the Prizes, which was justly given them, they designing to settle in this Island, but the Number of these did not exceed ten, which Loss was repaired by thirty of the Crew (they had saved from perishing) coming in to him.

While they past their Time in all manner of Diversions the Place would afford them, as hunting, feasting, and visiting the Island, the King of *Mohila* made a Descent, and alarm'd the whole Country. *Misson* advised the Queen's Brother not to give him any Impediment, but let him get into the Heart of the Island, and he would take Care to intercept their Return; but the Prince answered, should he follow his Advice the Enemy would do him and the Subjects an irreparable Damage, in destroying the Cocoa Walks, and for that Reason he must endeavour to stop his Progress. Upon this Answer he asked the *English* who were not under his Command, if they were willing to join him in repelling the Enemies of their common Host, and one and all consenting, he gave them Arms, and mixed them with his own Men, and about the same Number of *Johannians*, under the Command of

Caraccioli and the Queen's Brother, and arming out all his Boats, he went himself to the Westward of the Island, where they made their Descent. The Party which went by Land, fell in with, and beat the *Mohilians* with great Ease, who were in the greatest Consternation, to find their Retreat cut off by *Misson*'s Boats. The *Johannians*, whom they had often molested, were so enraged, that they gave Quarter to none, and out of 300 who made the Descent, if *Misson* and *Caraccioli* had not interposed, not a Soul had escaped; 113 were taken Prisoners by his Men, and carried on Board his Ships. These he sent fate to *Mohila*, with a Message to the King, to desire he would make Peace with his Friend and Ally the King of *Johanna*; but that Prince, little affected with the Service done him in the Preservation of his Subjects, sent him Word he took Laws from none, and knew when to make War and Peace without his Advice, which he neither asked nor wanted. *Misson*, irritated by this rude Answer, resolved to transfer the War into his own Country, and accordingly set sail for *Mohila*, with about 100 *Johanna* Men. The Shoar, on Sight of the Ships, was filled with Men to hinder a Descent if intended, but the great Guns soon dispersed this Rabble, and under their Cover he landed the *Johannians*, and an equal Number of *French* and *English*. They were met by about 700 *Mohilians*, who pretended to stop their Passage, but their Darts and Arrows were of little avail against *Misson*'s Fuzils; the first Discharge made a great Slaughter, and about 20 Shells which were thrown among them, put them to a confus'd Flight. The Party of *Europeans* and *Johannians* then marched to their Metropolis, without Resistance, which they reduced to Ashes, and the *Johannians* cut down all the Cocoa Walks that they could for the Time, for towards Evening they returned to their Ships, and stood off to Sea.

At their Return to *Johanna* the Queen made a Festival, and magnified the Bravery and Service of her Guests, Friends, and Allies. This Feast lasted four Days, at the Expiration of which Time the Queen's Brother proposed to Captain *Misson* the making another Descent, in which he would go in Person, and did not doubt subjecting the *Mohilians*; but this was not the Design of *Misson*, who had Thoughts of fixing a Retreat on the North West Side of *Madagascar*, and look'd upon the Feuds between these two Islands advantageous to his Views, and therefore no way his Interest to suffer the one to overcome the other; for while the Variance was kept up, and their Forces pretty much upon a Level, it was evident their Interest would make both Sides caress him; he therefore answer'd, that they ought to deliberate on the Consequences, for they might be deceived in their Hopes, and find the Conquest less easy than they imagined. That the King of *Mohilia* would be more upon his Guard, and not only intrench himself, but gall them with frequent Ambuscades, by which they must inevitably lose a Number of Men; and, if they were forced to retire with Loss, raise the Courage of the *Mohilians*, and make them irreconcilable Enemies to the *Johannians*, and intirely deprive him of the Advantages with which he might now make a Peace, having twice defeated them: That he could not be always with them, and at his leaving *Johanna* he might expect the King of *Mohilia* would endeavour to take a bloody Revenge for the late Damages. The Queen gave intirely into *Misson's* Sentiments.

While this was in Agitation four *Mohilians* arrived as Ambassadors to propose a Peace. They finding the *Johannians* upon high Terms, one of them spoke to this Purpose; O ye Johannians, *do not conclude from your late Success, that Fortune will be always favourable; she will not always give you the Protection of the* Europeans, *and without their Help its possible you might now sue for a Peace, which you seem averse to. Remember the Sun rises, comes to its Meridian Height, and stays not there, but declines in a Moment. Let this admonish you to reflect on the constant Revolution of all sublunary Affairs, and the greater is your Glory, the nearer you are to your Declension. We are taught by every Thing we see, that there is no Stability in the World, but Nature is in continual Movement. The Sea, which o'er flows the Sands has its Bounds set, which it cannot pass, which the Moment it has reached, without abiding, returns back to the Bottom of the Deep. Every Herb, every Shrub and Tree, and even our own Bodies, teach us this Lesson, that nothing is durable, or can be counted upon. Time passes away insensibly, one Sun follows another, and brings its Changes with it. To-Day's Globe of Light sees you strengthened by these* Europeans *elate with victory, and we, who have been used to conquer you, come to ask a Peace. To Morrow's Sun may see you deprived of your present Succours, and the* Johannians *petitioning us; as therefore we cannot say what to Morrow may bring forth, it would be unwise on uncertain Hopes to forego a certain Advantage, as surely Peace ought to be esteem'd by every wise Man.*

Having said this, the Ambassadors withdrew, and were treated by the Queen's Orders. After the Council had concluded, they were again call'd upon, and the Queen told them, that by the Advice of her good Friends, the *Europeans*, and those of her Council, she agreed to make a

Peace, which she wish'd might banish all Memory of former Injuries That they must own the War was begun by them, and that she was far from being the Agressor; she only defended her self in her own Kingdom, which they had often invaded, though, till within few Days, she had never molested their Coasts. If then they really desired to live amicably with her, they must resolve to send two of the King's Children, and ten of the first Nobility, as Hostages, that they might, when they pleased, return, for that was the only Terms on which she would desist prosecuting the Advantages she now had, with the utmost Vigour.

The Ambassadors returned with this Answer, and, about ten Days after, the two Ships appearing upon their Coasts, they sent off to give Notice, that their King comply'd with the Terms proposed, would send the Hostages, and desired a Cessation of all Hostility, and, at the same Time, invited the Commanders on Shoar. The *Johanna* Men on Board disswaded their accepting the Invitation; but *Misson* and *Caraccioli*, fearing nothing, went, but arm'd their Boat's Crew. They were received by the King with Demonstrations of Friendship, and they dined with him under a Tamerane Tree; but when they parted from him, and were returning to their Boats, they were inclosed by, at least, 100 of the *Mohilians*, who set upon them with the utmost Fury, and, in the first Flight of Arrows, wounded both the Captains, and killed four of their Boat's Crew of eight, who were with them; they, in return, discharged their Pistols with some Execution, and fell in with their Cutlasses; but all their Bravery would have stood them in little Stead, had not the Report of their Pistols alarm'd and brought the rest of their Friends to their Assistance, who took their Fuzils, and coming up while they were engaged, discharged a Volley on the Back of the Assailants, which laid twelve of them dead on the Spot. The Ships hearing this Fire, sent immediately the Yawls and Long-Boats well mann'd. Though the Islanders were a little damp'd in their Courage by this Fire of the Boats Crew, yet they did not give over the Fight, and one of them desperately threw himself upon *Caraccioli*, and gave him a deep Wound in his Side, with a long Knife, but he paid for the Rashness of the Attempt with his Life, one of the Crew cleaving his Skull. The Yawls and Long-Boats now arrived, and being guided by the Noise, reinforced their Companions, put the Traytors to Flight, and brought off their dead and wounded. The *Europeans* lost by this Treachery seven slain outright, and eight wounded, six of which recovered.

The Crew were resolved to revenge the Blood of their Officers and Comrades the next Day, and were accordingly on the Point of Landing, when two Canoes came off with two Men bound, the pretended Authors of this Treason, without the King's Knowledge, who had sent 'em that they might receive the Punishment due to their Villany. The *Johanna* Men on Board were call'd for Interpreters, who having given this Account, added, that the King only sacrificed these Men, but that they should not believe him, for he certainly had given Orders for assassinating the *Europeans*; and the better Way was to kill all the *Mohilians* that came in the Canoes as well as the two Prisoners; go back to *Johanna*, take more of their Countrymen, and give no Peace to Traytors; but *Misson* was for no such violent Measures, he was averse to every Thing that bore the Face of Cruelty and thought a bloody Revenge, if Necessity did not enforce it, spoke a groveling and timid Soul; he, therefore, sent those of the Canoes back, and bid them tell their King, if before the Evening he sent the Hostages agreed upon, he should give Credit to his Excuse, but if he did not, he should believe him the Author of the late vile Attempt on his Life.

The Canoes went off but returned not with an Answer, wherefore, he bid the *Johanna* Men tell the two Prisoners that they should be set on Shore the next Morning, and order'd them to acquaint their King, he was no Executioner to put those to Death whom he had condemn'd, but that he should find, he knew how to revenge himself of his Treason. The Prisoners being unbound, threw themselves at his Feet, and begg'd that he would not send them ashore, for they should be surely put to Death, for the Crime they had committed, was, the dissuading the barbarous Action of which they were accused as Authors.

Next Day the two Ships landed 200 Men, under the Cover of their Canon; but that Precaution of bringing their Ships close to the Shore they found needless; not a soul appearing, they march'd two Leagues up the Country, when they saw a Body of Men appear behind some Shrubs; *Caraccioli's* Lieutenant, who commanded the right Wing, with fifty Men made up to them, but found he had got among Pit Falls artificially cover'd, several of his Men falling into them, which made him halt, and not pursue those *Mohilians* who made a feint Retreat to ensnare him, thinking it dangerous to proceed farther; and seeing no Enemy would face them, they retired the same Way they came, and getting into their Boats, went on Board the Ships, resolving to return with a strong Reinforcement, and make Descents at one and the same Time in different Parts of the Island. They ask'd the two Prisoners how the Country lay, and what the Soil was on the North Side the Island; and they answer'd it was morass, and the most dangerous Part to attempt, it being a Place where they shelter on any imminent Danger.

The Ships return'd to *Johanna*, where the greatest Tenderness and Care was shown for the Recovery and Cure of the two Captains and of their Men; they lay six Weeks before they were able to walk the Decks, for neither of them would quit his Ship. Their *Johanna* Wives expressed a Concern they did not think them capable of, nay, a Wife of one of the wounded Men who died, stood some Time looking upon the Corpse as motionless as a Statue, then embracing it, without shedding a Tear, desired she might take it ashore to wash and bury it; and at the same Time, by an Interpreter, and with a little Mixture of *European* Language, she had, begg'd her late Husband's Friends would take their Leave of him the next Day.

Accordingly a Number went ashore, and carried with them the Dividend, which fell to his Share, which the Captain order'd to be given his Widow; when she saw the Money, she smil'd, and ask'd if all, all that was for her? Being answered in the affirmative, and what Good will all that shining Dirt do me, if I could with it purchase the Life of my Husband, and call him back from the Grave, I would accept it with Pleasure, but as it is not sufficient to allure him back to this World, I have no Use for it; do with it what you please. Then she desired they would go with her and perform the last Ceremonies to her Husband's dead Body, after their Country Fashion, least he should be displeased, that she could not stay with them, to be a Witness, because she was in haste to go and be married again. She startled the *Europeans* who heard this latter Part of her Speech so dissonant from the Beginning; however, they followed her, and she led them into a Plantane Walk, where they found a great many *Johanna* Men and Women, sitting under the Shade of Plantanes, round the Corpse, which lay (as they all sate) on the Ground, covered with Flowers. She embraced them round, and then the *Europeans*, one by one, and after these Ceremonies, she poured out a Number of bitter Imprecations against the *Mohila* Men, whose Treachery had darken'd her Husband's Eyes, and made him insensible of her Caresses, who was her first Love, to whom she had given her Heart, with her Virginity. She then proceeded in his Praises, calling him the Joy of Infants, the Love of Virgins, the Delight of the old, and the Wonder of the young, adding, he was strong and beautiful as the Cedar, brave as the Bull, tender as the Kid, and loving as the Ground Turtle; having finished this Oration, not unlike those of the *Romans*, which the nearest Relation of the deceas'd used to pronounce from the Rostrum, she laid her down by the Side of her Husband, embracing him, and sitting up again, gave herself a deep Wound under the left Breast with a Bayonet, and fell dead on her Husband's Corpse.

The *Europeans* were astonished at the Tenderness and Resolution of the Girl, for she was not, by what Her Mien spoke her, past seventeen; and they now admired, as much as they had secretly detested her, for saying she was in haste to be married again, the Meaning of which they did not understand.

After the Husband and Wife were buried, the Crew return'd on Board, and gave an Account of what had pass'd; the Captains Wives (for *Misson* and his were on Board the *Bijoux*, the Name they had given their Prize from her Make and Gilding) seem'd not in the least surprized, and *Caraccioli's* Lady only said, she must be of noble Descent, for none but the Families of the Nobility had the Privilege allowed them of following their Husbands on pain, if they transgressed, of being thrown into the Sea, to be eat by Fish; and they knew, that their Souls could not rest as long as any of the Fish, who fed upon them, lived. *Misson* asked, if they intended to have done the same Thing had they died? We should not, answer'd his Wife, have disgraced our Families; nor is our Tenderness for our Husbands inferior to hers whom you seem to admire.

After their Recovery, *Misson* proposes a Cruize, on the Coast of *Zangueber*, which being agreed to, he and *Caraccioli* took Leave of the Queen and her Brother, and would have left their Wives on the Island, but they could by no Means be induced to the Separation; it was in vain to urge the Shortness of the Time they were to Cruize; they answer'd it was farther than *Mohila* they intended to go, and if they were miserable in that short Absence, they could never support a longer; and if they would not allow them to keep them Company the Voyage, they must not expect to see them at their Return, if they intended one.

In a Word they were obliged to yield to them, but told them, if the Wives of their Men should insist as strongly on following their Example, their Tenderness, would be their Ruin, and make them a Prey to their Enemies; they answer'd the Queen should prevent that, by ordering no Woman should go on board, and if any were in the Ships, they should return on Shore: This Order was accordingly made, and they set Sail for the River of *Mozembique*. In about ten Days Cruize after they had left *Johanna*, and about 15 Leagues to the Eastward of this River, they fell in with a stout *Portuguese* Ship of 60 Guns, which engaged them from Break of Day till Two in the Afternoon, when the Captain being killed, and a great Number of Men lost, she struck: This proved a very rich Prize, for she had the Value of 250000 *L.* Sterling on Board, in Gold- Dust. The two Women never quitted the Decks all the Time of the Engagement, neither gave they the least Mark of Fear, except for their Husbands: This Engagement cost them thirty Men, and *Caraccioli* lost his right Leg; the Slaughter fell mostly on the *English,* for of the above Number, twenty were of that Nation: The *Portuguese* lost double the Number. *Caraccioli's* Wound made them resolve to make the best of their Way for *Johanna* where the greatest Care was taken of their wounded, not one of whom died, tho' their Number amounted to Twenty seven.

Caraccioli kept his Bed two Months, but *Misson* seeing him in a fair way of Recovery, took what Hands could be spar'd from the *Bijoux,* leaving her sufficient for Defence, and went out, having mounted ten of the *Portuguese* Guns, for he had hitherto carried but thirty, though he had Ports for forty. He stretched over to *Madagascar,* and coasted along this Island to the Northward, as far as the most northerly Point, when turning back, he enter'd a Bay to the northward of *Diego Suares.* He run ten Leagues up this Bay, and on the larboard Side found it afforded a large, and safe, Harbour, with plenty of fresh Water. He came here to an Anchor, went ashore and examined into the Nature of the Soil, which he found rich, the Air wholesome, and the Country level. He told his Men, that this was an excellent Place for an Asylum, and that he determined here to fortify and raise a small Town, and make Docks for Shipping, that they might have some Place to call their own; and a Receptacle, when Age or Wounds had render'd them incapable of Hardship, where they might enjoy the Fruits of their Labour, and go to their Graves in Peace. That he would not, however, set about this, till he had the Approbation of the whole Company; and were he sure they would all approve this Design, which he hoped, it being evidently for the general Good, he should not think it adviseable to begin any Works, lest the Natives should, in his Absence, destroy them; but however, as they had nothing upon their Hands, if they were of his Opinion, they might begin to fall and square Timber, ready for the raising a wooden Fort, when they return'd with their Companions.

The Captain's Motion was universally applauded, and in ten Days they fell'd and rough hew'd a hundred and fifty large Trees, without any Interruption from, or seeing any of, the Inhabitants. They fell'd their Timber at the Waters Edge, so that they had not the Trouble of hawling them any way, which would have employ'd a great deal more Time: They returned again, and acquainted their Companions with what they had seen and done, and with the Captain's Resolution, which they one and all came into.

Captain *Misson* then told the Queen, as he had been serviceable to her in her War with the Island of *Mohila*, and might continue to be of farther Use, he did not question her lending him Assistance in the settling himself on the Coast of *Madagascar*, and to that end, furnish him with 300 Men, to help in his Buildings; the Queen answered, she could do nothing without Consent of Council, and that she would assemble her Nobility, and did not question their agreeing to any Thing he could reasonably define, for they were sensible of the Obligations the *Johanians* had to him. The Council was accordingly called, and *Misson*'s Demand being told, one of the eldest said, he did not think it expedient to comply with it, nor safe to refuse; that they should in agreeing to give him that Assistance, help to raise a Power, which might prove formidable to themselves, by the being so near a Neighbour; and these Men who had lately protected, might, when they found it for their Interest, enslave them. On the other hand, if they did not comply, they had the Power to do them great Damage. That they were to make choice of the least of two possible Evils, for he could prognosticate no Good to *Johanna*, by their settling near it. Another answered, that many of them had *Johanna* Wives, that it was not likely they would make Enemies of the *Johanna* Men at first settling, because their Friendship might be of Use to them; and from their Children there was nothing to be apprehended in the next Generation, for they would be half their own Blood; that in the mean while, if they comply'd with the Request, they might be sure of an Ally, and Protector, against the King of *Mohila*; wherefore, he was for agreeing to the Demand.

After a long Debate, in which every Inconvenience, and Advantage, was maturely considered, it was agreed to send with him the Number of Men he required, on Condition he should send them back in four Moons, make an Alliance with them, and War against *Mohila*; this being agreed to, they staid till *Caraccioli* was thoroughly recovered, then putting the *Johannians* on board the *Portuguese* Ship with 40 *French* and *English* and 15 *Portuguese* to work her, and setting Sail, they arrived at the Place where *Misson* designed his Settlement, which he called *Libertalia*, and gave the Name of *Liberi* to his People, desiring in that might be drown'd the distingush'd Names of *French*, *English*, *Dutch*, *Africans*, &c.

The first Thing they sat about was, the raising a Fort on each Side the Harbour, which they made of an octogon Figure, and having finished and mounted them with 40 Guns taken out of the *Portuguese*, they raised a Battery on an Angle of ten Guns, and began to raise Houses and Magazines under the Protection of their Forts and Ships; the *Portuguese* was unrigg'd, and all her Sails and Cordage carefully laid up. While they were very busily employed in the raising a Town, a Party which had often hunted and rambled four or five Leagues off their Settlement, resolved to venture farther into the Country. They made themselves some Huts, at about 4 Leagues distance from their Companions, and travell'd East South East, about 5 Leagues farther into the Country, when they came up with a Black, who was arm'd with a Bow, Arrows, and a Javelin; they with a friendly Appearance engaged the Fellow to lay by his Fear and go with them. They carried him to their Companions, and there entertained him three Days with a great Deal of Humanity, and then returned with him near the Place they found him, made him a Present of a Piece of scarlet Baze, and an Ax; he appeared overjoy'd at the Present, and left them with seeming Satisfaction.

The Hunters imagined that there might be some Village not far off, and observing that he look'd at the Sun, and then took his Way direct South, they travell'd on the same Point of the Compass, and from the Top of a Hill they spied a pretty large Village, and went down to it; the Men came out with their Arms, such as before described, Bows, Arrows, and Javelins, but upon two only of the Whites advancing, with Presents of Axes, and Baze in their Hands, they sent only four to meet them. The Misfortune was, that they could not understand one another, but by their pointing to the Sun, and holding up one Finger, and making one of them go forward, and return again with shewing their Circumcision, and pointing up to Heaven with one Finger, they apprehended, they gave them to understand, there was but one God, who had sent one Prophet, and concluded from thence, and their Circumcision they were *Mahometans*; the Presents were carried to their Chief, and he seem'd to receive them kindly, and by Signs invited the Whites into their Village; but they, remembring the late Treachery of the *Mohilians*, made Signs for Victuals to be brought them where they were.

More of the History of these Adventurers in another Place.

DICKORY CRONKE

THE
DUMB PHILOSOPHER,
OR,
GREAT BRITAIN'S WONDER;
CONTAINING:

I. A faithful and very surprising Account how Dickory Cronke, a Tinner's son, in the County of Cornwall, was born Dumb, and continued so for Fifty-eight years; and how, some days before he died, he came to his Speech; with Memoirs of his Life, and the Manner of his Death.

II. A Declaration of his Faith and Principles in Religion; with a Collection of Select Meditations, composed in his Retirement.

III. His Prophetical Observations upon the Affairs of Europe, more particularly of Great Britain, from 1720 to 1729. The whole extracted from his Original Papers, and confirmed by unquestionable Authority.

TO WHICH IS ANNEXED HIS ELEGY,
WRITTEN BY A YOUNG CORNISH GENTLEMAN, OF
EXETER COLLEGE IN OXFORD.
WITH
AN EPITAPH BY ANOTHER HAND.

"Non quis, sed quid."

PREFACE

The formality of a preface to this little book might have been very well omitted, if it were not to gratify the curiosity of some inquisitive people, who, I foresee, will be apt to make objections against the reality of the narrative.

Indeed the public has too often been imposed upon by fictitious stories, and some of a very late date, so that I think myself obliged by the usual respect which is paid to candid and impartial readers, to acquaint them, by way of introduction, with what they are to expect, and what they may depend upon, and yet with this caution too, that it is an indication of ill nature or ill manners, if not both, to pry into a secret that is industriously concealed.

However, that there may be nothing wanting on my part, I do hereby assure the reader, that the papers from whence the following sheets were extracted, are now in town, in the custody of a person of unquestionable reputation, who, I will be bold to say, will not only be ready, but proud, to produce them upon a good occasion, and that I think is as much satisfaction as the nature of this case requires.

As to the performance, it can signify little now to make an apology upon that account, any farther than this, that if the reader pleases he may take notice that what he has now before him was collected from a large bundle of papers, most of which were writ in shorthand, and very ill-digested. However, this may be relied upon, that though the language is something altered, and now and then a word thrown in to help the expression, yet strict care has been taken to speak the author's mind, and keep as close as possible to the meaning of the original. For the design, I think there is nothing need be said in vindication of that. Here is a dumb philosopher introduced to a wicked and degenerate generation, as a proper emblem of virtue and morality; and if the world could be persuaded to look upon him with candour and impartiality, and then to copy after him, the editor has gained his end, and would think himself sufficiently recompensed for his present trouble.

PART I

Among the many strange and surprising events that help to fill the accounts of this last century, I know none that merit more an entire credit, or are more fit to be preserved and handed to posterity than those I am now going to lay before the public.

Dickory Cronke, the subject of the following narrative, was born at a little hamlet, near St. Columb, in Cornwall, on the 29th of May, 1660, being the day and year in which King Charles the Second was restored. His parents were of mean extraction, but honest, industrious people, and well beloved in their neighbourhood. His father's chief business was to work at the tin mines; his mother stayed at home to look after the children, of which they had several living at the same time. Our Dickory was the youngest, and being but a sickly child, had always a double portion of her care and tenderness.

It was upwards of three years before it was discovered that he was born dumb, the knowledge of which at first gave his mother great uneasiness, but finding soon after that he had his hearing, and all his other senses to the greatest perfection, her grief began to abate, and she resolved to have him brought up as well as their circumstances and his capacity would permit.

As he grew, notwithstanding his want of speech, he every day gave some instance of a ready genius, and a genius much superior to the country children, insomuch that several gentlemen in the neighbourhood took particular notice of him, and would often call him Restoration Dick, and give him money, &c.

When he came to be eight years of age, his mother agreed with a person in the next village, to teach him to read and write, both which, in a very short time, he acquired to such perfection, especially the latter, that he not only taught his own brothers and sisters, but likewise several young men and women in the neighbourhood, which often brought him in small sums, which he always laid out in such necessaries as he stood most in need of.

In this state he continued till he was about twenty, and then he began to reflect how scandalous it was for a young man of his age and circumstances to live idle at home, and so resolves to go with his father to the mines, to try if he could get something towards the support of himself and the family; but being of a tender constitution, and often sick, he soon perceived that sort of business was too hard for him, so was forced to return home and continue in his former station; upon which he grew exceeding melancholy, which his mother observing, she comforted him in the best manner she could, telling him that if it should please God to take her away, she had something left in store for him, which would preserve him against public want.

This kind assurance from a mother whom he so dearly loved gave him some, though not an entire satisfaction; however, he resolves to acquiesce under it till Providence should order something for him more to his content and advantage, which, in a short time happened according to his wish. The manner was thus:—

One Mr. Owen Parry, a Welsh gentleman of good repute, coming from Bristol to Padstow, a little seaport in the county of Cornwall, near the place where Dickory dwelt, and hearing much of this dumb man's perfections, would needs have him sent for; and finding, by his significant gestures and all outward appearances that he much exceeded the character that the country gave of him, took a mighty liking to him, insomuch that he told him, if he would go with him into Pembrokeshire, he would be kind to him, and take care of him as long as he lived.

This kind and unexpected offer was so welcome to poor Dickory, that without any farther consideration, he got a pen and ink and writ a note, and in a very handsome and submissive manner returned him thanks for his favour, assuring him he would do his best to continue and improve it; and that he would be ready to wait upon him whenever he should be pleased to command.

To shorten the account as much as possible, all things were concluded to their mutual satisfaction, and in about a fortnight's time they set forward for Wales, where Dickory, notwithstanding his dumbness, behaved himself with so much diligence and affability, that he not only gained the love of the family where he lived, but of everybody round him.

In this station he continued till the death of his master, which happened about twenty years afterwards; in all which time, as has been confirmed by several of the family, he was never observed to be any ways disguised by drinking, or to be guilty of any of the follies and irregularities incident to servants in gentlemen's houses. On the contrary, when he had any spare time, his constant custom was to retire with some good book into a private place within call, and there employ himself in reading, and then writing down his observations upon what he read.

After the death of his master, whose loss afflicted him to the last degree, one Mrs. Mary Mordant, a gentlewoman of great virtue and piety, and a very good fortune, took him into her service, and carried him with her, first to Bath, and then to Bristol, where, after a lingering distemper, which continued for about four years, she died likewise.

Upon the loss of his mistress, Dickory grew again exceeding melancholy and disconsolate; at length, reflecting that death is but a common debt which all mortals owe to nature, and must be paid sooner or later, he became a little better satisfied, and so determines to get together what he had saved in his service, and then to return to his native country, and there finish his life in privacy and retirement.

Having been, as has been mentioned, about twenty-four years a servant, and having, in the interim, received two legacies, viz., one of thirty pounds, left him by his master, and another of fifteen pounds by his mistress, and being always very frugal, he had got by him in the whole upwards of sixty pounds. This, thinks he, with prudent management, will be enough to support me as long as I live, and so I'll e'en lay aside all thoughts of future business, and make the best of my way to Cornwall, and there find out some safe and solitary retreat, where I may have liberty to meditate and make my melancholy observations upon the several occurrences of human life.

This resolution prevailed so far, that no time was let slip to get everything in readiness to go with the first ship. As to his money, he always kept that locked up by him, unless he sometimes lent it to a friend without interest, for he had a mortal hatred to all sorts of usury or extortion. His books, of which he had a considerable quantity, and some of them very good ones, together with his other equipage, he got packed up, that nothing might be wanting against the first opportunity.

In a few days he heard of a vessel bound to Padstow, the very port he wished to go to, being within four or five miles of the place where he was born. When he came thither, which was in less than a week, his first business was to inquire after the state of his family. It was some time before he could get any information of them, until an old man that knew his father and mother, and remembered they had a son was born dumb, recollected him, and after a great deal of difficulty, made him understand that all his family except his youngest sister were dead, and that she was a widow, and lived at a little town called St. Helen's, about ten miles farther in the country.

This doleful news, we must imagine, must be extremely shocking, and add a new sting to his former affliction; and here it was that he began to exercise the philosopher, and to demonstrate himself both a wise and a good man. All these things, thinks he, are the will of Providence, and must not be disputed; and so he bore up under them with an entire resignation, resolving that, as soon as he could find a place where he might deposit his trunk and boxes with safety, he would go to St. Helen's in quest of his sister.

How his sister and he met, and how transported they were to see each other after so long an interval, I think is not very material. It is enough for the present purpose that Dickory soon recollected his sister, and she him; and after a great many endearing tokens of love and tenderness, he wrote to her, telling her that he believed Providence had bestowed on him as much as would support him as long as he lived, and that if she thought proper he would come and spend the remainder of his days with her.

The good woman no sooner read his proposal than she accepted it, adding, withal, that she could wish her entertainment was better; but if he would accept of it as it was, she would do her best to make everything easy, and that he should be welcome upon his own terms, to stay with her as long as he pleased.

This affair being so happily settled to his full satisfaction, he returns to Padstow to fetch the things he had left behind him, and the next day came back to St. Helen's, where, according to his own proposal, he continued to the day of his death, which happened upon the 29th of May, 1718, about the same hour in which he was born.

Having thus given a short detail of the several periods of his life, extracted chiefly from the papers which he left behind him, I come in the next place to make a few observations how he managed himself and spent his time toward the latter part of it.

His constant practice, both winter and summer, was to rise and set with the sun; and if the weather would permit, he never failed to walk in some unfrequented place, for three hours, both morning and evening, and there it is supposed he composed the following meditations. The chief part of his sustenance was milk, with a little bread boiled in it, of which in the morning, after his walk, he would eat the quantity of a pint, and sometimes more. Dinners he never eat any; and at night he would only have a pretty large piece of bread, and drink a draught of good spring water; and after this method he lived during the whole time he was at St. Helen's. It is observed of him that he never slept out of a bed, nor never lay awake in one; which I take to be an argument, not only of a strong and healthful constitution, but of a mind composed and calm, and entirely free from the ordinary disturbances of human life. He never gave the least signs of complaint or dissatisfaction at anything, unless it was when he heard the tinners swear, or saw them drunk; and then, too, he would get out of the way as soon as he had let them see, by some significant signs, how scandalous and ridiculous they made themselves; and against the next time he met them, would be sure to have a paper ready written, wherein he would represent the folly of drunkenness, and the dangerous consequences that generally attended it.

Idleness was his utter aversion, and if at any time he had finished the business of the day, and was grown weary of reading and writing, in which he daily spent six hours at least, he would certainly find something either within doors or without, to employ himself.

Much might be said both with regard to the wise and regular management, and the prudent methods he took to spend his time well towards the declension of his life; but, as his history may perhaps be shortly published at large by a better hand, I shall only observe in the general, that he was a person of great wisdom and sagacity. He understood nature beyond the ordinary capacity, and, if he had had a competency of learning suitable to his genius, neither this nor the former ages would have produced a better philosopher or a greater man.

I come next to speak of the manner of his death and the consequences thereof, which are, indeed, very surprising, and, perhaps, not altogether unworthy a general observation. I shall relate them as briefly as I can, and leave every one to believe or disbelieve as he thinks proper.

Upon the 26th of May, 1718, according to his usual method, about four in the afternoon, he went out to take his evening walk; but before he could reach the place he intended, he was siezed with an apoplectic fit, which only gave him liberty to sit down under a tree, where, in an instant, he was deprived of all manner of sense and motion, and so he continued, as appears by his own confession afterwards, for more than fourteen hours.

His sister, who knew how exact he was in all his methods, finding him stay a considerable time beyond the usual hour, concludes that some misfortune must needs have happened to him, or he would certainly have been at home before. In short, she went immediately to all the places he was wont to frequent, but nothing could be heard or seen of him till the next morning, when a young man, as he was going to work, discovered him, and went home and told his sister that her brother lay in such a place, under a tree, and, as he believed had been robbed and murdered.

The poor woman, who had all night been under the most dreadful apprehensions, was now frightened and confounded to the last degree. However, recollecting herself, and finding there was no remedy, she got two or three of her neighbours to bear her company, and so hastened with the young man to the tree, where she found her brother lying in the same posture that he had described.

The dismal object at first view startled and surprised everybody present, and filled them full of different notions and conjectures. But some of the company going nearer to him, and finding that he had lost nothing, and that there were no marks of any violence to be discovered about him, they conclude that it must be an apoplectic or some other sudden fit that had surprised him in his walk, upon which his sister and the rest began to feel his hands and face, and observing that he was still warm, and that there were some symptoms of life yet remaining, they conclude that the best way was to carry him home to bed, which was accordingly done with the utmost expedition.

When they had got him into the bed, nothing was omitted that they could think of to bring him to himself, but still he continued utterly insensible for about six hours. At the sixth hour's end he began to move a little, and in a very short time was so far recovered, to the great astonishment of everybody about him, that he was able to look up, and to make a sign to his sister to bring him a cup of water.

After he had drunk the water he soon perceived that all his faculties were returned to their former stations, and though his strength was very much abated by the length and rigour of the fit, yet his intellects were as strong and vigorous as ever.

His sister observing him to look earnestly upon the company, as if he had something extraordinary to communicate to them, fetched him a pen and ink and a sheet of paper, which, after a short pause, he took, and wrote as follows:——

"Dear sister,

"I have now no need of pen, ink, and paper, to tell you my meaning. I find the strings that bound up my tongue, and hindered me from speaking, are unloosed, and I have words to express myself as freely and distinctly as any other person. From whence this strange and unexpected event should proceed, I must not pretend to say, any farther than this, that it is doubtless the hand of Providence that has done it, and in that I ought to acquiesce. Pray let me be alone for two or three hours, that I may be at liberty to compose myself, and put my thoughts in the best order I can before I leave them behind me."

The poor woman, though extremely startled at what her brother had written, yet took care to conceal it from the neighbours, who, she knew, as well as she, must be mightily surprised at a thing so utterly unexpected. Says she, my brother desires to be alone; I believe he may have something in his mind that disturbs him. Upon which the neighbours took their leave and returned home, and his sister shut the door, and left him alone to his private contemplations.

After the company were withdrawn he fell into a sound sleep, which lasted from two till six, and his sister, being apprehensive of the return of his fit, came to the bedside, and, asking softly if he wanted anything, he turned about to her and spoke to this effect: Dear sister, you see me not only recovered out of a terrible fit, but likewise that I have the liberty of speech, a blessing that I have been deprived of almost sixty years, and I am satisfied you are sincerely joyful to find me in the state I now am in; but, alas! it is but a mistaken kindness. These are things but of short duration, and if they were to continue for a hundred years longer, I can't see how I should be anyways the better.

I know the world too well to be fond of it, and am fully satisfied that the difference between a long and a short life is insignificant, especially when I consider the accidents and company I am to encounter. Do but look seriously and impartially upon the astonishing notion of time and eternity, what an immense deal has run out already, and how infinite it is still in the future; do but seriously and deliberately consider this, and you will find, upon the whole, that three days and three ages of life come much to the same measure and reckoning.

As soon as he had ended his discourse upon the vanity and uncertainty of human life, he looked steadfastly upon her. Sister, says he, I conjure you not to be disturbed at what I am going to tell you, which you will undoubtedly find to be true in every particular. I perceive my glass is run, and I have now no more to do in this world but to take my leave of it; for to-morrow about this time my speech will be again taken from me, and, in a short time, my fit will return; and the next day, which I understand is the day on which I came into this troublesome world, I shall exchange it for another, where, for the future, I shall for ever be free from all manner of sin and sufferings.

The good woman would have made him a reply, but he prevented her by telling her he had no time to hearken to unnecessary complaints or animadversions. I have a great many things in my mind, says he, that require a speedy and serious consideration. The time I have to stay is but short, and I have a great deal of important business to do in it. Time and death are both in my view, and seem both to call aloud to me to make no delay. I beg of you, therefore, not to disquiet yourself or me. What must be, must be. The decrees of Providence are eternal and unalterable; why, then, should we torment ourselves about that which we cannot remedy?

I must confess, my dear sister, I owe you many obligations for your exemplary fondness to me, and do solemnly assure you I shall retain the sense of them to the last moment. All that I have to request of you is, that I may be alone for this night. I have it in my thoughts to leave some short observations behind me, and likewise to discover some things of great weight which have been revealed to me, which may perhaps be of some use hereafter to you and your friends. What credit they may meet with I cannot say, but depend the consequence, according to their respective periods, will account for them, and vindicate them against the supposition of falsity and mere suggestion.

Upon this, his sister left him till about four in the morning, when coming to his bedside to know if he wanted anything, and how he had rested, he made her this answer; I have been taking a cursory view of my life, and though I find myself exceedingly deficient in several particulars, yet I bless God I cannot find I have any just grounds to suspect my pardon. In short, says he, I have spent this night with more inward pleasure and true satisfaction than ever I spent a night through the whole course of my life.

After he had concluded what he had to say upon the satisfaction that attended an innocent and well-spent life, and observed what a mighty consolation it was to persons, not only under the apprehension, but even in the very agonies of death itself, he desired her to bring him his usual cup of water, and then to help him on with his clothes, that he might sit up, and so be in a better posture to take his leave of her and her friends.

When she had taken him up, and placed him at a table where he usually sat, he desired her to bring him his box of papers, and after he had collected those he intended should be preserved, he ordered her to bring a candle, that he might see the rest burnt. The good woman seemed at first to oppose the burning of his papers, till he told her they were only useless trifles, some unfinished observations which he had made in his youthful days, and were not fit to be seen by her, or anybody that should come after him.

After he had seen his papers burnt, and placed the rest in their proper order, and had likewise settled all his other affairs, which was only fit to be done between himself and his sister, he desired her to call two or three of the most reputable neighbours, not only to be witnesses of his will, but likewise to hear what he had farther to communicate before the return of his fit, which he expected very speedily.

His sister, who had beforehand acquainted two or three of her confidants with all that had happened, was very much rejoiced to hear her brother make so unexpected a concession; and accordingly, without any delay or hesitation, went directly into the neighbourhood, and brought home her two select friends, upon whose secrecy and sincerity she knew she might depend upon all accounts.

In her absence he felt several symptoms of the approach of his fit, which made him a little uneasy, lest it should entirely seize him before he had perfected his will, but that apprehension was quickly removed by her speedy return. After she had introduced her friends into his chamber, he proceeded to express himself in the following manner; Dear sister, you now see your brother upon the brink of eternity; and as the words of dying persons are commonly the most regarded, and make deepest impressions, I cannot suspect but you will suffer the few I am about to say to have always some place in your thoughts, that they may be ready for you to make use of upon any occasion.

Do not be fond of anything on this side of eternity, or suffer your interest to incline you to break your word, quit your modesty, or to do anything that will not bear the light, and look the world in the face. For be assured of this; the person that values the virtue of his mind and the dignity of his reason, is always easy and well fortified both against death and misfortune, and is perfectly indifferent about the length or shortness of his life. Such a one is solicitous about nothing but his own conduct, and for fear he should be deficient in the duties of religion, and the respective functions of reason and prudence.

Always go the nearest way to work. Now, the nearest way through all the business of human life, are the paths of religion and honesty, and keeping those as directly as you can, you avoid all the dangerous precipices that often lie in the road, and sometimes block up the passage entirely.

Remember that life was but lent at first, and that the remainder is more than you have reason to expect, and consequently ought to be managed with more than ordinary diligence. A wise man spends every day as if it were his last; his hourglass is always in his hand, and he is never guilty of sluggishness or insincerity.

He was about to proceed, when a sudden symptom of the return of his fit put him in mind that it was time to get his will witnessed, which was no sooner done but he took it up and gave it to his sister, telling her that though all he had was hers of right, yet he thought it proper, to prevent even a possibility of a dispute, to write down his mind in the nature of a will, wherein I have given you, says he, the little that I have left, except my books and papers, which, as soon as I am dead, I desire may be delivered to Mr. Anthony Barlow, a near relation of my worthy master, Mr. Owen Parry.

This Mr. Anthony Barlow was an old contemplative Welsh gentleman, who, being under some difficulties in his own country, was forced to come into Cornwall and take sanctuary among the tinners. Dickory, though he kept himself as retired as possible, happened to meet him one day upon his walks, and presently remembered that he was the very person that used frequently to come to visit his master while he lived in Pembrokeshire, and so went to him, and by signs made him understand who he was.

The old gentleman, though at first surprised at this unexpected interview, soon recollected that he had formerly seen at Mr. Parry's a dumb man, whom they used to call the dumb philosopher, so concludes immediately that consequently this must be he. In short, they soon made themselves known to each other; and from that time contracted a strict friendship and a correspondence by letters, which for the future they mutually managed with the greatest exactness and familiarity.

But to leave this as a matter not much material, and to return to our narrative. By this time Dickory's speech began to falter, which his sister observing, put him in mind that he would do well to make some declaration of his faith and principles of religion, because some reflections had been made upon him upon the account of his neglect, or rather his refusal, to appear at any place of public worship.

"Dear sister," says he, "you observe very well, and I wish the continuance of my speech for a few moments, that I might make an ample declaration upon that account. But I find that cannot be; my speech is leaving me so fast that I can only tell you that I have always lived, and now die, an unworthy member of the ancient catholic and apostolic church; and as to my faith and principles, I refer you to my papers, which, I hope, will in some measure vindicate me against the reflections you mention."

He had hardly finished his discourse to his sister and her two friends, and given some short directions relating to his burial, but his speech left him; and what makes the thing the more remarkable, it went away, in all appearance, without giving him any sort of pain or uneasiness.

When he perceived that his speech was entirely vanished, and that he was again in his original state of dumbness, he took his pen as formerly and wrote to his sister, signifying that whereas the sudden loss of his speech had deprived him of the opportunity to speak to her and her friends what he intended, he would leave it for them in writing, and so desired he might not be disturbed till the return of his fit, which he expected in six hours at farthest. According to his desire they all left him, and then, with the greatest resignation imaginable, he wrote down the meditations following:

PART II

An Abstract of his Faith, and the Principles of his Religion &c., which begins thus:

Dear Sister; I thank you for putting me in mind to make a declaration of my faith, and the principles of my religion. I find, as you very well observe, I have been under some reflections upon that account, and therefore I think it highly requisite that I set that matter right in the first place. To begin, therefore, with my faith, in which I intend to be as short and as comprehensive as I can:

I. I most firmly believe that it was the eternal will of God, and the result of his infinite wisdom, to create a world, and for the glory of his majesty to make several sorts of creatures in order and degree one after another; that is to say, angels, or pure immortal spirits; men, consisting of immortal spirits and matter, having rational and sensitive souls; brutes, having mortal and sensitive souls; and mere vegetatives, such as trees, plants, &c.; and these creatures so made do, as it were, clasp the higher and lower world together.

2. I believe the holy Scriptures, and everything therein contained, to be the pure and essential word of God; and that, according to these sacred writings, man, the lord and prince of the creation, by his disobedience in Paradise, forfeited his innocence and the dignity of his nature, and subjected himself and all his posterity to sin and misery.

3. I believe and am fully and entirely satisfied, that God the Father, out of his infinite goodness and compassion to mankind, was pleased to send his only Son, the second person in the holy and undivided Trinity, to meditate for him, and to procure his redemption and eternal salvation.

4. I believe that God the Son, out of his infinite love, and for the glory of the Deity, was pleased voluntarily and freely to descend from heaven, and to take our nature upon him, and to lead an exemplary life of purity, holiness, and perfect obedience, and at last to suffer an ignominious death upon the cross, for the sins of the whole world, and to rise again the third day for our justification.

5. I believe that the Holy Ghost out of his infinite goodness was pleased to undertake the office of sanctifying us with his divine grace, and thereby assisting us with faith to believe, will to desire, and power to do all those things that are required of us in this world, in order to

entitle us to the blessings of just men made perfect in the world to come.

6. I believe that these three persons are of equal power, majesty, and duration, and that the Godhead of the Father, of the Son, and of the Holy Ghost is all one, and that they are equally uncreate, incomprehensible, eternal, and almighty; and that none is greater or less than the other, but that every one hath one and the same divine nature and perfections.

These, sister, are the doctrines which have been received and practised by the best men of every age, from the beginning of the Christian religion to this day, and it is upon this I ground my faith and hopes of salvation, not doubting but, if my life and practice have been answerable to them, that I shall be quickly translated out of this kingdom of darkness, out of this world of sorrow, vexation and confusion, into that blessed kingdom, where I shall cease to grieve and to suffer, and shall be happy to all eternity.

As to my principles in religion, to be as brief as I can, I declare myself to be a member of Christ's church, which I take to be a universal society of all Christian people, distributed under lawful governors and pastors into particular churches, holding communion with each other in all the essentials of the Christian faith, worship, and discipline; and among these I look upon the Church of England to be the chief and best constituted.

The Church of England is doubtless the great bulwark of the ancient Catholic or Apostolic faith all over the world; a church that has all the spiritual advantages that the nature of a church is capable of. From the doctrine and principles of the Church of England, we are taught loyalty to our prince, fidelity to our country, and justice to all mankind; and therefore, as I look upon this to be one of the most excellent branches of the Church Universal, and stands, as it were, between superstition and hypocrisy, I therefore declare, for the satisfaction of you and your friends, as I have always lived so I now die, a true and sincere, though a most unworthy member of it. And as to my discontinuance of my attendance at the public worship, I refer you to my papers, which I have left with my worthy friend, Mr. Barlow. And thus, my dear sister, I have given you a short account of my faith, and the principles of my religion. I come, in the next place, to lay before you a few meditations and observations I have at several times collected together, more particularly those since my retirement to St. Helen's.

Meditations and Observations relating to the Conduct of Human Life in general.

1. Remember how often you have neglected the great duties of religion and virtue, and slighted the opportunities that Providence has put into your hands; and, withal, that you have a set period assigned you for the management of the affairs of human life; and then reflect seriously that, unless you resolve immediately to improve the little remains, the whole must necessarily slip away insensibly, and then you are lost beyond recovery.

2. Let an unaffected gravity, freedom, justice, and sincerity shine through all your actions, and let no fancies and chimeras give the least check to those excellent qualities. This is an easy task, if you will but suppose everything you do to be your last, and if you can keep your passions and appetites from crossing your reason. Stand clear of rashness, and have nothing of insincerity or self-love to infect you.

3. Manage all your thoughts and actions with such prudence and circumspection as if you were sensible you were just going to step into the grave. A little thinking will show a man the vanity and uncertainty of all sublunary things, and enable him to examine maturely the manner of dying; which, if duly abstracted from the terror of the idea, will appear nothing more than an unavoidable appendix of life itself, and a pure natural action.

4. Consider that ill-usage from some sort of people is in a manner necessary, and therefore do not be disquieted about it, but rather conclude that you and your enemy are both marching off the stage together, and that in a little time your very memories will be extinguished.

5. Among your principal observations upon human life, let it be always one to take notice what a great deal both of time and ease that man gains who is not troubled with the spirit of curiosity, who lets his neighbours' affairs alone, and confines his inspections to himself, and only takes care of honesty and a good conscience.

6. If you would live at your ease, and as much as possible be free from the incumbrances of life, manage but a few things at once, and let those, too, be such as are absolutely necessary. By this rule you will draw the bulk of your business into a narrow compass, and have the double pleasure of making your actions good, and few into the bargain.

7. He that torments himself because things do not happen just as he would have them, is but a sort of ulcer in the world; and he that is selfish, narrow-souled, and sets up for a separate interest, is a kind of voluntary outlaw, and disincorporates himself from mankind.

8. Never think anything below you which reason and your own circumstances require, and never suffer yourself to be deterred by the ill-grounded notions of censure and reproach; but when honesty and conscience prompt you to say or do anything, do it boldly; never balk your resolution or start at the consequence.

9. If a man does me an injury, what is that to me? It is his own action, and let him account for it. As for me, I am in my proper station, and only doing the business that Providence has allotted; and withal, I ought to consider that the best way to revenge, is not to imitate the injury.

10. When you happen to be ruffled and put out of humour by any cross accident, retire immediately into your reason, and do not suffer your passion to overrule you a moment; for the sooner you recover yourself now, the better you will be able to guard yourself for the future.

11. Do not be like those ill-natured people that, though they do not love to give a good word to their contemporaries, yet are mighty fond of their own commendations. This argues a perverse and unjust temper, and often exposes the authors to scorn and contempt.

12. If any one convinces you of an error, change your opinion and thank him for it: truth and information are your business, and can never hurt anybody. On the contrary, he that is proud and stubborn, and wilfully continues in a mistake, it is he that receives the mischief.

13. Because you see a thing difficult, do not instantly conclude it to be impossible to master it. Diligence and industry are seldom defeated. Look, therefore, narrowly into the thing itself, and what you observe proper and practicable in another, conclude likewise within your own power.

14. The principal business of human life is run through within the short compass of twenty-four hours; and when you have taken a deliberate view of the present age, you have seen as much as if you had begun with the world, the rest being nothing else but an endless round of the same thing over and over again.

15. Bring your will to your fate, and suit your mind to your circumstances. Love your friends and forgive your enemies, and do

justice to all mankind, and you will be secure to make your passage easy, and enjoy most of the comforts human life is capable to afford you.

16. When you have a mind to entertain yourself in your retirements, let it be with the good qualifications of your friends and acquaintance. Think with pleasure and satisfaction upon the honour and bravery of one, the modesty of another, the generosity of a third, and so on; there being nothing more pleasant and diverting than the lively images and the advantages of those we love and converse with.

17. As nothing can deprive you of the privileges of your nature, or compel you to act counter to your reason, so nothing can happen to you but what comes from Providence, and consists with the interest of the universe.

18. Let people's tongues and actions be what they will, your business is to have honour and honesty in your view. Let them rail, revile, censure, and condemn, or make you the subject of their scorn and ridicule, what does it all signify? You have one certain remedy against all their malice and folly, and that is, to live so that nobody shall believe them.

19. Alas, poor mortals! did we rightly consider our own state and condition, we should find it would not be long before we have forgot all the world, and to be even, that all the world will have forgot us likewise.

20. He that would recommend himself to the public, let him do it by the candour and modesty of his behaviour, and by a generous indifference to external advantages. Let him love mankind, and resign to Providence, and then his works will follow him, and his good actions will praise him in the gate.

21. When you hear a discourse, let your understanding, as far as possible, keep pace with it, and lead you forward to those things which fall most within the compass of your own observations.

22. When vice and treachery shall be rewarded, and virtue and ability slighted and discountenanced; when ministers of state shall rather fear man than God, and to screen themselves run into parties and factions; when noise and clamour, and scandalous reports shall carry everything before them, it is natural to conclude that a nation in such a state of infatuation stands upon the brink of destruction, and without the intervention of some unforeseen accident, must be inevitably ruined.

23. When a prince is guarded by wise and honest men, and when all public officers are sure to be rewarded if they do well, and punished if they do evil, the consequence is plain; justice and honesty will

flourish, and men will be always contriving, not for themselves, but for the honour and interest of their king and country.

24. Wicked men may sometimes go unpunished in this world, but wicked nations never do; because this world is the only place of punishment of wicked nations, though not for private and particular persons.

25. An administration that is merely founded upon human policy must be always subject to human chance; but that which is founded on the divine wisdom can no more miscarry than the government of heaven. To govern by parties and factions is the advice of an atheist, and sets up a government by the spirit of Satan. In such a government the prince can never be secure under the greatest promises, since, as men's interest changes, so will their duty and affections likewise.

26. It is a very ancient observation, and a very true one, that people generally despise where they flatter, and cringe to those they design to betray; so that truth and ceremony are, and always will be, two distinct things.

27. When you find your friend in an error, undeceive him with secrecy and civility, and let him see his oversight first by hints and glances; and if you cannot convince him, leave him with respect, and lay the fault upon your own management.

28. When you are under the greatest vexations, then consider that human life lasts but for a moment; and do not forget but that you are like the rest of the world, and faulty yourself in many instances; and withal, remember that anger and impatience often prove more mischievous than the provocation.

29. Gentleness and good humour are invincible, provided they are without hypocrisy and design; they disarm the most barbarous and savage tempers, and make even malice ashamed of itself.

30. In all the actions of life let it be your first and principal care to guard against anger on the one hand, and flattery on the other, for they are both unserviceable qualities, and do a great deal of mischief in the government of human life.

31. When a man turns knave or libertine, and gives way to fear, jealousy, and fits of the spleen; when his mind complains of his fortune, and he quits the station in which Providence has placed him, he acts perfectly counter to humanity, deserts his own nature, and, as it were, runs away from himself.

32. Be not heavy in business, disturbed in conversation, nor impertinent in your thoughts. Let your judgment be right, your actions

friendly, and your mind contented; let them curse you, threaten you, or despise you; let them go on; they can never injure your reason or your virtue, and then all the rest that they can do to you signifies nothing.

33. The only pleasure of human life is doing the business of the creation; and which way is that to be compassed very easily? Most certainly by the practice of general kindness, by rejecting the importunity of our senses, by distinguishing truth from falsehood, and by contemplating the works of the Almighty.

34. Be sure to mind that which lies before you, whether it be thought, word, or action; and never postpone an opportunity, or make virtue wait for you till to-morrow.

35. Whatever tends neither to the improvement of your reason nor the benefit of society, think it below you; and when you have done any considerable service to mankind, do not lessen it by your folly in gaping after reputation and requital.

36. When you find yourself sleepy in a morning, rouse yourself, and consider that you are born to business, and that in doing good in your generation, you answer your character and act like a man; whereas sleep and idleness do but degrade you, and sink you down to a brute.

37. A mind that has nothing of hope, or fear, or aversion, or desire, to weaken and disturb it, is the most impregnable security. Hither we may with safety retire and defy our enemies; and he that sees not this advantage must be extremely ignorant, and he that forgets it unhappy.

38. Do not disturb yourself about the faults of other people, but let everybody's crimes be at their own door. Have always this great maxim in your remembrance, that to play the knave is to rebel against religion; all sorts of injustice being no less than high treason against Heaven itself.

39. Do not contemn death, but meet it with a decent and religious fortitude, and look upon it as one of those things which Providence has ordered. If you want a cordial to make the apprehensions of dying go down a little the more easily, consider what sort of world and what sort of company you will part with. To conclude, do but look seriously into the world, and there you will see multitudes of people preparing for funerals, and mourning for their friends and acquaintances; and look out again a little afterwards, and you will see others doing the very same thing for them.

40. In short, men are but poor transitory things. To-day they are busy and harassed with the affairs of human life; and to-morrow life

itself is taken from them, and they are returned to their original dust and ashes.

PART III

Containing prophetic observations relating to the affairs of Europe and of Great Britain, more particularly from 1720 to 1729.

1. In the latter end of 1720, an eminent old lady shall bring forth five sons at a birth; the youngest shall live and grow up to maturity, but the four eldest shall either die in the nursery, or be all carried off by one sudden and unexpected accident.

2. About this time a man with a double head shall arrive in Britain from the south. One of these heads shall deliver messages of great importance to the governing party, and the other to the party that is opposite to them. The first shall believe the monster, but the last shall discover the impostor, and so happily disengage themselves from a snare that was laid to destroy them and their posterity. After this the two heads shall unite, and the monster shall appear in his proper shape.

3. In the year 1721, a philosopher from Lower Germany shall come, first to Amsterdam in Holland, and afterwards to London. He will bring with him a world of curiosities, and among them a pretended secret for the transmutation of metals. Under the umbrage of this mighty secret he shall pass upon the world for some time; but at length he shall be detected, and proved to be nothing but an empiric and a cheat, and so forced to sneak off, and leave the people he has deluded, either to bemoan their loss, or laugh at their own folly. N.B.—This will be the last of his sect that will ever venture in this part of the world upon the same errand.

4. In this year great endeavours will be used for procuring a general peace, which shall be so near a conclusion that public rejoicings shall be made at the courts of several great potentates upon that account; but just in the critical juncture, a certain neighbouring prince shall come to a violent death, which shall occasion new war and commotion all over Europe; but these shall continue but for a short time, and at last terminate in the utter destruction of the first aggressors.

5. Towards the close of this year of mysteries, a person that was born blind shall have his sight restored, and shall see ravens perch upon the heads of traitors, among which the head of a notorious prelate shall stand upon the highest pole.

6. In the year 1722, there shall be a grand congress, and new overtures of peace offered by most of the principal parties concerned in

the war, which shall have so good effect that a cessation of arms shall be agreed upon for six months, which shall be kept inviolable till a certain general, either through treachery or inadvertency, shall begin hostilities before the expiration of the term; upon which the injured prince shall draw his sword, and throw the scabbard into the sea, vowing never to return it till he shall obtain satisfaction for himself, and done justice to all that were oppressed.

7. At the close of this year, a famous bridge shall be broken down, and the water that runs under it shall be tinctured with the blood of two notorious malefactors, whose unexpected death shall make mighty alterations in the present state of affairs, and put a stop to the ruin of a nation, which must otherwise have been unavoidable.

8. 1723 begins with plots, conspiracies, and intestine commotions in several countries; nor shall Great Britain itself be free from the calamity. These shall continue till a certain young prince shall take the reins of government into his own hands; and after that, a marriage shall be proposed, and an alliance concluded between two great potentates, who shall join their forces, and endeavour, in good earnest, to set all matters upon a right foundation.

9. This year several cardinals and prelates shall be publicly censured for heretical principles, and shall narrowly escape from being torn to pieces by the common people, who still look upon them as the grand disturbers of public tranquillity, perfect incendiaries, and the chief promoters of their former, present, and future calamities.

10. In 1724-5 there will be many treaties and negociations, and Great Britain, particularly, will be crowded with foreign ministers and ambassadors from remote princes and states. Trade and commerce will begin to flourish and revive, and everything will have a comfortable prospect, until some desperadoes, assisted by a monster with many heads, shall start new difficulties, and put the world again into a flame; but these shall be but of short duration.

11. Before the expiration of 1725, an eagle from the north shall fly directly to the south, and perch upon the palace of a prince, and first unravel the bloody projects and designs of a wicked set of people, and then publicly discover the murder of a great king, and the intended assassination of another greater than he.

12. In 1726, three princes will be born that will grow up to be men, and inherit the crowns of three of the greatest monarchies in Europe.

13. About this time the pope will die, and after a great many intrigues and struggles, a Spanish cardinal shall be elected, who shall decline the dignity, and declare his marriage with a great lady, heiress of one of the chief principalities in Italy, which may occasion new troubles in Europe, if not timely prevented.

14. In 1727, new troubles shall break out in the north, occasioned by the sudden death of a certain prince, and the avarice and ambition of another. Poor Poland seems to be pointed at; but the princes of the south shall enter into a confederacy to preserve her, and shall at length restore her peace, and prevent the perpetual ruin of her constitution.

15. Great endeavours will be used about this time for a comprehension in religion, supported by crafty and designing men, and a party of mistaken zealots, which they shall artfully draw in to join with them; but as the project is ill-concerted, and will be worse managed, it will come to nothing; and soon afterwards an effectual mode will be taken to prevent the like attempt for the future.

16. 1728 will be a year of inquiry and retrospection. Many exorbitant grants will be reassumed, and several persons who thought themselves secure will be called before the senate, and compelled to disgorge what they have unjustly pillaged either from the crown or the public.

17. About this time a new scaffold will be erected upon the confines of a certain great city, where an old count of a new extraction, that has been of all parties and true to none, will be doomed by his peers to make his first appearance. After this an old lady who has often been exposed to danger and disgrace, and sometimes brought to the very brink of destruction, will be brought to bed of three daughters at once, which they shall call Plenty, Peace, and Union; and these three shall live and grow up together, be the glory of their mother, and the comfort of posterity for many generations.

* * * * *

This is the substance of what he either writ or extracted from his papers in the interval between the loss of his speech and the return of his fit, which happened exactly at the time he had computed.

Upon the approach of his fit, he made signs to be put to bed, which was no sooner done but he was seized with extreme agonies, which he bore up under with the greatest steadfastness, and after a severe conflict, that lasted near eight hours, he expired.

Thus lived and thus died this extraordinary person; a person, though of mean extraction and obscure life, yet when his character comes to be fully and truly known, it will be read with pleasure, profit, and admiration.

His perfections at large would be the work of a volume, and inconsistent with the intention of these papers. I will, therefore, only add, for a conclusion, that he was a man of uncommon thought and judgment, and always kept his appetites and inclinations within their just limits.

His reason was strong and manly, his understanding sound and active, and his temper so easy, equal, and complaisant, that he never fell out, either with men or accidents. He bore all things with the highest affability, and computed justly upon their value and consequence, and then applied them to their proper uses.

A LETTER FROM OXFORD

Sir,

Being informed that you speedily intend to publish some memoirs relating to our dumb countryman, Dickory Cronke, I send you herewith a few lines, in the nature of an elegy, which I leave you to dispose of as you think fit. I knew and admired the man; and if I were capable, his character should be the first thing I would attempt.

Yours. &c.

AN ELEGY,
IN MEMORY OF DICKORY CRONKE,
THE DUMB PHILOSOPHER.

> Vitiis nemo sine nascitur; optimus ille est,
> Qui minimus urgetur.
> —HORACE.

If virtuous actions emulation raise,
Then this good man deserves immortal praise.
When nature such extensive wisdom lent,
She sure designed him for our precedent.
Such great endowments in a man unknown,
Declare the blessings were not all his own;
But rather granted for a time to show
What the wise hand of Providence can do.
In him we may a bright example see
Of nature, justice, and morality;
A mind not subject to the frowns of fate,
But calm and easy in a servile state.
He always kept a guard upon his will
And feared no harm because he knew no ill.
A decent posture and an humble mien,
In every action of his life were seen.
Through all the different stages that he went,
He still appeared both wise and diligent:
Firm to his word, and punctual to his trust,
Sagacious, frugal, arable, and just.

No gainful views his bounded hopes could sway,
No wanton thought led his chaste soul astray.
In short, his thoughts and actions both declare,
Nature designed him her philosopher;
That all mankind, by his example taught,
Might learn to live, and manage every thought.
Oh! could my muse the wondrous subject grace,
And, from his youth, his virtuous actions trace;
Could I in just and equal numbers tell
How well he lived, and how devoutly fell,
I boldly might your strict attention claim,
And bid you learn, and copy out the man.

J. P.
Exeter College, August 25th, 1719.

EPITAPH

The occasion of this epitaph was briefly thus:—A gentleman, who had heard much in commendation of this dumb man, going accidentally to the churchyard where he was buried, and finding his grave without a tombstone, or any manner of memorandum of his death, he pulled out his pencil, and writ as follows:—

PAUPER UBIQUE JACET.

Near to this lonely unfrequented place,
Mixed with the common dust, neglected lies
The man that every muse should strive to grace,
And all the world should for his virtue prize.
Stop, gentle passenger, and drop a tear,
Truth, justice, wisdom, all lie buried here.

What, though he wants a monumental stone,
The common pomp of every fool or knave,
Those virtues which through all his actions shone
Proclaim his worth, and praise him in the grave.
His merits will a bright example give,
Which shall both time and envy too outlive.

Oh, had I power but equal to my mind,
A decent tomb should soon this place adorn,
With this inscription: Lo, here lies confined
A wondrous man, although obscurely born;
A man, though dumb, yet he was nature's care,
Who marked him out her own philosopher.

THE

TRUE-BORN ENGLISHMAN:

A

SATIRE.

Statuimus pacem, et securitatem et concordiam judicum et justiciam
inter Anglos et Normannos, Francos et Britanes, Walliæ, et Cornubiæ,
Pictos et Scotos, Albaniæ, similiter inter Francos et insulanos provincias
et patrias, quæ pertinent ad coronam nostram, et inter omnes nobis
subjectos firmiter et inviolabiliter observare.

> --Charta Regis Gullielmi Conquisitoris de Pacis Publica, cap. i.

AN

EXPLANATORY PREFACE.

It is not that I see any reason to alter my opinion in any thing I have writ, which occasions this epistle; but I find it necessary for the satisfaction of some persons of honour, as well as wit, to pass a short explication upon it; and tell the world what I mean, or rather, what I do not mean, in some things wherein I find I am liable to be misunderstood.

I confess myself something surpris'd to hear that I am taxed with bewraying my own nest, and abusing our nation, by discovering the meanness of our original, in order to make the English contemptible abroad and at home; in which, I think, they are mistaken: for why should not our neighbours be as good as we to derive from? And I must add, that had we been an unmix'd nation, I am of opinion it had been to our disadvantage: for to go no farther, we have three nations about us as clear from mixtures of blood as any in the world, and I know not which of them I could wish ourselves to be like; I mean the Scots, the Welsh, and the Irish; and if I were to write a reverse to the Satire, I would examine all the nations of Europe, and prove, that those nations which are most mix'd, are the best, and have least of barbarism and brutality among them; and abundance of reasons might be given for it, too long to bring into a Preface.

But I give this hint, to let the world know, that I am far from thinking, 'tis a Satire upon the English nation, to tell them, they are derived from all the nations under heaven; that is, from several nations. Nor is it meant to undervalue the original of the English, for we see no reason to like them worse, being the relicts of Romans, Danes, Saxons and Normans, than we should have done if they had remain'd Britons, that is, than if they had been all Welshmen.

But the intent of the Satire is pointed at the vanity of those who talk of their antiquity, and value themselves upon their pedigree, their ancient families, and being true-born; whereas 'tis impossible we should be true-born: and if we could, should have lost by the bargain.

These sort of people, who call themselves true-born, and tell long stories of their families, and like a nobleman of Venice, think a foreigner ought not to walk on the same side of the street with them, are own'd to be meant in this Satire. What they would infer from their long original, I know not, nor is it easy to make out whether they are the better or the worse for their ancestors: our English nation may value themselves for their wit, wealth and courage, and I believe few nations will dispute it with them; but for long originals, and ancient true-born families of English, I would advise them to wave the discourse. A true Englishman is one that deserves a character, and I have nowhere lessened him, that I know of; but as for a true-born Englishman, I confess I do not understand him.

From hence I only infer, that an Englishman, of all men, ought not to despise foreigners as such, and I think the inference is just, since what they are to-day, we were yesterday, and to-morrow they will be like us. If foreigners misbehave in their several stations and employments, I have nothing to do with that; the laws are open to punish them equally with natives, and let them have no favour.

But when I see the town full of lampoons and invectives against Dutchmen, only because they are foreigners, and the king reproached and insulted by insolent pedants, and ballad-making poets, for employing foreigners, and for being a foreigner himself, I confess myself moved by it to remind our nation of their own original, thereby to let them see what a banter is put upon ourselves in it; since speaking of Englishmen *ab origine*, we are really all foreigners ourselves.

I could go on to prove it is also impolitic in us to discourage foreigners; since it is easy to make it appear that the multitudes of foreign nations who have taken sanctuary here, have been the greatest additions to the wealth and strength of the nation; the essential whereof is the number of its inhabitants; nor would this nation ever have arrived to the degree of wealth and glory it now boasts of, if the addition of foreign nations, both as to manufactures and arms, had not been helpful to it. This is so plain, that he who is ignorant of it, is too dull to be talked with.

The Satire therefore I must allow to be just, till I am otherwise convinced; because nothing can be more ridiculous than to hear our people boast of that antiquity, which if it had been true, would have left us in so much worse a condition than we are in now: whereas we ought rather to boast among our neighbours, that we are part of themselves, of the same original as they, but bettered by our climate, and like our language and manufactures, derived from them, and improved by us to a perfection greater than they can pretend to.

This we might have valued ourselves upon without vanity; but to disown our descent from them, talk big of our ancient families, and long originals, and stand at a distance from foreigners, like the enthusiast in religion, with a Stand off, I am more holy than thou: this is a thing so ridiculous, in a nation derived from foreigners, as we are, that I could not but attack them as I have done.

And whereas I am threatened to be called to a public account for this freedom; and the publisher of this has been newspapered into gaol already for it; tho' I see nothing in it for which the government can be displeased; yet if at the same time those people who with an unlimited arrogance in print, every day affront the king, prescribe the parliament, and lampoon the government, may be either punished or restrained, I am content to stand and fall by the public justice of my native country, which I am not sensible I have anywhere injured.

Nor would I be misunderstood concerning the clergy; with whom, if I have taken any license more than becomes a Satire, I question not but those gentlemen, who are men of letters, are also men of so much candor, as to allow me a loose at the crimes of the guilty, without thinking the whole profession lashed who are innocent. I profess to have very mean thoughts of those gentlemen who have deserted their own principles, and exposed even their morals as well as loyalty; but not at all to think it affects any but such as are concerned in the fact.

Nor would I be misrepresented as to the ingratitude of the English to the king and his friends; as if I meant the English as a nation, are so. The contrary is so apparent, that I would hope it should not be suggested of me: and, therefore when I have brought in Britannia speaking of the king, I suppose her to be the representative or mouth of the nation, as a body. But if I say we are full of such who daily affront the king, and abuse his friends; who print scurrilous pamphlets, virulent lampoons, and reproachful public banters, against both the king's person and his government; I say nothing but what is too true; and that the Satire is directed at such, I freely own; and cannot say, but I should think it very hard to be censured for this Satire, while such remain unquestioned and tacitly approved. That I can mean none but such, is plain from these few lines,

Ye heavens regard! Almighty Jove, look down,
And view thy injured monarch on the throne.
On their ungrateful heads due vengeance take,
Who sought his aid, and then his part forsake.

If I have fallen rudely upon our vices, I hope none but the vicious will be angry. As for writing for interest, I disown it; I have neither place, nor pension, nor prospect; nor seek none, nor will have none: if matter of fact justifies the truth of the crimes, the Satire is just. As to the poetic liberties, I hope the crime is pardonable; I am content to be stoned, provided none will attack me but the innocent.

If my countrymen would take the hint, and grow better natured from my ill-natured poem as some call it; I would say this of it, that though it is far from the best Satire that ever was wrote, it would do the most good that ever Satire did.

And yet I am ready to ask pardon of some gentlemen too; who though they are Englishmen, have good nature enough to see themselves reproved, and can hear it. These are gentlemen in a true sense, that can bare to be told of their *faux pas*, and not abuse the reprover. To such I must say, this is no Satire; they are exceptions to the general rule; and I value my performance from their generous approbation, more than I can from any opinion I have of its worth.

The hasty errors of my verse I made my excuse for before; and since the time I have been upon it has been but little, and my leisure less, I have all along strove rather to make the thoughts explicit, than the poem correct. However, I have mended some faults in this edition, and the rest must be placed to my account.

As to answers, banters, true English Billingsgate, I expect them till nobody will buy, and then the shop will be shut. Had I wrote it for the gain of the press, I should have been concerned at its being printed again, and again, by pirates, as they call them, and paragraph-men; but would they but do it justice, and print it true, according to the copy, they are welcome to sell it for a penny, if they please.

The pence, indeed, is the end of their works. I will engage if nobody will buy, nobody will write: and not a patriot poet of them all, now will in defence of his native country, which I have abused, they say, print an answer to it, and give it about for God's sake.

PREFACE.

The end of satire is reformation: and the author, though he doubt the work of conversion is at a general stop, has put his hand in the plough. I expect a storm of ill language from the fury of the town. And especially from those whose English talent it is to rail: and, without being taken for a conjuror, I may venture to foretel, that I shall be cavilled at about my mean style, rough verse, and incorrect language, things I indeed might have taken more care in. But the book is printed; and though I see some faults, it is too late to mend them. And this is all I think needful to say to them.

Possibly somebody may take me for a Dutchman; in which they are mistaken: but I am one that would be glad to see Englishmen behave themselves better to strangers, and to governors also, that one might not be reproached in foreign countries for belonging to a nation that wants manners.

I assure you, gentlemen, strangers use us better abroad; and we can give no reason but our ill-nature for the contrary here.

Methinks an Englishman who is so proud of being called a good fellow, should be civil. And it cannot be denied, but we are, in many cases, and particularly to strangers, the most churlish people alive.

As to vices, who can dispute our intemperance, while an honest drunken fellow is a character in a man's praise? All our reformations are banters, and will be so till our magistrates and gentry reform themselves, by way of example; then, and not till then, they may be expected to punish others without blushing.

As to our ingratitude, I desire to be understood of that particular people, who pretending to be Protestants, have all along endeavoured to reduce the liberties and religion of this nation into the hands of King James and his Popish powers: together with such who enjoy the peace and protection of the present government, and yet abuse and affront the king who procured it, and openly profess their uneasiness under him: these, by whatsoever names or titles they are dignified or distinguished, are the people aimed at; nor do I disown, but that it is so much the temper of an Englishman to abuse his benefactor, that I could be glad to see it rectified.

They who think I have been guilty of any error, in exposing the crimes of my own countrymen to themselves, may, among many honest instances of the like nature, find the same thing in Mr. Cowley, in his imitation of the second Olympic Ode of Pindar; his words are these:—

But in this thankless world, the givers
Are envied even by the receivers.
'Tis now the cheap and frugal fashion,
Rather to hide than pay an obligation.
Nay, 'tis much worse than so;
It now an artifice doth grow,
Wrongs and outrages they do,
Lest men should think we owe.

THE INTRODUCTION.

Speak, Satire, for there's none can tell like thee,
Whether 'tis folly, pride, or knavery,
That makes this discontented land appear
Less happy now in times of peace, than war:
Why civil feuds disturb the nation more,
Than all our bloody wars have done before.

Fools out of favour grudge at knaves in place,
And men are always honest in disgrace:
The court preferments make men knaves in course:
But they which wou'd be in them wou'd be worse.
'Tis not at foreigners that we repine,
Wou'd foreigners their perquisites resign:
The grand contention's plainly to be seen,
To get some men put out, and some put in.
For this our Senators make long harangues.
And florid Ministers whet their polish'd tongues.
Statesmen are always sick of one disease;
And a good pension gives them present ease.
That's the specific makes them all content
With any King and any government.
Good patriots at court abuses rail,
And all the nation's grievances bewail:
But when the sov'reign balsam's once apply'd,
The zealot never fails to change his side;
And when he must the golden key resign,
The railing spirit comes about again.

Who shall this bubbl'd nation disabuse,
While they their own felicities refuse?
Who at the wars have made such mighty pother,
And now are falling out with one another:
With needless fears the jealous nations fill,
And always have been sav'd against their will:
Who fifty millions sterling have disburs'd

To be with peace, and too much plenty, curs'd;
Who their old monarch eagerly undo,
And yet uneasily obey the new.
Search, Satire, search; a deep incision make:
The poison's strong, the antidote's too weak.
'Tis pointed truth must manage this dispute,
And down-right English, Englishmen confute.

Whet thy just anger at the nation's pride;
And with keen phrase repel the vicious tide,
To Englishmen their own beginnings show,
And ask them, why they slight their neighbours so:
Go back to elder times, and ages past,
And nations into long oblivion cast;
To elder Britain's youthful days retire,
And there for true-born Englishmen inquire,
Britannia freely will disown the name,
And hardly knows herself from whence they came;
Wonders that they of all men should pretend
To birth, and blood, and for a name contend.
Go back to causes where our follies dwell,
And fetch the dark original from hell:
Speak, Satire, for there's none like thee can tell.

THE

TRUE-BORN ENGLISHMAN.

PART I.

Wherever God erects a house of prayer,
The Devil always builds a chapel there:
And 'twill be found upon examination,
The latter has the largest congregation:
For ever since he first debauch'd the mind,
He made a perfect conquest of mankind.
With uniformity of service, he
Reigns with general aristocracy.
No non-conforming sects disturb his reign,
For of his yoke, there's very few complain.
He knows the genius and the inclination,
And matches proper sins for ev'ry nation.
He needs no standing army government;
He always rules us by our own consent:
His laws are easy, and his gentle sway
Makes it exceeding pleasant to obey.
The list of his vicegerents and commanders,
Out-does your Cæsars, or your Alexanders.
They never fail of his infernal aid,
And he's as certain ne'er to be betray'd.
Thro' all the world they spread his vast command,
And death's eternal empire is maintain'd.
They rule so politicly and so well,
As if they were Lords Justices of hell;
Duly divided to debauch mankind,
And plant infernal dictates in his mind.

Pride, the first peer, and president of hell,
To his share, Spain, the largest province fell.
The subtle Prince thought fittest to bestow

On these the golden mines of Mexico,
With all the silver mountains of Peru;
Wealth which in wise hands would the world undo;
Because he knew their genius was such,
Too lazy and too haughty to be rich:
So proud a people, so above their fate,
That, if reduced to beg, they'll beg in state:
Lavish of money, to be counted brave,
And proudly starve, because they scorn to save;
Never was nation in the world before,
So very rich, and yet so very poor.

Lust chose the torrid zone of Italy,
Where blood ferments in rapes and sodomy:
Where swelling veins o'erflow with living streams,
With heat impregnate from Vesuvian flames;
Whose flowing sulphur forms infernal lakes,
And human body of the soil partakes.
There nature ever burns with hot desires,
Fann'd with luxuriant air from subterranean fires:
Here undisturbed, in floods of scalding lust,
Th' infernal king reigns with infernal gust.

Drunkenness, the darling favourite of hell,
Chose Germany to rule; and rules so well,
No subjects more obsequiously obey,
None please so well, or are so pleased as they;
The cunning artist manages so well,
He lets them bow to heav'n, and drink to hell.
If but to wine and him they homage pay,
He cares not to what deity they pray;
What god they worship most, or in what way.
Whether by Luther, Calvin, or by Rome,
They sail for heaven, by wine he steers them home.

Ungovern'd passion settled first in France,
Where mankind lives in haste, and thrives by chance;
A dancing nation, fickle and untrue,
Have oft undone themselves, and others too;
Prompt the infernal dictates to obey,

And in hell's favour none more great than they.

The pagan world he blindly leads away,
And personally rules with arbitrary sway:
The mask thrown off, plain devil, his title stands;
And what elsewhere he tempts, he there commands;
There, with full gust, th' ambition of his mind,
Governs, as he of old in heaven design'd:
Worshipp'd as God, his Paynim altars smoke,
Imbrued with blood of those that him invoke.

The rest by deputies he rules so well,
And plants the distant colonies of hell;
By them his secret power he firm maintains,
And binds the world in his infernal chains.

By zeal the Irish, and the Russ by folly,
Fury the Dane, the Swede by melancholy;
By stupid ignorance, the Muscovite;
The Chinese, by a child of hell, call'd wit;
Wealth makes the Persian too effeminate;
And poverty the Tartar desperate:
The Turks and Moors, by Mah'met he subdues;
And God has given him leave to rule the Jews:
Rage rules the Portuguese, and fraud the Scotch;
Revenge the Pole, and avarice the Dutch.

Satire, be kind, and draw a silent veil,
Thy native England's vices to conceal:
Or, if that task's impossible to do,
At least be just, and show her virtues too;
Too great the first, alas! the last too few.

England, unknown, as yet unpeopled lay,—
Happy, had she remain'd so to this day,
And still to ev'ry nation been a prey.
Her open harbours, and her fertile plains,
The merchant's glory these, and those the swain's,
To ev'ry barbarous nation have betray'd her;
Who conquer her as oft as they invade her,

So beauty, guarded out by Innocence,
That ruins her which should be her defence.

Ingratitude, a devil of black renown,
Possess'd her very early for his own:
An ugly, surly, sullen, selfish spirit,
Who Satan's worst perfections does inherit;
Second to him in malice and in force,
All devil without, and all within him worse.

He made her first-born race to be so rude,
And suffer'd her to be so oft subdued;
By sev'ral crowds of wandering thieves o'er-run,
Often unpeopled, and as oft undone;
While ev'ry nation that her powers reduced,
Their languages and manners introduced;
From whose mix'd relics our compounded breed,
By spurious generation does succeed;
Making a race uncertain and uneven,
Derived from all the nations under heaven.

The Romans first with Julius Cæsar came,
Including all the nations of that name,
Gauls, Greek, and Lombards; and, by computation,
Auxiliaries or slaves of ev'ry nation.
With Hengist, Saxons; Danes with Sweno came,
In search of plunder, not in search of fame.
Scots, Picts, and Irish from th' Hibernian shore;
And conq'ring William brought the Normans o'er.

All these their barb'rous offspring left behind,
The dregs of armies, they of all mankind;
Blended with Britons, who before were here,
Of whom the Welch ha' blest the character.

From this amphibious, ill-born mob began,
That vain ill-natured thing, an Englishman.
The customs, sirnames, languages, and manners,
Of all these nations, are their own explainers;
Whose relics are so lasting and so strong,

They've left a Shiboleth upon our tongue;
By which, with easy search, you may distinguish
Your Roman, Saxon, Danish, Norman, English.

The great invading Norman let us know
What conquerors in after-times might do.
To every musqueteer he brought to town,
He gave the lands which never were his own;
When first the English crown he did obtain,
He did not send his Dutchmen home again.
No re-assumptions in his reign were known,
Davenant might there ha' let his book alone.
No parliament his army could disband;
He raised no money, for he paid in land.
He gave his legions their eternal station,
And made them all freeholders of the nation.
He canton'd out the country to his men,
And every soldier was a denizen.
The rascals thus enrich'd, he called them lords,
To please their upstart pride with new-made words,
And doomsday book his tyranny records.

And here begins the ancient pedigree
That so exalts our poor nobility.
'Tis that from some French trooper they derive,
Who with the Norman bastard did arrive:
The trophies of the families appear;
Some show the sword, the bow, and some the spear,
Which their great ancestor, forsooth, did wear.
These in the herald's register remain,
Their noble mean extraction to explain,
Yet who the hero was no man can tell,
Whether a drummer or a colonel:
The silent record blushes to reveal
Their undescended dark original.

But grant the best. How came the change to pass;
A true-born Englishman of Norman race?
A Turkish horse can show more history,
To prove his well-descended family.

Conquest, as by the moderns 'tis express'd,
May give a title to the lands possess'd;
But that the longest sword should be so civil,
To make a Frenchman English, that's the devil.

These are the heroes that despise the Dutch,
And rail at new-come foreigners so much;
Forgetting that themselves are all derived
From the most scoundrel race that ever lived;
A horrid crowd of rambling thieves and drones
Who ransack'd kingdoms, and dispeopled towns;
The Pict and painted Briton, treach'rous Scot,
By hunger, theft, and rapine, hither brought;
Norwegian pirates, buccaneering Danes,
Whose red-hair'd offspring everywhere remains;
Who, join'd with Norman French, compound the breed
From whence your true-born Englishmen proceed.

And lest, by length of time, it be pretended,
The climate may this modern breed have mended;
Wise Providence, to keep us where we are,
Mixes us daily with exceeding care;
We have been Europe's sink, the jakes, where she
Voids all her offal out-cast progeny;
From our fifth Henry's time the strolling bands,
Of banish'd fugitives from neighb'ring lands,
Have here a certain sanctuary found:
The eternal refuge of the vagabond,
Where in but half a common age of time,
Borrowing new blood and manners from the clime,
Proudly they learn all mankind to contemn,
And all their race are true-born Englishmen.

Dutch Walloons, Flemmings, Irishmen, and Scots,
Vaudois, and Valtolins, and Hugonots,
In good Queen Bess's charitable reign,
Supplied us with three hundred thousand men:
Religion—God, we thank thee!—sent them hither,
Priests, Protestants, the devil, and all together;
Of all professions, and of ev'ry trade,

All that were persecuted or afraid:
Whether for debt, or other crimes, they fled,
David at Hackelah was still their head.

The offspring of this miscellaneous crowd,
Had not their new plantations long enjoy'd,
But they grew Englishmen, and raised their votes,
At foreign shoals of interloping Scots;
The royal branch from Pict-land did succeed,
With troops of Scots and scabs from north of Tweed;
The seven first years of his pacific reign,
Made him and half his nation Englishmen.
Scots from the northern frozen banks of Tay,
With packs and plods came whigging all away,
Thick as the locusts which in Egypt swarm'd,
With pride and hungry hopes completely arm'd;
With native truth, diseases, and no money,
Plunder'd our Canaan of the milk and honey;
Here they grew quickly lords and gentlemen,
And all their race are true-born Englishmen.

The civil wars, the common purgative,
Which always use to make the nation thrive,
Made way for all that strolling congregation,
Which throng'd in pious Charles's restoration.
The royal refugee our breed restores,
With foreign courtiers, and with foreign whores:
And carefully re-peopled us again,
Throughout his lazy, long, lascivious reign,
With such a blest and true-born English fry,
As much illustrates our nobility.
A gratitude which will so black appear,
As future ages must abhor to bear:
When they look back on all that crimson flood,
Which stream'd in Lindsey's, and Caernarvon's blood;
Bold Strafford, Cambridge, Capel, Lucas, Lisle,
Who crown'd in death his father's fun'ral pile.
The loss of whom, in order to supply
With true-born English nobility,
Six bastard dukes survive his luscious reign,

The labours of Italian Castlemain,
French Portsmouth, Tabby Scott, and Cambrian;
Besides the num'rous bright and virgin throng,
Whose female glories shade them from my song.
This offspring if our age they multiply,
May half the house with English peers supply:
There with true English pride they may contemn
Schomberg and Portland, new-made noblemen.

French cooks, Scotch pedlars, and Italian whores,
Were all made lords or lords' progenitors.
Beggars and bastards by this new creation
Much multiplied the peerage of the nation;
Who will be all, ere one short age runs o'er,
As true-born lords as those we had before.

Then to recruit the commons he prepares,
And heal the latent breaches of the wars;
The pious purpose better to advance,
He invites the banish'd Protestants of France;
Hither for God's sake, and their own, they fled
Some for religion came, and some for bread:
Two hundred thousand pair of wooden shoes,
Who, God be thank'd, had nothing left to lose;
To heaven's great praise did for religion fly,
To make us starve our poor in charity.
In ev'ry port they plant their fruitful train,
To get a race of true-born Englishmen;
Whose children will, when riper years they see,
Be as ill-natured, and as proud as we;
Call themselves English, foreigners despise,
Be surly like us all, and just as wise.

Thus from a mixture of all kinds began,
That heterogeneous thing, an Englishman:
In eager rapes, and furious lust begot,
Betwixt a painted Briton and a Scot:
Whose gend'ring offspring quickly learn'd to bow,
And yoke their heifers to the Roman plough;
From whence a mongrel half-bred race there came,

With neither name nor nation, speech or fame,
In whose hot veins new mixtures quickly ran,
Infused betwixt a Saxon and a Dane;
While their rank daughters, to their parents just,
Received all nations with promiscuous lust.
This nauseous brood directly did contain
The well-extracted blood of Englishmen.

Which medley, canton'd in a heptarchy,
A rhapsody of nations to supply,
Among themselves maintain'd eternal wars,
And still the ladies loved the conquerors.

The Western Angles all the rest subdued,
A bloody nation, barbarous and rude;
Who by the tenure of the sword possess'd
One part of Britain, and subdued the rest:
And as great things denominate the small,
The conquering part gave title to the whole;
The Scot, Pict, Briton, Roman, Dane, submit,
And with the English Saxon all unite:
And these the mixture have so close pursued,
The very name and memory's subdued;
No Roman now, no Briton does remain;
Wales strove to separate, but strove in vain:
The silent nations undistinguish'd fall,
And Englishman's the common name for all.
Fate jumbled them together, God knows how;
Whate'er they were, they're true-born English now.

The wonder which remains is at our pride,
To value that which all wise men deride;
For Englishmen to boast of generation
Cancels their knowledge, and lampoons the nation,
A true-born Englishman's a contradiction,
In speech an irony, in fact a fiction:
A banter made to be a test of fools,
Which those that use it justly ridicules;
A metaphor intended to express,
A man a-kin to all the universe.

For as the Scots, as learned men have said,
Throughout the world their wand'ring seed have spread,
So open-handed England, 'tis believed,
Has all the gleanings of the world received.

Some think of England, 'twas our Saviour meant,
The Gospel should to all the world be sent:
Since when the blessed sound did hither reach,
They to all nations might be said to preach.

'Tis well that virtue gives nobility,
Else God knows where had we our gentry,
Since scarce one family is left alive,
Which does not from some foreigner derive.
Of sixty thousand English gentlemen,
Whose names and arms in registers remain,
We challenge all our heralds to declare
Ten families which English Saxons are.

France justly boasts the ancient noble line
Of Bourbon, Montmorency, and Lorraine.
The Germans too, their house of Austria show,
And Holland, their invincible Nassau.
Lines which in heraldry were ancient grown,
Before the name of Englishman was known.
Even Scotland, too, her elder glory shows,
Her Gordons, Hamiltons, and her Monro's;
Douglas', Mackays, and Grahams, names well known,
Long before ancient England knew her own.

But England, modern to the last degree,
Borrows or makes her own nobility,
And yet she boldly boasts of pedigree;
Repines that foreigners are put upon her,
And talks of her antiquity and honour:
Her Sackvills, Savils, Cecils, Delamers,
Mohuns, Montagues, Duras, and Veeres,
Not one have English names, yet all are English peers.
Your Houblons, Papillons, and Lethuliers,

Pass now for true-born English knights and squires,
And make good senate-members, or lord-mayors.
Wealth, howsoever got, in England makes
Lords of mechanics, gentlemen of rakes.
Antiquity and birth are needless here;
'Tis impudence and money makes a peer.

Innumerable city knights we know,
From Blue-coat Hospitals, and Bridewell flow.
Draymen and porters fill the city chair,
And foot-boys magisterial purple wear.
Fate has but very small distinction set
Betwixt the counter and the coronet.
Tarpaulin lords, pages of high renown,
Rise up by poor men's valour, not their own;
Great families of yesterday we show,
And lords, whose parents were the Lord knows who.

PART II.

The breed's described: now, Satire, if you can,
Their temper show, for manners make the man.
Fierce as the Briton, as the Roman brave,
And less inclined to conquer than to save;
Eager to fight, and lavish of their blood,
And equally of fear and forecast void.
The Pict has made them sour, the Dane morose,
False from the Scot, and from the Norman worse.
What honesty they have, the Saxon gave them,
And that, now they grow old, begins to leave them.
The climate makes them terrible and bold:
And English beef their courage does uphold:
No danger can their daring spirit dull,
Always provided when their belly's full.

In close intrigues, their faculty's but weak;
For, gen'rally, whate'er they know they speak.
And often their own councils undermine
By their infirmity, and not design.
From whence, the learned say, it does proceed,
That English treason never can succeed:
For they're so open-hearted, you may know
Their own most secret thoughts, and others too.

The lab'ring poor, in spite of double pay,
Are saucy, mutinous, and beggarly;
So lavish of their money and their time,
That want of forecast is the nation's crime.
Good drunken company is their delight;
And what they get by day they spend by night.
Dull thinking seldom does their heads engage,
But drink their youth away, and hurry on old age.
Empty of all good husbandry and sense;
And void of manners most when void of pence.
Their strong aversion to behaviour's such,
They always talk too little or too much.
So dull, they never take the pains to think;
And seldom are good natured but in drink.

In English ale their dear enjoyment lies,
For which they starve themselves and families.
An Englishman will fairly drink as much,
As will maintain two families of Dutch:
Subjecting all their labours to the pots;
The greatest artists are the greatest sots.
The country poor do by example live;
The gentry lead them, and the clergy drive;
What may we not from such examples hope?
The landlord is their god, the priest their pope;
A drunken clergy, and a swearing bench,
Has given the reformation such a drench,
As wise men think, there is some cause to doubt,
Will purge good manners and religion out.

Nor do the poor alone their liquor prize,
The sages join in this great sacrifice;
The learned men who study Aristotle,
Correct him with an explanation bottle:
Praise Epicurus rather than Lysander,
And Aristippus more than Alexander;
The doctors too their Galen here resign,
And generally prescribe specific wine;
The graduate's study's grown an easy task,
While for the urinal they toss the flask;
The surgeon's art grows plainer every hour,
And wine's the balm which into wounds they pour.

Poets long since Parnassus have forsaken,
And say the ancient bards were all mistaken.
Apollo's lately abdicate and fled,
And good king Bacchus reigneth in his stead:
He does the chaos of the head refine,
And atom thoughts jump into words by wine:
The inspiration's of a finer nature,
As wine must needs excel Parnassus water.

Statesmen their weighty politics refine,
And soldiers raise their courages by wine.

Cecilia gives her choristers their choice,
And lets them all drink wine to clear the voice.

Some think the clergy first found out the way,
And wine's the only spirit by which they pray.
But others, less profane than so, agree,
It clears the lungs, and helps the memory:
And, therefore, all of them divinely think,
Instead of study, 'tis as well to drink.

And here I would be very glad to know,
Whether our Asgilites may drink or no;
The enlightening fumes of wine would certainly
Assist them much when they begin to fly;
Or if a fiery chariot should appear,
Inflamed by wine, they'd have the less to fear.

Even the gods themselves, as mortals say,
Were they on earth, would be as drunk as they:
Nectar would be no more celestial drink,
They'd all take wine, to teach them how to think.
But English drunkards, gods and men outdo,
Drink their estates away, and senses too.
Colon's in debt, and if his friend should fail
To help him out, must die at last in jail:
His wealthy uncle sent a hundred nobles,
To pay his trifles off, and rid him of his troubles:
But Colon, like a true-born Englishman,
Drunk all the money out in bright champaign,
And Colon does in custody remain.
Drunk'ness has been the darling of the realm,
E'er since a drunken pilot had the helm.

In their religion, they're so uneven,
That each man goes his own byway to heaven.
Tenacious of mistakes to that degree,
That ev'ry man pursues it sep'rately,
And fancies none can find the way but he:
So shy of one another they are grown,
As if they strove to get to heaven alone.

Rigid and zealous, positive and grave,
And ev'ry grace, but charity, they have;
This makes them so ill-natured and uncivil,
That all men think an Englishman the devil.

Surly to strangers, froward to their friend,
Submit to love with a reluctant mind,
Resolved to be ungrateful and unkind.
If, by necessity, reduced to ask,
The giver has the difficultest task:
For what's bestow'd they awkwardly receive,
And always take less freely than they give;
The obligation is their highest grief,
They never love where they accept relief;
So sullen in their sorrows, that 'tis known
They'll rather die than their afflictions own;
And if relieved, it is too often true,
That they'll abuse their benefactors too;
For in distress their haughty stomach's such,
They hate to see themselves obliged too much;
Seldom contented, often in the wrong,
Hard to be pleased at all, and never long.

If your mistakes there ill opinion gain,
No merit can their favour re-obtain:
And if they're not vindictive in their fury,
'Tis their inconstant temper does secure ye:
Their brain's so cool, their passion seldom burns;
For all's condensed before the flame returns:
The fermentation's of so weak a matter,
The humid damps the flame, and runs it all to water;
So though the inclination may be strong,
They're pleased by fits, and never angry long:

Then, if good-nature show some slender proof,
They never think they have reward enough;
But, like our modern Quakers of the town,
Expect your manners, and return you none.

Friendship, th' abstracted union of the mind,

Which all men seek, but very few can find;
Of all the nations in the universe,
None can talk on't more, or understand it less;
For if it does their property annoy,
Their property their friendship will destroy.
As you discourse them, you shall hear them tell
All things in which they think they do excel:
No panegyric needs their praise record,
An Englishman ne'er wants his own good word.
His first discourses gen'rally appear,
Prologued with his own wond'rous character:
When, to illustrate his own good name,
He never fails his neighbour to defame.
And yet he really designs no wrong,
His malice goes no further than his tongue.
But, pleased to tattle, he delights to rail,
To satisfy the letch'ry of a tale.
His own dear praises close the ample speech,
Tells you how wise he is, that is, how rich:
For wealth is wisdom; he that's rich is wise;
And all men learned poverty despise:
His generosity comes next, and then
Concludes, that he's a true-born Englishman;
And they, 'tis known, are generous and free,
Forgetting, and forgiving injury:
Which may be true, thus rightly understood,
Forgiving ill turns, and forgetting good.

Cheerful in labour when they've undertook it,
But out of humour, when they're out of pocket.
But if their belly and their pocket's full,
They may be phlegmatic, but never dull:
And if a bottle does their brains refine,
It makes their wit as sparkling as their wine.

As for the general vices which we find,
They're guilty of in common with mankind,
Satire forbear, and silently endure,
We must conceal the crimes we cannot cure;
Nor shall my verse the brighter sex defame,

For English beauty will preserve her name;
Beyond dispute agreeable and fair,
And modester than other nations are;
For where the vice prevails, the great temptation
Is want of money more than inclination;
In general this only is allow'd,
They're something noisy, and a little proud.

An Englishman is gentlest in command,
Obedience is a stranger in the land:
Hardly subjected to the magistrate;
For Englishmen do all subjection hate.
Humblest when rich, but peevish when they're poor,
And think whate'er they have, they merit more.

The meanest English plowman studies law,
And keeps thereby the magistrates in awe,
Will boldly tell them what they ought to do,
And sometimes punish their omissions too.

Their liberty and property's so dear,
They scorn their laws or governors to fear;
So bugbear'd with the name of slavery,
They can't submit to their own liberty.
Restraint from ill is freedom to the wise!
But Englishmen do all restraint despise.
Slaves to the liquor, drudges to the pots;
The mob are statesmen, and their statesmen sots.

Their governors, they count such dang'rous things,
That 'tis their custom to affront their kings:
So jealous of the power their kings possess'd,
They suffer neither power nor kings to rest.
The bad with force they eagerly subdue;
The good with constant clamours they pursue,
And did King Jesus reign, they'd murmur too.
A discontented nation, and by far
Harder to rule in times of peace than war:
Easily set together by the ears,
And full of causeless jealousies and fears:

Apt to revolt, and willing to rebel,
And never are contented when they're well.
No government could ever please them long,
Could tie their hands, or rectify their tongue.
In this, to ancient Israel well compared,
Eternal murmurs are among them heard.

It was but lately, that they were oppress'd,
Their rights invaded, and their laws suppress'd:
When nicely tender of their liberty,
Lord! what a noise they made of slavery.
In daily tumults show'd their discontent,
Lampoon'd their king, and mock'd his government.
And if in arms they did not first appear,
'Twas want of force, and not for want of fear.
In humbler tone than English used to do,
At foreign hands for foreign aid they sue.

William, the great successor of Nassau,
Their prayers heard, and their oppressions saw;
He saw and saved them: God and him they praised
To this their thanks, to that their trophies raised.
But glutted with their own felicities,
They soon their new deliverer despise;
Say all their prayers back, their joy disown,
Unsing their thanks, and pull their trophies down;
Their harps of praise are on the willows hung;
For Englishmen are ne'er contented long.

The reverend clergy too, and who'd ha' thought
That they who had such non-resistance taught,
Should e'er to arms against their prince be brought
Who up to heav'n did regal power advance;
Subjecting English laws to modes of France
Twisting religion so with loyalty,
As one could never live, and t'other die;
And yet no sooner did their prince design
Their glebes and perquisites to undermine,
But all their passive doctrines laid aside,
The clergy their own principles denied;

Unpreach'd their non-resisting cant, and pray'd
To heav'n for help, and to the Dutch for aid;
The church chimed all her doctrines back again,
And pulpit-champions did the cause maintain;
Flew in the face of all their former zeal,
And non-resistance did at once repeal.

The Rabbi's say it would be too prolix,
To tie religion up to politics,
The churches' safety is *suprema lex*.
And so by a new figure of their own,
Their former doctrines all at once disown;
As laws *post facto* in the parliament,
In urgent cases have attained assent;
But are as dangerous precedents laid by,
Made lawful only by necessity.

The rev'rend fathers then in arms appear,
And men of God became the men of war:
The nation, fired by them, to arms apply,
Assault their antichristian monarchy;
To their due channel all our laws restore,
And made things what they should have been before.
But when they came to fill the vacant throne,
And the pale priests look'd back on what they'd done,
How England liberty began to thrive,
And Church of England loyalty outlive;
How all their persecuting days were done,
And their deliv'rer placed upon the throne:
The priests, as priests are wont to do, turn'd tail,
They're Englishmen, and nature will prevail;
Now they deplore their ruins they have made,
And murmur for the master they betray'd;
Excuse those crimes they could not make him mend,
And suffer for the cause they can't defend;
Pretend they'd not have carried things so high,
And proto-martyrs make for popery.

Had the prince done as they design'd the thing,
High set the clergy up to rule the king:

Taken a donative for coming hither,
And so have left their king and them together;
We had, say they, been now a happy nation;
No doubt we had seen a blessed reformation:
For wise men say 'tis as dangerous a thing,
A ruling priesthood, as a priest-rid king;
And of all plagues with which mankind are curst,
Ecclesiastic tyranny's the worst.

If all our former grievances were feign'd,
King James has been abused, and we trepann'd;
Bugbear'd with popery and power despotic,
Tyrannic government, and leagues exotic;
The revolution's a fanatic plot,
William's a tyrant, King James was not;
A factious army and a poison'd nation,
Unjustly forced King James's abdication.

But if he did the subjects' rights invade,
Then he was punish'd only, not betrayed;
And punishing of kings is no such crime,
But Englishmen have done it many a time.

When kings the sword of justice first lay down,
They are no kings, though they possess the crown.
Titles are shadows, crowns are empty things,
The good of subjects is the end of kings;
To guide in war, and to protect in peace,
Where tyrants once commence the kings do cease;
For arbitrary power's so strange a thing,
It makes the tyrant and unmakes the king:
If kings by foreign priests and armies reign,
And lawless power against their oaths maintain,
Then subjects must have reason to complain:
If oaths must bind us when our kings do ill,
To call in foreign aid is to rebel:
By force to circumscribe our lawful prince,
Is wilful treason in the largest sense:
And they who once rebel, must certainly
Their God, and king, and former oaths defy;

If ye allow no mal-administration
Could cancel the allegiance of the nation,
Let all our learned sons of Levi try,
This ecclesiastic riddle to untie;
How they could make a step to call the prince,
And yet pretend the oath and innocence.

By th' first address they made beyond the seas,
They're perjur'd in the most intense degrees;
And without scruple for the time to come,
May swear to all the kings in Christendom:
Nay, truly did our kings consider all,
They'd never let the clergy swear at all,
Their politic allegiance they'd refuse,
For whores and priests do never want excuse.

But if the mutual contract was dissolved,
The doubt's explain'd, the difficulty solved;
That kings, when they descend to tyranny,
Dissolve the bond, and leave the subject free;
The government's ungirt when justice dies,
And constitutions are nonentities.
The nation's all a mob, there's no such thing,
As lords, or commons, parliament, or king;
A great promiscuous crowd the Hydra lies,
Till laws revive and mutual contract ties;
A chaos free to choose for their own share,
What case of government they please to wear;
If to a king they do the reins commit,
All men are bound in conscience to submit;
But then the king must by his oath assent,
To *Postulata's* of the government;
Which if he breaks he cuts off the entail,
And power retreats to its original.

This doctrine has the sanction of assent
From nature's universal Parliament:
The voice of nations, and the course of things,
Allow that laws superior are to kings;
None but delinquents would have justice cease,

Knaves rail at laws, as soldiers rail at peace:
For justice is the end of government,
As reason is the test of argument:
No man was ever yet so void of sense,
As to debate the right of self-defence;
A principle so grafted in the mind,
With nature born, and does like nature bind;
Twisted with reason, and with nature too,
As neither one nor t'other can undo.

Nor can this right be less when national,
Reason which governs one should govern all;
Whate'er the dialect of courts may tell,
He that his right demands can ne'er rebel;
Which right, if 'tis by governors denied,
May be procured by force or foreign aid;
For tyranny's a nation's term of grief,
As folks cry fire to hasten in relief;
And when the hated word is heard about,
All men should come to help the people out.

Thus England groan'd, Britannia's voice was heard,
And great Nassau to rescue her appear'd:
Call'd by the universal voice of fate,
God and the people's legal magistrate:
Ye heavens regard! Almighty Jove look down,
And view thy injured monarch on the throne;
On their ungrateful heads due vengeance take
Who sought his aid, and then his part forsake:
Witness, ye powers! it was our call alone,
Which now our pride makes us ashamed to own;
Britannia's troubles fetch'd him from afar,
To court the dreadful casualties of war;
But where requital never can be made,
Acknowledgment's a tribute seldom paid.

He dwelt in bright Maria's circling arms,
Defended by the magic of her charms,
From foreign fears and from domestic harms;
Ambition found no fuel for her fire,

He had what God could give or man desire,
Till pity roused him from his soft repose,
His life to unseen hazards to expose;
Till pity moved him in our cause to appear,
Pity! that word which now we hate to hear;
But English gratitude is always such,
To hate the hand that does oblige too much.

Britannia's cries gave birth to his intent,
And hardly gain'd his unforeseen assent;
His boding thoughts foretold him he should find
The people fickle, selfish, and unkind;
Which thought did to his royal heart appear
More dreadful than the dangers of the war;
For nothing grates a generous mind so soon,
As base returns for hearty service done.

Satire, be silent! awfully prepare
Britannia's song, and William's praise to hear;
Stand by, and let her cheerfully rehearse
Her grateful vows in her immortal verse.
Loud fame's eternal trumpet let her sound,
Listen, ye distant poles, and endless round,
May the strong blast the welcome news convey,
As far as sound can reach or spirit fly!
To neighb'ring worlds, if such there be, relate
Our heroes fame for theirs to imitate;
To distant worlds of spirits let her rehearse,
For spirits without the helps of voice converse:
May angels hear the gladsome news on high,
Mix'd with their everlasting symphony;
And hell itself stand in surprise to know,
Whether it be the fatal blast or no.

BRITANNIA.

The fame of virtue 'tis for which I sound,
And heroes with immortal triumphs crown'd;
Fame built on solid virtue swifter flies,
Than morning light can spread the eastern skies:
The gath'ring air returns the doubling sound;
And loud repeating thunders force it round;
Echoes return from caverns of the deep,
Old Chaos dreams on't in eternal sleep:
Time hands it forward to its latest urn,
From whence it never, never shall return:
Nothing is heard so far, or lasts so long,
'Tis heard by ev'ry ear, and spoke by every tongue.

My hero, with the sails of honour furl'd,
Rises like the great genius of the world;
By fate and fame wisely prepared to be
The soul of war and life of victory;
He spreads the wings of virtue on the throne,
And ev'ry wind of glory fans them on;
Immortal trophies dwell upon his brow,
Fresh as the garlands he has won but now.

By different steps the high ascent he gains,
And differently that high ascent maintains:
Princes for pride and lust of rule make war,
And struggle for the name of conqueror;
Some fight for fame, and some for victory,
He fights to save, and conquers to set free.

Then seek no phrase his titles to conceal,
And hide with words what actions must reveal;
No parallel from Hebrew stories take,
Of godlike kings my similies to make;
No borrowed names conceal my living theme,
But names and things directly I proclaim;
His honest merit does his glory raise,
Whom that exalts let no man fear to praise;
Of such a subject no man need be shy,

Virtue's above the reach of flattery;
He needs no character but his own fame,
Nor any flattering titles but his own name.

William's the name that's spoke by every tongue,
William's the darling subject of my song;
Listen, ye virgins, to the charming sound,
And in eternal dances hand it round;
Your early offerings to this altar bring,
Make him at once a lover and a king;
May he submit to none but to your arms,
Nor ever be subdued, but by your charms;
May your soft thoughts for him be all sublime,
And ev'ry tender vow be made for him;
May he be first in ev'ry morning thought,
And heav'n ne'er hear a prayer where he's left out;
May every omen, every boding dream,
Be fortunate by mentioning his name;
May this one charm infernal powers affright,
And guard you from the terror of the night;
May ev'ry cheerful glass as it goes down
To William's health, be cordials to your own:
Let ev'ry song be chorust with his name,
And music pay her tribute to his fame;
Let ev'ry poet tune his artful verse,
And in immortal strains his deeds rehearse:
And may Apollo never more inspire
The disobedient bard with his seraphic fire
May all my sons their grateful homage pay,
His praises sing, and for his safety pray.

Satire, return to our unthankful isle,
Secured by heaven's regards, and William's toil:
To both ungrateful, and to both untrue,
Rebels to God, and to good nature too.

If e'er this nation be distress'd again,
To whomsoe'er they cry, they'll cry in vain;
To heav'n they cannot have the face to look,
Or, if they should, it would but heav'n provoke;

To hope for help from man would be too much,
Mankind would always tell 'em of the Dutch:
How they came here our freedoms to maintain,
Were paid, and cursed, and hurried home again;
How by their aid we first dissolved our fears,
And then our helpers damn'd for foreigners:
'Tis not our English temper to do better,
For Englishmen think ev'ry one their debtor.

'Tis worth observing, that we ne'er complain'd
Of foreigners, nor of the wealth we gain'd,
Till all their services were at an end:
Wise men affirm it is the English way,
Never to grumble till they come to pay;
And then they always think, their temper's such,
The work too little, and the pay too much.

As frighted patients, when they want a cure,
Bid any price, and any pain endure:
But when the doctor's remedies appear,
The cure's too easy, and the price too dear:
Great Portland near was banter'd when he strove,
For us his master's kindest thoughts to move:
We ne'er lampoon'd his conduct, when employ'd
King James's secret councils to divide:
Then we caress'd him as the only man,
Who could the doubtful oracle explain;
The only Hushai, able to repel
The dark designs of our Achitophel:
Compared his master's courage to his sense,
The ablest statesman, and the bravest prince;
On his wise conduct we depended much,
And liked him ne'er the worse for being Dutch:
Nor was he valued more than he deserved,
Freely he ventured, faithfully he served;
In all King William's dangers he has shared,
In England's quarrels always he appear'd:
The revolution first, and then the Boyne,
In both, his counsels and his conduct shine;
His martial valour Flanders will confess,

And France regrets his managing the peace;
Faithful to England's interest and her king,
The greatest reason of our murmuring:
Ten years in English service he appear'd,
And gain'd his master's and the world's regard;
But 'tis not England's custom to reward,
The wars are over, England needs him not;
Now he's a Dutchman, and the Lord knows what.

Schonbergh, the ablest soldier of his age,
With great Nassau did in our cause engage;
Both join'd for England's rescue and defence,
The greatest captain and the greatest prince;
With what applause his stories did we tell,
Stories which Europe's volumes largely swell!
We counted him an army in our aid,
Where he commanded, no man was afraid;
His actions with a constant conquest shine,
From Villa Vitiosa to the Rhine;
France, Flanders, Germany, his fame confess,
And all the world was fond of him but us:
Our turn first served, we grudged him the command,
Witness the grateful temper of the land.

We blame the King, that he relies too much,
On Strangers, Germans, Hugonots, and Dutch;
And seldom does his great affairs of state,
To English counsellors communicate:
The fact might very well be answer'd thus:
He had so often been betray'd by us,
He must have been a madman to rely,
On English gentlemen's fidelity;
For, laying other argument aside:
This thought might mortify our English pride;
That foreigners have faithfully obey'd him,
And none but Englishmen have e'er betray'd him:
They have our ships and merchants bought and sold,
And barter'd English blood for foreign gold;
First to the French they sold our Turkey fleet,
And injured Talmarsh next at Cameret;

The king himself is shelter'd from their snares,
Not by his merits, but the crown he wears;
Experience tells us 'tis the English way,
Their benefactors always to betray.

And, lest examples should be too remote,
A modern magistrate of famous note,
Shall give you his own history by rote;
I'll make it out, deny it he that can,
His worship is a true-born Englishman;
By all the latitude that empty word,
By modern acceptation's understood:
The parish books his great descent record,
And now he hopes ere long to be a lord;
And truly, as things go, it would be pity,
But such as he bore office in the city;
While robb'ry for burnt-offering he brings,
And gives to God what he has stole from kings;
Great monuments of charity he raises,
And good St. Magnus whistles out his praises;
To city jails he grants a jubilee,
And hires huzza's from his own mobile.

Lately he wore the golden chain and gown,
With which equipp'd he thus harangued the town.

HIS FINE SPEECH, &c.

With clouted iron shoes, and sheep-skin breeches,
More rags than manners, and more dirt than riches,
From driving cows and calves to Leyton market,
While of my greatness there appear'd no spark yet,
Behold I come to let you see the pride,
With which exalted beggars always ride.

Born to the needful labours of the plough,
The cart-whip graced me, as the chain does now.
Nature and fate in doubt what course to take,
Whether I should a lord or plough-boy make;
Kindly at last resolv'd they would promote me,
And first a knave, and then a knight they vote me.
What fate appointed, nature did prepare,
And furnish'd me with an exceeding care,
To fit me for what they design'd to have me;
And every gift but honesty they gave me.

And thus equipp'd, to this proud town I came,
In quest of bread, and not in quest of fame.
Blind to my future fate, an humble boy,
Free from the guilt and glory I enjoy.
The hopes which my ambition entertain'd,
Where in the name of foot-boy, all contain'd.
The greatest heights from small beginnings rise;
The gods were great on earth, before they reach'd the skies.

Backwell, the generous temper of whose mind,
Was always to be bountiful inclin'd:
Whether by his ill fate or fancy led,
First took me up, and furnish'd me with bread:
The little services he put me to,
Seem'd labours, rather than were truly so.
But always my advancement he design'd;
For 'twas his very nature to be kind:
Large was his soul, his temper ever free;

The best of masters and of men to me:
And I who was before decreed by fate,
To be made infamous as well as great,
With an obsequious diligence obey'd him,
Till trusted with his all, and then betray'd him.

All his past kindnesses I trampled on,
Ruin'd his fortunes to erect my own:
So vipers in the bosom bred begin,
To hiss at that hand first which took them in;
With eager treach'ry I his fall pursu'd,
And my first trophies were ingratitude.

Ingratitude's the worst of human guilt,
The basest action mankind can commit;
Which, like the sin against the Holy Ghost,
Has least of honour, and of guilt the most;
Distinguished from all other crimes by this,
That 'tis a crime which no man will confess;
That sin alone, which should not be forgiv'n
On earth, altho' perhaps it may in heaven.

Thus my first benefactor I o'erthrew;
And how shou'd I be to a second true?
The public trust came next into my care,
And I to use them scurvily prepare:
My needy sov'reign lord I play'd upon,
And lent him many a thousand of his own;
For which great interest I took care to charge,
And so my ill-got wealth became so large.

My predecessor Judas was a fool,
Fitter to have been whipt and sent to school,
Than sell a Saviour: had I been at hand,
His Master had not been so cheap trepann'd;
I would have made the eager Jews have found,
For thirty pieces, thirty thousand pound.

My cousin Ziba, of immortal fame,
(Ziba and I shall never want a name:)

First-born of treason, nobly did advance
His Master's fall, for his inheritance:
By whose keen arts old David first began
To break his sacred oath to Jonathan:
The good old king 'tis thought was very loth
To break his word, and therefore broke his oath.
Ziba's a traitor of some quality,
Yet Ziba might have been inform'd by me:
Had I been there, he ne'er had been content
With half th' estate, nor half the government.

In our late revolution 'twas thought strange,
That I of all mankind should like the change,
But they who wonder'd at it never knew,
That in it I did my old game pursue:
Nor had they heard of twenty thousand pound,
Which ne'er was lost, yet never could be found.

Thus all things in their turn to sale I bring,
God and my master first, and then the king;
Till by successful villanies made bold,
I thought to turn the nation into gold;
And so to forgery my hand I bent,
Not doubting I could gull the Government;
But there was ruffl'd by the Parliament.
And if I 'scaped th' unhappy tree to climb,
'Twas want of law, and not for want of crime;

But my old friend,[1] who printed in my face
A needful competence of English brass;
Having more business yet for me to do,
And loth to lose his trusty servant so,
Managed the matter with such art and skill,
As sav'd his hero, and threw out the Bill.

And now I'm grac'd with unexpected honours,
For which I'll certainly abuse the donors:
Knighted, and made a tribune of the people,

---

[1] The Devil.

Whose laws and properties I'm like to keep well:
The custos rotulorum of the city,
And captain of the guards of their banditti.
Surrounded by my catchpoles, I declare
Against the needy debtor open war.
I hang poor thieves for stealing of your pelf,
And suffer none to rob you, but myself.

The king commanded me to help reform ye,
And how I'll do't, Miss —— shall inform ye.
I keep the best seraglio in the nation,
And hope in time to bring it into fashion;
No brimstone whore need fear the lash from me,
That part I'll leave to Brother Jefferey:
Our gallants need not go abroad to Rome,
I'll keep a whoring jubilee at home;
Whoring's the darling of my inclination;
An't I a magistrate for reformation?
For this my praise is sung by ev'ry bard,
For which Bridewell wou'd be a just reward.
In print my panegyric fills the street,
And hired gaol-birds their huzzas repeat;
Some charities contriv'd to make a show,
Have taught the needy rabble to do so;
Whose empty noise is a mechanic fame,
Since for Sir Beelzebub they'd do the same.

THE CONCLUSION.

Then let us boast of ancestors no more,
Or deeds of heroes done in days of yore,
In latent records of the ages past,
Behind the rear of time, in long oblivion plac'd;
For if our virtues must in lines descend,
The merit with the families would end,
And intermixtures would most fatal grow;
For vice would be hereditary too;
The tainted blood would of necessity,
Involuntary wickedness convey.

Vice, like ill-nature, for an age or two,
May seem a generation to pursue;
But virtue seldom does regard the breed,
Fools do the wise, and wise men fools succeed.

What is't to us, what ancestors we had?
If good, what better? or what worse, if bad?
Examples are for imitation set,
Yet all men follow virtue with regret.

Could but our ancestors retrieve their fate,
And see their offspring thus degenerate;
How we contend for birth and names unknown,
And build on their past actions, not our own;
They'd cancel records, and their tombs deface,
And openly disown the vile degenerate race:
For fame of families is all a cheat,
It's personal virtue only makes us great.

THE Military Memoirs

OF

Capt. *George Carleton*

FROM THE
DUTCH WAR, 1672.

In which he Serv'd, to the

Conclusion of the Peace at
UTRECHT, 1713.

Illustrating
Some of the most Remarkable TRANSACTIONS, both by Sea
and Land, during the Reigns of King *Charles* and King
James II. hitherto unobserved by all the Writers of those
times.

Together with

An exact Series of the War in *Spain*; and a particular Description
of the several Places of the Author's Residence in
many Cities, Towns, and Countries; their Customs,
Manners, &c. Also Observations on the Genius of the
Spaniards (among whom he continued some Years a
Prisoner) their Monasteries and Nunneries (especially that
fine one at *Montserat*) and on their publick Diversions;
more particularly their famous BULL-FEASTS.

TO THE RIGHT HONOURABLE
Spencer Lord *Wilmington,*
Knight of the Bath, *and one of his Majesty's most Honourable Privy Council.*

'Twas my fortune, my Lord, in my juvenile Years, *Musas cum Marte commutare,* and truly I have Reason to blush, when I consider the small Advantage I have reap'd from that Change. But lest it should be imputed to my Want of Merit, I have wrote these Memoirs, and leave the World to judge of my Deserts. They are not set forth by any fictitious Stories, nor imbelished with rhetorical Flourishes; plain Truth is certainly most becoming the Character of an old Soldier. Yet let them be never so meritorious, if not protected by some noble Patron, some Persons may think them to be of no Value.

To you therefore, my Lord, I present them; to you, who have so eminently distinguished your self, and whose Wisdom has been so conspicuous to the late Representatives of *Great Britain,* that each revolving Age will speak in your Praise; and if you vouchsafe to be the *Mecoenas* of these Memoirs, your Name will give them sufficient Sanction.

An old Soldier I may truly call my self, and my Family allows me the Title of a Gentleman; yet I have seen many Favourites of Fortune, without being able to discern why they should be so happy, and my self so unfortunate; but let not that discourage your Lordship from receiving these my Memoirs into your Patronage; for the Unhappy cannot expect Favour but from those who are endued with generous Souls.

Give me Leave, my Lord, to congratulate this good Fortune, that neither Whig nor Tory (in this complaining Age) have found fault with your Conduct. Your Family has produced Heroes, in defence of injured Kings; and you, when 'twas necessary, have as nobly adher'd to the Cause of Liberty.

My LORD,
Your Lordship's
Most obedient
And most devoted
Humble Servant,
G. CARLETON.

TO THE READER

The Author of these Memoirs began early to distinguish himself in martial Affairs, otherwise he could not have seen such Variety of Actions both by Sea and Land. After the last Dutch War he went into Flanders, where he not only serv'd under the Command of his Highness the Prince of Orange, whilst he was Generalissimo of the Dutch Forces, but likewise all the time he reign'd King of Great Britain. Most of the considerable Passages and Events, which happened during that time, are contained in the former Part of this Book.

In the Year 1705, the Regiment in which he serv'd as Captain was order'd to embark for the West Indies; and he, having no Inclination to go thither, chang'd with an half-pay Captain; and being recommended to the Earl of Peterborow by the late Lord Cutts, went with him upon that noble Expedition into Spain.

When the Forces under his Lordship's Command were landed near Barcelona, the Siege of that Place was thought by several impracticable, not only for want of experienc'd Engineers, but that the Besieged were as numerous as the Besiegers; yet the Courage of that brave Earl surmounted those Difficulties, and the Siege was resolv'd upon.

Our Author having obtain'd, by his long Service, some Knowledge of the practick Part of an Engineer, and seeing at that critical Time the great Want of such, readily acted as one, which gave him the greater Opportunity of being an Eye-Witness of his Lordship's Actions; and consequently made him capable of setting them forth in these his Memoirs.

It may not be perhaps improper to mention that the Author of these Memoirs was born at Ewelme in Oxfordshire, descended from an ancient and an honourable Family. The Lord Dudley Carleton, who died Secretary of State to King Charles I. was his Great Uncle; and in the same Reign his Father was Envoy at the Court of Madrid, whilst his Uncle, Sir Dudley Carleton, was Embassador to the States of Holland, Men in those Days respected both for their Abilities and Loyalty.

MEMOIRS
OF AN
English Officer, &c.

In the year one Thousand six Hundred seventy two, War being proclaimed with *Holland*, it was looked upon among Nobility and Gentry, as a Blemish, not to attend the Duke of *York* aboard the Fleet, who was then declared Admiral. With many others, I, at that Time about twenty Years of Age, enter'd my self a Voluntier on board the *London*, commanded by Sir *Edward Sprage*, Vice-Admiral of the *Red*.

The Fleet set Sail from the *Buoy of the Nore* about the beginning of *May*, in order to join the *French* Fleet, then at Anchor in St. *Hellen's Road*, under the Command of the *Count de Estrée*. But in executing this Design we had a very narrow Escape: For *De Ruyter*, the Admiral of the *Dutch* Fleet, having Notice of our Intentions, waited to have intercepted us at the Mouth of the River, but by the Assistance of a great Fog we pass'd *Dover* before he was aware of it; and thus he miscarried, with the poor Advantage of taking only one small Tender.

A Day or two after the joining of the *English* and *French*, we sailed directly towards the *Dutch* Coast, where we soon got sight of their Fleet; a Sand called the *Galloper* lying between. The *Dutch* seem'd willing there to expect an Attack from us: But in regard the *Charles* Man of War had been lost on those Sands the War before; and that our Ships drawing more Water than those of the Enemy, an Engagement might be render'd very disadvantageous; it was resolv'd in a Council of War to avoid coming to a Battle for the present, and to sail direftly for *Solebay*, which was accordingly put in Execution.

We had not been in *Solebay* above four or five Days, when *De Ruyter*, hearing of it, made his Signal for sailing in order to surprize us; and he had certainly had his Aim, had there been any Breeze of Wind to favour him. But though they made use of all their Sails, there was so little Air stirring, that we could see their Fleet making towards us long before they came up; notwithstanding which, our Admirals found difficulty enough to form their Ships into a Line of Battle, so as to be ready to receive the Enemy.

It was about Four in the Morning of the 28th of *May*, being *Tuesday* in *Whitson Week*, when we first made the Discovery; and about Eight the same Morning the Blue Squadron, under the Command of the Earl of *Sandwich*, began to engage with Admiral *Van Ghent*, who commanded the *Amsterdam* Squadron; and about Nine the whole Fleets were under a general Engagement. The Fight lasted till Ten at Night, and with equal Fury on all Sides, the *French* excepted, who appeared stationed there rather as Spectators than Parties; and as unwilling to be too much upon the Offensive, for fear of offending themselves.

During the Fight the *English* Admiral had two Ships disabled under him; and was obliged about Four in the Afternoon to remove himself a third Time into the *London*, where he remain'd all the rest of the Fight, and till next Morning. Nevertheless, on his Entrance upon the *London*, which was the Ship I was in, and on our Hoisting the Standard, *De Ruyter* and his Squadron seem'd to double their Fire upon her, as if they resolv'd to blow her out of the Water. Notwithstanding all which, the Duke of *York* remain'd all the time upon Quarter Deck, and as the Bullets plentifully whizz'd around him, would often rub his Hands, and cry, *Sprage, Sprage, they follow us still.* I am very sensible later Times have not been over favourable in their Sentiments of that unfortunate Prince's Valour, yet I cannot omit the doing a Piece of Justice to his Memory, in relating a Matter of Fact, of which my own Eyes were Witnesses, and saying, That if Intrepidity, and Undauntedness, may be reckon'd any Parts of Courage, no Man in the Fleet better deserv'd the Title of Couragious, or behav'd himself with more Gallantry than he did.

The *English* lost the *Royal James*, commanded by the Earl of *Sandwich*, which about Twelve (after the strenuous Endeavours of her Sailors to disengage her from two *Dutch* Fire Ships plac'd on her, one athwart her Hawsers, the other on her Star-board Side) took Fire, blew up, and perish'd; and with her a great many brave Gentlemen, as well as Sailors; and amongst the rest the Earl himself, concerning whom I shall further add, that in my Passage from *Harwich* to the *Brill*, a Year or two after, the Master of the Pacquet Boat told me, That having observ'd a great Flock of Gulls hovering in one particular Part of the Sea, he order'd his Boat to make up to it; when discovering a Corpse, the Sailors would have return'd it to the Sea, as the Corpse of a *Dutch Man*; but keeping it in his Boat, it proved to be that of the Earl of *Sandwich*. There was found about him between twenty and thirty Guineas, some Silver, and his Gold Watch; restoring which to his Lady, she kept the Watch, but rewarded their Honesty with all the Gold and Silver.

This was the only Ship the *English* lost in this long Engagement. For although the *Katherine* was taken, and her Commander, Sir *John Chicheley*, made Prisoner, her Sailors soon after finding the Opportunity they had watch'd for, seiz'd all the *Dutch* Sailors, who had been put in upon them, and brought the Ship back to our own Fleet, together with all the *Dutch Men* Prisoners; for which, as they deserv'd, they were well rewarded. This is the same Ship which the Earl of *Mulgrave* (afterwards Duke of *Buckingham*) commanded the next Sea Fight, and has caus'd to be painted in his House in St. *James's Park*.

I must not omit one very remarkable Occurrence which happened in this Ship, There was a Gentleman aboard her, a Voluntier, of a very fine Estate, generally known by the Name of *Hodge Vaughan*. This Person receiv'd, in the beginning of the Fight, a considerable Wound, which the great Confusion, during the Battle, would not give them leave to inquire into; so he was carried out of the Way, and disposed of in the Hold. They had some Hogs aboard, which the Sailor, under whose Care they were, had neglected to feed; these Hogs, hungry as they were, found out, and fell upon the wounded Person, and between dead and alive eat him up to his very Scull, which, after the Fight was over, and the Ship retaken, as before, was all that could be found of him.

Another Thing, less to be accounted for, happen'd to a Gentleman Voluntier who was aboard the same Ship with my self. He was of known personal Courage, in the vulgar Notion of it, his Sword never having fail'd him in many private Duels. But notwithstanding all his Land-mettle, it was observ'd of him at Sea, that when ever the Bullets whizz'd over his Head, or any way incommoded his Ears, he immediately quitted the Deck, and ran down into the Hold. At first he was gently reproach'd; but after many Repetitions he was laugh'd at, and began to be despis'd; sensible of which, as a Testimonial of his Valour, he made it his Request to be ty'd to the Main Mast. But had it been granted him, I cannot see any Title he could have pleaded from hence, to true Magnanimity; since to be ty'd from running away can import nothing less, than that he would have still continued these Signs of Cowardice, if he had not been prevented. There is a Bravery of Mind which I fansy few of those Gentlemen Duellists are possess'd of. True Courage cannot proceed from what Sir *Walter Raleigh* finely calls *the Art* or *Philosophy of Quarrel*. No! It must be the Issue of Principle, and can have no other Basis than a steady Tenet of Religion. This will appear more plain, if those Artists in Murder will give themselves leave cooly to consider, and answer me this Question, Why he that had ran so many Risques at his Sword's Point, should be so shamefully intimidated at the Whiz of a Cannon Ball?

The Names of those English Gentlemen who lost their Lives, as I remember, in this Engagement.

Commissioner Cox, Captain of the *Royal Prince*, under the Command of the Admiral; and Mr. *Travanian*, Gentleman to the Duke of *York*; Mr. *Digby*, Captain of the *Henry*, second Son to the Earl of *Bristol*; Sir *Fletchvile Hollis*, Captain of the *Cambridge*, who lost one of his Arms in the War before, and his Life in this; Captain *Saddleton*, of the *Dartmouth*; the Lord *Maidstone*, Son to the Earl of *Winchelsea*, a Voluntier on board the *Charles*, commanded by Sir *John Harman*, Vice-Admiral of the Red.

Sir *Philip Carteret*, Mr. *Herbert*, Mr. *Cotterel*, Mr. *Peyton*, Mr. *Gose*, with several other Gentlemen unknown to me, lost their Lives with the Earl of *Sandwich*, on board the *Royal James*; Mr. *Vaughan*, on board the *Katherine*, commanded by Sir *John Chicheley*.

In this Engagement, Sir *George Rook* was youngest Lieutenant to Sir *Edward Sprage*; Mr. *Russel*, afterwards Earl of *Orford*, was Captain of a small Fifth Rate, called the *Phnix*; Mr. *Herbert*, afterwards Earl of *Torrington*, was Captain of a small Fourth Rate, called the *Monck*; Sir *Harry Dutton Colt*, who was on board the *Victory*, commanded by the Earl of *Offery*, is the only Man now living that I can remember was in this Engagement.

But to proceed, the *Dutch* had one Man of War sunk, though so near the Shore, that I saw some part of her Main Mast remain above Water, with their Admiral *Van Ghent*, who was slain in the close Engagement with the Earl of *Sandwich*. This Engagement lasted fourteen Hours, and was look'd upon the greatest that ever was fought between the *English* and the *Hollander*.

I cannot here omit one Thing, which to some may seem trifling; though I am apt to think our Naturalists may have a different Opinion of it, and find it afford their Fansies no undiverting Employment in more curious, and less perilous Reflections. We had on board the *London* where, as I have said, I was a Voluntier, a great Number of Pidgeons, of which our Commander was very fond. These, on the first firing of our Cannon, dispers'd, and flew away, and were seen no where near us during the Fight. The next Day it blew a brisk Gale, and drove our Fleet some Leagues to the Southward of the Place where they forsook our Ship, yet the Day after they all returned safe aboard; not in one Flock, but in small Parties of four or five at a Time. Some Persons at that Time aboard the Ship admiring at the Manner of their Return, and speaking of it with some Surprize, Sir *Edward Sprage* told them, That he brought those Pidgeons with him from the *Streights*; and that when, pursuant to his Order, he left the *Revenge* Man of War, to go aboard the *London*, all those Pidgeons, of their own accord, and without the Trouble or Care of carrying, left the *Revenge* likewise, and removed with the Sailors on board the *London*, where I saw them; All which many of the Sailors afterwards confirm'd to me. What Sort of Instinct this could proceed from, I leave to the Curious.

Soon after this Sea Engagement I left the Fleet. And the Parliament, the Winter following, manifesting their Resentments against two of the Plenipotentiaries, *viz. Buckingham* and *Arlington*, who had been sent over into *Holland*; and expressing, withal, their great Umbrage taken at the prodigious Progress of the *French* Arms in the *United Provinces*; and warmly remonstrating the inevitable Danger attending *England* in their Ruin. King *Charles* from all this, and for want of the expected Supplies, found himself under a Necessity of clapping up a speedy Peace with *Holland*.

This Peace leaving those youthful Spirits, that had by the late Naval War been rais'd into a generous Ferment, under a perfect Inactivity at Home; they found themselves, to avoid a Sort of Life that was their Aversion, oblig'd to look out for one more active, and more suitable to their vigorous Tempers Abroad.

I must acknowledge my self one of that Number; and therefore in the Year 1674, I resolv'd to go into *Flanders*, in order to serve as Voluntier in the Army commanded by his Highness the Prince of *Orange*. I took my Passage accordingly at *Dover* for *Calais*, and so went by way of *Dunkirk* for *Brussels*.

Arriving at which Place, I was inform'd that the Army of the Confederates lay encamp'd not far from *Nivelle*; and under the daily Expectation of an Engagement with the Enemy. This News made me press forward to the Service; for which Purpose I carry'd along with me proper Letters of Recommendation to Sir *Walter Vane*, who was at that time a Major-General. Upon further Enquiry I understood, that a Party of Horse, which was to guard some Waggons that were going to Count *Montery's* Army, were to set out next Morning; so I got an *Irish* Priest to introduce me to the Commanding Officer, which he readily oblig'd me in; and they, as I wish'd them, arriv'd in the Camp next day.

I had scarce been there an Hour, when happen'd one of the most extraordinary Accidents in Life. I observ'd in the East a strange dusty colour'd Cloud, of a pretty large Extent, riding, not before the Wind (for it was a perfect Calm) with such a precipitate Motion, that it was got over our Heads almost as soon as seen. When the Skirts of that Cloud began to cover our Camp, there suddenly arose such a terrible Hurricaine, or Whirlwind, that all the Tents were carry'd aloft with great Violence into the Air; and Soldiers' Hats flew so high and thick, that my Fansy can resemble it to nothing better than those Flights of Rooks, which at Dusk of Evening, leaving the Fields, seek their roosting Places. Trees were torn up by the very Roots; and the Roofs of all the Barns, &c. belonging to the Prince's Quarters, were blown quite away. This lasted for about half an Hour, until the Cloud was wholly past over us, when as suddenly ensued the same pacifik Calm as before the Cloud's Approach. Its Course was seemingly directly West; and yet we were soon after inform'd, that the fine Dome of the great Church at *Utrecht* had greatly suffer'd by it the same Day. And, if I am not must mistaken, Sir *William Temple*, in his Memoirs, mentions somewhat of it, which he felt at *Lillo*, on his Return from the Prince of *Orange's* Camp, where he had been a Day or two before.

As soon after this, as I could get an Opportunity, I deliver'd, at his Quarters, my recommendatory Letters to Sir *Walter Vane*; who receiv'd me very kindly, telling me at the same time, that there were six or seven *English* Gentlemen, who had enter'd themselves Voluntiers in the Prince's own Company of Guards: And added, that he would immediately recommend me to Count *Solmes*, their Colonel. He was not worse than his Word, and I was enter'd accordingly. Those six Gentlemen were as follows, ——— *Clavers*, who since was better known by the Title of Lord *Dundee*; Mr. *Collier*, now Lord *Portmore*; Mr. *Rooke*, since Major-General; Mr. *Hales*, who lately died, and was for a long time Governor of *Chelsea-Hospital*; Mr. *Venner*, Son of that *Venner* remarkable for his being one of the Fifth-Monarchy Men; and Mr. *Boyce*. The four first rose to be very eminent; but Fortune is not to all alike favourable.

In about a Week's Time after, it was resolv'd in a Council of War, to march towards *Binch*, a small wall'd Town, about four Leagues from *Nivelle*; the better to cut off the Provisions from coming to the Prince of *Condé's* Camp that Way.

Accordingly, on the first Day of *August*, being *Saturday*, we began our March; and the *English* Voluntiers had the Favour of a Baggage Waggon appointed them. Count *Souches*, the Imperial General, with the Troops of that Nation, led the Van; the main Body was compos'd of *Dutch*, under the Prince of *Orange*. as Generalissimo; and the *Spaniards*, under Prince *Vaudemont*, with some Detachments, made the Rear Guard.

As we were upon our March, I being among those Detachments which made up the Rear Guard, observ'd a great Party of the Enemy's Horse upon an Ascent, which, I then imagin'd, as it after prov'd, to be the Prince of *Condé* taking a View of our Forces under March. There were many Defiles, which our Army must necessarily pass; through which that Prince politickly enough permitted the *Imperial* and *Dutch* Forces to pass unmolested. But when Prince *Vaudemont*, with the *Spaniards*, and our Detachments, thought to have done the like, the Prince of *Condé* fell on our Rear Guard; and, after a long and sharp Dispute, entirely routed 'em; the Marquiss of *Assentar*, a *Spanish* Lieutenant-General, dying upon the spot.

Had the Prince of *Condé* contented himself with this Share of good Fortune, his Victory had been uncontested: But being pushed forward by a vehement Heat of Temper (which he was noted for) and flush'd with this extraordinary Success, he resolv'd to force the whole Confederate Army to a Battle. In order to which, he immediately led his Forces between our Second Line, and our Line of Baggage; by which means the latter were entirely cut off; and were subjected to the Will of the Enemy, who fell directly to plunder; in which they were not a little assisted by the routed *Spaniards* themselves, who did not disdain at that time to share with the Enemy in the plundering of their Friends and Allies.

The *English* Voluntiers had their Share of this ill Fortune with the rest; their Waggon appointed them being among those intercepted by the Enemy; and I, for my Part, lost every Thing but Life, which yet was saved almost as unaccountably as my Fellow-Soldiers had lost theirs. The Baggage, as I have said, being cut off, and at the Mercy of the Enemy, every one endeavour'd to escape through, or over the Hedges. And as in all Cases of like Confusion, one endeavours to save himself upon the Ruins of others: So here, he that found himself stopt by another in getting over the Cap of a Hedge, pull'd him back to make way for himself, and perhaps met with the same Fortune from a Third, to the Destruction of all. I was then in the Vigour of my Youth, and none of the least active, and perceiving how it had far'd with some before me, I clapt my left Leg upon the Shoulders of one who was thus contending with another, and with a Spring threw my self over both their Heads and the Hedge at the same time. By this Means I not only sav'd my Life (for they were all cut to Pieces that could not get over) but from an Eminence, which I soon after attain'd, I had an Opportunity of seeing, and making my Observations upon the remaining Part of that glorious Conflict.

It was from that advantageous Situation, that I presently discover'd that the Imperialists, who led the Van, had now join'd the main Body. And, I confess, it was with an almost inexpressible Pleasure, that I beheld, about three a-Clock, with what intrepid Fury they fell upon the Enemy. In short, both Armies were universally engag'd, and with great Obstinacy disputed the Victory till Eleven at Night. At which Time the *French*, being pretty well surfeited, made their Retreat. Nevertheless, to secure it by a Stratagem, they left their lighted Matches hanging in the Hedges, and waving with the Air, to conceal it from the Confederate Army.

About two Hours after, the Confederate Forces follow'd the Example of their Enemies, and drew off. And tho' neither Army had much Reason to boast; yet as the Prince of *Orange* remained last in the Field; and die *French* had lost what they before had gain'd, the Glory of the Day fell to the Prince of *Orange*; who, altho' but twenty-four Years of Age, had the Suffrage of Friend and Foe, of having play'd the Part of an old and experienc'd Officer.

There were left that Day on the Field of Battle, by a general Computation, not less than eighteen Thousand Men on both Sides, over and above those, who died of their Wounds: The Loss being pretty equal, only the *French* carried off most Prisoners. Prince *Waldeck* was shot through the Arm, which I was near enough to be an Eye-witness of; And my much lamented Friend, Sir *Walter Vane*, was carried off dead. A Wound in the Arm was all the Mark of Honour, that I as yet could boast of, though our Cannon in the Defiles had slain many near me.

The Prince *of Condé* (as we were next Day inform'd) lay all that Night under a Hedge, wrapp'd in his Cloke: And either from the Mortification of being disappointed in his Hopes of Victory; or from a Reflection of the Disservice, which is own natural over Heat of Temper had drawn upon him, was almost inconsolable many Days after. And thus ended the famous Battle of *Seneff*.

But though common Vogue has given it the Name of a Battle, in my weak Opinion, it might rather deserve that of a confus'd Skirmish; all Things having been forcibly carried on without Regularity, or even Design enough to allow it any higher Denomination: For, as I have said before, notwithstanding I was advantagiously stationed for Observation, I found it very often impossible to distinguish one Party from another. And this was more remarkably evident on the Part of the Prince of *Orange*, whose Valour and Vigour having led him into the Middle of the Enemy, and being then sensible of his Error, by a peculiar Presence of Mind, gave the Word of Command in *French*, which he spoke perfectly well. But the *French* Soldiers, who took him for one of their own Generals, making Answer, that their Powder was all spent, it afforded Matter of Instruction to him to persist in his Attack; at the same Time, that it gave him a Lesson of Caution, to withdraw himself, as soon as he could, to his own Troops.

However, the Day after the Prince of *Orange* thought proper to march to *Quarignan*, a Village within a League of *Mons*; where he remain'd some Days, till he could be supply'd from *Brussells* with those Necessaries which his Army stood in need of.

From thence we march'd to *Valenciennes*, where we again encamp'd, till we could receive Things proper for a Siege. Upon the Arrival whereof, the Prince gave Orders to decamp, and march'd his Army with a Design to besiege *Aeth*. But having Intelligence on our March, that the Mareschal *De Humiers* had reinforc'd that Garrison, we march'd directly to *Oudenard*, and immediately invested it.

This Siege was carried on with such Application and Success, that the Besiegers were in a few Days ready for a Storm; but the Prince of *Condé* prevented them, by coming up to its Relief. Upon which the Prince of *Orange*, pursuant to the Resolution of a Council of War the Night before, drew off his Forces in order to give him Battle; and to that purpose, after the laborious Work of filling up our Lines of Contravallation, that the Horse might pass more freely, we lay upon our Arms all Night. Next Morning we expected the Imperial General, Count *Souches*, to join us; but instead of that, he sent back some very frivolous Excuses, of the Inconveniency of the Ground for a Battle; and after that, instead of joining the Prince, marched off quite another way; the Prince of *Orange*, with the *Dutch* and *Spanish* Troops, marched directly for *Ghent*; exclaiming publickly against the Chicanery of *Souches*, and openly declaring, That he had been advertis'd of a Conference between a *French* Capuchin and that General, the Night before. Certain it is, that that General lay under the Displeasure of his Master, the Emperor, for that Piece of Management; and the Count *de Sporck* was immediately appointed General in his Place.

The Prince of *Orange* was hereupon leaving the Army in great Disgust, till prevail'd upon by the Count *de Montery*, for the general Safety, to recede from that Resolution. However, seeing no likelihood of any Thing further to be done, while *Souches* was in Command, he resolv'd upon a Post of more Action, though more dangerous; wherefore ordering ten Thousand Men to march before, he himself soon after foliow'd to the Siege of *Grave*.

The *Grave*, a strong Place, and of the first Moment to the *Hollanders*, had been block'd up by the *Dutch* Forces all the Summer; the Prince of *Orange* therefore leaving the main Army under Prince *Waldeck* at *Ghent*, follow'd the Detachment he had made for the Siege of that important Place, resolving to purchase it at any Rate. On his Arrival before it, Things began to find new Motion; and as they were carried on with the utmost Application and Fury, the Besieged found themselves, in a little Time, oblig'd to change their haughty Summer Note for one more suitable to the Season.

The Prince, from his first coming, having kept those within hotly ply'd with Ball, both from Cannon and Mortars, Monsieur *Chamilly*, the Governor, after a few Days, being weary of such warm Work, desired to capitulate; upon which Hostages were exchanged, and Articles agreed on next Morning. Pursuant to which, the Garrison march'd out with Drums beating and Colours flying, two Days after, and were conducted to *Charleroy*.

By the taking this Place, which made the Prince of *Orange* the more earnest upon it, the *French* were wholly expell'd their last Year's astonishing Conquests in *Holland*. And yet there was another Consideration, that render'd the Surrender of it much more considerable. For the *French* being sensible of the great Strength of this Place, had there deposited all their Cannon and Ammunition, taken from their other Conquests in *Holland*, which they never were able to remove or carry off, with tolerable Prospect of Safety, after that Prince's Army first took the Field.

The Enemy being march'd out, the Prince enter'd the Town, and immediately order'd public Thanksgivings for its happy Reduction. Then having appointed a Governor, and left a sufficient Garrison, he put an End to that Campaign, and return'd to the *Hague*, where he had not been long before he fell ill of the Small Pox. The Consternation this threw the whole Country into, is not to be express'd; Any one that had seen it would have thought, that the *French* had made another Inundation greater than the former. But when the Danger was over, their Joy and Satisfaction, for his Recovery, was equally beyond Expression.

The Year 1675 yielded very little remarkable in our Army. *Limburgh* was besieged by the *French*, under the Command of the Duke of *Enguien*, which the Prince of *Orange* having Intelligence of, immediately decamp'd from his fine Camp at *Bethlem*, near *Louvain*, in order to raise the Siege. But as we were on a full March for that purpose, and had already reach'd *Ruremond*, Word was brought, that the Place had surrender'd the Day before. Upon which Advice, the Prince, after a short Halt, made his little Army (for it consisted not of more than thirty Thousand Men) march back to *Brabant*. Nothing of moment, after this, occurr'd all that Campaign.

In the Year 1676, the Prince of *Orange* having, in concert with the *Spaniards*, resolv'd upon the important Siege of *Maestrich* (the only Town in the *Dutch* Provinces, then remaining in the Hands of the *French*) it was accordingly invested about the middle of *June*, with an Army of twenty Thousand Men, under the Command of his Highness Prince *Waldeck*, with the grand Army covering the Siege. It was some Time before the heavy Cannon, which we expected up the *Maes*, from *Holland*, arrived; which gave Occasion to a Piece of Raillery of Monsieur *Calvo*, the Governor, which was as handsomely repartec'd. That Governor, by a Messenger, intimating his Sorrow to find, we had pawn'd our Cannon for Ammunition Bread. Answer was made, That in a few Days we hoped to give him a Taste of the Loaves, which he should find would be sent him into the Town in extraordinary plenty. I remember another Piece of Raillery, which pass'd some Days after between the *Rhingrave* and the same *Calvo*. The former sending Word, that he hoped within three Weeks to salute that Governor's Mistress within the Place. *Calvo* reply'd, He'd give him leave to kiss her all over, if he kiss'd her any where in three Months.

But our long expected Artillery being at last arriv'd, all this Jest and Merriment was soon converted into earnest. Our Trenches were immediately open'd towards the *Dauphin* Bastion, against which were planted many Cannon, in order to make a Breach; my self as a Probationer being twice put upon the forlorn Hope to facilitate that difficult Piece of Service. Nor was it long before such a Breach was effected, as was esteem'd practicable, and therefore very soon after it was ordered to be attack'd.

The Disposition for the Attack was thus ordered; two Serjeants with twenty Grenadiers, a Captain with fifty Men, my self one of the

Number; then a Party carrying Wool Sacks, and after them two Captains with one Hundred Men more; the Soldiers in the Trenches to be ready to sustain them, as Occasion should require.

The Signal being given, we left our Trenches accordingly, having about one Hundred Yards to run, before we could reach the Breach, which we mounted with some Difficulty and Loss; all our Batteries firing at the same instant to keep our Action in countenance, and favour our Design. When we were in Possession of the Bastion, the Enemy fir'd most furiously upon us with their small Cannon through a thin brick Wall, by which, and their hand Grenadoes, we lost more Men than we did in the Attack it self.

But well had it been had our ill Fortune stopp'd there; for as if Disaster must needs be the Concomitant of Success, we soon lost what we had thus gotten, by a small, but very odd Accident. Not being furnished with such Scoopes as our Enemies made use of, in tossing their hand Grenadoes some distance off, one of our own Soldiers aiming to throw one over the Wall into the Counterscarp among the Enemy, it so happen'd that he unfortunately miss'd his Aim, and the Grenade fell down again on our side the Wall, very near the Person who fir'd it. He starting back to save himself, and some others who saw it fall, doing the like, those who knew nothing of the Matter fell into a sudden Confusion, and imagining some greater danger than there really was, every body was struck with a panick Fear, and endeavour'd to be the first who should quit the Bastion, and secure himself by a real Shame from an imaginary Evil. Thus was a Bastion, that had been gloriously gain'd, inadvertently deserted; and that too, with the Loss of almost as many Men in the Retreat, as had been slain in the Onset, and the Enemy most triumphantly again took Possession of it.

Among the Slain on our Side in this Action, was an Ensign of Sir *John Fenwick*'s Regiment; and as an Approbation of my Services his Commission was bestowed upon me.

A few Days after it was resolv'd again to storm that Bastion, as before; out of three *English*, and one *Scotch* Regiment, then in the Camp, a Detachment was selected for a fresh Attack. Those Regiments were under the Command of Sir *John Fenwick* (who was afterwards beheaded) Colonel *Ralph Widdrington*, and Colonel *Ashley*, of the *English*; and Sir *Alexander Collier*, Father of the present Lord *Portmore*, of the *Scotch*. Out of every of these four Regiments, as before, were detach'd a Captain, a Lieutenant, and an Ensign, with fifty

Men: Captain *Anthony Bamwell*, of Sir *John Fenwick's* Regiment, who was now my Captain, commanding that Attack.

At break of Day the Attack was begun with great Resolution; and though vigorously maintain'd, was attended with the desir'd Success. The Bastion was again taken, and in it the commanding Officer, who in Service to himself, more than to us, told us, that the Center of the Bastion would soon be blown up being to his Knowledge undermin'd for that purpose. But this Secret prov'd of no other use, than to make us, by way of Precaution, to keep as much as we could upon the Rampart. In this Attack Captain *Barnwell* lost his Life; and it happened my new Commission was wetted (not, as too frequently is the Custom, with a Debauch) but with a Bullet through my Hand, and the Breach of my Collar Bone with the Stroke of a Halberd.

After about half an hour's Possession of the Bastion, the Mine under it, of which the *French* Officer gave us warning, was sprung; the Enemy at the same Time making a furious Sally upon us. The Mine did a little, though the less, Execution, for being discovered; but the Sally no way answer'd their End, for we beat them back, and immediately fix'd our Lodgment; which we maintain'd during the Time of the Siege. But to our double Surprize, a few Days after they fir'd another Mine under, or aside, the former, in which they had plac'd a quantity of Grenadoes, which did much more Execution than the other: Notwithstanding all which, a Battery of Guns was presently erected upon that Bastion, which very considerably annoy'd the Enemy.

The Breach for a general Storm was now render'd almost practicable; yet before that could be advisably attempted, there was a strong Horn-work to be taken. Upon this Exploit the *Dutch* Troops only were to signalize themselves; and they answered the Confidence repos'd in them; for though they were twice repuls'd, at the third Onset they were more successful, and took Possession; which they likewise kept to the Raising of the Siege.

There was a Stratagem lay'd at this Time, which in its own Merit one would have thought should not have fail'd of a good Effect; but to shew the Vanity of the highest human Wisdom it miscarry'd. On the other side of the *Maes*, opposite to *Maestrich*, lies the strong Fortress of *Wyck*, to which it is join'd by a stone Bridge of six fair Arches. The design was, by a false Attack on that regular Fortification to draw the Strength of the Garrison to its Defence, which was but very natural to imagine would be the Consequence. Ready to attend that well concerted false Attack, a large flat bottom'd Boat, properly furnish'd with Barrels of Gun-Powder, and other Necessaries, was to fall down under one of the middle Arches, and when fix'd there, by firing the Powder to have blown up the Bridge, and by that means to have prevented the Return of the Garrison to oppose a real Attack at that instant of Time to be made upon the Town of *Maestrich* by the whole Army.

The false Attack on *Wyck* was accordingly made, which, as propos'd, drew the Main of the Garrison of *Maestrich* to its Defence, and the Boat so furnish'd fell down the River as projected, but unfortunately, before it could reach the Arch, from the Darkness of the Night, running upon a Shoal, it could not be got off; for which Reason the Men in the Boat were glad to make a hasty Escape for fear of being discovered; as the Boat was, next Morning; and the whole Design laid open.

This Stratagem thus miscarrying, all Things were immediately got ready for a general Storm, at the main Breach in the Town; and the rather, because the Prince of *Orange* had receiv'd incontestable Intelligence, That Duke *Schomberg*, at the Head of the *French* Army, was in full march to relieve the Place. But before every Thing could be rightly got ready for the intended Storm (though some there were who pretended to say, that a Dispute rais'd by the *Spaniards* with the *Dutch*, about the Propriety of the Town, when taken, was the Cause of that Delay) we heard at some distance several Guns fir'd as Signals of Relief; upon which we precipitately, and, as most imagin'd, shamefully drew off from before the Place, and join'd the grand Army under Prince *Waldeck*. But it was Matter of yet greater Surprize to most on the Spot, that when the Armies were so joyn'd, we did not stay to offer the Enemy Battle. The well known Courage of the Prince, then Generalissimo, was so far from solving this Riddle, that it rather puzzled all who thought of it; however, the prevailing Opinion was, that it was occasion'd by some great Misunderstanding between the *Spaniards* and the *Dutch*. And Experience will evince, that this was not the only Disappointment of that Nature, occasion'd by imperfect Understandings.

Besides the Number of common Soldiers slain in this Attack, which was not inconsiderable, we lost here the brave *Rhingrave*, a Person much lamented on account of his many other excellent Qualifications, as well as that of a General. Colonel *Ralph Widdrington*, and Colonel *Doleman* (who had not enjoy'd *Widdrington's* Commission above a Fortnight). Captain *Douglas*, Captain *Barnwell*, and Captain *Lee*, were of the Slain among the

English; who, indeed, had born the whole brunt of the Attack upon the *Dauphin*'s Bastion.

I remember the Prince of *Orange*, during the Siege, receiv'd a Shot through his Arm; which giving an immediate Alarm to the Troops under his Command, he took his Hat off his Head with the wounded Arm, and smiling, wav'd it, to shew them there was no danger. Thus, after the most gallant Defence against the most couragious Onsets, ended the Siege of *Maestrich*; and with it all that was material that Campaign.

Early in the Spring, in the Year 1677, the *French* Army, under the Duke of *Orleans*, besieged at once, both *Cambray* and *Saint Omers*. This last the Prince of *Orange* seem'd very intent and resolute to relieve. In order to which, well knowing by sad Experience, it would be to little purpose to wait the majestick Motions of the *Spaniards*, that Prince got together what Forces he could, all in *Dutch* Pay, and marching forward with all speed, resolv'd, even at the Hazard of a Battle, to attempt the Raising the Siege. Upon his appearing the Duke of *Orleans*, to whose particular Conduct the Care of that Siege was committed, drew off from before the Place, leaving scarce enough of his Men to defend the Trenches. The Prince was under the Necessity of marching his Forces over a Morass; and the Duke, well knowing it, took care to attack him near *Mont Cassel*, before half his little Army were got over. The Dispute was very sharp, but the Prince being much out number'd, and his Troops not able, by the Straitness of the Passage, to engage all at once, was oblig'd at last to retreat, which he did in pretty good Order. I remember the *Dutch* Troops did not all alike do their Duty; and the Prince seeing one of the Officers on his fullest speed, call'd to him over and over to halt; which the Officer in too must haste to obey, the Prince gave him a Slash over the Face, saying, *By this Mark I shall know you another Time*. Soon after this Retreat of the Prince, Saint *Omers* was surrender'd.

Upon this Retreat the Prince marching back, lay for some time among the Boors, who from the good Discipline, which he took care to make his Troops observe, did not give us their customary boorish Reception. And yet as secure as we might think our selves, I met with a little Passage that confirm'd in me the Notions, which the generality as well as I, had imbib'd of the private Barbarity of those People, whenever an Opportunity falls in their Way. I was stroling at a Distance from my Quarters, all alone, when I found my self near one of their Houses; into which, the Doors being open, I ventur'd to enter. I saw no body when I came in, though the House was, for that Sort of People, well enough furnish'd, and in pretty decent Order. I call'd, but no body answering, I had the Curiosity to advance a little farther, when, at the Mouth of the Oven, which had not yet wholly lost its Heat, I spy'd the Corpse of a Man so bloated, swoln and parch'd, as left me little room to doubt, that the Oven had been the Scene of his Destiny. I confess the Sight struck me with Horror; and as much Courage and Security as I enter'd with, I withdrew in haste, and with quite different Sentiments, and could not fansy my self out of Danger till I had reach'd our Camp. A wise Man should not frame an Accusation on Conjectures; but, on Inquiry, I was soon made sensible, that such barbarous Usage is too common among those People; especially if they meet with a Straggler, of what Nation soever.

This made me not very sorry when we decamp'd, and we soon after receiv'd Orders to march and invest *Charleroy*; before which Place we stay'd somewhat above a Week, and then drew off. I remember very well, that I was not the only Person then in the Camp that was at a Loss to dive into the Reason of this Investiture and Decampment: But since I at that time, among the Politicians of the Army, never heard a good one, I shall not venture to offer my Sentiments at so great a Distance.

We, after this march'd towards *Mons*; and, in our March, pass'd over the very Grounds on which the Battle of *Seneff* had been fought three Years before. It was with no little Pleasure, that I re-survey'd a Place, that had once been of so much Danger to me; and where my Memory and Fansy now repeated back all those Observations I had then made under some unavoidable Confusion. Young as I was, both in Years and Experience, from my own Reflections, and the Sentiments of others, after the Fight was over, methought I saw visibly before me the well order'd Disposition of the Prince of *Condé*; the inexpressible Difficulties which the Prince of *Orange* had to encounter with; while at the same Moment I could not omit to repay my Debt to the Memory of my first Patron, Sir *Walter Vane*, who there loosing his Life, left me a solitary Wanderer to the wide World of Fortune.

But these Thoughts soon gave place to new Objects, which every Hour presented themselves in our continu'd March to *Enghien*, a Place famous for the finest Gardens in all *Flanders*, near which we encamp'd, on the very same Ground which the *French* chose some Years after at the Battle of *Steenkirk*: of which I shall speak in its proper Place. Here the Prince of *Orange* left our Army, as we afterwards found, to pass into *England*; where he marry'd the Princess *Mary*, Daughter of the

Duke of *York*. And after his Departure, that Campaign ended without any thing further material.

Now began the Year 1678, famous for the Peace, and no less remarkable for an Action previous to it, which has not fail'd to employ the Talents of Men, variously, as they stood affected. Our Army, under the Prince of *Orange*, lay encamp'd at *Soignies*, where it was whisper'd that the Peace was concluded. Notwithstanding which, two Days after, being *Sunday* the 17th Day of *August*, the Army was drawn out, as most others as well as my self apprehended, in order to *feux de Joye*; but in lieu of that, we found our March order'd towards St. *Dennis*, where the Duke of *Luxembourg* lay, as he imagin'd, safe in inaccessible Entrenchments.

About three of the Clock our Army arriv'd there, when we receiv'd Orders to make the Attack. It began with a most vigorous Spirit, that promis'd no less than the Success which ensu'd. The three *English* and three *Scotch* Regiments, under the Command of the ever renown'd Earl of *Ossory*, together with the Prince of *Orange*'s Guards, made their Attack at a Place call'd the *Château*, where the *French* took their Refuge among a Parcel of Hop-Poles; but their Resource was as weak as their Defence; and they were soon beaten out with a very great Slaughter.

It was here that a *French* Officer having his Pistol directed at the Breast of the Prince, Monsieur *D'Auverquerque* interpos'd, and shot the Officer dead upon the Spot.

The Fight lasted from three in the Afternoon till Nine at Night; when growing dark, the Duke of *Luxembourg* forsook his Entrenchments, into which we march'd next Morning. And to see the sudden Change of Things! that very Spot of Ground, where nothing but Fire and Fury appear'd the Day before, the yest saw solac'd with the Proclamation of a Peace.

About an Hour before the Attack began, the Duke of *Monmouth* arriv'd in the Army, being kindly receiv'd by the Prince of *Orange*, bravely fighting by his Side, all that Day. The Woods and the Unevenness of the Ground, render'd the Cavalry almost useless; yet I saw a Standard, among some others, which was taken from the Enemy, being richly embroidered with Gold and Silver, bearing the Sun in the Zodiack, with these haughty Words, *Nihil obstabit eunte*. On the News of this unexpected Victory, the States of *Holland* sent to congratulate the Prince; and to testify how much they valued his Preservation, they presented Monsieur *D'Auverquerque*, who had so bravely rescued him, with a Sword, whose Handle was of massy Gold set with Diamonds. I forgot to mention that this Gentleman receiv'd a Shot on his Head at the Battle of *Seneff,* and truly in all Actions, which were many, he nobly distinguished himself by his Bravery. He was Father of this present Earl of *Grantham.*

    The Names of the English Officers which I knew to be killed in this Action.

Lieut. Col. Archer, Capt. Pemfield,
Capt. Charleton, Lieut. Charleton,
Capt. Richardson, Lieut. Barton,
Capt. Fisher, Ensign Colville.
With several others, whose Names I have forgot.

    Lieut. Col. *Babington,* who began the Attack, by beating the *French* out of the Hop Garden, was taken Prisoner. Col. *Hales,* who was a long time Governor of *Chelsea College,* being then a Captain, received a Shot on his Leg, of which he went lame to his dying Day.

    The War thus ended by the Peace of *Nimeugen,* The Regiment in which I serv'd, was appointed to be in Garrison at the *Grave.* We lay there near four Years, our Soldiers being mostly employ'd about the Fortifications. It was here, and by that Means, that I imbib'd the Rudiments of Fortification, and the practick Part of an Enginier, which in my more advanc'd Years was of no small Service to me.

    Nevertheless, in the Year 1684, our Regiment receiv'd Orders to march to *Haren,* near *Brussels,* where, with other Forces, we encamp'd, till we heard that *Luxemburg,* invaded by the *French,* in a Time of the profoundest Peace, had surrender'd to them. Then we decamp'd, and march'd to *Mechlin;* where we lay in the Field till near *November.* Not that there was any War proclaim'd; but as not knowing, whether those who had committed such Acts of Hostility in time of Peace might not take it in their Heads to proceed yet further. In *November* we march'd into that Town, where Count *Nivelle* was Governor: The Marquiss *de Grana,* at the same time, governing the *Netherlands* in the Jurisdiction of *Spain.*

    Nothing of any Moment happen'd after this, till the Death of King *Charles* II. The Summer after which, the three *English* and three *Scotch* Regiments receiv'd Orders to pass over into *England,* upon the Occasion of *Monmouth's* Rebellion; where, upon our Arrival, we receiv'd Orders to encamp on *Hounslow-Heath.* But that Rebellion being soon stifled, and King *James* having no farther Need of us, those Regiments were order'd to return again to *Holland,* into the proper Service of those who paid them.

Tho' I am no stiff Adherer to the Doctrine of Predestination, yet to the full Assurance of a Providence I never could fail to adhere. Thence came it, that my natural Desire to serve my own native Country prevail'd upon me to quit the Service of another, though its Neighbour and Allie. Events are not always to direct the Judgment; and therefore whether I did best in following those fondling Dictates of Nature, I shall neither question nor determine.

However, it was not long after my Arrival in *England* before I had a Commission given me by King *James*, to be a Lieutenant in a new rais'd Regiment under the Command of Colonel *Tufton*, Brother to the Earl of *Thanet*. Under this Commission I sojourn'd out two peaceable Campaigns on *Hounslow-Heath;* where I was an Eye-Witness of one mock Siege of *Buda*. After which our Regiment was order'd to *Berwick*, where I remained till the Revolution.

King *James* having abdicated the Throne, and the Prince of *Orange* accepting the Administration, all Commissions were order'd to be renew'd in his Name. The Officers of our Regiment, as well as others, severally took out theirs accordingly, a very few excepted, of which Number was our Colonel; who refusing a Compliance, his Commission was given to Sir *James Lesley*.

The Prince of *Orange* presently after was declar'd and proclaim'd King, and his Princess Queen, with a conjunctive Power. Upon which our Regiment was order'd into *Scotland*, where Affairs appear'd under a Face of Disquietude. We had our Quarters at *Leith*, till the Time the Castle of *Edinburgh*, then under the Command of the Duke of *Gordon*, had surrender'd. After which, pursuant to fresh Orders, we march'd to *Inverness*, a Place of no great Strength, and as little Beauty; though yet I think I may say, without the least Danger of an *Hyperbole*, that it is as pleasant as most Places in that Country. Here we lay two long Winters, perpetually harrass'd upon Parties, and hunting of somewhat wilder than their wildest Game, namely, the *Highlanders,* who were, if not as nimble footed, yet fully as hard to be found.

But General *Mackay* having receiv'd Orders to build a Fort at *Inverlochy*, our Regiment, among others, was commanded to that Service. The two Regiments appointed on the same Duty, with some few Dragoons, were already on their March, which having join'd, we march'd together through *Louquebar*. This sure is the wildest Country in the *Highlands*, if not in the World. I did not see one House in all our March; and their Oeconomy, if I may call it such, is much the same with that of the *Arabs* or *Tartars*. Hutts, or Cabins of Trees and Trash, are their Places of Habitation; in which they dwell, till their half-horn'd Cattle have devour'd the Grass, and then remove, staying no where longer than that Convenience invites them.

In this March, or rather, if you please, most dismal Peregrination, we could be very rarely go two on a Breast; and oftner, like Geeze in a String, one after another. So that our very little Army had sometimes, or rather most commonly, an Extent of many Miles; our Enemy, the *Highlanders*, firing down upon us from their Summits all the Way. Nor was it possible for our Men, or very rarely at least, to return their Favours with any Prospect of Success; for as they pop'd upon us always on a sudden, they never stay'd long enough to allow any of our Soldiers a Mark; or even time enough to fire: And for our Men to march, or climb up those Mountains, which to them were natural Champion, would have been as dangerous as it seem'd to us impracticable. Nevertheless, under all these disheartning Disadvantages, we arriv'd at *Inverlochy*, and there perform'd the Task appointed, building a Fort on the same Spot where *Cromwell* had rais'd one before. And which was not a little remarkable, we had with us one *Hill*, a Colonel, who had been Governor in *Oliver's* Time, and who was now again appointed Governor by General *Mackay*. Thus the Work on which we were sent being effected, we march'd back again by the Way of *Gillycrancky*, where that memorable Battle under *Dundee* had been fought the Year before.

Some time after, Sir *Thomas Levingston*, afterwards Earl of *Tiviot*, having receiv'd Intelligence that the *Highlanders* intended to fall down into the lower Countries, in a considerable Body, got together a Party of about five Hundred (the Dragoons, call'd the *Scotch Greys*, inclusive) with which he resolv'd, if possible, to give them a Meeting. We left *Inverness* the last Day of *April*, and encamp'd near a little Town call'd *Forrest*, the Place where, as Tradition still confidently avers, the Witches met *Mackbeth*, and greeted him with their diabolical Auspices. But this Story is so naturally display'd in a Play of the immortal *Shakespear*, that I need not descend here to any farther Particulars.

Here Sir *Thomas* receiv'd Intelligence, that the *Highlanders* design'd to encamp upon the *Spey*, near the Laird of *Grant's* Castle. Whereupon we began our March about Noon; and the next Day, about the Break thereof, we came to that River, where we soon discover'd the *Highlanders* by their Fires. Sir *Thomas* immediately, on Sight of it, issued his Orders for our fording the River, and falling upon them as soon after as possible. Both were accordingly perform'd, and with so good Order, Secrecy and Success, that *Cannon* and *Balfour*, their Commanders, were obliged to make their Escape naked.

They were about one Thousand in Number, of which were kill'd about three Hundred; we pursued them, till they got up *Crowdale-Hill*, where we lost them in a Fog. And, indeed so high is that Hill, that they, who perfectly knew it, assured me that it never is without a little dark Fog hanging over it. And to me, at that Instant of Time, they seem'd rather to be People receiv'd up into Clouds, than flying from an Enemy.

Near this there was an old Castle, call'd *Lethendy*, into which about Fifty of them made their Retreat, most of them Gentlemen, resolving there to defend themselves to the last. Sir *Thomas* sent a Messenger to them, with an Offer of Mercy, if they would surrender: But they refus'd the profer'd Quarter, and fir'd upon our Men, killing two of our Grenadiers, and wounding another. During my Quarters at the *Grave*, having learnt to throw a Grenado, I took three or four in a Bag, and crept down by the Side of a Ditch, or Dyke, to an old thatch'd House near the Castle, imagining, on my mounting the same, I might be near enough to throw them, so as to do execution. I found all Things answer my Expectation; and the Castle wanting a Cover, I threw in a Grenado, which put the Enemy immediately into Confusion. The Second had not so good Success, falling short, and the Third burst as soon as it was well out of my Hand, though without Damage to my self. But throwing the Fourth in at a Window, it so increas'd the Confusion, which the first had put them into, that they immediately call'd out to me, upon their Parole of Safety, to come to them.

Accordingly I went up to the Door, which they had barricaded, and made up with great Stones; when they told me they were ready to surrender upon Condition of obtaining Mercy. I return'd to Sir *Thomas*; and telling him what I had done, and the Consequence of it, and the Message they had desir'd me to deliver (a great many of the *Highland* Gentlemen, not of this Party, being with him) Sir *Thomas*, in a high Voice, and broad *Scotch*, best to be heard and understood, order'd me back to tell 'em, *He would cut them all to Pieces, for their Murder of two of his Grenadiers, after his Proffer of Quarter.*

I was returning full of these melancholy Tidings, when Sir *Thomas*, advancing after me a little Distance from the rest of the Company; *Hark ye, Sir*, says he, *I believe there may be among 'em some of our old Acquaintance* (for we had serv'd together in the Service of the *States* in *Flanders*) *therefore tell them they shall have good Quarter.*

I very willingly carry'd back a Message to much chang'd to my Mind; and upon delivering of it, without the least Hesitation, they threw down the Barricado, open'd the Door, and out came one *Brody*, who, as he then told me, had had a Piece of his Nose taken off by one of my Grenadoes. I carry'd him to Sir *Thomas*, who confirming my Message, they all came out, and surrendered themselves Prisoners. This happen'd on *May Day* in the Morning; for which Reason we return'd to *Inverness* with our Prisoners, and Boughs in our Hats; and the *Highlanders* never held up their Heads so high after this Defeat.

Upon this Success Sir *Thomas* wrote to Court, giving a full Account of the whole Action. In which being pleas'd to make mention of my Behaviour, with some Particularities, I had soon after a Commission order'd me for a Company in the Regiment under the Command of Brigadier *Tiffin*.

My Commission being made out, sign'd, and sent to me, I repair'd immediately to *Portsmouth*, where the Regiment lay in Garrison. A few Days after I had been there, Admiral *Russel* arriv'd with the Fleet, and anchor'd at St. *Hellen's*, where he remain'd about a Week. On the 18th of *May* the whole Fleet set Sail; and it being my Turn the same Day to mount the Main Guard, I was going the Rounds very early, when I heard great shooting at Sea. I went directly to acquaint the Governor, and told him my Sentiments, that the two contending Fleets were actually engag'd, which indeed prov'd true; for that very Night a Pinnace, which came from our Fleet, brought News that Admiral *Russel* had engag'd the *French* Admiral *Turvile*; and, after a long and sharp Dispute, was making after them to their own Coasts.

The next Day, towards Evening, several other Expresses arriv'd, one after another, all agreeing in the Defeat of the *French* Fleet, and in the Particulars of the burning their *Rising Sun*, together with many other of their Men of War, at *la Hogue*. All which Expresses were immediately forwarded to Court by Mr. *Gibson*, our Governor.

About two Months after this, our Regiment, among many others, was, according to Order, shipp'd off on a Secret Expedition, under the Command of the Duke of *Leinster*, no Man knowing to what Place we were going, or on what Design; no, not the Commander himself. However, when we were out at Sea, the General, according to Instructions, opening his Commission, we were soon put out of our Suspence, and inform'd, that our Orders were to attack *Dunkirk*. But what was so grand a Secret to those concern'd in the Expedition, having been intrusted to a Female Politician on Land, it was soon discover'd to the Enemy; for which Reason our Orders were countermanded, before we reach'd the Place of Action, and our Forces receiv'd Directions to land at *Ostend.*

Soon after this happen'd that memorable Battle at *Steenkirk,* which as very few at that Time could dive into the Reason of, and mistaken Accounts of it have pass'd for authentick, I will mention somewhat more particularly: The Undertaking was bold; and, as many thought, bolder than was consistent with the Character of the wise Undertaker. Nevertheless, the *French* having taken *Namure*; and, as the Malecontents alledg'd, in the very Sight of a superior Army; and nothing having been done by Land of any moment, Things were blown into such a dangerous Fermentation, by a malicious and lying Spirit, that King *William* found himself under a Necessity of attempting something that might appease the Murmurs of the People. He knew very well, though spoke in the Senate, that it was not true, that his Forces at the Siege of *Namure* exceeded those of the Enemy; no Man could be more afflicted than he at the overflowing of the *Mehaigne,* from the continual Rains, which obstructed the Relief he had designed for that important Place; yet since his Maligners made an ill Use of these false Topicks, to insinuate that he had no Mind to put an End to the War, he was resolv'd to evince the contrary, by shewing them that he was not afraid to venture his Life for the better obtaining what was so much desired.

To that Purpose, receiving Intelligence that the Duke of *Luxemburg* lay strongly encamp'd at *Steenkirk,* near *Enghien* (tho' he was sensible he must pass through many Defiles to engage him; and that the many Thickets between the two Armies would frequently afford him new Difficulties) he resolv'd there to attack him. Our Troops at first were forc'd to hew out their Passage for the Horse; and there was no one difficulty that his Imagination had drawn that was lessen'd by Experience; and yet so prosperous were his Arms at the Beginning, that our Troops had made themselves Masters of several Pieces of the Enemy's Cannon. But the farther he advanc'd, the Ground growing straiter, so strait as not to admit his Army's being drawn up in Battalia, the Troops behind could not give timely Succour to those engag'd, and the Cannon we had taken was forcibly left behind in order to make a good Retreat. The *French* had lost all their Courage in the Onset; for though they had too fair an Opportunity, they did not think fit to pursue it; or, at least, did it very languidly. However, the Malecontents at Home, I remember, grew very well pleas'd after this; for so long as they had but a Battle for their Money, like true *Englishmen*, lost or won, they were contented.

Several Causes, I remember, were assign'd for this Miscarriage, as they call'd it; Some there were who were willing to lay it upon the *Dutch*; and alledge a Saying of one of their Generals, who receiving Orders to relieve some *English* and *Scotch* that were over-power'd, was heard to say, *Dam 'em, since they love Fighting let 'em have their Bellies full.* But I should rather impute the Disappointment to the great Loss of so many of our bravest Officers at the very first Onset. General *Mackay*, Colonel *Lanier*, the Earl of *Angus*, with both his Field-Officers, Sir *Robert Douglas*, Colonel *Hodges*, and many others falling, it was enough to put a very considerable Army into Confusion. I remember one particular Action of Sir *Robert Douglas*, that I should think my self to blame should I omit: Seeing his Colours on the other Side the Hedge, in the Hands of the Enemy, he leap'd over, slew the Officer that had them, and then threw them over the Hedge to his Company; redeeming his Colours at the Expense of his Life. Thus the *Scotch* Commander improv'd upon the *Roman* General; for the brave *Posthumius* cast his Standard in the Middle of the Enemy for his Soldiers to retrieve, but *Douglas* retriev'd his from the Middle of the Enemy, without any Assistance, and cast it back to his Soldiers to retain, after he had so bravely rescued it out of the Hands of the Enemy.

From hence our Regiment receiv'd Orders to march to *Dixmuyd*, where we lay some time employ'd in fortifying that Place. While we were there, I had one Morning stedfastly fix'd my Eyes upon some Ducks, that were swimming in a large Water before me; when all on a sudden, in the Midst of a perfect Calm, I observ'd such a strange and strong Agitation in the Waters, that prodigiously surpriz'd me. I was at the same Moment seiz'd with such a Giddiness in my Head, that, for a Minute or two, I was scarce sensible, and had much a-do to keep on my Legs. I had never felt any thing of an Earthquake before, which, as I soon after understood from others, this was; and it left, indeed, very apparent Marks of its Force in a great Rent in the Body of the great Church, which remains to this Day.

Having brought the intended Fortifications into some tolerable Order, we receiv'd a Command out of hand to reimbarque for *England.* And, upon our Landing, Directions met us to march for *Ipswich*, where we had our Quarters all that Winter. From thence we were order'd up to *London*, to do Duty in the *Tower.* I had not been there long, before an Accident happen'd, as little to be accounted for, without a divine Providence, as some would make that Providence to be, that only can account for it.

There was at that Time, as I was assur'd by my Lord *Lucas*, Constable of it, upwards of twenty Thousand Barrels of Gun-powder, in that they call the *White-Tower*, when all at once the middle Flooring did not only give way, or shrink, but fell flat down upon other Barrels of Powder, together with many of the same combustible Matter which had been placed upon it. It was a Providence strangely neglected at that Time, and hardly thought of since; But let any considerate Man consult the Consequences, if it had taken fire; perhaps to the Destruction of the whole City, or, at least, as far as the *Bridge* and Parts adjacent. Let his Thoughts proceed to examine, why, or how, in that precipitate Fall, not one Nail, nor one Piece of Iron, in that large Fabrick, should afford one little Spark to enflame that Mass of sulphurous Matter it was loaded with; and if he is at a loss to find a Providence, I fear his Friends will be more at a loss to find his Understanding. But the Battle of *Landen* happening while our Regiment was here on Duty, we were soon remov'd to our Satisfaction from that pacifick Station, to one more active in *Flanders*.

Notwithstanding that fatal Battle the Year preceding, namely, *A.D.* 1694, the Confederate Army under King *William* lay encamp'd at *Mont. St. André*, an open Place, and much expos'd; while the *French* were entrench'd up to their very Teeth, at *Vignamont*, a little Distance from us. This afforded Matter of great Reflection to the Politicians of those Times, who could hardly allow, that if the Confederate Army suffer'd so much, as it really did in the Battle of *Landen*, it could consist with right Conduct to tempt, or rather dare a new Engagement. But those sage Objectors had forgot the well-known Courage of that brave Prince, and were as little capable of fathoming his Designs. The Enemy, who to their Sorrow had by Experience been made better Judges, was resolv'd to traverse both; for which Purpose they kept close within their Entrenchments; so that after all his Efforts, King *William* finding he could no way draw them to a Battle, suddenly decamp'd, and march'd directly to *Pont Espiers*, by long Marches, with a Design to pass the *French* Lines at that Place.

But notwithstanding our Army march'd in a direct Line, to our great Surprize, we found the Enemy had first taken possession of it. They gave this the Name of the *Long March*, and very deservedly; for though our Army march'd upon the String, and the Enemy upon the

Bow, sensible of the Importance of the Post, and the Necessity of securing it, by double horseing with their Foot, and by leaving their Weary and Weak in their Garrisons, and supplying their Places with fresh Men out of them, they gain'd their Point in disappointing us. Though certain it is, that March cost 'em as many Men and Horses as a Battle. However their Master, the *French* King, was so pleas'd with their indefatigable and auspicious Diligence, that he wrote, with his own Hand, a Letter of Thanks to the Officers, for the great Zeal and Care they had taken to prevent the Confederate Army from entring into *French Flanders*.

King *William*, thus disappointed in that noble Design, gave immediate Orders for his whole Army to march through *Oudenard*, and then ecamp'd at *Rofendale*; after some little Stay at that Camp we were remov'd to the *Camerlins*, between *Newport* and *Ostend*, once more to take our Winter Quarters there among the Boors.

We were now in the Year 1695 when the strong Fortress of *Namur*, taken by the *French* in 1692 and since made by them much stronger, was invested by the Earl of *Athlone*. After very many vigorous Attacks, with the Loss of many Men, the Town was taken, the Garrison retiring into the Castle. Into which soon after, notwithstanding all the Circumspection of the Besiegers, Mareschal *Boufflers* found means, with some Dragoons, to throw himself.

While King *William* was thus engag'd in that glorious and important Siege, Prince *Vaudemont* being posted at *Watergaem*, with about fifty Battallions, and as many Squadrons, the Mareschal *Villeroy* laid a Design to attack him with the whole *French* Army. The Prince imagin'd no less, therefore he prepar'd accordingly, giving us Orders to fortify our Camp, as well as the little time we had for it would permit. Those Orders were pursu'd; nevertheless, I must confess, it was beyond the Reach of my little Reason to account for our so long Stay in the Sight of an Army so much superior to ours. The Prince in the Whole could hardly muster thirty Thousand; and *Villeroy* was known to value himself upon having one Hundred Thousand effective Men. However, the Prince provisionally sent away all our Baggage that very Morning to *Ghent*, and still made shew as if he resolv'd to defend himself to the last Extremity in our little Entrenchments. The enemy on their Side began to surround us; and in their Motions for that Purpose, blew up little Bags of Gun-powder, to give the readier Notice how far they had acomplish'd it. Another Captain, with my self, being plac'd on the Right, with one Hundred Men (where I found Monsieur *Montal* endeavouring, if possible, to get behind us) I could easily observe, they had so far attain'd their Aim of encompassing us, as to the very Fashion of a Horse's Shoe. This made me fix my Eyes so intently upon the advancing Enemy, that I never minded what my Friends were doing behind me; though I afterwards found that they had been fileing off so very artfully and privately, by that narrow Opening of the Horse-Shoe, that when the Enemy imagin'd us past a Possibility of Escape, our little Army at once, and of a sudden, was ready to disappear. There was a large Wood on the Right of our Army, through which lay the Road to *Ghent*, not broader than to admit of more than Four to march a breast. Down this the Prince had slid his Forces, except to that very small Party which the Captain and my self commanded, and which was designedly left to bring up the Rear. Nor did we stir till Captain *Collier*, then *Aid de Camp* to his Brother, now Earl of *Portmore*, came with the Word of Command for us to draw off.

When *Villeroy* was told of our Retreat, he was much surpriz'd, as thinking it a Thing utterly impossible. However, at last, being sensible of the Truth of it, he gave Orders for our Rear to be attack'd; but we kept fireing from Ditch to Ditch, and Hedge to Hedge, till Night came upon us; and so our little Army got clear of its gigantick Enemy with very inconsiderable Loss. However, the *French* fail'd not, in their customary Way, to express the Sense of their vexation, at this Disappointment, with Fire and Sword in the Neighbourhood round. Thus Prince *Vaudemont* acquir'd more Glory by that Retreat than an intire Victory could have given him; and it was not, I confess, the least Part of Satisfaction in Life, that my self had a Share of Honour under him to bring off the Rear at that his glorious Retreat at *Arfeel.*

However, in further Revenge of this political Chicane of the Prince of *Vaudemont*, and to oblige, if possible, King *William* to raise the Siege from before *Namur*, *Villeroy* enter'd into the Resolution of Bombarding *Brussells.* In order to which he encamp'd at *Anderleck*, and then made his Approaches as near as was convenient to the Town. There he caus'd to be planted thirty Mortars, and rais'd a Battery of ten Guns to shoot hot Bullets into the Place.

But before they fir'd from either, *Villeroy*, in complement to the Duke of *Bavaria*, sent a Messenger to know in what Part of the Town his Dutchess chose to reside, that they might, as much as possible, avoid incommoding her, by directing their Fire to other Parts. Answer was return'd that she was at her usual Place of Residence, the Palace; and accordingly their fireing from Battery or Mortars little incommoded them that Way.

Five Days the Bombardment continu'd; and with such Fury, that the Centre of that noble City was quite lay'd in Rubbish. Most of the Time of Bombarding I was upon the Counterscarp, where I could best see and distinguish; and I have often counted in the Air, at one time, more than twenty Bombs; for they shot whole Vollies out of their Mortars all together. This, as it must needs be terrible, threw the Inhabitants into the utmost Confusion. Cartloads of Nuns, that for many Years before had never been out of the Cloister, were now hurry'd about from Place to Place, to find Retreats of some Security. In short, the Groves, and Parts remote, were all crowded; and the most spacious Streets had hardly a Spectator left to view their Ruins. Nothing was to be seen like that Dexterity of our People in extinguishing the Fires; for where the red-hot Bullets fell, and rais'd new Conflagrations, not Burghers only, but the vulgar Sort, stood stareing, and with their Hands impocketed, beheld their Houses gradually consume; and without offering prudent or charitable Hand to stop the growing Flames.

But after they had almost thus destroy'd that late fair City, *Villeroy*, finding he could not raise the Siege of *Namur*, by that vigorous Attack upon *Brussels*, decamp'd at last from before it, and put his Army on the March, to try if he could have better Success by exposing to Show his Pageant of one Hundred Thousand Men. Prince *Vaudemont* had timely Intelligence of the Duke's Resolution and Motion; and resolv'd, if possible to get there before him. Nor was the Attempt fruitless: He fortunately succeeded, though with much Fatigue, and no little Difficulty, after he had put a Trick upon the Spies of the Enemy, by pretending to encamp, and so soon as they were gone ordering a full March.

The Castle of *Namur* had been all this Time under the Fire of the Besieger's Cannon; and soon after our little Army under the Prince was arriv'd, a Breach, that was imagin'd practicable, being made in the *Terra Nova* (which, as the Name imports, was a new Work, rais'd by the *French*, and added to the Fortifications, since it fell into their Hands in 1692 and which very much increas'd the Strength of the Whole) a Breach, as I have said, being made in this *Terra Nova*, a Storm, in a Council of War, was resolv'd upon. Four entire Regiments, in conjunction with some Draughts made out of several others, were order'd for that Work, my self commanding that Part of 'em which had been drawn out of Colonel *Tiffins*. We were all to rendevouze at the

Abbey of *Salsines*, under the Command of the Lord Cutts; the Signal, when the Attack was to be made, being agreed to be the blowing up of a Bag of Gun-powder upon the Bridge of Boats that lay over the *Sambre*.

So soon as the Signal was made, we march'd up to the Breach with a decent Intrepidity, receiving all the Way we advanc'd the full Fire of the *Cohorn* Fort. But as soon as we came near enough to mount, we found it vastly steep and rugged. Notwithstanding all which, several did get up, and enter'd the Breach; but not being supported as they ought to have been, they were all made Prisoners. Which, together with a Wound my Lord *Cutts* receiv'd, after he had done all that was possible for us, necessitated us to retire with the Loss of many of our Men.

VILLEROY all this while lay in fight, with his Army of One Hundred Thousand Men, without making the least Offer to incommode the Besiegers; or even without doing any thing more than make his Appearance in favour of the Besieged, and reconnoitring our Encampment: And, at last, seeing, or imagining that he saw, the Attempt would be to little purpose, with all the good Manners in the World, in the Night, he withdrew that terrible Meteor, and reliev'd our poor Horses from feeding on Leaves, the only Inconvenience he had put us to.

This Retreat leaving the Garrison without all Hope of Relief, they in the Castle immediately capitulated. But after one of the Gates had been, according to Articles, delivered up and Count *Guiscard* was marching out at the Head of the Garrison, and *Bouflers* at the Head of the Dragoons; the latter was, by order of King *William*, arrested, in reprize of the Garrison of *Dixmuyd* (who, contrary to the *Cartel*, had been detain'd Prisoners) and remain'd under Arrest till they were set free.

At the very Beginning of the Year 1696 was discover'd a Plot, fit only to have had its Origin from Hell or *Rome*. A Plot, which would have put *Hottentots* and Barbarians out of Countenance. This was call'd the *Assassination Plot*, from the Design of it, which was to have assassinated King *William* a little before the Time of his usual leaving *England* to head the Army of the Confederates in *Flanders*. And as nothing could give a nobler Idea of the great Character of that Prince than such a nefarious Combination against him; so, with all considerate Men, nothing could more depreciate the Cause of his inconsiderate Enemies. If I remember what I have read, the Sons of ancient *Rome*, though Heathens, behav'd themselves against an Enemy in a quite different Manner. Their Historians afford us more Instances than a few of their generous Intimations to Kings and Generals, under actual Hostilities, of barbarous Designs upon their Lives. I proceed to this of our own Countrymen.

Soon after the Discovery had been made, by Persons actually engag'd in that inhuman Design, the Regiment, in which I served, with some others then in *Flanders*, receiv'd Orders, with all Expedition, to embarque for *England*; though, on our Arrival at *Gravesend*, fresh Orders met us to remain on board the Transports, till we had surther Directions.

On my going to *London*, a few Days after, I was told, that two Regiments only were now design'd to come a-shore; and that the rest would be remanded to *Flanders*, the Danger apprehended being pretty well over. I was at *White Hall* when I receiv'd this Notice; where meeting my Lord *Cutts* (who had ever since the storming of the *Terra Nova* at *Namur* allow'd me a Share in his Favour) he express'd himself in the most obliging Manner; and at parting desir'd he might not fail of seeing me next Morning at his House; for he had somewhat of an extraordinary Nature to communicate to me.

At the time appointed, I waited on his Lorship, where I met Mr. *Steel* (now Sir *Richard*, and at that time his Secretary) who immediately introduc'd me. I found in company with him three Gentlemen; and after common Salutations, his Lordship deliver'd into my Hands, an Order from the King in Council to go along with Captain *Porter*, Mr. *de la Rue*, and Mr. *George Harris* (who prov'd to be those three with him) to search all the Transports at *Gravesend*, in order to prevent any of the Conspirators getting out of *England* that Way. After answering, that I was ready to pay Obedience, and receiving, in private, the further necessary Instructions, we took our Leave, and Oars soon after for *Gravesend*. 'Twas in our Passage down, that I understood that they had all been of the Conspiracy, but now reluctant, were become Witnesses.

When we came to *Gravesend*, I produc'd my Authority to the Commanding Officer, who very readily paid Obedience, and gave Assistance; But after our most diligent Search, finding nothing of what we look'd for, we return'd that very Night to *London*.

Next Day a Proclamation was to come out for the apprehending three of four Troopers, who were sent over by King *James*, with a thousand Pounds Reward for each: Mr. *George Harris*, who was the fourth, being the only Evidence against the other three. No sooner were we return'd from *Gravesend*, but *Harris* had Intelligence brought him, that *Cassells*, one of the three, was at Mr. *Allens* in the *Savoy*, under the

Name of *Green*. Upon which we went directly to the Place; and enquiring for Mr. *Green*, we were told he lodg'd there, and was in his Room.

I was oblig'd by my Order to go along with them, and assist 'em; and very well was it that I was so: For in consideration of the Reward in the Proclamation, which, as I have said, was to come out the next Day, *Harris* and the rest were for deferring his Seizure, till the coming out of that Proclamation; but making answer, that in case of his Escape that Night, I must be responsible to my Superiors; who, under the most favourable Aspect, would construe it a Neglect of Duty, they were forc'd to comply; and so he was taken up, and his Name that Night struck out of the Proclamation. It is very true, by this faithful Discharge of my Trust, I did save the Government one Thousand Pounds; but it is equally so, that I never had of my Governors one Farthing Consideration for what others term'd an over-officious Piece of Service; though in Justice it must be own'd a Piece of exact and disinterested Duty.

Some few Days after, attending by Direction at the Secretary's Office, with Mr. *Harris*, there came in a *Dutchman*, spluttering and making a great Noise, that he was sure he could discover one of the Conspirators; but the Mein and the Behaviour of the Man, would not give any Body Leave to give him any Credit or Regard. However, the Man persisting in his Assertions, I spoke to Mr. *Harris* to take him aside, and ask him what Sort of a Person he was; *Harris* did so; and the *Dutchman* describing him, says *Harris*, returning to me, I'll be hang'd if it be not *Blackburn*. Upon which we had him question'd somewhat more narrowly; when having no room to doubt, and understanding where he was, Colonel *Rivet* of the Guards was sent for, and order'd to go along with us to seize him. We went accordingly; and it proving to be *Blackburn*, the *Dutchman* had five Hundred Pounds, and the Colonel and others the Remainder. *Cassels* and *Blackburn*, if still alive, are in *Newgate*, confin'd by Act of Parliament, one only Witness, which was *Harris*, being producible against them.

When *Blackburn* was seiz'd, I found in the Chamber with him, one *Davison*, a Watch-maker, living in *Holbourn*. I carry'd him along with me to the Secretary of State; but nothing on his Examination appearing against him, he was immediately discharg'd. He offer'd afterwards to present me with a fine Watch of his own making, which I refus'd; and he long after own'd the Obligation.

So soon as the Depth of this Plot was fathom'd, and the intended Evil provided against, as well as prevented, King *William* went over into *Flanders*, and our Regiment thereupon receiv'd Orders for their immediate Return. Nothing of any Moment occurr'd till our Arrival at our old Quarters, the *Camerlins*, where we lay dispers'd amongst the Country Boors or Farmers, as heretofore. However, for our better Security in those Quarters, and to preserve us from the Excursions of the neighbouring Garrison of Furnes, we were oblig'd to keep an Out-guard at a little Place call'd *Shoerbeck*. This Guard was every forty-eight Hours chang'd, and remounted with a Captain, a Lieutenant, an Ensign, and threescore Men.

When it came to my Turn to relieve that Guard, and for that Purpose I was arriv'd at my Post, it appear'd to me with the Face of a Place of Debauch, rather than Business; there being too visible Tokens, that the hard Duty of both Officers and Soldiers had been that of hard Drinking, the foulest Error that a Soldier can commit, especially when on his Guard.

To confirm my Apprehensions, a little after I had taken Possession of my Guard, the Man of the House related to me such Passages, and so many of'em, that satisfy'd me, that if ten sober Men had made the Attack, they might have fairly knock'd all my Predecessors of the last Guard on the Head, without much Difficulty. However, his Account administer'd Matter of Caution to me, and put me upon taking a narrower View of our Situation. In consequence whereof, at Night I plac'd a Centinel a Quarter of a Mile in the Rear, and such other Centinels as I thought necessary and convenient in other Places; with Orders, that upon Sight of an Enemy the Centinel near should fire; and that upon hearing that, all the other Centinels, as well as he, should hasten in to strengthen our Main Guard.

What my Jealousy, on my Landlord's Relation, had suggested, happen'd accordingly: For about one in the Morning I was alarm'd with the Cry of one of my Centinels, *Turn out for God's sake*; which he repeated, with Vehemence, three or four times over. I took the Alarm, got up suddenly; and with no little Difficulty got my Men into their Ranks, when the Person who made the Outcry came running in, almost spent, and out of Breath. It was the Centinel, that I had luckily plac'd about a Quarter of a Mile off, who gave the Alarm, and his Musket flashing in the Pan, without going off, he endeavour'd to supply with his Voice the Defect of his Piece. I had just got my Men into their Ranks, in order to receive the Enemy, when by the Moonlight, I discover'd a Party advancing upon us. My out Centinel challeng'd 'em, and as I had precaution'd, they answer'd, *Hispanioli*; though I knew 'em to be *French*.

However, on my Survey of our Situation by Day-light, having mark'd in my Mind a proper Place for drawing up my Men in Case of an Attack, which was too narrow to admit of more than two on a Breast; and which would secure between us and the Enemy a Ditch of Water: I resolv'd to put in practice what had entertain'd me so well in the Theory. To that Purpose I order'd my first Rank to keep their Post, stand still and face the Enemy, while the other two Ranks stooping should follow me to gain the intended Station; which done, the first Rank had Orders to file off and fall behind. All was perform'd in excellent Order; and I confess it was with no little Pleasure, that I beheld the Enemy, for the best Part of an Hour, in Consultation whether they should attack us or no. The result, nevertheless, of that Consultation ended in this; that, seeing us so well upon our Guard, it was most adviseable to draw off. They soon put their Resolution into practice, which I was very glad to see; on Examination a little before having found that my Predecessor, as in other Things, had fail'd of Conduct in leaving me a Garrison without Ammunition.

Next Morning I was very pleasingly surpriz'd with a handsome Present of Wine, and some other necessary Refreshments. At first I made a little Scruple and Hesitation whether or no to receive 'em; till the Bearer assur'd me, that they were sent me from the Officers of the next Garrison, who had made me a Visit the Night before, as a candid Acknowledgment of my Conduct and good Behaviour. I return'd their Compliment, that I hop'd I should never receive Men of Honour otherwise than like a Man of Honour; which mightily pleas'd them. Every of which Particulars the *Ghent Gazettier* the Week after publish'd.

We had little to do except Marching and Counter-marching all the Campaign after; till it was resolv'd in a Council of War, for the better preserving of *Brussels* from such Insults, as it had before sustain'd from the *French*, during the Siege of *Namur*, to fortify *Anderlech*; upon which our Regiment, as well as others, were commanded from our more pacifick Posts to attend that Work. Our whole Army was under Movement to cover that Resolution; and the Train fell to my Care and Command in the March. There accompany'd the Train a Fellow, seemingly ordinary, yet very officious and courteous, being ready to do any thing for any Person, from the Officer to the common Soldier. He travell'd along and mov'd with the Train, sometimes on Foot, and sometimes getting a Ride in some one or other of the Waggons; but ever full of his Chit-chat and Stories of Humour. By these insinuating Ways he had screw'd himself into the general good Opinion; but the Waggoners especially grew particularly fond of him. At the End of our March all our Powder-Waggons were plac'd breast a-breast, and so close, that one miscarrying would leave little doubt of the Fate of all the rest. This in the Camp we commonly call *the Park*; and here it was that our new Guest, like another *Phaeton*, though under Pretence of Weariness, not Ambition, got Leave of the very last Carter to the Train to take a Nap in his Waggon. One who had entertain'd a Jealousy of him, and had watch'd him, gave Information against him; upon which he was seiz'd and brought to me as Captain of the Guard. I caus'd him to be search'd; and upon search, finding Match, Touchwood, and other dangerous Materials upon him; I sent him and them away to the Provoe. Upon the Whole, a Council of War was call'd, at which, upon a strict Examination, he confess'd himself a hir'd Incendiary; and as such receiv'd his Sentence to be burnt in the Face of the Army. The Execution was a Day or two after: When on the very Spot, he further acknowledged, that on Sight or Noise of the Blow, it had been concerted, that the *French* Army should fall upon the Confederates under those lamentable Circumstances.

The Peace of *Riswick* soon after taking place, put an End to all Incendiarisms of either Sort. So that nothing of a Military Kind, which was now become my Province, happen'd of some Years after. Our Regiment was first order'd into *England*; and presently after into *Ireland*. But as these Memoirs are not design'd for the Low Amuzement of a Tea-Table, but rather of the Cabinet, a Series of inglorious Inactivity can furnish but very little towards 'em.

Yet as little as I admir'd a Life of Inactivity, there are some Sorts of Activity, to which a wise Man might almost give Supineness the Preference: Such is that of barely encountring Elements, and wageing War with Nature; and such, in my Opinion, would have been the spending my Commission, and very probably my Life with it, in the *West Indies*. For though the Climate (as some would urge) may afford a Chance for a very speedy Advance in Honour, yet, upon revolving in my Mind, that those Rotations of the Wheel of Fortune are often so very quick, as well as uncertain, that I my self might as well be the First as the Last; the Whole of the Debate ended in somewhat like that Couplet of the excellent *Hudibras*:

Then he, that ran away and fled,
Must lie in Honour's Truckle-bed.

However, my better Planets soon disannull'd those melancholy Ideas, which a Rumour of our being sent into the *West Indies* had crowded my Head and Heart with: For being call'd over into *England*, upon the very Affairs of the Regiment, I arriv'd there just after the Orders for their Transportation went over; by which Means the Choice of going was put out of my Power, and the Danger of Refusing, which was the Case of many, was very luckily avoided.

It being judg'd, therefore, impossible for me to return soon enough to gain my Passage, one in Power propos'd to me, that I should resign to an Officer then going over; and with some other contingent Advantages, to my great Satisfaction, I was put upon the Half-pay List. This was more agreeable, for I knew, or at least imagin'd my self wise enough to foretel, from the over hot Debate of the House of Commons upon the Partition Treaty, that it could not be long before the present Peace would, at least, require patching.

Under this Sort of uncertain Settlement I remain'd with the Patience of a *Jew*, though not with Judaical Absurdity, a faithful Adherer to my Expectation. Nor did the Consequence fail of answering, a War was apparent, and soon after proclaim'd. Thus waiting for an Opportunity, which I flatter'd my self would soon present, the little Diversions of *Dublin*, and the moderate Conversation of that People, were not of Temptation enough to make my Stay in *England* look like a Burden.

But though the War was proclaim'd, and Preparations accordingly made for it, the Expectations from all receiv'd a sudden Damp, by the as sudden Death of King *William.* That Prince, who had stared Death in the Face in many Sieges and Battles, met with his Fate in the Midst of his Diversions, who seiz'd his Prize in an Hour, to human Thought, the least adapted to it. He was a Hunting (his customary Diversion) when, by an unhappy Trip of his Horse, he fell to the Ground; and in the Fall displac'd his Collar-bone. The News of it immediately alarm'd the Court, and all around; and the sad Effects of it soon after gave all *Europe* the like Alarm. *France* only, who had not disdain'd to seek it sooner by ungenerous Means, receiv'd new Hope, from what gave others Motives for Despair. He flatter'd himself, that that long liv'd Obstacle to his Ambition thus remov'd, his Successor would never fall into those Measures, which he had wisely concerted for the Liberties of *Europe*; but he, as well as others of his Adherents, was gloriously deceiv'd; that God-like Queen, with a Heart entirely *English*, prosecuted her royal Predecessor's Counsels; and to remove all the very Faces of Jealousy, immediately on her Accession dispatch'd to every Court of the great Confederacy, Persons adequate to the Importance of the Message, to give Assurances thereof.

This gave new Spirit to a Cause, that at first seem'd to languish in its Founder, as it struck its great Opposers with a no less mortifying Terror; And well did the great Successes of her Arms answer the Prayers and Efforts of that royal Soul of the Confederacies; together with the Wishes of all, that, like her, had the Good, as well as the Honour of their Country at Heart, in which the Liberties of *Europe* were included. The first Campaign gave a noble Earnest of the Future. *Bon, Keyserwaert, Venlo,* and *Ruremond,* were sound Forerunners only of *Donawert, Hochstet,* and *Blenheim.* Such a March of *English* Forces to the Support of the tottering Empire, as it gloriously manifested the ancient Genius of a warlike People; so was it happily celebrated with a Success answerable to the Glory of the Undertaking, which concluded in Statues and princely Donatives to an *English* Subject, from the then only Emperor in *Europe.* A small Tribute, it's true, for ransom'd Nations and captiv'd Armies, which justly enough inverted the Exclamations of a *Roman* Emperor to the *French* Monarch, who deprecated his Legions lost pretty near the same Spot; but to a much superior Number, and on a much less glorious Occasion.

But my good Fortune not allowing me to participate in those glorious Appendages of the *English* Arms in *Flanders,* nor on the *Rhine,* I was resolv'd to make a Push for it the first Opportunity, and waste my Minutes no longer on Court Attendances. And my Lord *Cutts* returning with his full Share of Laurels, for his never to be forgotten Services at *Venlo, Ruremond,* and *Hochstet,* found his active Genius now to be repos'd, under the less agreeable Burden of unhazardous Honour, where Quiet must provide a Tomb for one already past any Danger of Oblivion; deep Wounds and glorious Actions having anticipated all that could be said in Epitaphs or litteral Inscriptions. Soon after his Arrival from *Germany,* he was appointed General of all her Majesty's Forces in *Ireland;* upon which going to congratulate him, he was pleas'd to enquire of me several Things relating to that Country; and particularly in what Part of *Dublin* I would recommend his Residence; offering at the same time, if I would go over with him, all the Services that should fall in his Way.

But Inactivity was a Thing I had too long lamented; therefore, after I had, as decently as I could, declin'd the latter Part, I told his Lordship, that as to a Place of Residence, I was Master of a House in *Dublin*, large enough, and suitable to his great Quality, which should be at his Service, on any Terms he thought fit. Adding withal, that I had a Mind to see *Spain*, where my Lord *Peterborow* was now going; and that if his Lordship would favour me with a Recommendation, it would suit my present Inclinations much better than any further tedious Recess. His Lordship was so good to close with both my Overtures; and spoke so effectually in my Favour, that the Earl of *Peterborow*, then General of all the Forces order'd on that Expedition, bad me speedily prepare my self; and so when all Things were ready I embarqu'd with that noble Lord for *Spain*, to pursue his well concerted Undertaking; which, in the Event, will demonstrate to the World, that little Armies, under the Conduct of auspicious Generals, may sometimes produce prodigious Effects.

The *Jews*, in whatever Part of the World, are a People industrious in the increasing of *Mammon*; and being accustom'd to the universal Methods of Gain, are always esteem'd best qualify'd for any Undertaking, where that bears a Probability of being a Perquisite. Providing Bread, and other Requisites for an Army, was ever allow'd to carry along with it a Profit answerable; and *Spain* was not the first Country where that People had engag'd in such an Undertaking. Besides, on any likely Appearance of great Advantage, it is in the Nature as well as Practice of that Race, strenuously to assist one another; and that with the utmost Confidence and prodigious Alacrity. One of that Number, both competent and willing enough to carry on an Undertaking of that kind, fortunately came at that Juncture to solicit the Earl of *Peterborow* to be employ'd as Proveditor to the Army and Troops, which were, or should be sent into *Spain*.

It will easily be admitted, that the Earl, under his present Exigencies, did not decline to listen. And a very considerable Sum being offer'd, by way of Advance, the Method common in like Cases was pursu'd, and the Sum propos'd accepted; by which Means the Earl of *Peterborow* found himself put into the happy Capacity of proceeding upon his first concerted Project. The Name of the *Jew*, who sign'd the Contract, was *Curtisos*; and he and his Friends, with great Punctuality, advanc'd the expected Sum of One Hundred Thousand Pounds Sterling, or very near it; which was immediately order'd into the Hands of the Pay-master of the Forces. For though the Earl took Money of the *Jews*, it was not for his own, but public Use. According to Agreement, Bills were drawn for the Value from *Lisbon*, upon the Lord *Godolphin* (then Lord Treasurer) all which were, on that Occasion, punctually comply'd with.

The Earl of *Peterborow* having thus fortunately found Means to supply himself with Money, and by that with some Horse, after he had obtain'd Leave of the Lord *Galoway* to make an Exchange of two Regiments of Foot, receiv'd the Arch-Duke, and all those who would follow him, aboard the Fleet; and, at his own Expense, transported him and his whole Retinue to *Barcelona*: For all which prodigious Charge, as I have been very lately inform'd, from very good Hands, that noble Earl never to this Day receiv'd any Consideration from the Government, or any Person whatsoever.

We sail'd from *Lisbon*, in order to join the Squadron under Sir *Cloudsley Shovel:* Meeting with which at the appointed Station off *Tangier*, the Men of War and Transports thus united, made the best of their Way for *Gibraltar.* There we stay'd no longer than to take aboard two Regiments out of that Garrison, in lieu of two out of our Fleet. Here we found the Prince of *Hesse*, who immediately took a Resolution to follow the Arch-Duke in this Expedition. He was a Person of great Gallantry; and having been Vice-Roy of *Catalonia*, was receiv'd on board the Fleet with the utmost Satisfaction, as being a Person capable of doing great Service in a Country where he was well known, and as well belov'd.

Speaking *Latin* then pretty fluently, it gave me frequent Opportunies of conversing with the two Father Confessors of the Duke of *Austria*; and upon that Account I found my self honour'd with some Share in the Favour of the Arch-Duke himself. I mention this, not to gratify any vain Humour, but as a corroborating Circumstance, that my Opportunities of Information, in Matters of Consequence, could not thereby be suppos'd to be lessen'd; but that I might more reasonably be imagin'd to arrive at Intelligence, that not very often, or at least not so soon, came to the Knowledge of others.

From *Gibraltar* we sail'd to the Bay of *Altea*, not far distant from the City of *Valencia*, in the Road of which we continu'd for some Days. While we were there, as I was very credibly inform'd, the Earl of *Peterborow* met with some fresh Disappointment; but what it was, neither I nor any Body else, as far as I could perceive, could ever dive into: Neither did it appear by any outward Tokens, in that noble

General, that it lay so much at his Heart, as those about him seem'd to assure me it did.

However, while we lay in *Altea* Bay, two Bomb-Vessels, and a small Squadron, were order'd against *Denia*, which had a small Castle; but rather fine than strong. And accordingly, upon our Offer to bring to bear with our Cannon, and preparing to fix our Bomb-Vessels, in order to bombard the Place, it surrender'd; and acknowledg'd the Arch-Duke as lawful King of *Spain*, and so proclaim'd him. From this time, therefore, speaking of that Prince, it shall be under that Title. General *Ramos* was left Commander here; a Person who afterwards acted a very extraordinary Part in the War carry'd on in the Kingdom of *Valencia*.

But notwithstanding no positive Resolutions had been taken for the Operations of the Campaign, before the Arch Duke's Departure from *Lisbon*, the Earl of *Peterborow*, ever solicitous of the Honour of his Country, had premeditated another Enterprize, which, had it been embrac'd, would in all Probability, have brought that War to a much more speedy Conclusion; and at the same time have obviated all those Difficulties, which were but too apparent in the Siege of *Barcelona*. He had justly and judiciously weigh'd, that there were no Forces in the Middle Parts of *Spain*, all their Troops being in the extream Parts of the Kingdom, either on the Frontiers of *Portugal*, or in the City of *Barcelona*; that with King *Philip*, and the royal Family at *Madrid*, there were only some few Horse, and those in a bad Condition, and which only serv'd for Guards: if therefore, as he rightly projected within himself, by the taking of *Valencia*, or any Sea-Port Town, that might have secur'd his Landing, he had march'd directly for *Madrid*; what could have oppos'd him? But I shall have occasion to dilate more upon this Head a few Pages hence; and therefore shall here only say, that though that Project of his might have brought about a speedy and wonderful Revolution, what he was by his Orders afterwards oblig'd to, against his Inclinations, to pursue, contributed much more to his great Reputation, as it put him under a frequent Necessity of overcoming Difficulties, which, to any other General, would have appear'd unsurmountable.

VALENCIA is a City towards the Centre of *Spain*, to the Seaward, seated in a rich and most populous Country, just fifty Leagues from *Madrid*. It abounds in Horses and Mules; by reason of the great Fertility of its Lands, which they can, to great Advantage, water when, and as they please. This City and Kingdom was as much inclin'd to the Interest of King *Charles* as *Catalonia* it self; for even on our first

Appearance, great Numbers of People came down to the Bay of *Altea*, with not only a bare Offer of their Services, but loaded with all Manner of Provisions, and loud Acclamations of *Viva Carlos tercero, Viva*. There were no regular Troops in any of the Places round about it, or in the City it self. The nearest were those few Horse in *Madrid*, one hundred and fifty Miles distant; nor any Foot nearer than *Barcelona*, or the Frontiers of *Portugal*.

On the contrary, *Barcelona* is one of the largest and most populous Cities in all *Spain*, fortify'd with Bastions; one Side thereof is secur'd by the Sea; and the other by a strong Fortification call'd *Monjouick*. The Place is of so large a Circumference, that thirty thousand Men would scarce suffice to form the Lines of Circumvallation. It once resisted for many Months an Army of that Force; and is almost at the greatest Distance from *England* of any Place belonging to that *Monarchy*.

This short Description of these two Places will appear highly necessary, if it be consider'd, that no Person without it would be able to judge of the Design which the Earl of *Peterborow* intended to pursue, when he first took the Arch-Duke aboard the Fleet. Nevertheless the Earl now found himself under a Necessity of quitting that noble Design, upon his Receipt of Orders from *England*, while he lay in the Bay of *Altea*, to proceed directly to *Catalonia*; to which the Arch-Duke, as well as many Sea and Land Officers, were most inclin'd; and the Prince of *Hesse* more than all the rest.

On receiving those Orders, the Earl of *Peterborow* seem'd to be of Opinion, that from an Attempt, which he thought under a Probability of Success, he was condemn'd to undertake what was next to an Impossibility of effecting; since nothing appear'd to him so injudicious as an Attempt upon *Barcelona*. A Place at such a Distance from receiving any Reinforcement or Relief; the only Place in which the *Spaniards* had a Garrison of regular Forces; and those in Number rather exceeding the Army he was to undertake the Siege with, was enough to cool the Ardour of a Person of less Penetration and Zeal than what the Earl had on all Occasions demonstrated. Whereas if the General, as he intended, had made an immediate March to *Madrid*, after he had secur'd *Valencia*, and the Towns adjacent, which were all ready to submit and declare for King *Charles*; or if otherwise inclin'd, had it not in their Power to make any considerable Resistance; to which, if it be added, that he could have had Mules and Horses immediately provided for him, in what Number he pleas'd, together with Carriages necessary for Artillery, Baggage, and Ammunition; in few Days he could have forc'd King *Philip* out of *Madrid*, where he had so little Force to oppose him. And as there was nothing in his Way to prevent or obstruct his marching thither, it is hard to conceive any other Part King *Philip* could have acted in such an Extremity, than to retire either towards *Portugal* or *Catalonia*. In either of which Cases he must have left all the middle Part of *Spain* open to the Pleasure of the Enemy; who in the mean time would have had it in their Power to prevent any Communication of those Bodies at such opposite Extreams of the Country, as were the Frontiers of *Portugal* and *Barcelona*, where only, as I said before, were any regular Troops.

And on the other Side, as the Forces of the Earl of *Peterborow* were more than sufficient for an Attempt where there was so little Danger of Opposition; so if their Army on the Frontiers of *Portugal* should have march'd back upon him into the Country; either the *Portugueze* Army could have enter'd into *Spain* without Opposition; or, at worst, supposing the General had been forc'd to retire, his Retreat would have been easy and safe into those Parts of *Valencia* and *Andahzia*, which he previously had secur'd. Besides, *Gibraltar*, the strongest Place in *Spain*, if not in the whole World, was already in our Possession, and a great Fleet at Hand ready to give Assistance in all Places near the Sea. From all which it is pretty apparent, that in a little time the War on our Side might have been supported without entering the *Mediterranean*; by which Means all Reinforcements would have been much nearer at Hand, and the Expences of transporting Troops and Ammunition very considerably diminish'd.

But none of these Arguments, though every one of them is founded on solid Reason, were of Force enough against the prevailing Opinion for an Attempt upon *Catalonia*. Mr. *Crow*, Agent for the Queen in those Parts, had sent into *England* most positive Assurances, that nothing would be wanting, if once our Fleet made an invasion amongst the *Catalans*. The Prince of *Hesse* likewise abounded in mighty Offers and prodigious Assurances; all which enforc'd our Army to that Part of *Spain*, and that gallant Prince to those Attempts in which he lost his Life. Very much against the Inclination of our General, who foresaw all those Difficulties, which were no less evident afterwards to every one; and the Sense of which occasion'd those Delays, and that Opposition to any Effort upon *Barcelona*, which ran thro' so many successive Councils of War.

However, pursuant to his Instructions from *England*, the repeated Desires of the Arch-Duke, and the Importunities of the Prince of *Hesse*, our General gave Orders to sail from *Altea* towards the Bay of *Barcelona*, the chief City of *Catalonia*. Nevertheless, when we arriv'd there, he was very unwilling to land any of the Forces, till he saw some Probability of that Assistance and Succour so must boasted of, and so often promis'd. But as nothing appear'd but some small Numbers of Men, very indifferently arm'd, and without either Gentlemen or Officers at the Head of them; the Earl of *Peterborow* was of Opinion, this could not be deem'd sufficient Encouragement for him to engage in an Enterprize, which carry'd so poor a Face of Probability of Success along with it. In answer to this it was urg'd, that till a Descent was made, and the Affairs thoroughly engag'd in, it was not to be expected that any great Numbers would appear, or that Persons of Condition would discover themselves. Upon all which it was resolv'd the Troops should be landed.

Accordingly, our Forces were disembark'd, and immediately encamp'd; notwithstanding which the Number of Succours increas'd very slowly, and that after the first straggling Manner. Nor were those that did appear any way to be depended on; coming when they thought fit, and going away when they pleas'd, and not to be brought under any regular Discipline. It was then pretended, that until they saw the Artillery landed as well as Forces, they would not believe any Siege actually intended. This brought the General under a sort of Necessity of complying in that also. Though certainly so to do must be allow'd a little unreasonable, while the Majority in all Councils of War declar'd the Design to be impracticable; and the Earl of *Peterborow* had positive Orders to proceed according to such Majorities.

At last the Prince of *Hesse* was pleas'd to demand Pay for those Stragglers, as Officers and Soldiers, endeavouring to maintain, that it could not be expected that Men should venture their Lives for nothing. Thus we came to *Catalonia* upon Assurances of universal Assistance; but found, when we came there, that we were to have none unless we paid for it. And as we were sent thither without Money to pay for any thing, it had certainly been for us more tolerable to have been in a Country where we might have taken by Force what we could not obtain any other way.

However, to do the *Miquelets* all possible Justice, I must say, that notwithstanding the Number of 'em, which hover'd about the Place, never much exceeded fifteen Hundred Men; if sometimes more, oftner less; and though they never came under any Command, but planted themselves where and as they pleas'd; yet did they considerable Service in taking Possession of all the Country Houses and Convents, that lay between the Hills and the Plain of *Barcelona*; by means whereof they render'd it impossible for the Enemy to make any *Sorties* or Sallies at any Distance from the Town.

And now began all those Difficulties to bear, which long before by the General had been apprehended. The Troops had continu'd under a State of Inactivity for the Space of three Weeks, all which was spent in perpetual Contrivances and Disputes amongst our selves, not with the Enemy. In six several Councils of War the Siege of *Barcelona*, under the Circumstances we then lay, was rejected as a Madness and Impossibility. And though the General and Brigadier *Stanhope* (afterward Earl *Stanhope*) consented to some Effort should be made to satisfy the Expectation of the World, than with any Hopes of Success. However, no Consent at all could be obtain'd from any Council of War; and the *Dutch* General in particular declar'd, that he would not obey even the Commands of the Earl of *Peterborow*, if he should order the Sacrifice of the Troops under him in so unjustifiable a Manner, without the Consent of a Council of War.

And yet all those Officers, who refus'd their Consent to the Siege of *Barcelona*, offer'd to march into the Country, and attempt any other Place, that was not provided with so strong and numerous a Garrison; taking it for granted, that no Town in *Catalonia, Barcelona* excepted, could make long Resistance; and in case the Troops in that Garrison should pursue them, they then might have an Opportunity of fighting them at less Disadvantage in the open Field, than behind the Walls of a Place of such Strength. And, indeed, should they have issu'd out on any such Design, a Defeat of those Troops would have put the Province of *Catalonia*, together with the Kingdoms of *Aragon* and *Valencia,* into the Hands of King *Charles* more effectually than the taking of *Barcelona* it self.

Let it be observ'd, *en passant,* that by those Offers of the Land Officers in a Council of War, it is easy to imagine what would have been the Success of our Troops, had they march'd directly from *Valencia* to *Madrid.* For if after two Months Alarm, it was thought reasonable, as well as practicable, to march into the open Country rather than attempt the Siege of *Barcelona*, where Forces equal, if not superior in Number, were ready to follow us at the Heels; what might not have been expected from an Invasion by our Troops when and where they could meet with little Opposition? But leaving the Consideration of what might have been, I shall now endeavour at least with great Exactness to set down some of the most remarkable Events from our taking to the Relief of *Barcelona*.

The repeated Refusals of the Councils of War for undertaking the Siege of so strong a Place, with a Garrison so numerous, and those Refusals grounded upon such solid Reasons, against a Design so rash, reduc'd the General to the utmost Perplexity. The Court of King *Charles* was immerg'd in complaint; all belonging to him lamenting the hard Fate of that Prince, to be brought into *Catalonia* only to return again, without the Offer of any one Effort in his Favour. On the other Hand, our own Officers and Soldiers were highly dissatisfy'd, that they were reproach'd, because not dispos'd to enter upon and engage themselves in Impossibilities. And, indeed, in the Manner that the Siege was propos'd and insisted upon by the Prince of *Hesse*, in every of the several Councils of War, after the Loss of many Men, thrown away to no other purpose, but to avoid the Shame (as the Expression ran) of coming like Fools and going away like Cowards, it could have ended in nothing but a Retreat at last.

It afforded but small Comfort to the Earl to have foreseen all these Difficulties, and to have it in his Power to say, that he would never have taken the Arch-Duke on Board, nor have propos'd to him the Hopes of a Recovery of the *Spanish* Monarchy from King *Philip*, if he could have imagin'd it probable, that he should not have been at liberty to pursue his own Design, according to his own Judgment. It must be allow'd very hard for him, who had undertaken so great a Work, and that without any Orders from the Government; and by so doing could have had no Justification but by Success; I say, it must be allow'd to be very hard (after the Undertaking had been approv'd in *England*) that he should find himself to be directed in this Manner by those at a Distance, upon ill grounded and confident Reports from Mr. *Crow*; and compell'd, as it were, though General, to follow the Sentiments of Strangers, who either had private Views of Ambition, or had no immediate Care or Concern for the Troops employ'd in this Expedition.

Such were the present unhappy Circumstanches of the Earl of *Peterborow* in the Camp before *Barcelona*. Impossibilities propos'd; no Expedients to be accepted; a Court reproaching; Councils of War rejecting; and the *Dutch* General refusing the Assistance of the Troops under his Command; and what surmounted all, a Despair of bringing such Animosities and differing Opinions to any tolerable Agreement. Yet all these Difficulties, instead of discouraging the Earl, set every Faculty of his more afloat; and, at last, produc'd a lucky Thought, which was happily attended with Events extraordinary, and Scenes of Success much beyond his Expectation; such, as the General himself was heard to confess, it had been next to Folly to have look'd for; as certainly, *in prima facie*, it would hardly have born proposing, to take by Surprize a Place much stronger than *Barcelona* it self. True it is, that his only Hope of succeeding consisted in this: That no Person could suppose such an Enterprize could enter into the Imagination of Man; and without doubt the General's chief Dependence lay upon what he found true in the Sequel; that the Governor and Garrison of *Monjouick*, by reason of their own Security, would be very negligent, and very little upon their Guard.

However, to make the Experiment, he took an Opportunity, unknown to any Person but an *Aid de Camp* that attended him, and went out to view the Fortifications: And there being no Horse in that strong Fortress; and the *Miquelets* being possess'd of all the Houses and Gardens in the Plain, it was not difficult to give himself that Satisfaction, taking his Way by the Foot of the Hill. The Observation he made of the Place it self, the Negligence and Supineness of the Garrison, together with his own uneasy Circumstances, soon brought the Earl to a Resolution of putting his first Conceptions in Execution, satisfy'd as he was, from the Situation of the Ground between *Monjouick* and the Town, that if the first was in our Possession, the Siege of the latter might be undertaken with some Prospect of Success.

From what has been said, some may be apt to conclude that the Siege afterward succeeding, when the Attack was made from the Side of *Monjouick*, it had not been impossible to have prevail'd, if the Effort had been made on the East Side of the Town, where our Forces were at first encamp'd, and where only we could have made our Approaches, if *Monjouick* had not been in our Power. But a few Words will convince any of common Experience of the utter Impossibility of Success upon the East Part of the Town, although many almost miraculous Accidents made us succeed when we brought our Batteries to bear upon that Part of *Barcelona* towards the West. The Ground to the East was a perfect Level for many Miles, which would have necessitated our making our Approaches in a regular Way; and consequently our Men must have been expos'd to the full Fire of their whole Artillery. Besides, the Town is on that Side much stronger than any other; there is an Out-work just under the Walls of the Town, flank'd by the Courtin and the Faces of two Bastions, which might have cost us half our Troops to possess, before we could have rais'd a Battery against the Walls. Or supposing, after all, a competent Breach had been made, what a wise Piece of Work must it have been to have attempted a Storm against double the Number of regular Troops within?

On the contrary, we were so favoured by the Situation, when we made the Attack from the Side of *Monjouick*, that the Breach was made and the Town taken without opening of Trenches, or without our being at all incommoded by any Sallies of the Enemy; as in truth they made not one during the whole Siege. Our great Battery, which consisted of upwards of fifty heavy Cannon, supply'd from the Ships, and manag'd by the Seamen, were plac'd upon a Spot of rising Ground, just large enough to contain our Guns, with two deep hollow Ways on each Side the Field, at each End whereof we had rais'd a little Redoubt, which serv'd to preserve our Men from the Shot of the Town. Those little Redoubts, in which we had some Field Pieces, flank'd the Battery, and render'd it intirely secure from any Surprize of the Enemy. There were several other smaller Batteries rais'd upon the Hills adjacent, in Places not to be approach'd, which, in a manner, render'd all the Artillery of the Enemy useless, by reason their Men could not play 'em, but with the utmost Danger; whereas ours were secure, very few being kill'd, and those mostly by random Shot.

But to return to the General; forc'd, as he was, to take this extraordinary Resolution, he concluded, the readiest Way to surprize his Enemies was to elude his Friends. He therefore call'd a Council of War a-shore, of the Land Officers; and aboard, of the Admirals and Sea Officers: In both which it was resolv'd, that in case the Siege of *Barcelona* was judg'd impracticable, and that the Troops should be re-imbark'd by a Day appointed, an Effort should be made upon the Kingdom of *Naples*. Accordingly, the Day affix'd being come, the heavy Artillery landed for the Siege was return'd aboard the Ships, and every thing in appearance prepar'd for a Re-imbarkment. During which, the General was oblig'd to undergo all the Reproaches of a dissatisfy'd Court; and what was more uneasy to him, the Murmurings of the Sea Officers, who, not so competent Judges in what related to Sieges, were one and all inclin'd to a Design upon *Barcelona*; and the rather, because as the Season was so far spent, it was thought altogether improper to engage the Fleet in any new Undertaking. However, all Things were so well disguis'd by our seeming Preparations for a Retreat, that the very

Night our Troops were in March towards the Attack of *Monjouick*, there were publick Entertainments and Rejoicings in the Town for the raising of the Siege.

The Prince of *Hesse* had taken large Liberties in complaining against all the Proceedings in the Camp before *Barcelona*; even to Insinuations, that though the Earl gave his Opinion for some Effort in public, yet us'd he not sufficient Authority over the other General Officers to incline them to comply; throwing out withal some Hints, that the General from the Beginning had declar'd himself in favour of other Operations, and against coming to *Catalonia*; the latter Part whereof was nothing but Fact. On the other Side, the Earl of *Peterborow* complain'd, that the boasted Assistance was no way made good; and that in failure thereof, his Troops were to be sacrificed to the Humours of a Stranger; one who had no Command; and whose Conduct might bear a Question whether equal to his Courage. These Reproaches of one another had bred so much ill Blood between those two great Men, that for above a Fortnight they had no Correspondence, nor ever exchang'd one Word.

The Earl, however, having made his proper Dispositions, and deliver'd out his Orders, began his March in the Evening with twelve Hundred Foot and two Hundred Horse, which of necessity were to pass by the Quarters of the Prince of *Hesse*. That Prince, on their Appearance, was told that the General was come to speak with him; and being brought into his Apartment, the Earl acquainted him, that he had at last resolv'd upon an Attempt against the Enemy; adding, that now, if he pleas'd, he might be a Judge of their Behaviour, and see whether his Officers and Soldiers had deserv'd that Character which he had so liberally given 'em. The Prince made answer, that he had always been ready to take his Share; but could hardly believe, that Troops marching that way could make any Attempt against the Enemy to satisfaction. However, without further Discourse he call'd for his Horse.

By this we may see what Share Fortune has in the greatest Events. In all probability the Earl of *Peterborow* had never engag'd in such a dangerous Affair in cold Blood and unprovok'd; and if such an Enterprize had been resolv'd on in a regular Way, it is very likely he might have given the Command to some of the General Officers; since it is not usual, nor hardly allowable, for one, that commands in chief, to go in Person on such kind of Services. But here we see the General and Prince, notwithstanding their late indifferent Harmony, engag'd together in this most desperate Undertaking.

Brigadier *Stanhope* and Mr. *Methuen* (now Sir *Paul*) were the General's particular Friends, and those he most consulted, and most confided in; yet he never imparted this Resolution of his to either of them; for he was not willing to engage them in a Design so dangerous, and where there was so little Hope of Success; rather choosing to reserve them as Persons most capable of giving Advice and Assistance in the Confusion, great enough already, which yet must have been greater, if any Accident had happen'd to himself. And I have very good Reason to believe, that the Motive, which mainly engag'd the Earl of *Peterborow* in this Enterprize, was to satisfy the Prince of *Hesse* and the World, that his Diffidence proceeded from his Concern for the Troops committed to his Charge, and not for his own Person. On the other Hand, the great Characters of the two Gentlemen just mention'd are so well known, that it will easily gain Credit, that the only Way the General could take to prevent their being of the Party, was to conceal it from them, as he did from all Mankind, even from the Archduke himself. And certainly there never was a more universal Surprize than when the firing was heard next Morning from *Monjouick*.

But I now proceed to give an exact Account of this great Action; of which no Person, that I have heard of, ever yet took upon him to deliver to Posterity the glorious Particulars; and yet the Consequences and Events, by what follows, will appear so great, and so very extraordinary, that few, if any, had they had it in their Power, would have deny'd themselves the Pleasure or the World the Satisfaction of knowing it.

The Troops, which march'd all Night along the Foot of the Mountains, arriv'd two Hours before Day under the Hill of *Monjouick*, not a Quarter of a Mile from the outward Works: For this Reason it was taken for granted, whatever the Design was which the General had propos'd to himself, that it would be put in Execution before Day-light; but the Earl of *Peterborow* was now pleas'd to inform the Officers of the Reasons why he chose to stay till the Light appear'd. He was of opinion that any Success would be impossible, unless the Enemy came into the outward Ditch under the Bastions of the second Enclosure; but that if they had time allow'd them to come thither, there being no Palisadoes, our Men, by leaping in upon them, after receipt of their first Fire, might drive 'em into the upper Works; and following them close, with some Probability, might force them, under that Confusion, into the inward Fortifications.

Such were the General's Reasons then and there given; after which, having promis'd ample Rewards to such as discharg'd their Duty well, a Lieutenant, with thirty Men, was order'd to advance towards the Bastion nearest the Town; and a Captain, with fifty Men, to support him. After the Enemy's Fire they were to leap into the Ditch, and their Orders were to follow 'em close, if they retir'd into the upper Works: Nevertheless, not to pursue 'em farther, if they made into the inner Fort; but to endeavour to cover themselves within the Gorge of the Bastion.

A Lieutenant and a Captain, with the Like Number of Men and the same Orders, were commanded to a Demi-Bastion at the Extremity of the Fort towards the West, which was above Musket-Shot from the inward Fortification. Towards this Place the Wall, which was cut into the Rock, was not fac'd for about twenty Yards; and here our own Men got up; where they found three Pieces of Cannon upon a Platform, without many Men to defend them.

Those appointed to the Bastion towards the Town were sustain'd by two hundred Men; with which the General and Prince went in Person. The like Number, under the Directions of Colonel *Southwell*, were to sustain the Attack towards the West; and about five hundred Men were left under the Command of a *Dutch* Colonel, whose Orders were to assist, where, in his own Judgment, he should think most proper; and these were drawn up between the two Parties appointed to begin the Assault. My Lot was on the Side where the Prince and Earl were in Person; and where we sustain'd the only Loss from the first Fire of the Enemy.

Our men, though quite expos'd, and though the Glacis was all escarp'd upon the live Rock, went on with an undaunted Courage; and immediately after the first Fire of the Enemy, all, that were not kill'd or wounded, leap'd in, *pel-mel*, amongst the Enemy; who, being thus boldly attack'd, and seeing others pouring in upon 'em, retir'd in great Confusion; and some one Way, some another, ran into the inward Works.

There was a large Port in the Flank of the principal Bastion, towards the North-East, and a cover'd Way, through which the General and the Prince of *Hesse* follow'd the flying Forces; and by that Means became possess'd of it. Luckily enough here lay a Number of great Stones in the Gorge of the Bastion, for the Use of the Fortification; with which we made a Sort of Breast-Work, before the Enemy recover'd of their Amaze, or made any considerable Fire upon us from their inward Fort, which commanded the upper Part of that Bastion.

We were afterwards inform'd, that the Commander of the Citadel, expecting but one Attack, had call'd off the Men from the most distant and western Part of the Fort, to that Side which was next the Town; upon which our Men got into a Demi-Bastion in the most extream Part of the Fortification. Here they got Possession of three Pieces of Cannon, with hardly any Opposition; and had Leisure to cast up a little Retrenchment, and to make use of the Guns they had taken to defend it. Under this Situation, the Enemy, when drove into the inward Fort, were expos'd to our Fire from those Places we were possess'd of, in case they offer'd to make any Sally, or other Attempt against us. Thus we every Moment became better and better prepar'd against any Effort of the Garrison. And as they could not pretend to assail us without evident Hazard; so nothing remain'd for us to do, till we could bring up our Artillery and Mortars. Now it was that the General sent for the thousand Men under Brigadier *Stanhope's* Command, which he had posted at a Convent, halfway between the Town and *Monjouick.*

There was almost a total Cessation of Fire, the Men on both Sides being under Cover. The General was in the upper Part of the Bastion; the Prince of *Hesse* below, behind a little Work at the Point of the Bastion, whence he could only see the Heads of the Enemy over the Parapet of the inward Fort. Soon after an Accident happen'd which cost that gallant Prince his Life.

The Enemy had Lines of Communication between *Barcelona* and *Monjouick.* The Governor of the former, upon hearing the firing from the latter, immediately sent four hundred Dragoons on Horseback, under Orders, that two Hundred dismounting should reinforce the Garrison, and the other two Hundred should return with their Horses back to the Town.

When those two Hundred Dragoons were accordingly got into the inward Fort, unseen by any of our Men, the *Spaniards,* waving their Hats over their Heads, repeated over and over, *Viva el Rey, Viva.* This the Prince of *Hesse* unfortunately took for a Signal of their Desire to surrender. Upon which, with too much Warmth and Precipitancy, calling to the Soldiers following, *They surrender, they surrender,* he advanc'd with near three Hundred Men (who follow'd him without any Orders from their General) along the Curtain which led to the Ditch of the inward Fort. The Enemy suffered them to come into the Ditch, and there surrounding 'em, took two Hundred of them Prisoners, at the same time making a Discharge upon the rest, who were running back the Way they came. This firing brought the Earl of *Peterborow* down from the upper Part of the Bastion, to see what was doing below. When he had just turn'd the Point of the Bastion, he saw the Prince of *Hesse* retiring, with the Men that had so rashly advanc'd. The Earl had exchang'd a very few Words with him, when, from a second Fire, that Prince receiv'd a Shot in the great Artery of the Thigh, of which he died immediately, falling down at the General's Feet, who instantly gave Orders to carry off the Body to the next Convent.

Almost the same Moment an Officer came to acquaint the Earl of *Peterborow*, that a great Body of Horse and Foot, at least three Thousand, were on their March from *Barcelona* towards the Fort. The Distance is near a Mile, all uneven Ground; so that the Enemy was either discoverable, or not to be seen, just as they were marching on the Hills or in the Vallies. However, the General directly got on Horseback, to take a View of those Forces from the rising Ground without the Fort, having left all the Posts, which were already taken, well secur'd with the allotted Numbers of Officers and Soldiers.

But the Event will demonstrate of what Consequence the Absence or Presence of one Man may prove on great Occasions; No sooner was the Earl out of the Fort, the Care of which he had left under the Command of the Lord *Charlemont* (a Person of known Merit and undoubted Courage, but somewhat too flexible in his Temper) when a panick Fear (tho' the Earl, as I have said, was only gone to take a View of the Enemy) seiz'd upon the Soldiery, which was a little too easily comply'd with by the Lord *Charlemont*, then commanding Officer. True it is; for I heard an Officer, ready enough to take such Advantages, urge to him, that none of all those Posts we were become Masters of, were tenable; that to offer at it would be no better than wilfully sacrificing human Lives to Caprice and Humour; and just like a Man's knocking his Head against Stone Walls, to try which was hardest. Having over-heard this Piece of Lip-Oratory, and finding by the Answer that it was too likely to prevail, and that all I was like to say would avail nothing. I slipt away as fast as I could, to acquaint the General with the Danger impending.

As I pass'd along, I took notice that the Panick was upon the Increase, the general Rumor affirming, that we should be all cut off by the Troops that were come out of *Barcelona*, if we did not immediately gain the Hills, or the Houses possess'd by the *Miquelets*. Officers and Soldiers, under this prevailing Terror, quitted their Posts; and in one united Body (the Lord *Charlemont* at the Head of them) march'd, or rather hurry'd out of the Fort; and were come halfway down the Hill before the Earl of *Peterborow* came up to them. Though on my acquainting him with the shameful and surprizing Accident he made no Stay, but answering, with a good deal of Vehemence, *Good God, is it possible?* hastened back as fast as he could.

I never thought my self happier than in this Piece of Service to my Country. I confess I could not but value it, as having been therein more than a little instrumental in the glorious Successes which succeeded; since immediately upon this Notice from me, the Earl gallop'd up the Hill, and lighting when he came to Lord *Charlemont*, he took his Half-pike out of his Hand; and turning to the Officers and Soldiers, told them, if they would not face about and follow him, they should have the Scandal and eternal Infamy upon them of having deserted their Posts, and abandon'd their General.

It was surprizing to see with what Alacrity and new Courage they fac'd about and follow'd the Earl of *Peterborow*. In a Moment they had forgot their Apprehensions; and, without doubt, had they met with any Opposition, they would have behav'd themselves with the greatest Bravery. But as these Motions were unperceiv'd by the Enemy, all the Posts were regain'd, and anew possess'd in less than half an Hour, without any Loss: Though, had our Forces march'd half Musket-shot farther, their Retreat would have been perceiv'd, and all the Success attendant on this glorious Attempt must have been intirely blasted.

Another Incident which attended this happy Enterprize was this: The two hundred Men which fell into the Hands of the Enemy, by the unhappy Mistake of the Prince of *Hesse*, were carry'd directly into the Town. The Marquis of *Risburg*, a Lieutenant-General, who commanded the three thousand Men which were marching from the Town to the Relief of the Fort, examin'd the Prisoners, as they pass'd by; and they all agreeing that the General and the Prince of *Hesse* were in Person with the Troops that made the Attack on *Monjouick*, the Marquis gave immediate Orders to retire to the Town; taking it for granted, that the main Body of the Troops attended the Prince and General; and that some Design therefore was on foot to intercept his Return, in case he should venture too far. Thus the unfortunate Loss of our two hundred Men turn'd to our Advantage, in preventing the Advance of the Enemy, which must have put the Earl of *Peterborow* to inconceivable Difficulties.

The Body of one Thousand, under Brigadier *Stanhope*, being come up to *Monjouick*, and no Interruption given us by the Enemy, our Affairs were put into very good Order on this Side; while the Camp on the other Side was so fortify'd, that the Enemy, during the Siege, never made one Effort against it. In the mean time, the Communication between the two Camps was secure enough; although our Troops were obliged to a tedious March along the Foot of the Hills, whenever the General thought fit to relieve those on Duty on the Side of the Attack, from those Regiments encamp'd on the West Side of *Barcelona*.

The next Day, after the Earl of *Peterborow* had taken Care to secure the first Camp to the Eastward of the Town, he gave Orders to the Officers of the Fleet to land the Artillery and Ammunition behind the Fortress to the Westward. Immediately upon the Landing whereof, two Mortars were fix'd; from both which we ply'd the Fort of *Monjouick* furiously with our Bombs. But the third or fourth Day, one of our Shells fortunately lighting on their Magazine of Powder, blew it up; and with it the Governor, and many principal Officers who were at Dinner with him. The Blast, at the same Instant, threw down a Face of one of the smaller Bastions; which the vigilant *Miquelets*, ready enough to take all Advantages, no sooner saw (for they were under the Hill, very near the Place) but they readily enter'd, while the Enemy were under the utmost Confusion. If the Earl, no less watchful than they, had not at the same Moment thrown himself in with some regular Troops, and appeas'd the general Disorder, in all probability the Garrison had been put to the Sword. However, the General's Presence not only allay'd the Fury of the *Miquelets*; but kept his own Troops under strictest Discipline: So that in a happy Hour for the frighted Garrison, the General gave Officers and Soldiers Quarters, making them Prisoners of War.

How critical was that Minute wherein the General met his retreating Commander? a very few Steps farther had excluded us our own Conquests, to the utter Loss of all those greater Glories which ensu'd. Nor would that have been the worst; for besides the Shame attending such an ill concerted Retreat from our Acquests on *Monjouick*, we must have felt the accumulative Disgrace of infamously retiring aboard the Ships that brought us; but Heaven reserv'd for our General amazing Scenes both of Glory and Mortification.

I cannot here omit one Singularity of Life, which will demonstrate Men's different Way of Thinking, if not somewhat worse; when many Years after, to one in Office, who seem'd a little too dead to my

Complaints, and by that Means irritating my human Passions, injustice to my self, as well as Cause, I urged this Piece of Service, by which I not only preserv'd the Place, but the Honour of my Country, that *Minister petite*, to mortify my Expectations and baffle my Plea, with a Grimace as odd as his Logick, return'd, that, in his Opinion, the Service pretended was a Disservice to the Nation; since Perseverance had cost the Government more Money than all our Conquests were worth, could we have kept 'em. So irregular are the Conceptions of Man, when even great Actions thwart the Bent of an interested Will!

The Fort of *Monjouick* being thus surprizingly reduc'd, furnish'd a strange Vivacity to Mens Expectations, and as extravagantly flatter'd their Hopes; for as Success never fails to excite weaker Minds to pursue their good Fortune, though many times to their own Loss; so is it often too apt to push on more elevated Spirits to renew the Encounter for atchieving new Conquests, by hazarding too rashly all their former Glory. Accordingly, every Body now began to make his utmost Efforts; and look'd upon himself as a Drone, if he was not employ'd in doing something or other towards pushing forward the Siege of *Barcelona* it self, and raising proper Batteries for that Purpose. But, after all, it must in Justice be acknowledg'd, that notwithstanding this prodigious Success that attended this bold Enterprize, the Land Forces of themselves, without the Assistance of the Sailors, could never have reduc'd the Town. The Commanders and Officers of the Fleet had always evinc'd themselves Favourers of this Project upon *Barcelona*. A new Undertaking so late in the Year, as I have said before, was their utter Aversion, and what they hated to hear of. Elated therefore with a Beginning so auspicious, they gave a more willing Assistance than could have been ask'd, or judiciously expected. The Admirals forgot their Element, and acted as General Officers at Land: They came every Day from their Ships, with a Body of Men form'd into Companies, and regularly marshall'd and commanded by Captains and Lieutenants of their own. Captain *Littleton* in particular, one of the most advanced Captains in the whole Fleet, offer'd of himself to take care of the Landing and Conveyance of the Artillery to the Camp. And answerable to that his first Zeal was his Vigour all along, for finding it next to an Impossibility to draw the Cannon and Mortars up such vast Precipices by Horses, if the Country had afforded them, he caus'd Harnesses to be made for two hundred Men; and by that Means, after a prodigious Fatigue and Labour, brought the Cannon and Mortars necessary for the Siege up to the very Batteries.

In this Manner was the Siege begun; nor was it carry'd on with any less Application; the Approaches being made by an Army of Besiegers, that very little, if at all, exceeded the Number of the Besieg'd; not altogether in a regular Manner, our few Forces would not admit it; but yet with Regularity enough to secure our two little Camps, and preserve a Communication between both, not to be interrupted or incommoded by the Enemy. We had soon erected three several Batteries against the Place, all on the West Side of the Town, *viz.* one of nine Guns, another of Twelve, and the last of upwards of Thirty. From all which we ply'd the Town incessantly, and with all imaginable Fury; and very often in whole Vollies.

Nevertheless it was thought not only adviseable, but necessary, to erect another Battery, upon a lower Piece of Ground under a small Hill; which lying more within Reach, and opposite to those Places where the Walls were imagin'd weakest, would annoy the Town the more; and being design'd for six Guns only, might soon be perfected. A *French* Engeneer had the Direction; and indeed very quickly perfected it. But when it came to be consider'd which way to get the Cannon to it, most were of opinion that it would be absolutely impracticable, by reason of the vast Descent; tho' I believe they might have added a stronger Reason, and perhaps more intrinsick, that it was extremely expos'd to the Fire of the Enemy.

Having gain'd some little Reputation in the Attack of *Monjouick*, this Difficulty was at last to be put upon me; and as some, not my Enemies, suppos'd, more out of Envy than good Will. However, when I came to the Place, and had carefully taken a View of it, though I was sensible enough of the Difficulty, I made my main Objection as to the Time for accomplishing it; for it was then between Nine and Ten, and the Guns were to be mounted by Day-light. Neither could I at present see any other Way to answer their Expectations, than by casting the Cannon down the Precipice, at all Hazards, to the Place below, where that fourth Battery was erected.

This wanted not Objections to; and therefore to answer my Purpose, as to point of Time, sixty Men more were order'd me, as much as possible to facilitate the Work by Numbers; and accordingly I set about it. Just as I was setting all Hands to work, and had given Orders to my Men to begin some Paces back, to make the Descent more gradual, and thereby render the Task a little more feasible, Major *Collier*, who commanded the Train, came to me; and perceiving the Difficulties of the Undertaking, in a Fret told me, I was impos'd upon;

and vow'd he would go and find out Brigadier *Petit*, and let him know the Impossibility, as well as the Unreasonableness of the Task I was put upon. He had scarce utter'd those Words, and turn'd himself round to perform his Promise, when an unlucky Shot with a Musket-Ball wounded him through the Shoulder; upon which he was carry'd off, and I saw him not till some considerable time after.

By the painful Diligence, and the additional Compliment of Men, however, I so well succeeded (such was my great good Fortune) that the Way was made, and the Guns, by the Help of Fascines, and other lesser Preparations below, safely let down and mounted; so that that fourth Battery began to play upon the Town before Break of Day; and with all the Success that was propos'd.

In short, the Breach in a very few Days after was found wholly practicable; and all Things were got ready for a general Storm. Which Don *Valasco* the Governor being sensible of, immediately beat a Parley; upon which it was, among other Articles, concluded, that the Town should be surrender'd in three Days; and the better to ensure it, the Bastion, which commanded the Port St. *Angelo*, was directly put into our Possession.

But before the Expiration of the limited three Days, a very unexpected Accident fell out, which hasten'd the Surrender. Don *Valasco*, during his Government, had behav'd himself very arbitrarily, and thereby procur'd, as the Consequence of it, a large Proportion of ill will, not only among the Townsmen, but among the *Miquelets*, who had, in their Zeal to King *Charles*, flock'd from all Parts of *Catalonia* to the Siege of their Capital; and who, on the Signing of the Articles of Surrender, had found various Ways, being well acquainted with the most private Avenues, to get by Night into the Town: So that early in the Morning they began to plunder all that they knew Enemies to King *Charles*, or thought Friends to the Prince his Competitor.

Their main Design was upon *Valasco* the Governor, whom, if they could have got into their Hands, it was not to be question'd, but as far as his Life and Limbs would have serv'd, they would have sufficiently satiated their Vengeance upon. He expected no less; and therefore concealed himself, till the Earl of *Peterborow* could give Orders for his more safe and private Conveyance by Sea to *Alicant.*

Nevertheless, in the Town all was in the utmost Confusion; which the Earl of *Peterborow*, at the very first hearing, hastened to appease; with his usual Alacrity he rid all alone to Port St. *Angelo*, where at that time my self happen'd to be; and demanding to be admitted, the Officer of the Guard, under Fear and Surprise, open'd the Wicket, through which the Earl enter'd, and I after him.

Scarce had we gone a hundred Paces, when we saw a Lady of apparent Quality, and indisputable Beauty, in a strange, but most affecting Agony, flying from the apprehended Fury of the *Miquelets*; her lovely Hair was all flowing about her Shoulders, which, and the Consternation she was in, rather added to, than any thing diminish'd from the Charms of an Excess of Beauty. She, as is very natural to People in Distress, made up directly to the Earl, her Eyes satisfying her he was a Person likely to give her all the Protection she wanted. And as soon as ever she came near enough, in a Manner that declar'd her Quality before she spoke, she crav'd that Protection, telling him, the better to secure it, who it was that ask'd it. But the generous Earl presently convinc'd her, he wanted no Intreaties, having, before he knew her to be the Dutchess of *Popoli*, taken her by the Hand, in order to convey her through the Wicket which he enter'd at, to a Place of Safety without the Town.

I stay'd behind, while the Earl convey'd the distress'd Dutchess to her requested *Asylum*; and I believe it was much the longest Part of an Hour before he return'd. But as soon as ever he came back, he, and my self, at his Command, repair'd to the Place of most Confusion, which the extraordinary Noise full readily directed us to; and which happened to be on the Parade before the Palace. There it was that the *Miquelets* were making their utmost Efforts to get into their Hands the almost sole Occasion of the Tumult, and the Object of their raging Fury, the Person of Don *Valasco*, the late Governor.

It was here that the Earl preserv'd that Governor from the violent, but perhaps too just Resentments of the *Miquelets*; and, as I said before, convey'd him by Sea to *Alicant*. And, indeed, I could little doubt the Effect, or be any thing surpriz'd at the Easiness of the Task, when I saw, that wherever he appear'd the popular Fury was in a Moment allay'd, and that every Dictate of that General was assented to with the utmost Chearfulness and Deference. *Valasco*, before his Embarkment, had given Orders, in Gratitude to his Preserver, for all the Gates to be deliver'd up, tho' short of the stipulated Term; and they were accordingly so delivered, and our Troops took Possession so soon as ever that Governor was aboard the Ship that was to convey him to *Alicant*.

During the Siege of *Barcelona*, Brigadier *Stanhope* order'd a Tent to be pitch'd as near the Trenches as possibly could be with Safety;

where he not only entertain'd the chief Officers who were upon Duty, but likewise the *Catalonian* Gentlemen who brought *Miquelets* to our Assistance. I remember I saw an old Cavalier, having his only Son with him, who appear'd a fine young Gentleman, about twenty Years of Age, go into the Tent, in order to dine with the Brigadier. But whilst they were at Dinner, an unfortunate Shot came from the Bastion of St. *Antonio*, and intirely struck off the Head of the Son. The father immediately rose up, first looking down upon his headless Child, and then lifting up his Eyes to Heaven, whilst the Tears ran down his Cheeks, he cross'd himself, and only said, *Fiat voluntas tua*, and bore it with a wonderful Patience. 'Twas a sad Spectacle, and truly it affects me now whilst I am writing.

The Earl of *Peterborow*, tho' for some time after the Revolution he had been employ'd in civil Affairs, return'd to the military Life with great Satisfaction, which was ever his Inclination. Brigadier *Stanhope*, who was justly afterwards created an Earl, did well deserve this Motto, *Tam Marte quam Mercurio*; for truly he behav'd, all the time he continu'd in *Spain*, as if he had been inspir'd with Conduct; for the Victory at *Almanar* was intirely owing to him; and likewise at the Battle of *Saragosa* he distinguish'd himself with great Bravery. That he had not Success at *Bruhega* was not his Fault; for no Man can resist Fate; for 'twas decreed by Heaven that *Philip* should remain King of *Spain*, and *Charles* to be Emperor of *Germany*. Yet each of these Monarchs have been ungrateful to the Instruments which the Almighty made use of to preserve them upon their Thrones; for one had not been King of *Spain* but for *France*; and the other had not been Emperor but for *England*.

Barcelona, the chief Place in *Catalonia*, being thus in our Hands, as soon as the Garrison, little inferior to our Army, had march'd out with Drums beating, Colours flying, &c. according to the Articles, *Charles* the Third made his publick Entry, and was proclaim'd King, and receiv'd with the general Acclamations, and all other Demonstrations of Joy suitable to that great Occasion.

Some Days after which, the Citizens, far from being satiated with their former Demonstrations of their Duty, sent a Petition to the King, by proper Deputies for that Purpose appointed, desiring Leave to give more ample Instances of their Affections in a public *Cavalcade*. The King granted their Request, and the Citizens, pursuant thereto, made their Preparations.

On the Day appointed, the King, plac'd in a Balcony belonging to the House of the Earl of *Peterborow*, appear'd ready to honour the

Show. The Ceremonial, to speak nothing figuratively, was very fine and grand: Those of the first Rank made their Appearance in decent Order, and upon fine Horses; and others under Arms, and in Companies, march'd with native Gravity and Grandeur, all saluting his Majesty as they pass'd by, after the *Spanish* Manner, which that Prince return'd with the Movement of his Hand to his Mouth; for the Kings of *Spain* are not allow'd to salute, or return a Salute, by any Motion to, or of, the Hat.

After these follow'd several Pageants; the first of which was drawn by Mules, set off to the Height with stateliest Feathers, and adorn'd with little Bells. Upon the Top of this Pageant appear'd a Man dress'd all in Green; but in the Likeness of a Dragon. The Pageant making a Stop just over-against the Balcony where the King sate, the Dragonical Representative diverted him with great Variety of Dancings, the Earl of *Peterborow* all the time throwing out Dollars by Handfuls among the Populace, which they as constantly receiv'd with the loud Acclamation and repeated Cries of *Viva, Viva, Carlos Terceros, Viva la Casa d'Austria.*

When that had play'd its Part, another Pageant, drawn as before, made a like full Stop before the same Balcony. On this was plac'd a very large Cage, or Aviary, the Cover of which, by Springs contriv'd for that Purpose, immediately flew open, and out of it a surprizing Flight of Birds of various Colours. These, all amaz'd at their sudden Liberty, which I took to be the Emblem intended, hover'd a considerable space of time over and about their Place of Freedom, chirping, singing, and otherwise testifying their mighty Joy for their so unexpected Enlargement.

There were many other Pageants; but having little in them very remarkable, I have forgot the Particulars. Nevertheless, every one of them was dismiss'd with the like Acclamations of *Viva, Viva;* the Whole concluding with Bonfires and Illuminations common on all such Occasions.

I cannot here omit one very remarkable Instance of the Catholick Zeal of that Prince, which I was soon after an Eye-witness of. I was at that time in the Fruit-Market, when the King passing by in his Coach, the Host (whether by Accident or Contrivance I cannot say) was brought, at that very Juncture, out of the great Church, in order, as I after understood, to a poor sick Woman's receiving the Sacrament. On Sight of the Host the King came out of his Coach, kneel'd down in the Street, which at that time prov'd to be very dirty, till the Host pass'd by;

then rose up, and taking the lighted Flambeau from him who bore it, he follow'd the Priest up a streight nasty Alley, and there up a dark ordinary Pair of Stairs, where the poor sick Woman lay. There he stay'd till the whole Ceremony was over, when, returning to the Door of the Church, he very faithfully restor'd the lighted Flambeau to the Fellow he had taken it from, the People all the while crying out *Viva, Viva*; an Acclamation, we may imagine, intended to his Zeal, as well as his Person.

Another remarkable Accident, of a much more moral Nature, I must, injustice to the Temperance of that, in this truly inimitable People, recite. I was one Day walking in one of the most populous Streets of that City, where I found an uncommon Concourse of People, of all Sorts, got together; and imagining so great a Croud could not be assembled on a small Occasion, I prest in among the rest; and after a good deal of Struggling and Difficulty, reach'd into the Ring and Centre of that mix'd Multitude. But how did I blush? with what Confusion did I appear? when I found one of my own Countrymen, a drunken Granadier, the attractive Loadstone of all that high and low Mob, and the Butt of all their Merriment? It will be easily imagin'd to be a Thing not a little surprizing to one of our Country, to find that a drunken Man should be such a wonderful Sight; However, the witty Sarcasms that were then by high and low thrown upon that senseless Creature, and as I interpreted Matters, me in him, were so pungent, that if I did not curse my Curiosity, I thought it best to withdraw my self as fast as Legs could carry me away.

BARCELONA being now under King *Charles*, the Towns of *Gironne, Tarragona, Tortosa*, and *Lerida*, immediately declar'd for him. To every one of which Engeneers being order'd, it was my Lot to be sent to *Tortosa*. This Town is situated on the Side of the River *Ebro*, over which there is a fair and famous Bridge of Boats. The Waters of this River are always of a dirty red Colour, somewhat fouler than our Moorish Waters; yet is it the only Water the Inhabitants drink, or covet to drink; and every House providing for its own Convenience Cisterns to preserve it in, by a few Hours standing it becomes as clear as the clearest Rock-water, but as soft as Milk. In short, for Softness, Brightness, and Pleasantness of Taste, the Natives prefer it to all the Waters in the World. And I must declare in favour of their Opinion, that none ever pleas'd me like it.

This Town was of the greater Moment to our Army, as opening a Passage into the Kingdom of *Valencia* on one Side, and the Kingdom of *Arragon* on the other: And being of it self tolerably defensible, in human Appearance might probably repay a little Care and Charge in its Repair and Improvement. Upon this Employ was I appointed, and thus was I busy'd, till the Arrival of the Earl of *Peterborow* with his little Army, in order to march to *Valencia*, the Capital of that Province. Here he left in Garrison Colonel *Hans Hamilton's* Regiment; the Place, nevertheless, was under the Command of a *Spanish* Governor, appointed by King *Charles*.

While the Earl stay'd a few Days at this Place, under Expectation of the promis'd Succours from *Barcelona*, he receiv'd *a Proprio* (or Express) from the King of *Spain*, full of Excuses, instead of Forces. And yet the very same Letter, in a paradoxical Manner, commanded him, at all Events, to attempt the Relief of *Santo Mattheo*, where Colonel *Jones* commanded, and which was then under Siege by the *Conde de los Torres* (as was the Report) with upwards of three thousand Men. The Earl of *Peterborow* could not muster above one thousand Foot, and about two hundred Horse; a small Force to make an Attempt of that Nature upon such a superior Power: Yet the Earl's Vivacity (as will be occasionally further observ'd in the Course of these Memoirs) never much regarded Numbers, so there was but room, by any Stratagem, to hope for Success. True it is, for his greater Encouragement and Consolation, the same Letter intimated, that a great Concourse of the Country People being up in Arms, to the Number of many Thousands, in Favour of King *Charles*, and wanting only Officers, the Enterprize would be easy and unattended with much Danger. But upon mature Enquiry, the Earl found that great Body of Men all *in nubibus*; and that the *Conde*, in the plain Truth of the Matter, was much stronger than the Letter at first represented.

Santo Mattheo was a Place of known Importance; and that from its Situation, which cut off all Communication between *Catalonia* and *Valencia*; and, consequently, should it fall into the Hands of the Enemy, the Earl's Design upon the latter must inevitably have been postpon'd. It must be granted, the Commands for attempting the Relief of it were pressing and peremptory; nevertheless, the Earl was very conscious to himself, that as the promis'd Reinforcements were suspended, his Officers would not approve of the Attempt upon the Foot of such vast Inequalities; and their own declar'd Sentiments soon confirm'd the Dictates of the Earl's Reason. He therefore addresses himself to those Officers in a different Manner: He told 'em he only desir'd they would be passive, and leave it to him to work his own Way.

Accordingly, the Earl found out and hired two *Spanish* Spies, for whose Fidelity (as his great Precaution always led him to do) he took sufficient Security; and dispatch'd 'em with a Letter to Colonel *Jones*, Governor of the Place, intimating his Readiness, as well as Ability, to relieve him; and, above all, exhorting him to have the *Miquelets* in the Town ready, on Sight of his Troops, to issue out, pursue, and plunder; since that would be all they would have to do, and all he would expect at their Hands. The Spies were dispatch'd accordingly; and, pursuant to Instructions, one betray'd and discover'd the other who had the Letter in charge to deliver to Colonel *Jones*. The Earl, to carry on the Feint, having in the mean time, by dividing his Troops, and marching secretly over the Mountains, drawn his Men together, so as to make their Appearance on the Height of a neighbouring Mountain, little more than Cannot-shot from the Enemy's Camp. The Tale of the Spies was fully confirm'd, and the *Conde* (though an able General) march'd off with some Precipitation with his Army; and by that Means the Earl's smaller Number of twelve Hundred had Liberty to march into the Town without Interruption. I must not let slip an Action of Colonel *Jones*'s just before the Earl's Delivery of them: The *Conde*, for want of Artillery, had set his Miners to work; and the Colonel, finding they had made some dangerous Advances, turned the Course of a Rivulet, that ran through the Middle of the Town, in upon them, and made them quit a Work they thought was brought to Perfection.

SANTO *Mattheo* being reliev'd, as I have said, the Earl, though he had so far gain'd his Ends, left not the flying Enemy without a Feint of Pursuit; with such Caution, nevertheless, that in case they should happen to be better inform'd of his Weakness, he might have a Resource either back again to *Santo Mattheo*, or to *Vinaros* on the Sea-side; or some other Place, as occasion might require. But having just before receiv'd fresh Advice, that the Reinforcements he expected were anew countermanded; and that the Duke of *Anjou* had increas'd his Troops to twelve thousand Men; the Officers, not enough elated with the last Success to adventure upon new Experiments, resolv'd, in a Council of War, to advise the Earl, who had just before receiv'd a discretionary Commission in lieu of Troops, so to post the Forces under him, as not to be cut off from being able to assist the King in Person; or to march to the Defence of *Catalonia*, in case of Necessity.

Pursuant to this Resolution of the Council of War, the Earl of *Peterborow*, tho' still intent upon his Expedition into *Valencia* (which had been afresh commanded, even while his Supplies were countermanded) orders his Foot, in a truly bad Condition, by tedious Marches Day and Night over the Mountains, to *Vinaros*; and with his two hundred Horse, set out to prosecute his pretended Design of pursuing the flying Enemy; resolv'd, if possible, notwithstanding all seemingly desperate Circumstances, to perfect the Security of that Capital.

To that Purpose, the Earl, with his small Body of Patrolers, went on frightning the Enemy, till they came under the Walls of *Nules*, a Town fortify'd with the best Walls, regular Towers, and in the best Repair of any in that Kingdom. But even here, upon the Appearance of the Earl's Forlorn (if they might not properly at that time all have pass'd under that Character) under the same Panick they left that sensible Town, with only one Thousand of the Town's People, well arm'd, for the Defence of it. Yet was it scarce to be imagin'd, that the Earl, with his small Body of two hundred Horse, should be able to gain Admission; or, indeed, under such Circumstances, to attempt it. But bold as the Undertaking was, his good Genius went along with him; and so good a Genius was it, that it rarely left him without a good Effect. He had been told the Day before, that the Enemy, on leaving *Nules*, had got Possession of *Villa Real*, where they put all to the Sword. What would have furnish'd another with Terror, inspir'd his Lordship with a Thought as fortunate as it was successful. The Earl rides up to the very Gates of the Town, at the Head of his Party, and peremptorily demands the chief Magistrate, or a Priest, immediately to be sent out to him; and that under Penalty of being all put to the Sword, and us'd as the Enemy had us'd those at *Villa-Real* the Day or two before. The Troops, that had so lately left the Place, had left behind 'em more Terror than Men; which, together with the peremptory Demand of the Earl, soon produc'd some Priests to wait upon the General. By their Readiness to obey, the Earl very justly imagin'd Fear to be the Motive; wherefore, to improve their Terror, he only allow'd them six Minutes time to resolve upon a Surrender, telling them, that otherwise, so soon as his Artillery was come up, he would lay them under the utmost Extremities. The Priests return'd with this melancholy Message into the Place; and in a very short time after the Gates were thrown open. Upon the Earl's Entrance he found two hundred Horse, which were the Original of his Lordship's forming that Body of Horse, which afterwards prov'd the saving of *Valencia*.

The News of the taking of *Nules* soon overtook the flying Enemy; and so increas'd the Apprehensions of their Danger, that they renew'd their March, the same Day; though what they had taken before would have satisfy'd them much better without it. On the other hand, the Earl was so well pleas'd with his Success, that leaving the Enemy to fly before their Fears, he made a short Turn towards *Castillon de la Plana*, a considerable, but open Town, where his Lordship furnish'd himself with four hundred Horses more; and all this under the Assurance that his Troops were driving the Enemy before them out of the Kingdom. Hence he sent Orders to Colonel *Pierce's* Regiment at *Vinaros* to meet him at *Oropesa*, a Place at no great Distance; where, when they came, they were very pleasingly surpriz'd at their being well mounted, and furnish'd with all Accoutrements necessary. After which, leaving 'em canton'd in wall'd Towns, where they could not be disturb'd without Artillery, that indefatigable General, leaving them full Orders, went on his way towards *Tortosa*.

At *Vinaros* the Earl met with Advice, that the *Spanish* Militia of the Kingdom of *Valencia* were assembled, and had already advanc'd a Day's March at least into that Country. Upon which, collecting, as fast as he could, the whole Corps together, the Earl resolv'd to penetrate into *Valencia* directly; notwithstanding this whole collected Body would amount to no more than six hundred Horse and two thousand Foot.

But there was a strong Pass over a River, just under the Walls of *Molviedro*, which must be first disputed and taken. This Brigadier *Mahoni*, by the Orders of the Duke of *Arcos*, who commanded the Troops of the Duke of *Anjou* in the Kingdom of *Valencia*, had taken care to secure. *Molviedro*, though not very strong, is a wall'd Town, very populous of it self; and had in it, besides a Garrison of eight hundred Men, most of *Mahoni's* Dragoons. It lies at the very Bottom of a high Hill; on the upper Part whereof they shew the Ruins of the once famous SAGUNTUM; famous sure to Eternity, if Letters shall last so long, for an inviolable Fidelity to a negligent Confederate, against an implacable Enemy. Here yet appear the visible *Vestigia* of awful Antiquity, in half standing Arches, and the yet unlevell'd Walls and Towers of that once celebrated City. I could not but look upon all these with the Eyes of Despight, in regard to their Enemy *Hannibal*; with those of Disdain, in respect to the uncommon and unaccountable Supineness of its Confederates, the *Romans*; but with those of Veneration, as to the Memory of a glorious People, who rather than stand reproach'd with a Breach of Faith, or the Brand of Cowardice, chose to sacrifice themselves, their Wives, Children, and all that was dear to them, in the Flames of their expiring City.

In *Molviedro*, as I said before, *Mahoni* commanded, with eight hundred Men, besides Inhabitants; which, together with our having but little Artillery, induc'd the Officers under the Earl of *Peterborow* reasonably enough to imagine and declare, that there could be no visible Appearance of surmounting such Difficulties. The Earl, nevertheless, instead of indulging such Despondencies, gave them Hope, that what Strength serv'd not to accomplish, Art might possibly obtain. To that Purpose he proposed an Interview between himself and *Mahoni*; and accordingly sent an Officer with a Trumpet to intimate his Desire. The Motion was agreed to; and the Earl having previously station'd his Troops to advantage, and his little Artillery at a convenient Distance, with Orders they should appear on a slow March on the Side of a rising Hill, during the time of Conference, went to the Place appointed; only, as had been stipulated, attended with a small Party of Horse. When they were met, the Earl first offer'd all he could to engage *Mahoni* to the Interest of King *Charles*; proposing some Things extravagant enough (as *Mahoni* himself some time after told me) to stagger the Faith of a Catholick; but all to little Purpose: *Mahoni* was inflexible, which oblig'd the Earl to new Measures.

Whereupon the Earl frankly told him, that he could not however but esteem the Confidence he had put in him; and therefore, to make some Retaliation, he was ready to put it in his Power to avoid the Barbarities lately executed at *Villa-Real*.

"My Relation to you," continued the General, "inclines me to spare a Town under your Command. You see how near my Forces are; and can hardly doubt our soon being Masters of the Place: What I would therefore offer you, said the Earl, is a Capitulation, that my Inclination may be held in Countenance by my Honour. Barbarities, however justified by Example, are my utter Aversion, and against my Nature; and to testify so much, together with my good Will to your Person, was the main Intent of this Interview."

This Frankness so far prevail'd on *Mahoni*, that he agreed to return an Answer in half an Hour. Accordingly, an Answer was returned by a *Spanish* Officer, and a Capitulation agreed upon; the Earl at the same time endeavouring to bring over that Officer to King *Charles*, on much the same Topicks he us'd with *Mahoni*. But finding this equally fruitless, whether it was that he tacitly reproach'd the Officer with a Want of Consideration in neglecting to follow the Example of his

Commander, or what else, he created in that Officer such a Jealousy of *Mahoni*, that was afterward very serviceable to him in his further Design.

To forward which to a good Issue, the Earl immediately made choice of two Dragoons, who, upon promise of Promotion, undertook to go as Spies to the Duke of *Arcos*, whose Forces lay not far off, on the other Side a large Plain, which the Earl must unavoidably pass, and which would inevitably be attended with almost insuperable Dangers, if there attack'd by a Force so much superior. Those Spies, according to Instructions, were to discover to the Duke, that they over-heard the Conference between the Earl and *Mahoni*; and at the same time saw a considerable Number of Pistoles deliver'd into *Mahoni*'s Hands, large Promises passing at that Instant reciprocally: But above all, that the Earl had recommended to him the procuring the March of the Duke over the Plain between them. The Spies went and deliver'd all according to Concert; concluding, before the Duke, that they would ask no Reward, but undergo any Punishment, if *Mahoni* did not very soon send to the Duke a Request to march over the Plain, in order to put the concerted Plot in execution. It was not long after this pretended Discovery before *Mahoni* did send indeed an Officer to the Duke, desiring the March of his Forces over the Plain; but, in reality, to obstruct the Earl's Passage, which he knew very well must be that and no other way. However, the Duke being prepossess'd by the Spies, and what those *Spanish* Officers that at first escap'd had before infus'd, took Things in their Sense; and as soon as *Mahoni*, who was forc'd to make the best of his way over the Plain before the Earl of *Peterborow*, arriv'd at his Camp, he was put under Arrest and sent to *Madrid*. The Duke having thus imbib'd the Venom, and taken the Alarm, immediately decamp'd in Confusion, and took a different Rout than at first he intended; leaving that once formidable Plain open to the Earl, without an Enemy to obstruct him. In some little time after he arriv'd at *Madrid*, *Mahoni* made his Innocence appear, and was created a General; while the Duke of *Arcos* was recall'd from his Post of Honour.

The Day after we arriv'd at *Valencia*, the Gates of which fine City were set open to us with the highest Demonstrations of Joy. I call'd it a fine City; but sure it richly deserves a brighter Epithet, since it is a common Saying among the *Spaniards*, that the Pleasures of *Valencia* would make a *Jew* forget *Jerusalem*. It is most sweetly situated in a very beautiful Plain, and within half a League of the *Mediterranean* Sea. It never wants any of the Fragrancies of Nature, and always has something to delight the most curious Eye. It is famous to a Proverb for fine Women; but as infamous, and only in that so, for the Race of Bravoes, the common Companions of the Ladies of Pleasure in this Country. These Wretches are so Case-hardened, they will commit a Murder for a Dollar, tho' they run their Country for it when they have done. Not that other Parts of this Nation are uninfested with this sort of Animals; but here their Numbers are so great, that if a Catalogue was to be taken of those in other Parts of that Country, perhaps nine in ten would be found by Birth to be of this Province.

But to proceed, tho' the Citizens, and all Sorts of People, were redundant in their various Expressions of Joy, for an Entry so surprizing, and utterly lost to their Expedition, whatever it was to their Wishes, the Earl had a secret Concern for the Publick, which lay gnawing at his Heart, and which yet he was forced to conceal. He knew that he had not four thousand Soldiers in the Place, and not Powder or Ammunition for those; nor any Provisions lay'd in for any thing like a Siege. On the other Hand, the Enemy without were upwards of seven Thousand, with a Body of four Thousand more, not fifteen Leagues off, on their March to join them. Add to this, the Marechal de *Thesse* was no farther off than *Madrid*, a very few Days' March from *Valencia*; a short Way indeed for the Earl (who, as was said before, was wholly unprovided for a Siege, which was reported to be the sole End of the Mareschal's moving that Way.) But the Earl's never-failing Genius resolv'd again to attempt that by Art, which the Strength of his Forces utterly disallow'd him. And in the first Place, his Intelligence telling him that sixteen twenty-four Pounders, with Stores and Ammunition answerable for a Siege, were ship'd off for the Enemy's Service at *Alicant*, the Earl forthwith lays a Design, and with his usual Success intercepts 'em all, supplying that way his own Necessities at the Expence of the Enemy.

The four thousand Men ready to reinforce the Troops nearer *Valencia*, were the next Point to be undertaken; but *hic labor, hoc opus;* since the greater Body under the Conde *de las Torres* (who, with *Mahoni*, was now reinstated in his Post) lay between the Earl and those Troops intended to be dispers'd. And what inhaunc'd the Difficulty, the River *Xucar* must be passed in almost the Face of the Enemy. Great Disadvantages as these were, they did not discourage the Earl. He detach'd by Night four hundred Horse and eight hundred Foot, who march'd with such hasty Silence, that they surpriz'd that great Body, routed 'em, and brought into *Valencia* six hundred Prisoners very safely, notwithstanding they were oblig'd, under the same Night-Covert, to pass very near a Body of three Thousand of the Enemy's Horse. Such a prodigious Victory would hardly have gain'd Credit in that City, if the Prisoners brought in had not been living Witnesses of the Action as well as the Triumph. The Conde *de las Torres*, upon these two military Rebuffs, drew off to a more convenient Distance, and left the Earl a little more at ease in his new Quarters.

Here the Earl of *Peterborow* made his Residence for some time. He was extreamly well belov'd, his affable Behaviour exacted as much from all; and he preserv'd such a good Correspondence with the Priests and the Ladies, that he never fail'd of the most early and best Intelligence, a thing by no means to be slighted in the common Course of Life; but much more commendable and necessary in a General, with so small an Army, at open War, and in the Heart of his Enemy's Country.

The Earl, by this Means, some small time after, receiving early Intelligence that King *Philip* was actually on his March to *Barcelona*, with an Army of upwards of twenty five thousand Men, under the Command of a Mareschal of *France*, began his March towards *Catalonia*, with all the Troops that he could gather together, leaving in *Valencia* a small Body of Foot, such as in that Exigence could best be spar'd. The whole Body thus collected made very little more than two thousand Foot and six hundred Horse; yet resolutely with these he sets out for *Barcelona*: In the Neighbourhood of which, as soon as he arriv'd, he took care to post himself and his diminutive Army in the Mountains which inviron that City; where he not only secur'd 'em against the Enemy; but found himself in a Capacity of putting him under perpetual Alarms. Nor was the Mareschal, with his great Army, capable of returning the Earl's Compliment of Disturbance; since he himself, every six or eight Hours, put his Troops into such a varying Situation, that always when most arduously fought, he was farthest off from being found. In this Manner the General bitterly harrass'd the Troops of the Enemy; and by these Means struck a perpetual Terror into the Besiegers. Nor did he only this way annoy the Enemy; the Precautions he had us'd, and the Measures he had taken in other Places, with a View to prevent their Return to *Madrid*, though the Invidious endeavour'd to bury them in Oblivion, having equally contributed to the driving of the Mareschal of *France*, and his Catholick King, out of the *Spanish* Dominions.

But to go on with the Siege: The Breaches in the Walls of that City, during its Siege by the Earl, had been put into tolerable Repair; but those of *Monjouick*, on the contrary, had been as much neglected. However, the Garrison made shift to hold out a Battery of twenty-three Days, with no less than fifty Pieces of Cannon; when, after a Loss of the Enemy of upwards of three thousand Men (a Moiety of the Army employ'd against it when the Earl took it) they were forc'd to surrender at Discretion. And this cannot but merit our Observation, that a Place, which the *English* General took in little more than an Hour, and with inconsiderable Loss, afforded the Mareschal of *France* a Resistance of twenty-three Days.

Upon the taking of Fort *Monjouick*, the Mareschal *de Thess* gave immediate Orders for Batteries to be rais'd against the Town. Those Orders were put in Execution with all Expedition; and at the same time his Army fortify'd themselves with such Entrenchments, as would have ruin'd the Earl's former little Army to have rais'd, or his present much lesser Army to have attempted the forcing them. However, they sufficiently demonstrated their Apprehensions of that watchful General, who lay hovering over their Heads upon the Mountains. Their main Effort was to make a Breach between Port St. *Antonio* and that Breach which our Forces had made the Year before; to effect which they took care to ply them very diligently both from Cannon and Mortars; and in some few Days their Application was answer'd with a practicable Breach for a Storm. Which however was prudently deferr'd for some time, and that thro' fear of the Earl's falling on the Back of them whenever they should attempt it; which, consequently, they were sensible might put them into some dangerous Disorder.

And now it was that the Earl of *Peterborow* resolv'd to put in practice the Resolution he had some time before concerted within himself. About nine or ten Days before the Raising of the Siege, he had receiv'd an Express from Brigadier *Stanhope* (who was aboard Sir *John Leake's* Fleet appointed for the Relief of the Place, with the Reinforcements from *England*) acquainting the Earl, that he had us'd all possible Endeavours to prevail on the Admiral to make the best of his way to *Barcelona*. But that the Admiral, however, persisted in a positive Resolution not to attempt the *French* Fleet before that Place under the Count *de Thoulouse*, till the Ships were join'd him which were expected from *Ireland*, under the Command of Sir *George Bing*. True it was, the Fleet under Admiral *Leake* was of equal Strength with that under the *French* Admiral; but jealous of the Informations he had receiv'd, and too ready to conclude that People in Distress were apt to make Representations too much in their own Favour; he held himself, in point of Discretion, oblig'd not to hazard the Queen's Ships, when a Reinforcement of both cleaner and larger were under daily Expectation.

This unhappy Circumstance (notwithstanding all former glorious Deliverances) had almost brought the Earl to the Brink of Despair; and to increase it, the Earl every Day receiv'd such Commands from the King within the Place, as must have sacrificed his few Forces, without the least Probability of succeeding. Those all tended to his forcing his Way into the Town; when, in all human Appearance, not one Man of all that should make the Attempt could have done it, with any Hope or Prospect of surviving. The *French* were strongly encamp'd at the Foot of the Mountains, distant two Miles from *Barcelona*; towards the Bottom of those Hills, the Avenues into the Plain were possess'd and fortify'd by great Detachments from the Enemy's Army. From all which it will be evident, that no Attempt could be made without giving the Enemy time to draw together what Body of Foot they pleas'd. Or supposing it feasible, under all these difficult Circumstances, for some of them to have forc'd their Passage, the Remainder, that should have been so lucky to have escap'd their Foot, would have found themselves expos'd in open Field to a Pursuit of four thousand Horse and Dragoons; and that for two Miles together; when in case of their inclosing them, the bravest Troops in the World, under such a Situation, would have found it their best way to have surrender'd themselves Prisoners of War.

Nevertheless, when Brigadier *Stanhope* sent that Express to the Earl, which I just now mention'd, he assur'd him in the same, that he would use his utmost Diligence, both by Sea and Land, to let him have timely Notice of the Conjunction of the Fleets, which was now all they had to depend upon. Adding withal, that if the Earl should at any time receive a Letter, or Paper, though directed to no Body, and with nothing in it, but a half Sheet of Paper cut in the Middle, he, the Earl, might certainly depend upon it, that the two Fleets were join'd, and making the best of their Way for *Barcelona*. It will easily be imagin'd the Express was to be well paid; and being made sensible that he ran little or no Hazard in carrying a Piece of blank Paper, he undertook it, and as fortunately arriv'd with it to the Earl, at a Moment when Chagrin and Despair might have hurry'd him to some Resolution that might have prov'd fatal. The Messenger himself, however, knew nothing of the Joining of the Fleets, or the Meaning of his Message.

As soon as the Earl of *Peterborow* receiv'd this welcome Message from Brigadier *Stanhope*, he march'd the very same Night, with his whole little Body of Forces, to a Town on the Sea-Shore, call'd *Sigeth*. No Person guess'd the Reason of his March, or knew any thing of what the Intent of it was. The Officers, as formerly, obey'd without Enquiry; for they were led to it by so many unaccountable Varieties of Success, that Affiance became a second Nature, both in Officer and Soldier.

The Town of *Sigeth* was about seven Leagues to the Westward of *Barcelona*; where, as soon as the Earl with his Forces arriv'd, he took care to secure all the small Fishing-Boats, *Feluccas*, and *Sattées*; nay, in a Word, every Machine in which he could transport any of his Men: So that in two Days' time he had got together a Number sufficient for the Conveyance of all his Foot.

But a Day or two before the Arrival of the *English* Fleet off *Sigeth*, The Officers of his Troops were under a strange Consternation at a Resolution their General had taken. Impatient of Delay, and fearful of the Fleets passing by without his Knowledge, the Earl summon'd them together a little before Night, at which time he discover'd to the whole Assembly, that he himself was oblig'd to endeavour to get aboard the *English* Fleet; and that, if possible, before the *French* Scouts should be able to make any Discovery of their Strength: That finding himself of no further Use on Shore, having already taken the necessary Precautions for their Transportation and Security, they had nothing to do but to pursue his Orders, and make the best of their Way to *Barcelona*, in the Vessels which he had provided for them: That they might do this in perfect Security when they saw the *English* Fleet pass by; or if they should pass by in the Night, an Engagement with the *French*, which would give them sufficient Notice what they had to do further.

This Declaration, instead of satisfying, made the Officers ten times more curious: But when they saw their General going with a Resolution to lie out all Night at Sea, in an open Boat, attended with only one Officer; and understood that he intended to row out in his *Felucca* five or six Leagues distance from the Shore, it is hardly to be express'd what Amazement and Concern surpriz'd them all. Mr. *Crow*, the Queen's Minister, and others, express'd a particular Dislike and Uneasiness; but all to no purpose, the Earl had resolv'd upon it. Accordingly, at Night he put out to Sea in his open *Felucca*, all which he spent five Leagues from Shore, with no other Company than one Captain and his Rowers.

In the Morning, to the great Satisfaction of all, Officers and others, the Earl came again to Land; and immediately began to put his Men into the several Vessels which lay ready in Port for that Purpose. But at Night their Amaze was renew'd, when they found their General ready to put in execution his old Resolution, in the same Equipage, and with the same Attendance. Accordingly, he again *felucca'd* himself; and they saw him no more till they were landed on the Mole in *Barcelona*.

When the Earl of *Peterborow* first engag'd himself in the Expedition to *Spain*, he propos'd to the Queen and her Ministry, that Admiral *Shovel* might be join'd in Commission with him in the Command of the Fleet. But this Year, when the Fleet came through the Straites, under Vice-Admiral *Leake*, the Queen had sent a Commission to the Earl of *Peterborow* for the full Command, whenever he thought fit to come aboard in Person. This it was that made the General endeavour, at all Hazards, to get aboard the Fleet by Night; for he was apprehensive, and the Sequel prov'd his Apprehensions too well grounded, that *Admiral Leake* would make his Appearance with the whole Body of the Fleet, which made near twice the Number of the Ships of the Enemy; in which Case it was natural to suppose, that the Count *de Tholouse*, as soon as ever the *French* Scouts should give Notice of our Strength, would cut his Cables and put out to Sea, to avoid an Engagement. On the other hand, the Earl was very sensible, that if a Part of his Ships had kept a-stern, that the Superiority might have appear'd on the *French* Side, or rather if they had bore away in the Night towards the Coast of *Africa*, and fallen to the Eastward of *Barcelona* the next Day, a Battle had been inevitable, and a Victory equally certain; since the Enemy by this Means had been tempted into an Engagement, and their Retreat being cut off, and their whole Fleet surrounded with almost double their Number, there had hardly been left for any of them a Probability of Escaping.

Therefore, when the Earl of *Peterborow* put to Sea again the second Evening, fearful of loosing such a glorious Opportunity, and impatient to be aboard to give the necessary Orders, he order'd his Rowers to obtain the same Station, in order to discover the *English* Fleet. And according to his Wishes he did fall in with it; but unfortunately the Night was so far advanc'd, that it was impossible for him then to put his Project into practice. Captain *Price*, a Gentleman of *Wales*, who commanded a Third Rate, was the Person he first came aboard of; but how amaz'd was he to find, in an open Boat at open Sea, the Person who had Commission to command the Fleet? So soon as he was enter'd the Ship, the Earl sent the Ship's Pinnace with Letters to Admiral *Leake*, to acquaint him with his Orders and Intentions; and to Brigadier *Stanhope* with a Notification of his safe Arrival; but the Darkness of the Night prov'd so great an Obstacle, that it was a long time before the Pinnace could reach the Admiral. When Day appear'd, it was astonishing to the whole Fleet to see the *Union* Flag waving at the Main-top-mast Head. No body could trust his own Eyes, or guess at the Meaning, till better certify'd by the Account of an Event so singular and extraordinary.

When we were about six Leagues Distance from *Barcelona*, the Port we aim'd at, one of the *French* Scouts gave the Alarm, who making the Signal to another, he communicated it to a Third, and so on, as we afterward sorrowfully found, and as the Earl had before apprehended: The *French* Admiral being thus made acquainted with the Force of our Fleet, hoisted sail, and made the best of his Way from us, either pursuant to Orders, or under the plausible Excuse of a Retreat.

This favourable Opportunity thus lost, there remain'd nothing to do but to land the Troops with all Expedition; which was executed accordingly: The Regiments, which the Earl of *Peterborow* embark'd the Night before, being the first that got into the Town. Let the Reader imagine how pleasing such a Sight must be to those in *Barcelona*, reduc'd as they were to the last Extremity. In this Condition, to see an Enemy's Fleet give way to another with Reinforcements from *England*, the Sea at the same Instant cover'd with little Vessels crouded with greater Succours; what was there wanting to compleat the glorious Scene, but what the General had projected, a Fight at Sea, under the very Walls of the invested City, and the Ships of the Enemy sinking, or tow'd in by the victorious *English*? But Night, and a few Hours, defeated the latter Part of that well intended Landskip.

King *Philip*, and the Mareschal of *France*, had not fail'd to push on the Siege with all imaginable Vigour; but this Retreat of the Count *de Tholouse*, and the News of those Reinforcements, soon chang'd the Scene. Their Courage without was abated proportionably, as theirs within was elated. In these Circumstances, a Council of War being call'd, it was unanimously resolv'd to raise the Siege. Accordingly, next Morning, the first of *May*, 1706, while the Sun was under a total Eclipse, in a suitable Hurry and Confusion, they broke up, leaving behind them most of their Cannon and Mortars, together with vast Quantities of all sorts of Ammunition and Provisions, scarce stopping to look back till they had left all but the very Verge of the disputed Dominion behind them.

King *Charles* look'd with new Pleasure upon this lucky Effort of his old Deliverers. Captivity is a State no way desirable to Persons however brave, of the most private Station in Life; but for a King, within two Days of falling into the Hands of his Rival, to receive so seasonable and unexpected a Deliverance, must be supposed, as it really did, to open a Scene to universal Rejoicing among us, too high for any Words to express, or any Thoughts to imagine, to those that were not present and Partakers of it. He forthwith gave Orders for a Medal to be struck suitable to the Occasion; one of which, set round with Diamonds, he presented to Sir *John Leake*, the *English* Admiral. The next Orders were for re-casting all the damag'd brass Cannon which the Enemy had left; upon every one of which was, by order, a Sun eclyps'd, with this Motto under it: *Magna parvis obscurantur.*

I have often wonder'd that I never heard any Body curious enough to enquire what could be the Motives to the King of *Spain's* quitting his Dominions upon the raising of this Siege; very certain it is that he had a fine Army, under the Command of a Mareschal of *France*, not very considerably decreas'd, either by Action or Desertion: But all this would rather increase the Curiosity than abate it. In my Opinion then, though Men might have Curiosity enough, the Question was purposely evaded, under an Apprehension that an honest Answer must inevitably give a higher Idea of the General than their Inclinations led them to. At first View this may carry the Face of a Paradox; yet if the Reader will consider, that in every Age Virtue has had its Shaders or Maligners, he will himself easily solve it, at the same time that he finds himself compell'd to allow, that those, who found themselves unable to prevent his great Services, were willing, in a more subtil Manner, to endeavour at the annulling of them by Silence and Concealment.

This will appear more than bare Supposition, if we compare the present Situation, as to Strength, of the two contending Powers: The *French*, at the Birth of the Siege, consisted of five thousand Horse and Dragoons, and twenty-five thousand Foot, effective Men. Now grant, that their kill'd and wounded, together with their Sick in the Hospitals, might amount to five Thousand; yet as their Body of Horse was entire, and in the best Condition, the Remaining will appear to be an Army of twenty-five Thousand at least. On the other Side, all the Forces in *Barcelona*, even with their Reinforcements, amounted to no more than seven thousand Foot and four hundred Horse. Why then, when they rais'd their Siege, did not they march back into the Heart of *Spain*, with their so much superior Army? or, at least, towards their Capital? The Answer can be this, and this only; Because the Earl of *Peterborow* had taken such provident Care to render all secure, that it was thereby render'd next to an Impossibility for them so to do. That General was satisfy'd, that the Capital of *Catalonia* must, in course, fall into the Hands of the Enemy, unless a superior Fleet remov'd the Count *de Tholouse*, and threw in timely Succours into the Town: And as that could not depend upon him, but others, he made it his chief Care and assiduous Employment to provide against those Strokes of Fortune to which he found himself again likely to be expos'd, as he often had been; and therefore had he Resource to that Vigilance and Precaution which had often retriev'd him, when to others his Circumstances seem'd to be most desperate.

The Generality of Mankind, and the *French* in particular, were of opinion that the taking *Barcelona* would prove a decisive Stroke, and put a Period to the War in *Spain*; and yet at that very Instant I was inclin'd to believe, that the General flatter'd himself it would be in his Power to give the Enemy sufficient Mortification, even though the Town should be oblig'd to submit to King *Philip*. The wise Measures taken induc'd me so to believe, and the Sequel approv'd it; for the Earl had so well expended his Caution, that the Enemy, on the Disappointment, found himself under a Necessity of quitting *Spain*; and the same would have put him under equal Difficulties had he carry'd the Place. The *French* could never have undertaken that Siege without depending on their Fleet, for their Artillery, Ammunition, and Provisions; since they must be inevitably forc'd to leave behind them the strong Towns of *Tortosa*, *Lerida*, and *Taragona*. The Earl, therefore, whose perpetual Difficulties seem'd rather to render him more sprightly and vigorous, took care himself to examine the whole Country between the *Ebro* and *Barcelona*; and, upon his doing so, was pleasingly, as well as sensibly satisfy'd, that it was practicable to render their Return into the Heart of *Spain* impossible, whether they did or did not succeed in the Siege they were so intent to undertake.

There were but three Ways they could attempt it: The first of which was by the Sea-side, from *Taragona* towards *Tortosa*; the most barren, and consequently the most improper Country in the Universe to sustain an Army; and yet to the natural, the Earl had added such artificial Difficulties, as render'd it absolutely impossible for an Army to subsist or march that Way.

The middle Way lay through a better Country indeed, yet only practicable by the Care which had been taken to make the Road so. And even here there was a Necessity of marching along the Side of a Mountain, where by vast Labour and Industry, a high Way had been cut for two Miles at least out of the main Rock. The Earl therefore, by somewhat of the same Labour, soon made it impassable. He employ'd to that End many Thousands of the Country People, under a few of his own Officers and Troops, who cutting up twenty several Places, made so many Precipices, perpendicular almost as a Wall, which render'd it neither safe, or even to be attempted by any single Man in his Wits, much less by an Army. Besides, a very few Men, from the higher Cliffs of the Mountain, might have destroy'd an Army with the Arms of Nature only, by rolling down large Stones and Pieces of the Rock upon the Enemy passing below.

The last and uppermost Way, lay thro' the hilly Part of *Catalonia*, and led to *Lerida*, towards the Head of the *Ebro*, the strongest Place we had in all *Spain*, and which was as well furnish'd with a very good Garrison. Along this Road there lay many old Castles and little Towns in the Mountains, naturally strong; all which would not only have afforded Opposition, but at the same time had entertain'd an Enemy with variety of Difficulties; and especially as the Earl had given Orders and taken Care that all Cattle, and every Thing necessary to sustain an Army, should be convey'd into Places of Security, either in the Mountains or thereabouts. These three Ways thus precautiously secur'd, what had the Earl to apprehend but the Safety of the Arch-Duke; which yet was through no Default of his, if in any Danger from the Siege?

For I well remember, on Receipt of an Express from the Duke of *Savoy* (as he frequenly sent such to enquire after the Proceedings in *Spain*) I was shew'd a Letter, wrote about this time by the Earl of *Peterborow* to that Prince, which rais'd my Spirits, though then at a very low Ebb. It was too remarkable to be forgot; and the Substance of it was, That his Highness might depend upon it, that he (the Earl) was in much better Circumstances than he was thought to be: That the *French* Officers, knowing nothing of the Situation of the Country, would find themselves extreamly disappointed, since in case the Siege was rais'd, their Army should be oblig'd to abandon *Spain*: Or in case the Town was taken, they should find themselves shut up in that Corner of *Catalonia*, and under an Impossibility of forcing their Way back, either through *Aragon* or *Valencia*: That by this Means all *Spain*, to the *Ebro*, would be open to the Lord *Galoway*, who might march to *Madrid*, or any where else, without Opposition. That he had no other Uneasiness or Concern upon him, but for the Person of the Arch-Duke, whom he had nevertheless earnestly solicited not to remain in the Town on the very first Appearance of the intended Siege.

BARCELONA being thus reliev'd, and King *Philip* forc'd out of *Spain*, by these cautious Steps taken by the Earl of *Peterborow*, before we bring him to *Valencia*, it will be necessary to intimate, that as it always was the Custom of that General to settle, by a Council of War, all the Measures to be taken, whenever he was oblig'd for the Service to leave the Arch-Duke; a Council of War was now accordingly held, where all the General Officers, and those in greatest Employments at Court assisted. Here every thing was in the most solemn Manner concerted and resolv'd upon; here Garrisons were settled for all the strong Places, and Governors appointed: But the main Article then agreed upon was, that King *Charles* should immediately begin his Journey to *Madrid*, and that by the Way of *Valencia*. The Reason assign'd for it was, because that Kingdom being in his Possession, no Difficulties could arise which might occasion Delay, if his Majesty took that Rout. It was likewise agreed in the same Council, that the Earl of *Peterborow* should embark all the Foot, not in Garrisons, for their more speedy, as well as more easy Conveyance to *Valencia*. The same Council of War agreed, that all the Horse in that Kingdom should be drawn together, the better to insure the Measures to be taken for the opening and facilitating his Majesty's Progress to *Madrid*.

Accordingly, after these Resolutions were taken, the Earl of *Peterborow* embarks his Forces and sails for *Valencia*, where he was doubly welcom'd by all Sorts of People upon Account of his safe Arrival, and the News he brought along with it. By the Joy they express'd, one would have imagin'd that the General had escap'd the same Danger with the King; and, in truth, had their King arriv'd with him in Person, the most loyal and zealous would have found themselves at a loss how to have express'd their Satisfaction in a more sensible Manner.

Soon after his Landing, with his customary Vivacity, he apply'd himself to put in execution the Resolutions taken in the Councils of War at *Barcelona*; and a little to improve upon them, he rais'd an intire Regiment of Dragoons, bought them Horses, provided them Cloaths, Arms, and Acoutrements; and in six Weeks time had them ready to take the Field; a thing though hardly to be parallell'd, is yet scarce worthy to be mentioned among so many nobler Actions of his; yet in regard to another General it may merit Notice, since while he had *Madrid* in Possession near four Months, he neither augmented his Troops, nor lay'd up any Magazines; neither sent he all that time any one Express to concert any Measures with the Earl of *Peterborow*, but lay under a perfect Inactivity, or which was worse, negotiating that unfortunate Project of carrying King *Charles* to *Madrid* by the roundabout and ill-concerted Way of *Aragon*; a Project not only contrary to the solemn Resolutions of the Council of War; but which in reality was the Root of all our succeeding Misfortunes; and that only for the wretched Vanity of appearing to have had some Share in bringing the King to his Capital; but how minute a Share it was will be manifest, if it be consider'd that another General had first made the Way easy, by driving the Enemy out of *Spain*; and that the French General only stay'd at *Madrid* till the Return of those Troops which were in a manner driven out of *Spain*.

And yet that Transaction, doughty as it was, took up four most precious Months, which most certainly might have been much better employ'd in rendering it impossible for the Enemy to re-enter *Spain*; nor had there been any Great Difficulty in so doing, but the contrary, if the General at *Madrid* had thought convenient to have join'd the Troops under the Earl of *Peterhorow*, and then to have march'd directly towards *Pampelona*, or the Frontiers of *France*. To this the Earl of *Peterborow* solicited the King, and those about him; he advis'd, desir'd, and intreated him to lose no time, but to put in Execution those Measures resolv'd on at *Barcelona*. A Council of War in *Valencia* renew'd the same Application; but all to no Purpose, his Rout was order'd him, and that to meet his Majesty on the Frontiers of *Arragon*. There, indeed, the Earl did meet the King; and the *French* General an Army, which, by Virtue of a decrepid Intelligence, he never saw or heard of till he fled from it to his Camp at *Guadalira*. Inexpressible with the Confusion in this fatal Camp: The King from *Arragon*, The Earl of *Peterborow* from *Valencia* arriving in it the same Day, almost the same Hour that the Earl of *Galoway* enter'd under a hasty Retreat before the *French* Army.

But to return to Order, which a Zeal of Justice has made me somewhat anticipate; the Earl had not been long at *Valencia* before he gave Orders to Major-General *Windham* to march with all the Forces he had, which were not above two thousand Men, and lay Siege to *Requina*, a Town ten Leagues distant from *Valencia*, and in the Way to

Madrid. The Town was not very strong, nor very large; but sure the odliest fortify'd that ever was. The Houses in a Circle connectively compos'd the Wall; and the People, who defended the Town, instead of firing from Hornworks, Counterscarps, and Bastions, fir'd out of the Windows of their Houses.

Notwithstanding all which, General *Windham* found much greater Opposition than he at first imagin'd; and therefore finding he should want Ammunition, he sent to the Earl of *Peterborow* for a Supply; at the same time assigning, as a Reason for it, the unexpected Obstinacy of the Town. So soon as the Earl receiv'd the Letter he sent for me; and told me I must repair to *Requifia*, where they would want an Engineer; and that I must be ready next Morning, when he should order a Lieutenant, with thirty Soldiers and two Matrosses, to guard some Powder for that Service. Accordingly, the next Morning we set out, the Lieutenant, who was a *Dutchman*, and Commander of the Convoy, being of my Acquaintance.

We had reach'd Saint *Jago*, a small Village about midway between *Valencia* and *Requina*, when the Officer, just as he was got without the Town, resolving to take up his Quarters on the Spot, order'd the Mules to be unloaded. The Powder, which consisted of forty-five Barrels, was pil'd up in a Circle, and cover'd with Oil-cloth, to preserve it from the Weather; and though we had agreed to sup together at my Quarters within the Village, yet being weary and fatigu'd, he order'd his Field-Bed to be put up near the Powder, and so lay down to take a short Nap. I had scarce been at my Quarters an Hour, when a sudden Shock attack'd the House so violently, that it threw down Tiles, Windows, Chimneys and all. It presently came into my Head what was the Occasion; and as my Fears suggested so it prov'd: For running to the Door I saw a Cloud ascending from the Spot I left the Powder pitch'd upon. In haste making up to which, nothing was to be seen but the bare Circle upon which it had stood. The Bed was blown quite away, and the poor Lieutenant all to pieces, several of his Limbs being found separate, and at a vast Distance each from the other; and particularly an Arm, with a Ring on one of the Fingers. The Matrosses were, if possible, in a yet worse Condition, that is, as to Manglement and Laceration. All the Soldiers who were standing, and any thing near, were struck dead. Only such as lay sleeping on the Ground escap'd, and of those one assur'd me, that the Blast remov'd him several Foot from his Place of Repose. In short, enquiring into this deplorable Disaster, I had this Account: That a Pig running out of the Town, the Soldiers endeavour'd to intercept its Return; but driving it upon the Matrosses, one of them, who was jealous of its getting back into the Hands of the Soldiers, drew his Pistol to shoot it, which was the Source of this miserable Catastrophe. The Lieutenant carry'd along with him a Bag of Dollars to pay the Soldiers' Quarters, of which the People, and the Soldiers that were say'd, found many; but blown to an inconceivable Distance.

With those few Soldiers that remain'd alive, I proceeded, according to my Order, to *Requina*; where, when I arriv'd, I gave General *Windham* an Account of the Disaster at St. *Jago*. As such it troubled him, and not a little on account of the Disappointment. However, to make the best of a bad Market, he gave Orders for the forming of a Mine under an old Castle, which was part of the Wall. As it was order'd, so it was begun, more *in Terrorem*, than with any Expectation of Success from it as a Mine. Nevertheless, I had scarce began to frame the Oven of the Mine, when those within the Town desir'd to capitulate. This being all we could aim at, under the Miscarriage of our Powder at St. *Jago* (none being yet arriv'd to supply that Defect) Articles were readily granted them; pursuant to which, that Part of the Garrison, which was compos'd of *Castilian* Gentry, had Liberty to go wherever they thought best, and the rest were made Prisoners of War. *Requina* being thus reduc'd to the Obedience of *Charles* III a new rais'd Regiment of *Spaniards* was left in Garrison, the Colonel of which was appointed Governor; and our Supply of Powder having at last got safe to us, General *Windham* march'd his little Army to *Cuenca*.

CUENCA is a considerable City and a Bishoprick; therefore to pretend to sit down before it with such a Company of Forragers, rather than an Army, must be plac'd among the hardy Influences of the Earl of *Peterborow*'s auspicious Administration. On the out Part of *Cuenca* there stood an old Castle, from which, upon our Approach, they play'd upon us furiously: But as soon as we could bring two Pieces of our Cannon to bear, we answered their Fire with so good Success, that we soon oblig'd them to retire into the Town. We had rais'd a Battery of twelve Guns against the City, on their Rejection of the Summons sent them to come under the Obedience of King *Charles*; going to which from the old Castle last reduc'd, I receiv'd a Shot on the Toe of one of my Shoes, which carry'd that Part of the Shoe intirely away, without any further Damage.

When I came to that Battery we ply'd them warmly (as well as from three Mortars) for the Space of three Days, their Nights included;

but observing, that in one particular House, they were remarkably busy; People thronging in and out below; and those above firing perpetually out of the Windows, I was resolv'd to have one Shot at that Window, and made those Officers about me take Notice of it. True it was, the Distance would hardly allow me to hope for Success; yet as the Experiment could only be attended with the Expence of a single Ball, I made it. So soon as the Smoak of my own Cannon would permit it, we could see Clouds of Dust issuing from out of the Window, which, together with the People's crouding out of Doors, convinc'd the Officers, whom I had desir'd to take Notice of it, that I had been no bad Marksman.

Upon this, two Priests were sent out of the Place with Proposals; but they were so triflingly extravagant, that as soon as ever the General heard them, he order'd their Answer in a fresh Renewal of the Fire of both Cannon and Mortars. And it happen'd to be with so much Havock and Execution, that they were soon taught Reason; and sent back their Divines, with much more moderate Demands. After the General had a little modell'd these last, they were accepted; and according to the Articles of Capitulation, the City was that very Day surrender'd into our Possession. The Earl of *Duncannon's* Regiment took Guard of all the Gates; and King *Charles* was proclaim'd in due Form.

The Earl of *Peterborow*, during this Expedition, had left *Valencia*, and was arriv'd at my Lord *Galway's* Camp at *Guadalaxara*; who for the Confederates, and King *Charles* in particular, unfortunately was order'd from *Portugal*, to take the Command from a General, who had all along been almost miraculously successful, and by his own great Actions pay'd the Way for a safe Passage to that his Supplanter.

Yet even in this fatal Place the Earl of *Peterborow* made some Proposals, which, had they been embrac'd, might, in all Probability, have secur'd *Madrid* from falling into the Hands of the Enemy; But, in opposition thereto, the Lord *Galway*, and all his *Portugueze* Officers, were for forcing the next Day the Enemy to Battle. The almost only Person against it was the Earl of *Peterborow*; who then and there took the Liberty to evince the Impossibility of coming to an Engagement. This the next Morning too evidently made apparent, when upon the first Motion of our Troops towards the River, which they pretended to pass, and must pass, before they could engage, they were so warmly saluted from the Batteries of the Enemy, and their small Shot, that our Regiments were forc'd to retire in Confusion to their Camp. By which

Rebuff all heroical Imaginations were at present laid aside, to consider how they might make their Retreat to *Valencia*.

The Retreat being at last resolv'd on, and a Multiplicity of Generals rendering our bad Circumstances much worse, the Earl of *Peterborow* met with a fortunate Reprieve, by Solicitations from the Queen, and Desires tantamount to Orders, that he would go with the Troops left in *Catalonia* to the Relief of the Duke of *Savoy*. It is hardly to be doubted that that General was glad to withdraw from those Scenes of Confusion, which were but too visible to Eyes even less discerning than his. However, he forebore to prepare himself to put her Majesty's Desires in execution, as they were not peremptory, till it had been resolv'd by the unanimous Consent of a Council of War, where the King, all the Generals and Ministers were present. That it was expedient for the Service that the Earl of *Peterborow*, during the Winter Season, should comply with her Majesty's Desires, and go for *Italy*; since he might return before the opening of the Campaign, if it should be necessary. And return indeed he did, before the Campaign open'd, and brought along with him one hundred thousand Pounds from *Genoa*, to the great Comfort and Support of our Troops, which had neither Money nor Credit. But on his Return, that noble Earl found the Lord *Galway* had been near as successful against him, as he had been unsuccessful against the Enemy. Thence was the Earl of *Peterborow* recall'd to make room for an unfortunate General, who the next Year suffer'd himself to be decoy'd into that fatal Battle of *Almanza*.

The Earl of *Peterborow*, on his leaving *Valencia*, had order'd his Baggage to follow him to the Camp at *Guadalaxara*; and it arriv'd in our little Camp, so far safe in its way to the greater at *Guadalaxara*. I think it consisted of seven loaded Waggons; and General *Windham* gave Orders for a small Guard to escorte it; under which they proceeded on their Journey: But about eight Leagues from *Cuenca*, at a pretty Town call'd *Huette*, a Party from the Duke of *Berwick's* Army, with Boughs in their Hats, the better to appear what they were not (for the Bough in the Hat is the Badge of the *English*, as white Paper is the Badge of the *French*) came into the Town, crying all the way, *Viva Carlos Tercero, Viva*. With these Acclamations in their Mouths, they advanc'd up to the very Waggons; when attacking the Guards, who had too much deluded themselves with Appearances, they routed 'em, and immediately plunder'd the Waggons of all that was valuable, and then march'd off.

The Noise of this soon reach'd the Ears of the Earl of *Peterborow* at *Guadalaxara*. When leaving my Lord *Galways* Camp, pursuant to the Resolutions of the Council of War, with a Party only of fourscore of *Killigrew's* Dragoons, he met General *Windham's* little Army within a League of *Huette*, the Place where his Baggage had been plunder'd. The Earl had strong Motives of Suspicion, that the Inhabitants had given Intelligence to the Enemy; and, as is very natural, giving way to the first Dictates of Resentment, he resolv'd to have lay'd the Town in Ashes: But when he came near it, the Clergy and Magistrates upon their Knees, disavowing the Charge, and asserting their Innocence, prevail'd on the good Nature of that generous Earl, without any great Difficulty, to spare the Town, at least not to burn it.

We march'd however into the Town, and that Night took up our Quarters there; and the Magistrates, under the Dread of our avenging our selves, on their part took Care that we were well supplied. But when they were made sensible of the Value of the Loss, which the Earl had sustain'd; and that on a moderate Computation it amounted to at least eight thousand Pistoles; they voluntarily presented themselves next Morning, and of their own accord offer'd to make his Lordship full Satisfaction, and that, in their own Phrase, *de Contado, in Ready Money.* The Earl was not displeas'd at their Offer; but generously made Answer, That he was just come from my Lord *Galway's* Camp at *Chincon,* where he found they were in a likelihood of wanting Bread; and as he imagin'd it might be easier to them to raise the Value in Corn, than in ready Money; if they would send to that Value in Corn to the Lord *Galway's* Camp, he would be satisfy'd. This they with Joy embrac'd, and immediately complied with.

I am apt to think the last Century (and I very much fear the Current will be as deficient) can hardly produce a parallel Instance of Generosity and true public Spiritedness; And the World will be of my Opinion, when I have corroborated this with another Passage some Years after. The Commissioners for Stating the Debts due to the Army, meeting daily for that Purpose at their House in *Darby* Court in *Channel Row,* I there mentioned to Mr. *Read,* Gentleman to his Lordship, this very just and honourable Claim upon the Government, as Monies advanced for the Use of the Army. Who told me in a little Time after, that he had mention'd it to his Lordship, but with no other Effect than to have it rejected with a generous Disdain.

While we stayed at *Huette* there was a little Incident in Life, which gave me great Diversion. The Earl, who had always maintain'd a good Correspondence with the fair Sex, hearing from one of the Priests of the Place, That on the Alarm of burning the Town, one of the finest Ladies in all *Spain* had taken Refuge in the Nunnery, was desirous to speak with her.

The Nunnery stood upon a small rising Hill within the Town; and to obtain the View, the Earl had presently in his Head this Stratagem; he sends for me, as Engineer, to have my Advice, how to raise a proper Fortification upon that Hill out of the Nunnery. I waited upon his Lordship to the Place, where declaring the Intent of our coming, and giving plausible Reasons for it, the Train took, and immediately the Lady Abbess, and the fair Lady, came out to make Intercession, That his Lordship would be pleas'd to lay aside that Design. The divine Oratory of one, and the beautiful Charms of the other, prevail'd; so his Lordship left the Fortification to be the Work of some future Generation.

From *Huette* the Earl of *Peterborow* march'd forwards for *Valencia*, with only those fourscore Dragoons, which came with him from *Chincon*, leaving General *Windham* pursuing his own Orders to join his Forces to the Army then under the Command of the Lord *Galway*. But stopping at *Campilio*, a little Town in our Way, his Lordship had Information of a most barbarous Fact committed that very Morning by the *Spaniards*, at a small *Villa*, about a League distant, upon some *English* Soldiers.

A Captain of the *English* Guards (whose Name has slip'd my Memory, tho' I well knew the Man) marching in order to join the Battalion of the Guards, then under the Command of General *Windham*, with some of his Soldiers, that had been in the Hospital, took up his Quarters in that little *Villa*. But on his marching out of it, next Morning, a Shot in the Back laid that Officer dead upon the Spot: And as it had been before concerted, the *Spaniards* of the Place at the same Time fell upon the poor, weak Soldiers, killing several; not even sparing their Wives. This was but a Prelude to their Barbarity; their savage Cruelty was only whetted, not glutted. They took the surviving few; hurried and dragg'd them up a Hill, a little without the *Villa*. On the Top of this Hill there was a Hole, or Opening, somewhat like the Mouth of one of our Coal-Pits, down this they cast several, who, with hideous Shrieks and Cries, made more hideous by the Ecchoes of the Chasm, there lost their Lives.

This Relation was thus made to the Earl of *Peterborow*, at his Quarters at *Campilio*; who immediately gave Orders for to sound to

Horse. At first we were all surpriz'd; but were soon satisfy'd, that it was to revenge, or rather, do Justice, on this barbarous Action.

As soon as we enter'd the *Villa* we found that most of the Inhabitants, but especially the most Guilty, had withdrawn themselves on our Approach. We found, however, many of the dead Soldiers Cloaths, which had been convey'd into the Church, and there hid. And a strong Accusation being laid against a Person belonging to the Church, and full Proof made, that he had been singularly Industrious in the Execution of that horrid Piece of Barbarity on the Hill, his Lordship commanded him to be hang'd up at the Knocker of the Door.

After this piece of military Justice, we were led up to the fatal Pit or Hole, down which many had been cast headlong. There we found one poor Soldier alive, who, upon his throwing in, had catch'd fast hold of some impending Bushes, and sav'd himself on a little Jutty within the Concavity. On hearing us talk *English* he cry'd out; and Ropes being let down, in a little Time he was drawn up; when he gave us an ample Detail of the whole Villany. Among other Particulars, I remember he told me of a very narrow Escape he had in that obscure Recess. A poor Woman, one of the Wives of the Soldiers, who were thrown down after him, struggled, and roared so much, that they could not, without all their Force, throw her cleaverly in the Middle; by which means falling near the Side, in her Fall she almost beat him from his Place of Security.

Upon the Conclusion of this tragical Relation of the Soldier thus saved, his Lordship gave immediate Orders for the Firing of the *Villa*, which was executed with due Severity: After which his Lordship march'd back to his Quarters at *Campilio*; from whence, two Days after, we arriv'd at *Valencia*, Where, the first Thing presented to that noble Lord, was all the Papers taken in the Plunder of his Baggage, which the Duke of *Berwick* had generously order'd to be return'd him, without waste or opening.

It was too manifest, after the Earl's arrival at this City, that the Alteration in the Command of the *English* Forces, which before was only receiv'd as a Rumour, had deeper Grounds for Belief, than many of his Friends in that City could have wish'd. His Lordship had gain'd the Love of all by a Thousand engaging Condescensions; even his Gallantries being no way prejudicial, were not offensive; and though his Lordships did his utmost to conceal his Chagrin, the Sympathy of those around him made such Discoveries upon him, as would have disappointed a double Portion of his Caution. They had seen him un-elated under Successes, that were so near being unaccountable, that in a

Country of less Superstition than *Spain*, they might almost have pass'd for miraculous; they knew full well, that nothing, but that Series of Successes had pav'd a Passage for the General that was to supersede him; those only having removed all the Difficulties of his March from *Portugal* to *Madrid*; they knew him the older General; and therefore not knowing, that in the Court he came from, Intrigue was too often the Soul of Merit, they could not but be amazed at a Change, which his Lordship was unwilling any body should perceive by himself.

It was upon this Account, that, as formerly, he treated the Ladies with Balls, and to pursue the Dons in their own Humour, order'd a *Tawridore* or *Bull-Feast*. In *Spain* no sort of public Diversions are esteemed equal with this. But the Bulls provided at *Valencia*, not being of the right Breed, nor ever initiated in the Mysteries, did not acquit themselves at all masterly; and consequently, did not give the Diversion, or Satisfaction expected. For which Reason I shall omit giving a Description of this Bull-Feast; and desire my Reader to suspend his Curiosity till I come to some, which, in the *Spanish* Sense, were much more entertaining; that is, attended with much greater Hazards and Danger.

But though I have said, the Gallantries of the General were mostly political at least very inoffensive; yet there happen'd about this Time, and in this Place, a piece of Gallantry, that gave the Earl a vast deal of Offence and Vexation; as a Matter, that in its Consequences might have been fatal to the Interest of King *Charles*, if not to the *English* Nation in general; and which I the rather relate, in that it may be of use to young Officers, and others; pointing out to them the Danger, not to say Folly, of inadvertent and precipitate Engagements, under unruly Passions.

I have said before, that *Valencia* is famous for fine Women. It indeed abounds in them; and among those, are great Numbers of Courtezans not inferior in Beauty to any. Nevertheless, two of our *English* Officers, not caring for the common Road, however safe, resolv'd to launch into the deeper Seas, though attended with much greater Danger. Amours, the common Failing of that fair City, was the Occasion of this Accident, and two Nuns the Objects. It is customary in that Country for young People in an Evening to resort to the Grates of the Nunneries, there to divert themselves, and the Nuns, with a little pleasant and inoffensive Chit-chat. For though I have heard some relate a World of nauseous Passages at such Conversations, I must declare, that I never saw, or heard any Thing unseemly; and therefore whenever

I have heard any such from such Fabulists, I never so much wrong'd my Judgment as to afford them Credit.

Our two Officers were very assiduous at the Grates of a Nunnery in this Place; and having there pitch'd upon two Nuns, prosecuted their Amours with such Vigour, that, in a little time, they had made a very great Progress in their Affections, without in the least considering the Dangers that must attend themselves and the Fair; they had exchang'd Vows, and prevail'd upon the weaker Vessels to endeavour to get out to their Lovers. To effect which, soon after, a Plot was lay'd; the Means, the Hour, and every thing agreed upon.

It is the Custom of that Nunnery, as of many others, for the Nuns to take their weekly Courses in keeping the Keys of all the Doors. The two Love-sick Ladies giving Notice to their Lovers at the Grate, that one of their Turns was come, the Night and Hour was appointed, which the Officers punctually observing, carry'd off their Prey without either Difficulty or Interruption.

But next Morning, when the Nuns were missing, what an Uproar was there over all the City? The Ladies were both of Quality; and therefore the Tidings were first carry'd to their Relations. They receiv'd the News with Vows of utmost Vengeance; and, as is usual in that Country, put themselves in Arms for that Purpose. There needed no great canvassing for discovering who were the Aggressors: The Officers had been too frequent, and too publick, in their Addresses, to leave any room for question. Accordingly, they were complain'd of and sought for, but sensible at last of their past Temerity, they endeavour'd, and with a great deal of Difficulty perfected their Escape.

Less fortunate were the two fair Nuns; their Lovers, in their utmost Exigence, had forsaken them; and they, poor Creatures, knew not where to fly. Under this sad Dilemma they were taken; and, as in like Offences, condemn'd directly to the Punishment of *immuring*. And what greater Punishment is there on Earth than to be confin'd between four narrow Walls, only open at the Top; and thence to be half supported with Bread and Water, till the Offenders gradually starve to Death?

The Earl of *Peterborow*, though highly exasperated at the Proceedings of his Officers, in compassion to the unhappy Fair, resolv'd to interpose by all the moderate Means possible. He knew very well, that no one Thing could so much prejudice the *Spaniard* against him, as the countenancing such an Action; wherefore he inveigh'd against the Officers, at the same time that he endeavour'd to mitigate in favour of the Ladies: But all was in vain; it was urg'd against those charitable Intercessions, that they had broke their Vows; and in that had broke in upon the Laws of the Nunnery and Religion; the Consequence of all which could be nothing less than the Punishment appointed to be inflicted. And which was the hardest of all, the nearest of their Relations most oppos'd all his generous Mediations; and those, who according to the common Course of Nature should have thank'd him for his Endeavours to be instrumental in rescuing them from the impending Danger, grew more and more enrag'd, because he oppos'd them in their Design of a cruel Revenge.

Notwithstanding all which the Earl persever'd; and after a deal of Labour, first got the Penalty suspended; and, soon after, by the Dint of a very considerable Sum of Money (a most powerful Argument, which prevails in every Country) sav'd the poor Nuns from immuring; and at last, though with great Reluctance, he got them receiv'd again into the Nunnery. As to the Warlike Lovers, one of them was the Year after slain at the Battle of *Almanza*; the other is yet living, being a Brigadier in the Army.

While the Earl of *Peterborow* was here with his little Army of great Hereticks, neither Priests nor People were so open in their superstitious Fopperies, as I at other times found them. For which Reason I will make bold, and by an Antichronism in this Place, a little anticipate some Observations that I made some time after the Earl left it. And as I have not often committed such a Transgression, I hope it may be the more excusable now, and no way blemish my Memoirs, that I break in upon the Series of my Journal.

VALENCIA is a handsome City, and a Bishoprick; and is considerable not only for the Pleasantness of its Situation and beautiful Ladies; but (which at some certain Times, and on some Occasions, to them is more valuable than both those put together) for being the Birth-place of Saint *Vincent*, the Patron of the Place; and next for its being the Place where *Santo Domingo*, the first Institutor of the *Dominican* Order had his Education. Here, in honour of the last, is a spacious and very splendid Convent of the *Dominicans*. Walking by which, I one Day observ'd over the Gate, a Figure of a man in stone; and near it a Dog with a lighted Torch in his Mouth. The Image I rightly enough took to intend that of the Saint; but inquiring of one of the Order, at the Gate, the Meaning of the Figures near it, he very courteously ask'd me to walk in, and then entertain'd me with the following Relation:

When the Mother of *Santo Domingo*, said that Religious, was with Child of that future Saint, she had a Dream which very much afflicted her. She dreamt that she heard a Dog bark in her Belly; and inquiring (at what Oracle is not said) the Meaning of her Dream, she was told, *That that Child should bark out the Gospel* (excuse the Bareness of the Expression, it may run better in *Spanish*; tho', if I remember right, *Erasmus* gives it in *Latin* much the same Turn) *which should thence shine out like that lighted Torch*. And this is the Reason, that wherever you see the Image of that Saint, a Dog and a lighted Torch is in the Group.

He told me at the same time, that there had been more Popes and Cardinals of that Order than of any, if not all the other. To confirm which, he led me into a large Gallery, on each Side whereof he shew'd me the Pictures of all the Popes and Cardinals that had been of that Order; among which, I particularly took Notice of that of Cardinal *Howard*, great Uncle to the present Duke of *Norfolk*. But after many *Encomiums* of their Society, with which he interspers'd his Discourse, he added one that I least valu'd it for; That the sole Care and Conduct of the Inquisition was intrusted with them.

Finding me attentive, or not so contradictory as the *English* Humour generally is, he next brought me into a fair and large Cloister, round which I took several Turns with him; and, indeed, The Place was too delicious to tire, under a Conversation less pertinent or courteous than that he entertain'd me with. In the Middle of the Cloister was a small but pretty and sweet Grove of Orange and Lemon-trees; these bore Fruit ripe and green, and Flowers, all together on one Tree; and their Fruit was so very large and beautiful, and their Flowers so transcendently odoriferous, that all I had ever seen of the like Kind in *England* could comparatively pass only for Beauty in Epitome, or Nature imitated in Wax-work. Many Flocks also of pretty little Birds, with their chearful Notes, added not a little to my Delight. In short, in Life I never knew or found three of my Senses at once so exquisitely gratify'd.

Not far from this, Saint *Vincent*, the Patron, as I said before, of this City, has a Chapel dedicated to him. Once a Year they do him Honour in a sumptuous Procession. Then are their Streets all strow'd with Flowers, and their Houses set off with their richest Tapestries, every one strives to excel his Neighbour in distinguishing himself by the Honour he pays to that Saint; and he is the best Catholick, as well as the best Citizen, in the Eye of the *religious*, who most exerts himself on this Occasion.

The Procession begins with a Cavalcade of all the Friars of all the Convents in and about the City. These walk two and two with folded Arms, and Eyes cast down to the very Ground, and with the greatest outward Appearance of Humility imaginable; nor, though the Temptation from the fine Women that fill'd their Windows, or the rich Tapestries that adorn'd the Balconies might be allow'd sufficient to attract, could I observe that any one of them all ever mov'd them upwards.

After the Friars is borne, upon the Shoulders of twenty Men at least, an Imagine of that Saint of solid Silver, large as the Life; It is plac'd in a great Chair of Silver likewise; the Staves that bear him up, and upon which they bear him, being of the same Metal. The whole is a most costly and curious Piece of Workmanship, such as my Eyes never before or since beheld.

The Magistrates follow the Image and its Supporters, dress'd in their richest Apparel, which is always on this Day, and on this Occasion, particularly sumptuous and distinguishing. Thus is the Image, in the greatest Splendor, borne and accompany'd round that fine City; and at last convey'd to the Place from whence it came: And so concludes that annual Ceremony.

The *Valencians*, as to the Exteriors of Religion, are the most devout of any in *Spain*, though in common Life you find them amorous, gallant, and gay, like other People; yet on solemn Occasions there shines out-right such a Spirit as proves them the very Bigots of Bigotry: As a Proof of which Assertion, I will now give some Account of such Observations, as I had time to make upon them, during two *Lent* Seasons, while I resided there.

The Week before the *Lent* commences, commonly known by the Name of *Carnaval Time*, the whole City appears a perfect *Bartholomew* Fair; the Streets are crouded, and the Houses empty; nor is it possible to pass along without some Gambol or Jack-pudding Trick offer'd to you; Ink, Water, and sometimes Ordure, are sure to be hurl'd at your Face or Cloaths; and if you appear concern'd or angry, they rejoyce at it, pleas'd the more, the more they displease; for all other Resentment is at that time out of Season, though at other times few in the World are fuller of Resentment or more captious.

The younger Gentry, or Dons, to express their Gallantry, carry about them Egg-shells, fill'd with Orange or other sweet Water, which they cast at Ladies in their Coaches, or such other of the fair Sex as they happen to meet in the Streets.

But after all, if you would think them extravagant to Day, as much transgressing the Rules of common Civility, and neither regarding Decency to one another, nor the Duty they owe to Almighty God; yet when *Ash-Wednesday* comes you will imagine them more unaccountable in their Conduct, being then as much too excessive in all outwards Indications of Humility and Repentance. Here you shall meet one, bare-footed, with a Cross on his Shoulder, a Burden rather fit for somewhat with four Feet, and which his poor Two are ready to sink under, yet the vain Wretch bears and sweats, and sweats and bears, in hope of finding Merit in an Ass's Labour.

Others you shall see naked to their Wastes, whipping themselves with Scourges made for the Purpose, till the Blood follows every Stroke; and no Man need be at a Loss to follow them by the very Tracks of Gore they shed in this frentick Perambulation. Some, who from the Thickness of their Hides, or other Impediments, have not Power by their Scourgings to fetch Blood of themselves, are follow'd by Surgeons with their Lancets, who at every Turn, make use of them, to evince the Extent of their Patience and Zeal by the Smart of their Folly. While others, mingling Amour with Devotion, take particular Care to present themselves all macerated before the Windows of their Mistresses; and even in that Condition, not satisfy'd with what they have barbarously done to themselves, they have their Operators at hand, to evince their Love by the Number of their Gashes and Wounds; imagining the more Blood they lose, the more Love they shew, and the more they shall gain. These are generally Devoto's of Quality; though the Tenet is universal, that he that is most bloody is most devout.

After these Street-Exercises, these ostentatious Castigations are over, these Self-sacrificers repair to the great Church, the bloodier the better; there they throw themselves, in a Condition too vile for the Eye of a Female, before the Image of the Virgin *Mary*; though I defy all their Race of Fathers, and their infallible holy Father into the Bargain, to produce any Authority to fit it for Belief, that she ever delighted in such sanguinary Holocausts.

During the whole Time of *Lent*, you will see in every Street some Priest or Frier, upon some Stall or Stool, preaching up Repentance to the People; and with violent Blows on his Breast crying aloud, *Mia Culpa, mia maxima Culpa*, till he extract reciprocal Returns from the Hands of his Auditors on their own Breasts.

When *Good Friday* is come they entertain it with the most profound Show of Reverence and Religion, both in their Streets and in their Churches. In the last, particularly, they have contriv'd about twelve a-Clock suddenly to darken them, so as to render them quite gloomy. This they do to intimate the Eclipse of the Sun, which at that time happen'd. And to signify the Rending of the Vail of the Temple, you are struck with a strange artificial Noise at the very same Instant.

But when *Easter* Day appears, you find it in all Respects with them a Day of Rejoicing; for though Abstinence from Flesh with them, who at no time eat much, is not so great a Mortification as with those of the same Persuasion in other Countries, who eat much more, yet there is a visible Satisfaction darts out at their Eyes, which demonstrates their inward Pleasure in being set free from the Confinement of Mind to the Dissatisfaction of the Body. Every Person you now meet greets you with a *Resurrexit Jesus*; a good Imitation of the primitive Christians, were it the real Effect of Devotion. And all Sorts of the best Musick (which here indeed is the best in all *Spain*) proclaim an auspicious Valediction to the departed Season of superficial Sorrow and stupid Superstition. But enough of this: I proceed to weightier Matters.

While we lay at *Valencia*, under the Vigilance and Care of the indefatigable Earl, News was brought that *Alicant* was besieg'd by General *Gorge* by Land, while a Squadron of Men of War batter'd it from the Sea; from both which the Besiegers play'd their Parts so well, and so warmly ply'd them with their Cannon, that an indifferent practicable Breach was made in a little time.

Mahoni commanded in the Place, being again receiv'd into Favour; and clear'd as he was of those political Insinuations before intimated, he now seem'd resolv'd to confirm his Innocence by a resolute Defence. However, perceiving that all Preparations tended towards a Storm, and knowing full well the Weakness of the Town, he withdrew his Garrison into the Castle, leaving the Town to the Defence of its own Inhabitants.

Just as that was doing, the Sailors, not much skill'd in Sieges, nor at all times capable of the coolest Consideration, with a Resolution natural to them, storm'd the Walls to the Side of the Sea; where not meeting with much Opposition (for the People of the Town apprehended the least Danger there) they soon got into the Place; and, as soon as got in, began to Plunder. This oblig'd the People, for the better Security of themselves, to open their Gates, and seek a Refuge under one Enemy, in opposition to the Rage of another.

General *Gorge*, as soon as he enter'd the Town, with a good deal of seeming Lenity, put a stop to the Ravages of the Sailors; and ordered Proclamation to be made throughout the Place, that all the Inhabitants should immediately bring in their best Effects into the great Church for their better Security. This was by the mistaken Populace, as readily comply'd with; and neither Friend nor Foe at all disputing the Command, or questioning the Integrity of the Intention; the Church was presently crouded with Riches of all sorts and sizes. Yet after some time remaining there, they were all taken out, and disposed of by those, that had as little Property in 'em, as the Sailors, they were pretended to be preserv'd from.

The Earl of *Peterborow* upon the very first News of the Siege had left *Valencia*, and taken Shipping for *Alicant*; where he arrived soon after the Surrender of the Town, and that Outcry of the Goods of the Townsmen. Upon his Arrival, *Mahoni*, who was block'd up in the Castle, and had experienced his indefatigable Diligence, being in want of Provisions, and without much hope of Relief, desired to capitulate. The Earl granted him honourable Conditions, upon which he delivered up the Castle, and *Gorge* was made Governor.

Upon his Lordship's taking Ship at *Valencia*, I had an Opportunity of marching with those Dragoons, which escorted him from *Castile*, who had received Orders to march into *Murcia*. We quarter'd the first Night at *Alcira*, a Town that the River *Segra* almost surrounds, which renders it capable of being made a Place of vast Strength, though now of small Importance.

The next Night we lay at *Xativa*, a Place famous for its steadiness to King *Charles*. General *Basset*, a *Spaniard*, being Governor; it was besieg'd by the Forces of King *Philip*; but after a noble Resistance, the Enemy were beat off, and the Siege raised; for which Effort, it is supposed, that on the Retirement of King *Charles* out of this Country, it was depriv'd of its old Name *Xativa*, and is now called *San Felippo*; though to this day the People thereabouts much dissallow by their Practice, that novel Denomination.

We march'd next Morning by *Monteza*; which gives Name to the famous Title of Knights of *Monteza*. It was at the Time that Colonel *O Guaza*, an *Irish-man*, was Governor, besieg'd by the People of the Country, in favour of King *Charles*; but very ineffectually, so it never chang'd its Sovereign. That Night we quarter'd at *Fonte dalas Figuras*, within one League of *Almanza*; where that fatal and unfortunate Battle, which I shall give an Account of in its Place, was fought the Year after, under the Lord *Galway*.

On our fourth days March we were oblig'd to pass *Villena*, where the Enemy had a Garrison. A Party of *Mahoni's* Dragoons made a part of that Garrison, and they were commanded by Major *O. Rairk* an *Irish* Officer, who always carried the Reputation of a good Soldier, and a brave Gentleman.

I had all along made it my Observation, that Captain *Matthews*, who commanded those Dragoons, that I march'd with, was a Person of much more Courage than Conduct; and he us'd as little Precaution here, though just marching under the Eye of the Enemy, as he had done at other Times. As I was become intimately acquainted with him, I rode up to him, and told him the Danger, which, in my Opinion, attended our present March. I pointed out to him just before *Villena* a jutting Hill, under which we must unavoidably pass; at the turning whereof, I was apprehensive the Enemy might he, and either by Ambuscade or otherwise, surprize us; I therefore intreated we might either wait the coming of our Rear Guard; or at least march with a little more leisure and caution. But he taking little notice of all I said, kept on his round March; seeing which, I press'd forward my Mule, which was a very good one, and rid as fast as her Legs could carry her, till I had got on the top of the Hill. When I came there, I found both my Expectation, and my Apprehensions answered: For I could very plainly discern three Squadrons of the Enemy ready drawn up, and waiting for Us at the very winding of the Hill.

Hereupon I hastened back to the Captain with the like Speed, and told him the Discovery I had made; who nevertheless kept on his March, and it was with a good deal of Difficulty, that I at last prevail'd on him to halt, till our Rear Guard of twenty Men had got up to us. But those joining us, and a new Troop of *Spanish* Dragoons, who had march'd towards us that Morning, appearing in Sight; our Captain, as if he was afraid of their rivalling him in his Glory, at the very turn of the Hill, rode in a full Gallop, with Sword in Hand, up to the Enemy. They stood their Ground, till we were advanc'd within two hundred Yards of them, and then in Confusion endeavoured to retire into the Town.

They were obliged to pass over a small Bridge, too small to admit of such a Company in so much haste; their crouding upon which obstructed their Retreat, and left all that could not get over, to the Mercy of our Swords, which spar'd none. However narrow as the Bridge was, Captain *Matthews* was resolved to venture over after the

Enemy; on doing which, the Enemy made a halt, till the People of the Town, and the very Priests came out to their Relief with fire Arms. On so large an Appearance, Captain *Matthews* thought it not adviseable to make any further Advances; so driving a very great flock of Sheep from under the Walls, he continued his March towards *Elda.* In this Action we lost Captain *Topham,* and three Dragoons.

I remember we were not marched very far from the Place, where this Rencounter happen'd; when an *Irish* Dragoon overtook the Captain, with a civil Message from Major *O Rairk,* desiring that he would not entertain a mean Opinion of him for the Defence that was made; since could he have got the *Spaniards* to have stood their Ground, he should have given him good Reason for a better. The Captain return'd a complimental Answer, and so march'd on. This Major *O Rairk,* or *O Roork,* was the next Year killed at *Alkay,* being much lamented, for he was esteemed both for his Courage and Conduct, one of the best of the *Irish* Officers in the *Spanish* Service. I was likewise informed that he was descended from one of the ancient Kings of *Ireland;* the Mother of the honourable Colonel *Paget,* one of the Grooms of the Bedchamber to his present Majesty, was nearly related to this Gallant Gentleman.

One remarkable Thing I saw in that Action, which affected and surprised me; A *Scotch* Dragoon, of but a moderate Size, with his large basket-hilted Sword, struck off a *Spaniard's* Head at one stroke, with the same ease, in appearance, as a Man would do that of a Poppy.

When we came to *Elda* (a Town much in the Interest of King *Charles,* and famous for its fine Situation, and the largest Grapes in *Spain*) the Inhabitants received us in a manner as handsome as it was peculiar; all standing at their Doors with lighted Torches; which considering the Time we enter'd was far from an unwelcome or disagreeable Sight.

The next Day several requested to be the Messengers of the Action at *Villena* to the Earl of *Peterborow* at *Alicant;* but the Captain return'd this Answer to all, that in consideration of the Share that I might justly claim in that Day's Transactions, he could not think of letting any other Person be the Bearer. So giving me his Letters to the Earl, I the next Day deliver'd them to him at *Alicant.* At the Delivery, Colonel *Killigrew* (whose Dragoons they were) being present, he expressed a deal of Satisfaction at the Account, and his Lordship was pleased at the same time to appoint me sole Engineer of the Castle of *Alicant.*

Soon after which, that successful General embark'd for *Genoa*, according to the Resolutions of the Council of War at *Guadalaxara*, on a particular Commission from the Queen of *England*, another from *Charles* King of *Spain*, and charged at the same time with a Request of the Marquiss *das Minas*, General of the *Portugueze* Forces, to negotiate Bills for one hundred thousand Pounds for the use of his Troops. In all which, tho' he was (as ever) successful; yet may it be said without a figure, that his Departure, in a good measure, determin'd the Success of the confederate Forces in that Kingdom. True it is, the General return'd again with the fortunate, Fruits of those Negotiations; but never to act in his old auspicious Sphere: And therefore, as I am now to take leave of this fortunate General, let me do it with Justice, in an Appeal to the World, of the not to be parallel'd Usage (in these latter Ages, at least) that he met with for all his Services; such a vast variety of Enterprizes, all successful, and which had set all *Europe* in amaze; Services that had given occasion to such solemn and public Thanksgivings in our Churches, and which had received such very remarkable Approbations, both of Sovereign and Parliament; and which had been represented in so lively a Manner, in a Letter wrote by the King *of Spain*, under his own Hand, to the Queen of *England*, and communicated to both Houses in the Terms following:

Madam, my Sister,

I should not have been so long e'er I did my self the Honour to repeat the Assurances of my sincere Respects to you, had I not waited for the good Occasion which I now acquaint you with, that the City of *Barcelona* is surrendered to me by Capitulation. I doubt not but you will receive this great News with intire Satisfaction, as well, because this happy Success is the Effect of your Arms, always glorious, as from the pure Motives of that Bounty and maternal Affection you have for me, and for every Thing which may contribute to the Advancement of my Interest.

I must do this Justice to all the Officers and common Soldiers, and particularly to my Lord *Peterborow*, that he has shown in this whole Expedition, a Constancy, Bravery, and Conduct, worthy of the Choice that your Majesty has made of him, and that he could no ways give me better Satisfaction than he has, by the great Zeal and Application, which he has equally testified for my Interest, and for the Service of my Person. I owe the same Justice to Brigadier *Stanhope*, for his great Zeal, Vigilance, and very wise Conduct, which he has given Proofs of upon all Occasions: As also to all your Officers of the Fleet, particularly to your worthy Admiral *Shovel*, assuring your Majesty, that he has assisted me in this Expedition, with an inconceivable Readiness and Application, and that no Admiral will be ever better able to render me greater Satisfaction, than he has done. During the Siege of *Barcelona*, some of your Majesty's Ships, with the Assistance of the Troops of the Country, have reduc'd the Town of *Tarragona*, and the officers are made Prisoners of War. The Town of *Girone* has been taken at the same time by Surprize, by the Troops of the Country. The Town of *Lerida* has submitted, as also that of *Tortosa* upon the *Ebro*; so that we have taken all the Places of *Catalonia*, except *Roses*. Some Places in *Aragon* near *Sarrogosa* have declared for me, and the Garrison of the Castle of *Denia* in *Valencia* have maintained their Post, and repulsed the Enemy; 400 of the Enemies Cavalry have enter'd into our Service, and a great number of their Infantry have deserted.

This, Madam, is the State that your Arms, and the Inclination of the People have put my Affairs in. It is unnecessary to tell you what stops the Course of these Conquests, it is not the Season of the Year, nor the Enemy; these are no Obstacles to your Troops, who desire nothing more than to act under the Conduct that your Majesty has appointed them. The taking of Barcelona, with so small a Number of Troops, is very remarkable; and what has been done in this Siege is almost without Example; that with seven or eight thousand Men of your Troops, and two hundred Miquelets, we should surround and invest a Place, that thirty thousand *French* could not block up.

After a March of thirteen Hours, the Troops climb'd up the Rocks and Precipices, to attack a Fortification stronger than the Place, which the Earl of *Peterborow* has sent you a Plan of; two Generals, with the Grenadiers, attack'd it Sword in Hand. In which Action the Prince of *Hesse* died gloriously, after so many brave Actions: I hope his Brother and his Family will always have your Majesty's Protection. With eight hundred Men they forc'd the cover'd Way, and all the Intrenchments and Works, one after another, till they came to the last Work which surrounded it, against five hundred Men of regular Troops which defended the Place, and a Reinforcement they had receiv'd; and three Days afterwards we became Masters of the Place. We afterwards attack'd the Town on the Side of the Castle. We landed again our Cannon, and the other Artillery, with inconceivable Trouble, and form'd two Camps, distant from each other three Leagues, against a Garrison almost as numerous as our Army, whose Cavalry was double the Strength of ours. The first Camp was so well intrench'd, that 'twas defended by two thousand Men and the Dragoons; whilst we attack'd the Town with the rest of our Troops. The Breach being made, we prepar'd to make a general Assault with all the Army. These are Circumstances, Madam, which distinguish this Action, perhaps, from all others.

Here has happen'd an unforeseen Accident. The Cruelty of the pretended Viceroy, and the Report spread abroad, that he would take away the Prisoners, contrary to the Capitulation, provok'd the Burghers, and some of the Country People, to take up Arms against the Garrison, whilst they were busy in packing up their Baggage, which was to be sent away the next Day; so that every thing tended to Slaughter: But your Majesty's Troops, entering into Town with the Earl of *Peterborow*, instead of seeking Pillage, a Practice common upon such Occasions, appeas'd the Tumult, and have say'd the Town, and even the Lives of their Enemies, with a Discipline and Generosity without Example.

What remains is, that I return you my most hearty Thanks for sending so great a Fleet, and such good and valiant Troops to my Assistance. After so happy a Beginning, I have thought it proper, according to the Sentiments of your Generals and Admirals, to support, by my Presence, the Conquests that we have made; and to shew my Subjects, so affectionate to my Person, that I cannot abandon them. I receive such succours from your Majesty, and from your generous Nation, that I am loaded with your Bounties; and am not a little concern'd to think that the Support of my Interest should cause so great an Expence. But, Madam, I sacrifice my Person, and my Subjects in Catalonia expose also their Lives and Fortunes, upon the Assurances they have of your Majesty's generous Protection. Your Majesty and your Council knows better than we do, what is necessary for our Conservation. We shall then expect your Majesty's Succours, with an entire Confidence in your Bounty and Wisdom. A further Force is necessary: We give no small Diversion to *France*, and without doubt they will make their utmost Efforts against me as soon as possible; but I am satisfy'd, that the same Efforts will be made by my Allies to defend me. Your Goodness, Madam, inclines you, and your Power enables you, to support those that the Tyranny of France would oppress. All that I can insinuate to your Wisdom, and that of your Allies, is, that the Forces employ'd in this Country will not be unprofitable to the public Good, but will be under an Obligation and Necessity to act with the utmost Vigour against the Enemy. I am,

With an inviolable Affection,
Respect, and most
Sincere Acknowledgment,
Madam, my Sister,
Your most affectionate
Brother,
CHARLES.

And yet, after all, was this noble General not only recall'd, the
Command of the Fleet taken from him, and that of the Army given to
my Lord *Galway*, without Assignment of Cause; but all Manner of
Falsities were industriously spread abroad, not only to dimish, if they
could, his Reputation, but to bring him under Accusations of a
malevolent Nature. I can hardly imagine it necessary here to take
Notice, that afterward he disprov'd all those idle Calumnies and ill-
invented Rumours; or to mention what Compliments he receiv'd, in the
most solemn Manner, from his Country, upon a full Examination and
thorough canvassing of his Actions in the House of Lords. But this is
too notorious to be omitted, That all Officers coming from *Spain* were
purposely intercepted in their Way to *London*, and craftily examin'd
upon all the idle Stories which had pass'd tending to lessen his
Character: And when any Officers had asserted the Falsity of those
Inventions (as they all did, except a military Sweetner or two) and that
there was no Possibility of laying any thing amiss to the Charge of that
General—they were told, that they ought to be careful however, not to
speak advantagiously of that Lord's Conduct, unless they were willing
to fall Martyrs in his Cause—A Thing scarce to be credited even in a
popish Country. But *Scipio* was accus'd—tho' (as my Author finely
observes) by Wretches only known to Posterity by that stupid
Accusation.

As a mournful Valediction, before I enter upon any new Scene,
the Reader will pardon this melancholy Expostulation. How mortifying
must it be to an *Englishman*, after he has found himself solac'd with a
Relation of so many surprising Successes of her Majesty's Arms, under
the Earl of *Peterborow*; Successes that have lay'd before our Eyes
Provinces and Kingdoms reduc'd, and Towns and Fortresses taken and
reliev'd; where we have seen a continu'd Series of happy Events, the
Fruits of Conduct and Vigilance; and Caution and Foresight preventing
Dangers that were held, at first View, certain and unsurmountable: to
change this glorious Landskip, I say, for Scenes every way different,

even while our Troops were as numerous as the Enemy, and better provided, yet always baffled and beaten, and flying before the Enemy till fatally ruin'd in the Battle of *Almanza*. How mortifying must this be to any Lover of his Country! But I proceed to my Memoirs.

ALICANT is a Town of the greatest Trade of any in the Kingdom of *Valencia*, having a strong Castle, being situated on a high Hill, which commands both Town and Harbour. In this Place I resided a whole Year; but it was soon after my first Arrival, that Major *Collier* (who was shot in the Back at *Barcelona*, as I have related in the Siege of that Place) hearing of me, sought me out at my Quarters; and, after a particular Enquiry into the Success of that difficult Task that he left me upon, and my answering all his Questions to satisfaction (all which he receiv'd with evident Pleasure) he threw down a Purse of Pistoles upon the Table; which I refusing, he told me, in a most handsome Manner, his Friendship was not to be preserved but by my accepting it.

After I had made some very necessary Repairs, I pursu'd the Orders I had receiv'd from the Earl of *Peterborow*, to go upon the erecting a new Battery between the Castle and the Town. This was a Task attended with Difficulties, neither few in Number, nor small in Consequence; for it was to be rais'd upon a great Declivity, which must render the Work both laborious and precarious. However, I had the good Fortune to effect it much sooner than was expected; and it was call'd *Gorge's* Battery, from the Name of the Governor then commanding; who, out of an uncommon Profusion of Generosity, wetted that Piece of Gossiping with a distinguishing Bowl of Punch. Brigadier *Bougard*, when he saw this Work some time after, was pleas'd to honour it with a singular Admiration and Approbation, for its Compleatness, notwithstanding its Difficulties.

This Work, and the Siege of *Cartagena*, then in our Possession, by the Duke of *Berwick*, brought the Lord *Galway* down to this place. *Cartagena* is of so little Distance from *Alicant*, that we could easily hear the Cannon playing against, and from it, in our Castle, where I then was. And I remember my Lord *Galway*, on the fourth Day of the Siege, sending to know if I could make any useful Observations, as to the Success of it; I return'd, that I was of Opinion the Town was surrender'd, from the sudden Cessation of the Cannon, which, by our News next Day from the Place, prov'd to be fact. *Cartagena* is a small Sea-Port Town in *Murcia*; but has so good an Harbour, that when the famous Admiral *Doria* was ask'd, which were the three best Havens in the *Mediterranean*, he readily return'd, *June, July,* and *Cartagena*.

Upon the Surrender of this Place, a Detachment of Foot was sent by the Governor, with some Dragoons, to *Elsha*; but it being a Place of very little Strength they were soon made Prisoners of War.

The Siege of *Cartagena* being over, the Lord *Galway* return'd to his Camp; and the Lord *Duncannon* dying in *Alicant*, the first Guns that were fir'd from *Gorge's* Battery, were the Minute-Guns for his Funeral. His Regiment had been given to the Lord *Montandre*, who lost it before he had Possession, by an Action as odd as it was scandalous.

That Regiment had received Orders to march to the Lord *Galway's* Camp, under the Command of their Lieutenant-Colonel *Bateman*, a Person before reputedly a good Officer, tho' his Conduct here gave People, not invidious, too much Reason to call it in Question. On his March, he was so very careless and negligent (though he knew himself in a Country surrounded with Enemies, and that he was to march through a Wood, where they every Day made their Appearance in great Numbers) that his Soldiers march'd with their Muskets slung at their Backs, and went one after another (as necessity had forc'd us to do in *Scotland*) himself at the Head of 'em, in his Chaise, riding a considerable way before.

It happened there was a Captain, with threescore Dragoons, detach'd from the Duke of *Berwick's* Army, with a Design to intercept some Cash, that was order'd to be sent to Lord *Galway's* Army from *Alicant*. This Detachment, missing of that intended Prize, was returning very disconsolately, *Re infecta*; when their Captain, observing that careless and disorderly March of the *English*, resolv'd, boldly enough, to attack them in the Wood. To that Purpose he secreted his little Party behind a great Barn; and so soon as they were half passed by, he falls upon 'em in the Center with his Dragoons, cutting and slashing at such a violent Rate, that he soon dispersed the whole Regiment, leaving many dead and wounded upon the Spot. The three Colours were taken; and the gallant Lieutenant-Colonel taken out of his Chaise, and carried away Prisoner with many others; only one Officer who was an Ensign, and so bold as to do his Duty, was kill'd.

The Lieutenant who commanded the Granadiers, received the Alarm time enough to draw his Men into a House in their way; where he bravely defended himself for a long Time; but being killed, the rest immediately surrender'd. The Account of this Action I had from the Commander of the Enemy's Party himself, some Time after, while I was a Prisoner. And Captain *Mahoni*, who was present when the News was brought, that a few *Spanish* Dragoons had defeated an *English* Regiment, which was this under *Bateman*, protested to me, that the Duke of *Berwick* turn'd pale at the Relation; and when they offer'd to bring the Colours before him, he would not so much as see them. A little before the Duke went to Supper, *Bateman* himself was brought to him, but the Duke turn'd away from him without any further Notice than coldly saying, that *he thought he was very strangely taken*. The Wags of the Army made a thorough jest of him, and said his military Conduct was of a piece with his Oeconomy, having two Days before this March, sent his young handsome Wife into *England*, under the Guardship of the young Chaplain of the Regiment.

April 15. In the Year 1707, being *Easter Monday*, we had in the Morning a flying Report in *Alicant*, that there had been the Day before a Battle at *Almanza*, between the Army under the Command of the Duke of *Berwick*, and that of the *English*, under Lord *Galway*, in which the latter had suffer'd an entire Defeat. We at first gave no great Credit to it: But, alas, we were too soon woefully convinced of the Truth of it, by Numbers that came flying to us from the conquering Enemy. Then indeed we were satisfied of Truths, too difficult before to be credited. But as I was not present in that calamitous Battle, I shall relate it, as I received it from an Officer then in the Duke's Army.

To bring the Lord *Galway* to a Battle, in a Place most commodious for his purpose, the Duke made use of this Stratagem: He ordered two *Irishmen*, both Officers, to make their way over to the Enemy as Deserters; putting this Story in their Mouths, that the Duke of *Orleans* was in a full March to join the Duke of *Berwick* with twelve thousand Men; that this would be done in two Days, and that then they would find out the Lord *Galway*, and force him to Fight, where-ever they found him.

Lord *Galway*, who at this Time lay before *Villena*, receiving this Intelligence from those well instructed Deserters, immediately rais'd the Siege; with a Resolution, by a hasty March, to force the Enemy to Battle, before the Duke of *Orleans* should be able to join the Duke of *Berwick*. To effect this, after a hard March of three long *Spanish* Leagues in the heat of the Day; he appears a little after Noon in the face of the Enemy with his fatigu'd Forces. Glad and rejoyc'd at the Sight, for he found his Plot had taken; *Berwick*, the better to receive him, draws up his Army in a half Moon, placing at a pretty good Advance three Regiments to make up the Centre, with express Order, nevertheless, to retreat at the very first Charge. All which was punctually observ'd, and had its desired Effect; For the three Regiments, at the first Attack gave way, and seemingly fled towards their Camp; the *English*, after their customary Manner, pursuing them with Shouts and Hollowings. As soon as the Duke of *Berwick* perceiv'd his Trap had taken, he order'd his right and left Wings to close; by which Means, he at once cut off from the rest of their Army all those who had so eagerly pursu'd the imaginary Runaways. In short, the Rout was total, and the most fatal Blow that ever the *English* receiv'd during the whole War with *Spain*. Nor, as it is thought, with a great probability of Reason, had those Troops that made their Retreat to the Top of the Hills, under Major General *Shrimpton*, met with any better Fate than those on the Plain, had the *Spaniards* had any other General in the Command than the Duke of *Berwick*; whose native Sympathy gave a check to the Ardour of a victorious Enemy. And this was the sense of the *Spaniards* themselves after the Battle. Verifying herein that noble Maxim, *That Victory to generous Minds is only an Inducement to Moderation.*

The Day after this fatal Battle (which gave occasion to a *Spanish* piece of Wit, *that the English General had routed the French*) the Duke of *Orleans* did arrive indeed in the Camp, but with an Army of only fourteen Attendants.

The fatal Effects of this Battle were soon made visible, and to none more than those in *Alicant*. The Enemy grew every Day more and more troublesome; visiting us in Parties more boldly than before: and often hovering about us so very near, that with our Cannon we could hardly teach 'em to keep a proper Distance. *Gorge* the Governor of *Alicant* being recall'd into *England*, Major General *Richards* was by King *Charles* appointed Governor in his Place. He was a Roman Catholick, and very much belov'd by the Natives on that Account; tho' to give him his due, he behaved himself extremely well in all other Respects. It was in his Time, that a Design was laid of surprising *Guardamere*, a small Sea-port Town, in *Murcia*. But the military Bishop (for he was in a literal Sense excellent *tam Marte, quam Mercurio*, among his many others Exploits), by a timely Expedition, prevented that.

Governor *Richards*, my Post being always in the Castle, had sent to desire me to give notice whenever I saw any Parties of the Enemy moving. Pursuant to this Order, discovering one Morning a considerable body of Horse towards *Elsha*, I went down into the Town, and told the Governor what I had seen; and without any delay he gave his Orders, that a Captain with threescore Men should attend me to an old House about a Mile distance. As soon as we had got into it, I set about barricading all the open Places, and Avenues, and put my Men in a Posture ready to receive an Enemy, as soon as he should appear; upon which the Captain, as a feint, ordered a few of his men to shew themselves on a rising Ground just before the House. But we had like to have caught a Tartar: For tho' the Enemy took the Train I had laid, and on sight of our small Body on the Hill, sent a Party from their greater Body to intercept them, before they could reach the Town; yet the Sequel prov'd, we had mistaken their Number and it soon appeared to be much greater than we at first imagin'd. However our Out-scouts, as I may call 'em, got safe into the House; and on the Appearance of the Party, we let fly a full Volly, which laid dead on the Spot three Men and one Horse. Hereupon the whole Body made up to the House, but stood a-loof upon the Hill without reach of our Shot. We soon saw our Danger from the number of the Enemy: And well for us it was, that the watchful Governor had taken notice of it, as well as we in the House. For observing us surrounded with the Enemy, and by a Power so much superior, he marched himself with a good part of the Garrison to our Relief. The Enemy stood a little time as if they would receive 'em; but upon second thoughts they retir'd; and to our no little Joy left us at Liberty to come out of the House and join the Garrison.

Scarce a Day pass'd but we had some visits of the like kind attended sometimes with Rencounters of this Nature; in so much that there was hardly any stirring out in Safety for small Parties, tho' never so little away. There was within a little Mile of the Town, an old Vineyard, environed with a loose stone Wall: An Officer and I made an Agreement to ride thither for an Airing. We did so, and after a little riding, it came into my Head to put a Fright upon the Officer. And very lucky for us both was that unlucky Thought of mine; pretending to see a Party of the Enemy make up to us, I gave him the Alarm, set Spurs to my Horse, and rid as fast as Legs could carry me. The Officer no way bated of his Speed; and we had scarce got out of the Vineyard but my Jest prov'd Earnest, twelve of the Enemy's Horse pursuing us to the very Gates of the Town. Nor could I ever after prevail upon my Fellow-Traveller to believe that he ow'd his Escape to Merriment more than Speed.

Soon after my Charge, as to the Fortifications, was pretty well over, I obtain'd Leave of the Governor to be absent for a Fortnight, upon some Affairs of my own at *Valencia*. On my Return from whence, at a Town call'd *Venissa*, I met two Officers of an *English* Regiment, going to the Place from whence I last came. They told me, after common Congratulations, that they had left Major *Boyd*, at a little Place call'd *Capel*, hiring another Mule, that he rode on thither having tir'd and fail'd him; desiring withal, that if I met him, I would let him know that they would stay for him at that Place. I had another Gentleman in my Company, and we had travell'd on not above a League further, whence, at a little Distance, we were both surpriz'd with a Sight that seem'd to have set all Art at defiance, and was too odd for any thing in Nature. It appear'd all in red, and to move; but so very slowly, that if we had not made more way to that than it did to us, we should have made it a Day's Journey before we met it. My Companion could as little tell what to make of it as I; and, indeed, the nearer it came the more monstrous it seem'd, having nothing of the Tokens of Man, either Walking, Riding, or in any Posture whatever. At last, coming up with this strange Figure of a Creature (for now we found it was certainly such) what, or rather who, should it prove to be, but Major *Boyd*? He was a Person of himself far from one of the least Proportion, and mounted on a poor little Ass, with all his warlike Accoutrements upon it, you will allow must make a Figure almost as odd as one of the old *Centaurs*. The Morocco Saddle that cover'd the Ass was of Burden enough for the Beast without its Master; and the additional Holsters and Pistols made it much more weighty. Nevertheless, a Curb Bridle of the largest Size cover'd his little Head, and a long red Cloak, hanging down to the Ground, cover'd Jackboots, Ass, Master and all. In short, my Companion and I, after we could specifically declare it to be a Man, agreed we never saw a Figure so comical in all our Lives. When we had merrily greeted our Major (for a *Cynick* could not have forborn Laughter) He excus'd all as well as he could, by saying he could get no other Beast. After which, delivering our Message, and condoling with him for his present Mounting, and wishing him better at his next Quarters, he settled into his old Pace, and we into ours, and parted.

We lay that Night at *Altea*, famous for its Bay for Ships to water at. It stands on a high Hill; and is adorn'd, not defended, with an old Fort.

Thence we came to *Alicant*, where having now been a whole Year, and having effected what was held necessary, I once more prevail'd upon the Governor to permit me to take another Journey. The Lord *Galway* lay at *Tarraga*, while *Lerida* lay under the Siege of the Duke of *Orleans*; and having some Grounds of Expectation given me, while he was at *Alicant*, I resolv'd at least to demonstrate I was still living. The

Governor favour'd me with Letters, not at all to my Disadvantage; so taking Ship for *Barcelona*, just at our putting into the Harbour, we met with the *English* Fleet, on its Return from the Expedition to *Toulon* under Sir *Cloudsly Shovel*.

I stay'd but very few Days at *Barcelona*, and then proceeded on my intended Journey to *Tarraga*; arriving at which Place I deliver'd my Packet to the Lord *Galway*, who receiv'd me with very great Civility; and to double it, acquainted me at the same time, that the Governor of *Alicant* had wrote very much in my Favour: But though it was a known Part of that noble Lord's Character, that the first Impression was generally strongest, I had Reason soon after to close with another Saying, equally true, *That general Rules always admit of some Exception.* While I was here we had News of the taking of the Town of *Lerida*; the Prince of *Hesse* (Brother to that brave Prince who lost his Life before *Monjouick*) retiring into the Castle with the Garrison, which he bravely defended a long time after.

When I was thus attending my Lord *Galway* at *Tarraga*, he receiv'd Intelligence that the Enemy had a Design to lay Siege to *Denia*; whereupon he gave me Orders to repair there as Engineer. After I had receiv'd my Orders, and taken Leave of his Lordship, I set out, resolving, since it was left to my Choice, to go by way of *Barcelona*, and there take Shipping for the Place of my Station; by which I propos'd to save more time than would allow me a full Opportunity of visiting *Montserat*, a Place I had heard much Talk of, which had fill'd me with a longing Desire to see it. To say Truth, I had been told such extravagant Things of the Place, that I could hardly impute more than one half of it to any thing but *Spanish* Rhodomontado's, the Vice of extravagant Exaggeration being too natural to that Nation.

MONTSERAT is a rising lofty Hill, in the very Middle of a spacious Plain, in the Principality of *Catalonia*, about seven Leagues distant from *Barcelona* to the Westward, somewhat inclining to the North. At the very first Sight, its Oddness of Figure promises something extraordinary; and given at that Distance the Prospect makes somewhat of a grand Appearance: Hundreds of aspiring Pyramids presenting themselves all at once to the Eye, look, if I may be allowed so to speak, like a little petrify'd Forrest; or, rather, like the awful Ruins of some capacious Structure, the Labour of venerable Antiquity. The nearer you approach the more it affects; but till you are very near you can hardly form in your Mind any thing like what you find it when you come close to it. Till just upon it you would imagine it a perfect Hill of

Steeples; but so intermingled with Trees of Magnitude, as well as Beauty, that your Admiration can never be tir'd, or your Curiosity surfeited. Such I found it on my Approach; yet much less than what I found it, was so soon as I enter'd upon the very Premisses.

Now that stupendious Cluster of Pyramids affected me in a Manner different to all before; and I found it so finely group'd with verdant Groves, and here and there interspers'd with aspiring, but solitary Trees, that it no way lessened my Admiration, while it increased my Delight. Those Trees, which I call solitary, as standing single, in opposition to the numerous Groves, which are close and thick (as I observ'd when I ascended to take a View of the several Cells) rise generally out of the very Clefts of the main Rock, with nothing, to Appearance, but a Soil or bed of Stone for their Nurture. But though some few Naturalists may assert, that the Nitre in the Stone may afford a due Proportion of Nourishment to Trees and Vegetables; these, in my Opinion, were all too beautiful, their Bark, Leaf, and Flowers, carry'd too fair a Face of Health, to allow them even to be the Foster-children of Rock and Stone only.

Upon this Hill, or if you please, Grove of Rocks, are thirteen Hermits Cells, the last of which lies near the very Summit. You gradually advance to every one, from Bottom to Top, by a winding Ascent; which to do would otherwise be Impossible, by reason of the Steepness; but though there is a winding Ascent to every Cell, as I have said, I would yet set at defiance the most observant, if a Stranger, to find it feasible to visit them in order, if not precaution'd to follow the poor *Borigo*, or old Ass, that with Paniers hanging on each Side of him, mounts regularly, and daily, up to every particular Cell. The Manner is as follows:

In the Paniers there are thirteen Partitions; one for every Cell. At the Hour appointed, the Servant having plac'd the Paniers on his Back, the Ass, of himself, goes to the Door of the Convent at the very Foot of the Hill, where every Partition is supply'd with their several Allowances of Victuals and Wine. Which, as soon as he has receiv'd, without any further Attendance, or any Guide, he mounts and takes the Cells gradually, in their due Course, till he reaches the very uppermost. Where having discharg'd his Duty, he descends the same Way, lighter by the Load he carry'd up. This the poor stupid Drudge fails not to do, Day and Night, at the stated Hours.

Two Gentlemen, who had join'd me on the Road, alike led by Curiosity, seem'd alike delighted, that the End of it was so well answer'd. I could easily discover in their Countenances a Satisfaction, which, if it did not give a Sanction to my own, much confirm'd it, while they seem'd to allow with me that these reverend Solitaries were truly happy Men; I then thought them such; and a thousand times since, reflecting within my self, have wish'd, bating their Errors, and lesser Superstitions, my self as happily station'd: For what can there be wanting to a happy Life, where all things necessary are provided without Care? Where the Days, without Anxiety or Troubles, may be gratefully passed away, with an innocent Variety of diverting and pleasing Objects, and where their Sleep sand Slumbers are never interrupted with any thing more offensive, than murmuring Springs, natural Cascades, or the various Songs of the pretty feather'd Quiristers.

But their Courtesy to Strangers is no less engaging than their Solitude. A recluse Life, for the Fruits of it, generally speaking, produces Moroseness; Pharisaical Pride too often sours the Temper; and a mistaken Opinion of their own Merit too naturally leads such Men into a Contempt of others; But on the contrary, these good Men (for I must call them as I thought them) seem'd to me the very Emblems of Innocence; so ready to oblige others, that at the same Instant they seem'd laying Obligations upon themselves. This is self-evident, in that Affability and Complaisance they use in shewing the Rarities of their several Cells; where, for fear you should slip any thing worthy Observation, they endeavour to instil in you as quick a Propensity of asking, as you find in them a prompt Alacrity in answering such Questions of Curiosity as their own have inspir'd.

In particular, I remember one of those reverend old Men, when we were taking Leave at the Door of his Cell, to which out of his great Civility he accompany'd us, finding by the Air of our Faces, as well as our Expressions, that we thought ourselves pleasingly entertain'd; to divert us afresh, advanc'd a few Paces from the Door, when giving a Whistle with his Mouth, a surprising Flock of pretty little Birds, variegated, and of different Colours, immediately flock'd around him. Here you should see some alighting upon his Shoulders, some on his awful Beard; others took Refuge on his snow-like Head, and many feeding, and more endeavouring to feed out of his Mouth; each appearing emulous and under an innocent Contention, how best to express their Love and Respect to their no less pleased Master.

Nor did the other Cells labour under any Deficiency of Variety: Every one boasting in some particular, that might distinguish it in something equally agreeable and entertaining. Nevertheless, crystal

Springs spouting from the solid Rocks were, from the highest to the lowest, common to them all; and, in most of them, they had little brass Cocks, out of which, when turn'd, issu'd the most cool and crystalline Flows of excellent pure Water. And yet what more affected me, and which I found near more Cells than one, was the natural Cascades of the same transparent Element; these falling from one Rock to another, in that warm, or rather hot Climate, gave not more delightful Astonishment to the Eye, than they afforded grateful Refreshment to the whole Man. The Streams falling from these, soften, from a rougher tumultuous Noise, into such affecting Murmurs, by Distance, the Intervention of Groves, or neighbouring Rocks, that it were impossible to see or hear them and not be chann'd.

Neither are those Groves grateful only in a beautiful Verdure; Nature renders them otherwise delightful, in loading them with Clusters of Berries of a perfect scarlet Colour, which, by a beautiful Intermixture, strike the Eye with additional Delight. In short, it might nonplus a Person of the nicest Taste, to distinguish or determine, whether the Neatness of their Cells within, or the beauteous Varieties without, most exhaust his Admiration. Nor is the Whole, in my Opinion, a little advantag'd by the frequent View of some of those pyramidical Pillars, which seem, as weary of their own Weight, to recline and seek Support from others in the Neighbourhood.

When I mention'd the outside Beauties of their Cells, I must be thought to have forgot to particularize the glorious Prospects presented to your Eye from every one of them; but especially from that nearest the Summit. A Prospect, by reason of the Purity of the Air, so extensive, and so very entertaining that to dilate upon it properly to one that never saw it, would baffle Credit; and naturally to depaint it, would confound Invention. I therefore shall only say, that on the *Mediterranean* Side, after an agreeable Interval of some fair Leagues, it will set at defiance the strongest Opticks; and although *Barcelona* bounds it on the Land, the Eyes are feasted with the Delights of such an intervening Champion (where beauteous Nature does not only smile, but riot) that the Sense must be very temperate, or very weak, that can be soon or easily satisfy'd.

Having thus taken a View of all their refreshing Springs, their grateful Groves, and solitary Shades under single Trees, whose Clusters prov'd that even Rocks were grown fruitful; and having ran over all the Variety of Pleasures in their several pretty Cells, decently set off with Gardens round the, equally fragrant and beautiful, we were brought down again to the Convent, which, though on a small Ascent, lies very near the Foot of this terrestrial Paradise, there to take a Survey of their sumptuous Hall, much more sumptuous Chapel, and its adjoining Repository; and feast our Eyes with Wonders of a different Nature; and yet as entertaining as any, or all, we had seen before.

Immediately on our Descent, a Priest presented himself at the Door of the Convent, ready to shew us the hidden Rarities. And though, as I understood, hardly a Day passes without the Resort of some Strangers to gratify their Curiosity with the Wonders of the Place; yet is there, on every such Occasion, a superior Concourse of Natives ready to see over again, out of meer Bigotry and Superstition, what they have seen, perhaps, a hundred times before. I could not avoid taking notice, however, that the Priest treated those constant Visitants with much less Ceremony, or more Freedom, if you please, than any of the Strangers of what Nation soever; or, indeed, he seem'd to take as much Pains to disoblige those, as he did Pleasure in obliging us.

The Hall was neat, large and stately; but being plain and unadorn'd with more than decent Decorations, suitable to such a Society, I hasten to the other.

When we enter'd the Chapel, our Eyes were immediately attracted by the Image of our Lady of *Montserat* (as they call it) which stands over the Altar-Piece. It is about the natural Stature; but as black and shining as Ebony it self. Most would imagine it made of that Material; though her Retinue and Adorers will allow nothing of the Matter. On the contrary, Tradition, which with them is, on some Occasions, more than tantamount to Religion, has assur'd them, and they relate it as undoubted Matter of Fact, that her present Colour, if I may so call it, proceeded from her Concealment, in the Time of the *Moors*, between those two Rocks on which the Chapel is founded; and that her long lying in that dismal Place chang'd her once lovely White into its present opposite. Would not a Heretick here be apt to say, That it was greaty pity that an Image which still boasts the Power of acting so many Miracles, could no better conserve her own Complexion? At least it must be allow'd, even by a good Catholick, to carry along with it Matter of Reproach to the fair Ladies, Natives of the Country, for their unnatural and excessive Affection of adulterating, if not defacing, their beautiful Faces, with the ruinating Dauberies of *Carmine*?

As the Custom of the Place is (which is likewise allow'd to be a distinguishing Piece of Civility to Strangers) when we approach the black Lady (who, I should have told you, bears a Child in her Arms; but whether maternally Black, or of the *Mulatto* Kind, I protest I did not mind) the Priest, in great Civility, offers you her Arm to salute; at which Juncture, I, like a true blue Protestant, mistaking my Word of Command, fell foul on the fair Lady's Face. The Displeasure in his Countenance (for he took more Notice of the Rudeness than the good Lady her self) soon convinc'd me of my Error; However, as a greater Token of his Civility, having admitted no *Spaniards* along with my Companions and me, is pass'd off the better; and his after Civilities manifested, that he was willing to reform my Ignorance by his Complaisance.

To demonstrate which, upon my telling him that I had a Set of Beads, which I must entreat him to consecrate for me, he readily, nay eagerly comply'd; and having hung them on her Arm for the Space of about half, or somewhat short of a whole Minute, he return'd me the holy Baubles with a great deal of Address and most evident Satisfaction. The Reader will be apt to admire at this curious Piece of Superstition of mine, till I have told him, that even rigid Protestants have, in this Country, thought it but prudent to do the like; and likewise having so done, to carry them about their Persons, or in their Pockets: For Experience has convinc'd us of the Necessity of this most Catholick Precaution; since those who have here, travelling or otherwise, come to their Ends, whether by Accident, Sickness, or the Course of Nature, not having these sanctifying Seals found upon them, have ever been refus'd Christian Burial, under a superstitious Imagination, that the Corps of a Heretick will infect every thing near it.

Two instances of this kind fell within my Knowledge; one before I came to *Montserat*, the other after. The first was of one *Slunt*, who had been *Bombardier* at *Monjouick*; but being kill'd while we lay at *Campilio*, a Priest, whom I advis'd with upon the Matter, told me, that if he should be buried where any Corn grew, his Body would not only be taken up again, but ill treated, in revenge of the Destruction of so much Corn, which the People would on no account be persuaded to touch; for which Reason we took care to have him lay'd in a very deep Grave, on a very barren Spot of Ground. The other was of one Captain *Bush*, who was a Prisoner with me on the Surrender of *Denia*; who being sent, as I was afterwards, to Saint *Clemente la Mancha*, there dy'd; and, as I was inform'd, tho' he was privately, and by Night, bury'd in a Corn-Field, he was taken out of his Grave by those superstitious People, as soon as ever they could discover the Place where his Body was deposited. But I return to the Convent at *Montserat*.

Out of the Chapel, behind the High-Altar, we descended into a spacious Room, the Repository of the great Offerings made to the Lady. Here, though I thought in the Chapel it self I had seen the Riches of the Universe, I found a prodigious Quantity of more costly Presents, the superstitious Tribute of most of the Roman-Catholick Princes in *Europe*. Among a Multitude of others, they show'd me a Sword set with Diamonds, the Offering of *Charles* the Third, then King of *Spain*, but now Emperor of *Germany*. Though I must confess, being a Heretick, I could much easier find a Reason for a fair Lady's presenting such a Sword to a King of *Spain*, than for a King of *Spain's* presenting such a Sword to a fair Lady: And by the Motto upon it, *Pulchra tamen nigra*, it was plain such was his Opinion. That Prince was so delighted with the Pleasure's of this sweet Place, that he, as well as I, stay'd as long as ever he could; though neither of us so long as either could have wish'd.

But there was another Offering from a King of *Portugal*, equally glorious and costly; but much better adapted; and therefore in its Propriety easier to be accounted for. That was a Glory for the Head of her Ladiship, every Ray of which was set with Diamonds, large at the Bottom, and gradually lessening to the very Extremity of every Ray. Each Ray might be about half a Yard Long; and I imagin'd in the Whole there might be about one Hundred of them. In short, if ever her Ladiship did the Offerer the Honour to put it on, I will though a Heretick, venture to aver, she did not at that present time look like a humane Creature.

To enumerate the rest, if my Memory would suffice, would exceed Belief. As the upper Part was a plain Miracle of Nature, the lower was a compleat Treasury of miraculous Art.

If you ascend from the lowest Cell to the very Summit, the last of all the thirteen, you will perceive a continual Contention between Pleasure and Devotion; and at last, perhaps, find your self at a Loss to decide which deserves the Preheminence: For you are not here to take Cells in the vulgar Acceptation, as the little Dormitories of solitary Monks: No! Neatness, Use, and Contrivance appear in every one of them; and though in an almost perfect Equality, yet in such Perfection, that you will find it difficult to discover in any one of them any thing wanting to the Pleasure of Life.

If you descend to the Convent near the Foot of that venerable Hill; you may see more, much more of the Riches of the World; but less, far less Appearance of a celestial Treasure. Perhaps, it might be only the Sentiment of a Heretick; but that Awe and Devotion, which I found in my Attendant from Cell to Cell grew languid, and lost in meer empty Bigotry and foggy Superstition, when I came below. In short, there was not a great Difference in their Heights, than in the Sentiments they inspir'd me with.

Before I leave this Emblem of the beatific Vision, I must correct some thing like a Mistake, as to the poor *Borigo*. I said at the Beginning that his Labour was daily; but the *Sunday* is to him a Day of rest, as it is to the Hermits, his Masters, a Day of Refection. For to save the poor faithful Brute the hard Drudgery of that Day, the thirteen Hermits, if Health permit, descend to their *Canobium*, as they call it; that is, to the Hall of the Convent; where they dine in common with the Monks of the Order, who are *Benedictines*.

After seven Days Variety of such innocent Delight (the Space allow'd for the Entertainment of Strangers), I took my Leave of this pacifick Hermitage, to pursue the more boisterous Duties of my Calling. The Life of a Soldier is in every Respect the full *Antithesis* to that of a Hermit; and I know not, whether it might not be a Sense of that, which inspir'd me with very great Reluctancy at parting. I confess, while on the Spot, I over and over bandy'd in my Mind the Reasons which might prevail upon *Charles* the Fifth to relinquish his Crown; and the Arguments on his Side never fail'd of Energy, I could persuade my self that this, or some like happy Retreat, was the Reward of abdicated Empire.

Full of these Contemplations (for they lasted there) I arriv'd at *Barcelona*; where I found a Vessel ready to sail, on which I embarked for *Denia*, in pursuance of my Orders. Sailing to the Mouth of the *Mediterranean*, no Place along the *Christian* Shore affords a Prospect equally delightful with the Castle of *Denia*. It was never designed for a Place of great Strength, being built, and first design'd, as a Seat of Pleasure to the Great Duke of *Lerma*. In that Family it many Years remain'd; tho', within less than a Century, that with two other Dukedoms, have devolv'd upon the Family of the Duke *de Medina Celi*, the richest Subject at this time in all *Spain*.

DENIA was the first Town, that in our Way to *Barcelona*, declar'd for King *Charles*; and was then by his Order made a Garrison. The Town is but small, and surrounded with a thin Wall; so thin, that I have known a Cannon-Ball pierce through it at once.

When I arriv'd at *Denia*, I found a *Spaniard* Governor of the Town, whose Name has slipt my Memory; tho' his Behaviour merited everlasting Annals. Major *Percival*, an *Englishman*, commanded in the Castle, and on my coming there, I understood, it had been agreed between 'em, that in case of a Siege, which they apprehended, the Town should be defended wholly by *Spaniards*, and the Castle by the *English*.

I had scarce been there three Weeks before those Expectations were answered. The Place was invested by Count *D'Alfelt*, and Major General *Mahoni*; two Days after which, they open'd Trenches on the East Side of the Town. I was necessitated upon their so doing, to order the Demolishment of some Houses on that Side, that I might erect a Battery to point upon their Trenches, the better to annoy them. I did so; and it did the intended Service; for with that, and two others, which I rais'd upon the Castle (from all which we fir'd incessantly, and with great Success) the Besiegers were sufficiently incommoded.

The Governor of the Town (a *Spaniard* as I said before, and with a *Spanish* Garrison) behav'd very gallantly; insomuch, that what was said of the Prince of *Hesse*, when he so bravely defended *Gibraltar* against the joint Forces of *France* and *Spain*, might be said of him, that he was Governor, Engineer, Gunner, and Bombardier all in one; For no Man could exceed him, either in Conduct or Courage; nor were the *Spaniards* under him less valiant or vigilant; for in case the Place was taken, expecting but indifferent Quarter, they fought with Bravery, and defended the Place to Admiration.

The Enemy had answer'd our Fire with all the Ardour imaginable; and having made a Breach, that, as we thought was practicable, a Storm was expected every Hour. Preparing against which to the great Joy of all the Inhabitants, and the Surprize of the whole Garrison, and without our being able to assign the least Cause, the Enemy suddenly raised the Siege, and withdrew from a Place, which those within imagined in great Danger.

The Siege thus abdicated (if I may use a modern Phrase) I was resolved to improve my Time, and make the best Provision I could against any future Attack. To that purpose I made several new Fortifications, together with proper Casemets for our Powder, all which render'd the Place much stronger, tho' Time too soon show'd me that Strength it self must yield to Fortune.

Surveying those works, and my Workmen, I was one Day standing on the great Battery, when casting my Eye toward the *Barbary* Coast, I observ'd an odd sort of greenish Cloud making to the *Spanish* Shoar. Not like other Clouds with Rapidity or Swiftness, but with a Motion so slow, that Sight itself was a long time before it would allow it such.

At last, it came just over my Head, and interposing between the Sun and me, so thickened the Air, that I had lost the very Sight of Day. At this moment it had reach'd the Land; and tho' very near me in my Imagination, it began to dissolve, and lose of its first Tenebrity, when all on a sudden there fell such a vast multitude of Locusts, as exceeded the thickest storm of Hail or Snow that I ever saw. All around me was immediately cover'd with those crauling Creatures; and they yet continu'd to fall so thick, that with the swing of my Cane I knock'd down thousands. It is scarce imaginable the Havock I made in a very little space of time; much less conceivable is the horrid Desolation which attended the Visitation of those *Animalcula.* There was not in a Day or two's time, the least Leaf to be seen upon a Tree, nor any green Thing in a Garden. Nature seem'd buried in her own Ruins; and the vegetable World to be Supporters only to her Monument. I never saw the hardest Winter, in those Parts, attended with any equal Desolation. When, glutton like, they had devoured all that should have sustained them, and the more valuable Part of God's Creation (whether weary with gorging, or over thirsty with devouring, I leave to Philosophers) they made to Ponds, Brooks, and standing Pools, there revenging their own Rape upon Nature, upon their own vile Carkasses. In every of these you might see them lie in Heaps like little Hills; drown'd indeed, but attended with Stenches so noisome, that it gave the distracted Neighbourhood too great Reason to apprehend yet more fatal Consequences. A Pestilential Infection is the Dread of every Place, but especially of all Parts upon the *Mediterranean.* The Priests therefore repair'd to a little Chapel, built in the open Fields, to be made use of on such like Occasions, there to deprecate the miserable Cause of this dreadful Visitation. In a Week's time, or there abouts, the Stench was over, and every Thing but verdant Nature in its pristin Order.

Some few Months after this, and about eight Months from the former Siege, Count *D'Alfelt* caus'd *Denia* to be again invested; and being then sensible of all the Mistakes he had before committed, he now went about his Business with more Regularity and Discretion. The first Thing he set upon, and it was the wisest Thing he could do, was to cut off our Communication with the Sea. This he did, and thereby obtained what he much desired. Next, he caus'd his Batteries to be erected on the West side of the Town, from which he ply'd it so furiously, that in five Days' time a practicable Breach was made; upon which they stormed and took it. The Governor, who had so bravely defended it in the former Seige, fortunately for him had been remov'd;

and *Francis Valero*, now in his Place, was made Prisoner of War with all his Garrison.

After the taking the Town, they erected Batteries against the Castle, which they kept ply'd with incessant Fire, both from Cannon and Mortars. But what most of all plagu'd us, and did us most Mischief, was the vast showers of Stones sent among the Garrison from their Mortars. These, terrible in Bulk and Size, did more Execution than all the rest put together. The Garrison could not avoid being somewhat disheartened at this uncommon way of Rencounter; yet, to a Man, dedar'd against hearkening to any Proposals of Surrender, the Governor excepted; who having selected more Treasure than he could properly, or justly call his own, was the only Person that seem'd forward for such a Motion. He had more than once thrown out Expressions of such a Nature, but without any effect. Nevertheless, having at last secretly obtained a peculiar Capitulation for himself, Bag, and Baggage; the Garrison was sacrific'd to his private Interest, and basely given up Prisoners of War. By these Means indeed he saved his Money, but lost his Reputation; and soon after, Life it self. And sure every Body will allow the latter loss to be least, who will take Pains to consider, that it screened him from the consequential Scrutinies of a Council of War, which must have issued as the just Reward of his Demerits.

The Garrison being thus unaccountably delivered up and made Prisoners, were dispersed different ways: Some into *Castile*, others as far as *Oviedo*, in the Kingdom of *Leon*. For my own part, having received a Contusion in my Breast; I was under a necessity of being left behind with the Enemy, till I should be in a Condition to be remov'd, and when that time came, I found my self agreeably ordered to *Valencia*.

As Prisoner of War I must now bid adieu to the active Part of the military Life; and hereafter concern my self with Descriptions of Countries, Towns, Palaces, and Men, instead of Battles. However, if I take in my way Actions of War, founded on the best Authorities, I hope my Interspersing such will be no disadvantage to my now more pacifick MEMOIRS.

So soon as I arriv'd at *Valencia*, I wrote to our Pay-master Mr. *Mead*, at *Barcelona*, letting him know, that I was become a Prisoner, wounded, and in want of Money. Nor could even all those Circumstances prevail on me to think it long before he returned a favourable Answer, in an Order to Monsieur *Zoulicafre*, a Banker, to pay me on Sight fifty Pistoles. But in the same Letter he gave me to understand, that those fifty Pistoles were a Present to me from General (afterward Earl) *Stanhope*; and so indeed I found it, when I return'd into *England*, my Account not being charged with any part of it: But this was not the only Test I received of that generous Earl's Generosity. And where's the Wonder, as the World is compell'd to own, that Heroick Actions and Largeness of Soul ever did discover and amply distinguish the genuine Branches of that illustrious Family.

This Recruit to me however was the more generous for being seasonable. Benefits are always doubled in their being easily conferr'd and well tim'd; and with such an Allowance as I constantly had by the order of King *Philip*, as Prisoner of War, *viz.* eighteen Ounces of Mutton *per diem* for my self, and nine for my Man, with Bread and Wine in proportion, and especially in such a Situation; all this I say was sufficient to invite a Man to be easy, and almost forget his want of Liberty, and much more so to me if it be consider'd, that, that want of Liberty consisted only in being debarr'd from leaving the pleasantest City in all *Spain*.

Here I met with the *French* Engineer, who made the Mine under the Rock of the Castle at *Alicant*. That fatal Mine, which blew up General *Richards*, Colonel *Syburg*, Colonel *Thornicroft*, and at least twenty more Officers. And yet by the Account, that Engineer gave me, their Fate was their own choosing: The General, who commanded at that Siege being more industrious to save them, than they were to be say'd: He endeavour'd it many ways: He sent them word of the Mine, and their readiness to spring it; he over and over sent them Offers of Leave to come, and take a view of it, and inspect it: Notwithstanding all which, tho' Colonel *Thornicroft*, and Captain *Page*, a *French* Engineer, in the Service of King *Charles*, pursued the Invitation, and were permitted to view it, yet would they not believe; but reported on their Return, that it was a sham Mine, a feint only to intimidate 'em to a Surrender, all the Bags being fill'd with Sand instead of Gun-powder.

The very Day on which the Besiegers design'd to spring the Mine, they gave Notice of it; and the People of the Neighbourhood ran up in Crowds to an opposite Hill in order to see it: Nevertheless, altho' those in the Castle saw all this, they still remain'd so infatuated, as to imagine it all done only to affright 'em. At length the fatal Mine was sprung, and all who were upon that Battery lost their Lives; and among them those I first mentioned. The very Recital hereof made me think within my self, *who can resist his Fate?*

That Engineer added further, that it was with an incredible Difficulty, that he prepar'd that Mine; that there were in the Concavity thirteen hundred Barrels of Powder; notwithstanding which, it made no great Noise without, whatever it might do inwardly; that only taking away what might be not improperly term'd an Excrescence in the Rock, the Heave on the Blast had render'd the Castle rather stronger on that Side than it was before, a Crevice or Crack which had often occasioned Apprehensions being thereby wholly clos'd and firm.

Some further Particulars I soon after had from Colonel *Syburg's* Gentleman; who seeing me at the Play-house, challenged me, tho' at that Time unkown to me. He told me, that the Night preceeding the unfortunate Catastrophe of his Master, he was waiting on him in the Casemet, where he observed, sometime before the rest of the Company took notice of it, that General *Richards* appeared very pensive and thoughtful, that the whole Night long he was pester'd with, and could not get rid of a great Flie, which was perpetually buzzing about his Ears and Head, to the vexation and disturbance of the rest of the Company, as well as the General himself; that in the Morning, when they went upon the Battery, under which the Mine was, the General made many offers of going off; but Colonel *Syburg*, who was got a little merry, and the rest out of a Bravado, would stay, and would not let the General stir; that at last it was propos'd by Colonel *Syburg* to have the other two Bottles to the Queen's Health, after which he promised they would all go off together.

Upon this my Relator, *Syburg's* Gentleman, said, he was sent to fetch the stipulated two Bottles; returning with which, Captain *Daniel Weaver*, within thirty or forty Yards of the Battery, ran by him, vowing, he was resolv'd to drink the Queen's Health with them; but his Feet were scarce on the Battery, when the Mine was sprung, which took him away with the rest of the Company; while Major *Harding* now a Justice in *Westminster* coming that very Moment off Duty, exchang'd Fates.

If Predestination, in the Eyes of many, is an unaccountable Doctrine, what better Account can the wisest give of this Fatality? Or to what else shall we impute the Issue of this whole Transaction? That Men shall be solicited to their Safety; suffered to survey the Danger they were threatened with; among many other Tokens of its approaching Certainty, see such a Concourse of People crowding to be Spectators of their impending Catastrophe; and after all this, so infatuated to stay on the fatal Spot the fetching up of the other two Bottles; whatever it may to such as never think, to such as plead an use of Reason, it must administer Matter worthy of the sedatest Consideration.

Being now pretty well recover'd of my Wounds, I was by Order of the Governor of *Valencia*, removed to *Sainte Clemente de la Mancha*, a Town somewhat more Inland, and consequently esteem'd more secure than a Semi-Seaport. Here I remain'd under a sort of Pilgrimage upwards of three Years. To me as a Stranger divested of Acquaintance or Friend (for at that instant I was sole Prisoner there) at first it appear'd such, tho' in a very small compass of Time, I luckily found it made quite otherwise by an agreeable Conversation.

SAINTE *Clemente de la Mancha*, is rendered famous by the renown'd *Don Michael Cerviantes*, who in his facetious but satyrical Romance, has fix'd it the Seat and Birth Place of his Hero *Don Quixot.*

The Gentlemen of this Place are the least Priest-ridden or Sons of Bigotry, of any that I met with in all *Spain*; of which in my Conversation with them I had daily Instances. Among many others, an Expression that fell from *Don Felix Pacheco*, a Gentleman of the best Figure thereabout, and of a very plentiful Fortune, shall now suffice. I was become very intimate with him; and we us'd often to converse together with a Freedom too dangerous to be common in a Country so enslav'd by the Inquisition. Asking me one Day in a sort of a jocose manner, who, in my Opinion, had done the greatest Miracles that ever were heard of? I answer'd, Jesus Christ.

"It is very true," says he, "Jesus Christ did great Miracles, and a great one it was to feed five Thousand People with two or three small Fishes, and a like number of Loaves: But *Saint Francis*, the Founder of the *Franciscan* Order, has found out a way to feed daily one hundred Thousand Lubbards with nothing at all"; meaning the *Franciscans*, the Followers of Saint *Francis*, who have no visible Revenues; yet in their way of Living come up to, if they do not exceed any other Order.

Another Day talking of the Place, it naturally led us into a Discourse of the Knight of *la Mancha, Don Quixot.* At which time he told me, that in his Opinion, that Work was a perfect Paradox, being the best and the worst Romance, that ever was wrote.

"For," says he, "tho' it must infallibly please every Man, that has any taste of Wit; yet has it had such a fatal Effect upon the Spirits of my Countrymen, that every Man of Wit must ever resent; for," continu'd he, "before the Appearance in the World of that Labour of *Cerviantes*, it was next to an Impossibility for a Man to walk the Streets with any Delight, or without Danger. There were seen so many Cavaliero's prancing and curvetting before the Windows of their Mistresses, that a Stranger would have imagin'd the whole Nation to have been nothing less than a Race of Knight Errants. But after the World became a little acquainted with that notable History; the Man that was seen in that once celebrated Drapery, was pointed at as a *Don Quixot*, and found himself the Jest of High and Low. And I verily believe," added he, "that to this, and this only we owe that dampness and poverty of Spirit, which has run thro' all our Councils for a Century past, so little agreeable to those nobler Actions of our famous Ancestors."

After many of these lesser sorts of Confidences, *Don Felix* recommended me to a Lodging next Door to his own. It was at a Widow's, who had one only Daughter, her House just opposite to a *Francisan* Nunnery. Here I remain'd somewhat upwards of two Years; all which time, lying in my Bed, I could hear the Nuns early in the Morning at their *Matins*, and late in the Evening at their *Vespers*, with Delight enough to my self, and without the least Indecency in the World in my Thoughts of them. Their own Divine Employ too much employ'd every Faculty of mine to entertain any Thing inconsentaneous or offensive.

This my Neighbourhood to the Nunnery gave me an opportunity of seeing two Nuns invested; and in this I must do a Justice to the whole Country, to acknowledge, that a Stranger who is curious (I would impute it rather to their hopes of Conversion, than to their Vanity) shall be admitted to much greater Freedoms in their religious Pageantries, than any Native.

One of these Nuns was of the first Quality, which render'd the Ceremony more remarkably fine. The manner of investing them was thus: In the Morning her Relations and Friends all met at her Father's House; whence, she being attir'd in her most sumptuous Apparel, and a Coronet plac'd on her Head, they attended her, in Cavalcade, to the Nunnery, the Streets and Windows being crowded, and fill'd with Spectators of all sorts.

So soon as she enter'd the Chapel belonging to the Nunnery, she kneel'd down, and with an appearance of much Devotion, saluted the Ground; then rising up, she advanced a Step or two farther, when on her Knees she repeated the Salutes: This done she approached to the Altar, where she remained till Mass was over: After which, a Sermon was preach'd by one of the Priests in Praise, or rather in an exalted Preference of a single Life. The Sermon being over, the Nun elect fell down on her Knees before the Altar; and after some short mental Oraisons, rising again, she withdrew into an inner Room, where stripping off all her rich Attire, she put on her Nun's Weeds: In which making her Appearance, she, again kneeling, offer'd up some private Devotions; which being over, she was led to the Door of the Nunnery, where the Lady and the rest of the Nuns stood ready to receive her with open Arms. Thus enter'd, the Nuns conducted her into the Quire, where after they had entertained her with Singing, and playing upon the Organ, the Ceremony concluded, and every one departed to their proper Habitations.

The very same Day of the Year ensuing the Relations and Friends of the fair Novitiate meet again in the Chapel of the Nunnery, where the Lady Abbess brings her out, and delivers her to them. Then again is there a Sermon preach'd on the same Subject as at first; which being over, she is brought up to the Altar, in a decent, but plain Dress, the fine Apparel, which she put off on her Initiation, being deposited on one side of the Altar, and her Nun's Weeds on the other. Here the Priest in Latin cries, *Utrum horum mavis, accipe*: to which she answers, as her Inclination, or as her Instruction directs her. If she, after this her Year of Probation, show any Dislike, she is at Liberty to come again into the World: But if aw'd by Fear (as too often is the Case) or won by Expectation, or present real Inclination, she makes choice of the Nun's Weeds, she is immediately invested, and must never expect to appear again in the World out of the Walls of the Nunnery. The young Lady I thus saw invested was very beautiful, and sang the best of any in the Nunnery.

There are in the Town three Nunneries, and a Convent to every one of them; *viz.* one of *Jesuits*, one of *Carmelites*, and the other of *Franciscans*. Let me not be so far mistaken to have this taken by way of Reflection. No! Whatever some of our Rakes of the Town may assert, I freely declare, that I never saw in any of the Nunneries (of which I have seen many both in *Spain* and other Parts of the World) any thing like indecent Behaviour, that might give occasion for Satyr or Disesteem. It is true, there may be Accidents, that may lead to a Misinterpretation, of which I remember a very untoward Instance in *Alicant*.

When the *English* Forces first laid Siege to that Town, the Priests, who were apprehensive of it, having been long since made sensible of the profound Regard to Chastity and Modesty of us Hereticks, by the ignominious Behaviour of certain Officers at *Rota* and *Porta St. Maria*, the Priests, I say, had taken care to send away privately all the Nuns to *Majorca*. But that the Heretick Invaders might have no Jealousy of it, the fair *Curtezans* of the Town were admitted to supply their Room.

The Officers, both of Land and Sea, as was by the Friars pre-imagin'd, on taking the Town and Castle, immediately repair'd to the Grates of the Nunnery, toss'd over their Handkercheifs, Nosegays, and other pretty Things; all which were, doubtless, very graciously received by those imaginary Recluses. Thence came it to pass, that in the space of a Month or less, you could hardly fall into Comany of any one of our younger Officers, of either sort, but the Discourse, if it might deserve the Name, was concerning these beautiful Nuns; and you wou'd have imagin'd the Price of these Ladies as well known as that of Flesh in their common Markets. Others, as well as my self, have often endeavour'd to disabuse those Glorioso's, but all to little purpose, till more sensible Tokens convinced them, that the Nuns, of whose Favours they so much boasted, could hardly be perfect Virgins, tho' in a Cloyster. And I am apt to think, those who would palm upon the World like vicious Relations of Nuns and Nunneries, do it on much like Grounds. Not that there are wanting Instances of Nunneries disfranchis'd, and even demolish'd, upon very flagrant Accounts; but I confine myself to *Spain*.

In this Town of *la Mancha* the *Corrigidore* always has his Presidence, having sixteen others under his Jurisdiction, of which *Almanza* is one. They are changed every three Years, and their Offices are the Purchase of an excessive Price; which occasions the poor People's being extravagantly fleeced, nothing being to be sold but at the Rates they impose; and every Thing that is sold paying the *Corrigidore* an Acknowledgment in specie, or an Equivalent to his liking.

While I was here, News came of the Battle of *Almanar* and *Saragosa*; and giving the Victory to that Side, which they espous'd (that of King *Philip*) they made very great Rejoycings. But soon, alas, for them, was all that Joy converted into Sorrow: The next Courier evincing, that the Forces of King *Charles* had been victorious in both Engagements. This did not turn to my present Disadvantage: For Convents and Nunneries, as well as some of those Dons, whom afore I had not stood so well with, strove now how most to oblige me; not doubting, but if the victorious Army should march that way, it might be in my Power to double the most signal of their Services in my Friendship.

Soon after an Accident fell out, which had like to have been of an unhappy Consequence to me. I was standing in Company, upon the Parade, when a most surprizing flock of Eagles flew over our Heads, where they hover'd for a considerable time. The Novelty struck them all with Admiration, as well as my self. But I, less accustomed to like Spectacles, innocent saying, that in my Opinion, it could not bode any good to King *Philip*, because the Eagle compos'd the Arms of *Austria*; some busie Body, in hearing, went and inform'd the *Corrigidore* of it. Those most magisterial Wretches embrace all Occasions of squeezing Money; and more especially from Strangers. However finding his Expectations disappointed in me, and that I too well knew the length of his Foot, to let my Money run freely; he sent me next Day to *Alercon*; but the Governor of that Place having had before Intelligence, that the *English* Army was advancing that way, refus'd to receive me, so I return'd as I went; only the Gentlemen of the Place, as they had condol'd the first, congratulated the last; for that *Corrigidore* stood but very indifferently in their Affections. However, it was a warning to me ever after, how I made use of *English* Freedom in a *Spanish* Territory.

As I had attain'd the Acquaintance of most of the Clergy, and Religious of the Place; so particularly I had my aim in obtaining that of the Provincial of the *Carmelites*. His Convent, tho' small, was exceeding neat; but what to me was much more agreeable, There were very large Gardens belonging to it, which often furnished me with Sallading and Fruit, and much oftner with Walks of Refreshment, the most satisfactory Amusement in this warm Climate. This Acquaintance with the Provincial was by a little Incident soon advanced into a Friendship; which was thus: I was one Day walking, as I us'd to do, in the long Gallery of the Convent, when observing the Images of the Virgin *Mary*, of which there was one at each end; I took notice that one had an Inscription under it, which was this, *Ecce, Virgo peperit filium*: but the other had no Inscription at all; upon which, I took out my Pencil, and wrote underneath, this Line:

Sponsa Dei, patrisque parens, & filia filii.

The Friars, who at a little distance had observed me, as soon as I was gone, came up and read what I had writ; reporting which to the Provincial, he order'd them to be writ over in Letters of Gold, and plac'd just as I had put 'em; saying, doubtless, such a fine Line you'd proceed from nothing less than Inspiration. This secur'd me ever after his and their Esteem; the least advantage of which, was a full Liberty of their Garden for all manner of Fruit, Sallading, or whatever I pleased: And as I said before, the Gardens were too fine not to render such a Freedom acceptable.

They often want Rain in this Country: To supply the Defect of which, I observed in this Garden, as well as others, an Invention not unuseful. There is a Well in the Middle of the Garden, and over that a Wheel with many Pitchers, or Buckets, one under another, which Wheel being turned round by an Ass, the Pitchers scoop up the Water on one Side, and throw it out on the other into a Trough, that by little Channels conveys it, as the Gardiner directs, into every part of the Garden. By this Means their Flowers and their Sallading are continually refresh'd, and preserved from the otherwise over-parching Beams of the Sun.

The Inquisition, in almost every Town in *Spain* (and more especially, if of any great Account) has its Spies, or Informers, for treacherous Intelligence. These make it their Business to ensnare the simple and unguarded; and are more to be avoided by the Stranger, than the Rattle Snake. Nature have appointed no such happy Tokens in the former to foreshew the Danger. I had Reason to believe, that one of those Vermin once made his Attack upon me in this place: And as they are very rarely, if ever known to the Natives themselves, I being a Stranger, may be allowed to make a guess by Circumstances.

I was walking by my self, when a Person, wholly unknown to me, giving me the civil Salute of the Day, endeavour'd to draw me into Conversation. After Questions had passed on general Heads, the fellow ensnaringly asked me, how it came to pass, that I show'd so little Respect to the Image of the crucify'd Jesus, as I pass'd by it in such a Street, naming it? I made Answer, that I had, or ought to have him always in my Heart crucified. To that he made no Reply: But proceeding in his Interrogatories, question'd me next, whether I believ'd a Purgatory? I evaded the Question, as I took it to be ensnaring; and only told him, that I should be willing to hear him offer any Thing that might convince me of the Truth, or Probability of it. Truth? He reply'd in a Heat: There never yet was Man so Holy as to enter Heaven without first passing through Purgatory. In my Opinion, said I, there will be no Difficulty in convincing a reasonable Man to the contrary. What mean you by that, cry'd the Spy? I mean, said I, that I can name one, and a great Sinner too, who went into Bliss without any Visit to Purgatory. Name him, if you can, reply'd my Querist. What think you of the Thief upon the Cross, said I? to whom our dying Saviour said, *Hodie eris mecum in Paradiso.* At which being silenced tho' not convicted, he turned from me in a violent Rage, and left me to my self.

What increas'd my first Suspicion of him was, that a very short time after, my Friend the Provincial sent to speak with me; and repeating all Passages between the holy Spy and me, assur'd me that he had been forc'd to argue in my Favour, and tell him that I had said nothing but well: *For* says he, *all ought to have the Holy Jesus crucified in their Hearts.*

"Nevertheless," continu'd he, "it is a commendable and good Thing to have him represented in the high Ways: For, suppose," said he, "a Man was going upon some base or profligate Design, the very Sight of a crucified Saviour may happen to subvert his Resolution, and deter him from committing Theft, Murder, or any other of the deadly Sins." And thus ended that Conference.

I remember upon some other occasional Conversation after, the Provincial told me, that in the *Carmelite* Nunnery next to his Convent, and under his Care, there was a Nun, that was Daughter to *Don Juan* of *Austria*; if so, her Age must render her venerable, as her Quality.

Taking notice one Day, that all the People of the Place fetch'd their Water from a Well without the Town, altho' they had many seemingly as good within; I spoke to *Don Felix* of it, who gave me, under the Seal of Secrecy, this Reason for it:

"When the Seat of the War," said he, "lay in these Parts, the *French* Train of Artillery was commonly quarter'd in this Place; the Officers and Soldiers of which were so very rampant and rude, in attempting to debauch our Women, that there is not a Well within the Town, which has not some *French* Mens Bones at the bottom of it; therefore the Natives, who are sensible of it, choose rather to go farther a field."

By this Well there runs a little Rivulet, which gives head to that famous River call'd the *Guadiana*; which running for some Leagues under Ground, affords a pretence for the Natives to boast of a Bridge on which they feed many Thousands of Sheep. When it rises again, it is a fine large River, and after a Currency of many Leagues, empties it self into the *Atlantick* Ocean.

As to military Affairs, *Almanar* and *Saragosa* were Victories so compleat, that no Body made the least doubt of their settling the Crown of *Spain* upon the Head of *Charles* the Third, without a Rival. This was not barely the Opinion of his Friends, but his very Enemies resign'd all Hope or Expectation in favour of King *Philip*. The *Castilians*, his most faithful Friends, entertain'd no other Imagination; for after they had advis'd, and prevail'd that the Queen with the Prince of *Asturias* should be sent to *Victoria*; under the same Despondency, and a full Dispiritedness, they gave him so little Encouragement to stay in *Madrid*, that he immediately quitted the Place, with a Resolution to retire into his Grandfather's Dominions, the Place of his Nativity.

In his way to which, even on the last Day's Journey, it was his great good Fortune to meet the Duke of *Vendome*, with some few Troops, which his Grandfather *Lewis* XIV. of *France* had order'd to his Succour, under that Duke's Command. The Duke was grievously affected at such an unexpected Catastrophe; nevertheless, he left nothing unsaid or undone, that might induce that Prince to turn back; and at length prevailing, after a little Rest, and a great deal of Patience, by the Coming in of his scatter'd Troops, and some few he could raise, together with those the Duke brought with him, he once more saw himself at the Head of twenty thousand Men.

While Things were in this Manner, under Motion in King *Philip's* Favour, *Charles* the third, with his victorious Army, advances forward, and enters into *Madrid*, of which he made General *Stanhope* Governor. And even here the *Castilians* gave full Proof of their Fidelity to their Prince; even at the Time when, in their Opinion, his Affairs were past all Hopes of Retrieve, they themselves having, by their Advice, contributed to his Retreat. Instead of prudential Acclamations therefore, such as might have answered the Expectations of a victorious Prince, now entering into their Capital, their Streets were all in a profound Silence, their Balconies unadorn'd with costly Carpets, as was customary on like Occasions; and scarce an Inhabitant to be seen in either Shop or Window.

This doubtless was no little Mortification to a conquering Prince; however his Generals were wife enough to keep him from shewing any other Tokens of Resentment, than marching through the City with Unconcern, and taking up his Quarters at *Villa-verda*, about a League from it.

Nevertheless King *Charles* visited, in his March, the Chapel of the Lady *de Atocha*, where finding several *English* Colours and Standards, taken in the Battle of *Almanza*, there hung up; he ordered 'em to be taken down, and restor'd 'em to the *English* General.

It was the current Opinion then, and almost universal Consent has since confirm'd it, that the falsest Step in that whole War was this Advancement of King *Charles* to *Madrid*. After those two remarkable Victories at *Almanar* and *Saragosa*, had he directed his March to *Pampeluna*, and obtain'd Possession of that Place, or some other near it, he had not only stopt all Succours from coming out of *France*, but he would, in a great Measure, have prevented the gathering together of any of the routed and dispers'd Forces of King *Philip.* And it was the general Notion of the *Spaniards,* I convers'd with while at *Madrid,* that had King *Philip* once again set his Foot upon *French* Land, *Spain* would never have been brought to have re-acknowledged him.

King *Charles* with his Army having stay'd some Time about *Madrid,* and seeing his Expectations of the *Castilians* joining him not at all answered, at last resolved to decamp, and return to *Saragosa.* Accordingly with a very few Troops that Prince advanced thither; while the main Body, under the Command of the Generals *Stanhope* and *Staremberg,* passing under the very Walls of *Madrid,* held on their March towards *Aragon.*

After about three Days' March, General *Stanhope* took up his Quarters at *Breuhiga,* a small Town half wall'd; General *Staremberg* marching three Leagues farther, to *Cisuentes.* This choice of Situation of the two several Armies not a little puzzled the Politicians of those Times, who could very indifferently account for the *English* General's lying expos'd in an open Town, with his few *English* Forces, of which General *Harvey's* Regiment of fine Horse might be deem'd the Main; and General *Staremberg* encamping three Leagues farther off the Enemy. But to see the Vicissitudes of Fortune, to which the Actions of the bravest, by an untoward Sort of Fatality, are often forced to contribute! None, who had been Eye-witnesses of the Bravery of either of those Generals at the Battles of *Almanar* and *Saragosa,* could find Room to call in question either their Conduct or their Courage; and yet in this March, and this Encampment will appear a visible ill Consequence to the Affairs of the Interest they fought for.

The Duke of *Vendome* having increas'd the Forces which he brought from *France,* to upwards of twenty thousand Men, marches by *Madrid* directly for *Breuhiga,* where his Intelligence inform'd him General *Stanhope* lay, and that so secretly as well as swiftly, that that General knew nothing of it, nor could be persuaded to believe it, till the very Moment their Bullets from the Enemy's Cannon convinc'd him of the Truth. *Breuhiga,* I have said, was wall'd only on one Side, and yet on that very side the Enemy made their Attack. But what could a Handful do against a Force so much superior, though they had not been in want of both Powder and Ball; and in want of these were forc'd to make use of Stones against all Sorts of Ammunition, which the Enemy ply'd them with? The Consequence answered the Deficiency; they were all made Prisoners of War, and *Harvey's* Regiment of Horse among the rest; which, to augment their Calamity, was immediately remounted by the Enemy, and march'd along with their Army to attack General *Staremberg*.

That General had heard somewhat of the March of *Vendome*; and waited with some Impatience to have the Confirmation of it from General *Stanhope*, who lay between, and whom he lay under an Expectation of being joined with: However he thought it not improper to make some little Advance towards him; and accordingly breaking up from his Camp at *Cisuentes*, he came back to *Villa viciosa*, a little Town between *Cisuentes* and *Breuhiga*; there he found *Vendome* ready to attack him, before he could well be prepared for him, but no *English* to join him, as he had expected; nevertheless, the Battle was hot, and obstinately fought; although *Staremberg* had visibly the Advantage, having beat the Enemy at least a League from their Cannon; at which Time hearing of the Misfortune of *Breuhiga*, and finding himself thereby frustrated of those expected Succours to support him, he made a handsome Retreat to *Barcelona*, which in common Calculation is about one hundred Leagues, without any Disturbance of an Enemy that seem'd glad to be rid of him. Nevertheless his Baggage having fallen into the Hands of the Enemy, at the Beginning of the Fight, King *Philip* and the Duke of *Vendome* generously returned it unopen'd, and untouched, in acknowledgement of his brave Behaviour.

I had like to have omitted one material Passage, which I was very credibly informed of; That General *Carpenter* offered to have gone, and have join'd General *Staremberg* with the Horse, which was refus'd him. This was certainly an Oversight of the highest Nature; since his going would have strengthen'd *Staremberg* almost to the Assurance of an intire Victory; whereas his Stay was of no manner of Service, but quite the contrary: For, as I said before, the Enemy, by re-mounting the *English* Horse (which perhaps were the compleatest of any Regiment in the World) turn'd, if I may be allowed the Expression, the Strength of our Artillery upon our Allies.

Upon this Retreat of *Staremberg*, and the Surprize at *Breuhiga*, there were great Rejoicings at *Madrid*, and everywhere else, where King *Philip's* Interest prevailed. And indeed it might be said, from that Day the Interest of King *Charles* look'd with a very lowering Aspect. I was still a Prisoner at *la Mancha*, when this News arriv'd; and very sensibly affected at that strange Turn of Fortune. I was in bed, when the Express pass'd through the Town, in order to convey it farther; and in the Middle of the Night I heard a certain *Spanish* Don, with whom, a little before, I had had some little Variance, thundering at my Door, endeavouring to burst it open, with, as I had Reason to suppose, no very favourable Design upon me. But my Landlady, who hitherto had always been kind and careful, calling Don *Felix*, and some others of my Friends together, sav'd me from the Fury of his Designs, whatever they were.

Among other Expressions of the general Joy upon this Occasion, there was a Bull-Feast at *la Mancha*; which being much beyond what I saw at *Valencia*, I shall here give a Description of. These Bull-Feasts are not so common now in *Spain* as formerly, King *Philip* not taking much Delight in them. Nevertheless, as soon as it was publish'd here, that there was to be one, no other Discourse was heard; and in the Talk of the Bulls, and the great Preparations for the Feast, Men seem'd to have lost, or to have lay'd aside, all Thoughts of the very Occasion. A Week's time was allow'd for the Building of Stalls for the Beasts, and Scaffolds for the Spectators; and other necessary Preparations for the setting off their Joy with the most suitable Splendour.

On the Day appointed for the bringing the Bulls into Town, the *Cavalieroes* mounted their Horses, and, with Spears in their Hands, rode out of Town about a League, or somewhat more to meet them: If any of the Bulls break from the Drove, and make an Excursion (as they frequently do) the *Cavaliero* that can make him return again to his Station among his Companions, is held in Honour, suitable to the Dexterity and Address he performs it with. On their Entrance into the Town, all the Windows are fill'd with Spectators; a Pope passing in grand Procession could not have more; for what can be more than all? And he or she who should neglect so rare a Show, would give Occasion to have his or her Legitimacy call'd in Question.

When they come to the *Plaza*, where the Stalls and Scaffolds are built, and upon which the Feats of Chivalry are to be performed, it is often with a great deal of Difficulty that the Brutes are got in; for there are twelve Stalls, one for every Bull, and as their Number grows less by the enstalling of some, the Remainder often prove more untractable and unruly: In these Stalls they are kept very dark, to render them fiercer for the Day of Battle.

On the first of the Days appointed (for a Bull-Feast commonly lasts three) all the Gentry of the Place, or near adjacent, resort to the *Plaza* in their most gaudy Apparel, every one vieing in making the most glorious Appearance. Those in the lower Ranks provide themselves with Spears, or a great many small Darts in their Hands, which they fail not to cast or dart, whenever the Bull by his Nearness gives them an

Opportunity. So that the poor Creature may be said to fight, not only with the Tauriro (or Bullhunter, a Person always hired for that Purpose) but with the whole Multitude in the lower Class at least.

All being seated, the uppermost Door is open'd first; and as soon as ever the Bull perceives the Light, out he comes, snuffing up the Air, and stareing about him, as if in admiration of his attendants; and with his Tail cock'd up, he spurns the Ground with his Forefeet, as if he intended a Challenge to his yet unappearing Antagonist. Then at a Door appointed for that purpose, enters the Tauriro all in white, holding a Cloak in one Hand, and a sharp two edged Sword in the other. The Bull no sooner sets Eyes upon him, but wildly staring, he moves gently towards him; then gradually mends his pace, till he is come within about the space of twenty Yards of the Tauriro; when, with a sort of Spring, he makes at him with all his might. The Tauriro knowing by frequent Experience, that it behoves him to be watchful, slips aside just when the Bull is at him; when casting his Cloak over his Horns, at the same Moment he gives him a slash or two, always aiming at the Neck, where there is one particular Place, which if he hit, he knows he shall easily bring him to the Ground. I my Self observ'd the truth of this Experiment made upon one of the Bulls, who receiv'd no more than one Cut, which happening upon the fatal Spot, so stun'd him, that he remain'd perfectly stupid, the Blood flowing out from the Wound, till after a violent Trembling he dropt down stone dead.

But this rarely happens, and the poor Creature oftner receives many Wounds, and numberless Darts, before he dies. Yet whenever he feels a fresh Wound either from Dart, Spear, or Sword, his Rage receives addition from the Wound, and he pursues his Tauriro with an Increase of Fury and Violence. And as often as he makes at his Adversary, the Tauriro takes care with the utmost of his Agility to avoid him, and reward his kind Intention with a new Wound.

Some of their Bulls will play their Parts much better than others: But the best must die. For when they have behav'd themselves with all the commendable Fury possible; if the Tauriro is spent, and fail of doing Execution upon him, they set Dogs upon him: Hough him and stick him all over with Darts, till with very loss of Blood he puts an end to their present Cruelty.

When dead, a Man brings in two Mules dress'd out with Bells and Feathers, and fastening a Rope about his Horns, draws off the Bull with the Shouts and Acclamations of the Spectators; as if the Infidels had been drove from before *Ceuta*.

I had almost forgot another very common piece of barbarous Pleasure at these Diversions. The Tauriro will sometimes stick one of their Bull Spears fast in the Ground, aslant, but levell'd as near as he can at his Chest; then presenting himself to the Bull, just before the point of the Spear, on his taking his run at the Tauriro, which, as they assur'd me, he always does with his Eyes closed, the Tauriro slips on one side, and the poor Creature runs with a violence often to stick himself, and sometimes to break the Spear in his Chest, running away with part of it till he drop.

This *Tauriro* was accounted one of the best in *Spain*; and indeed I saw him mount the back of one of the Bulls, and ride on him, slashing and cutting, till he had quite wearied him; at which time dismounting, he kill'd him with much Ease, and to the acclamatory Satisfaction of the whole Concourse: For variety of Cruelty, as well as Dexterity, administers to their Delight.

The *Tauriroes* are very well paid; and in Truth so they ought to be; for they often lose their Lives in the Diversion, as this did the Year after in the way of his Calling. Yet is it a Service of very great Profit when they perform dextrously: For when ever they do any Thing remarkable, deserving the Notice of the Spectators, they never fail of a generous Gratification, Money being thrown down to 'em in plenty.

This Feast (as they generally do) lasted three Days; the last of which was, in my Opinion, much before either of the other. On this, a young Gentleman, whose Name was *Don Pedro Ortega*, a Person of great Quality, perform'd the Exercise on Horseback. The Seats, if not more crowded, were filled with People of better Fashion, who came from Places at a distance to grace the noble *Tauriro*.

He was finely mounted, and made a very graceful Figure; but as when the Foot *Tauriro* engages, the Bull first enters, so in the Contest the *Cavaliero* always makes his Appearance on the *Plaza* before the Bull. His Steed was a manag'd Horse; mounted on which he made his Entry, attended by four Footmen in rich Liveries; who, as soon as their Master had rid round, and paid his Devoirs to all the Spectators, withdrew from the Dangers they left him expos'd to. The *Cavaliero* having thus made his Bows, and received the repeated Vivas of that vast Concourse, march'd with a very stately Air to the very middle of the *Plaza*, there standing ready to receive his Enemy at coming out.

The Door being open'd, the Bull appeared; and as I thought with a fiercer and more threatning Aspect that any of the former. He star'd around him for a considerable time, snuffing up the Air, and spurning the Ground, without in the least taking notice of his Antagonist. But at last fixing his Eyes upon him, he made a full run at the *Cavaliero*, which he most dexterously avoided, and at the same moment of time, passing by, he cast a Dart that stuck in his Shoulders. At this the Shouts and *Vivas* were repeated; and I observed a Handkerchief wav'd twice or thrice, which, as I afterwards understood, was a Signal from the Lady of his Affections, that she had beheld him with Satisfaction. I took notice that the *Cavaliero* endeavour'd all he could to keep aside the Bull, for the Advantage of the Stroke, when putting his Horse on a full Career, he threw another Dart, which fix'd in his Side, and so enrag'd the Beast, that he seem'd to renew his Attacks with greater Fury. The *Cavaliero* had behav'd himself to Admiration, and escap'd many Dangers; with the often repeated Acclamations of *Viva, Viva*; when at last the enraged Creature getting his Horns between the Horse's hinder Legs, Man and Horse came both together to the Ground.

I expected at that Moment nothing less than Death could be the Issue; when to the general Surprize, as well as mine, the very civil Brute, Author of all the Mischief, only withdrew to the other Side of the *Plaza*, where he stood still, staring about him as if he knew nothing of the Matter.

The *Cavaliero* was carry'd off not much hurt, but his delicate Beast suffer'd much more. However I could not but think afterward, that the good natur'd Bull came short of fair Play. If I may be pardon'd the Expression, he had us'd his Adversary with more Humanity than he met with; at least, since, after he had the *Cavaliero* under, he generously forsook him; I think he might have pleaded, or others for him, for better Treatment than he after met with.

For as the *Cavaliero* was disabled and carry'd off, the Foot *Tauriro* enter'd in white Accoutrements, as before; but he flatter'd himself with an easier Conquest than he found: there is always on these Occasions, when he apprehends any imminent Danger, a Place of Retreat ready for the Foot *Tauriro*; and well for him there was so; this Bull oblig'd him over and over to make Use of it. Nor was he able at last to dispatch him, without a general Assistance; for I believe I speak within Compass, when I say, he had more than an hundred Darts stuck in him. And so barbarously was he mangled, and flash'd besides, that, in my Mind, I could not but think King *Philip* in the Right, when he said, *That it was a Custom deserv'd little Encouragement.*

Soon after this *Tauridore*, or Bull-Feast was over, I had a Mind to take a pleasant Walk to a little Town, call'd *Minai*, about three Leagues off; but I was scarce got out of *la Mancha*, when an Acquaintance meeting me, ask'd where I was going? I told him to *Minar*; when taking me by the Hand, *Friend* Gorgio, says he in *Spanish, Come back with me; you shall not go a Stride further; there are* Picarons *that Way; you shall not go*. Inquiring, as we went back, into his Meaning, he told me, that the Day before, a Man, who had received a Sum of Money in Pistoles at *la Mancha*, was, on the road, set upon by some, who had got notice of it, and murdered him; that not finding the Money expected about him (for he had cautiously enough left it in a Friend's Hands at *la Mancha*) they concluded he had swallowed it; and therefore they ript up his Belly, and open'd every Gut; but all to as little Purpose. This diverted my Walk for that time.

But some little Time after, the same Person inviting me over to the same Place, to see his Melon-Grounds, which in that Country are wonderful fine and pleasant; I accepted his Invitation, and under the Advantage of his Company, went thither. On the Road I took notice of a Cross newly erected, and a Multitude of small stones around the Foot of it: Asking the Meaning whereof, my Friend told me, that it was rais'd for a Person there murder'd (as is the Custom throughout *Spain*) and that every good Catholick passing by, held it his Duty to cast a Stone upon the Place, in Detestation of the Murder. I had often before taken Notice of many such Crosses: but never till then knew the Meaning of their Erection, or the Reason of the Heaps of Stones around them.

There is no Place in all *Spain* more famous for good Wine than *Sainte Clemente de la Mancha*; nor is it any where sold cheaper: For as it is only an inland Town, near no navigable River, and the People temperate to a Proverb, great Plenty, and a small Vend must consequently make it cheap. The Wine here is so famous, that, when I came to *Madrid*, I saw wrote over the Doors of host Houses that sold Wine, *Vino Sainte Clemente*. As to the Temperance of the People, I must say, that notwithstanding those two excellent Qualities of good and cheap, I never saw, all the three Years I was Prisoner there, any one Person overcome with Drinking.

It is true, there may be a Reason, and a political one, assign'd for that Abstemiousness of theirs, which is this, That if any Man, upon any Occasion, should be brought in as an Evidence against you, if you can prove that he was ever drunk, it will invalidate his whole Evidence. I could not but think this a grand Improvement upon the *Spartans*. They made their Slaves purposely drunk, to shew their Youth the Folly of the Vice by the sottish Behaviour of their Servants under it: But they never reach'd to that noble height of laying a Penalty upon the Aggressor, or of discouraging a voluntary Impotence of Reason by a disreputable Impotence of Interest. The *Spaniard* therefore, in my Opinion, in this exceeds the *Spartan*, as much as a natural Beauty exceeds one procured by Art; for tho' Shame may somewhat influence some few, Terrour is of force to deter all. A Man, we have seen it, may shake Hands with Shame; but *Interest*, says another Proverb, *will never lye*. A wise Institution therefore doubtless is this of the *Spaniard*; but such as I fear will never take Place in *Germany, Holland, France*, or *Great Britain*.

But though I commend their Temperance, I would not be thought by any Means to approve of their Bigotry. If there may be such a Thing as Intemperance in Religion, I much fear their Ebriety in that will be found to be over-measure. Under the notion of Devotion, I have seen Men among 'em, and of Sense too, guilty of the grossest Intemperancies. It is too common to be a rarity to see their Dons of the prime Quality as well as those of the lower Ranks, upon meeting a Priest in the open Streets, condescend to take up the lower part of his Vestment, and salute it with Eyes erected as if they look'd upon it as the Seal of Salvation.

When the *Ave-Bell* is heard, the Hearer must down on his Knees upon the very Spot; nor is he allowed the small Indulgence of deferring a little, till he can recover a clean Place; Dirtiness excuses not, nor will dirty Actions by any means exempt. This is so notorious, that even at the Play-house, in the middle of a Scene, on the first sound of the Bell, the Actors drop their Discourse, the Auditors supersede the indulging of their unsanctified Ears, and all on their Hearts, quite a different way, to what they just before had been employ'd in. In short, tho' they pretend in all this to an extraordinary Measure of Zeal and real Devotion; no Man, that lives among them any time, can be a Proselyte to them without immolating his Senses and his Reason: Yet I must confess, while I have seen them thus deludeing themselves with *Ave Marias*, I you'd not refrain throwing up my Eyes to the only proper Object of Adoration, in commiseration of such Delusions.

The Hours of the *Ave Bell*, are eight and twelve in the Morning, and six in the Evening. They pretend at the first to fall down in beg that God would be pleas'd to prosper them in all things they go about that Day. At twelve they return Thanks for their Preservation to that time; and at six for that of the whole Day. After which, one would think that they imagine themselves at perfect Liberty; and their open Gallantries perfectly countenance the Imagination: for tho' Adultery is look'd upon as a grievous Crime, and punish'd accordingly; yet Fornication is softened with the title of a Venial Sin, and they seem to practise it under that Persuasion.

I found here, what *Erasmus* ridicules with so much Wit and Delicacy, the custom of burying in a *Franciscan's* Habit, in mighty request. If they can for that purpose procure an old one at the price of a new one; the Purchaser wil look upon himself a provident Chap, that has secur'd to his deceased Friend or Relation, no less than Heaven by that wise Bargain.

The Evening being almost the only time of Enjoyment of Company, or Conversation, every body in *Spain* then greedily seeks it; and the Streets are at that time crowded like our finest Gardens or most private Walks. On one of those Occasions, I met a Don of my Acquaintance walking out with his Sisters; and as I thought it became an *English* Cavalier, I saluted him: But to my Surprize he never return'd the Civility. When I met him the Day after, instead of an Apology, as I had flattered my self, I received a Reprimand, tho' a very civil one; telling me it was the Custom in *Spain*, nor well taken of any one, that took Notice of any who were walking in the Company of Ladies at Night.

But a Night or two after, I found by Experience, that if the Men were by Custom prohibited taking Notice, Women were not. I was standing at the Door, in the cool of the Evening, when a Woman seemingly genteel, passing by, call'd me by my Name, telling me she wanted to speak with me: She had her *Mantilio* on; so that had I had Day-light, I could have only seen one Eye of her. However I walk'd with her a good while, without being able to discover any thing of her Business, nor pass'd there between us any thing more than a Conversation upon indifferent Matters. Nevertheless, at parting she told me she should pass by again the next Evening; and if I would be at the Door, she would give me the same Advantage of a Conversation, That seem'd not to displease me. Accordingly the next Night she came, and as before we walk'd together in the privatest parts of the Town: For tho' I knew her not, her Discourse was always entertaining and full of Wit, and her Enquiries not often improper. We had continu'd this Intercourse many Nights together, when my Landlady's Daughter having taken Notice of it, stopt me one Evening, and would not allow me to stand at the usual Post of Intelligence, saying, with a good deal of heat, *Don Gorgio, take my Advice; go no more along with that Woman: You may soon be brought home deprived of your Life if you do.* I cannot say, whether she knew her; but this I must say, she was very agreeable in Wit as well as Person. However my Landlady and her Daughter took that Opportunity of giving me so many Instances of the fatal Issues of such innocent Conversations, (for I could not call it an Intrigue) that apprehensive enough of the Danger, on laying Circumstances together, I took their Advice, and never went into her Company after.

Sainte Clemente de la Mancha, where I so long remain'd a Prisoner of War, lies in the Road from *Madrid* to *Valencia;* and the Duke of *Vendome* being ordered to the latter, great Preparations were made for his Entertainment, as he pass'd through. He stay'd here only one Night, where he was very handsomely treated by the *Corrigidore.* He was a tall fair Person, and very fat, and at the time I saw him wore a long black Patch over his left Eye; but on what Occasion I could not learn. The afterwards famous *Alberoni* (since made a Cardinal) was in his Attendance; as indeed the Duke was very rarely without him. I remember that very Day three Weeks, they return'd through the same Place; the Duke in his Herse, and *Alberoni* in a Coach, paying his last Duties. That Duke was a prodigious Lover of Fish, of which having eat over heartily at *Veneros,* in the Province of *Valencia,* he took a Surfeit, and died in three Days' time. His Corps was carrying to the *Escurial,* there to be buried in the *Panthæon* among their Kings.

The *Castilians* have a Privilege by Licence from the Pope, which, if it could have been converted into a Prohibition, might have sav'd that Duke's Life: In regard their Country is wholly inland, and the River *Tagus* famous for its Poverty, or rather Barrenness; their Holy Father indulges the Natives with the Liberty, in lieu of that dangerous Eatable, of eating all Lent time the Inwards of Cattle. When I first heard this related, I imagin'd, that the Garbidge had been intended, but I was soon after this rectify'd, *by Inwards* (for so expressly says the Licence it self) *is meant the Heart, the Liver, and the Feet.*

They have here as well as in most other Parts of *Spain, Valencia* excepted, the most wretched Musick in the Universe. Their *Guitars,* if not their *Sole,* are their darling Instruments, and what they most delight in: Tho' in my Opinion our *English* Sailors are not much amiss in giving them the Title of *Strum Strums.* They are little better than our *Jews-harps,* tho' hardly half so Musical. Yet are they perpetually at Nights disturbing their Women with the Noise of them, under the notion and name of Serenadoes. From the Barber to the Grandee the Infection spreads, and very often with the same Attendant, Danger:

Night Quarrels and Rencounters being the frequent Result. The true born *Spaniards* reckon it a part of their Glory, to be jealous of their Mistresses, which is too often the Forerunner of Murders; at best attended with many other very dangerous Inconveniences. And yet bad as their Musick is, their Dancing is the reverse. I have seen a Country Girl manage her Castanets with the graceful Air of a Dutchess, and that not to common Musick; but to Peoples beating or druming a Tune with their Hands on a Table. I have seen half a Dozen couple at a time dance to the like in excellent order.

I just now distinguish'd, by an Exception, the Music of *Valencia*, where alone I experienced the use of the Violin; which tho' I cannot, in respect to other Countries, call good; yet in respect to the other parts of *Spain*, I must acknowledge it much the best. In my Account of that City, I omitted to speak of it; therefore now to supply that Defect, I will speak of the best I heard, which was on this unfortunate Occasion: Several Natives of that Country having received Sentence of Death for their Adherence to King *Charles*, were accordingly ordered to the Place of Execution. It is the Custom there, on all such Occasions, for all the Musick of the City to meet near the Gallows, and play the most affecting and melancholy Airs, to the very approach of the Condemn'd; and really the Musick was so moving, it heightened the Scene of Sorrow, and brought Compassion into the Eyes of even Enemies.

As to the Condemn'd, they came stript of their own Cloaths, and cover'd with black Frocks, in which they were led along the Streets to the Place of Execution, the Friars praying all the way. When they came through any Street, were any public Images were fix'd, they stay'd before 'em some reasonable time in Prayer with the Friars. When they are arriv'd at the fatal Place, those Fathers leave 'em not, but continue praying and giving them ghostly Encouragement, standing upon the rounds of the Ladder till they are turn'd off. The Hangman always wears a silver Badge of a Ladder to distinguish his Profession: But his manner of executing his Office had somewhat in it too singular to allow of Silence. When he had ty'd fast the Hands of the Criminal, he rested his Knee upon them, and with one Hand on the Criminal's Nostrils, to stop his Breath the sooner, threw himself off the Ladder along with the dying Party. This he does to expedite his Fate; tho' considering the Force, I wonder it does not tear Head and Body asunder; which yet I never heard that it did.

But to return to *la Mancha*; I had been there now upwards of two Years, much diverted with the good Humour and Kindness of the

Gentlemen, and daily pleased with the Conversation of the Nuns of the Nunnery opposite to my Lodgings; when walking one Day alone upon the *Plaza*, I found my self accosted by a *Clerico*. At the first Attack, he told me his Country: But added, that he now came from *Madrid* with a *Potent*, that was his Word, from *Pedro de Dios*, Dean of the Inquisition, to endeavour the Conversion of any of the *English* Prisoners; that being an *Irish-man*, as a sort of a Brother, he had conceived a Love for the *English*, and therefore more eagerly embraced the Opportunity which the Holy Inquisition had put into his Hands for the bringing over to Mother Church as many Hereticks as he could; that having heard a very good Character of me, he should think himself very happy, if he could be instrumental in my Salvation;

"It is very true, continu'd he, I have lately had the good Fortune to convert many; and besides the Candour of my own Disposition, I must tell you, that I have a peculiar knack at Conversion, which very few, if any, ever could resist. I am going upon the same work into *Murcia*; but your good Character is fix'd me in my Resolution of preferring your Salvation to that of others."

To this very long, and no less surprising Address, I only return'd, that it being an Affair of moment, it would require some Consideration; and that by the time he return'd from *Murcia*, I might be able to return him a proper Answer. But not at all satisfy'd with this Reply;

"Sir," says he, "God Almighty is all-sufficient: This moment is too precious to be lost; he can turn the Heart in the twinkling of an Eye, as well as in twenty Years. Hear me then; mind what I say to you: I will convince you immediately. You Hereticks do not believe in Transubstantiation, and yet did not our Saviour say in so many Words, *Hoc est corpus meum?* And if you don't believe him, don't you give him the Lye? Besides, does not one of the Fatherss ay, *Deus, qui est omnis Veritas, non potest dicere falsum?*"

He went on at the same ridiculous rate; which soon convinced me, he was a thorough Rattle. However, as a *Clerico*, and consequently in this Country, a Man dangerous to disoblige, I invited him home to Dinner; where when I had brought him, I found I had no way done an unacceptable thing; for my Landlady and her Daughter, seeing him to be a Clergyman, receiv'd him with a vast deal of Respect and Pleasure.

Dinner being over, he began to entertain me with a Detail of the many wonderful Conversions he had made upon obstinate Hereticks; that he had convinced the most Stubborn, and had such a *Nostrum*, that he would undertake to convert any one. Here he began his old round, intermixing his Harangue with such scraps and raw sentences of fustian *Latin*, that I grew weary of his Conversation; so pretending some Business of consequence, I took leave, and left him and my Landlady together.

I did not return till pretty late in the Evening, with Intent to give him Time enough to think his own Visit tedious; but to my great Surprize, I found my *Irish* Missionary still on the Spot, ready to dare me to the Encounter, and resolv'd, like a true Son of the Church militant, to keep last on the Field of Battle. As soon as I had seated my self, he began again to tell me, how good a Character my Landlady had given me, which had prodigiously increased his Ardour of saving my Soul; that he could not answer it to his own Character, as well as mine, to be negligent; and therefore he had enter'd into a Resolution to stay my Coming, though it had been later. To all which, I return'd him Abundance of Thanks for his good Will, but pleading Indisposition and want of Rest, after a good deal of civil Impertinence, I once more got rid of him; at least, I took my Leave, and went to Bed, leaving him again Master of the Field; for I understood next Morning, that he stay'd some Time after I was gone, with my good Landlady.

Next Morning the Nuns of the Nunnery opposite, having taken Notice of the *Clerico's* Ingress, long Visit, and late Egress, sent to know whether he was my Countryman; with many other Questions, which I was not then let into the Secret of. To all which I return'd, that he was no Countryman of mine, but an *Irish-man*, and so perfectly a Stranger to me, that I knew no more of him than what I had from his own Mouth, that he was going into *Murcia*. What the Meaning of this Enquiry was, I could never learn; but I could not doubt, but it proceeded from their great Care of their *Vicino*, as they call'd me; a Mark of their Esteem, and of which I was not a little proud.

As was my usual Custom, I had been taking my Morning Walk, and had not been long come home in order to Dinner, when in again drops my *Irish Clerico*; I was confounded, and vexed, and he could not avoid taking Notice of it; nevertheless, without the least Alteration of Countenance, he took his Seat; and on my saying, in a cold and indifferent Tone, that I imagin'd he had been got to *Murcia* before this; he reply'd, with a natural Fleer, that truely he was going to *Murcia*, but his Conscience pricked him, and he did find that he could not go away with any Satisfaction, or Peace of Mind, without making me a perfect Convert; that he had plainly discovered in me a good Disposition, and had, for that very Reason, put himself to the Charge of Man and Mule, to the Bishop of *Cuenca* for a Licence, under his Hand, for my Conversion: For in *Spain*, all private Missionaries are obliged to ask Leave of the next Bishop, before they dare enter upon any Enterprize of this Nature.

I was more confounded at this last Assurance of the Man than at all before; and it put me directly upon reflecting, whether any, and what Inconveniences might ensue, from a Rencounter that I, at first, conceiv'd ridiculous, but might now reasonably begin to have more dangerous Apprehensions of. I knew, by the Articles of War, all Persons are exempted from any Power of the Inquisition; but whether carrying on a Part in such a Farce, might not admit, or at least be liable to some dangerous Construction, was not imprudently now to be considered. Though I was not fearful, yet I resolv'd to be cautious. Wherefore not making any Answer to his Declaration about the Bishop, he took Notice of it; and to raise a Confidence, he found expiring, began to tell me, that his Name was *Murtough Brennan*, that he was born near *Kilkenny*, of a very considerable Family. This last part indeed, when I came to *Madrid*, I found pretty well confirm'd in a considerable Manner. However, taking Notice that he had alter'd his Tone of leaving the Town, and that instead of it, he was advancing somewhat like an Invitation of himself to Dinner the next Day, I resolv'd to show my self shy of him; and thereupon abruptly, and without taking any Leave, I left the Room, and my Landlady and him together.

Three or four Days had passed, every one of which, he never fail'd my Lodgings; not at Dinner Time only, but Night and Morning too; from all which I began to suspect, that instead of my Conversion, he had fix'd upon a Re-conversion of my Landlady. She was not young, yet, for a black Woman, handsom enough; and her Daughter very pretty: I entered into a Resolution to make my Observations, and watch them all at a Distance; nevertheless carefully concealing my Jealousy. However, I must confess, I was not a little pleas'd, that any Thing could divert my own Persecution. He was now no longer my Guest, but my Landlady's, with whom I found him so much taken up, that a little Care might frustrate all his former impertinent Importunities on the old Topick.

But all my Suspicions were very soon after turn'd into Certainties, in this Manner: I had been abroad, and returning somewhat weary, I went to my Chamber, to take, what in that Country they call, a *Cesto*, upon my Bed: I got in unseen, or without seeing any Body, but had scarce laid my self down, before my young Landlady, as I jestingly us'd to call the Daughter, rushing into my Room, threw her self down on the Floor, bitterly exclaiming. I started off my Bed, and immediately running to the Door, who should I meet there but my *Irish Clerico*, without his Habit, and in his Shirt? I could not doubt, by *the Dishabillé* of the *Clerico*, but the young Creature had Reason enough for her Passion, which render'd me quite unable to master mine; wherefore as he stood with his Back next the Door, I thrust him in that ghostly Plight into the open Street.

I might, with leisure enough, have repented that precipitate Piece of Indiscretion; if it had not been for his bad Character, and the favourable Opinion the Town had conceived of me; for he inordinately exclaim'd against me, calling me Heretick, and telling the People, who were soon gathered round him, that coming to my Lodgings on the charitable work of Conversion, I had thus abus'd him, stript him of his Habit, and then turn'd him out of Doors. The Nuns, on their hearing the Outcries he made, came running to their Grates, to enquire into the Matter, and when they understood it, as he was pleas'd to relate it; though they condemn'd my Zeal, they pity'd my Condition. Very well was it for me, that I stood more than a little well in the good Opinion of the Town; among the Gentry, by my frequent Conversation, and the inferior Sort by my charitable Distributions; for nothing can be more dangerous, or a nearer Way to violent Fate, than to insult one of the Clergy in *Spain*, and especially, for such an one as they entitle a Heretick.

My old Landlady (I speak in respect to her Daughter) however formerly my seeming Friend, came in a violent Passion, and wrenching the Door out of my Hands, opened it, and pull'd her *Clerico* in; and so soon as she had done this, she took his Part, and railed so bitterly at me, that I had no Reason longer to doubt her thorough Conversion, under the full Power of his Mission. However the young one stood her Ground, and by all her Expressions, gave her many Inquirers Reason enough to believe, all was not Matter of Faith that the *Clerico* had advanced. Nevertheless, holding it adviseable to change my Lodgings, and a Friend confirming my Resolutions, I removed that Night.

The *Clerico* having put on his upper Garments, was run away to the *Corrigidor*, in a violent Fury, resolving to be early, as well knowing, that he who tells his Story first, has the Prospect of telling it to double Advantage. When he came there, he told that Officer a thousand idle Stories, and in the worst Manner; repeating how I had abus'd him, and not him only, but my poor Landlady, for taking his Part. The *Corrigidor* was glad to hear it all, and with an officious Ear fish'd for a great deal more; expecting, according to Usage, at last to squeeze a Sum of Money out of me. However he told the *Clerico*, that, as I was a Prisoner of War, he had no direct Power over me; but if he would immediately write to the President *Ronquillo*, at *Madrid*, he would not fail to give his immediate Orders, according to which he would as readily act against me.

The *Clerico* resolv'd to pursue his old Maxim and cry out first; and so taking the *Corrigidor's* Advice, he wrote away to *Madrid* directly. In the mean Time the People in the Town, both high and low, some out of Curiosity, some out of Friendship, pursu'd their Enquiries into the Reality of the Facts. The old Landlady they could make little of to my Advantage; but whenever the young one came to the Question, she always left them with these Words in her Mouth, *El Diabolo en forma del Clerico*, which rendring Things more than a little cloudy on the *Clerico's* Side, he was advis'd and press'd by his few Friends, as fast as he could to get out of Town; Nuns, Clergy, and every Body taking Part against him, excepting his new Convert, my old Landlady.

The Day after, as I was sitting with a Friend at my new Quarters, *Maria* (for that was the Name of my Landlady's Daughter) came running in with these Words in her Mouth, *El Clerico, el Clerico, passa la Calle*. We hasten'd to the Window, out of which we beheld the *Clerico, Murtough Brennan*, pitifully mounted on the Back of a very poor Ass (for they would neither let, nor lend him a Mule through all the Town) his Legs almost rested on the Ground, for he was lusty, as his Ass was little; and a Fellow with a large Cudgel march'd a-foot, driving his Ass along. Never did *Sancha Pancha*, on his Embassage to *Dulcinea*, make such a despicable, out of the way Figure, as our *Clerico* did at this Time. And what increas'd our Mirth was, their telling me, that our *Clerico*, like that Squire (tho' upon his own Priest-Errantry) was actually on his March to *Toboso*, a Place five Leagues off, famous for the Nativity of *Dulcinea*, The Object of the Passion of that celebrated Hero *Don Quixot*. So I will leave our *Clerico* on his Journey to *Murcia*, to relate the unhappy Sequel of this ridiculous Affair.

I have before said, that, by the Advice of the *Corrigidor, our Clerico* had wrote to *Don Ronquillo* at *Madrid*. About a Fortnight after his Departure from *la Mancha*, I was sitting alone in my new Lodgings, when two *Alguizils* (Officers under the *Corrigidor*, and in the Nature of our Bailiffs) came into my Room, but very civilly, to tell me, that they had Orders to carry me away to Prison; but at the same Moment they advis'd me, not to be afraid; for they had observed, that the whole Town was concern'd at what the *Corrigidor* and *Clerico* had done; adding, that it was their Opinion, that I should find so general a Friendship, that I need not be apprehensive of any Danger. With these plausible Speeches, though I afterwards experienced the Truth of them, I resign'd my self, and went with them to a much closer Confinement.

I had not been there above a Day or two, before many Gentlemen of the Place sent to me, to assure me, they were heartily afflicted at my Confinement, and resolv'd to write in my Favour to *Madrid*; but as it was not safe, nor the Custom in *Spain*, to visit those in my present Circumstances, they hoped I would not take it amiss, since they were bent to act all in their Power towards my Deliverance; concluding however with their Advice, that I would not give one *Real of Plata* to the *Corrigidor*, whom they hated, but confide in their assiduous Interposal, Don *Pedro de Ortega* in particular, the Person that perform'd the Part of the *Tauriro* on Horseback, sometime before, sent me Word, he would not fail to write to a Relation of his, of the first Account in *Madrid*, and so represent the Affair, that I should not long be debarr'd my old Acquaintance.

It may administer, perhaps, Matter of Wonder, that *Spaniards*, Gentlemen of the stanchest Punctilio, should make a Scruple and execute themselves from visiting Persons under Confinement, when, according to all Christian Acceptation, such a Circumstance would render such a Visit, not charitable only but generous. But though Men of vulgar Spirits might, from the Narrowness of their Views, form such insipid Excuses, those of these Gentlemen, I very well knew, proceeded from much more excusable Topicks. I was committed under the Accusation of having abus'd a sacred Person, one of the Clergy; and though, as a Prisoner of War, I might deem my self exempt from the Power of the Inquisition; yet how far one of that Country, visiting a Person, so accused, might be esteemed culpable, was a consideration in that dangerous Climate, far from deserving to be slighted. To me therefore, who well knew the Customs of the Country, and the Temper of its Countrymen, their Excuses were not only allowable, but acceptable also; for, without calling in Question their Charity, I verily believ'd I might falsely confide in their Honour.

Accordingly, after I had been a close Prisoner one Month to a Day, I found the Benefit of these Gentlemen's Promises and Solicitations. Pursuant to which, an Order was brought for my immediate Discharge; notwithstanding, the new Convert, my old Landlady, did all she could to make her appearing against me effectual, to the Height of her Prejudice and Malice, even while the Daughter, as sensible of my Innocence, and acting with a much better Conscience, endeavoured as much to justify me, against both the Threats and Persuasions of the *Corrigidor*, and his few Accomplices, though her own Mother made one.

After Receipt of this Order for my Enlargement, I was mightily press'd by Don *Felix*, and others of my Friends, to go to *Madrid*, and enter my Complaint against the *Corrigidor* and the *Clerico*, as a Thing highly essential to my own future Security. Without asking Leave therefore of the *Corrigidor*, or in the least acquainting him with it, I set out from *la Mancha*, and, as I afterwards understood, to the terrible Alarm of that griping Officer; who was under the greatest Consternation, when he heard I was gone; for as he knew very well, that he had done more than he could justify, he was very apprehensive of any Complaint; well knowing, that as he was hated as much as I was beloved, he might assure himself of the Want of that Assistance from the Gentlemen, which I had experienced.

So soon as I arrived at *Madrid*, I made it my Business to enquire out, and wait upon Father *Fahy*, Chief of the *Irish College*. He received me very courteously; but when I acquainted him with the Treatment I had met with from *Brennan*, and had given him an Account of his other scandalous Behaviour, I found he was no Stranger to the Man, or his Character; for he soon confirm'd to me the Honour *Brennan* first boasted of, his considerable Family, by saying, that scarce an Assize passed in his own Country, without two or three of that Name receiving at the Gallows the just Reward of their Demerits. In short, not only Father *Fahy*, but all the Clergy of that Nation at *Madrid*, readily subscribed to this Character of him, *That he was a Scandal to their Country*.

After this, I had nothing more to do, but to get that Father to go with me to *Pedro de Dios*, who was the Head of the *Dominican* Cloyster, and Dean of the Inquisition. He readily granted my Request, and when we came there, in a Manner unexpected, represented to the Dean, that having some good Dispositions towards Mother-Church, I had been diverted from them, he feared, by the evil Practices of one *Murtough Brennan*, a Countryman of his, tho' a Scandal to his Country; that under a Pretence of seeking my Conversion, he had lay'd himself open in a most beastly Manner, such as would have set a

Catholick into a vile Opinion of their Religion, and much more one that was yet a Heretick. The Dean had hardly Patience to hear Particulars; but as soon as my Friend had ended his Narration, he immediately gave his Orders, prohibiting *Murtough's* saying any more Masses, either in *Madrid*, or any other Place in *Spain*. This indeed was taking away the poor Wretches sole Subsistence, and putting him just upon an Equality with his Demerits.

I took the same Opportunity to make my Complaints of the *Corrigidor*; but his Term expiring very soon, and a Process being likely to be chargeable, I was advised to let it drop. So having effected what I came for, I returned to my old Station at *la Mancha*.

When I came back, I found a new *Corrigidor*, as I had been told there would, by the Dean of the Inquisition, who, at the same Time, advised me to wait on him. I did so, soon after my Arrival, and then experienced the Advice to be well intended; the Dean having wrote a Letter to him, to order him to treat me with all Manner of Civility. He show'd me the very Letter, and it was in such particular and obliging Terms, that I could not but perceive he had taken a Resolution, if possible, to eradicate all the evil impressions, that *Murtough's* Behaviour might have given too great Occasion for. This serv'd to confirm me in an Observation that I had long before made, That a Protestant, who will prudently keep his Sentiments in his own Breast, may command any Thing in *Spain*; where their stiff Bigotry leads 'em naturally into that other Mistake, That not to oppose, is to assent. Besides, it is generally among them, almost a work of Supererogation to be even instrumental in the Conversion of one they call a Heretick. To bring any such back to what they call Mother Church, nothing shall be spar'd, nothing thought too much: And if you have Insincerity enough to give them Hopes, you shall not only live in Ease, but in Pleasure and Plenty.

I had entertain'd some thoughts on my Journey back, of taking up my old Quarters at the Widow's; but found her so intirely converted by her *Clerico*, that there wou'd be no room to expect Peace: For which Reason, with the help of my fair *Vicinos*, and *Don Felix*, I took another, where I had not been long, before I received an unhappy Account of *Murtough's* Conduct in *Murcia*. It seems he had kept his Resolution in going thither; where meeting with some of his own Countrymen, though he found 'em stanch good Catholics, he so far inveigled himself into 'em, that he brought them all into a foul chance for their Lives. There were three of 'em, all Soldiers, in a *Spanish*

Regiment, but in a fit of ambitious, though frantick, Zeal: *Murtough* had wheedled them to go along with him to *Pedro de Dios*, Dean of the Inquisition, to declare and acknowledge before him, that they were converted and brought over to Mother Church, and by him only. The poor Ignorants, thus intic'd, had left their Regiment, of which the Colonel, having notice, sent after them, and they were overtaken on the Road, their *Missionair* with them. But notwithstanding all his Oratory, nay, even the Discovery of the whole Farce, one of them was hang'd for an Example to the other two.

It was not long after my Return before News arriv'd of the Peace; which though they receiv'd with Joy, they could hardly entertain with Belief. Upon which, the new *Corrigidor*, with whom I held a better Correspondence than I had done with the old one, desired me to produce my Letters from *England*, that it was true. Never did People give greater Demonstrations of Joy, than they upon this Occasion. It was the common cry in the Streets, *Paz con Angleterra, con todo Mundo Guerra*; And my Confirmation did them as much Pleasure as it did Service to me; for is possible, they treated me with more Civility than before.

But the Peace soon after being proclaimed, I received Orders to repair to *Madrid*, where the rest of the Prisoners taken at *Denia* had been carried; when I, by reason of my Wounds, and want of Health, had been left behind. Others I understood lay ready, and some were on their March to *Bayone* in *France*; where Ships were ordered for their Transportation into *England*. So after a Residence of three Years and three Months; having taken leave of all my Acquaintance, I left a Place, that was almost become natural to me, the delicious *Sainte Clemente de la Mancha*.

Nothing of Moment, or worth observing, met I with, till I came near *Ocanna*; and there occurred a Sight ridiculous enough. The Knight of the Town, I last came from, the ever renown'd *Don Quixot*, never made such a Figure as a *Spaniard*, I there met on the Road. He was mounted on a Mule of the largest size, and yet no way unsizeable to his Person: He had two Pistols in his Holsters, and one on each side stuck in his Belt; a sort of large Blunderbuss in one of his Hands, and the fellow to it slung over his Shoulders hung at his Back. All these were accompany'd with a right *Spanish Spado*, and an Attendant *Stiletto*, in their customary Position. The Muletier that was my guide, calling out to him in *Spanish*, told him he was very well arm'd; to which, with a great deal of Gravity, the Don returned Answer, *by Saint Jago a Man cannot be too well arm'd in such dangerous Times.*

I took up my Quarters that Night at *Ocanna*, a large, neat, and well built Town. Houses of good Reception, and Entertainment, are very scarce all over *Spain*; but that, where I then lay, might have pass'd for good in any other Country. Yet it gave me a Notion quite different to what I found: for I imagined it to proceed from my near Approach to the Capital. But instead of that, contrary to all other Countries, the nearer I came to *Madrid*, the Houses of Entertainment grew worse and worse; not in their Rates do I mean (for that with Reason enough might have been expected) but even in their Provision, and Places and way of Reception, I could not however forbear smiling at the Reason given by my Muletier, that it proceeded from a piece of Court Policy, in Order to oblige all Travellers to hasten to *Madrid*.

Two small Leagues from *Ocanna* we arrived at *Aranjuez*, a Seat of Pleasure, which the Kings of *Spain* commonly select for their place of Residence during the Months of *April and May*. It is distant from *Madrid* about seven Leagues; and the Country round is the pleasantest in all *Spain, Valencia* excepted. The House it self makes but a very indifferent Appearance; I have seen many a better in *England*, with an Owner to it of no more than five hundred Pounds *per Annum*; yet the Gardens are large and fine; or as the *Spaniards* say, the finest in all *Spain*, which with them is all the World. They tell you at the same Time, that those of *Versailles*, in their most beautiful Parts, took their Model from these. I never saw those at *Versailles*. But in my Opinion, the Walks at *Aranjuez*, tho' noble in their length, lose much of their Beauty by their Narrowness.

The Water-works here are a great Curiosity; to which the River *Tagus* running along close by, does mightily contribute. That River is let into the Gardens by a vast number of little Canals, which with their pleasing *Mæanders* divert the Eye with inexpressible Delight. These pretty Wanderers by Pipes properly plac'd in them, afford Varieties scarce to be believ'd or imagin'd; and which would be grateful in any Climate; but much more, where the Air, as it does here, wants in the Summer Months perpetual cooling.

To see a spreading Tree, as growing in its natural Soil, distinguish'd from its pineing Neighbourhood by a gentle refreshing Shower, which appears softly distilling from every Branch and Leaf thereof, while Nature all around is smiling, without one liquid sign of Sorrow, to me appear'd surprizingly pleasing. And the more when I observ'd that its Neighbours receiv'd not any the least Benefit of that plentiful Effusion; And yet a very few Trees distant, you should find a dozen together under the same healthful *Sudor*. Where art imitates Nature well, Philosophers hold it a Perfection: Then what must she exact of us, where we find her transcendent in the Perfections of Nature?

The watry Arch is nothing less surprizing; where Art contending with Nature, acts against the Laws of Nature, and yet is beautiful. To see a Liquid Stream vaulting it self from the space of threescore Yards into a perfect Semi-Orb, will be granted by the Curious to be rare and strange: But sure to walk beneath that Arch, and see the Waters flowing over your Head, without your receiving the minutest Drop, is stranger, if not strange enough to stagger all Belief.

The Story of *Actæon*, pictur'd in Water Colours, if I may so express my self, tho' pretty, seem'd to me, but trifling to the other. Those seem'd to be like Nature miraculously displayed; this only Fable in Grotesque. The Figures indeed were not only fine, but extraordinary; yet their various Shapes were not at all so entertaining to the Mind, however refreshing they might be found to the Body.

I took notice before of the straitness of their Walks: But tho' to me it might seem a Diminution of their Beauty: I am apt to believe to the *Spaniard*, for and by whom they were laid out, it may seem otherwise. They, of both Sexes, give themselves so intolerably up to Amouring, that on that Account the Closeness of the Walks may be look'd upon as an Advantage rather than a Defect. The grand Avenue to the House is much more stately, and compos'd as they are, of Rows of Trees, somewhat larger than our largest Limes, whose Leaves are all of a perfect Pea bloom Colour, together with their Grandeur, they strike the Eye with a pleasing Beauty. At the Entrance of the Grand Court we see the Statue of *Philip* the Second; to intimate to the Spectators, I suppose, that he was the Founder.

Among other Parks about *Aranjuez* there is one intirely preserved for Dromedaries; an useful Creature for Fatigue, Burden, and Dispatch; but the nearest of kin to Deformity of any I ever saw. There are several other enclosures for several sorts of strange and wild Beasts, which are sometimes baited in a very large Pond, that was shown me about half a League from hence. This is no ordinary Diversion: but when the Court is disposed that way, the Beast, or Beasts, whether Bear, Lyon, or Tyger, are convey'd into a House prepar'd for that purpose; whence he can no other way issue than by a Door over the Water, through, or over, which forcing or flinging himself, he gradually finds himself descend into the very depth of the Pond by a wooden Declivity. The Dogs stand ready on the Banks, and so soon as ever they spye their Enemy, rush all at once into the Water, and engage him. A Diversion less to be complain'd of than their *Tauridores*; because attended with less Cruelty to the Beast, as well as Danger to the Spectators.

When we arrived at *Madrid*, a Town much spoken of by Natives, as well as Strangers, tho' I had seen it before, I could hardly restrain my self from being surprized to find it only environ'd with Mud Walls. It may very easily be imagin'd, they were never intended for Defence, and yet it was a long time before I could find any other use, or rather any use at all in 'em. And yet I was at last convinc'd of my Error by a sensible Increase of Expence. Without the Gates, to half a League without the Town, you have Wine for two Pence the Quart; but within the Place, you drink it little cheaper than you may in *London*. The Mud Walls therefore well enough answer their Intent of forcing People to reside there, under pretence of Security; but in reality to be tax'd, for other Things are taxable, as well as Wine, tho' not in like Proportion.

All Embassadors have a Claim or Privilege, of bringing in what Wine they please Tax-free; and the King, to wave it, will at any Time purchase that Exemption of Duty at the price of five hundred Pistoles *per Annum*. The Convents and Nunneries are allowed a like Licence of free Importation; and it is one of the first Advantages they can boast of; for, under that Licence having a liberty of setting up a Tavern near them, they make a prodigious Advantage of it. The Wine drank and sold in this Place, is for the most part a sort of white Wine.

But if the Mud Walls gave me at first but a faint Idea of the Place; I was pleasingly disappointed, as soon as I enter'd the Gates. The Town then show'd itself well built, and of Brick, and the Streets wide, long, and spacious. Those of *Atocha*, and *Alcala*, are as fine as any I ever saw; yet is it situated but very indifferently: For tho' they have what they call a River, to which they give the very fair Name of *la Mansuera*, and over which they have built a curious, long, and large Stone Bridge; yet is the Course of it, in Summer time especially, mostly dry. This gave occasion to that piece of Railery of a Foreign Embassador, *That the King would have don wisely to have bought a River, before he built the Bridge.* Nevertheless, that little Stream of a River which they boast of, they improve as much as possible; since down the Sides, as far as you can see, there are Coops, or little Places hooped in, for People to wash their Linen (for they very rarely wash in their own Houses) nor is it really an unpleasing Sight, to view the regular Rows of them at that cleanly Operation.

The King has here two Palaces; one within the Town, the other near adjoining. That in the Town is built of Stone, the other which is called *Bueno Retiro*, is all of Brick. From the Town to this last, in Summer time, there is a large covering of Canvas, propt up with tall Poles; under which People walk to avoid the scorching heats of the Sun.

As I was passing by the Chapel of the *Carmelites*, I saw several blind Men, some led, some groping the Way with their Sticks, going into the Chapel. I had the curiosity to know the Reason; I no sooner enter'd the Door, but was surprized to see such a number of those unfortunate People, all kneeling before the Altar, some kissing the Ground, others holding up their Heads, crying out *Misericordia*. I was informed 'twas Saint *Lucy's* Day, the Patroness of the Blind; therefore all who were able, came upon that Day to pay their Devotion: So I left them, and directed my Course towards the King's Palace.

When I came to the outward Court, I met with a *Spanish* Gentleman of my Acquaintance, and we went into the *Piazza's*; whilst we were talking there, I saw several Gentlemen passing by having Badges on their Breasts; some white, some red, and others green: My Friend informed me that there were five Orders of Knighthood in *Spain*. That of the Golden Fleece was only given to great Princes, but the other four to private Gentlemen, *viz.* That of *Saint Jago, Alacantara, Saint Salvador de Montreal,* and *Monteza.*

He likewise told me, that there were above ninety Places of Grandees, but never filled up; who have the Privilege of being cover'd in the Presence of the King, and are distinguished into three Ranks. The first is of those who cover themselves before they speak to the King. The second are those who put on their Hats after they have begun to speak. The third are those who only put on their Hats, having spoke to him. The Ladies of the Grandees have also great Respect show'd them. The Queen rises up when they enter the Chamber, and offers them Cushions.

No married Man except the King lies in the Palace, for all the Women who live there are Widows, or Maids of Honour to the Queen. I saw the Prince of *Asturia's* Dinner carried through the Court up to him, being guarded by four Gentlemen of the Guards, one before, another behind, and one on each Side, with their Carbines shoulder'd; the Queen's came next, and the King's the last, guarded as before, for they always dine separately. I observed that the Gentlemen of the

Guards, though not on Duty, yet they are obliged to wear their Carbine Belts.

SAINT Isodore, who from a poor labouring Man, by his Sanctity of Life arrived to the Title of *Saint*, is the Patron of *Madrid*, and has a Church dedicated to him, which is richly adorned within. The Sovereign Court of the Inquisition is held at *Madrid*, the President whereof is called the Inquisitor General. They judge without allowing any Appeal for four Sorts of Crimes, *viz.* Heresy, Polygamy, Sodomy and Witchcraft, and when any are convicted, 'tis called the Act of Faith.

Most People believe that the King's greatest Revenue consists in the Gold and Silver brought from the West Indies (which is a mistake) for most Part of that Wealth belongs to Merchants and others, that pay the Workmen at the Golden Mines of *Potosi*, and the Silver Mines at *Mexico*; yet the King, as I have been informed, receives about a Million and a half of Gold.

The *Spaniards* have a Saying, that the finest Garden of Fruit in *Spain* is in the middle of *Madrid*, which is the *Plaza* or Market Place, and truly the Stalls there are set forth with such variety of delicious fruit, that I must confess I never saw any Place comparable to it; and which adds to my Admiration, there are no Gardens or Orchards of Fruit within some Leagues.

They seldom eat Hares in *Spain* but whilst the Grapes are growing, and then they are so exceeding fat, they are knocked down with Sticks. Their Rabits are not so good as ours in *England*, they have great plenty of Patridges, which are larger and finer feather'd than ours. They have but little Beef in *Spain*, because there is no Grass, but they have plenty of Mutton, and exceeding good, because their Sheep feed only upon wild Potherbs; their Pork is delicious, their Hogs feeding only upon Chestnuts and Acorns.

MADRID and *Valladolid*, though Great, yet are only accounted Villages: In the latter *Philip* the Second, by the persuasion of *Parsons* an *English* Jesuit, erected an *English* Seminary; and *Philip* the Fourth built a most noble Palace, with extraordinary fine Gardens. They say that *Christopher Columbus*, who first discover'd the West Indies, dyed there, tho' I have heard he lies buried, and has a Monument at *Sevil*.

The Palace in the Town stands upon eleven Arches, under every one of which there are Shops, which degrade it to a meer Exchange. Nevertheless, the Stairs by which you ascend up to the Guard Room (which is very spacious too) are stately, large, and curious. So soon as you have pass'd the Guard Room, you enter into a long and noble

Gallery, the right Hand whereof leads to the King's Apartment, the left to the Queen's. Entring into the King's Apartment you soon arrive at a large Room, where he keeps his *Levee*; on one side whereof (for it takes up the whole Side) is painted the fatal Battle of *Almanza*. I confess the View somewhat affected me, tho' so long after; and brought to Mind many old Passages. However, the Reflection concluded thus in favour of the *Spaniard*, that we ought to excuse their Vanity in so exposing under a *French* General, a Victory, which was the only material one the *Spaniards* could ever boast of over an *English* Army.

In this State Room, when the King first appears, every Person present, receives him with a profound Homage: After which turning from the Company to a large Velvet Chair, by which stands the Father Confessor, he kneels down, and remains some Time at his Devotion; which being over, he rising crosses himself, and his Father Confessor having with the motion of his Hand intimated his Benediction, he then gives Audience to all that attend for that purpose. He receives every Body with a seeming Complaisance; and with an Air more resembling the French than the *Spanish* Ceremony. Petitions to the King, as with us, are delivered into the Hands of the Secretary of State: Yet in one Particular they are, in my Opinion, worthy the Imitation of other Courts; the Petitioner is directly told, what Day he must come for an Answer to the Office; at which Time he is sure, without any further fruitless Attendance, not to fail of it. The Audience being over, the King returns through the Gallery to his own Apartment.

I cannot here omit an accidental Conversation, that pass'd between General *Mahoni* and my self in this Place. After some talk of the Bravery of the *English* Nation, he made mention of General *Stanhope*, with a very peculiar *Emphasis*.

"But," says he, "I never was so put to the Nonplus in all my Days, as that General once put me in. I was on the road from *Paris to Madrid*, and having notice, that that General was going just the Reverse, and that in all likelyhood we should meet the next day: Before my setting out in the Morning, I took care to order my gayest Regimental Apparel, resolving to make the best Appearance I could to receive so great a Man. I had not travell'd above four Hours before I saw two Gentlemen, who appearing to be *English*, it induc'd me to imagine they were Forerunners, and some of his Retinue. But how abash'd and confounded was I? when putting the Question to one of 'em, he made answer, *Sir, I am the Person*. Never did Moderation put Vanity more out of Countenance: Tho' to say Truth, I cou'd not but think his Dress as much too plain for General *Stanhope*, as I at that juncture thought my own too gay for *Mahoni.* But," added he, "that great Man had too many inward great Endowments to stand in need of any outside Decoration."

Of all Diversions the King takes most delight in that of Shooting, which he performs with great Exactness and Dexterity. I have seen him divert himself at Swallow shooting (by all, I think allow'd to be the most difficult) and exceeding all I ever saw. The last time I had the Honour to see him, was on his Return from that Exercise. He had been abroad with the Duke of *Medina Sidonia*, and alighted out of his Coach at a back Door of the Palace, with three or four Birds in his Hand, which according to his usual Custom, he carried up to the Queen with his own Hands.

There are two Play-houses in *Madrid*, at both which they act every Day; but their Actors, and their Music, are almost too indifferent to be mentioned. The Theatre at the *Bueno Retiro* is much the best; but as much inferior to ours at *London*, as those at *Madrid* are to that. I was at one Play, when both King and Queen were present. There was a splendid Audience, and a great Concourse of Ladies; but the latter, as is the Custom there, having Lattices before them, the Appearance lost most of its Lustre. One very remarkable Thing happen'd, while I was there; the *Ave-Bell* rung in the Middle of an Act, when down on their Knees fell every Body, even the Players on the Stage, in the Middle of their Harangue. They remained for some Time at their Devotion; then up they rose, and returned to the Business they were before engag'd in, beginning where they left off.

The Ladies of Quality make their Visits in grand State and Decorum. The Lady Visitant is carry'd in a Chair by four Men; the two first, in all Weathers, always bare. Two others walk as a Guard, one on each Side; another carrying a large Lanthorn for fear of being benighted; then follows a Coach drawn by six Mules, with her Women, and after that another with her Gentlemen; several Servants walking after, more or less, according to the Quality of the Person. They never suffer their Servants to over load a Coach, as is frequently seen with us, neither do Coachmen or Chairmen go or drive as if they carried Midwives in lieu of Ladies. On the contrary, they affect a Motion so slow and so stately, that you would rather imagine the Ladies were every one of them near their Time, and very apprehensive of a Miscarriage.

I remember not to have seen here any Horses in any Coach, but in the King's, or an Embassador's; which can only proceed from Custom; for certainly finer Horses are not to be found in the World.

At the Time of my being here, Cardinal *Giudici* was at *Madrid*; he was a tall, proper, comely Man, and one that made the best Appearance. *Alberoni* was there at the same Time, who, upon the Death of the Duke of *Vendome*, had the good Fortune to find the Princess *Ursini* his Patroness. An Instance of whose Ingratitude will plead Pardon for this little Digression. That Princess first brought *Alberoni* into Favour at Court. They were both of *Italy*, and that might be one Reason of that Lady's espousing his Interest: tho' some there are, that assign it to the Recommendation of the Duke of *Vendome*; with whom *Alberoni* had the Honour to be very intimate, as the other was always distinguish'd by that Princess. Be which it will, certain it is, she was *Alberoni's* first, and sole Patroness; which gave many People afterwards a very smart Occasion of reflecting upon him, both as to his Integrity and Gratitude. For, when *Alberoni*, upon the Death of King *Philip's* first Queen, had recommended this present Lady, who was his Countrywoman, (she of *Parma*, and he of *Placentia*, both in the same Dukedom) and had forwarded her Match with the King, with all possible Assiduity; and when that Princess, pursuant to the Orders she had received from the King, passed over into *Italy* to accompany the Queen Elect into her own Dominions; *Alberoni*, forgetful of the Hand that first advanced him, sent a Letter to the present Queen, just before her Landing, that if she resolved to be Queen of *Spain*, she must banish the Princess *Ursini*, her Companion, and never let her come to Court. Accordingly that Lady, to evince the Extent of her Power, and the Strength of her Resolution, dipatch'd that Princess away, on her very Landing, and before she had seen the King, under a Detachment of her own Guards, into *France*; and all this without either allowing her an Opportunity of justifying her self, or assigning the least Reason for so uncommon an Action. But the same *Alberoni* (though afterwards created Cardinal, and for some Time King *Philip's* Prime Minion) soon saw that Ingratitude of his rewarded in his own Disgrace, at the very same Court.

I remember, when at *la Mancha*, Don *Felix Pachero*, in a Conversation there, maintain'd, that three Women, at that Time, rul'd the World, *viz.* Queen Anne, Madam *Mantenon*, and this Princess *Ursini*.

Father *Fahy's* Civilities, when last at *Madrid*, exacting of me some suitable Acknowledgment, I went to pay him a Visit; as to render him due Thanks for the past, so to give him a further Account of his Countryman *Brennan*; but I soon found he did not much incline to hear any Thing more of *Murtough*, not expecting to hear any Good of him; for which Reason, as soon as I well could, I changed the Conversation to another Topick. In which some Word dropping of the Count *de Montery*, I told him, that I heard he had taken Orders, and officiated at Mass: He made answer, it was all very true. And upon my intimating, that I had the Honour to serve under him in *Flanders*, on my first entring into Service, and when he commanded the *Spanish* Forces at the famous Battle of *Seneff*; and adding, that I could not but be surprized, that he, who was then one of the brightest *Cavalieroes* of the Age, should now be in Orders; and that I should look upon it as a mighty Favour barely to have, if it might be, a View of him; he very obligingly told me, that he was very well acquainted with him, and that if I would come the next Day, he would not fail to accompany me to the Count's House.

Punctually at the Time appointed, I waited on Father *Fahy*, who, as he promised, carry'd me to the Count's House: He was stepping into his Coach just as we got there; but seeing Father *Fahy*, he advanced towards us. The Father deliver'd my Desire in as handsom a Manner as could be, and concluding with the Reason of it, from my having been in that Service under him; he seem'd very well pleas'd, but added, that there were not many beside my self living, who had been in that Service with him. After some other Conversation, he call'd his Gentleman to him, and gave him particular Orders to give us a *Frescari*, or in *English*, an Entertainment; so taking leave, he went into his Coach, and we to our *Frescari*.

Coming from which, Father *Fahi* made me observe, in the open Street, a Stone, on which was a visible great Stain of somewhat reddish and like Blood.

"This," said he, "was occasion'd by the Death of a Countryman of mine, who had the Misfortune to overset a Child, coming out of that House (pointing to one opposite to us) the Child frighted, though not hurt, as is natural, made a terrible Outcry; upon which its Father coming out in a violent Rage (notwithstanding my Countryman beg'd Pardon, and pleaded Sorrow as being only an Accident) stabb'd him to the Heart, and down he fell upon that Stone, which to this Day retains the Mark of innocent Blood, so rashly shed".

He went on, and told me, the *Spaniard* immediately took Sanctuary in the Church, whence some Time after he made his Escape.

But Escapes of that Nature are so common in *Spain*, that they are not worth wondering at. For even though it were for wilful and premeditated Murder, if the Murderer have taken Sanctuary, it was never known, that he was delivered up to Justice, though demanded; but in some Disguise he makes his Escape, or some Way is secured against all the Clamours of Power or Equity. I have observed, that some of the greatest Quality stop their Coaches over a stinking nasty Puddle, which they often find in the Streets, and holding their Heads over the Door, snuff up the nasty Scent which ascends, believing that 'tis extream healthful; when I was forced to hold my Nose, passing by. 'Tis not convenient to walk out early in the Morning, they having no necessary Houses, throw out their Nastiness in the Middle of the Street.

After I had taken Leave of Father *Fahy*, and return'd my Thanks for all Civilities, I went to pay a Visit to Mr. *Salter*, who was Secretary to General *Stanhope*, when the *English* Forces were made Prisoners of War at *Breuhiga*; going up Stairs, I found the Door of his Lodgings a-jar; and knocking, a Person came to the Door, who appeared under some Surprize at Sight of me. I did not know him, but inquiring if Mr. *Salter* was within; He answered, as I fancy'd, with some Hesitation, that he was but was busy in an inner Room. However, though unask'd, I went in, resolving, since I had found him at home, to wait his Leisure. In a little Time Mr. *Salter* enter'd the Room; and after customary Ceremonies, asking my Patience a little longer, he desired I would sit down and bear Ensign *Fanshaw* Company (for so he call'd him) adding at going out, he had a little Business that required Dispatch; which being over, he would return, and join Company.

The Ensign, as he call'd him, appear'd to me under a *Dishabileé*; and the first Question he ask'd me, was, if I would drink a Glass of *English* Beer? Misled by his Appearance, though I assented, it was with a Design to treat; which he would be no Means permit; but calling to a Servant, ordered some in. We sat drinking that Liquor, which to me was a greater Rarity than all the Wine in *Spain*; when in dropt an old Acquaintance of mine, Mr. *Le Noy*, Secretary to Colonel *Nevil*. He sat down with us, and before the Glass could go twice round, told Ensign *Fanshaw*, That his Colonel gave his humble Service to him, and ordered him to let him know, that he had but threescore Pistoles by him, which he had sent, and which were at his Service, as what he pleas'd more should be, as soon as it came to his Hands.

At this I began to look upon my Ensign as another guess Person than I had taken him for; and *Le Noy* imagining, by our setting cheek by joul together, that I must be in the Secret, soon after gave him the Title of Captain. This soon convinc'd me, that there was more in the Matter than I was yet Master of; for laying Things together, I could not but argue within my self, that as it seem'd at first, a most incredible Thing, that a Person of his Appearance should have so large Credit, with such a Complement at the End of it, without some Disguise, and as from an Ensign he was risen to be a Captain, in the taking of one Bottle of *English* Beer; a little Patience would let me into a Farce, in which, at present, I had not the Honour to bear any Part but that of a Mute.

At last *Le Noy* took his leave, and as soon as he had left us, and the other Bottle was brought in, Ensign *Fanshaw* began to open his Heart, and tell me, who he was. "I am necessitated," said he, "to be under this Disguise, to conceal my self, especially in this Place.

"For you must know," continued he, "that when our Forces were Lords of this Town, as we were for a little while, I fell under an Intrigue with another Man's Wife; Her Husband was a Person of considerable Account; nevertheless the Wife show'd me all the Favours that a Soldier, under a long and hard Campaigne, could be imagined to ask. In short, her Relations got acquainted with our Amour, and knowing that I was among the Prisoners taken at *Breuhiga*, are now upon the Scout and Enquiry, to make a Discovery that may be of fatal Consequence. This is the Reason of my Disguise; this the unfortunate Occasion of my taking upon me a Name that does not belong to me."

He spoke all this with such an Openness of Heart, that in return of so much Confidence, I confess'd to him, that I had heard of the Affair, for that it had made no little Noise all over the Country; that it highly behoved him to take great Care of himself, since as the Relations on both Sides were considerable, he must consequently be in great Danger; That in Cases of that Nature, no People in the World carry Things to greater Extremities, than the *Spaniards*. He return'd me Thanks for my good Advice, which I understood, in a few Days after, he, with the Assistance of his Friends, had taken Care to put in Practice; for he was convey'd away secretly, and afterwards had the Honour to be made a Peer of *Ireland*.

My Passport being at last sign'd by the Count *de las Torres*, I prepared for a Journey, I had long and ardently wish'd for, and set out from *Madrid*, in the Beginning of *September*, 1712, in Order to return to my native Country.

Accordingly I set forward upon my Journey, but having heard, both before and since my being in *Spain*, very famous Things spoken of the *Escurial*; though it was a League out of my Road, I resolved to make it a Visit. And I must confess, when I came there, I was so far from condemning my Curiosity, that I chose to congratulate my good Fortune, that had, at half a Day's Expence, feasted my Eyes with Extraordinaries, which would have justify'd a Twelve-months' Journey on purpose.

The Structure is intirely magnificent, beyond any Thing I ever saw, or any Thing my Imagination could frame. It is composed of eleven several Quadrangles, with noble Cloisters round every one of them. The Front to the West is adorn'd with three stately Gates; every one of a different Model, yet every one the Model of nicest Architecture. The Middlemost of the three leads into a fine Chapel of the *Hieronomites*, as they call them; in which are entertain'd one hundred and fifty Monks. At every of the four Corners of this august Fabrick, there is a Turret of excellent Workmanship, which yields to the Whole an extraordinary Air of Grandure. The King's Palace is on the North, nearest that Mountain, whence the Stone it is built of was hew'n; and all the South Part is set off with many Galleries, both beautiful and sumptuous.

This prodigious Pile, which, as I have said, exceeds all that I ever saw; and which would ask, of it self, a Volume to particularize, was built by *Philip* the Second. He lay'd the first Stone, yet liv'd to see it finished; and lies buryed in the *Panthæon*, a Part of it, set apart for the Burial-place of succeeding Princes, as well as himself. It was dedicated to Saint *Laurence*, in the very Foundation; and therefore built in the Shape of a Gridiron, the Instrument of that Martyr's Execution; and in Memory of a great Victory obtained on that Saint's Day. The Stone of which it is built, contrary to the common Course, grows whiter by Age; and the Quarry, whence it was dug, lies near enough, if it had Sense or Ambition, to grow enamour'd of its own wonderful Production. Some there are, who stick not to assign this Convenience, as the main Cause of its Situation; and for my Part, I must agree, that I have seen many other Parts of *Spain*, where that glorious Building would have shone with yet far greater Splendour.

There was no Town of any Consequence presented it self in my Way to *Burgos*. Here I took up my Quarters that Night; where I met with an *Irish* Priest, whose Name was *White*. As is natural on such Rencounters, having answered his Enquiry, whither I was going; he very kindly told me, he should be very glad of my Company as far as *Victoria*, which lay in my Road; and I with equal Frankness embrac'd the Offer.

Next Morning, when we had mounted our Mules, and were got a little Distance from *Burgos*; he began to relate to me a great many impious Pranks of an *English* Officer, who had been a Prisoner there a little before I came; concluding all, with some Vehemence, that he had given greater Occasion of Scandal and Infamy to his native Country, than would easily be wiped off, or in a little Time. The Truth of it is, many Particularly, which he related to me, were too monstrously vile to admit of any Repetition here; and highly meriting that unfortunate End, which that Officer met with some time after. Nevertheless the just Reflection made by that Father, plainly manifested to me the Folly of those Gentlemen, who, by such Inadvertencies, to say no worse, cause the Honour of the Land of their Nativity to be called in question. For tho', no doubt, it is a very false Conclusion, from a singular, to conceive a general Character; yet in a strange Country, nothing is more common, A Man therefore, of common Sense, would carefully avoid all Occasions of Censure, if not in respect to himself, yet out of a human Regard to such of his Countrymen as may have the Fortune to come after him; and, it's more than probable, may desire to hear a better and juster Character of their Country, and Countrymen, than he perhaps might incline to leave behind him.

As we travelled along, Father *White* told me, that near the Place of our Quartering that Night, there was a Convent of the *Carthusian* Order, which would be well worth my seeing. I was doubly glad to hear it, as it was an Order most a Stranger to me; and as I had often heard from many others, most unaccountable Relations of the Severity of their Way of Life, and the very odd Original of their Institution.

The next Morning therefore, being *Sunday*, we took a Walk to the Convent. It was situated at the Foot of a great Hill, having a pretty little River running before it. The Hill was naturally cover'd with Evergreens of various Sorts; but the very Summit of the Rock was so impending, that one would at first Sight be led to apprehend the Destruction of the Convent, from the Fall of it. Notwithstanding all which, they have very curious and well ordered Gardens; which led me to observe, that, what ever Men may pretend, Pleasure was not incompatible with the most austere Life. And indeed, if I may guess of others by this, no Order in that Church can boast of finer Convents. Their Chapel was completely neat, the Altar of it set out with the utmost Magnificence, both as to fine Paintings, and other rich Adornments. The Building was answerable to the rest; and, in short, nothing seem'd omitted, that might render it beautiful or pleasant.

When we had taken a full Survey of all; we, not without some Regret, return'd to our very indifferent Inn; Where the better to pass away the Time, Father *White* gave me an ample Detail of the Original of that Order. I had before-hand heard somewhat of it; nevertheless, I did not care to interrupt him, because I had a Mind to hear how his Account would agree with what I had already heard.

"*Bruno*," said the Father, "the Author or Founder of this Order, was not originally of this, but of another. He had a holy Brother of the same Order, that was his Cell-mate, or Chamber-fellow, who was reputed by all that ever saw or knew him, for a Person of exalted Piety, and of a most exact holy Life. This man, *Bruno* had intimately known for many years; and agreed in his Character, that general Consent did him no more than Justice, having never observed any Thing in any of his Actions, that, in his Opinion, could be offensive to God or Man. He was perpetually at his Devotions; and distinguishably remarkable, for never permitting any Thing but pious Ejaculations to proceed out of his Mouth. In short, he was reputed a Saint upon Earth.

"This Man at last dies, and, according to Custom, is removed into the Chapel of the Convent, and there plac'd with a Cross fix'd in his Hands: Soon after which, saying the proper Masses for his Soul, in the Middle of their Devotion, the dead Man lifts up his Head, and with an audible Voice, cry'd out, *Vocatus sum.* The pious Brethren, as any one will easily imagine, were most prodigiously surprised at such an Accident, and therefore they earnestly redoubled their Prayers; when hfting up his Head a second Time, the dead Man cried aloud, *Judicatus sum.* Knowing his former Piety, the pious Fraternity could not then entertain the least doubt of his Felicity; when, to their great Consternation and Confusion, he lifted up his Head a third Time, crying out in a terrible Tone, *Damnatus sum;* upon which they incontinently removed the Corps out of the Chapel, and threw it upon the Dunghill.

"Good *Bruno*, pondering upon these Passages, could not fail of drawing this Conclusion; That if a Person to all Appearance so holy and devout, should miss of Salvation, it behov'd a wise Man to contrive some Way more certain to make his Calling and Election sure. To that Purpose he instituted this strict and severe Order, with an Injunction to them sacred as any Part, that every Professor should always wear Hair

Cloth next his Skin, never eat any Flesh; nor speak to one another, only as passing by, to say, *Memento mori.*"

This Account I found to agree pretty well with what I had before heard; but at the same Time, I found the Redouble of it made but just the same Impression, it had at first made upon my Heart. However having made it my Observation, that a Spirit the least contradictory, best carries a Man through *Spain*, I kept Father White Company, and in Humour, 'till we arrived at *Victoria.* Where he added one Thing, by Way of Appendix, in Relation to the *Carthusians*, That every Person of the Society, is oblig'd every Day to go into their Place of Burial, and take up as much Earth, as he can hold at a Grasp with one Hand, in order to prepare his Grave.

Next Day we set out for *Victoria.* It is a sweet, delicious, and pleasant Town. It received that Name in Memory of a considerable Victory there obtained over the *Moors.* Leaving this Place, I parted with Father *White*; he going where his Affairs led him; and I to make the best of my Way to *Bilboa.*

Entring into *Biscay*, soon after I left *Victoria*, I was at a Loss almost to imagine, what Country I was got into. By my long Stay in *Spain*, I thought my self a tolerable Master of the Tongue; yet here I found my self at the utmost Loss to understand Landlord, Landlady, or any of the Family. I was told by my Muletier, that they pretend their Language, as they call it, has continued uncorrupted from the very Confusion of *Babel*; though if I might freely give my Opinion in the Matter, I should rather take it to be the very Corruption of all that Confusion. Another *Rhodomontado* they have, (for in this they are perfect *Spaniards*) that neither *Romans, Carthaginians, Vandals, Goths*, or *Moors*, ever totally subdued them. And yet any Man that has ever seen their Country, might cut this Knot without a Hatchet, by saying truly, that neither *Roman, Carthaginian*, nor any victorious People, thought it worth while to make a Conquest of a Country, so mountainous and so barren.

However, *Bilboa* must be allowed, tho' not very large, to be a pretty, clean and neat Town. Here, as in *Amsterdam*, they allow neither Cart, nor Coach, to enter; but every Thing of Merchandize is drawn, and carried upon Sledges: And yet it is a Place of no small Account, as to Trade; and especially for Iron and Wooll. Here I hop'd to have met with an opportunity of Embarking for *England*; but to my Sorrow I found my self disappointed, and under that Disappointment, obliged to make the best of my Way to *Bayonne.*

Setting out for which Place, the first Town of Note that I came to, was *Saint Sebastian*. A very clean Town, and neatly pay'd; which is no little Rarity in *Spain*. It has a very good Wall about it, and a pretty Citadel. At this Place I met with two *English* Officers, who were under the same state with my self; one of them being a Prisoner of War with me at *Denia*. They were going to *Bayonne* to embark for *England* as well as my self; so we agreed to set out together for *Port Passage*. The Road from St. *Sebastian* is all over a well pav'd Stone Causeway; almost at the end whereof, there accosted us a great number of young Lasses. They were all prettily dress'd, their long Hair flowing in a decent manner over their Shoulders, and here and there decorated with Ribbons of various Colours, which wantonly play'd on their Backs with the Wind. The Sight surpriz'd my Fellow Travellers no less than me; and the more, as they advanced directly up to us, and seiz'd our Hands. But a little time undeceiv'd us, and we found what they came for; and that their Contest, tho' not so robust as our Oars on the *Thames*, was much of the same Nature; each contending who should have us for their Fare. For 'tis here a Custom of Time out of mind, that none but young Women should have the management and profit of that Ferry. And tho' the Ferry is over an Arm of the Sea, very broad, and sometimes very rough, those fair Ferriers manage themselves with that Dexterity, that the Passage is very little dangerous, and in calm Weather, very pleasant. In short, we made choice of those that best pleased us; who in a grateful Return, led us down to their Boat under a sort of Music, which they, walking along, made with their Oars, and which we all thought far from being disagreeable. Thus were we transported over to *Port Passage*; not undeservedly accounted the best Harbour in all the Bay of *Biscay*.

We stay'd not long here after Landing, resolving, if possible, to reach *Fonterabia* before Night; but all the Expedition we could use, little avail'd; for before we could reach thither the Gates were shut, and good Nature and Humanity were so lock'd up with them, that all the Rhetorick we were Masters of could not prevail upon the Governor to order their being opened; for which Reason we were obliged to take up our Quarters at the Ferry House.

When we got up the next Morning, we found the Waters so broad, as well as rough, that we began to enquire after another Passage; and were answer'd, that at the Isle of *Conference*, but a short League upwards, the Passage was much shorter, and exposed to less Danger. Such good Reasons soon determind's us: So, setting out we got there in a very little Time; and very soon after were landed in *France*. Here we found a House of very good Entertainment, a Thing we had long wanted, and much lamented the want of.

We were hardly well seated in the House before we were made sensible, that it was the Custom, which had made it the business of our Host, to entertain all his Guests at first coming in, with a prolix Account of that remarkable Interview between the two Kings of *France* and *Spain*. I speak safely now, as being got on *French* Ground: For the *Spaniard* in his own Country would have made me to know, that putting *Spain* after *France* had there been look'd upon as a meer Solecism in Speech. However, having refresh'd our selves, to show our deference to our Host's Relation, we agreed to pay our Respects to that famous little Isle he mention'd; which indeed, was the whole burden of the Design of our crafty Landlord's Relation.

When we came there, we found it a little oval Island, over-run with Weeds, and surrounded with Reeds and Rushes.

"Here," said our Landlord (for he went with us) "upon this little Spot, were at that juncture seen the two greatest Monarchs in the Universe. A noble Pavilion was erected in the very middle of it, and in the middle of that was placed a very large oval Table; at which was the Conference, from which the Place receiv'd its Title. There were two Bridges rais'd; one on the *Spanish* side, the Passage to which was a little upon a Descent by reason of the Hills adjacent; and the other upon the *French* side, which as you see, was all upon a Level. The Musick playing, and Trumpets sounding, the two Kings, upon a Signal agreed upon, set forward at the same time; the *Spanish* Monarch handing the *Infanta* his Daughter to the Place of Interview. As soon as they were enter'd the Pavilion, on each Side, all the Artillery fired, and both Annies after that made their several Vollies. Then the King of *Spain* advancing on his side the Table with the *Infanta*, the King of *France* advanced at the same Moment on the other; till meeting, he received the *Infanta* at the Hands of her Father, as his Queen; upon which, both the Artillery and small Arms fir'd as before. After this, was a most splendid and sumptuous Entertainment; which being over, both Kings retir'd into their several Dominions; the King of *France* conducting his new Queen to *Saint Jean de Luz*, where the Marriage was consummated; and the King of *Spain* returning to *Port Passage*."

After a Relation so very inconsistent with the present State of the Place; we took Horse (for Mule-mounting was now out of Fashion) and rode to *Saint Jean de Luz*, where we found as great a difference in our Eating and Drinking, as we had before done in our Riding. Here they might be properly call'd Houses of Entertainment; tho' generally speaking, till we came to this Place, we met with very mean Fare, and were poorly accommodated in the Houses where we lodged.

A Person that travels this way, would be esteem'd a Man of a narrow Curiosity, who should not desire to see the Chamber where *Louis le grand* took his first Night's Lodging with his Queen. Accordingly, when it was put into my Head, out of an Ambition to evince my self a Person of Taste, I asked the Question, and the Favour was granted me, with a great deal of *French* Civility. Not that I found any Thing here, more than in the Isle of *Conference*, but what Tradition only had rendered remarkable.

Saint Jean de Luz is esteem'd one of the greatest Village Towns in all *France*. It was in the great Church of this Place, that *Lewis* XIV according to Marriage Articles, took before the high Altar the Oath of Renunciation to the Crown of *Spain*, by which all the Issue of that Marriage were debarred Inheritance, if Oaths had been obligatory with Princes. The Natives here are reckon'd expert Seamen; especially in Whale fishing. Here is a fine Bridge of Wood; in the middle of which is a Descent, by Steps, into a pretty little Island; where is a Chapel, and a Palace belonging to the Bishop of *Bayonne*. Here the Queen Dowager of *Spain* often walks to divert herself; and on this Bridge, and in the Walks on the Island, I had the Honour to see that Princess more than once.

This *Villa* not being above four Leagues from *Bayonne*, we got there by Dinner time, where at an Ordinary of twenty *Sous*, we eat and drank in Plenty, and with a *gusto*, much better than in any part of *Spain*; where for eating much worse, we paid very much more.

BAYONNE is a Town strong by Nature; yet the Fortifications have been very much neglected, since the building of the Citadel, on the other Side the River; which not only commands the Town, but the Harbour too. It is a noble Fabrick; fair and strong, and rais'd on the side of a Hill, wanting nothing that Art could furnish, to render it impregnable. The Marshal *Bouflers* had the Care of it in its erection; and there is a fine Walk near it, from which he us'd to survey the Workmen, which still carries his Name. There are two noble Bridges here, tho' both of Wood, one over that River which runs on one side the Town; the other over that, which divides it in the middle, the Tide runs thro' both with vast Rapidity; notwithstanding which, Ships of Burden come up, and paying for it, are often fasten'd to the Bridge, while loading or unloading. While I was here, there came in four or five

English Ships laden with Corn, the first, as they told me, that had come in to unlade there, since the beginning of the War.

On that Side of the River where the new Citadel is built, at a very little distance lies *Pont d' Esprit*, a Place mostly inhabited by *Jews*, who drive a great Trade there, and are esteemed very rich, tho' as in all other Countries mostly very rogueish. Here the Queen Dowager of *Spain* has kept her Court ever since the Jealousy of the present King reclus'd her from *Madrid.* As Aunt to his Competitor *Charles* (now Emperor) he apprehended her Intrigueing; for which Reason giving her an Option of Retreat, that Princess made choice of this City, much to the Advantage of the Place, and in all Appearance much to her own Satisfaction. She is a Lady not of the lesser Size; and lives here in suitable Splendour, and not without the Respect due to a Person of her high Quality: Every time she goes to take the Air, the Cannon of the Citadel saluting her, as she passes over the Bridge; and to say Truth, the Country round is extremely pleasant, and abounds in plenty of all Provisions; especially in wild Fowl. *Bayonne* Hams are, to a Proverb, celebrated all over *France.*

We waited here near five Months before the expected Transports arrived from *England,* without any other Amusements, than such as are common to People under Suspence. Short Tours will not admit of great Varieties; and much Acquaintance could not be any way suitable to People, that had long been in a strange Country, and earnestly desired to return to our own. Yet one Accident befell me here, that was nearer costing me my Life, than all I had before encounter'd, either in Battle or Siege.

Going to my Lodgings one Evening, I unfortunately met with an Officer, who would needs have me along with him, aboard one of the *English* Ships, to drink a Bottle of *English* Beer. He had been often invited, he said; and I am afraid our Countryman, continued he, will hold himself slighted, if I delay it longer. *English* Beer was a great rarity, and the Vessel lay not at any great distance from my Lodgings; so without any further Persuasion I consented. When we came upon the Bridge, to which the Ship we were to go aboard was fastened, we found, as was customary, as well as necessary, a Plank laid over from the Ship, and a Rope to hold by, for safe Passage. The Night was very dark; and I had cautiously enough taken care to provide a Man with a Lanthorn to prevent Casualties. The Man with the Light went first, and out of his abundant Complaisance, my Friend, the Officer, would have me follow the Light: But I was no sooner stept upon the Plank after my Guide, but Rope and Plank gave way, and Guide and I tumbled both together into the Water.

The Tide was then running in pretty strong: However, my Feet in the Fall touching Ground, gave me an opportunity to recover my self a little; at which Time I catch'd fast hold of a Buoy, which was plac'd over an Anchor on one of the Ships there riding: I held fast, till the Tide rising stronger and stronger threw me off my Feet; which gave an Opportunity to the poor Fellow, our Lanthorn-bearer, to lay hold of one of my Legs, by which he held as fast as I by the Buoy. We had lain thus lovingly at Hull together, struggling with the increasing Tide, which, well for us, did not break my hold (for if it had, the Ships which lay breast a breast had certainly sucked us under) when several on the Bridge, who saw us fall, brought others with Ropes and Lights to our Assistance; and especially my Brother Officer, who had been Accessary as well as Spectator of our Calamity; tho' at last a very small Portion of our Deliverance fell to his share.

As soon as I could feel a Rope, I quitted my hold of the Buoy; but my poor Drag at my Heels would not on any account quit his hold of my Leg. And as it was next to an Impossibility, in that Posture to draw us up the Bridge to save both, if either of us, we must still have perished, had not the Alarm brought off a Boat or two to our Succour, who took us in.

I was carry'd as fast as possible, to a neighbouring House hard by, where they took immediate care to make a good Fire; and where I had not been long before our intended Host, the Master of the Ship, came in very much concern'd, and blaming us for not hailing the Vessel, before we made an Attempt to enter. For, says he, the very Night before, my Vessel was robb'd; and that Plank and Rope were a Trap design'd for the Thieves, if they came again; not imagining that Men in an honest way would have come on board without asking Questions. Like the wise Men of this World, I hereupon began to form Resolutions against a Thing, which was never again likely to happen; and to draw inferences of Instruction from an Accident, that had not so much as a Moral for its Foundation.

One Day after this, partly out of Business, and partly out of Curiosity, I went to see the Mint here, and having taken notice to one of the Officers, that there was a difference in the Impress of their Crown Pieces, one having at the bottom the Impress of a Cow, and the other none:

"Sir," reply'd that Officer, "you are much in the right in your Observation. Those that have the Cow, were not coin'd here, but at *Paw*, the chief City of *Navarr*; where they enjoy the Privilege of a Mint, as well as we. And Tradition tells," says he, "that the Reason of that Addition to the Impress was this: A certain King of *Navarr* (when it was a Kingdom distinct from that of *France*) looking out of a Window of the Palace, spy'd a Cow, with her Calf standing aside her, attack'd by a Lyon, which had got loose out of his Menagery. The Lyon strove to get the young Calf into his Paw; the Cow bravely defended her Charge; and so well, that the Lyon at last, tir'd and weary, withdrew, and left her Mistress of the Field of Battle; and her young one. Ever since which, concluded that Officer, by Order of that King, the Cow is plac'd at the bottom of the Impress of all the Money there coined."

Whether or no my Relator guess'd at the Moral, or whether it was Fact, I dare not determine; But to me it seem'd apparent, that it was no otherways intended, than as an emblematical Fable to cover, and preserve the Memory of the Deliverance of *Henry* the Fourth, then the young King of *Navarr*, at that eternally ignominious Slaughter, the Massacre of *Paris*. Many Historians, their own as well as others, agree, that the House of *Guise* had levell'd the Malice of their Design at that great Prince. They knew him to be the lawful Heir; but as they knew him bred, what they call'd a *Hugonot*, Barbarity and Injustice was easily conceal'd under the Cloak of Religion, and the Good of Mother Church, under the veil of Ambition, was held sufficient to postpone the Laws of God and Man. Some of those Historians have deliver'd it as Matter of Fact, that the Conspirators, in searching after that young King, press'd into the very Apartments of the Queen his Mother; who having, at the Toll of the Bell, and Cries of the Murder'd, taken the Alarm, on hearing 'em coming, plac'd her self in her Chair, and cover'd the young King her Son with her Farthingale, till they were gone. By which means she found an opportunity to convey him to a Place of more Safety; and so preserv'd him from those bloody Murderers, and in them from the Paw of the Lyon. This was only a private Reflection of my own at that Time; but I think carries so great a Face of Probability, that I can see no present Reason to reject it. And to have sought after better Information from the Officer of the Mint, had been to sacrifice my Discretion to my Curiosity.

While I stay'd at *Bayonne*, the Princess *Ursini* came thither, attended by some of the King of *Spain's* Guards. She had been to drink the Waters of some famous Spaw in the Neighbourhood, the Name of which has now slipt my Memory. She was most splendidly entertain'd by the Queen Dowager of *Spain*; and the Mareschal *de Montrevel* no less signaliz'd himself in his Reception of that great Lady, who was at that Instant the greatest Favourite in the *Spanish* Court; tho' as I have before related, she was some Time after basely undermined by a Creature of her own advancing.

BAYONNE is esteem'd the third *Emporium* of Trade in all *France*. It was once, and remain'd long so, in the Possession of the *English*; of which had History been silent, the Cathedral Church had afforded evident Demonstration; being in every respect of the *English* Model, and quite different to any of their own way of Building in *France*.

PAMPELONA is the Capital City of the *Spanish Navarr*, supposed to have been built by *Pompey*. 'Tis situated in a pleasant Valley, surrounded by lofty Hills. This Town, whether famous or infamous, was the Cause of the first Institution of the Order of the Jesuits. For at the Siege of this Place *Ignatius Loyola* being only a private Soldier, receiv'd a shot on his Thigh, which made him uncapable of following that Profession any longer; upon which he set his Brains to work, being a subtle Man, and invented the Order of the Jesuits, which has been so troublesome to the World ever since.

At *Saint Stephen* near *Lerida*, an Action happened between the *English* and *Spaniards*, in which Major General *Cunningham* bravely fighting at the Head of his Men, lost his Life, being extreamly much lamented. He was a Gentleman of a great Estate, yet left it, to serve his Country; *Dulce est pro Patria Mori.*

About two Leagues from *Victoria*, there is a very pleasant Hermitage plac'd upon a small rising Ground, a murmuring Rivulet running at the bottom, and a pretty neat Chapel standing near it, in which I saw *Saint Christopher* in a Gigantick Shape, having a *Christo* on his Shoulders. The Hermit was there at his Devotion, I ask'd him (tho' I knew it before) the reason why he was represented in so large a Shape: The Hermit answered with great Civility, and told me, he had his Name from *Christo Ferendo*, for when our Saviour was young, he had an inclination to pass a River, so *Saint Christopher* took him on his Shoulders in order to carry him over, and as the Water grew deeper and deeper, so he grew higher and higher.

At last we received News, that the *Gloucester* Man of War, with two Transports, was arrived at *Port Passage*, in order for the Transporting of all the remaining Prisoners of War into *England.*

Accordingly they march'd next Day, and there embark'd. But I having before agreed with a Master of a Vessel, which was loaded with Wine for *Amsterdam*, to set me ashoar at *Dover*, stay'd behind, waiting for that Ship, as did that for a fair Wind.

In three or four Days' Time, a fine and fair Gale presented; of which the Master taking due Advantage, we sail'd over the Bar into the Bay of *Biscay*. This is with Sailors, to a Proverb, reckon'd the roughest of Seas; and yet on our Entrance into it, nothing appear'd like it. 'Twas smooth as Glass; a Lady's Face might pass for young, and in its Bloom, that discover'd no more Wrinkles; Yet scarce had we sail'd three Leagues, before a prodigious Fish presented it self to our View. As near as we could guess, it might be twenty Yards in Length; and it lay sporting it self on the surface of the Sea, a great Part appearing out of the Water. The Sailors, one and all, as soon as they saw it, declar'd it the certain Forerunner of a Storm. However, our Ship kept on its Course, before a fine Gale, till we had near passed over half the Bay; when, all on a sudden, there was such a hideous Alteration, as makes Nature recoil on the very Reflection. Those Seas that seem'd before to smile upon us, with the Aspect of a Friend, now in a Moment chang'd their flattering Countenance into that of an open Enemy; and Frowns, the certain Indexes of Wrath, presented us with apparent Danger, of which little on this Side Death could be the Sequel. The angry Waves cast themselves up into Mountains, and scourg'd the Ship on every Side from Poop to Prow: Such Shocks from the contending Wind and Surges! Such Falls from Precipices of Water, to dismal Caverns of the same uncertain Element! Although the latter seem'd to receive us in Order to skreen us from the Riot of the former, Imagination could offer no other Advantage than that of a Winding-Sheet, presented and prepared for our approaching Fate. But why mention I Imagination? In me 'twas wholly dormant. And yet those Sons of stormy Weather, the Sailors, had theirs about them in full Stretch; for seeing the Wind and Seas so very boisterous, they lash'd the Rudder of the Ship, resolv'd to let her drive, and steer herself; since it was past their Skill to steer her. This was our Way of sojourning most Part of that tedious Night; driven where the Winds and Waves thought fit to drive us, with all our Sails quite lower'd and flat upon the Deck. If *Ovid*, in the little *Archipelagian* Sea, could whine out his *jam jam jacturus*, &c. in this more dismal Scene, and much more dangerous Sea (the Pitch-like Darkness of the Night adding to all our sad Variety of Woes) what Words in Verse or Prose could serve to paint our Passions, or our

Expectations? Alas! our only Expectation was in the Return of Morning; It came at last; yet even slowly as it came, when come, we thought it come too soon, a new Scene of sudden Death being all the Advantage of its first Appearance. Our Ship was driving full Speed, towards the *Breakers* on the *Cabritton* Shore, between *Burdeaux* and *Bayonne*; which filled us with Ideas more terrible than all before, since those were past, and these seemingly as certain. Beside, to add to our Distress, the Tide was driving in, and consequently must drive us fast to visible Destruction. A State so evident, that one of our Sailors, whom great Experience had render'd more sensible of our present Danger, was preparing to save one, by lashing himself to the main Mast, against the expected Minute of Desolation. He was about that melancholy Work, in utter Despair of any better Fortune, when, as loud as ever he could bawl, he cry'd out, *a Point, a Point of Wind.* To me, who had had too much of it, it appear'd like the Sound of the last Trump; but to the more intelligent Crew, it had a different Sound. With Vigour and Alacrity they started from their Prayers, or their Despair, and with all imaginable Speed, unlash'd the Rudder, and hoisted all their Sails. Never sure in Nature did one Minute produce a greater Scene of Contraries. The more skilful Sailors took Courage at this happy Presage of Deliverance. And according to their Expectation did it happen; that heavenly Point of Wind deliver'd us from the Jaws of those *Breakers*, ready open to devour us; and carrying us out to the much more wellcome wide Sea, furnished every one in the Ship with Thoughts, as distant as we thought our Danger.

We endeavoured to make *Port Passage*; but our Ship became unruly, and would not answer her Helm; for which Reason we were glad to go before the Wind, and make for the Harbour of *Saint Jean de Luz.* This we attain'd without any great Difficulty, and to the Satisfaction of all, Sailors as well as Passengers, we there cast Anchor, after the most terrible Storm (as all the oldest Sailors agreed) and as much Danger as ever People escap'd.

Here I took notice, that the Sailors buoy'd up their Cables with Hogsheads; enquiring into the Reason of which, they told me, that the Rocks at the Bottom of the Harbour were by Experience found to be so very sharp, that they would otherwise cut their Cables asunder. Our Ship was obliged to be drawn up into the Dock to be refitted; during which, I lay in the Town, where nothing of Moment, or worth reciting, happen'd.

I beg Pardon for my Errors; the very Movements of Princes must always be considerable, and consequently worth Recital. While the Ship lay in the Dock, I was one Evening walking upon the Bridge, with the little Island near it, (which I have before spoke of) and had a little *Spanish* Dog along with me, when at the further End I spy'd a Lady, and three or four Gentlemen in Company; I kept on my Pace of Leisure, and so did they; but when I came nearer, I found they as much out number'd me in the Dog, as they did in the human Kind. And I soon experienced to my Sorrow, that their Dogs, by their Fierceness and Ill-humour, were Dogs of Quality; having, without Warning, or the least Declaration of War, fallen upon my little Dog, according to pristine Custom, without any honourable Regard to Size, Interest or Number. However the good Lady, who, by the Privilege of her Sex, must be allow'd the most competent Judge of Inequalities, out of an Excess of Condescension and Goodness, came running to the Relief of oppressed poor *Tony*; and, in courtly Language, rated her own oppressive Dogs for their great Incivility to Strangers. The Dogs, in the Middle of their insulting Wrath, obey'd the Lady with a vast deal of profound Submission; which I could not much wonder at, when I understood, that it was a Queen Dowager of *Spain*, who had chid them.

Our Ship being now repaired, and made fit to go out again to Sea, we left the Harbour of *Saint Jean de Luz*, and with a much better Passage, as the last Tempest was still dancing in my Imagination, in ten Days' Sail we reach'd *Dover*. Here I landed on the last Day of *March*, 1713 having not, till then, seen or touch'd *English* Shoar from the Beginning of *May*, 1705.

I took Coach directly for *London*, where, when I arriv'd, I thought my self transported into a Country more foreign, than any I had either fought or pilgrimag'd in. Not foreign, do I mean, in respect to others, so much as to it self. I left it, seemingly, under a perfect Unanimity: The fatal Distinctions of *Whig* and *Tory* were then esteemed meerly nominal; and of no more ill Consequence or Danger, than a Bee robb'd of its Sting. The national Concern went on with Vigour, and the prodigious Success of the Queen's Arms, left every Soul without the least Pretence to a Murmur. But now on my Return, I found them on their old Establishment, perfect Contraries, and as unlikely to be brought to meet as direct Angles. Some arraigning, some extolling of a Peace; in which Time has shown both were wrong, and consequently neither could be right in their Notions of it, however an over prejudic'd Way of thinking might draw them into one or the other. But *Whig* and

Tory are, in my Mind, the compleatest Paradox in Nature, and yet like other Paradoxes, old as I am, I live in Hope to see, before I die, those seeming Contraries perfectly reconcil'd, and reduc'd into one happy Certainty, the Publick Good.

*****

Whilst I stay'd at *Madrid*, I made several Visits to my old Acquaintance General *Mahoni.* I remember that he told me, when the Earl of *Peterborow* and he held a Conference at *Morvidro*, his Lordship used many Arguments to induce him to leave the *Spanish* Service. *Mahoni* made several Excuses, especially that none of his Religion was suffer'd to serve in the *English* Army. My Lord reply'd, That he would undertake to get him excepted by an Act of Parliament. I have often heard him speak with great Respect of his Lordship, and was strangely surprized, that after so many glorious Successes he should be sent away.

He was likewise pleased to inform me, that at the Battle of *Saragoza*, 'twas his Fortune to make some of our Horse to give way, and he pursued them for a considerable time; but at his Return, he saw the *Spanish* Army in great Confusion: But it gave him the Opportunity of attacking our Battery of Guns; which he performed with great Slaughter, both of Gunners and Matrosses: He at the same time inquired, who 'twas that commanded there in chief. I informed him 'twas Col. *Bourguard*, one that understood the Oeconomy of the Train exceeding well. As for that, he knew nothing of; but that he would vouch, he behaved himself with extraordinary Courage, and defended the Battery to the utmost extremity, receiving several Wounds, and deserved the Post in which he acted. A Gentleman who was a Prisoner at *Gualaxara*, informed me, that he saw King *Philip* riding through that Town, being only attended with one of his Guards.

Saragoza, or *Cæsar Augusta*, lies upon the River *Ebro*, being the Capital of *Arragon*; 'tis a very ancient City, and contains fourteen great Churches, and twelve Convents. The Church of the Lady of the *Pillar* is frequented by Pilgrims, almost from all Countries; 'twas anciently a Roman Colony.

Tibi laus, tibi honor, tibi sit gloria, O gloriosa Trinitas, quia tu dedisti mihi hanc opportunitatem, omnes has res gestas recordandi. Nomen tuum sit benedictum, per sæcula sæculorum. Amen.

THE MEMOIRS OF
Majr. *Alexander Ramkins,*

A HIGHLAND OFFICER,
Now in Prison at *AVIGNON.*

BEING

An Account of several remarkable Adventures during about
Twenty Eight Years Service in *Scotland, Germany, Italy,
Flanders* and *Ireland;* exhibiting a very agreeable and instructive
Lesson of Human Life, both in a Publick and
Private Capacity, in several pleasant Instances of his
Amours, Gallantry, Oeconomy, &c.

THE PUBLISHER TO THE READER

I Think it proper to inform the Reader that these Papers were deliver'd into my Hands by a near Kinsman of the Authors, who lately came from the Southern Parts of France. *His Design in imparting these Memoirs to me, was (as I quickly perceiv'd) to know my Sentiments of the Performance. It seems the Gentleman had been sour'd by* French *Practises, and was willing that the World should be no longer a Stranger to what was the ground of his distast. The Author appears very well qualify d for his Task, and opens a Scene of Politicks which the good natur'd part of Mankind will scarce think human Race capable of. Those that are acquainted with the Person of Major Ramkins, assure me, that the late King fames never had a more active and diligent Servant, and that he was one never wanting in his Station. If I am of a contrary Opinion to the Publick in judging these Remarks worthy of the Press, 'tis what I do not at present find my self convinc'd of. One Benefit at least may be expected from 'em, that they will induce all true Britains to be cautious, and not imbark themselves in a foreign Interest for the future, if not for the sake of their Country, at least for their own Sakes. I will not anticipate the Contents, but only take the freedom to acquaint the Reader in General. That it will be one of the greatest Paradoxes in future Ages to read, that the Court of* St. Germains *should have been a Sleep, and impos'd upon for Twenty Eight Years successively, unless their being trick'd by the greatest of Politicians, be a Circumstance to take off from the Surprize.*

THE MEMOIRS OF
Alexander Ramkins, &c.

I was not above Seventeen Years of Age when the Battle of *Gillycranky* was fought between the Two Highland Generals, the Lord Viscount *Dundee* and *Mackay*. And being then a Stripling at the University of *Aberdeen* and understanding that several Clans were gathering into a Body in defence of King *James* III sold my Books and Furniture of my Lodgings, and equipp'd my self to observe the Martial Call, I found my self prompted with. I arriv'd in a few Days near the Field of Battle, and joyn'd my self with a broken Body of Men who were making up towards the Mountains to recover themselves after the Fatigue of Battle. The Noviceship I went through in the *Highlands*, was no improper Foundation for the course Method of living I have been since engag'd in for above Twenty Seven Years; during which Time, I have run through all those Hardships which are incident to one who seeks a Preferment in Fire and Smoak.

While I strolled about in the *Highlands*, it was my good Fortune to be under the Tuition of an old Officer, who let me into many of those little Secrets which are not unserviceable to such as Design to make the whole Earth the Theatre of their Life; but what I chiefly valued this old Gentleman's Conversation for, was the Happiness I had to be a Hearer of some of his Politick Lessons, of which he was a great Master, having furnish'd himself by Fifty Years Practice, with the best Idea's of that kind.

Upon a certain Day when our Party were out, some upon Foraging, and others to get Intelligence, I being alone in a Cottage with this old Captain, and being desirous to know his Opinion of the Affairs of *Europe* in general, as also what was like to be the Issue of that Cause we had undertaken. The old Captain willing to satisfy my Curiosity as far as his Skill would reach, pulled out some Remarks he had made upon the Year 1640. Observe, *says* he, Child what I say to you, 'tis a Maxim never to be neglected among Politicians to keep up Divisions in an Enemies Country; you may, perhaps, imagine that this will be a short Game that is a playing, but depend upon it my Grey Hairs will not see an end of it. I allow the King of *France* has declar'd himself a Friend to King *James* II; He is a very powerful Prince, and if he would turn his Forces this Way, and be upon the Defensive near Home, a few Months would bring the War to a Period. But that Monarch has things in his Head which I must not mention. There will be great Skirmishing in the Dominions of *Great Britain*, but no decisive Action if *Lewis le Grand* can hinder it. He takes Cardinal *Richlieu's* Conduct for a Precedent. It would have been no difficult Task for the *French* to have joyn'd their Forces with King *Charles* I. and have made a short Hand of that Contest between the King and Parliament; but that Politick Cardinal instead of this Method, had Emissaries in the *English* Cabinet to exaggerate Matters between them. The same Method has been observ'd by that Nation ever since; and if *Lewis le Grand* does not make a Politick Use of King *James* II. without doing him any real Service, I shall be very willing to correct my self, and cancel that Paragraph in my Observations.

This was the first Politick Lesson I was entertain'd with by my old Master; which, though at that time my want of Experience did not permit me thoroughly to comprehend, yet since, a Resemblance of Circumstances has often reviv'd it my Mind; nor could I ever be well reconcil'd to that Piece of Morality, That it was a laudable Practice to set People by the Ears together.

The hopes of being releas'd, is the best Support to Men in Misery, and our small Body of Three Hundred Men wou'd not have remain'd so long under Discipline, if Expectation had not been nourish'd with daily Alarms of Assistance from *France*. Our commanding Officer was Romantickly Loyal, and look'd upon every little Hill we scrambled over, as an impregnable Fortress, from whose Summit he often took occasion to Harangue us, as if the Eyes of all *Europe* were upon us, and the Fate of the Three Kingdoms hung at our Swords Points. But the Truth was, I believe, we were unknown to all Mankind, and if those Villages we march'd by you'd but secure the Cattle from us, the State was in no great Danger from our Quarter.

As for the Hopes of being assisted from *France*, though our Commander neglected no Pains to instill such a Belief into the Generality of the Soldiers, in order to prolong his Reign in that honourable Post he enjoy'd, yet I read it plainly in my old Captain's Forehead, that *France* was not accustom'd to open their Treasures in countenancing Chimerical Adventures, and that the most we could expect from thence, would be a small *Dunkirk* Privateer, with a Hogshead or two of Brandy to keep the Cause alive, while he was pushing on his Conquests in other Parts of the Globe, in which the Glory and Interest of *France* was more immediately concern'd. For my own Part, as I was resolv'd to pursue my Fortune in the way of Arms, and finding that there was no appearance of *Scotland's* being a Place of Action, so I advis'd with my old Master what course I should steer to answer the Ends of my Call. The old Gentleman, though he might have deterr'd me from such an Undertaking, by proposing himself as an Instance how little you'd be gain'd that way, having nothing to show for near Sixty Years Service in the War, but a Bundle of Politick Remarks drawn from the false Steps he and others have made in endeavouring to make their Fortune, yet since every Man must spin out his Thread of Life one way or other, and that that was most likely to succeed well to which a Person found himself most inclinable, so he humour'd my present Dispositions; but at the same time, counsell'd me to Transport my self over to the Continent, where I might meet with something worthy my Curiosity. Islands, *says he*, are commonly won and lost in a Day, nor will they afford you that variety of Stratagems which will make you perfect in the Art of War. After this I only waited for a fit Opportunity to quit the Service I was in, for though I was no farther engaged than in the Quality of a Gentleman Volunteer, yet a Strain of Honour would not permit me to forsake my Companions, unless some more plausible Reason occurr'd to me than what I could invent at that Time. But it was not long before an occasion offered it self to put my Project in Execution. By moving too and fro our little Army, I was within Twenty Miles of my Mother's House, (for my Father had been dead some Years) having therefor first communicated my Design to my old Master, whom I intended to invite along with me, if he approv'd of my Undertaking.

In conclusion, Things were order'd so, that the old Captain, with myself, and another, were detach'd out towards the Coast to get Intelligence, and that Night about Eleven we agreeably surpriz'd my Mother who had for several Months been lamenting the Loss of her darling Son, whom she suppos'd to be kill'd at the Battle of *Gillycranky;* for she had not justly inform'd herself of the precise Time I ran away from the College at *Aberdeen.*

I had Two elder Brothers, who both inherited the martial Spirit of our Family, had been a long time absent from Home; one of them was prefer'd in the Emperor's Army in *Hungary,* the other belonging to the Guards of King *James* II follow'd his Fate into *France* and *Ireland,* and afterwards was kill'd in *Ireland.* My father had three small Lordships, which we were equally to be Sharers of, allowing proportionably for my

Mothers maintenance, with a Thousand Pounds to be rais'd to marry our only Sister.

Now, as it was my Intention to Travel and gain Experience in the World, so my old Captain put it into my Head to raise a Sum of Money upon the Credit of my Land, assuring me it would prove my best Friend upon all Occasions, for that the World had but a very mean Opinion of Merit when strip'd of other Advantages to recommend it. This Affair took up more Time than my warm Temper could well bear, and the Lawyers threw in so many Delays, that had not the old Captain (who was well acquainted with Business) been at my Elbow to forward Things, I might have lost my Vocation of being a Soldier before any Agreement cou'd have been made. But after two Months were expir'd, I found my self Master of fifteen Hundred Pound, the Price of my share of Land after the Deductions made for my Mother and Sister; Twelve Hundred Pounds I lodg'd with a Banker at *Amsterdam*, the other Three was employ'd for an Equipage, and to supply my Necessities in the Tour I design'd to take. The old Captain I intended to take along with me to be my Guide as well as Adviser; for I saw so many Perfections in him, which the ungrateful World had neglected, That I judg'd it would be an honourable Omen in one that was beginning the World, not to let him leave the Stage of Life unrewarded: But as his Years had render'd him incapable to attend me in my Rambles, so Death came in to release him, and this worthy Person was taken from me about Ten Days before the Time I had fix'd for my Travels. However, I must not let his Memory die, but give the World an Account of him as far as I cou'd gather from the Gentleman when he was disposed to Answer to Questions concerning himself, in which he always behaved himself with a well guarded Modesty.

I learn'd from him, That his Father was the Head of a Clan which was one half cut off by *Oliver Cromwell*, and the other half Transported into the *West-Indies*, with the fifteen Hundred *Scots*, that were condemn'd thither to Slavery by the Protector. My Friend being at that time about Twelve Years old, chose rather to share his Fathers Fate, and view the Western parts of the Worlds, than fall into the Hands of a Person who would stain the Beauty of his tender Mind, by giving him an unsuitable Education. After he had buried his Father in *Virginia*, he took the Opportunity of a *French* Vessel to pass over to *Brest*, and so to *Paris*, who by the Assistance of a *Scotch* Nobleman, who was acquainted with his Family, he pick'd up a liberal Education, and made himself Master of the *French* and *Latin*, and having it in his

Election whether he wou'd engage himself to the Church or follow the Camp, he chose the latter, and after some Months spent in the Academy, he enter'd himself among the *Gens d'Arms*, and made very useful Observations in two or three Campaigns in *Germany*, in the last of which he was taken Prisoner and seduc'd into the Emperors Service by some of his Countrymen, who persuaded him the *Germans* were more accustom'd to advance Strangers than the *French*. In a little time he was observ'd by his Colonel to be a Person of Parts and Resolution, and so was gradually advanc'd from a Cornet to a Captain of Horse; and as a Man of Spirit and Action never wants Opportunity to shew himself, so this Gentleman met with many brave Adventures in the way of Soldiery, which some time he would occasionally recount to me, but they would be too tedious to insert in these Remarks. When King *James* II came to the Crown of *England*, he desired to throw up his Commission, it being suggested to him, that the Prince stood in need of some old experienc'd Officers to model an Army he was raising. Upon this Prospect he pass'd over to *England*, but being destitute of Acquaintance he loiter'd about the Court, till one of the Duke of *Berwick's* Retinue, who had heard of him at the Siege of *Buda*, made the King acquainted with him. So he was order'd down into *Scotland* with the Promise of a Colonels Commission, but the Revolution following soon after, he acted only as a Captain of Foot at the Battle of *Gillycranky*.

But to cut short this Digression, the time now drew near that I was to undertake my intended Ramble, and indeed it was high time; for it being whisper'd about in the Neighbourhood that I had been in Arms for King *James* II. *Home*, as the saying is, *was too hot a Place for me*; so I sent my Servant to enquire for a Conveniency to pass over to *Flanders*, and in two Days I was provided with a *Roterdam* Vessel, and so with very little Ceremony took leave of my Mother, who though she was unwilling to part with me, yet she prefer'd the lesser Danger to the greater, and rather wish'd me expos'd to the Waves, than to the Insults of my Enemies at Home.

The Wind blew very fresh, but tacking about too much to the *North East*, it drove us upon Shore with that violence that we were oblig'd to put in twice to Land, once at *Scarborough*, and again at *Yarmouth*.

At this latter Place, a Pragmatical Searcher came aboard us with an Air of Authority as if he design'd to visit my Trunks; but one of the Sailors informing me that this was stretching his Commission, for he ought not to search after any Goods unless the Cargo was design'd for that Port, so I ridded my self of this Spark with a Half-Crown Piece; for I had no mind to enter much into a Parley with him lest he might discover my *Highland* Expedition, for Fear never wants Apprehensions. After two Days stay in this Port, the Wind proving favourable, we were not very long in making a Trip to *Roterdam*, where I only refresh'd myself a few Hours, and pass'd on to *Amsterdam* to visit my Bank, and settle a Correspondence as to Returns of money.

I met with nothing in this City that made any Impression upon me to stay any longer than settling the small concern of Money I lodg'd there. The hurry of Business was too Mechanical an Entertainment, for one whose Head was filled with high Flights of Honour, Sieges, Battles, and other such like Sports. The *French* Army at this time lay upon the *Rhine*, and my Design was to make that Way. When I arriv'd there, I found they had surrounded *Mentz* in order to Besiege it. I was glad to begin my first Campaign with so glorious an Undertaking, not doubting, but a great deal of Bravery would be shown where the Flower of the Houshold was design'd for Action; but before I could make any Advantage of this Occurrence, I was to make my self known to some Person of Character who might introduce me so as to be a Spectator of that noble Siege. At last I met with a *Scotch* Gentleman, who rid in among the grand Molquetains, who being fully inform'd of my Warlike Dispositions, assur'd me he would put me into the readiest Method he cou'd to gain Experience; but when he inform'd me that I must not pretend to great Things on a sudden, and that I had at present only two Things in Election, either to carry a Musquet in a Common Foot Regiment, during the Siege, or which he wou'd rather advise me to (in case I had Money to be at that expence) to go to *Strasburgh* and put my self under Discipline for six Weeks or two Months among the *French* Cadets.

I must confess this was a great balk upon a double account: It not only depriv'd me of the Satisfaction of seeing the Siege carried on, but it was a sensible check to my aspiring Humour, to think what Drudgery I was to undergo before I could be regarded by the World; but when I reflected on what I had often heard the old Captain (I buried in the *Highlands*) say upon this Head, it made me easier under the Disappointment, and the next Day I went on to *Strasburg*, and enter'd my self among the Cadets. 'Tis in the Nature of a College, where young Gentlemen are instructed in the Rudiments of War.

During my stay at *Strasburg* I omitted no opportunity of improving myself as to the *French* and *High Dutch* Fortifications, and other Parts of the Mathematicks which were useful in War. I was also present at some Lectures of Politicks which were given to those more advanc'd in Years, in which they handled the Interest of Nations, and brought down their Reflections to the present Times. This I look'd upon as an excellent Method of educating young Officers; for it qualify'd them to be serviceable to their Country under a double Capacity; that is, as well to Argue as to Fight for it, and defend it equally with their Tongue and Sword.

I remember an Antient Marquis who had a Superintendency over this Academy, entertaining us one Day with the Motives of the present War, and running up the Cause to its Original, laid it before us in this manner: *That the Monarchs of France wou'd look upon themselves as injur'd by the rest of the Princes of* Europe, *till the imperial Diadem was restor'd to* France, *who were first Possessors of it in the Person of* Charles the Great; *that they had made several pushes in all Ages to recover it, but without Effect; that while the* English *had footing in* France, *they were too lazy to extend their Conquests upon the Empire of the* West; *and when they had chased out the* English, *and were rid of that Incumbrance, the House of* Austria, *by the vast Acquisitions of the* Low Countries, *and joint Power of* Spain, *sat so hard upon 'em, that* France *was not in a Capacity to make any Advances towards recovering their Right to the Empire: What therefore they had been upon these latter Years, was to make a strong Party among the Electoral Princes, and by degrees secure a Majority in the Imperial Diet, in order to set aside the House of* Austria, *and settle the Imperial Crown upon the* French *Line, as it was in the Beginning.* To this he added, *That this invincible Monarch,* Lewis XIV, *had made considerable Advances of late Years, especially in bringing over several Electors, and now the Chapter of* Cologn *to chuse Cardinal* Fustenberg *for their Archbishop, who though a Native of Germany, yet was a* Frenchman *by Interest, and had given his Word to be very Industrious in settling the Imperial Dignity upon the House of* Bourbon. *And this Election of Cardinal* Fustenberg *being contested by the Emperor and Pope Innocent* XI. *was the Motive of the present War; for they put up the Duke of* Bavaria's *Brother in opposition against him.*

This Account of the occasion of the present War, vary'd very much from the Idea we in *Scotland* had of Affairs. We were made to believe, That the King of *France* being a zealous Roman Catholick

Monarch, had engag'd himself in a War against the Allies, meerly upon a Religious Motive, to re-establish King *James*, who was dethron'd upon no other Account but because he was a Roman Catholick. But I have since found by comparing Matters, that the Revolution in *England* was not the Occasion, but the Consequence of the War between the *French* and the Allies; for the Emperor, *&c.* understanding that King *James* II. was drawn into a Scrape by the *French* King, and that he made a Property of him to carry on his Ambitious Designs; 'tis not to be wonder'd at, if they prefer'd the general Good of *Europe*, and immediate Safety of their own People to the private Good of King *James* II, who had been so indiscreet as to expose himself to Ruin by giving into a *French* Project. However this unpolitick Management proved very lucky to *France* upon a double Account; for tho' they had begun a War upon the disedifying bottom of Ambition, it was afterwards consecrated in mny Peoples Thoughts, under a Colour of justifying a dethron'd Roman Catholick Prince, besides the Advantage of causing a considerable Diversion by fomenting a War in the Three Kingdoms of *Great-Britain*; for as for re-establishing that unfortunate Prince in his Throne, though I was a long Time of Opinion *France* really design'd it; yet since I have been convinc'd by undeniable Arguments, that it neither was his Interest to bring it about, nor that he ever seriously attempted it. I must own it was never very Intelligible to me, not even in my very darkest State of Bigottry for the *French* Interest, that the Emperor, the King of *Spain*, and Duke of *Savoy*, with many other Roman Catholick Princes, nay, the Pope himself should all fail in their Duty and Zeal for Religion, and the King of *France* (who was remarkable upon other Occasions for sacrificing it to Politick ends) should be the only one in *Europe* that wou'd stand up for it. It was not so in the Infancy of the *Dutch* Republic, when *France* concurr'd with the Seven Provinces to have them torn from the *Spanish* Monarchy, and by the same Assistance, enabled 'em to make head against the Church. It was not so when a Frown of *Oliver Cromwell* cou'd oblige *France* to lay aside the charitable Maxim of Royal Protection, and send *Charles* II. and his Brother the Duke of *York*, out of their Territories by an Infamous Condescension. But *James* II. had forgotten the Affronts offer'd to the Duke of *York*, and I suppose had a Mind to make a second Tryal of *French* Hospitality, and whether they would be more obliging to him in his old Age, than they had been in his Youth. Neither is this plausible Pretence of defending a Prince injur'd upon the Score of Religion, very consistent with their Conduct, in regard of the

Turk. To maintain a Catholick Prince at St. *Germains,* and support the Enemy of Christianity at *Constantinople* with great Remittances of Moneys, and a constant Supply of Engineers; is a piece of State Casuistry above my Comprehension, and Prince *Eugene* had a great deal of Reason to knock his Breast, and hold up his Hands to Heaven, when he saw *French* Engineers dragg'd out of *Turkish* Mines in *Hungary* with *Agnus Dei*'s, and Relicks about their Necks as Ensigns of *Lewis* XIV's Christianity, and Zeal for the Church.

But to proceed to my own concerns. As soon as the Time was expir'd, I propos'd to my self to stay in the Academy at *Strasburgh,* I provided my self with the Equipage of a grand Musketeer, and for a Present of 50 Pistols, and the strength of good Recommendation from my Countrymen, I was admitted to ride among 'em. But here I had a fresh Difficulty to struggle with. My Countrymen finding me pretty flush of Money, and that I was very generous, was as observant as a Spaniel, and so very Officious both early and late, that I found it impracticable to steal an Hour of Privacy to recollect my self, in order to model my Conduct after the best Precedents I met with in the course of the Day; and what made me yet more uneasy, he was not content to visit me alone, but had often a second or third with him; who as they were very obliging in informing me of the Methods of living in a Camp, so they was always very *adroit,* and gave me the Preference upon all Occasions; but then as I engross'd all the Ceremony of the Day, so I was thrown into unavoidable Circumstances of paying them for their Attendance. This constant Charge, though in Time it would have made me weary of acting the Grand Signior, yet I could better have bore with it, had I not smelt a Design they had to strip me of my Bank I had at *Amsterdam*; for I was so unguarded in my Conduct as to have acquainted my Countrymen with my Money concerns, which he and his Associates had already devour'd in their Imagination, and wanted but a fit Opportunity to draw me in at Play, and so at once put me upon a Level with themselves and other Soldiers of Fortune: But being aware of the Trap that was laid for me, my whole Study was how to disengage myself from this Gang, so as to give no Suspicion that I understood their meaning; for this I imagin'd might be the ground of a Quarrel, and to perhaps have worse Consequences than if they really had strip'd me of my Substance. Arm'd with this Caution, I receiv'd 'em in the usual manner, but still kept off when a Motion was made either of high drinking or playing deep; for no Man is secure, when either Liquor or Passion gains the Ascendent over him. But this State of Violence could not continue long, sometimes I was at a loss for an Excuse to baffle their Importunity, other times I found them dispos'd to represent me as of an uncomplying Temper, so that there was no way left but either to draw or withdraw, for I saw plainly that if I staid among them a Quarrel would ensue. This Consideration, with the unheard of Devastation I saw in the Palatinate made by the *French* Troops, gave me a Surfeit of the *Rhine*. I am not Ignorant that no Part of the World is free from Sharpers, but I thought in another Place I might better resist their first Onset, and let them gain no ground upon me, while Rule I here neglected for want of Experience. And now I was oblig'd to make a Call upon my Banker at *Amsterdam* for Two Hundred Pounds, resolving not to break the remaining 1000 Pound Bulk, unless upon some extraordinary Emergency. I had sometime before intimated to my Officers and Comrades the Design I had to quit the Service upon the *Rhine*, assuring them it was not out of any Disobligation, having experienced their obliging Temper upon all Occasions; but as I understood King *James* was at the Head of his Army in *Ireland*, so I look'd upon my self in some Measure inexcusable if I serv'd in a foreign Army, when I might contribute more immediately to succour my Prince. My Reasons were applauded, and I not a little content to depart without giving Disgust. Without delay therefore I posted to *Paris*, where I design'd to make no very long stay, only what was necessary to recover my self from the Fatigue of the Campaign, and satisfy my Curiosity in taking a View of that noble City. I was happy in one thing during my stay here, that I was agreeably surpriz'd with the fight of my only Sister, whose Husband being under some malignant Court Influence, was oblig'd to withdraw with his Family out of *Scotland*. *Paris* is a Place like all other great Cities, where Persons of all Conditions and Characters may spend their Time agreeably, if that useful Trifle call'd Money be not wanting. Hitherto I had no occasion to be Melancholly upon that Score; for though I was not furnish'd to make any extraordinary Figure, yet being only a single Person, and as yet never launch'd out into any Extravagances, so within my narrow Sphere, I made a decent Appearance. But as no Man is prosperous at all Times, so it was not long before I found my self engag'd in an Affair which very much troubled my Repose, and which I would willingly have compounded for with my *Amsterdam* Bank. The Business was this, my Eldest Brother before he went with King *James* into *Ireland*, made some stay at *Paris* and *St. Germains*, where he was order'd to collect some Recruits of the Three Nations, which he was to conduct over in the Quality of a Route-Captain. Now as he was a Person who had seen very much of the World, and was somewhat addicted to Gallantry and Intriguing with the Fair Sex, so he could not remain long in a Place without Publishing some Marks of his Vocation that way. It happen'd that a young Lady who lodg'd in the same House with him, had occasion to pay a visit to her Acquaintance; my Brother observing her in a Posture to go out of the House alone, offer'd to usher her to the place she design'd for. The Lady with the usual *French* Freedom and obliging Air, made him a Courtsey, and accepted the Offer. When he complied with this Piece of Civility, he took his leave, and return'd to his Lodgings. From this Accident my Brother dated an Intrigue. The Ladies Carriage (which by the way was nothing but what is customary there upon a slender Acquaintance) encourag'd him to make Advances; the next Step he made was to drink Tea with her in her Chamber, and afterwards he invited her to the *Opera*. But the young Lady as she was strictly Virtuous, never gave way to none of these Freedoms, but in the Company of her Landlady or her Daughter, who were both Prudes. In the mean time a Relation of this Gentlewoman's, who was a Lieutenant in the Regiment of *Navarre* came up to *Paris*, and had not been long in Town before he was inform'd by some busy Noddle, that his Cousin was either upon the Point of being married, or what was rather suggested to him, that one Captain *Ramkins* a *Scotch* Officer, who lodg'd in the same House, had dishonourable Designs upon her. Now as Persons never want Arguments to induce them to take things in the worst Sense, (tho' I will not avouch for my Brothers Intention) so the *French* Officer being of a suspicious and also a fiery Temper, wanted no body to exasperate him. He took it for granted the Thing was so, and taking Coach he came to his Kinswoman, and after having attack'd her with a great deal of scurrilous Language, he waited not for her Reply, but flung away to find my Brother in order to cut his Throat. My Brother was then at St. *Germains* receiving his last Orders from the Secretary for his departure for *Ireland*, but return'd that Night to *Paris*. His Landlady at his Return gave him a Note, which she said was deliver'd to her by the Post. The Contents were a double Surprize to him, first a bold and daring Challenge, and again, he neither knew whom he was to meet, nor upon what Account, only the Time and Place were mention'd. Thus doubtful with himself what Course to take, he acquainted his Landlady with the Subject of the Letter, but she was also at a loss, having neither seen the Lady's Relation, nor heard that he was come to Town, otherwise it might have created some Suspicion.

But after Supper, according to Custom, she went up to have an Hours Chat with the young Lady, and among other Things, mention'd the odd Letter Captain *Ramkins* had receiv'd that Evening; the Lady suspecting what the matter really was, gave the Landlady sufficient Intimation by the Consternation she was in, that she was not unacquainted with the Occasion of that Letter. In the mean time, my Brother was gone to consult with some of his Acquaintance how he should behave himself in this juncture: Some advis'd him to neglect it as a sham Challenge, whereby some of his Acquaintance being merry dispos'd had a mind to divert themselves; others judg'd it might be a Design to Assassinate him upon account of some old Grudge now worn out of his Memory; in conclusion, 'twas order'd that he should present himself at the Place mention'd in the Challenge, and in case it was a real Thing, and that he escap'd with Life, a Horse should be ready to ride Post to *Brest*, whether he and his Recruits were order'd to take Shipping. But that he might not Alarm his Lodgings, he spent the remainder of the Night in the Tavern with his Friends, a fitter Preparation than praying for the Work he was about. About Five in the Morning he set out towards the Place of Battle, half a dozen of his Acquaintance following him at a convenient distance, to wait for the Issue, and to see Justice done in case he was assaulted against the usual Method of Duelling. When he came to the Place apointed, he saw a young Gentleman walking and musing under a Hedge with his Arms a Kimbo, whom he rightly judg'd to be his Man. When he came within Speech of him, the *French* Officer stop'd and ask'd him if his Name was not *Ramkins*, and whether he had not receiv'd a Note the Evening before upon such an Occasion? my Brother made no other Reply, but that he took himself to be the Person, and that he would indite an Answer with the Point of his Sword; for though, said he, I am a Stranger both to you and the occasion of this Trouble you have given me, yet as I take you to be a Man of Honour, so I suppose you think your self injur'd to that degree, that Satisfaction either cannot or will not be given any other way, and therefore I am here ready to make up this mysterious Quarrel after the Method you have made choice of. It sometimes happens that Peace is struck up between Two Nations Sword in Hand; but my Brother's Antagonist was too warm to stand a Parley and act the Part of a Plenipotentiary; upon which, without making the least Reply, he whips off his Cloaths into his Shirt, and open'd his Breast to show his Adversary he scorn'd to take any ungenerous Advantage. My Brother was also honourable upon the same score; for though he wore a short

Buff Waiscoat without Skirts according to the Fashions of those Times, and which might have deadened a Push, yet he threw it off and put himself upon the Level with his Adversary in all respects, so to it they went. My Brother found himself much superior in Strength and Vigour, and that in all probability he cou'd Command his Adversary's Sword, paried with him a considerable Time, and put by several Pushes without attempting the Gentleman's Life, but finding him Resolute, and that one of them must fall, he made one home Thrust, and drove his Sword quite through his Adversary's Body, falling upon him at the same time; and thus fell this unfortunate young Gentleman a Victim to his ungovernable Passion.

It appear'd afterwards, that this *French* Officer having been often play'd upon by several in his Regiment, that he had been two Years among them and never yet made any Experiment of his personal Courage, told them at his going up to *Paris*, That they should here in a little Time he had qualify'd himself by killing his Man. Now it is suppos'd he thought the *British* Nation, not being fam'd for their Skill in handling the Sword, he had an excellent opportunity of showing his Manhood, and the Advantage of making his escape when he had done the Fact, because little or no Enquiry wou'd be made after a Stranger. My Brother being convinc'd his Adversary was incapable to Rally, made haste to gather up his Cloaths, exchanging the Evangelical Advice of *burying* the dead, to that natural Precept of *Self-preservation*, and I must leave him pursuing his Journey towards *Brest*, to return to his Lodgings, and give an account how this Catastrophe came to affect me at my coming to *Paris*.

The young Lady who was the Innocent occasion of this unfortunate Accident, took little Rest after she was inform'd of the Contents of the Note left by her Kinsman, and her Concern grew upon her when she understood Captain *Ramkins* was out of his Lodgings all Night; thus she remain'd under great Inquietudes till Three a Clock the next Day, when she, with her Landlady and Daughter, took a Coach privately and drove directly to the Place where the Gentlemen were to meet according to the Contents of the Letter. They discharg'd their Coach upon a pretence of taking a Walk in the Fields, and after a small Tour the Landlady's Daughter put her Foot into a Cake of clotted Blood, but it was so chang'd, as to the Colour, that she could not well distinguish what it was, but at a little distance finding a Glove, and several Blades of Grass ting'd with a Vermillion Dye, being press'd down and ruffled as it were with some Cattle weltring and tumbling about. They had a strong Suspicion one of the Gentlemen had ended his Days upon the Spot, and to clear their Suspicion, they walk'd back into the City till they arrived at the *Petite Chastelet*, which is a publick Room in the Nature of a Guard Bed, where all Corps are expos'd to view and whither People usually go in quest of any of their Friends, or Acquaintance that are wanting. And here the young Gentlewoman was quickly satisfy'd that her Cousin's Rashness had brought him to his End. This Accident happening not long before I came to *Paris*, the Discourse of it was very fresh, and what occasion'd me to have an account of it at my first Arrival, was my Lodging at the same House with my Brother, it being the usual Lodgings for *English* and *Scotch*. 'Tis true that Landlady and her Daughter where remov'd to *Orleans*, where they had an *Estate* belonging to their Family, but the young Lady, Cousin to the deceas'd Officer, was still in her old Apartment. I had not been above three Days, but my Name began to be known as well by the Direction of some Letters I receiv'd out of *Germany*, as by other means there are of having such Things divulg'd. The young Lady was not so struck with the Horror of the Name of her Cousins Murtherer, as not to have the Curiosity to peep at me as I came in and out of my Lodgings, and the more, because I had so great a Resemblance to him both as to Figure and Features, that without any extraordinary Skill in Physiognomy, she might conclude I was either his Brother or some near Relation. Now whether my Brother's Cavaliers Carriage had left an Idea in the Lady's Head which she could not conveniently part with, or her Inquisitiveness after me was only a Female Curiosity, I am not able to determine, but it was very unfortunate to me to have been so near a Kin to one she admired in case it was so, or that her Inquisitiveness should make me so publick; for I had not been in *Paris* above Eight Days, but the Archers or City Guards took me out of my Bed at Four a Clock in the Morning, and carried me to Prison upon strong Suspicion of being that very Captain *Ramkins* who had kill'd the *French* Officer in a Duel. Captain *Ramkins* I certainly was call'd at my own Request, having taken that Travelling Name as all Independent Gentlemen do, who cannot tell well what Title to give themselves upon the Road. My case had no very good Aspect at the beginning. There were so many Circumstances to render me suspected, that though I was satisfy'd my Life was not in Danger, yet it was an easy Thing to perceive it wou'd be both a troublesome, and also a chargeable Spot of Work. The first Thing I did was to send for my Brother-in-law, whom I employ'd as my Solicitor, to lay a true

Narration of the Fact before the King's Attorney. My Counsel advis'd me to *Subpoena* the young Lady, who wou'd be a material Witness that I was not the Captain *Ramkins* chargeable with the Fact, which she seem'd willingly to acquiesce to; but some of the deceased Friends endeavour'd to invalidate her *Affidavit*, upon a pretence, that there was too great an Intimacy between her and Captain *Ramkins*. However, to put the Contest upon an Issue which would allow of no Reply, I procured the Testimonies of several Officers in the Army, that I was actually upon the *Rhine* when the Duel was fought at *Paris*, besides the corroborating Evidence of several *Irish* Gentlemen who liv'd in *Paris* and at *St. Germains*, who were ready to offer their Oaths I was not the Man. 'Tis incredible to think what Pains the deceas'd Gentleman's Relations took to destroy me, though I have the Charity to think they judg'd I was the Person they sought after, though it is somewhat unintelligible they wou'd not Credit the young Lady their Cousin. This Affair help'd me off with the greatest Part of my ready Money, for 'tis a Blessing which attends all Law-Suits, that the Gainer is oblig'd to refund to the Lawyers what he recovers from his Adversary, and for my part, I pay'd pretty dear for an Authentick Copy of my Innocence; and the Carriage of the Court to me was such, as if I had been particularly favour'd in not being hang'd instead of my Brother.

After this troublesome Business was over, I began to enjoy my self a little in the Diversions of *Paris*; and by the Assistance of my Brother-in-law, I had a good Guide in him to view several of the Curiosities that City abounds with, though I cannot say I took any extraordinary relish that way, for my Thoughts being chiefly upon War, I digested other Matters as a nice Appetite does improper Food. It was my Intention to go over to *Ireland*, and to made that undertaking less chargeable to me, I endeavour'd to procure a Commission, which was no difficult matter at that Time, especially to one who was provided with a little Money to facilitate the Grant. I did not stick much upon the Nature of the Commission, for my Years, and small Experience could make no very extraordinary Demands; so I was Registred as a Lieutenant, which I, according to the usual Custom, upon receival dexterously improv'd into Captain. Indeed I had very lofty Expectations, and the Affairs of King *James* went so well at that time in *Ireland*, that there was not a Footman who follow'd that Prince, but look'd upon his Fortune as made.

These Considerations put me and some others upon a Project of transporting our selves to the *North* of *England*, where King *James* had a very strong Party, and we were inform'd that immediately upon the

Reduction of *Ireland*, as before, the whole Strength of his Army wou'd power in upon *England* that way. A Day was fix'd to put my Design in Execution, but falling into Discourse a little after with a Person of Experience, he intimated that the Business wou'd not be so near over in *Ireland* as I imagin'd; for I can assure you, says he, Three Expresses have arrived lately at *Versailles*, to solicit the *French* Court for Cannon and Ammunition, without which it wou'd be impossible for King *James's* Forces to become Masters in *Ireland*, but that the *French* were so dilatory in this Affair upon some Politick Views, that it was great Odds that Nation wou'd be quickly recover'd by King *William's* Forces. This was a misterious Insinuation to one of my small Experience, for my shallow Brain told me, Expedition was the Business of War; whereas I found afterwards it was the Interest of *France* to spin on the *Irish* War, and to order Things so, that King *William* should always have an Army employ'd there; for they look'd upon it as a Chimerical Notion, that the War could be carry'd on into *England*, or that an *Irish* Army was capable to reduce *England*; for *France* knew very well their own Designs of not intending to send any *French* Troops to joyn them in *England*.

I own I never entirely forgot the Reflexion that Gentleman made upon the present Posture of Affairs; but yet I cannot say I assented to his Opinion, however, it wrought so much upon me as to alter my Resolutions of going directly into the *North* of *England*; for I govern'd my self by this Dilemma, that in Case *Ireland* was not reduc'd till I came there, I might have the Opportunity of having a share in the Reduction, but if it was, the Passage between the *North* of *Ireland* and *England* was very short. Upon this Bottom I began my Journey, I took Shipping at *Brest* and landed at *Cork*, pursuing the rest of my Journey by Land, upon account of the Danger I was inform'd of in going by Sea; for that several *English* Men of War guarded the narrow Seas between *Dublin* and *Holy-head*. When I came into King *James's* Army, my first Enquiry was after my Brother, whom you may be sure I entertain'd in the first place with the Consequence of his Duel at *Paris*; and though he often sigh'd to reflect upon his Misfortune in being the occasion of the *French* Officer's Death, which might have been honourably avoided; yet he laugh'd plentifully, when he heard the Part I had afterwards in that Melancholy Farce; and rally'd me home when I insisted upon Charges and desired to be reimburs'd with Sixty *Louis d'Ors*, which that Affair had cost me upon his Account; all the Satisfaction I could get was, that he thought I put a greater Value upon my being his Brother, than to think it over-rated at that trifling Sum:

The Life of a Brother, said he, is the only thing that can answer for a Brotherly Affection.

The Scene of Affairs in *Ireland* was very much alter'd upon raising the Siege of *London-derry*; Men and Arms were imported from *England* on all Sides to make Head against King *James*, and several bloody Skirmishes happen'd in several Parts of the Kingdom. It wou'd make a Volume to account the Marches and Counter-marches both Parties made in that irregular Country to attack and avoid one another. But where ever it was my Lot to engage, the general Complaint was a want of Money, Ammunition and Arms; this (as it cou'd not be otherwise) made us unsuccessful under many promising Advantages. We had Men enough, and those not destitute of Zeal or Courage; but to expose themselves Naked against Arms and Discipline, was a desperate way of Engaging. But *France* still went upon the old Politick Scheme to gain Advantages upon the Continent by dilatory Proceedings in King *James's* Affairs; for unless this was their Prospect, was it not a supine Piece of Management to suffer a Body of near Thirty Thousand brave Men to lie unarm'd in the Field above half a Year, when *France* had Magazines and Stores to furnish above a Million of Soldiers? But as King *James* was not only to be the *Dupe* of their great Monarch, but the Sport and Game of his Ministers, besides a general Topick of refusing him an Assistance upon the Politick Motive of prolonging the War. It seems the Chief Minister of State had some private Ends in these dilatory Proceedings, and King *James's* Cause in *Ireland* was also to be sacrific'd to this Gentleman's Resentments. The Case was this, *Lewis* XIV upon great Importunity, and to put a Gloss upon, and lay deep Colours upon his Politicks, condescended so far, as to order five or six Thousand despicable Foot Soldiers for King *James's* Service in *Ireland*, with a General at their Head, who had been more accustom'd to lead up a Country Dance than an Army, and better qualify'd to break a Jest than look in upon an Enemy. This General, however, was according to King *James's* own liking, though contrary to the Chief Minister's Design, who wanted that Post for a Relation of his own. This undesign'd Affront of King *James* in preferring *C.L.* to the Minister's Favourite, lost the Battle of the *Boyne*, and perhaps all *Ireland*; for the Chief Minister would neither send Arms nor Money to supply that brave Body of Men, but threw them into the Circumstances of either dying unreveng'd, or saving their Lives by Flight. The History of that Battle has so many Eye Witnesses still alive for me to dwell upon it; I shall only make bold to relate what my Fate was upon that unfortunate Day, and how inglorious *France* withdrew the sham Succours they sent *King* James. My Post was to Head a Company of *Fingalian* Granadiers, who were plac'd in an Orchard which hung over a Defilee, through which we expected the Enemy would march after they had pass'd the River. I make bold to stile my Company Granadiers, because they were design'd to be so when first rais'd, but were now arm'd rather like Pioneers than Grenadiers; we had not above a dozen Granadoes, no Bayonets, and several without any Fire-arms; and if the Chief Men of the Action were no better equipp'd, 'tis easy to guess how the Gross of the Army was provided. According to our Expectation, a Party of the Enemy fell into the Trap, and what Shot we had, we let it successively fly at them out of the Orchard; in the mean time, we heard a great Noise behind us, and turning my self about, I saw the Orchard almost surrounded with Horse, which I expected were some of our own Party coming up to support us, but found them to be a Squadron of the Enemy, who immediately summon'd us to yield, or we must expect the last Fate of War. There was no time to Parley, upon which I made a Sign to the Commanding Officer of the Enemy not to proceed to Slaughter, and so out of Twenty Two Men with which I defended that Post, Nine of us fell into the Enemies Hands, the rest dying bravely in the Engagement. Our Entertaintment was what is usually with Prisoners of War, Hunger and hard Lodgings, but in a little Time being remov'd to *Dublin*, Things were better with me; I had the Liberty of a large Prison and civil Usage. And here it was I met with an excellent Friend, who never fail'd those who make Application to him, I mean a small Bank of Money which my Brother left me, and which I had sent to *Dublin per* Bill from *Newry*, that I might run no hazard of being plunder'd in case of a Defeat, and in this I have often applauded my own Caution, that though I have frequently hazarded my Life, I never risqu'd my Substance; if Death happen'd, I was certain of being provided for; and if Imprisonment, I had what wou'd make my Captivity easy, and perhaps, purchase my Enlargement.

'Tis not a being in a Battle that makes a Person a capable Judge how to describe it; every Officer has his Post which he must not depart from, and though he may be able to describe the Situation of the Troops before an Engagement, yet afterwards during the Fight, there is so much Noise, Smoak and Confusion, that for my part, I scarce can give a true Narration of what happen'd within a dozen Yards compass. Upon this Account, I cannot tell in what manner the *French* Troops behav'd themselves, but I was inform'd they made a tollerable Stand against King *William*'s Army, but that they quickly chang'd it into a running Fight, and very dexterously convey'd both King *James* and themselves out of Danger, and in a little time out of the Kingdom, directing their March to the next Seaport Town, which was not in the Enemies Hands, from whence they found their way Home. If these Troops were serviceable at the *Boyne*, they certainly might have been much more useful, if they had remain'd and assisted the *Irish* the remainder of the War; but they had shown themselves, and that was enough to answer the politick Ends for which they were sent. 'Tis suppos'd after this Defeat at the *Boyne*, that King *James* was aware of the *French* Politics, and so would ne'er think of returning in Person again into *Ireland*, it being abundantly sufficient if he left two or three active Generals among 'em to Alarm the Enemy and do the Drudgery of the *French* Court, in making a Diversion to favour his Conquests in other Parts of the World. But to return to the Series of my own Story, I had now obtain'd Liberty of the City of *Dublin* upon Paroll, and spent my Life pretty agreeable, especially when I understood that a kind of a Cartel was fix'd, and there was no Danger of a Halter. My long stay in *Dublin* brought me acquainted with several General Officers of King *William*'s Army, who were my Countrymen and well acquainted with my Family. The great Respect they showed me, was, as I perceiv'd at long run, in order to debauch me from King *James*'s Service; but it was not in my power at that time, to remove the Scruples I was entangled in as to the Revolution; besides I had other Motives urgent enough not to engage in the *English* Service, till I had seen a little more Abroad. But in the midst of all the Disasters I met with, nothing affected me with a more sensible Grief than the Thoughts of *Lewis* the XIVth's Insincerity, for though it only rid my Mind in the Nature of a Scruple or first Impression, yet I found it grow daily more and more upon me, and often in the height of my Diversions it lay upon my Stomach like an indigested Meal; yet at the same time I durst not mutter the least of this Matter to the greatest Confident I had in the World; for I was sensible what would be the Consequence of such a Liberty of Speech, and that nothing less than perpetual Imprisonment in the *Bastile* must have atton'd for the Crime, and that King *James* wou'd have look'd upon himself as oblig'd to have justify'd the Conduct of *France*, though perhaps he lay under the same Jealousies with myself in regard of *French* Politics. How often have I, when I have been alone, exaggerated my Folly in engaging in a Cause, which the principal Agent never design'd to bring to an Issue? but then again I have corrected my self for giving way to a false Impression, and condemning the Conduct of so many Thousands who had more Experience than I could lay claim to, and yet willingly went all the Lengths of the *French* Court. Now as I always had a great Respect for Men of Years and Experience, so I was resolv'd to silence all the Scruples relating to *French* Politicks, and see an end of the *Irish* War, not so much under the Influence of a *French* Power (which never did any real Service to King *James* in *Ireland*) but because so many worthy Gentlemen eagerly pursue the Cause, whom I had Reason to think were better Judges of such high Matters than my self. And what in the next place I was to undertake, was how to be releas'd from my Confinement, in which I cou'd find no Difficulty besides a breach of Paroll, my Person being every Day at Liberty, but understanding that several Persons in the same Circumstances with my self, were partly conniv'd at when they made their Escape. I took the same Method, and rather chose to walk off, than wait to be exchang'd, or Bribe for my Enlargement. Perhaps the Reader will expect here to be entertain'd with the remaining Part of the *Irish* War, especially where I was employ'd; but he must be content to be inform'd in General, That as I made it a Law with my self ne'er to omit any Occasion of improving my self in the Art of War, so I took particular care not to be upon any Foreign Duty in the Day of Action. I was wounded at the Battle of *Aghram*, where I had one of my Legs broke, and lost two Fingers with the cut of a Sabre. I was at the first Siege of *Limerick*, and help'd to surprize the Enemy's flying Camp and Provisions they were carrying to supply the main Army that was carrying on the Siege. Afterwards I entred the Town, and remain'd there during the Siege, having the Liberty to pass over into *France* with the rest of the *Irish* Troops upon the Articles of *Limerick*; but there was one remarkable Passage happen'd to me during the Siege of that Town, which I cannot dispense with my self to pass over in Silence; it was rather a casual Matter, than a Design laid, however it equally answer'd the end. At one of the Sallies, in which we design'd to overthrow a Mount they had made to raise a Battery upon, after a smart Engagement, it being in the Night, I had the opportunity to step aside and strip a *Dutch* Granadier, and immediately putting on his Cloaths I mingled my self with the Enemy's Battalions as they drew back towards their Camp, thus unperceiv'd I had the opportunity the next Morning to view their Works and make my Remarks. But now I was somewhat at a loss how to make a hand of this Stratagem and get back into the Town, nor was I less concern'd how to avoid being discover'd as not belonging to the

Enemy; but the Confusion they were in the next Day in burying their Dead and repairing their Works, made me pass undiscover'd till Night, so about Nine at Night when it was throughly dark, I stole to that Side of the Town which lies next to the Sea, and swimming over undiscover'd, I crept under the Wall, and calling softly upon the next Centinel, I inform'd him who I was, bidding him call to the Captain of the next Guard, and bring a Rope and two or three Soldiers to hall me up. I was very welcome to the Garrison, for 'twas suppos'd, I was either kill'd or taken Prisoner in the Sally. This Stratagem, though I had no Design in it at our attacking the Enemy, it being only a sudden Thought, yet it had a very good Event; for the next Sally we made, as I had observ'd, the weakest Part of the Besiegers Works, so I lead a Party of Resolute Men that way, who lost no Time, but levell'd all their Works, and dragg'd a considerable Booty into the Town.

The Wars of *Ireland* being at an End, and the Articles of *Limerick* Sign'd, about 15000 regular Troops were Transported into *France*, besides several Thousands of others, who all proved as useful to the Monarch of *France* in his Wars in *Italy, Spain, Germany, &c.* as they had been in making a Three Years Diversion in *Ireland*, so happy was *France* in making a Politick use of King *James's* Misfortune, that *Lewis* XIV was much a greater Gainer by his being Banish'd, than if he had remain'd in the quiet Possession of his Throne. And now there were several Speculations, what Method the *French* King wou'd take to make the World believe he had a Design to reinstall King *James*. The most direct Means was to attempt a Descent, but this was impracticable by the way of *Ireland*; for if an Army of 30000 Men cou'd not keep it when they were actually in Possession of it, there was no likelyhood of their succeeding in a Descent, nor was it probable, that *France* would add more Force to them who had so often refus'd them when they were in Circumstances to receive. The most favourable Interpreters of the *French* King's Politicks, began now to think he had laid all Thoughts of a Restoration aside. King *James's* Troops were employ'd and scatter'd where they were useless upon that Design, and his Court was modell'd, as if nothing more should be attempted. However it was thought convenient still to carry the Juggle on, and several Methods were made use of to seduce the poor Jacobites in *England* and *St. Germains*, that their Work was still going on. Great Respect was shown to the Court of *St. Germains* by his Most Christian Majesty, with repeated Assurances to stand by them: In the mean time I was permitted to leave the Army, and solace my self for two or three Months at *Paris*, where, by the Assistance of my old Friend ready Money, I made my self very acceptable. It was my Happiness hitherto never to be engaged in an Intrigue with the Fair Sex; for though several of my Station have diverted themselves that way with much prejudice to their Business, yet I was always so bent upon War, that I cou'd never find spare Hours for such trifling Conversation, for that was the Notion I had of it. A general Whining and Pining away for a Trolloping Girl, was to me a very awker'd and inconsistent Piece of Pageantry; however, I had been often told by Persons of Experience, that no Man had so just an Idea of the World, as he that had been well hamper'd and sower'd by a Love Intrigue; for though Women appear to be only Spectators, and to bear no Sway in the Politicks of the World, yet underhand, the Fate of Kingdoms often hung at their Girdles, and the wisest of Princes often hazarded the Repose of his People for an Hours Dalliance with some Coquet and diverting Creature of the fair Sex. I cannot tell well how it happen'd, but I suppose by not resisting the first impressions of this kind, I found my self far gone in an Intrigue, and that without either Thought or Design; but I understood afterwards that a Breach of Idleness being espy'd in my Conduct, the Roving Deity seiz'd the Advantage and enter'd Sword in Hand. The Gentlewoman who drew me into this Snare, was no otherwise my Acquaintance than by an accidental Visit; but I was so much a Philosopher, as to know that where there is a Sympathy of Humours, all other Considerations are neglected, and a *Turk* with those Advantages, is as capable to make a Conquest as a *Christian*. I had at my first entrance upon the Stage of the World made a double Promise to my self, the one was never to hearken to a Love Affair till I had acquired a Stock of Experience, and Money to make that Passion Serviceable and of real Use in an honourable Way; the other was not to graft upon a Foreign Stock; but I was forc'd to humble my self under a violation of both these Purposes; for the Object of my Passion was a *Spanish* young Lady though of *Irish* Extraction, her Family Transporting themselves thither about the middle of Queen *Elizabeth*'s Reign. Now I had two or three Difficulties to struggle with relating to this Affair: in the first place, I had not as yet imparted the Secret to the young Lady; again, my Brother's Example gave me grounds to think I cou'd not avoid a Quarrel with some of her Relations; but what chiefly frighted me, was the Plague of Wedding, in case we were both of a Mind, for a keen Hound is not easily call'd off from a hot Scent, till he has either caught or lost his Game. In the midst of these Perplexities, I judg'd 'twou'd be a wise Part to disclose my self to some Persons of Experience in these Matters; for in all the Skirmishes and Sieges I had been at, they never threw me into such a Consternation and Absence of Thought; and accordingly I met with an old Adept in these Affairs. When he heard my Case, after two or three Turns he approach'd me with the serious Air of a Physician, and I thinking he had Design to feel my Pulse, I offer'd him my Hand, which he only shook very gently, saying, Young Man, all the Comfort I can give you is, that you must buy your Knowledge by Experience as I and many others have done before you. All Advice is lost upon a Person in Love. Should I advice you to quit the Enterprize, I know you would not do it. A Halter or an *East-India* Voyage may do you Service in Case you are refused. In a Word, whatever I advised you to you will certainly do the contrary; However, that you may be said to have lost your Time in coming hither, hasten to the young Lady, tell her in a Franck Cavalier way how Things are with you; give all the vent you can to your Passion; if it blows over, you will be a wary Man hereafter, if it ends in Wedlock, any Body will inform you of the Consequences. While the old Gentleman was entertaining me with this Lesson, my Head grew so dizy, as if some invisible Hand had turn'd it round like a Gigg, so I left him abruptly, and went directly to my Lodgings to Bed, but to this Day I cannot tell, whether I went a Foot or in a Coach my Head was in such a Confusion. The next Morning finding my ideas better rang'd, I propos'd to seize the first Opportunity to let the Lady understand the Difficulties I struggled under upon her Account; but the Nature of our Visits was such, that I cou'd not do it any otherwise than by Letter: Thus when I had once broke the Ice, and that too with a fair Prospect of making Advances, in the next Place I gain'd the Maid by the usual Methods that such Creatures are render'd Obsequious, and under her Conduct methoughts I sail'd prosperously on without the least Rub to my suppos'd Happiness; 'tis true I was at a constant Charge of Presents, Treats, and now and then a Serenade according to the *Spanish* Customs. But I remember at one of these Midnight Scenes of Gallantry, I saw something that gave me a great deal of Uneasiness; drawing up my Musick under the Lady's Window, besides her Face, which was at the Casement wide open, I saw the Reflexion of a Periwig move towards the Corner of the Window; this made me vehemently suspect somebody had a better place in her Affections than my self, for there was no Male kind belonging to the Family, her Father and Brother, as she told me at other Times, being in *Spain*, to take care of some Effects they expected by the Flota from the *West Indies*. However, I endeavour'd to smother this Impression of Jealousy, attributing the Mistake to the Circumstances of Night, Candle Light, or some other false Medium that might ground it, so I was resolv'd to take no notice of it at my next Visit. But it was not long before I met with another Occasion of Jealousy, which cou'd not so easily be banish'd out of my Head. Sitting in the Chocolate House, a young Gentleman was giving himself Airs with a Snuff-box, which to my Eye (and it was my Interest to observe it very narrowly) appear'd to be the very same I had some time before presented the Lady with, and as an aggravating Circumstance, in taking Notice of the Gentleman's Periwig, it had the same Form with the Reflexion I saw up in the Lady's Chamber Window, *vid.* a flat Top, neither rais'd nor parted in the Middle, which spoke it to be a Piece of *English* Furniture. The Sight of the snuff-box drew all my Blood into my Heart, and left my pale Cheeks to account for the Consternation, wherefore not able to contain my self had I kept my Ground, I flung out of the Chocolate House, not unobserv'd by the Company to be in some Disorder; but when they look'd out of the Window and saw me stand gazing in the middle of the Street, (for my Motion thither was purely Animal, having no thought whither I was going) it encreas'd their Surprise. However, at three Steps I was got again into the Chocolate House, and with a galliard Air, addressing my self to the Gentleman with the Snuff box, *Sir,* said I, *I confirm the Gift, and may all sniffling Fools that are in Love be serv'd like me.* I allow'd no Time for a Reply, but bolting again into the Street, it came into my Head that perhaps two Snuff-boxes might be so much alike, as not to observe the difference without confronting 'em. This Thought gave me a Curiosity to step into a Toyshop, where I desired to have a Sight of the newest fashion'd Snuff-boxes, and when among others, I saw above half a Dozen exactly like that I had made the Lady a Present of, a Secret Confusion spread it self over my Soul to have given way to such Suspicions. The Matyrdom accustom'd by such like Thoughts as these being the usual Entertainment of Persons in my Condition, and I having read in several Moralists, *That there can be no true Love without a Mixture of Jealousy, which two rose proportionably, and that Jealousy was the greatest Plague of Human Life.* These Considerations, I say, made me Struggle hard to throw off the Tyranny I groan'd under, and it happen'd very luckily for me that within a few Days after the young Lady was sent for into *Spain,* so that I had in Election either to throw up all my Expectations in *France,* and follow her, or Moralize a

Week or two; upon the Disappointment, and so recover my self again to my Senses, which I quickly did by spending my Time in a Treatise of Algebra and Fortifications. As for the Lady she parted without any Reluctance, and it mortify'd me sensibly, that what I had made a Study and Business of, was only her Diversion and Amusement; but I kept my Resolution never more to divert my self that way, till I was effectually tramell'd.

And now I was preparing to visit *Italy*, where some of the *Irish* Forces were then employ'd, and my Company expected me; but before I set out, I had a mind to inform my self better of a certain Report wisper'd at *St. Germains*, That in a little Time King *James* would make another Push, and that a Descent in *England* was certainly in Agitation. Now I was at a Loss how to be truly inform'd of this Matter; the King's Fleet rendevouzing upon the Coast of *Normandy*, and several Battalions marching that way, look'd something like a Descent, but this was not sufficient to convince me, who knew that such Alarms were often given upon a quite different Score, to what the Generality of People had in View. However, the *French* laid strong Colours upon this Preparative; first they gave out, That they had bribed most of the *English* Fleet, so there wou'd be no Danger from that Quarter nor Body to oppose the Descent; again, King *James* set forth a solemn Manifesto, inviting all his Subjects to rise and take Arms, granting an Amnesty only to such as were specify'd in his Proclamation, and to put the last Stroke to this Master-piece of Policy; the King himself was perswaded to appear at the Head of some Troops upon the Coast of *Normandy*. The Pill thus guilded, was swallow'd by every Body; I own I was my self charm'd with the Beauty of the Project, and it look'd so like the dawning of a Restoration, that I was resolv'd to make Interest with our General, that I might not return to my Company upon the Borders of *Italy*; but rather accompany my Prince, and contribute more immediately to conclude the happy Work. While these Matters were in Agitation, I had an Invitation to see the Palace and Gardens of St. *Clou*, from an old Acquaintance, whom I knew an Officer upon the *Rhine*, but now was one of the Duke of *Orlean*'s Secretaries. This Gentleman, as we walk'd in St. *Clou*'s Gardens, being inquisitive how I had spent my Time since our last parting, and how my Affairs stood at present, I gave him a short Narration of my Travels and Actions, telling him I was now a Captain of Foot, and had a Promise of a Lieutenant Colonels Commission the next Vacancy, but that I design'd to throw up my Pretensions, and accompany King *James*. The Gentleman surpriz'd at what I said, I suppose Sir, said he, you must have a fair Prospect of a Place at Court to put it at Ballance with a Lieutenant Colonels Commission, and then turning his Discourse into Raillery, or perhaps says he, you are so taken with the beautiful Enclosures of *Normandy*, as to think a Tour in that Country will recompence all other Losses. No Sir, said I, but I am in hopes, that as I am one who have been useful to his Majesty in several Capacities, so being near his Person in the Descent, if it prove Successful, as no Body seems to question, so I shall be more in his Majesty's Eye, and in fairer Prospect of climbing, than if I were doing him Service at a Distance. Well, Sir, said he, I am sorry our former Intimacy does oblige me to use the Freedom of disabusing you of this vulgar Error of most of King *James*'s Subjects. I cannot blame them for being desirous to return Home, but they are so Infatuated in their Zeal that way, that they imagine every Step our Monarch takes, tends immediately towards their Master's Restoration; believe me, old Friend, Kings have commonly long Heads, and 'tis well known *Lewis* XIV has led all *Europe* through so many Politick Mazes for these Forty or Fifty Years, that he never lets any Body know he is doing a Thing till 'tis in a manner done. All Masters in Politicks look one way and Row another. I own the Preparatives upon the Coast of *Normandy* look like a Descent, but there are false Attacks upon Kingdoms as well as upon Towns: You are not Ignorant that King *William* is now at the Head of a powerful Army in *Flanders*, and that our King is not so well provided there as he expected; Now if King *William* receives the Reinforcement he expects out of *England* and *Scotland*, it will give him that Superiority, that *France* will not be able to make the last stand on that Quarter; so that 'tis no Secret for us at *Versailles*, that all this Alarm of a Descent upon *England*, is a meer blind to make a Diversion, and to hinder the Transportation of the *British* Forces. But you Jacobites and *English* are so ragingly dispos'd, to give every Thing a favourable turn towards King *James*'s Cause, that I have frequently observ'd, there can scare be two Men of War sent out of any Port of *France*, let it be towards the *Indies, Mediterranean*, or other Places, but you make a Descent of it. But as I insinuated Sir, I am glad I have the Opportunity to set you to Rights as to this Affair, that you may not risque a seeming promising Fortune, by catching a Shadow. The Thoughts of having King *James* made such a Tool of, would not permit me immediately to be civil to the Gentleman, and return him Thanks for the seasonable Advice; however, after I had recollected my self, I did my Duty in that Respect: But the Idea he gave me of his Masters Politicks left a Deep Resentment on my Soul. Afterwards, as I return'd to *Paris*, I ruminated upon this Subject, and I saw a thousand Contradictions and Improbabilities in the pretended Descent. The Troops design'd for this Business was very few, and the worst in *France*; the King's own Subjects were not to be employ'd, unless a few Straglers; besides there were no Transportships, nor in fine, any Thing that look'd like an Attempt to Conquer three Potent Kingdoms. King *William* had in a manner the whole Kingdom in his Design at his Descent, he also had the *English* Army secur'd to him, he brought over 15000 Veterans in a Fleet of 600 Sail, but this sham Descent was destitute of all these Advantages. I don't question but *Lewis* XIV, as he proposed an End in this Politick Amusement, so it answer'd accordingly; but as for poor King *James*, I know no Benefit either He or his Friends reap'd from it, besides the Fatigue of a *Norman* Progress, and having all the Jacobites in *England* imprison'd, fin'd, and plunder'd; so that to gain a few Acres of Land to *France*, *England* must be exasperated to let all the Laws loose upon both Protestants and Roman Catholicks that were Well-wishers to King *James*. And yet though the French Court obtain'd their Ends in one Respect, they suffer'd from the Hand of Providence in another. I wou'd not be thought to pry with too much Curiosity into the hidden Paths of Providence, otherwise I should be apt to judge that the Destruction of the *French* Fleet at the *Hague*, look'd somewhat like a Judgment from Heaven for amusing an unfortunate Prince with a false Prospect of Happiness, and yet that loss has been sometimes objected to King *James*, as marr'd upon his Account, so dextrous are the *French* in turning Things to their own Credit.

After this you may well imagine I took a new Resolution not to part with the Prospect I had of making my Fortune in the Post I was in, joyning Company therefore with three or four more Officers who belong'd to the same Army in which I serv'd, we set out with all Expedition. I don't remember to have been better diverted upon the Road, since I first knew what it was to Travel; one of our Company was a *Provincial*, and the very Quintessence of Wit and Gaiety. There was not the most trivial Occurrence but he dexterously made use of it to divert us, particularly at a small Village within a Days Journey of *Lions*. The Bailiff of the Village coming to our Inn to gather a kind of Tax (as it happen'd to be a Day pitch'd upon for that end) for the Relief of the Poor, the *Provincial* Gentleman being deputed, the Steward of our Company, fell into some Discourse with the Bailiff in the Kitchin.

Among other Things, the Bailiff being mellow, gave him to understand, that though his Mien and Equipage was not extraordinary, yet he was the Chief Man in the Town, and immediately represented the King's Majesty, so that if any of the Company were of Quality, it was his Business to show them that Respect which was due to them. The *Provincial* had a good Cue to give us a Comical Scene, which all was contriv'd upon the Spot, to drive away a deep Melancholy from one of our Company, who had not spoke a Word in two Days. With that he took the Bailiff aside, Sir, said the Person, we all attend here on the Prince of——Eldest Son, who is going to Travel into *Italy*. Had there been a Garison here, it ought to have been drawn up at his Entrance, and the Keys of the Town deliver'd to him; but since you are not so provided, you may exert yourselves as much as you can; I suppose you have Musick in the Town? yes Sir said the Bailiff, we have three Violins, a grand Bass, and a Citherne. Do you never exhibit any Plays says the *Provincial*, or other Antick Performance? No replies the Bailiff, but we have a Sport that comes very near it, which we entertain the Country with twice a Year, *viz.* at *Easter* and *Whitsunday*, and the Parts are now fresh in the Actors Memory. This will do says the *Provincial*, but see all Things are ready to give the Young Prince the Diversion immediately after Supper, because he durst not sit up very late. As for the Prologue, wherein you are to Address your selves to his Highness, I will furnish you with the Method and Form in which it must be spoke by the School-master of the Town. Now all this was carried on in Privacy from us, tell we were call'd out one by one, all excepting the Chagrin Gentleman, who lay dozing in an two arm'd Chair, to whom we were instructed to pay a singular Respect to during Supper, to blind the Matter. And now the whole Village was drawn about the Inn, to have a Sight of the young Prince. After Supper all the Tables and Chairs were remov'd; the Bailiff enters with his Staff, and according to Information given him, Kneels down and pays his Respects to the suppos'd Prince; After him comes in the Actors in their proper Dresses; and then the School-master, who open'd the Farce with a Comical Address made by the *Provincial* Officer, which in every Line hinted at some Passage of the Melancholy Gentleman's Life, but with such an Ambiguous turn, and yet home to the Man, that it was an excellent Piece of Diversion, to observe the variety of Motions in the Princes Countenance, who thought all to be Witchcraft and Inchantment. The Force being over, and we left to our selves, the *Provincial* returning up Stairs from conducting his Troop to the Door,

Well, Gentlemen, says he, how do you relish your Diversion? *Et vous Monsieur le Prince*, if this will not bring you to your self, you shall be Dethron'd at *Lyons*, and put upon a Level with the rest of the Company; for he that pretends to put on a starch'd reserv'd Air upon a Journey, make himself a Prince by his Distance, and so must either lose his Dignity by being good Humour'd, or pay the Reckoning like a Prince, and that we have Decreed shall be your Choice the Remainder of the Journey. The *Provincial* gain'd his End, for either this comical Accident was the Occasion, or the Term of the Gentleman's Melancholy was expired; for afterwards he put on a gay Temper, and proved tollerable Company.

We cou'd not content our selves with a single Nights Lodging in *Lyons*, that City is furnish'd with too many Rarities for the amusement of Strangers, not to partake of a little more of their Money than any Vulgar Inn upon the Road. And as we none of us desired to carry more with us than what wou'd Answer our Travelling Expences, so we joyn'd in a Resolution to divert our selves one Week or ten Days in that Populous Place. I had a Recommendation from *Paris* to an *Irish* Clergyman, who was a Prepandary here, and a Person of Repute. This Gentleman wou'd oblige me to take a Bed with him during my stay there, which I was very unwilling to accept of upon Account of my Company, however, he said that would be no Inconvenience, since I might take my freedom with them all the Day, in case I wou'd favour him with my Company half an Hour before Bed time in the Evening. I perceiv'd this Goatly Clergyman was of a different Stamp to the Generality of his Countrymen, and had a true Idea of the *French* Politicks, for discoursing one Night upon the Subject of a Restoration, and finding I was a Person he might deliver his Mind freely to. Certainly, *said* he, never Prince was more the Game of Politicians and Fools than King *James* II. His own Friends at home threw him out of his Throne by their forward and indiscreet Management, and now he is bubbled with daily Hopes of Recovering it, when in reality there was never any Design to bring it about. But King *James* will always be King *James*, and Judge every Man Honest, who does but pretend to be so; for pray, gave me leave Sir, will it pass for a seizable Story in future Ages. That *Lewis* XIV should make War in order to Restore *James* II and keep above 40000 Men in constant Pay, and never employ any of them that way. Twenty thousand Horse would have laid the Three Kingdoms desolate in a few Weeks, but was there so much as one single Dragoon employ'd that way? Was not King *James* forced to melt his Canon and debase the Coin with it, whilst *Lewis* XIV could send vast Remittances to *Constantinople* to Support the *Turk*? Were not 300000 Men driven like Sheep from the Banks of the *Boyne* for want of Arms, while what wou'd have furnish'd a Million of Men, were Rusting in the Magazines of *France*? Were not the Highlanders constantly neglected, and fed with nothing but Promises, till they were reduc'd from a Victorious Army to a Troop of Banditti? Have not the Lives and Fortunes of Thousands in *England* payed very dear for these *French* Politics, by being encourag'd to rise up and Precipitate themselves into Ruin, by the Motions of Fleets and Armies upon sham Pretences of making Descents. I own Sir, I am transported when I find an Opportunity to vent my self upon this Subject. Had *Lewis* XIV been streightned by the Allies, he might have some pretence of not affording so much Assistance as otherwise he might; but in the last War, he was always Victorious both upon the *Rhine* and in *Flanders*, and if after the Battle of *Steenheer, Fleurs, Landen*, and Victories at Sea, besides the vast number of Towns he reduced, he did not think fit to employ his Arms towards restoring King *James*, I must take the Liberty to think the War was not begun upon his Account, nor that it can be judg'd the Interest of *France* (unless they act against their own interest, which they are too wise a Nation to do) to have him reestablish'd. But all this, Sir, I speak under the Rose; the Honour of the *French* Court is too much touch'd by such Reflections as these to suffer them to go unpunish'd if I should be discover'd. But I conclude from my worthy Friend at *Paris* who gave me your Character, that I might use any freedom in your Company. It may perhaps look like Ingratitude in me to reflect upon a Person by whose Benevolence I possess this Post I have in the Church, which does not only afford me a decent Maintenance, but the Opportunity of obliging a Friend, but as I was a greater sufferer in *Ireland*, by giving too much into *French* Projects, so I look upon both this or any other Kindness they can do me, as a piece of Restitution. The Frank and open Satyr of this Clergyman against the *French* Conduct was very agreeable to my Temper, and I was not backward in seconding him in the same Key. But while we were entertaining our selves with these dismal Reflections, a Servant knock'd at the Chamber Door, so the Gentleman step'd to know his Business, and after about half a Quarter of an Hour return'd again. I have been, says he, this Fortnight engaged in a very troublesome Affair, which is like to have an ill Consequence to the Party concern'd. Here is, says he in Town an *Englishman*, who has, as he informs me, been studying at a College of that Nation of *Rome*, but for want of

Health is oblig'd to break off his Studies, to have the Benefit of his own Country Air, which the Physicians prescribe to him as the only Remedy to patch up his decaying Constitution: But the poor Gentleman, about Three Leagues out of Town, as he was steering his Course towards *Paris*, and so Homeward, met with a very unfortunate Accident. Walking on the Road about half an Hour before Sun setting, he was overtaken by a Gentleman who kept pace with him, and ask'd him among other Things how far he design'd to Travel that Night, the *Englishman* told him he was a Stranger to the Stages upon the Road, but he believ'd he should take the Opportunity of the next Inn, for that it began to grow late. The *French* Man appear'd very obliging in his Conversation, and told him he should have been glad of his Company, but that he was oblig'd to turn off on the Right Hand to a Friends House, whither he was going to divert himself a Day or Two. They had not gone a Hundred Rood farther, but he stop'd and desired the *Englishman* if he wou'd take a pinch of Snuff, and then look'd backward and forward with an ominous Countenance, he Collar'd the *Englishman*, and drawing a small Pistol out of his Pocket, without any farther Ceremony, he cry'd *Ou la vie, ou la Bourse*. The Business was quickly over, and the *Englishman* robb'd of all his Stock, which was to the value of Nine Pounds *English*, besides a little Box of *Roman* Coin, which were small Pieces of Money he kept for Counters. The Foot-pad, after he had got his Booty, alters his Course, and turns back towards *Lyons*, charging the *Englishman* not to pursue him, nor yet go forward till he saw him out of Sight; for if he did, he wou'd certainly return upon him and deprive him of his Life as well as his Money. There was no arguing the Case, and the Surprize was so great, that had there been any way of escaping this Accident, 'tis probable it wou'd not have occurr'd at that time.

As soon as the Villain was out of sight, the *Englishman* loitered his Time too and fro till it was dark, and then return'd backward towards *Lyons*, hoping to meet either with Credit or Charity for a small Sum to bear his Charges home, but not being able to reach the Town that Night, he put in at a poor Cabaret, where he open'd his dismal Condition to the Master of the House, who being a very Compassionate Man, promis'd to entertain him *Gratis* that Night, and conduct him to *Lyons* the next Morning. His first Application was to me; I promis'd to get him some Relief in a Day or Two, and the mean Time I procur'd him a Lodging. The next Day coming up a Street which leads to my House, he accidently cast his Eyes into a

Habadasher's Shop, where he saw a Person sitting upon a Stool at the side of the Counter chaffering for a Hat; his Back, and a Silk Bag his Wigg was tied up in, had so much the Resemblance with the Person that rob'd him, that he stood gazing into the Shop so long, that the shop-keeper step'd to the Door, and call'd to him if he would come in and please to buy any Thing, upon which the Gentleman upon the Stool turning himself about to look out of the Shop, he was known to be the same Man who had committed the Robbery, and being in a Consternation to see the Person he had assaulted stand directly before the Shop, he threw down the Hat he had in his Hand, and leaving his Money upon the Counter, bolted out of the Door; but the *Englishman* immediately alarm'd the whole Street, and the Rogue was taken and carried before a Magistrate. In the mean time I was sent for to assist the *Englishman* in the Narrative of this Fact. At first the Foot-pad denied he ever saw the Person, and as for the Money it cou'd not be sworn too; but the Box with little Roman Pieces being found upon him, he cou'd not stand that Proof, besides, it appears he can give no Account where he was the Evening of the Robbery, and the Innkeeper upon the Road, is positive he was one of the Persons which pass'd by his House that Evening; and to compleat all, several Persons who came in to see him out of Curiosity, depos'd, that he is very like the Man, by Description, has follow'd that Road several Years. To conclude, the *Englishman* only stays in Town now to be Witness against this *Malhoneux*. Hanging is certainly his Doom; but if other Suspicions are made out, of his being that noted Offender, who had infested the Road for a considerable Time, it will be his Fate to be broke upon the Wheel. However, the *Englishman* has recover'd most of his Money, but he will be forc'd to expend it on Charges; but I will see to ease him in that Point. I was very much edify'd with this Clergyman's Generous and Christian Temper in being obliging and endeavouring to do good to every Body. But now the Time drew near that we were to leave *Lyons*, we had but one Day more to stay, and that the *Irish* Prebendary challenged to himself, desiring I and my Companions would accept of a small Treat and Dine with him. We had every thing that was good in its kind, but he wou'd not press his Wine upon us, for the Churchman's Character, was not to be Sacrific'd to the Soldiers Appetite; for he who urges the Glass too far, if he is not himself suspected of Insobriety, is certainly obnoxious to the immoral Part of the Ceremony.

When an Army is not upon Action, the Camp is a tedious Place to spend a Mans time in; but we, who are Subjects of *Great Britain*, had some additional Circumstances to make our Time lie heavy upon our Hands; For my own part, I always look'd upon my self as a banish'd Man, and my Thoughts always look'd homeward. There are a great many Charms in some sort of Delusions, especially, if they flatter Inclination. It was now almost grown into a settled Opinion with me, that *France* would never make any farther Attempt to restore King *James*, than by way of Amusement, to drive on some other Project; and yet upon the least Intimation of a Descent, my Inclinations willingly carry'd me over to another Belief: And of this my wavering Temper I soon after gave a very remarkable Instance. My Brother-in-law inform'd me by Letter from *Paris*, that there was a deep Design laid to make us all Happy in a little Time, so he advised me to make what haste I could, for that now the Sea was dividing, and the Children of *Israel* were upon their march to the *Land of Promise*. Immediately I answer'd the Summons, and gave into the Advice by taking Post, and had the Satisfaction to Sup with my Brother in five Days time. The very next Day I went to St. *Germains*, where I was glad to find every thing in such forwardness. The King was preparing himself to go to *Callis*, where a considerable Body of Men were Rendevouzing, as 'twas generally believ'd, in order to be transported into *England*; where in and about *London*, several Persons were privately engag'd, and ready with Arms to receive the King at Landing. In the Town of St. *Germains*, several Persons dispos'd of their Lodgings and Furniture and turn'd them into Money for this Expedition. The Day came that the King was to take leave of the Queen, and here I was resolv'd to play the Physiogminist, and observe in their Countenances, whether I cou'd see any thing that look'd like a Descent, for I did not think it improbable, but the King by this time might be so far habituated to the *French* Politicks, as to concur to be made a Fool of, and I was not the only one of that Opinion, that the King himself was let into the Secret, and knew very well his Journey to *Callis*; and hovering about the Coast, was only to keep back ten Thousand *English* and *Scotch*, whose Presence, that Campaign, would have done the *French* no kindness in *Flanders*. An old Project; and thus much I read both in the King and Queen's Face, for neither at parting, nor afterwards, did the Queen signify that Disturbance which she could not have conceal'd, had the Project been real. I need not give the Reader any farther Account of this Matter for it shewed it self upon the Kings returning to St. *Germains*. Had this Design been attended with no worse Circumstances than harassing a Monarch, and fooling his Subjects at *Paris*, and St. *Germains*, it might here be regarded as an Innocent stroke of Politicks, though very disobliging and improper; but if we look on the other side the Channel, it had occasion'd very Cruel and Barbarous Consequences. Those unfortunate Gentlemen who went upon the Strength of this sham Project to raise Men, provide Arms and Horses, and attempt seizing of King *William*'s Person, are dear Instances of *French* Policy; for 'tis not to be suppos'd that *Church, King*, Sir *William Perkins*, Sir *John Friend*, Sir *John Fenwick*, or half a hundred of their Adherents, wou'd either have attempted the Conquering of three Kingdoms, or been discover'd by any of the Confederacy, had not the *French* both encourag'd 'em and left 'em in the lurch.

It was observable after this Peregrination, that King *James* began to ride with a very loose Rein, and throwing the Bridle in the Neck, managed his Concerns with a great deal of Indifference. He saw clearly how fatal a Thing it was for one King to fall into the Hands of another; and that under the plausible Cloak of Hospitality, and Royal Protection, a Person might be lull'd a Sleep in the Arms of an Enslaver. When Princes are detain'd Prisoners, they generally wear all the Symptoms of their Royalty besides that of Freedom, which cannot be distinguish'd so much by the Eye as, the Judgment; and if some of King *James*'s Subjects regarded their Master with the same Compassion at the Castle of St. *Germains* as if he had been in the *Bastile*, there was very little Difference to be found besides the largeness of the Enclosure. And if King *James* has not often been heard to let drop Expressions as if he regarded himself no otherwise than a Politick Prisoner, I am very much misinform'd by those who constantly attended his Person. The denying him his own Guards, the number of Spies he had upon all his Actions, the Uneasiness he often shew'd that he cou'd enjoy no Privacy, are Circumstances that smell very strong of a Prison. However, the Pretence of protecting a Person in Distress, was a noble Sham, and so well dress'd up, that the Generallity ne'er look'd through the Disguise. The Salary allow'd him, and frequent Protestations of standing by him with unpolitick Heads, were look'd upon as undeniable Proofs of *Lewis* XIV.' Sincerity; but those who were better acquainted with *French* Stratagems, easily pull'd off the Vizard. King *James* fell into the Hands of *France*, and was a rich Opportunity in the *French* Hands, from whence they might raise a Thousand Advantages. He was too great a Treasure to be parted with only upon good Terms. A Tool no less useful to make a Diversion in time of War, than to obtain a beneficial Article at the Conclusion of Peace; and if upon the Foot of this Maxim he was not thrown into one side of the Scales at the Peace of *Reswick*, when *France* cou'd have no other Motive but being gratified with an Equivalent for the disclaim of his Title, I shall own my self a Stranger to the Spirit and Design of that Treaty. Two things surpris'd all *Europe* upon that Treaty, the first was, that *France* should be so inclinable to hearken to a Peace after a War, in which he had always been successful. The other was, that no regard shou'd be had to King *James*, not so much as to be admitted to speak, though *France* pretended to have undertaken the War meerly upon his Account, and that his Quarrel seem'd to be the only Circumstance to justify his Conduct in the War. The Hopes of gaining Time to work his Ends upon *Spain*, will easily account for his forwardness in clapping up a Peace, and giving up more Towns than he had been Master of by the War; for thus like a through pac'd Politician, he humbled himself by little Condescensions to the Feet of the Allies, and sacrifices these Excrescencies of his Glory, in hopes very speedily to make good all such Deficiences by the larger Acquisition of *Spain*. But nothing will answer the other Part of People's Expectations. *Lewis* XIV had often made solemn Protestations, that as the War was principally undertaking to do right to K. *James*, so Peace should not be made unless he was consider'd; and unless it were a few near the Person of *Lewis* XIV who were in the Secret concerning the Design upon *Spain*, there was not a Man in *France* but who had a better Opinion of their Monarch's Honour, than to think he wou'd desert King *James* the Second's Cause in so scandalous a Manner, as not to admit his Plenipotentiaries to speak at *Reswick*: Yes, so undefensible was the Conduct of *France* upon this Head, that they commonly own'd they were asham'd to look any that belong to the Court of St. *Germains* in the Face, since all their lofty Protestations for restoring King *James* ended in the self-ended Design of securing the *Spanish* Monarchy in the House of *Bourbon*. And thus poor King *James* had implicitely devoted himself to the *French* King's Politicks, first by suffering himself to be led blindfolded, and after he had pull'd off the Veil, (though some will have it he died with the Film upon his Eyes) caress'd the Opportunity, and made it a principal Ingredient among those Misfortunes which he was in hopes to raise his Merits hereafter, and if he question'd the *French* King's Sincerity, he either durst not tell him, or scrupled to publish his Insincerity.

These were the melancholly Meditations with which the more discerning part of King *James's* Friends often entertain'd themselves, but great care was taken that no such Language shou'd reach the *French*

Court. Their Honour was too nearly touch'd to pass over such Reflexions in that severity and remarkable Punishment. I took my self to be pretty Cautious upon such like Subjects, yet upon this last pretended Descent, King *James* being inform'd that I had express'd my self very improperly upon the Matter, so as to blame the Dilatory Methods of *France* upon his Account, I was order'd to be Prisoner in my Lodgings, but releas'd after two Days Confinement, with a threatening Charge, never more to reflect upon the *French* King's Conduct. I do not remember where I spoke the Words, or in what Company, but I believe I might make a loose upon their Management who prefer'd the *French* to the King's own Subjects upon this Expedition; adding withal, that it look'd as if such Persons had no Design the Project should take Effect, but this was enough to shew I had a jealous Mind.

About this Time my Company, with the rest of the Regiment, was order'd down into *Flanders*, and having been a considerable Time absent I was commanded to attend there. My Brother-in-law who was one of the Robe in his own Country, and unacquainted with the Wars, yet was moved with a certain Curiosity to see a Campaign, and tho' much against my Sister's Will, resolv'd to accompany me into *Flanders*; yet his Principal Motive was to make a Halt at *Doway*, whither he had been invited some time before by a near Relation belonging to the *Scotch* College in that University. We went together in the *Cambray* Coach, and after a short stay at *Doway*, we proceeded on to the Army, which then was under that expert and resolute General the Duke of *Luxembourg*. It was certainly a kind impulse of Heaven that gave me my Brother for a Companion upon this Occasion; for an Action happening soon after, viz. the famous Battle of *Launden*, where it was my Misfortune to be dangerously wounded. I had the Satisfaction of my Brother's Company and Assistance during a tedious Sickness, which was the Consequence of my Wounds. The *French* were no great Gainers by this Battle, though they at long run routed the Enemy, and kept the Field; for besides the great loss they sustain'd during the Attack, which far exceeded that of the Allies, the Victory was not well pursu'd. It was my Post to reinforce a Party of *French* Fusiliers, who were order'd to Storm the Intrenchment, in which Service a Bullet was lodg'd in my Shoulder, which besides disabling me on one Side, the loss of Blood I suffer'd was so great, that I was not able to support my self, but drop'd down and had been trampled to Death under my own Mens Feet, had not a strong Body'd Drummer hurried me out of the

Croud upon his Back; but he carried me off with such Precipitation, that one of the Enemies Troopers seeing me at a Distance, and thinking me to be somebody of Consequence, sprung after me upon his Gelding, and carried both me and the Drummer into a Village on the left Hand of the Attack, where several Squadrons were posted. The commanding Officer who was a Colonel of the *English* Guards, finding, I was of the *British* Nation, order'd me to be laid in a Barn with a Centinel to guard me, and the Surgeon of the Regiment was immediately call'd for to dress and tie up my Wounds. I had not been in that Lodging above an Hour, but the Village was attack'd by the *French* Gens d'Arms, and there was a Tryal of Skill between the Flower of both the Armies, in which Action the *French* at last were Superior, so I was releas'd, but it was equal to me in the Condition I was in whose Hands I fell into, for I had so many fainting Fits which succeeded one another, that I expected not to survive any of 'em. My Brother, whom I desired to go to *Loraine* during the Action had a Mind to be a little nearer, so remain'd with the Baggage, but met not with me till the next Day, that we both went in a Waggon to his Lodgings in *Loraine*, where I was confin'd three Months before I was able to Travel.

In this Retirement it was that I began to be very Serious: A Soldiers Life has many Occurrences which are not very reconcileable to strict Morality. To comprize my own Character in relation to Christianity, I was neither a Saint nor a Devil. The Pains I felt were very Sharp, and hindred my Rest; my Blood was heated and boiling up to a Fever, which being agitated with daily dressing my Wounds, it requir'd a skillful Physician and a good Regimen in the Patient, to stave off a Fit of Sickness. My Brother prov'd an excellent Nurse, and had he not us'd a great deal of Reason in keeping me from improper Nourishment, the Game would quickly have been up with me. I was also waited upon several times by a worthy Clergyman, who neglected not to give me Penitent Hints to have regard to the main Concern; I return'd him Thanks, and gave him to understand I would make use of him when there was more urgent Occasion. When I began to grow a Valetudinarian, and that my Wounds began to heel up, I had the Liberty to drink *Loraine* Beer, which is much celebrated in those Parts. As yet I had drank nothing but Tissans and such like Decoctions, which being very mild upon the Palate, did not give content to the inward dryness and thirst I felt by the loss of Blood. But I quickly repented this Indulgence of tasting the Beer, I took such deep Draughts that I relaps'd into a dangerous and most violent Fever, in which I acted all the Parts of a dying Man, besides making my Exit; I was delirious above three Days, which though it was but a melancholly Sight in it self, yet I behav'd my self so various in my rambling Discourse, that it occasion'd no small Diversion to such as were present, and had no immediate concern in my Welfare. I besieg'd Towns, rally'd scattered Forces, accepted Challenges, wandered over the *Alpes*, and pass'd over several Seas without Ships; I was in the Orchard at the Boyne, under the Walls of *London Derry*, and diverted with the fine Rode to *Lions*, and what I thought I should never have in my Head again, some amorous Ideas, though very faint one's, discover'd themselves, and I was heard to talk of Snuff-Boxes, Periwigs, and *Spanish* Ladies. My Brother who heard me, and to whom I had discover'd that Intrigue, burst out into a Laugh when he heard me name Snuff-Boxes; for this was enough to make him believe the Passion was not dead in me, which he horded up to rally me with.

During this Entertainment which I gave the Spectators, my Brother had sent for the Priest, but I was then in a very improper State to settle Accounts in Relation to the next World. However, the Gentleman approaching my Bed, and calling upon me to hear whether I could return a rational Answer. He bid me lift up my Heart to God, and call upon my Redeemer. But I, as I suppose, taking him to be one of my Sergeants, bid God—D—n him for a Rascal, why had he not been with me before? for the Colonel had order'd a Review shou'd be made at Eleven a Clock. The Priest shrugg'd up his Shoulders, sprinkled me with Holy Water, and retir'd to the Window, where my Brother and the Physician were attending my Fate. When my Delirious Fit was over, which was about an Hour afterwards, I turn'd my Eyes towards the other Side of the Room, where I saw three Persons leaning in the Window with their Backs towards me; and not being entirely recover'd from my Delirious State, I fancied my self a Prisoner at *Constantinople*, and that my Brother, the Physician, and the Priest, were three Mutes sent to Strangle me; but in an Instant or two I return'd to my self, and discover'd whose Hands I was in. This was a terrible Attack, and the Enemy had made such a Breach, that I desired to wisper a Word with the Priests, telling him I wou'd Capitulate next Morning about Eight a Clock. Afterwards I recover'd very leisurely, and took great Care not to be too bold with the *Lorain* Beer. My Phician advised me not to remove from that Place till I was perfectly establish'd, assuring me there was not better Air in all the *Netherlands*. I follow'd his Advice, for I cou'd not think him prompted to give it me through

Avarice, for he was so very moderate in his Fees, that I thought my self oblig'd at our parting to make him a handsome Present. My Brother who was a Man of Letters, and very curious in his Enquiries, had a good opportunity during our stay here to get acquainted with several learned Men of this University. One of the first account was Dr. *Martin* an *Irish* Clergyman, who had a lively Genious and was also a Person of great reading. In the mean time my Sister at *Paris* began to grow impatient for her Husband, but she bore his Absence the better when she understood how useful he had been to me during my Sickness. However, we made bold to Trespass a little further, by taking a turn round the Country. It was not a Journey entirely of Pleasure, for I was oblig'd to go to *Amsterdam*, there being a stop put to the Interest of my Mony, so I was resolved to see that Matter rectify'd. So having obtained a Pass from the Allies, under the Quality of two *Scotch* Merchants we began our Journey. When I came to *Amsterdam*, I was very much surpriz'd to understand the odd Occasion of my Money being stop'd. It seems a Countryman, of mine who had fish'd out something of my Concerns, and saw me fall at the Battle of *Launden*, had Counterfeited a Deed in the Nature of a Will, which imported, that all my Effects in *Amsterdam* were left to him, he being my Brother, and demanding it as his due. The Banker had the Deed perus'd by several Persons, it had a great appearance of being Authentick, and my Hand was so inimitably clap'd to it, that when compared with what was certainly known not to be Counterfeit, 'twas impossible to discover the Difference. Now the Banker desired this pretended Brother of mine to have Patience till he had an account from *Paris* whether or no I was dead, and the general Report being that I was kill'd at *Launden*, this was the occasion that the Money was neither paid to my Correspondent nor to my Sham Brother. This Point once clear'd, I was resolv'd to find out the Person who had personated my Brother, that I might bring him to condign Punishment, as also to clear a Suspicion I had, that my Servant had a Hand in it, for otherwise I thought it impossible one that was a Stranger should know whose Hands my Money was in. In the first place I cunningly interrogated my Servant at a distance, and found enough by his Countenance that he was not entirely Innocent, however, not being able to prove it upon him, I in the next place made a diligent Search after my Sham-Brother; for he had told the Banker at his last Visit that he wou'd return again in Seven or Eight Days, and Six of 'em were now expired. The Gentleman was as good as his World. He came to the Banker with a good Assurance, and demanded both Principal and Interest. I was then at my Lodging, but being sent for, I was strangely surpris'd to see the Clerk of my Company, who was also a Sergeant, metamorphos'd into my Brother. He shrunk two Inches lower at the Sight of me; but dissembling the matter, I am glad to see thee alive Sergeant said I, for I took it for granted you were kill'd at the Battle of *Launden*; and I, reply'd the impudent Villain, thought you had, otherwise I had not been here: but if you please, noble Captain, to walk into the next Tavern and give me leave to wait upon you, I will discover to you the occasion of my coming to *Amsterdam*. My Fears as to my Money being now all over, I comply'd with the Rascal, and went along with him. But he dress'd up such a Narrative in favour of his good Intention, and strengthen'd it with such plausible Circumstances, That he and my Servant, whom he confess'd to be one of the Party, had no other Intention but to get the Money out of the Banker's Hands for the Use of my Relations; for that they had Reason to suspect I had made no Will, and so no body wou'd have a Right to demand the Money. Now though this Stratagem was very probably all a Fiction, yet it wrought so much with me, that I did not Prosecute either of 'em; for as I was acquainted with both their Friends in *Scotland*, so I had some regard for them, and dismissed them to go home or whither they pleas'd, not thinking it safe to entertain Persons who had been involved in such mysterious Practices.

My Affairs being settled at *Amsterdam*, we had the Curiosity to see *Antwerp*, which is a City where a Stranger may employ his Time very agreeably, for a longer Term than we cou'd conveniently spend there. We lodg'd at a House where an *English* Nobleman also had an Apartment. He had been in that City about two Months, kept a handsome Equipage, was very young, and a well bred Gentleman, of great value among the Ladies, and had he been able to support the Character he bore at first appearance here, it would have convinced the World there is very little difference between a Footman and a Nobleman, where neither Sense nor Money are wanting to carry on the Resemblance. I must anticipate the dismal Exit of this unfortunate Gentleman which happen'd not till about two Years afterwards. While he was in his Splendour at *Antwerp*, and cou'd answer every bodies Expectations as to Money matters, it was not any Mans Business to pry into his Pedigree; but when his Conduct began to be observ'd, and taken Notice to be full of Shuffling and Demurs in the Payment of small Bills, there was a Jealousy spread about the Town that the Lord G——— would prove a Cheat, so his Credit began to sink in the Shops, but it held up still among the Ladies, where a handsome Personage, and a charming Tongue is often ready Money. But it was not long before he began also to be suspected from this Quarter; his Visits were not so frequent, his Treats much more sparing; and especially one Lady, who was his greatest Admirer, and most capable to make Him Happy on all Accounts, was oblig'd to expose him, and make this Phantom of Nobility evaporate. In the frequent Visits he pay'd this Lady, he had observ'd a very handsome Diamond Ring upon her Finger, which was no less remarkable for its uncommon Form, than intrinsick Value, at a low Estimate being judg'd to be worth 80*l.* Sterling. The Gentleman had often thrown out a great many Compliments upon it, which usually tended towards extolling the Ladies Judgment and Fancy in the choice and ordering of that Jewel, for she wanting to her self, let him and every body else know, it was a Thought of her own. The Gentleman in the midst of one of his Panegyricks upon this little Charmer, begg'd the Favour of the Lady that he might borrow it for a Day or two till he had shewn it a Jeweller, for he design'd to have one made in the same Form. The Lady was not a little pleas'd that her Fancy was like to become a Pattern to the Town, willingly drew it off her Finger, not in the least suspecting any Trick, for as yet his Fame was untouch'd. I think he made two or three Visits without returning the Ring, pretending the Workman was dilatory in taking a Pattern; but 'tis suppos'd he wanted time to prepare himself for a Flight, and brush off with the Ring. However, none of these Suspicions enter'd the Ladies Head, he not being her Aversion. About three or four Days after, a Lady visiting her, told her the *English* Nobleman had parted with his Chariot, pawn'd his best Suit of Cloaths, and that his Credit was not only very low, but it was suppos'd he wou'd in a Day or two be oblig'd to Decamp, or take up his Quarters in a Jail. 'Tis obvious to imagine that the first Thing that came into the Ladies Mind upon this Occasion was her Diamond Ring; but, as she confess'd afterwards to a Friend, the Compassion she had for the Gentleman's Circumstances had so large a Place in her Heart, that she does not remember to have had any concern upon her in Relation to the Jewel; from whence we may gather that Evil Fate that hangs over some Persons Heads, for had but this unfortunate Person pursu'd the Interest he had with that Lady, whilst he was in flourishing Circumstances, he might easily have carried it to the *non plus ultra*, and became Master, of 15000, as she her self own'd when she recover'd her Passion and began to think calmly. However, the Diamond Ring was not to be neglected, for though she had been willing to have parted with her Interest in it to Succour the Gentleman in Distress, it was too large an Alms, and would perhaps have been judg'd by the World rather an Instance of her Forwardness and Indiscretion than of her Charity. Her Friends before advis'd her to demand the Ring, which she did that Evening, but understood he had pawn'd it for the full Value; upon which she was (though much against her Inclination) oblig'd to Arrest him, and had him clap'd up in Prison: But however, she was a very kind Jailor. It is a Custom, having the Force of the Law in the *Netherlands*, that when a Debtor is kept in Prison, it shall be at the Charges of the Creditors; in which also they observe a kind of Proportion, that a Gentleman is to be allow'd like a Gentleman, and a Mechanick is to be content with a smaller Allowance. The Lady comply'd very willingly with the Custom, and her Prisoner being reputed a Person of Quality, it was an excellent Disguise to show her Liberality. But afterwards being weary of the Charge, and finding by the Information of several *Englishmen* that pass'd thro' *Antwerp*, that her Prisoner was not the Person he pretended to be, but a meer Sharper and Knight of the Post, she slacken'd in her Charity, and gradually brought him down to a common Allowance, and at last discharg'd him. His Life after that was a meer Romance; He first went into *Gaunt*, here he took up a large Apartment of four or five Rooms well furnish'd, which he sold after a Fortnight, taking an advantage of the Landlady's Abscence. With the strength of this Plunder, he made a Figure for two or three Months at *Brussels*, where he fought a Duel with *H.S.* an *English* Gentleman. This Accident drove him from *Brussels*, but finding he was not secure in the *Spanish Flanders*, he crossed the Lines, spent the remainder of his Substance at *Lisle*, and he directed his Course to *Dunkirk*, from whence 'tis said he design'd to take Shipping for *England*. But here he finish'd his Misfortunes as I was inform'd upon the Spot, by a Merchant who resided in that Town, and saw his Exit. This *English* Merchant walking upon the Key according to Custom, observ'd a young Gentleman walking in a Melancholy Posture, and thinking he knew him, though the poor Dress he was in would not suffer him to make a positive Judgment; however, he stept up towards him, and upon a nearer View, was convinc'd he was the Person he took him for. This Merchant had been acquainted with him at *Antwerp*, when he bore the Character of an *English* Nobleman and lived with great Splendor. The Gentleman more dash'd, as I suppose, to jump upon one who had heard of his Tricks, than for the meanness of his Circumstances, told the Merchant he was an unfortunate Man, and Things were now so desperate with him, that he had no way left to relieve himself but by a Halter. The Merchant having a charitable regard for his Circumstance, though he knew him to be a very undeserving Object, told him, he wou'd provide him with a Lodging and Diet till he had a Return of Money, the Gentleman answer'd frankly he expected no Returns, nor did he know of any Body that wou'd Assist him, nor you'd he make any Demands. This Account encourag'd the Merchant to be more Charitable, so he conducted him to an Inn, desiring the Master of the House to furnish him with Diet and Lodging till further Orders. Two Days after, the Merchant coming to Visit him about Ten in the Morning, when they imagin'd he was still in Bed, a Servant being sent up to call him, he was hang'd upon the Beam, in one Corner of his Chamber. The Merchant had a great Curiosity to find out the Pedigree of this Romantick Gentleman, but you'd get no Authentick Account. I told him I was inform'd at *Antwerp*, that he was Footman to a Person of Quality, and that he had robb'd his Master, and fled into the *Netherlands* to escape Justice, which made him always unwilling to think of returning Home.

The Peace of *Reswick* was a ratifying King *James's* Abdication, and enrolling in the *French* Archives, what was before declar'd in the Convention at *Westminster*. It was now no Time to expostulate with *Lewis* XIV. why he had concluded a Peace without mentioning the Person upon whose Account he had began the War? The Titular King of St. *Germains*, and the Real one at *Whitehall*, were not irreconcileable, and the continuation of the Pension was regarded as an unquestionable mark of the *French* King's Sincerity, and the unthinking Crew spoke well of the Master that cramm'd them, never dreaming that they were but fatten'd for Slaughter, and that under the Disguise of Succouring their Persons, he might Prey upon their Interest. The *Spanish* Monarchy was what *France* had in their Eye by the Peace of *Reswick*, and the Restoring of King *James* was decreed to be the Motive of a War when they came to a Rupture. Upon the Decease of the King of *Spain*, *Lewis* XIV diverted Europe with a fresh Scene of Politicks. He convinc'd 'em, that what he had done at *Reswick* was a meer Decoy to gain Time and Breath, and bring greater Designs about. The Allies saw clearly he had been jugling with two Sham Treaties of Partition, but was underhand working to engross the Whole, and that the Son and Father at St. *Germains* were always to serve to the same Purposes, and stand in the first Line of his *Manifesto*, to make the War plausible, and raise Factions in the Territories of *Great-Britain*. This was Fact, for no sooner were *Things* ready in *Spain* and *Flanders*, but

King *James* II departed this Life, which opportunity the *French* Monarch snatched, and in a studied Royal Transport, exalted the young Striplings Expectations at St. *Germains* by a solemn Protestation, that he wou'd never sheath his Sword till he saw him upon the Throne of his Ancestors, by which I suppose he understood no more than that titular Inauguration which was settled upon his Father at the Peace of *Reswick*. For had not the Affair of the *Spanish* Monarchy prompted *France* to this generous Declaration in Favour of the Son, 'tis highly probable the *Gallick* Sword wou'd have rusted in the Scabbard, as it was lock'd up by the Treaty of *Reswick*, nor had it been now drawn but upon a more beneficial Provocation, than restoring King *James*, for if it was the Interest of *France* to let the Father sit down quietly with the Title, nothing cou'd supervene to give the Son the Reality. Upon this Basis the War was renewed again on both Sides, and the Juggle was kept on with the Court of St. *James*'s, and great Pains were taken by the Emissaries of *France*, to buoy up King *James*'s Friends both at home and abroad, that *Lewis* XIV was Sincere, and wou'd exert himself sooner and later in their Cause.

The World needs not be put in Mind what Service King *James* II, Troops did to *France* during the War, every Action spoke their Bravery, but the grand Reform that was made upon the Peace was a sorry recompence for their Service. *France* wou'd not entertain 'em, and a Halter was their Doom if they return'd Home. This was an odd way of obliging King *James*; I speak not so much upon my own account, (though I was reduc'd at the same Time) because I had a Sufficiency elsewhere to keep me from Starving; but it was but a melancholly sight to behold poor Men strolling upon the Road, not knowing which way to direct their Course, and begging Alms through those Towns in which a little before they had Triumph'd in Victory. But the Rod is often thrown away and burnt after the Child is Whip'd. Upon this Occasion it was that I took leave of *Mars*, resolving to make use of this Interval of Peace, to satisfy an old Curiosity to see *England*, a Place as yet I never had beheld. Some Acquaintance I had contracted at *Dunkirk*, made me willing to take Shipping there, besides the hopes I had of decoying a pleasant Gentleman for my Companion, and upon my Arrival I found him in a good Humour, so we set Sail about three in the Morning, and came under *North Foreland Point* about seven the same Day. The Master of the Vessel, though he was an old Coaster, was not willing to trust himself among the Flats in a dark Moon, so we lay at Anchor all Night, and in the Morning by peep of Day, the Wind being pretty favourable, we weigh'd and pursu'd our Voyage up the River; but being a little too soon for the Tyde, we struck upon a Sand Bed, and oblig'd to remain ther till the Rise of the Water. I was all alone in the Master's Cabin when this Accident happen'd, but being very intent upon a Book, I was not sensible whether we mov'd or stood still. A Lady who was with the rest of the Passengers upon Deck coming hastily down, Sir, said she. Do you sit quietly here and we are struck upon a Sand-Bed? Madame, said I, I did suppose such a Thing, but the Tyde will cast us off. You suppos'd such a Thing, said she, Why, Sir, we shall certainly be drown'd, come let us to Prayers. I was not very much accustom'd to the Sea, yet I imagin'd there could be no great Danger as long as we had a flowing Tyde, and that it did not blow a Storm: Had the Water been ebbing and a Storm ensu'd upon it, 'tis probable our Ship, being none of the strongest, might have been beaten to Pieces among those Sands. However, I step'd upon Deck to see how Things went; there was a profound Silence every where, the Passengers were scatter'd here and there looking one at another, but not speaking a Word; the Master was walking with his Arms across without Fear, but not without Concern in his Countenance: I ask'd him how he came to be mistaken in the Tyde? he answer'd, Accidents would happen'd sometimes, but there was no Danger. Then running on in a Strain of Sailors Cant, he said, God was at Sea as well as at Land, that the Lord wou'd protect 'em if they did but put their Trust in him, and love him as they ought. In the middle of this moral Lesson, the Ship was gently wafted off the Sands by the Tyde, and Sails being abroad spread, the Ship sail'd merrily along. 'Twas surprizing to observe the Alteration in every bodies Countenance; the Women began to Laugh and Giggle; the Men began to rally one another for want of Courage; the Sailors began to raise their Note higher and higher, and the Master of the Ship turn'd his Sermon into a Volley of Oaths and Curses against his Crew; and thus in an instant, from a profound Silence we recover'd our selves again to Noise and Hurry. That Day brought us to *Gravesend,* where we took Boat, and so arriv'd safe at *London,* though I was not very well pleas'd with those small Boats People usually pass in from *Gravesend* to *London,* for I understood they were often Overset by sudden Gusts of Wind which blow from the Shoar.

London is a Place above my Description, and though I lost no Time the six Months I remain'd there, to view what Curiosities were to be seen, yet 'tis probable many Things worthy of Observation escaped my Diligence. I took a particular care not to make my self Public, but pass'd at my Lodgings under Disguise of a Merchant, yet abroad I acted the Marquess, not to be depriv'd of the Means of introducing my self into the best of Company. I found they were much divided in *England* as to the *French* Politicks; some were of Opinion that *Lewis* XIV was serious in King *James*'s Cause, but these were Persons who had no Notion of Foreign Affairs, and judg'd of Matters according to their first Appearance; for others who had studied the Interest of Nations, and how their Pretensions lie in regard of one another, had no Notion of the *French* King's Sincerity, either towards King *James*, or any other Prince he dealt with, and there is not one Instance I have mention'd in these Memoirs, in order to demonstrate the Infatuated State of the Court of St. *Germains*, but I heard it frequently urg'd to the same purpose, by the most intelligent Persons, as well Friends as Enemies to King *James*. While I was diverting my self at *London*, I receiv'd a Letter from *Paris*, that there was a Lieutenant Collonel's Place vacant, which I might easily be promoted to in Case I wou'd be at the trouble to, make use of what Interest I might reasonably Command. But I quickly understood, that by my Interest was meant my Money, so employing my *Amsterdam* Stock that way, I might very probably by a *French* Piece of Civility, live to want both my Money and a Commission. I return'd a thousand Thanks to my Friends for their Diligence in my Absence, but told 'em, I had rather wait till another War broke out, and their would be more choice of Promotions, and I might please my self, because I was somewhat curious what Regiment I engag'd in.

It was a tedious Journey to go into *Scotland* by Land, otherwise I was very much disposed to see my own Country once more, and apprehending besides, there might be some Danger upon account of being engaged in the *French* Service during this late War. I laid these Thoughts aside, and contented my self with making a small Tour Twenty or Thirty Miles distance from *London*, in which Progrination I saw *Windsor*, *Greenwich*, *Hampton-Court*, and some other Places of Note. But in one of these Jaunts, I had like to have paid very dear for my Curiosity. The Neighbourhood of *London* is much infested with Highwaymen, and if a Gentleman rides not with Pistols, 'tis very probable he will be attack'd. Unacquainted with these Customs, the Day I went to *Windsor*, I had in Company with me an *Irish* Gentleman; we made use of nothing but common Hacks, nor had any other Arms but our Swords; about the middle of *Honslow Heath* we met two Gentlemen well mounted, who pass'd by us unsuspected, but turning suddenly upon us again, with each of 'em a small Pistol cock'd, they very civilly demanded our Money. Gentlemen, said I, I am a Stranger; no Gentlemen said they, come quickly deliver what you have, we are in a publick Road, and can't stand arguing; but finding us a little Dilatory, they whip'd the Bridles from our Horfes, cut our Garths, and so dismounted us; and so I and my Companion were very dexterously strip'd of what they found in our Pockets, which was all I had about me, but my Friend reserv'd two or three Guineas in his Fob. When they had finish'd their Business, they gallop'd different ways cross the Heath, and left us like a couple of Asses, to drive our Horses to the next Town, and carry the Saddles under our Arms; but by the Invention of our Garters, and some other such like Tackle, we halter'd our Steeds till we cou'd refit our selves better. What we lost was but a Trifle, and 'twas done in so small a space of Time, that appear'd like a Dream or passing Thought. It was happy either for us or them, that this happen'd in the Morning when our Heads were cool, for had they attack'd us when warm'd up with good Liquor, I believe I should have had little regard to those Pop-guns they threatened us with. When we came to the next Town, and gave the People an account of our Disaster; the Landlord of the Inn ask'd us, if we had ever been upon that Road before, and we inform'd him this was the first time, then said I have Authority to enroll you as Freemen upon the small Fee of each a Bottle of Wine, and this I take to be no Imposition, because I am plac'd here in a convenient Part of the Country to advance a small sum to such as are robb'd of all they have, and cannot pursue their Journey; so Gentlemen, if that be your Condition, I have a couple of Guineas ready for you, which I will lend upon Honour, but in Case it be not a clean Robbery, what you have conceal'd from the Diligent Highwaymen is the Landlord's Fee as far as each a Bottle of Wine. This Merry Landlord I thought was very conveniently posted to divert People after their Misfortunes, we never went about to examine him, whether his Demand was customary, or only a Piece of shire Wit, and an extemporary Instance of his prolifick Genius, but sat down, and made our selves most immoderately drunk. The Landlord discanted very copiously upon the ancient and modern Practise of Robbing upon the Road, and seem'd very much inclin'd to lessen the Crime. Formerly, said he, no Body robb'd upon the Road but base scoundrel Fellows; but now 'tis become a Gentleman-like Employment, and young Brothers of very good Families are not asham'd to spend their time that way; besides the Practise is very much refin'd as to the manner, there's no Fighting or Hectoring during the Performance, but these Gentlemen approach you decently and submissive, with their Hat in their Hand to know your Pleasure, and what you can well afford to support them in that Dignity they live in: 'Tis true, says he, they often for Form sake have a Pistol in their Hand, which is part of their riding Furniture; but that is only in the Nature of a Petition, to let you know they are Orphans of Providence just fallen under your Protection. In a Word, demanding Money upon the Road, is now so agreeably perform'd, that 'tis much the same with asking an Alms. The poor Beggar wou'd rob you if he durst, and the Gentleman Beggar will not rob you if you will but give a decent Alms suitable to his Quality. I thought my time so well spent to hear this Landlord plead in favour of Padding, that I told my Companion I had often known the time that I wou'd have willingly have parted with more Money than I was strip'd of upon the Heath, to have some Melancholly Thoughts driven away by such a merry Companion.

The Time drawing near that I prescribed to my self to remain in *England,* we were now advis'd to return by the short Sea, which we perform'd without any Let or remarkable Accident. I have observ'd towards the beginning of these Memoirs, that the War begun in 1688, was undertaken in Defence of Cardinal *Fastenberg* to the Electorate of *Cologn*; the next War was for the Mornarchy of *Spain*, but the Restoration of King *James* was always a material Article, and a very useful Circumstance of the War. I need not acquaint the Reader how *France* was reduced in this last bloody War, her best Troops ruin'd, incapable to win a Battle, every Campaign carry'd two or three of their best Towns, the Nation dispirited, and Credit sunk, and nothing but a dismal Scene of Poverty and Misery: And yet in the midst of all this Misery, (as the *Spanish* Beggars are said to strut about in their Cloak and Bilboes at their Side) so this Gasping Monarch had the Assurance not only to talk of making a Descent, but actually equipp'd a small nimble Fleet with a Body of Men, and persuaded the Pretender to go upon the foolish Errand, as if he you'd have any prospect of Conquering the Three Kingdoms, who was in danger every Moment of having his Capital Sack'd and himself turn'd out of his Throne. Cou'd there be a more Romantick Undertaking, or more unintelligible in all its Circumstances, than the Pretender's Descent upon *Scotland*? The deluded Youth was carry'd to the Coast of *Scotland,* but upon what Design, is a Secret to this Day. He was made to believe at his departure from *Dunkirk,* that *Scotland* was dissatisfy'd to a Man upon account of the Union, and that it wou'd be an easie matter to Conquer *England* by putting himself at the Head of a *Scotch* Army; but when he desired to be landed to put the Project in Execution, the *French* General told him, he had Orders from his great Master, that there should be no Landing. Now whether this was part of the old Game, and only in Order to make a Diversion, or to surprize *Edinburgh* Castle, where most of the Specie of *Scotland* was said to be lodg'd at that time, is various alledg'd by Men of Speculation. That there was no appearance of succeeding in the main, is pretty plain from many Circumstances. *England* with their Allies at that Time were in a Capacity to spare 50000 Men, against which a few poor scrambling *Highland* Foot, wou'd but have made a very bad Resistance. I am not willing to think *France* would send Princes a Pilfering, or that the Pretender was design'd to steal the Money out of *Edinburgh* Castle, a Stratagem much more decently committed to some Partisan, or three or four *Dunkirk* Privateers. So I think it more suitable to the Prudence, and for the Honour of the *French* Court, to mention this design'd Descent only as a Diversion to amuse and employ the *British* Troops at Home, that they might not annoy the Enemy in *Flanders*. But how this Affair will be reconcil'd to that Affection and Friendship *Lewis* XIV. seem'd to have at that time for the Pretender, I am at a loss, with the rest of Mankind, to account for, since it was exposing him to the greatest of hazards for a Trifle, and throwing up the Cause at once, had he fallen into the Hands of his Enemies, and 'tis not the least Miracle of his Life that he escap'd them. I was invited to have gone abroad with the Pretender upon this Expedition, being than Free, but the Project appear'd to me so full of Inconsistencies, I have frequently since enlarg'd upon my own Politicks and Foresight in that Affair.

Thus much I must say for the Jacobite Party, never were Men more baffled and rallied oftner upon Projects or Hopes, but the unwholesome Diet never turn into the Substance, but infects the Body with peccant Humours, which now and then are discharg'd by Phlegbotomy, and then they turn to a Gangreen by Amputation. Jacobitism (I speak of it in relation to the strong Hopes they have of succeeding by a *French* Power) is an uncurable Distemper. I have often wonder'd to hear Persons, otherwise of great Penetration and Sense, grow constantly Delirious upon this Topick. The Wagers that have been lost upon that very Prospect wou'd have purchas'd him a little Kingdom. Time has open'd a great many People's Eyes; but there is a set of Men who are enslaved to the *French* Projects, and so far infatuated, that nothing can cure them. If fooling him with sham Descents, neglecting all Opportunities of assisting, if banishing him, excluding him by solemn Articles, will not satisfy 'em as to this Particular, 'tis my Opinion they wou'd not be convinc'd, if they should see *France* chaffering for his Head, and finish the Twenty Eight Years old Politicks with 100000*l.* being what is set upon it. There is no extraordinary difference between disposing of another Man's Right, and disposing of his Person. There was a Time when *France* gloried in the Ostentatious Title of being the Assylum of distress'd Monarchs, and I remember I was once dispos'd to have almost deify'd their Monarch upon that Score; but when I took the Frame of his Politics, and examin'd every Wheel and Spring by which they moved, I rescued my self from the Prejudices I had been nurs'd up in; and though I always pursu'd the same End, yet I was a constant Enemy to their Method, which I was convinc'd were all directed another Way, and that a Restoration upon a *French* Footing was a Chimerical Project, and that if it had taken Effect by their Arms, *England* must have had another Doomsday-Book, and have suffer'd once more under an Arbitary Discipline, more dreadful than that of *William the Conqueror*, from whom *England* has been struggling to retrieve her self ever since. I had formerly made a Resolution with my self not to hearken to a Love-Intrigue, but upon a Prospect of putting an end to such Amusements. The long time I had been out of the Army, gave me several Opportunities to make Enquiry after a Person who was capable of making me happy in that Respect. I took a singular Care when any Thing was offer'd that way, to consult my Reason more than my Passions, and had fix'd before my Eyes, the per-plex'd State I liv'd in those Weeks I held a Correspondence with the *Spanish* Lady. 'Tis a dangerous practice when a Person shuts his Eyes among Precipices, and neglects Consultation where the Choice is hazardous. There liv'd in *Paris* a Collonel's Widow, neither very young, nor very handsome. The intimacy I had with her Husband, who was kill'd in *Italy*, brought me first acquainted with her. Her discreet Carriage in a great variety of intricate Circumstances had often Charm'd me. There was no Difficulty in a marriage State, but she had struggled with it; a morose Husband, the Death of an only Child, the Gripes of Poverty when her Consort was in the Army and lavish'd away his Income, were great Tryals in which she always Triumph'd, and wore a stoical Constancy without any Reservedness. She had a large Pension allow'd her for Life, upon account of her Husband's Merits, who had done great Service during the Wars. Under these Circumstances I attack'd, rather like a Judicious than a Passionate Lover. The Method I took with her, was quite different to what I observ'd in pursuing my *Spanish* Mistress. There was no Balls, Treats, nor Serenading, we both knew the World too well, either She to expect, or I to offer her such Entertainments. In a Word, our whole Discourse when I visited ran upon Oeconomy and Morals. It was not long before she understood my Meaning, and that my repeated Visits tended towards Marriage. She alledg'd several Things to divert me from it; that she was tired with being an Officer's Wife, which oblig'd either to a rambling Method of Living, or to labour under great Inconveniences, and that I, perhaps, might not make the best of Husbands, that State being a Lottery full of Blanks. I had nothing more pertinent to alledge upon this Occasion, than to assure her, that during my Absence in the Army she should never be unprovided with what would make her easie, and for being a good Husband, I gave her all the Assurances that such a Matter was capable of, and at the same time made her the Compliment, that in case any misunderstanding should ever happen between us, her approv'd Conduct and Discretion would certainly declare me Guilty. In conclusion, I put on the Trummels, and never question'd but I had made the most prudential Choice that any Person could do; but there is something in Woman-kind which can never be found out by Study or Reflection. 'Tis only Experience that can School a Husband, and can give him a true Idea of that mysterious Creature; for in less than Twelve Months my Thousand Pounds which I had so carefully kept unbroke at *Amsterdam* was all dispos'd of, my Soldiers Pay being my only Subsistance for myself and Family, my Wife reserving her own Income for Pin-mony; my Credit very low, my Days very irksome upon many accounts, and I who had hitherto appear'd with Assurance in Company, because of my Money-merit, was now Neglected; for every Tradesman began to smell out my Poverty. I am of Opinion it would do Posterity no kindness, if I shou'd discover how I came to be ruin'd by a Prudent Wife, for no Body wou'd Credit me. If I should advise 'em to trust no Woman living, so as to give her full Scope upon an Opinion of her Conduct. I took my self to be as wise, upon this Head, as any Man living. It had been my Study above twenty Years. There is a secret Devil in every Woman, which is often Conjur'd down by a Husband's Temper; and though many Men may pass for bad Husbands by their Morose Carriage, 'tis less prejudicial, than that Indulgence which few Women have Discretion to make use of. My Wife's first Husband was represented as not very kind to her, whereas his less obliging Temper was the Effect of his Judgment, and a touch of

Skill he had in managing a Woman, whom Caresses wou'd have exalted into Impertinence, &c.

I would not be understood so upon this Subject, as if we lived unhappily as to our Affections; no, we regarded each other as two inseparable Companions, not only whose Interest it was not to be at variance, but we really did affectionately love each other. I cou'd not so much blame her as my self for if Children, Servants, &c. make a loose from their Duty, who are chiefly to be blam'd, but such gentle and restraining Methods did not curb 'em, but let 'em feel they had Reins in their Hands. Thus hamper'd in Wedlock, I had nothing to give me ease but that three parts of Mankind were in the same, if not in a much worse Condition. However, to make our Circumstances tollerable for the future, I perswaded my Consort to abridge her self of some superfluous Charge which we cou'd not well bear any longer. First we disposed of our Coach, and then our Acquaintance was reform'd of Course; by Degrees a multitude of modish Visitors dwindled away into two or three formal Matrons, which at last ended in a Decent Apartment in a Monastery, where she spent her Time agreeably enough when I was in the Camp. Hitherto the main matter which pall'd all my Joys, was the impossibility of a Restoration, which now was much lessen'd by the concurrence of Domestick Evils, and the Cares which attend a married State. Yet when I seriously reflected upon the Conduct of *France* in regard of King *James* and the Pretender, I have often observ'd my self to sweat and fret my self into a violent Fever with the very Thoughts of it; but I never was so sensibly touch'd upon this Head as after the Battle of *Malplacket.* which was follow'd with the Surrender of several Towns, so that there was nothing but the poor Barrier of *Landrecy* left to save the Capital, and by Consequence, the Kingdom of *France.* The *French* King having now play'd away all his Leading Cards, was now put to his Trumps. He attempts the Treacherous and Needy Ministers with long Bags of *Louisdo'rs,* which were all ineffectual when his Arms cou'd do no more.

'Tis fresh in every true *Britains* Memory, what strange Methods were taken to bring about the Peace, which quickly after ensued. I shall only mention as much of that Affair as is requisite to make it manifest, That *France* had no consideration for the Pretender's Interest during that Treaty. The War was begun upon account of the *Spanish* Monarchy; *France* was reduc'd to the last extremity, and could hold out no longer, now the Consequence shou'd have been for *France* to have surrender'd up King *Philip*'s Title; but on the contrary it was secur'd to him, and by what any one can conjecture on the Equivalent, that the Pretender should be banish'd *France*, and herafter neither directly nor indirectly be assisted by Force: Nay, so eagerly was *France* bent upon this Project of securing *Spain*, *France*, and neglecting the Pretender, that 'tis well known he refus'd to be concern'd with those in *England* who were willing to restore the Pretender. I shall not pretend to dive into the late Queen's Secrets, and how she was dispos'd that way. 'Tis well known she was not over real for the *Hanoverian* Succession, and that the Pretender's Interest was the only one in competition with it. But where was the *French* Zeal for the Pretender, when he had the Generalissimo and his Arms, the Secretary, the Treasurer, &c. all at his Devotion, and if the Pretender was not actually restor'd at that Juncture, the Remora cou'd be no where but on the *French* Side, who had a longer reach in their Politicks than the Restoration of the Pretender. They saw clearly bringing that about wou'd create a Civil War in *England*, and be an occasion of renewing in *Germany*; now their Business was a sudden Peace, and a quiet Possession of *Spain*. And this is the real Spirit of Politics that govern'd the *French* at the Peace of *Utrecht*.

This kind of Management so disconcerted all the Pretenders Party who then govern'd the Queen, that they flew all in Pieces, astonish'd not to find the *French* insist upon the Pretender's Right, as they had laid the Design. They inform against one another, and by their unseasonable and discontinued Animosities threw the Queen into an Agony of Fear, which afterwards usher'd in the Agony of Death. In the mean Time *France* smil'd at the disorder, and hugg'd themselves in the noble Project of having lost every Battle in that Bloody War, and yet obtain'd what they fought for, as they had always been Victorious, whilst the poor Pretender was so little consider'd by *France*, that tho' the Ministry was ready to assert his Title, yet *France* wav'd it and subscrib'd to his Banishment, least that Affair should ruin the Main Project.

But what I am in the next place going to observe, will make clear that *France* was not only unwilling to be active in assisting the Pretender, but that they were scrupulous upon the Point, and made it their Business to disswade him from any such Attempt. I remember I was my self in *Lorain*, when the News of the Queen's Decease was brought the Pretender by a Servant of *L.P.* He was no Stranger to the Interest he had just before with the Ministry, who still were most of 'em in Power. A Ship lay ready for him to waft him over, but he was arrested in his Journey by the *French* King's Orders, and threatened by *M.T.* with the Bastile, if he did not return forthwith to *Lorain*, otherwise considering the After-acts of the Gentlemen then in Play, he would very probably been at St. *James*'s several Days before King *George* left his Palace at *Hanover*. This was so shocking a Treatment from the grand Protector of distress'd Monarchs, that the Queen Mother then at *Chalonois* said this was a Key to all the mask Politics which had been acting 27 Years, and the very Thought of it threw her into such a Consternation, that she has never since recover'd it. I know 'tis pretended that *Lewis* XIV was now grown more scrupulous than formerly; he had been in sticking to the Letter of Treaties. I shall not dispute whether passing through the Country without assisting the Pretender, cou'd be wrested by any Logick to be acting in his Favour. But if *Lewis* XIV, was scrupulous, he ought to have been so when he grew nearer his End; for 'tis pretended by those who are willing to represent him as always a Friend to King *James*, that in despute of the Articles of *Utrecht*, he came into the Measures of the Duke of *Ormond*, Lord *Bolinbroke*, the Earl of *Mar*, &c. and had not Death in the mean time taken him off, wou'd have furnish'd 'em with all Things necessary to have made a Head against King *George*. This, I say, is confidently reported by *Lewis* XIV's Admirers. But then they will have the inconsistancy to account for, why he shou'd not scruple to raise an Army to succour the Pretender, who a little before scrupled to let him pass'd with a Couple of Servants, through his Country. For my own Part I am enclin'd to believe he never was so much his Friend, but died as he cou'd, a juggler, and that if he sign'd any thing in form of the late Insurrection 'twas in one of his delirious Fits which were not infrequent in his latter Years. If the Regent be a just Interpreter of his Actions.

And to come home to the present Time, has not *France* still the same regardless Dispositions towards the Pretender? Are they not ready to enter into any Engagement whatever to stand by the Articles of *Utrecht* to the greatest nicety? I know it has been aprised about, that *France* was in the Design against King *George*; but as the Regent reply'd very pertinently to the Earl of *Stairs*'s Memorial. There needs no more convincing Proof that *France* has not been meddling, than to understand that both in *Scotland* and *England*, the Rebels have been destitute both of Arms and Money? The Custom-house Officers of *Great-Britain*, have no Authority to search *French* Ships as they go out of their own Ports, and had it not been an easy Matter to have sent what Arms they pleas'd into *Scotland*? What occasion was their for the

Pretender to have sculk'd so long upon the Shoar, and stolen privately out of one of their Havens, if the Regent had encourag'd him.

It was no Secret to me and several others above Twenty Eight Years ago, that *France* was never sincere in this Affair; but as their Projects came nearer to a Conclusion, they took less care to conceal the Secret. Till they had a Prospect of settling the *Spanish* Monarchy in the House of *Bourbon*, they were loud and high in their Demands concerning King *James*; but the Hopes they conceiv'd that way, made 'em clap up a Peace at *Reswick*, and lay King *James*'s Interest to Sleep. When the *Spanish* Project was ripe, and the Wealth of the *Indies* ready to drop into their Lap, and that they were actually to be put into Possession of it, the Allies were amused with two Partition Treaties, and the Pretender sacrific'd to the same Politicks at the Treaty of *Utrecht*. Yes he was neglected, despised, banish'd out of *France*, forc'd out of *Lorain*, a free State, threaten'd at *Avignon*, a Sanction never yet violated, and now he and his Adherents are preparing themselves to be thrust into the Jaws of the *Turk*, unless the Regent out of Pity deliver him up in hope of the 100000*l.* and finish the Character of succouring distress'd Monarchs, by being the Occasion of losing his Head on *Tower-Hill*, rather than being Impail'd at *Constantinople*.

But before I dismiss this Matter, I am to account for several Things, which will argue the Court of St. *Germains* guilty of the greatest Ingratitude, unless they acknowledge the endless Obligations they lie under to *France*. Has he not fed a distressed People almost Twenty Years, and that two in a Royal and Princely Manner? Did he not entertain above 15000 *Irish* Troops who were dismiss'd *Ireland* by the Treaty of *Limerick*? Has he not constantly pay'd all the Respect imaginable to the Court of St. *Germains*? promis'd King *James* upon his Death-bed, he wou'd never desist? assur'd the Son he wou'd draw his Sword, and it should ne'er be sheath'd till he had fix'd him in his Throne? Has he not made several chargeable Attempts to make good his Promise? Such Panegyricks as these have often Rung in my Ears, when the *French* were bent upon extolling the Religious Disposition of the Monarch in protecting an unfortunate Prince; and the Expedient was not unserviceable in regard of the generality of the People who easily were blinded with the glaring Object. But let us take this Oeconomy to pieces, and examine every Wheel and Spring; for my part, I can regard this boasted Liberality no otherwise than a very imperfect Restitution. Did not K. *James* both Ruin himself and Thousands of Families meerly by going into *French* Measures. I heard the Court of

France was oblig'd to feed all the Posterity of that unfortunate misled Multitude, who have been deluded this Twenty Nine Years by their Politicks. 'Tis what I believe what the loosest of their Casuists wou'd not refuse to oblige 'em to upon a fair hearing of the Case. But that the Entertaining the *Irish* Troops shou'd be mention'd as an Instance of *French* Charity, is a very Remarkable piece of Assurance. The *Swiss* and other States are consider'd with large annual Pensions for the Privilege of Listing Men, besides double Pay during the Time of their Service; but the *Irish* and all the rest of King *James*'s Subjects, poor Fools, must think themselves happy to bear the brunt of every Siege and Engagement, for half Pay, be regarded as Beggars, living upon Charity, be reform'd and abandon'd when they are no further useful. The Honour purchas'd by these distress'd People at *Cremina, Luzara, Spireback, Almaza, Friburg, &c.* have merited better Articles, and the Blood they have lost is a large disbursement for the Expences at St. *Germains.* A few *French* Compliments paid once a Week at St. *Germains,* is but a poor recompence for a ruin'd People, especially when the Origin and Motive of their Misfortunes are look'd into. And the Gasconades and Politick, Promises made both to the Father and the Son of never sheathing the Sword with the Sham Attempts in their Favour, will be recorded in Antiquity, not as Arguments of his Christianity, but strong Lines of Policy how a Prince is to make use of all Occurrences to promote the welfare of his own People, nothing, being more successful in such junctures, than a Pretence of Religion, and assisting Persons in distress.

Having brought my Remarks to this Period, I design'd to have drop'd my Pen immediately, but considering that a Judicious Reader will expect I should advance something by way of Principle to justify the Reflexions I have made. I must add a Word or two more concerning the unjust, as well as unpolitick Proceedings of those who have been deluded by a Foreign Power to bring Destruction to their own native Country. And in the first place I must deliver my Thoughts as to the Cause in General. The Question of Hereditary, was not so well clear'd at the Revolution, but that many very discerning and well meaning Men might be drawn into a Belief, that lineal and immediate Right was part of the Divine Law, and so not dispensable. This was my Opinion in the Beginning, and it was a Principle which carried me through the Wars this Twenty Nine Years in Favour of King *James,* even at those Times, when I was fully convinc'd that *France* had no real Design to re-establish him. But afterwards when I began to look narrowly into the Question of Hereditary Right, and saw that the Notion of *Jure Divino* was only an assum'd Principle to buoy up the Faction. I by Degrees slacken'd in my Zeal, and having no other Nation of Government, then by submitting to the Supream National Power, where the Law of God was silent, I found this an effectual Means to quiet my Conscience. However I still persisted and follow'd the Pretender's Cause, the Success of the Roman-Catholick Interest provoking me to it: For I imagin'd that Salvo ought to weigh down in Practise, where other Matters relating to Succession were still under Controversy; but when I took under serious Consideration the Practise of our Ancestors, and how in all Ages both Church and State came frequently into Non-Hereditary Measures, where I run over the String of Disappointments King *James* had met withal by the Politic Management *of France.* When I reflected what Misery had befallen, and was like to befall these Kings by adhering to the besoted Notion of Hereditary Right, I put the whole Controversy upon the Issue of Religion, and it plainly appear'd to me, that no Roman Catholick was oblig'd to oppose the Revolutionary Measures in Conscience, much less in Policy. I was fully satisfy'd in the first Part of the Enquiry by that unanswerable Piece lately printed, call'd, *A Roman Catholick System of Allegiance.* As for the latter Part, let the Tory and Roman Catholick Party sum up their Losses since 1688, and it will convince 'em how foolishly they acted. Thus settled in my Principles in regard of Loyalty, I design'd to pay an intire and unlimited Obedience to the present Constitution; as to my Religion, which I own is not conformable to that by Law Established. I will make a discreet Use of that Indulgence the Government is pleas'd to allow; and if Providence thinks fit to make me Suffer upon that Score, no rational Man will blame my Zeal till he does convince me of my Mistake.

Vindication of the Press:

OR, AN ESSAY ON THE *Usefulness of Writing*,
ON CRITICISM, AND THE
Qualification of AUTHORS.
Wherein is shewn,

That 'tis for the Advantage of all Governments to encourage Writing; otherwise a Nation would never be secure from the Attempts of its most secret Enemies; Barbarous and prejudic'd Criticisms on Writings are detected, and Criticism is justly stated. With an Examination into what Genius's and Learning are necessary for an AUTHOR in all manner of Performances.

The very great Clamour against some late Performances or Authorship, and the unpresidented Criticisms introduc'd, render a Treatise on the Usefulness of Writing in general so absolutely necessary, that the Author of this Essay has not the least Apprehensions of Displeasure from the most inveterate, but on the contrary, doubts not an Approbation, even of the Great Mr. *Dennis*.

For the Usefulness of Writing in the Church, I shall trace back to the Annals of our Saviour and his Apostles. Had not Writing been at that Time in use, what Obscurity might we reasonably have expected the whole World would have labour'd under at this Day? when, notwithstanding the Infidels possess such vast Regions, and Religion in its Purity shines but in a small Quarter of the Globe. 'Tis easy-to imagine, that without the New-Testament every Person of excellency in Literature, and compleat in Hypocrisy, either out of Interest, or other worldly Views, would have taken the Liberty to deny the most Sacred Traditions, and to have impos'd upon the Populace as many Religions as they pleas'd, and that the ignorant Multitude would easily acquiesce, as they do in *Turkey*, and other distant Parts of the World, which deny the Divinity of our Saviour.

What fatal Errors, Schisms, and concomitant Evils would have been introduc'd, must be apparent to all Persons of the least Penetration. The Quakers might at this Time possibly have been our National Church, and our present Happiness, with regard to those Considerations, can no way be more lively and amply demonstrated than in taking a step at once from Mr. *Penn's* Conventicle to the Cathedral Church of St. *Pauls*.

The Regularity and heavenly Decorum of the latter, give an Awe and Transport to the Audience at the same time they ornament Religion; and the Confusion of the former fully shews, that as it only serves to amuse a Crowd of ignorant Wretches, unless meerly with temporal Views (Sectarists generally calculating Religion for their Interests) so it gives a License to all manner of Indecencies, and the Congregations usually resort thither with the same Regard as a Rake of the Town would do to Mother *Wybourn's*, or any publick Place of Diversion.

Whether it be not natural to have expected a Confusion in the Church, equal to that of the worst Sectaries in the World, had not the Use of Waiting been early attain'd and practis'd, I appeal to the Breast of every unprejudic'd Reader; and if so, how infinitely happy are we by the Use of our Sacred Writings, which clear up the Cloud of Ignorance and Error, and give a Sanction to our Religion, besides the Satisfaction we of the Church of *England* have in this felicitous Contemplation, that our Religion, since the Reformation, strictly observ'd, is the nearest that of our Saviour and his Apostles of any Profession of Faith upon Earth.

'Tis owing to Writing, that we enjoy the purest Religion in the World, and exclusive of it, there would have been no possibility of transmitting down entirely those valuable Maxims of *Solomon*, and the Sufferings of the Righteous *Job*, in the old Testament; which are so extensive to all Parts and Stations of Life, that as they are infinitely preferable to all other Writings of the Kind, so they afford the greatest Comfort and Repose in the Vicisitudes incident to Humane Nature.

How far Theology is improv'd from those inestimable Writings, I need not to enlarge, since it is highly conspicuous that they are the Foundation of all Divine Literature; and how ignorant and imperfect we should have been without them, is no great difficulty to explain; and who can sufficiently admire the Psalter of *David*, which fills the Soul with Rapture, and gives an Anticipation of sublimest Joys.
Besides the Advantages of Sacred Writings in the Cause of Religion;
'tis chiefly owing to Writing, that we have our most valuable
Liberties preserv'd; and 'tis observable, that the Liberty of the
Press is no where restrain'd but in Roman Catholick Countries, or
Kingdoms, or States Exercising an Absolute Power.

In the Kingdom of *France* Writings relating to the Church and State are prohibited upon the severest Penalties, and the Consequences of those Laws are very Obvious to all Persons of Discernment here; they serve to secure the Subject in the utmost Obscurity, and as it were

Effect an entire Ignorance, whereby an exorbitant Power is chearfully submitted to, and a perfect Obedience paid to Tyranny; and the Ignorance and Superstition of these People so powerfully prevail, that the greatest Oppressor is commonly the most entirely Belov'd, which I take to be sufficiently ently Illustrated in the late *Lewis* the Fourteenth, whose Arbitrary Government was so far from Diminishing the Affections of his Subjects, that it highten'd their Esteem for their Grand Monarch.

But of late the populace of *France* are not so perfectly enclouded with Superstition, and if a young Author can pretend to Divine, I think it is easy to foresee that the papal Power will in a very short space be considerably lessen'd if not in a great measure disregarded in that Kingdom, by the intestine Jarrs and Discords of their Parties for Religion, and the Desultory Judgments of the most considerable Prelates.

The best Support of an Arbitrary Power is undoubtedly Ignorance, and this cannot be better cultivated than by an Absolute Denial of Printing; the Oppressions of the Popularity cannot be thoroughly Stated, or Liberty in general Propagated without the use of the Press in some measure, and therefore the Subjects must inevitably submit to such Ordinances as an Ambitious or Ignorant Monarch and his Tyrannical Council shall think fit to impose upon them, how Arbitrary soever: And the Hands of the Patriots and Men of Eminence who should Illuminate the Age, and open the Eyes of the deluded People are thereby tied up, and the Infelicity of the Populace so compleat that they are incapable of either seeing their approaching Misery, or having a redress of present Grievances.

In *Constantinople* I think they have no such thing as Printing allow'd on any Account whatsoever; all their Publick Acts relating to the Church and State are recorded in Writing by expert Amanuensis's, so very strict are the Divan and great Council of the Sultan in prohibiting the Publication of all manner of Writings: They are very sensible had Persons a common Liberty of stating their own Cases, they might Influence the Publick so far, that the Yoke of Tyranny must sink if not be rendred insupportable; and this is regarded in all Kingdoms and Countries upon Earth Govern'd by a Despotick Power.

To what I have already offer'd in favour of the Press, there may be Exceptions taken by some Persons in the World; and as it is my Intentions to solve all Objections that may be rais'd to what I advance, as I proceed, I think I cannot too early make known, that I am apprehensive the following Observations may be made; *viz.* that a general License of the Press is of such a fatal Tendency, that it causes Uneasinesses in the State, Confusions in the Church, and is destructive sometimes even to Liberty, by putting the ruling Powers upon making Laws of Severity, on a Detection of ill Designs against the State, otherwise never intended.

In answer to which, I shall give the following Particulars: In respect to Uneasinesses in the State, it may not be amiss to premise, that it is esteem'd by Men of Penetration, no small Wisdom in the present Administration, to bestow Preferments on the brightest and most enterprising Authors of the Age; but whether it be so much out of a Regard to the Service they are capable of to the State in their Employs, as to their Writing for the Government, and to answer treasonable Pamphlets, poison'd Pens, &c. I do not take upon me to determine. I must confess, where a Faction prevails, it gives a sensible Monarch some Pain to see Disaffection propagated by the Press, without any manner of Restraint; but then, on the other Hand, such a Ruler is thereby let into the Secrets of the Faction, he may with facility penetrate into their deepest Intrigues, and be enabled to avert an impending Storm. Upon approach of a Rebellion, he will be thoroughly sensible from what Quarter his greatest Danger is to be expected, whereby it will be entirely his own Fault, if he be without a sufficient Guard against it, which he could not be appriz'd of (with any certainty) without a general Liberty of Writing: And tho' Slander must occasion a great deal of Uneasiness to a crown'd Head, the Power of bestowing Favours on Friends only is no small Satisfaction to the Prince, and a sufficient Punishment to his Enemies. And it is my Opinion, that the Grand Sultan, and other Eastern Potentates, would be in a great deal less danger of Deposing, (a Practice very frequent of late) if in some measure a Liberty of Writing was allow'd; for the Eyes of the People would be open, as well for as against their Prince, and their fearing a worse Evil should succeed, might make them easy under a present Oppression.

As for Confusion in the Church, I look upon this to be the greatest Objection that can be raised; but then it must be allow'd, that without Writing the Reformation (the Glory of our Religion) could never have been effected; and in respect to religious Controversies, tho' I own they are seldom attended with good Consequences, yet I must beg leave to observe, that as the Age we now live in, is more bright and shining in substantial Literature than any preceding Century, so the generality of Mankind are capable of judging with such an Exactness as to avoid a Bad; not but, I confess, I think many of the Persons concern'd in the Controversy lately on foot, with relation to the Bishop of *Bangor's* Sermon, preach'd before His Majesty, deserve to be stigmatiz'd, as well for their indecent Heat, as for the Latitude taken with regard to the Holy Scriptures. And for the last Objection, I never knew that Writing was any ways destructive to Liberty, unless it was in a Pamphlet, [entitled King-Killing no Murder] which 'tis said occasion'd the Death of *Oliver Cromwel.*

These are the Uses of Writings in the Church and the State, with Answers to such Objections as may be made against them, not to mention particularly in respect to the former, the Writings of the Fathers, and even of some Heathen Philosophers, such as *Seneca,* &c. And besides the valuable Performances of our most eminent Divines in all Ages, as Dr. *Taylor,* Bishop *Usher, Tillotson, Beveridge* &c. and *The whole Duty of Man,* &c. in our private Devotions. I now proceed to the Uses in Arts and Sciences.

How much Posterity will be oblig'd to the Great Sir *Isaac Newton* and Doctor *Flamstead* for their Mathematical Writings, is more easy to imagine than the Improvements which may be made from thence; there's a great deal of Reason to believe, that if a future Age produces a Successor to Sir *Isaac,* (at present I take it, there's none in the World) that not only the Longitude at Sea will be discover'd, but the perpetual Motion, so many Ages sought after, found out.

How much are the Gentlemen of the Law oblig'd to my Lord *Littleton's* Institutes and *Coke's* Commentaries thereupon? Writing in this Profession is esteem'd so Essential, that there's seldom a Judge quits the Stage of Life, without a voluminous Performance, as a Legacy to the World, and there's rarely a Term without some Production of the Press: The Numbers of these Writings are very much augmented by the various Reports of Cases from Time to Time made; and these seem to be entirely necessary by way of Precedent, as a discreet and cautious Justice will not take upon him to determine a Cause of difficulty without the Authority of a Precedent.

And in the Practice of Physick, are not the present Professors infinitely obliged to the Discoveries and Recipes of *Aristotle, Galen,* &c? How much the World is oblig'd to the Declamations of *Tully, Cicero,* for Oratory; to the famous Writings of *Milton* for the Foundation of Divine Poetry; Poetry in general is improv'd from the Writings of *Chaucer, Spencer,* and others; Dramatick Entertainments perfected by *Shakespear*, our Language and Poetry refin'd by *Dryden*, the Passions rais'd by *Otway*, the Inclination mov'd by *Cowley*, and the World diverted by *Hudibras*, (not to mention the Perfections of Mr. *Addison*, and several others of this Age) I leave to the Determination of every impartial Reader.

'Tis by Writing that Arts and Sciences are Cultivated, Navigation and Commerce (by which alone Wealth is attain'd) to the most distant parts of the World Improv'd, Geography Compleated, the Languages, Customs and Manners of Foreign Nations known; and there is scarce any one Mechanick calling of Note or Signification, but Treatises have been written upon, to transmit the valuable Observations of Ingenious Artificers to the latest Posterity.

There might be innumerable Instances given of the Advantages of Writings in all Cases, but I shall satisfy my self with the particulars already advanc'd, and proceed to such Objections, as I am apprehensive may be made relating to the Writings last mentioned. First, it may be Objected that the numerous Writings tend more to confound the Reader, than to inform him; to this I answer, that it is impossible there can be many Writings produced, but there must be some valuable Informations communicated, easy to be Collected by a judicious Reader; tho' there may be a great deal superfluous, and notwithstanding it is a considerable Charge to purchase a useful Library, (the greatest Grievance) yet we had better be at that Expence, than to have no Books publish'd, and consequently no Discoveries; the same Reason may be given where Books in the Law, Physick, &c. are imperfect in some Part, and tend to the misleading Persons; for of two Evils the old Maxim is, always chuse the least. The only Objection that I do not take upon me to Defend, is, that against Lewd and obscene Poetry in general; (for sometimes the very great Wit may make it excuseable) which in my Opinion will admit of but a slender Apology in its Defence.

The use of Writing is Illustrated in the following Lines, which conclude my first Head of this Essay.

By ancient Writing Knowledge is convey'd,
Of famous Arts the best Foundation laid;
By these the Cause of Liberty remains,
Are Nations free'd from Arbitrary Chains,
From Errors still our Church is purified,
The State maintained, with justice on its Side.

I now advance to my second Particular, *Criticism*.

The fatal Criticism or Damnation which the Writings of some Authors meet with thro' their Obscurity, want of Friends and Interest in the World, &c. is very discouraging to the Productions of Literature: It is the greatest difficulty immaginable, for an obscure Person to Establish a Reputation in any sort of Writing; he's a long time in the same Condition with *Sisyphus*, rolling a heavy Stone against an aspiring Mount which perpetually descends again; it must be to his benign Stars, some lucky Subject suiting the Humour of the Times, more than the Beauty of his Performance, which he will be oblig'd for his Rise: And in this Age Persons in general, are so Estrang'd from bare Merit, that an Author destitute of Patronage will be equally Unsuccessful to a Person without Interest at Court, (and you'll as rarely find the Friendship of an *Orestes*, as the Chastity of *Penelope*) When a Man of Fortune has no other Task, than to give out a stupid Performance to be of his own Composing, and he's immediately respected as a Celebrated Writer: And if a Man has the good Fortune to hit the capricious Humour of the Age; after he has attained a Reputation with the utmost Difficulty, he's sure to meet with the severest Treatment, from a herd of Malicious and Implacable Scriblers.

This was the Case of the late Mr. *Dryden*, a Man for Learning and universal Writing in Poetry, perhaps the Greatest that *England* has produc'd; he was Persecuted by Envy, with the utmost Inveteracy for many Years in Succession: And is the Misfortune at this Juncture of Mr. *Pope*, a Person tho' Inferior to Mr. *Dryden*, yet speaking Impartially has few Superiors in this Age: From these Considerations it is Evident, (tho' it seems a Paradox) that it is a Reputation to be Scandaliz'd, as a Person in all Cases of this Nature is allow'd some Merit, when Envy attacks him, and the World might not be sensible of it in General, without a publick Encounter in Criticism; and many Authors would be Buried in Oblivion were they not kept alive by Clamours against their Performances.

The Criticks in this Age are arriv'd to that consummate Pitch of ill-nature, that they'll by no means permit any Person the favour to Blunder but their mighty selves, and are in all respects, except the Office of a Critick, in some measure ill Writers; I have known an unnatural Brother of the Quill causless condemn Language in the Writings of other Persons, when his own has really been the meanest; to Accuse others of Inconsistency with the utmost Vehemence, when his own Works have not been without their Æra's, and to find fault with every

Line in a Poem, when he has been wholly at a loss to Correct, or at least not capable of Writing one single Page of it.

There are another sort of Criticks, which are equally ill-natur'd to these I have mention'd, tho' in all other respects vastly inferior to them: They are such as no sooner hear of a Performance compos'd by a Juvenile Author, or one not hitherto known in the way of Writing he has undertaken; but immediately without reading a Line give it a Stamp of Damnation; (not considering that the first Performance of an Author in any way of Writing done carefully, is oftentimes the best) and if they had thoroughly perus'd it, they were no ways capable of Judging of either the Sense, Language, or Beauty of any one Paragraph; and what is still worse, these ignorant Slanderers of Writings frequently take what other Persons report for Authority, who know as little, or perhaps are more Ignorant than themselves, so little Regard have they to the Reputation of an Author.

And sometimes you'll find a pert *Bookseller* give himself the Airs of Judging a Performance so far, as to Condemn the Correctness of what he knows nothing of these there's a pretender to Authorship in the City, who Rules the young Fry of Biblioples about the *Royal-Exchange*. But the *Booksellers* in general, (tho' they commonly Judge of the Goodness of Writings, by the greatness of the Sale,) are Very sensible that their greatest Security in respect to the Performance of any Work, is the Qualification of the Person that Composes it, the Confidence they can Repose in him; his Capacity, Industry and Veracity; And the Author's Reputation is so far concern'd in a Performance, which he owns that the *Bookseller* will sooner rely upon that, than his own Judgment.

To descend still to a lower Order of Criticks, you'll find very few Coffee-Houses in this opulent City without an illiterate Mechanick, Commenting upon the most material Occurrences, and Judging the Actions of the greatest Councils in *Europe*, and rarely a Victualing House, but you meet with a *Tinker, a Cobler, or a Porter,* Criticizing upon the Speeches of Majesty, or the Writings of the most celebrated Men of the Age.

This is entirely owing to Party, and there is such a Contagion diffuses it self thro' the greatest Part of the World at this Time, that it is impossible for a Man to acquire a universal Character in Writing, as it is inconsistent for him to engage in Writings for both Parties at one and the same Time, (whatever he may do alternately) without which such a Character is not attainable; and these contending Parties carry

Things to that Extremity, that they'll by no means allow the least Merit in the most perfect Author, who adheres to the opposite Side; his Performances will be generally unheeded, if not blasted, and frequently damn'd, as if, like *Coelus*, he were capable of producing nothing but Monsters; he shall be in all Respects depress'd and debas'd, at the same time an illiterate Scribler, an auspicious Ideot of their own (with whose Nonsense they are never sated) shall be extoll'd to the Skies: Herein, if a Man has all the Qualifications necessary in Poetry, as an Elegance of Style, an Excellency of Wit, and a Nobleness of Thought; were Master of the most surprizing Turns, fine Similies, and of universal Learning, yet he shall be despis'd by the Criticks, and rang'd amongst the damn'd Writers of the Times.

The Question first ask'd is, whether an Author is a Whig or a Tory; if he be a Whig, or that Party which is in Power, his Praise is resounded, he's presently cried up for an excellent Writer; if not, he's mark'd as a Scoundrel, a perpetual Gloom hangs over his Head; if he was Master of the sublime Thoughts of *Addison*, the easy flowing Numbers of *Pope*, the fine Humour of *Garth*, the beautiful Language of *Rowe*, the Perfection of *Prior*, the Dialogue of *Congreve*, and the Pastoral of *Phillips*, he must nevertheless submit to a mean Character, if not expect the Reputation of an Illitterate.

Writings for the Stage are of late so very much perverted by the Violence of Party, that the finest Performance, without Scandal, cannot be supported; *Shakespear* and *Ben Johnson*, were they, now living, would be wholly at a Loss in the Composure of a Play suitable to the Taste of the Town; without a promiscuous heap of Scurrility to expose a Party, or, what is more detestable, perhaps a particular Person, no Play will succeed, and the most execrable Language, in a Comedy, produc'd at this Time, shall be more applauded than the most beautiful Turns in a *Love for Love*: Such are the Hardships a Dramatick-Poet has to struggle with, that either Obscenity, Party, or Scandal must be his Theme, and after he has performed his utmost in either of these Ways, without a powerful Interest, he'll have more Difficulty in the bringing his Play upon the Theatre than in the Writing, and sometimes never be able to accomplish it.

These are the Inconveniencies which Writers for the Stage labour under, besides 'tis observable, that an obsequious prolifick Muse generally meets with a worse Reception than a petulant inanimate Author; and when a Poet has finished his Labours, so that he has brought his Play upon the Stage, the best Performance has oftentimes the worst Success, for which I need only instance Mr. *Congreve's Way of the World*, a Comedy esteem'd by most Persons capable of judging, no way inferior to any of his other Performances.

A Choice of Actors, next to Interest and Popularity, is the greatest Advantage to a new Play: If a Stage-Poet has the Misfortune not to have a sufficient Influence over the Managers of the Theatres to make a Nomination, his Performance must very much suffer; and if he cannot entirely Command his Theatre, and Season for bringing it on, it will be perfectly slaughter'd; and a certain Theatre has lately acquir'd the Name of a *Slaughter-House*, but whether more for the Stupidity of its Poets than its Actors, I do not pretend to determine; but certain it is, that Acting is the Life of all Dramatick-Performances. And tho' an indifferent Play may appear tolerable, with good Acting, it is impossible a bad one can afford any Entertainment, when perform'd by an incompleat Set of Comedians.

In respect to Writings in general, there is an unaccountable Caprice in abundance of Persons, to Condemn or Commend a Performance meerly by a Name. The Names of some Writers will effectually recommend, without making an Examination into the Merit of the Work; and the Names of other Persons, equally qualified for Writing, and perhaps of greater Learning than the Former, shall be sufficient to Damn it; and all this is owing either to some lucky Accident of writing apposite to the Humour of the Town, (wherein an agreeable Season and a proper Subject are chiefly to be regarded) or to Prejudice, but most commonly the Former.

It is a Misfortune to Authors both in Prose and Verse, who are reduc'd to a Necessity of constant writing for a Subsistence, that the numerous Performances, publish'd by them, cannot possibly be so correct as they might be, could more Time be afforded in the Composure. By this Means there is sometimes just room for Criticism upon the best of their Productions, and these Gentlemen, notwithstanding it be never so contrary to their Inclinations, are entirely oblig'd to prostrate their Pens to the Town, as Ladies of Pleasure do their Bodies; tho' herein, in respect to Party, it is to be observ'd, that a Bookseller and an Author may very well be allow'd occasionally to be of either Party, or at least, that they should be permitted the Liberty of Writing and Printing of either Side for Bread, free from Ignominy; and as getting Money is the chief Business of the World, so these Measures cannot by any means be esteem'd Unjust or Disreputable, with regard to the several Ways of accumulating Wealth, introduc'd in *Exchange-Alley*, and at the other End of the Town.

It is a common Practice with some Persons in the World, either to prefix the Name of a *Mecanas* in the Front of their Performances, or to obtain recommendatory Lines from some Person of excellency in Writing, as a Protection against Criticism; and there is nothing more frequent than to see a mean Performance (especially if it be done by a Man of Figure) with this Guard.

'Tis true, the worst Performances have the greatest occasion of these Ramparts, but then the Person who takes upon him to Recommend, must have such an absolute Authority and Influence over the generality of Mankind, as to silence all Objections, or else it will have a contrary Turn, by promoting a Criticism as well upon the Author as upon himself; for which Reason it is very hazardous for a Person in a middle Station (tho' he have never so great a Reputation in Writing) to engage in the Recommendation of the Writings of others.

The severe Treatment which the brightest Men of the Age have met with from the Criticks, is sufficient to deter all young Gentlemen from entring the Lists of Writing; and was not the World in general more good-natur'd and favourable to youthful Performances than the Criticks, there would be no such thing as a Succession of Writings; whereas, by that Means, and his present Majesty's Encouragement, Literature is in a flourishing Condition, and Poetry seems to improve more at this Time than it has done in any preceding Reign, except that of King *Charles* II. when there was a *Rochester*, a *Sidley*, a *Buckingham*, &c. And (setting aside Party) what the World may hope from a generous Encouragement of polite Writing, I take to be very conspicuous from Mr. *Pope's* Translation of *Homer*, notwithstanding the malicious and violent Criticisms of a certain Gentleman in its Disfavour.

In the religious Controversy of late depending, Criticisms have been carried to that height, that some Persons have pretended to fix false Grammer on one of the most celebrated Writers perhaps at this Time in *Europe*, but how justly, I leave to the Determination of those who have perused the Bishop's incomparable Answer; but admitting his Lordship had permitted an irregularity of Grammer to pass unobser'd [typo for "unobserv'd"?], he is not the first of his Sacred Character that has done it, and small Errors of this kind are easily looked over, where the Nominative Case is at a distance from the Verb, or a Performance is done in haste, the Case of the Bishop against so many powerful

Adversaries. Besides, it is apparent and well known, that a certain Person [*Mr.* Lessey, *now with the* Chevalier.] in the World, who has a very great Reputation in Writing, never regards the strict Rules of Grammer in any of his Performances.

It is a Satisfaction to Authors of tender Date, to see their Superiors thus roughly handled by the Criticks; a young Writer in Divinity will not think his Case desperate, when the shining *Bangor* has met with such malevolent Treatment; neither must a youthful Poet be uneasy at a severe Criticism, when the Great Mr. *Addison, Rowe* and *Pope* have been treated with the utmost Scurrility.

These Men of Eminence sitting easy with a load of Calumny, is a sufficient Consolation to Inferiors under the most despicable Usage, and there is this satisfactory Reflection, that perhaps the most perfect Work that ever was compos'd, if not so entirely correct, but there may be some room for Criticism by a Man of consummate Learning; for there is nothing more common than to find a Man, (if not wholly blind) over opiniated in respect to his own Performances, and too exact in a Scrutiny into the Writings of others.

The ill Nature attending Criticism I take to be greater now than in any Age past; a Man's Defects in Writing shall not only be expos'd, but all the personal Infamy heap'd upon him that is possible; his Descent and Education shall be scandaliz'd, (as if a fine Performance was the worse for the Author's Parentage) his good Name villified, a History of the Transactions of his whole Life, and oftentimes a great deal more, shall be written, as if the were a Candidate setting up in a Burough for Member of Parliament, not an airy[?] or loose Action shall be omitted, and neither the Sacred Gown, nor the greatest Dignity shall be exempted; but there is this Consideration which sways the sensible part of Mankind, *viz.* a Man of Excellency in Writing his being generally a Person of more Vivacity than the common Herd, and consequently the more extraordinary Actions in him are allowable; yet, nevertheless, I think it consistent with Prudence for an Author, when he has the good fortune to compose a Piece, which he's assur'd will occasion Envy and Criticism, to write his own Life at the same Time with it, tho' it be a little extravagant and the method is unusual, to prevent an ill-natur'd doing thereof by the Hand of another Person.

According to the old Maxim, *Get a Reputation, and lye a Bed,* not to mention how many lye a Bed before they can attain it, according to the humorous Turn of the late ingenious Mr. *Farqubar;* but there's at this Time a greater necessity for a Man to be wakeful, when he has acquir'd a Reputation, than at any Time before; he'll find abundantly more difficulty attend the Securing than the Attaining of the greatest Reputation; he'll meet with Envy from every Quarter; Malice will pursue him in all his undertakings, and if he makes any manner of Defence, he cannot commence it too soon, tho' it is not always prudential to shew an open Resentment, even to the utmost ill Treatment.

If a Man be so considerable as to be thought worthy of Criticism, a luducrous Reprimand is always preferable to a serious Answer; returning Scurrility with Comic-Satyr will gaul an ill-natur'd Adversary beyond any Treatment whatsoever; his Spleen will encrease equal to any Poison, his Rage keep within no Bounds, and at length his Passion will not only destroy his own Performance, but himself likewise: And this I take to be natural in our modern Criticks.

The Business of these Gentlemen is to set the ignorant Part of Mankind right, In correcting the Errors of pretending Authors, and exposing of Impositions, whereby who has Learning and Merit, and who has not, may be so apparent, that the World may not misplace their Favour; but unless they do it with more Impartiality, Temper and Candour than of late, they may, with equal prospect of Success, endeavour to turn the current of the Thames, as to pervert the Humour of this good-natur'd Town.

I presume to present them with these two Verses:
The learned Criticks learn not to be Civil,
In Spite and Malice personate the Devil.
Having now dispatch'd the two first Subjects of my Essay *(viz.)* The Usefulness of Writing, and Criticism, I come to my last Head, the Qualification of Authors.
I am not of the Opinion of a great many Persons in the World, that a Poet is entirely born such, and that Poetry is a particular Gift of Heaven, not but I confess there is a great deal in natural Genius, which I shall mention hereafter:

It is consistent with my Reason, that any Man having a share of Learning, and acquainted with the Methods of Writing, may by an assiduous Application, not only write good Poetry, but make a tollerable Figure in any sort of Writings whatsoever; and herein I could give numerous Instances of Authors who have written all manner of Ways with success. Neither can I acquiesce in the common Notion, that the Person who begins most early in Poetry always arrives to the greatest Perfection; for, in my Opinion, it is a Matter of no great difficulty, for a Person of any Age, before his Vivacity is too much abated, and Fire exhausted, to commence a Poet; the great Mr. *Dryden* not beginning to Write 'till he was above the Age of 30; and I doubt not but a great many Persons have lost themselves for want of putting their Genius's to the Trial, and making particular Writings their particular Studies.

Their is no Practice more frequent than for an Author to misapply his Genius; and there is nothing more common than for a Man, after numerous Trials in almost all sorts of Authorship, to make that his favourite Writing which he is least capable of performing; and too frequently Authors use their Genius's as Parents do their Children, place them to such Businesses as make the most considerable Figure in the World, without consulting their Qualifications.

There are many other Faults equal to these, as where Authors, through overmuch Timerity, or too great Opinion of their own Performances, permit their Writings to pass with egregious Errors; and I take it to be equally pernicious for a Man to be too diffident of his own Performances, as it is to be presuming: There are likewise some Gentlemen, who (by a lazy Disposition, or through over much Haste, an impatience in dispatch to gain an early Reputation) commit Blunders almost to their immediate Ruin; but many of these Errors are commonly excus'd in an Author by a condescending Printer, who is oblig'd to take the Errata upon himself.

In Prose a slight Examination of a Performance may suffice, but in Poetry it cannot be too often repeated; and in this way of Writing, haste is attended with a fatal Consequence. To compose your Lines in perfect Harmony, of easy flowing Numbers, fine Flights and Similies, and at the same Time retain a strong Sense, which make Poetry substantially Beautiful, is a Work of Time, and requires the most sedate Perusals: And though some Persons think, giving Poetry the Character of easy Lines to be a Disgrace, it is rightly considered the greatest Reputation and Honour they can do it; the utmost Difficulty attending this easy Writing, and there are very few Persons that can ever attain it.

But to leave these general Observations, I proceed to my Point in Hand, the Qualification of Authors; Though I shall first take Notice, that the Business of every Author is to please and inform his Readers; but how difficult it is to please, through the prevalence of Parties, Envy and Prejudice needs no Illustration, and some Persons in the World are so very perverse and obstinate, that they will not be inform'd by a Person they entertain no good Opinion of. For writing Prose a Man ought to have a tollerable Foundation of Learning, at least to be Master of the Latin Tongue, to be a good Historian, and to have a perfect Knowledge of the World; and besides these Qualifications, in Poetry as I have before observ'd, a Writer should be Master of the most refin'd and beautiful Language, surprizing Turns, fine adapted Similes, a sublimity of Thought, and to be a Person of universal Learning: Though I have often observ'd, both in Prose and Verse, that some Persons of strong Genius, well acquainted with the World, and but of little Learning, have made a better Figure in some kinds of Writings, than Persons of the most consummate Literature, not bless'd with natural Genius, and a Knowledge of Mankind.

The preference of Genius to Learning, is sufficiently Demonstrated in the Writings of the Author of the *True born English Man*; (a Poem that has Sold beyond the best Performance of any Ancient or Modern Poet of the greatest Excellency, and perhaps beyond any Poetry ever Printed in the *English* Language) This Author is Characteriz'd as a Person of little Learning, but of prodigious Natural Parts; and the immortal *Shakespear* had but a small share of Literature: It is likewise worthy Observation, that some of our most entertaining Comedies, Novels and Romances have been Written by the fair Sex, who cannot be suppos'd to have Learning in any Degree equal to Gentlemen of a University Education. And in *North Britain* where Literature shines amongst the Persons of middle Station, an Ounce of Natural Parts, (speaking in a common way of Comparison) is Esteem'd of greater Value, than a Pound of Learning.

A Person of Learning without Genius and Knowledge of the World, is like an *Architect's* Assistant, whose only Business is to Draw the Draught or Model of a Pile of Building; he's at a loss in the Materials necessary for compleating the Structure, tho' he can Judge of its Beauty when Perfected; and may be compared to a Man that has the theory in any Art or Science, but wants the Practice.

And a meer Scholar is the most unacceptable Companion upon Earth: He is Rude in his Manners, Unpolish'd in his Literature, and generally Ill-Natur'd to the last Degree; he's Company for a very few Persons, and Pleasing to None; his Pride exalts him in Self-Opinion beyond all Mankind: And some of the sucking Tribe of *Levi*, think the Gown and Cassock alone, Merit a Respect due to the greatest Personages, and that the broad Hat with the Rose should be Ador'd, tho' it covers a thick and brainless Skull.

But these are a few only; there are great Numbers of the Clergy who deserve the utmost Respect, and are justly paid more than they desire; and no Person can have a greater Regard for that sacred Body than my self, as I was not only intended for a Clergyman, but have several Relations now in being of that venerable Order; Tho' I am oblig'd to take Notice, that the Authors of the Gown in general, treat the World with greater Insolence and Incharity, than any Lay-Persons whatsoever.

There's nothing more frequent, than to find the Writings of many of our Modern Divines, not only Stiff and Harsh, but full of Rancour, and to find an easy Propensity and Complaisance in the Writings of the Laity; a Gentleman without the Gown commonly Writes with a genteel Respect to the World, abundance of good Temper and a condescension Endearing; when a brawny Priest, shall shew a great deal of Ill-nature, give indecent Reflections, and affrontive Language, and oftentimes be Dogmatical in all his Performances.

Whether this be owing more to Pride, than a want of an Easy, Free, and polite Conversation, I do not take upon me to Determine; but I believe it must be generally Imputed to the Former, as it cannot be suppos'd, that either of the Universities, are at any time without a polite Converse; tho' I take leave to observe, that there is a great deal of difference between a finish'd *Oxonian*, and a sprightly Senator.

This is Demonstrated in the Speeches from Time to Time, made in the Senate and the Synod; the Stile and Composure of the one, is no way to be compar'd to the other, tho' the Sense be equally strong; there's an Elegancy and Beauty of Expression in the Former, not to be met with in the Latter, Oratory no where to be exceeded, and an Affluence of Words not to be met with in any other Speeches whatsoever; and I believe it must be generally allow'd that there is a very great difference in the common Conversation, (particularly in point of Manners) of the Members of those August Assemblies.

A good Conversation is the greatest Advantage an Author can possibly Enjoy, by a variety of Converse, a Man is furnish'd with a perpetual Variety of Hints, and may acquire a greater Knowledge on some Subjects in the space of a few Minutes, than he can attain by Study, in a Succession of Weeks, (tho' I must allow Study to be the only Foundation for Writing) 'twas owing to a good Conversation, that those Entertaining Papers the *Tatlers* were publish'd by Sir *Richard Steel*, the *Examiner* carried on by Mr. *Oldsworth*; and 'tis impossible a perfect good Comedy can be written by any Person, without a constant

Resort to the best Conversation, whereby alone a Man will be Master of the best Thoughts.

In short, Conversation is the Aliment of the Genius, the Life of all airy Performances, as Learning is the Soul; the various Humours of Mankind, upon all Occasions, afford the most agreeable Subjects for all sorts of Writings, and I look upon any Performance, tho' done by a Person celebrated for Writing, without the use of Conversation, in some measure incompleat.

If an Author be enclin'd to write for Reformation of Manners, let him repair to St. *Pauls* or *Westminster-Abbey*, and observe the indecent Behaviour of multitudes of Persons, who make those Sacred Places Assignations of Vice; if you are enclin'd to lash the Follies and Vanities of the fair Sex, retire to the Tea Table and the Theatre; if your Business be to compose a Sermon, or you are engag'd in Theological Studies, resort to *Child's* Coffee-House in St. *Paul's* Church-Yard; if you are desirous to depaint the Cheat and the Trickster, I recommend ye to the *Royal-Exchange* and the Court End of the Town; and if you would write a Poem in imitation of *Rochester*, you need only go to the Hundreds of *Drury*, and you'll be sufficiently furnish'd with laudable Themes.

But Converse at home falls infinitely short of Conversation abroad, and the Advantages attending Travelling are so very great, that they are not to be express'd; this finishes Education in the most effectual manner, and enables a Man to speak and write on all Occasions with a Grace and Perfection, no other way to be attain'd. The Travels of a young Gentleman have not only the effect of transplation of Vegetables, in respect to the encrease of Stature, but also the Consequence of the most beautiful Pruning. How much the Gentlemen of *Scotland* owe their Capacities to Travelling, is very obvious, there being no Person of Quality in that Kingdom but expends the greatest part of his Fortune in other Countries, to reap the Benefit of it in personal Accomplishments; and a greater Commendation than this to the *Scots* is, the bestowing the best of Literature upon all manner of Youth educated amongst them.

Whilst the Men of Quality here very often neglect giving their Children the common and necessary Learning, and too frequently entrust their Education with lazy, ignorant, and incogitant Tutors, not to mention the Supineness of Schoolmasters in general throughout *England*; the *North-Britains* labour in this Particular indefatigably, as they are very sensible that Learning is the greatest Honour of their

Country, and the ancient *Britains* come so near the *Scots*, that amongst the common Persons, in some Parts of *Wales*, you may meet with a Ploughman that speaks tollerable Latin, and a Mason, like the famous *Ben Johnson*, with his *Horace* and a Trowel.

The want of a generous Education is an irretrieveable Misfortune, and the Negligence of an Inspector of the Literature of Youth ought to be unpardonable; how many Persons of Distinction have curs'd their aged Parents for not bestowing on them a liberal Education? And how many of the Commonalty have regretted the mispending of the precious Time of Youth? A Man arriv'd to Maturity has the Mortification of observing an Inferior in Circumstances superior in Literature, and wants the Satisfaction of giving a tollerable Reason for any Thing he says or does, or in any respect to judge of the Excellency of others; and, in my Opinion, a generous Education, with a bare Subsistence only, is to be preferr'd to the largest Patrimony, and a want of Learning.

Without Education it is impossible to Write or Read any Thing distinctly; without a frequent turning of the Dictionary, no Person can be compleat in the *English* Language, neither can he give Words their proper Accent and Pronunciation, or be any ways Master of Elocution; and a Man without Learning, though he appears tollerable in Conversation, (which I have known some Persons do by a constant enjoyment of good Company, and a strength of Memory) is like an *Empirick*, that takes Things upon trust: And whenever he comes to exercise the Pen, that the Subject is uncommon, and Study is requir'd, you'll find him oftentimes not capable of writing one single Line of Senfe, and scarcely one Word of *English*. And, on the other Hand, I have known some Persons who could talk Latin very fluently, who have us'd Phrases and Sentences perpetually in that Language, in Conversation, vulgar and deficient in the Mother-Tongue, and who have written most egregious Nonsense; from whence it is evident, that Writing is the only Test of Literature.

I have a little deviated from my Subject, in pursuing the Rules and Advantages of Education, which I take to be of that universal good Tendency, that they are acceptable in any Performance whatsoever: I shall offer nothing farther, but conclude this Essay with the following Particulars; that besides the Qualifications already mention'd, it is as necessary for a fine Writer to be endued with Modesty as for a beautiful Lady; that good Sense is of equal Consequence to an Author, as a good Soil for the Culture of the most noble Plants; that a Person writing a great deal on various Subjects, should be as cautious in owning all his Performances, as in revealing the Secrets of his most intimate Friend; and in respect to those Gentlemen, who have made no scruple to prostitute their Names, the following Similie may be judg'd well adapted:

As Musick soft, by constant use is forc'd
Grows harsh, and cloys, becomes at length the worst,
The Harmony amidst Confusion lost:
So finest Pens, employ'd in Writing still
Lose Strength and Beauty as the Folio's fill.

FINIS.

SECOND
THOUGHTS ARE BEST:
OR A
FURTHER IMPROVEMENT
Of a Late
SCHEME
TO PREVENT
STREET ROBBERIES:
BY WHICH

Our Streets will be strongly guarded, and so gloriously illuminated, that any part of London will be as safe and pleasant at Midnight as at Noonday; and Burglary totally impracticable:
With
Some Thoughts for suppressing Robberies in all the Public Roads of England, &c.
Humbly
Offered for the Good of his Country, submitted to the Consideration of the Parliament, and dedicated to his sacred Majesty King George II.

By Andrew Moreton, Esq.

TO THE
KING'S
Most Excellent
MAJESTY,
SACRED AND MOST AUGUST!

Permit a loyal subject, in the sincerity of his heart, to press through the crowds of courtiers who surround your royal person, and lay his little mite, humbly offered for the public welfare, at your majesty's feet.

Happy is it for me, as well as the whole kingdom, we have a king of such humanity and affability; a king naturalized to us, a king who loves us, a king in whose person as well as mind, the whole hero appears: the king of our hearts; the king of our wishes!

Those who are dissatisfied with such a monarch, deserve to be abandoned of God, and have the devil sent to reign over them. Yet such there are, (pity they should wear human forms, or breathe the free air of Britain!) who are so scandalously fickle, that if God himself was to reign, they would yearn after their darling monarch the prince of darkness.

These are they who fly in the face of majesty, who so abuse the liberty of the press, that from a benefit it becomes an evil, and demands immediate regulation.

Not against your majesty only, but against many of your loyal subjects, are arrows shot in the dark, by lurking villains who wound the reputations of the innocent in sport. Our public newspapers, which ought to contain nothing but what is instructive and communicative, being now become public nuisances, vehicles of personal, private slander, and scandalous pasquins.

Let the glory be yours, most gracious sovereign! to suppress this growing evil; and if any hints from your most faithful subject can be of the least use, I live but to serve, to admire, and pray for your majesty.

Who am,
Most gracious Sovereign,
Your Majesty's
Most loyal, most dutiful, most obedient
subject and servant,
Andrew Moreton.

THE PREFACE.

Nothing is more easy than to discover a thing already found out. This is verified in me and that anonymous gentleman, whom the public prints have lately complimented with a Discovery to Prevent Street Robberies; though, by the by, we have only his vain *ipse dixit*, and the ostentatious outcry of venal newswriters in his behalf.

But to strip him of his borrowed plumes, these are to remind the public, that about six months ago, in a treatise, entituled, Augusta Triumphans: or, the Way to make London the most flourishing City in the Universe, I laid down a plain and practicable scheme for the total suppression and prevention of street robberies, which scheme has been approved of by several learned and judicious persons.

Oh! but say the advocates of this second-hand schemist, our project is to be laid before the parliament. Does that make his better, or mine worse? Have not many silly projects been laid before parliaments ere now? Admit it be not the same (as I have but too much reason to fear it is,) cannot the members of both houses read print as well as written hand? Or does he think they are so prejudiced to dislike a thing the worse for being offered without view of gain? I trust Andrew Moreton's scheme, generously offered for the public good, will meet with as fair a reception as that of this hireling projector.

Mine is already published; let him generously follow my example, and no doubt, if his scheme be preferred, the government will reward him.

If my antagonist be necessitous, where is the merit? he does it for his own sake, not for the public. If he be not necessitous, what a sordid wretch is he to withhold his scheme for lucre? putting it up at public sale; so that if you do not give him his price you shall not have it.

Some people, indeed, are so fond of mysteries they run down everything that is plain and intelligible; they love darkness, whispers, and freemasonry, despising whatever comes in the shape of a pamphlet, be it never so useful or commendable. But in spite of prejudice, truth is the standard by which I hope all honest and impartial men will judge me.

Though I must confess I am not a little piqued to be jockeyed out of my labours, yet not to be behindhand with my gentleman in the clouds, who would have the parliament buy his pig in a poke, and build up his fortune at my expense, I have so amply enlarged and amended my scheme, that it is now scarce like the same. I have taken in everything possible of comprehension or practice; nor have I left him room to edge in one single hint. I have debated the objections of divers wise and learned men, and corrected my project accordingly; so that, on comparison, my first thoughts will appear but as a rude and imperfect sketch, only valuable in that it gave the idea of this more laboured and finished performance, on which I pledge my whole reputation, being ready to stand or fall by its success.

In order to which, I have presented copies of this book to the king and queen's most excellent majesties, to several of the lords spiritual, and divers honourable and worthy members of both houses, and time must show whose scheme shall have the precedence.

In the mean time I stand prepared for the sneers of those who despise everything and everybody but their own dear selves, as also the objections of the puzzle causes, who will turry-lugg a thing out of all sense and meaning, and by the cloudiness of their explanations darken what is most plain and obvious. My business is to go straight forward, and let the end crown the work. If men of sense approve me, I need not value the laughter of fools, whose very approbation is scandal; for if a thinking man is to be laughed out of every good intention or invention, nothing will ever be done for the public good.

SECOND THOUGHTS, &c.

The principal encouragement and opportunity given to our street robbers is, that our streets are so poorly watched; the watchmen, for the most part, being decrepit, superannuated wretches, with one foot in the grave and the other ready to follow; so feeble that a puff of breath can blow them down. Poor crazy mortals! much fitter for an almshouse than a watchhouse. A city watched and guarded by such animals is wretchedly watched indeed.

Nay, so little terror do they carry with them, that hardy thieves make a mere jest of them, and oftentimes oblige even the very watchman who should apprehend, to light them in their roguery. And what can a poor creature do, in terror of his life, surrounded by a pack of ruffians, and no assistance near?

Add to this, that our rogues are grown more wicked than ever, and vice in all kinds is so much winked at, that robbery is accounted a petty crime. We take pains to puff them up in their villany, and thieves are set out in so amiable a light in the Beggar's Opera, it has taught them to value themselves on their profession rather than to be ashamed of it.

There was some cessation of street robberies, from the time of Bunworth and Blewitt's execution, until the introduction of this pious opera. Now we find the Cartouchian villanies revived, and London, that used to be the most safe and peaceful city in the universe, is now become a scene of rapine and danger. If some of Cartouch's gang be not come over hither to instruct our thieves, we have, doubtless, a Cartouch of our own, and a gang which, if not suppressed, may be full as pernicious as was ever Cartouch's, and London may be as dangerous as Paris, if due care be not taken.

Not content with the mischief done by the Beggar's Opera, we must have a Quaker's Opera, forsooth, of much more evil tendency than the former; for in this Jack Shepherd is made the hero of the drama, and runs through such a scene of riot and success, that but too many weak minds have been drawn away, and many unwary persons so charmed with his appearance on the stage, dressed in that elegant manner, and his pockets so well lined, they have forthwith commenced street-robbers or housebreakers; so that every idle fellow, weary of honest labour, need but fancy himself a Macheath or a Shepherd, and there is a rogue made at once. Since, therefore, example, has such force, the stage ought to be reformed, and nothing exhibited but what might be represented before a bishop. They may be merry and wise: let them take the Provoked Husband for a pattern.

A good physician seeks the cause, and weighs the symptoms before he proceeds to prescribe; and if we trace this evil from its radix, we shall find a cause antecedent to the two operas aforesaid: namely, accursed Geneva, the bane and ruin of our lower class of people.

Those who deny an inferior class of people to be necessary in a body politic, contradict reason and experience itself; since they are most useful when industrious, and equally pernicious when lazy. By their industry our manufactures, trade, and commerce, are carried on. The merchant in his counting-house, and the captain in his cabin, would find but little employment, were it not that many hands carried on the different branches of the concerns they superintended.

But now so far are our common people infatuated with Geneva, that half the work is not done now as formerly. It debilitates and enervates them, nor are they near so strong and healthy as formerly.

So that if this abuse of Geneva be not stopped, we may go whoop for husbandmen, labourers, &c.; trade must consequently stand still, and the credit of the nation sink. Nor is the abatement of the excise, though very considerable, and most worthy notice, any ways comparable to the corruption of manners, destruction of health, and all the train of evils we are threatened with from pernicious Geneva.

We will suppose a man able to maintain himself and family by his trade, and at the same time to be a Geneva drinker. This fellow first makes himself incapable of working by being continually drunk; which runs him behindhand, so that he either pawns, or neglects his work, for which reason nobody will employ him. At last, fear of arrests, his own hunger, the cries of a family for bread, his natural desire to support an irregular life, and a propense hatred to labour, turn but too many an honest tradesman into an arrant desperate rogue. And these are commonly the means that furnish us with thieves and villains in general.

Thus is a man, who might be useful in a body politic, rendered obnoxious to the same: so that if this trade of wickedness goes on, they will increase upon us so much that we shall not dare to stir out of our habitations; nay, it will be well if they arrive not to the impudence of plundering our houses at noonday.

Where is the courage of the English nation, that a gentleman, with six or seven servants, shall be robbed by one single highwayman? Yet we have lately had instances of this; and for this we may thank our effeminacy, our toupee wigs, and powdered pates, our tea, and other scandalous fopperies; and, above all, the disuse of noble and manly sports, so necessary to a brave people, once in vogue, but now totally lost amongst us.

Let not the reader think I run from my subject if I search the bottom of the distemper before I propose a cure, which having done, though indeed but slightly, for this is an argument could be carried to a much greater length, I proceed to the purpose in manner following:—

Let the watch be composed of stout able-bodied men, and of those a sufficient number, that is to say, a watchman to every forty houses, twenty on one side of the way, and twenty on the other; for it is observable that a man cannot well see distinctly beyond the extent of twenty houses in a row; if it is a single row, and no opposite houses, the charge must be greater, or their safety less.

This man should be elected and paid by the housekeepers themselves, to prevent misapplication and abuse, so much complained of in the distribution of the public money.

He should be allowed ten shillings per annum by each housekeeper, which at forty houses, as above specified, amounts to 20*l.* per annum, almost treble to what is at present allowed; and yet most housekeepers are charged at least 2s. 6d. a quarter to the watch, whose beat is, generally speaking, little less than the compass of half a mile.

What a shame it is that at least 100*l.* should be collected in some beats, and the poor watchman should not have the one-tenth part of the money? And this I leave to the consideration of any housekeeper who will take the pains to inquire into the extent of a watchman's beat, and after that cast up what is collected in the said beat, as they say for the watch. But this is a small abuse in comparison of other parochial misapplications, for a proof of which I refer my reader to a treatise of mine, entituled, Parochial Tyranny.

This salary of 20*l.* per annum is something of encouragement, and a pretty settlement for a poor man, who with frugality may live decently thereon, and by due rest be enabled to give due and vigilant attendance; that is to say, from evening dusk to morning light.

If a housekeeper break, or a house is empty, the poor watchman ought not to suffer, the deficiency should be made up by the housekeepers remaining.

The watch thus stationed, strengthened, and encouraged, let every watchman be armed with firearms and sword; and let no watchman stand above twenty doors distant from his fellow.

This has already been put in practice in the parish of St. Giles's in the Fields, and has had so good an effect that it is hoped other parishes will follow their example, which redounds not a little to the credit of our project.

Let each watchman be provided with a horn, to sound an alarm, or in time of danger; and let it be made penal, if not felony, for any but a watchman to sound a horn in and about the city, from the time of their going on, to that of their going off.

I know an objection will be here made on account of the postboys, to obviate which, I had thoughts of a bell, but that would be too ponderous and troublesome for a watchman to carry, besides his arms and lantern; whereas a horn is portable, always ready, and most alarming.

Let the postboys therefore use some other signal, since this is most convenient to this more material purpose. They may carry a bell in a holster with ease, and give notice by that, as well as those who collect the letters.

That the watchmen may see from one end of their walks to the other, let a convenient number of lamps be set up, and those not of the convex kind, which blind the eyes, and are of no manner of use; they dazzle, but give no distinct light, and further, rather than prevent robberies. Many persons, deceived and blinded by these *ignes fatui*, have been run over by coaches, carts, &c., people stumbling more, even under these very lamps, than in the dark. In short, they are most unprofitable lights, and, in my opinion, rather abuses than benefits.

Besides, I see no reason why every ten housekeepers cannot find a lamp among themselves, which would be four lamps in a beat, and let their watchman dress it, rather than fatten a crew of directors.

But we are so fond of companies, it is a wonder we have not our shoes blacked by one, and a set of directors made rich at the expense of our very black-guards.

The watch ought to be in view, as well as in the hearing of each other, or they may be overpowered, and much danger may happen.

The streets being thus gloriously illuminated, and so strongly guarded by stout and able fellows, well armed and well paid, all within the view of one another, proceed we to secure all by-turnings, courts, alleys, lanes, &c., which may favour a street-robber's escape, and make our project ineffectual.

A street, court, lane, alley, or other place, where the number of houses or poverty of the inhabitants will not afford a watchman on the terms before mentioned, should be gated in, and the inhabitants let in and out by the watchman of the street.

Where there are even but twelve houses in a court, and the inhabitants people of credit, they may have a separate watch to themselves, as is practised in Boswell-court by Lincoln's-inn-fields, Angel-court in Throckmorton-street, and many other places in London.

This I think an unexceptionable way to secure the cities and suburbs of London and Westminster. The only difficulty I can conceive is, that persons after dark may now and then go a little way round about by keeping the street way, but the pleasantness and safety occasioned by the lights and watch aforesaid, make ample amends. Let those go through byways, and in the dark, whose deeds are so; I am for providing security for honest men, and obstacle for rogues.

And now we have put a stop to their roguery, let us endeavour to suppress the rogues themselves; in order to which I shall begin with their harlots, who are, generally speaking, the first motives to their villany, and egg them on to all manner of mischief.

And these are generally servant wenches, who stroll from place to place, and at last, weary of working, throw themselves on the public. To maintain these creatures, many a man turns rogue. It behoves the government, therefore, to oblige all young wenches to keep in service. Masters and mistresses ought likewise to see that servants of both sexes go not a rambling when sent to church, but that they keep good hours; for many have been ruined by junketing and staying out, instead of being at church or at home.

Our common women ought to be restrained in the liberties they have lately taken; they openly swear and talk so obscenely, it is a shame to a Christian country.

Having fully handled this topic in two treatises, viz., Everybody's Business is Nobody's Business, and Parochial Tyranny, I shall not tire my readers with repetition, but referring them to the treatises themselves, return to my subject, which is,—

After we have reformed the ladies, let us take their sparks in hand. And first, let all shoe-cleaners, I mean boys and sturdy vagrants, be suppressed, according to my scheme in Everybody's Business, &c.; as for link-boys, alias thieves with lights, there will be no need of them when the streets are illuminated, according to my project.

That sailors as well as soldiers may not give cause of suspicion, it is fit they should also be quartered after the same nature; and more to enforce it, surveyors of quarters should have rounds allotted them.

These surveyors should call at the quarters of every soldier or sailor at a limited hour, to see if they are there or no, and register them at home or absent accordingly; absence to be penal.

Every soldier or sailor leaving his quarters till morning, after he has been found at home and registered, should be punished.

I must be excused if I ward every obstacle, my design being to break up street-robbers, nest and egg.

And that thieves may not stroll about, under pretence of being destitute of lodging, barracks or barns should be built at convenient ends of the town, where all vagrants should be obliged to render themselves at a stated hour, where they should have clean straw allowed them, and be kept orderly and out of harm's way; they may be let loose if they have apparent means of honest livelihood, otherwise they should be sent to the workhouse of their respective parish, or to a general workhouse, of which there is great need; and of which more hereafter.

All publichouses and gin-shops, if they should be tolerated, should be shut up at ten.

If the government should think fit to tolerate gin-shops, I see no reason why they may not be subject to licenses, and come into the pot-act as well as alehouses; especially considering there is as much gin as ale consumed nowadays.

Night houses and cellars, above all, should be totally suppressed; these are the harbours and refuge of villains and strumpets; these are their houses of call where there hellish trade is carried on; it is here they wait for the signal of their scouts; here they cast their schemes, and bring in advices; here they encourage and initiate young thieves; here they barter and sell their stolen goods; these are their exchanges and asylums after mischief.

Hackney coach drivers next require our care; they are the scum of the people, and, generally speaking, the worst of rogues.

So many and such frequent robberies can never be committed without the connivance of these villains; and it is but too much to be feared, that at the same time they take up a fare they take up a robber, who is ready to mark his prey, and gets up either on the box or behind; and alights at a convenient place to perpetrate his hellish design. As for a 'snack of the coal' as they term it, no doubt but the coachman and he have proper understanding and rendezvous.

Many who go to the coach-office nowadays, may be mistaken in their hopes of redress, not but the commissioners to a man treat complainants with the utmost civility; but the penalty, which used to be on the renter, being now on the driver, the renter or owner of that figure is clear, and the driver has nothing to do but to be absent and laugh at the complainant, an instance of which take in the following case:—

A hackney coachman took eighteenpence of a gentleman for a twelvepenny fare; the gentleman took his number and complained; the driver appeared, and was fined fifteen shillings, but the renter escaped; what was the result? The driver absconded, the gentleman sits down at his loss of attendance and money; had robbery or assault been the complaint, the consequence had been the same, the gentleman is but where he was. He has since called several times at the office, but to no purpose; all the answer he can get is, the fellow cannot be found. I write this therefore to undeceive those persons, who think when they have taken the number of a coach they can punish the driver for insolence or extortion.

The law in this case ought to be turned into its old channel, that is to say, the owner of the figure should be answerable; he ought to employ a driver he can answer for, or drive himself.

Every renter therefore should be obliged to register, and respond for his driver; or commissioners, figures, and all other forms, are to little purpose.

Beggars should next be suppressed, who lounge about all day, to see where they can steal at night. It is a shame we should suffer real objects of charity to beg; and for those who are not so, it is a shame but they should work.

I shall close all with these observations:—

That the extortions and cabals of tradesmen, by enhancing the prices of provisions, is most detrimental to a state, and worthy the notice of its legislature; for men not being able to support their families by honest labour, and being made beggars by reason of the dearness of provisions, ofttimes grow desperate and turn rogues. This assertion is but too true, to prove which I appeal to the late conduct of

The coal merchants,

The bakers,

The butchers,

And, above all, the tallow chandlers.

The cabals of coal traders have for many years jockeyed us in the price of coals; they have raised and fell them at pleasure, and made mere stockjobbing work of it; but never so much as in his late majesty's reign; on a great impress for seamen, they, in less than a fortnight, raised the price of coals from twenty-three shillings to almost fifty. What a pinch must this be on the poor, who live only from hand to mouth, and buy their coals, poor souls! some by the half peck.

The bakers are yet more flagrant and vile; they turn plenty to famine, and push up the price of bread without rule or reason; they have already been detected in one bite, i.e., procuring some of the fraternity to buy a small quantity of corn much above the market price, and then, by making oath thereof, abuse a well-intended law, and raise the price of bread accordingly.

Thus are the poor ground to dust, in order to fatten a pack of misers, who know no mercy. But I hope the government will make them honest, even against their will.

The butchers are now so extravagant in their way of living, that usual and moderate profit will not content them; they cannot drink malt liquor, and the poor must pay for the wine, which they swill down at an unmerciful rate.

The price of meat should therefore be regulated according to the price of cattle, but not according to the baker's rule afore mentioned.

But as for the tallow-chandlers, their oppressions call aloud for redress. To what an exorbitant pitch have they raised candles; just double what it was some years ago: nay, they threaten to have them at tenpence per pound. How can the poor work when candles are so dear? But we may thank our own luxury for these impositions. I see no reason why we should not humble these upstarts by making our own candles; aye, and our own bread too, as our forefathers have done before us.

The tallow-chandlers, to excuse themselves, lay the fault on the melters. The melters shift it from themselves to the butchers; and so the game goes round.

Oh but, say they, the government will lose part of its revenue: to which I answer, that rather than they shall raise candles to double their value, on pretence of paying a penny per pound excise; in case the parliament will take off the duty on candles for the ease of the poor, I will present them with a project gratis, which shall bring in almost double the money now levied by candles, and that without the least hardship on the subject.

Having, I hope, taken sufficient care of street-robbers, I proceed now to clear the roads from highwaymen, footpads, &c.

Let parties of horse be stationed at all the outgoings from the city of London; so that if a coach, wagon, &c., want a convoy, two, three, or more may be detached by the commanding officer; these shall be registered, and answerable for their charge; and for encouragement shall receive so much per mile, or in the whole, convoy money.

This may be likewise practised from town to town all over England, so that the roads will be as safe as the streets; and they who scruple the trifle of convoy money above proposed, merit not safety.

For those who walk on foot to the adjacent villages, parties of foot may be stationed in like manner; so that not only the subject will be free from danger, but the soldier employed and prevented from corrupt measures by this additional perquisite to his pay.

Nothing remains but that robbers be prosecuted at the public charge; the trials fixed to respective days, that prosecutors may not lose so much time, and the rewards paid in court without deduction or delay; nor should any robber be admitted an evidence after he is taken, or pardoned after conviction.

AN APPEAL

TO

HONOUR AND JUSTICE,
THOUGH IT BE OF HIS WORST ENEMIES,

BY

DANIEL DE FOE;

BEING
A TRUE ACCOUNT OF HIS CONDUCT IN PUBLIC
AFFAIRS.

"Come and let us smite him with the tongue, and let us not give heed to any of his words."

--Jeremiah, xviii. 18.

APPEAL, &c.

I hope the time is come at last when the voice of moderate principles may be heard. Hitherto the noise has been so great, and the prejudices and passions of men so strong, that it had been but in vain to offer at any argument, or for any man to talk of giving a reason for his actions; and this alone has been the cause why, when other men, who, I think, have less to say in their own defence, are appealing to the public, and struggling to defend themselves, I alone have been silent under the infinite clamours and reproaches, causeless curses, unusual threatenings, and the most unjust and injurious treatment in the world.

I hear much of people's calling out to punish the guilty, but very few are concerned to clear the innocent. I hope some will be inclined to judge impartially, and have yet reserved so much of the Christian as to believe, and at least to hope, that a rational creature cannot abandon himself so as to act without some reason, and are willing not only to have me defend myself, but to be able to answer for me where they hear me causelessly insulted by others, and, therefore, are willing to have such just arguments put into their mouths as the cause will bear.

As for those who are prepossessed, and according to the modern justice of parties are resolved to be so, let them go; I am not arguing with them, but against them; they act so contrary to justice, to reason, to religion, so contrary to the rules of Christians and of good manners, that they are not to be argued with, but to be exposed, or entirely neglected. I have a receipt against all the uneasiness which it may be supposed to give me, and that is, to contemn slander, and think it not worth the least concern; neither should I think it worth while to give any answer to it, if it were not on some other accounts of which I shall speak as I go on. If any young man ask me why I am in such haste to publish this matter at this time, among many other good reasons which I could give, these are some:—

I. I think I have long enough been made *Fabula Vulgi*, and borne the weight of general slander; and I should be wanting to truth, to my family, and to myself, if I did not give a fair and true state of my conduct, for impartial men to judge of, when I am no more in being to answer for myself.

2. By the hints of mortality, and by the infirmities of a life of sorrow and fatigue, I have reason to think I am not a great way off from, if not very near to, the great ocean of eternity, and the time may not be long ere I embark on the last voyage. Wherefore, I think I should even accounts with this world before I go, that no actions (slanders) may lie against my heirs, executors, administrators, and assigns, to disturb them in the peaceable possession of their father's (character) inheritance.

3. I fear—God grant I have not a second-sight in it—that this lucid interval of temper and moderation, which shines, though dimly too, upon us at this time, will be but of short continuance, and that some men, who know not how to use the advantage God has put into their hands with moderation, will push, in spite of the best prince in the world, at such extravagant things, and act with such an intemperate forwardness, as will revive the heats and animosities which wise and good men were in hopes should be allayed by the happy accession of the king to the throne.

It is and ever was my opinion, that moderation is the only virtue by which the peace and tranquillity of this nation can be preserved. Even the king himself—I believe his majesty will allow me that freedom—can only be happy in the enjoyment of the crown by a moderative administration. If his majesty should be obliged, contrary to his known disposition, to join with intemperate councils, if it does not lessen his security, I am persuaded it will lessen his satisfaction. It cannot be pleasant or agreeable, and I think it cannot be safe, to any just prince, to rule over a divided people, split into incensed and exasperated parties. Though a skilful mariner may have courage to master a tempest, and goes fearless through a storm, yet he can never be said to delight in the danger; a fresh, fair gale, and a quiet sea, is the pleasure of his voyage, and we have a saying worth notice to them that are otherwise minded, *Qui amat periculum, periebat in illo.*

To attain at the happy calm, which, as I say, is the safety of Britain, is the question which should now move us all; and he would merit to be called the nation's physician that could prescribe the specific for it. I think I may be allowed to say, a conquest of parties will never do it; a balance of parties may. Some are for the former; they talk high of punishments, letting blood, revenging the treatment they have met with, and the like. If they, not knowing what spirit they are of, think this the course to be taken, let them try their hands; I shall give them up for lost, and look for their downfall from that time; for the ruin of all such tempers slumbereth not.

It is many years that I have professed myself an enemy to all precipitations in public administrations; and often I have attempted to show, that hot councils have ever been destructive to those who have made use of them. Indeed, they have not always been a disadvantage to the nation, as in king James II.'s reign, when, as I have often said in print, his precipitation was the safety of us all: and if he had proceeded temperately and politicly, we had been undone. *Felix quem faciunt.*

But these things have been spoken when your ferment has been too high for anything to be heard; whether you will hear it now or no, I know not; and therefore it was that I said, I fear the present cessation of party arms will not hold long. These are some of the reasons why I think this is the proper juncture for me to give some account of myself, and of my past conduct to the world; and that I may do this as effectually as I can, being perhaps never more to speak from the press, I shall, as concisely as I can, give an abridgment of my own history during the few unhappy years I have employed myself, or been employed, in public in the world.

Misfortunes in business having unhinged me from matters of trade, it was about the year 1694 when I was invited by some merchants, with whom I had corresponded abroad, and some also at home, to settle at Cadiz, in Spain, and that with offers of very good commissions. But Providence, which had other work for me to do, placed a secret aversion in my mind to quitting England upon any account, and made me refuse the best offers of that kind, to be concerned with some eminent persons at home in proposing ways and means to the government, for raising money to supply the occasions of the war then newly begun. Some time after this I was, without the least application of mine, and being then seventy miles from London, sent for to be accountant to the commissioners of the glass duty, in which service I continued to the determination of their commission.

During this time there came out a vile abhorred pamphlet in very ill verse, written by one Mr. Tutchin, and called The Foreigners, in which the author—who he was I then knew not—fell personally upon the king himself, and then upon the Dutch nation; and after having reproached his majesty with crimes that his worst enemy could not think of without horror, he sums up all in the odious name of foreigner.

This filled me with a kind of rage against the book, and gave birth to a trifle, which I never could hope should have met with so general an acceptation as it did; I mean The True-born Englishman. How this poem was the occasion of my being known to his majesty; how I was afterwards received by him; how employed; and how, above my capacity of deserving, rewarded, is no part of the present case, and is only mentioned here, as I take all occasions to do, for the expressing the honour I ever preserved for the immortal and glorious memory of that greatest and best of princes, and whom it was my honour and advantage to call master, as well as sovereign; whose goodness to me I never forgot, neither can forget; and whose memory I never patiently heard abused, nor ever can do so; and who, had he lived, would never have suffered me to be treated as I have been in the world. But Heaven for our sins removed him in judgment. How far the treatment he met with from the nation he came to save, and whose deliverance he finished, was admitted by Heaven to be a means of his death, I desire to forget for their sakes who are guilty; and if this calls any of it to mind, it is mentioned to move them to treat him better who is now, with like principles of goodness and clemency, appointed by God and the constitution to be their sovereign, lest He that protects righteous princes avenge the injuries they receive from an ungrateful people by giving them up to the confusions their madness leads them to.

And in their just acclamations at the happy accession of his present majesty to the throne, I cannot but advise them to look back and call to mind who it was that first guided them to the family of Hanover, and to pass by all the popish branches of Orleans and Savoy; recognising the just authority of parliament in the undoubted right of limiting the succession, and establishing that glorious maxim of our settlement, viz., that it is inconsistent with the constitution of this protestant kingdom to be governed by a popish prince. I say, let them call to mind who it was that guided their thoughts first to the protestant race of our own kings in the house of Hanover; and that it is to king William, next to Heaven itself, to whom we owe the enjoying a protestant king at this time. I need not go back to the particulars of his majesty's conduct in that affair; his journey in person to the country of Hanover and the court of Zell; his particular management of the affair afterwards at home, perfecting the design by naming the illustrious family to the nation, and bringing about a parliamentary settlement to effect it; entailing the crown thereby in so effectual a manner as we see has been sufficient to prevent the worst designs of our Jacobite people in behalf of the pretender; a settlement, together with the subsequent acts which followed it, and the Union with Scotland, which made it unalterable, that gave a complete satisfaction to those who knew and understood it, and removed those terrible apprehensions of the pretender (which some entertained) from the minds of others, who were yet as zealous against him as it was possible for any to be. Upon this settlement, as I shall show presently, I grounded my opinion, which I often expressed, viz., that I did not see it possible the Jacobites could ever set up their idol here, and I think my opinion abundantly justified in the consequences; of which by and by.

This digression, as a debt to the glorious memory of king William, I could not in justice omit; and as the reign of his present majesty is esteemed happy, and looked upon as a blessing from heaven by us, it will most necessarily lead us to bless the memory of king William, to whom we owe so much of it. How easily could his majesty have led us to other branches, whose relation to the crown might have had large pretences! What prince but would have submitted to have educated a successor of his race in the protestant religion for the sake of such a crown? But the king, who had our happiness in view, and saw as far into it as any human sight could penetrate; who knew we were not to be governed by inexperienced youths; that the protestant religion was not to be established by political converts; and that princes, under French influence, or instructed in French politics, were not proper instruments to preserve the liberties of Britain, fixed his eyes upon the family which now possesses the crown, as not only having an undoubted relation to it by blood, but as being first and principally zealous and powerful asserters of the protestant religion and interest against popery; and, secondly, stored with a visible succession of worthy and promising branches, who appeared equal to the weight of government, qualified to fill a throne and guide a nation, which, without reflection, are not famed to be the most easy to rule in the world.

Whether the consequence has been a credit to king William's judgment I need not say. I am not writing panegyrics here, but doing justice to the memory of the king my master, whom I have had the honour very often to hear express himself with great satisfaction in having brought the settlement of the succession to so good an issue; and, to repeat his majesty's own words, that he knew no prince in Europe so fit to be king of England as the elector of Hanover. I am persuaded, without any flattery, that if it should not every way answer the expectations his majesty had of it, the fault will be our own. God grant the king may have more comfort of his crown than we suffered king William to have!

The king being dead, and the queen proclaimed, the hot men of that side, as the hot men of all sides do, thinking the game in their own hands, and all other people under their feet, began to run out into those mad extremes, and precipitate themselves into such measures as, according to the fate of all intemperate councils, ended in their own confusion, and threw them at last out of the saddle.

The queen, who, though willing to favour the high-church party, did not thereby design the ruin of those whom she did not employ, was soon alarmed at their wild conduct, and turned them out, adhering to the moderate counsels of those who better understood, or more faithfully pursued, her majesty's and the country's interest. In this turn fell sir Edward Seymour's party, for so the high men were then called; and to this turn we owe the conversion of several other great men, who became whigs on that occasion, which it is known they were not before; which conversion afterwards begat that unkind distinction of old whig and modern whig, which some of the former were with very little justice pleased to run up afterwards to an extreme very pernicious to both.

But I am gone too far in this part. I return to my own story.

In the interval of these things, and during the heat of the first fury of highflying, I fell a sacrifice for writing against the rage and madness of that high party, and in the service of the dissenters. What justice I met with, and, above all, what mercy, is too well known to need repetition.

This introduction is made that it may bring me to what has been the foundation of all my further concern in public affairs, and will produce a sufficient reason for my adhering to those whose obligations upon me were too strong to be resisted, even when many things were done by them which I could not approve; and for this reason it is that I think it necessary to distinguish how far I did or did not adhere to, or join in or with, the persons or conduct of the late government; and those who are willing to judge with impartiality and charity, will see reason to use me the more tenderly in their thoughts, when they weigh the particulars.

I will make no reflections upon the treatment I met with from the people I suffered for, or how I was abandoned even in my sufferings, at the same time that they acknowledged the service I had been to their cause; but I must mention it to let you know that while I lay friendless and distressed in the prison of Newgate, my family ruined, and myself without hope of deliverance, a message was brought me from a person of honour, who, till that time, I had never had the least acquaintance with, or knowledge of, other than by fame, or by sight, as we know men of quality by seeing them on public occasions. I gave no present answer to the person who brought it, having not duly weighed the import of the message. The message was by word of mouth thus:—"Pray, ask that gentleman what I can do for him?" But in return to this kind and generous message, I immediately took my pen and ink, and wrote the story of the blind man in the gospel, who followed our Saviour, and to whom our blessed Lord put the question, "What wilt thou that I should do unto thee?" Who, as if he had made it strange that such a question should be asked, or as if he had said that I am blind, and yet ask me what thou shalt do for me? My answer is plain in my misery, "Lord, that I may receive my sight?"

I needed not to make the application. And from this time, although I lay four months in prison after this, and heard no more of it, yet from this time, as I learned afterwards, this noble person made it his business to have my case represented to her majesty, and methods taken for my deliverance.

I mention this part, because I am no more to forget the obligation upon me to the queen, than to my first benefactor.

When her majesty came to have the truth of the case laid before her, I soon felt the effects of her royal goodness and compassion. And first, her majesty declared, that she left all that matter to a certain person, and did not think he would have used me in such a manner. Probably these words may seem imaginary to some, and the speaking them to be of no value, and so they would have been had they not been followed with further and more convincing proofs of what they imported, which were these, that her majesty was pleased particularly to inquire into my circumstances and family, and by my lord treasurer Godolphin to send a considerable supply to my wife and family, and to send to me the prison money to pay my fine and the expenses of my discharge. Whether this be a just foundation let my enemies judge. Here is the foundation on which I built my first sense of duty to her majesty's person, and the indelible bond of gratitude to my first benefactor.

Gratitude and fidelity are inseparable from an honest man. But, to be thus obliged by a stranger, by a man of quality and honour, and after that by the sovereign under whose administration I was suffering, let any one put himself in my stead, and examine upon what principles I could ever act against either such a queen, or such a benefactor; and what must my own heart reproach me with, what blushes must have covered my face when I had looked in, and called myself ungrateful to him that saved me thus from distress, or her that fetched me out of the dungeon, and gave my family relief? Let any man who knows what principles are, what engagements of honour and gratitude are, make his case his own, and say what I could have done more or less than I have done.

I must go on a little with the detail of the obligation, and then I shall descend to relate what I have done, and what I have not done, in the case.

Being delivered from the distress I was in, her majesty, who was not satisfied to do me good by a single act of her bounty, had the goodness to think of taking me into her service, and I had the honour to be employed in several honourable, though secret services, by the interposition of my first benefactor, who then appeared as a member in the public administration.

I had the happiness to discharge myself in all these trusts so much to the satisfaction of those who employed me, though oftentimes with difficulty and danger, that my lord treasurer Godolphin, whose memory I have always honoured, was pleased to continue his favour to me, and to do me all good offices with her majesty, even after an unhappy breach had separated him from my first benefactor, the particulars of which may not be improper to relate; and as it is not an injustice to any, so I hope it will not be offensive.

When, upon that fatal breach, the secretary of state was dismissed from the service, I looked upon myself as lost; it being a general rule in such cases, when a great officer falls, that all who came in by his interest fall with him; and resolving never to abandon the fortunes of the man to whom I owed so much of my own, I quitted the usual applications which I had made to my lord treasurer.

But my generous benefactor, when he understood it, frankly told me that I should by no means do so; "For," said he, in the most engaging terms, "my lord treasurer will employ you in nothing but what is for the public service, and agreeably to your own sentiments of things; and besides, it is the queen you are serving, who has been very good to you. Pray, apply yourself as you used to do; I shall not take it ill from you in the least."

Upon this, I went to wait on my lord-treasurer, who received me with great freedom, and told me, smiling, he had not seen me a long while. I told his lordship very frankly the occasion—that the unhappy breach that had fallen out made me doubtful whether I should be acceptable to his lordship. That I knew it was usual when great persons fall, that all who were in their interest fell with them. That his lordship knew the obligations I was under, and that I could not but fear my interest in his lordship was lessened on that account. "Not at all, Mr. De Foe," replied his lordship, "I always think a man honest till I find to the contrary."

Upon this, I attended his lordship as usual; and being resolved to remove all possible ground of suspicion that I kept any secret correspondence, I never visited, or wrote to, or any way corresponded with my principal benefactor for above three years; which he so well knew the reason of, and so well approved that punctual behaviour in me, that he never took it ill from me at all.

In consequence of this reception, my lord Godolphin had the goodness not only to introduce me for the second time to her majesty, and to the honour of kissing her hand, but obtained for me the continuance of an appointment which her majesty had been pleased to make me, in consideration of a formal special service I had done, and in which I had run as much risk of my life as a grenadier upon the counterscarp; and which appointment, however, was first obtained for me at the intercession of my said first benefactor, and is all owing to that intercession and her majesty's bounty. Upon this second introduction, her majesty was pleased to tell me, with a goodness peculiar to herself, that she had such satisfaction in my former services, that she had appointed me for another affair, which was something nice, and that my lord treasurer should tell me the rest; and so I withdrew.

The next day, his lordship having commanded me to attend, told me that he must send me to Scotland, and gave me but three days to prepare myself. Accordingly, I went to Scotland, where neither my business, nor the manner of my discharging it, is material to this tract; nor will it be ever any part of my character that I reveal what should be concealed. And yet, my errand was such as was far from being unfit for a sovereign to direct, or an honest man to perform; and the service I did upon that occasion, as it is not unknown to the greatest man now in the nation under the king and the prince, so, I dare say, his grace was never displeased with the part I had in it, and I hope will not forget it.

These things I mention upon this account, and no other, viz., to state the obligation I have been in all along to her majesty personally, and to my first benefactor principally; by which I say, I think I was at least obliged not to act against them, even in those things which I might not approve. Whether I have acted with them further than I ought, shall be spoken of by itself.

Having said thus much of the obligations laid on me, and the persons by whom, I have this only to add, that I think no man will say, a subject could be under greater bonds to his prince, or a private person to a minister of state; and I shall ever preserve this principle, that an honest man cannot be ungrateful to his benefactor.

But let no man run away now with the notion, that I am now intending to plead the obligation that was laid upon me from her majesty, or from any other person, to justify my doing anything that is not otherwise to be justified in itself.

Nothing would be more injurious than such a construction; and therefore I capitulate for so much justice as to explain myself by this declaration, viz., that I only speak of those obligations as binding me to a negative conduct, not to fly in the face of, or concern myself in disputes with those to whom I was under such obligations, although I might not, in my judgment, join in many things that were done. No obligation could excuse me in calling evil good, or good evil; but I am of the opinion, that I might justly think myself obliged to defend what I thought was to be defended, and to be silent in anything which I might think was not.

If this is a crime, I must plead guilty, and give in the history of my obligation above mentioned as an extenuation at least, if not a justification of my conduct.

Suppose a man's father was guilty of several things unlawful and unjustifiable; a man may heartily detest the unjustifiable thing, and yet it ought not to be expected that he should expose his father. I think the case on my side exactly the same, nor can the duty to a parent be more strongly obliging than the obligation laid on me; but I must allow the case on the other side not the same.

And this brings me to the affirmative, and inquire what the matters of fact are; what I have done, or have not done, on account of these obligations which I am under.

It is a general suggestion, and is affirmed with such assurance, that they tell me it is in vain to contradict it, that I have been employed by the earl of Oxford, late lord treasurer, in the late disputes about public affairs, to write for him, or, to put it into their own particulars, have written by his directions taken the materials from him, been dictated to or instructed by him, or by other persons from him, by his order, and the like; and that I have received a pension, or salary, or payment from his lordship for such services as these. It was impossible, since these things have been so confidently affirmed, but that, if I could put it into words that would more fully express the meaning of these people, I profess I would do it. One would think that some evidence might be produced, some facts might appear, some one or other might be found that could speak of certain knowledge. To say things have been carried too closely to be discovered, is saying nothing, for then they must own that it is not discovered; and how then can they affirm it as they do, with such an assurance as nothing ought to be affirmed by honest men, unless they were able to prove it?

To speak, then, to the fact. Were the reproach upon me only in this particular, I should not mention it. I should not think it a reproach to be directed by a man to whom the queen had at that time entrusted the administration of the government. But, as it is a reproach upon his lordship, justice requires that I do right in this case. The thing is true or false. I would recommend it to those who would be called honest men, to consider but one thing, viz., what if it should not be true? Can they justify the injury done to that person, or to any person concerned? If it cannot be proved, if no vestiges appear to ground it upon, how can they charge men upon rumours and reports, and join to run down men's characters by the stream of clamour?

Sed quo rapit impetus undæ.

In answer to the charge, I bear witness to posterity, that every part of it is false and forged. And I do solemnly protest, in the fear and presence of Him that shall judge us all, both the slanderers and the slandered, that I have not received any instructions, directions, orders, or let them call it what they will, of that kind, for the writing of any part of what I have written, or any materials for the putting together for the forming any book or pamphlet whatsoever, from the said earl of Oxford, late lord treasurer, or from any person by his order or direction, since the time that the late earl of Godolphin was lord treasurer. Neither did I ever show, or cause to be shown to his lordship, for his approbation, correction, alteration, or for any other cause, any book, paper, or pamphlet which I have written and published, before the same was worked off at the press and published.

If any man living can detect me of the least prevarication in this, or in any part of it, I desire him to do it by all means; and I challenge all the world to do it. And if they cannot, then I appeal, as in my title, to the honour and justice of my worst enemies, to know upon what foundation of truth or conscience they can affirm these things, and for what it is that I bear these reproaches.

In all my writing, I ever capitulated for my liberty to speak according to my own judgment of things; I ever had that liberty allowed me, nor was I ever imposed upon to write this way or that against my judgment by any person whatsoever.

I come now historically to the point of time when my lord Godolphin was dismissed from his employment, and the late unhappy division broke out at court. I waited on my lord the day he was displaced, and humbly asked his lordship's direction what course I should take? His lordship's answer was, "that he had the same goodwill to assist me, but not the same power; that I was the queen's servant, and that all he had done for me was by her majesty's special and particular direction; and that whoever should succeed him, it was not material to me; he supposed I should be employed in nothing relating to the present differences. My business was to wait till I saw things settled, and then apply myself to the ministers of state, to receive her majesty's commands from them."

It occurred to me immediately, as a principle for my conduct, that it was not material to me what ministers her majesty was pleased to employ; my duty was to go along with every ministry, so far as they did not break in upon the constitution, and the laws and liberties of my country; my part being only the duty of a subject, viz., to submit to all lawful commands, and to enter into no service which was not justifiable by the laws; to all which I have exactly obliged myself.

By this, I was providentially cast back upon my original benefactor, who, according to his wonted goodness, was pleased to lay my case before her majesty; and thereby I preserved my interest in her majesty's favour, but without any engagement of service.

As for consideration, pension, gratification, or reward, I declare to all the world I have had none, except only that old appointment which her majesty was pleased to make me in the days of the ministry of my lord Godolphin; of which I have spoken already, and which was for services done in a foreign country some years before. Neither have I been employed, directed, or ordered by my lord treasurer aforesaid to do, or not to do, anything in the affairs of the unhappy differences which have so long perplexed us, and for which I have so many, and such unjust reproaches.

I come next to enter into the matters of fact, and what it is I have done, or not done, which may justify the treatment I have met with; and first, for the negative part, what I have not done.

The first thing in the unhappy breaches which have fallen out, is the heaping up scandal upon the persons and conduct of men of honour on one side as well as the other; those unworthy methods of falling upon one another by personal calumny and reproach. This I have often in print complained of as an unchristian, ungenerous, and unjustifiable practice. Not a word can be found in all I have written reflecting on the persons or conduct of any of the former ministry. I served her majesty under their administration; they acted honourably and justly in every transaction in which I had the honour to be concerned with them, and I never published or said anything dishonourable of any of them in my life; nor can the worst enemy I have produce any such thing against me. I always regretted the change, and looked upon it as a great disaster to the nation in general, I am sure it was so to me in particular; and the divisions and feuds among parties which followed that change were doubtless a disaster to us all.

The next thing that followed the change was the peace: no man can say that ever I once said in my life that I approved of the peace. I wrote a public paper at that time, and there it remains upon record against me. I printed it openly, and that so plainly as others durst not do, that I did not like the peace; neither that which was made, nor that which was before making; that I thought the protestant interest was not taken care of in either; and that the peace I was for was such as should neither have given the Spanish monarchy to the house of Bourbon nor to the house of Austria, but that this bone of contention should have been broken to pieces, that it might not be dangerous to Europe; and that the protestant powers, viz., Britain and the States, should have so strengthened and fortified their interest by their sharing the commerce and strength of Spain, as should have made them no more afraid of France or the emperor: so that the protestant interest should have been superior to all the powers of Europe, and been in no more danger of exorbitant powers whether French or Austrian. This was the peace I always argued for, pursuant to the design of king William in the Treaty of Partition, and pursuant to that article of the grand alliance which was directed by the same glorious hand at the beginning of this last war, viz., that all we should conquer in the Spanish West Indies should be our own.

This was the true design, that England and Holland should have turned their naval power, which was eminently superior to that of France, to the conquest of the Spanish West Indies, by which the channel of trade and return of bullion, which now enriches the enemies of both, had been ours; and as the wealth, so the strength of the world had been in protestant hands. Spain, whoever had it, must then have been dependent upon us. The house of Bourbon would have found it so poor without us, as to be scarce worth fighting for: and the people so averse to them, for want of their commerce, as not to make it ever likely that France could keep it.

This was the foundation I ever acted upon with relation to the peace. It is true, that when it was made, and could not be otherwise, I thought our business was to make the best of it, and rather to inquire what improvements were to be made of it, than to be continually exclaiming at those who made it; and where the objection lies against this part, I cannot yet see.

While I spoke of things in this manner, I bore infinite reproaches from clamouring pens, of being in the French interest, being hired and bribed to defend a bad peace, and the like; and most of this was upon a supposition of my writing, or being the author of, abundance of pamphlets which came out every day, and which I had no hand in. And indeed, as I shall observe again by and by, this was one of the greatest pieces of injustice that could be done me, and which I labour still under without any redress; that whenever any piece comes out which is not liked, I am immediately charged with being the author; and very often the first knowledge I have had of a book being published, has been from seeing myself abused for being the author of it, in some other pamphlet published in answer to it.

Finding myself treated in this manner, I declined writing at all, and for a great part of a year never set pen to paper, except in the public paper called the Review. After this I was long absent in the north of England; and, observing the insolence of the jacobite party, and how they insinuated fine things into the heads of the common people, of the right and claim of the pretender, and of the great things he would do for us if he were to come in; of his being to turn a protestant, of his being resolved to maintain our liberties, support our friends, give liberty to dissenters, and the like; and finding that the people began to be deluded, and that the jacobites gained ground among them by these insinuations, I thought it the best service I could do the protestant interest, and the best way to open people's eyes of the protestant succession, if I took some course effectually to alarm the people with what they really ought to expect, if the pretender should come to be king. And this made me set pen to paper again.

And this brings me to the affirmative part, or to what really I have done; and in this, I am sorry to say, I have one of the foulest, most unjust, and unchristian clamours to complain of, that any man has suffered, I believe, since the days of the tyranny of king James II. The fact is thus:—

In order to detect the influence of jacobite emissaries, as above, the first thing I wrote was a small tract, called A Seasonable Caution; a book sincerely written to open the eyes of the poor, ignorant country people, and to warn them against the subtle insinuations of the emissaries of the pretender; and that it might be effectual to that purpose, I prevailed with several of my friends to give them away among the poor people, all over

England, especially in the north; and several thousands were actually given away, the price being reduced so low, that the bare expense of paper and press was only preserved, that every one might be convinced that nothing of gain was designed, but a sincere endeavour to do a public good, and assist to keep the people entirely in the interest of the protestant succession.

Next to this, and with the same sincere design, I wrote two pamphlets, one entituled, What if the Pretender should come? the other, Reasons against the Succession of the House of Hanover.

Nothing can be more plain than that the titles of these books were amusements, in order to put the books into the hands of those people whom the jacobites had deluded, and to bring them to be read by them.

Previous to what I shall further say of these books, I must observe that all these books met with so general a reception and approbation among those who were most sincere for the protestant succession, that they sent them all over the kingdom, and recommended them to the people as excellent and useful pieces; insomuch that about seven editions of them were printed, and they were reprinted in other places. And I do protest, had his present majesty, then elector of Hanover, given me a thousand pounds to have written for the interest of his succession, and to expose and render the interest of the pretender odious and ridiculous, I could have done nothing more effectual to those purposes than these books were.

And that I may make my worst enemies, to whom this is a fair appeal, judges of this, I must take leave, by and by, to repeat some of the expressions in these books, which were direct and need no explanation, which I think no man that was in the interest of the pretender, nay, which no man but one who was entirely in the interest of the Hanover succession, could write.

Nothing can be severer in the fate of a man than to act so between two parties, that both sides should be provoked against him. It is certain, the jacobites cursed those tracts and the author, and when they came to read them, being deluded by the titles according to the design, they threw them by with the greatest indignation imaginable. Had the pretender ever come to the throne, I could have expected nothing but death, and all the ignominy and reproach that the most inveterate enemy of his person and claim could be supposed to suffer.

On the other hand, I leave it to any considering man to judge, what a surprise it must be to me to meet with all the public clamour that informers could invent, as being guilty of writing against the Hanover succession, and as having written several pamphlets in favour of the pretender.

No man in this nation ever had a more rivetted aversion to the pretender, and to all the family he pretended to come of, than I; a man that had been in arms under the duke of Monmouth, against the cruelty and arbitrary government of his pretended father; that for twenty years had to my utmost opposed him (king James) and his party after his abdication; and had served king William to his satisfaction, and the friends of the revolution after his death, at all hazards and upon all occasions; that had suffered and been ruined under the administration of high-fliers and jacobites, of whom some at this day counterfeit whigs. It could not be! The nature of the thing could by no means allow it; it must be monstrous; and that the wonder may cease, I shall take leave to quote some of the expressions out of these books, of which the worst enemy I have in the world is left to judge whether they are in favour of the pretender or no; but of this in its place. For these books I was prosecuted, taken into custody, and obliged to give 800*l.* bail.

I do not in the least object here against, or design to reflect upon, the proceedings of the judges which were subsequent to this. I acknowledged then, and now acknowledge again, that upon the information given, there was a sufficient ground for all they did; and my unhappy entering upon my own vindication in print, while the case was before their lordships in a judicial way, was an error which I did not understand, and which I did not foresee; and therefore, although I had great reason to reflect upon the informers, yet I was wrong in making that defence in the manner and time I then made it; and which when I found, I made no scruple afterwards to petition the judges, and acknowledge they had just ground to resent it. Upon which petition and acknowledgment their lordships were pleased, with particular marks of goodness, to release me, and not to take the advantage of an error of ignorance, as if it had been considered and premeditated.

But against the informers I think I have great reason to complain; and against the injustice of those writers who, in many pamphlets, charged me with writing for the pretender, and the government with pardoning an author who wrote for the pretender. And, indeed, the justice of these men can be in nothing more clearly stated than in this case of mine; where the charge, in their printed papers and public discourse, was brought; not that they themselves believed me guilty of the crime, but because it was necessary to blacken the man, that a general reproach might serve for an answer to whatever he should say that was not for their turn. So that it was the person, not the crime, they fell upon; and they may justly be said to persecute for the sake of persecution, as will thus appear.

This matter making some noise, people began to inquire into it, and ask what De Foe was prosecuted for, seeing the books were manifestly written against the pretender, and for the interest of the house of Hanover. And my friends expostulated freely with some of the men who appeared in it, who answered with more truth than honesty, that they knew this book had nothing in it, and that it was meant another way; but that De Foe had disobliged them in other things, and they were resolved to take the advantage they had, both to punish and expose him. They were no inconsiderable people who said this; and had the case come to a trial, I had provided good evidence to prove the words.

This is the christianity and justice by which I have been treated, and this in justice is the thing I complain of.

Now, as this was the plot of a few men to see if they could brand me in the world for a jacobite, and persuade rash and ignorant people that I was turned about for the pretender, I think they might as easily have proved me to be a mahometan;

therefore, I say, this obliges me to state the matter as it really stands, that impartial men may judge whether those books were written for or against the pretender. And this cannot be better done than by the account of what followed after the information, which, in a few words, was this:—

Upon the several days appointed, I appeared at the Queen's Bench bar to discharge my bail; and at last had an indictment for high crimes and misdemeanors exhibited against me by her majesty's attorney-general, which, as I was informed, contained two hundred sheets of paper.

What was the substance of the indictment I shall not mention here, neither could I enter upon it, having never seen the particulars; but I was told that I should be brought to trial the very next term.

I was not ignorant that in such cases it is easy to make any book a libel, and that the jury must have found the matter of fact in the indictment, viz., that I had written such books, and then what might have followed I knew not. Wherefore, I thought it was my only way to cast myself on the clemency of her majesty, of whose goodness I had so much experience many ways; representing in my petition, that I was far from the least intention to favour the interest of the pretender, but that the books were all written with a sincere design to promote the interest of the house of Hanover; and humbly laid before her majesty, as I do now before the rest of the world, the books themselves to plead in my behalf; representing further, that I was maliciously informed against by those who were willing to put a construction upon the expressions different from my true meaning; and therefore, flying to her majesty's goodness and clemency, I entreated her gracious pardon.

It was not only the native disposition of her majesty to acts of clemency and goodness that obtained me this pardon; but, as I was informed, her majesty was pleased to express it in the council, "She saw nothing but private pique in the first prosecution." And therefore I think I cannot give a better and clearer vindication of myself; than what is contained in the preamble to the pardon which her majesty was pleased to grant me; and I must be allowed to say to those who are still willing to object, that I think what satisfied her majesty might be sufficient to satisfy them; and I can assure them that this pardon was not granted without her majesty's being specially and particularly acquainted with the things alleged in the petition, the books also being looked into, to find the expressions quoted in the petition. The preamble to the patent for a pardon, as far as relates to the matters of fact, runs thus:—

"Whereas, in the term of the Holy Trinity last past, our attorney-general did exhibit an information, in our court of Queen's Bench at Westminster, against Daniel De Foe, late of London, gent., for writing, printing, and publishing, and causing to be written, printed, and published, three libels, the one entituled, Reasons against the Succession of the House of Hanover; with an Inquiry how far the Abdication of King James, supposing it to be legal, ought to affect the person of the Pretender. One other, entituled, And what if the Pretender should come? or, Some Considerations of the Advantages and real Consequences of the Pretender's possessing the Crown of Great Britain. And one other, entituled, An Answer to a Question that nobody thinks of, viz., What if the Queen should die?

"And whereas the said Daniel De Foe hath by his humble petition represented to us, that he, with a sincere design to propagate the interest of the Hanover succession, and to animate the people against the designs of the pretender, whom he always looked on as an enemy to our sacred person and government, did publish the said pamphlets: in all which books, although the titles seemed to look as if written in favour of the pretender, and several expressions, as in all ironical writing it must be, may be wrested against the true design of the whole, and turned to a meaning quite different from the intention of the author, yet the petitioner humbly assures us, in the solemnest manner, that his true and only design in all the said books was, by an ironical discourse of recommending the pretender, in the strongest and most forcible manner to expose his designs, and the ruinous consequences of his succeeding therein; which, as the petitioner humbly represents, will appear to our satisfaction by the books themselves, where the following expressions are very plain: viz:, 'That the pretender is recommended as a person proper to amass the English liberties into his own sovereignty; supply them with the privilege of wearing wooden shoes; easing them of the trouble of choosing parliaments; and the nobility and gentry of the hazard and expense of winter journeys, by governing them in that more righteous method, of his absolute will, and enforcing the laws by a glorious standing army; paying all the nation's debts at once by stopping the funds and shutting up the exchequer; easing and quieting their differences in religion, by bringing them to the union of popery, or leaving them at liberty to have no religion at all:' that these were some of the very expressions in the said books, which the petitioner sincerely designed to expose and oppose, and as far as in him lies, the interest of the pretender, and with no other intention; nevertheless, the petitioner, to his great surprise, has been misrepresented, and his said books misconstrued, as if written in favour of the pretender; and the petitioner is now under prosecution for the same; which prosecution, if further carried on, will be the utter ruin of the petitioner and his family. Wherefore, the petitioner, humbly assuring us of the innocence of his design as aforesaid, flies to our clemency, and most humbly prays our most gracious and free pardon.

"We, taking the premises and the circumstances of the petitioner into our royal consideration, are graciously pleased to extend our royal mercy to the petitioner. Our will and pleasure therefore is, that you prepare a bill for our royal signature, to pass our great seal, containing our gracious and free pardon unto him, the said Daniel De Foe, of the offences aforementioned, and of all indictments, convictions, pains, penalties, and forfeitures incurred thereby; and you are to insert therein all such apt beneficial clauses as you shall deem requisite to make this our intended pardon more full, valid, and effectual; and for so doing, this shall be your warrant. Given at our castle at Windsor, the twentieth day of November, 1713, in the twentieth year of our reign. By her majesty's command.

Bolingbroke.

Let any indifferent man judge whether I was not treated with particular malice in this matter; who was, notwithstanding this, reproached in the daily public prints with having written treasonable books in behalf of the pretender; nay, and in some of those books, as before, the queen herself was reproached with having granted her pardon to an author who writ for the pretender.

I think I might with much more justice say, I was the first man that ever was obliged to seek a pardon for writing for the Hanover succession, and the first man that these people ever sought to ruin for writing against the pretender. For, if ever a book was sincerely designed to further and propagate the affection and zeal of the nation against the pretender, nay, and was made use of, and that with success too, for that purpose, these books were so; and I ask no more favour of the world to determine the opinion of honest men for or against me, than what is drawn constructively from these books. Let one word, either written or spoken by me, either published or not published, be produced, that was in the least disrespectful to the protestant succession, or to any branch of the family of Hanover, or that can be judged to be favourable to the interest or person of the pretender, and I will be willing to waive her majesty's pardon, and render myself to public justice, to be punished for it, as I should well deserve.

I freely and openly challenge the worst of my enemies to charge me with any discourse, conversation, or behaviour, in my whole life, which had the least word in it injurious to the protestant succession, unbecoming or disrespectful to any of the persons of the royal family of Hanover, or the least favourable word of the persons, the designs, or friends of the pretender. If they can do it, let them stand forth and speak; no doubt but that they may be heard; and I, for my part, will relinquish all pleas, pardons, and defences, and cast myself into the hands of justice.

Nay, to go further, I defy them to prove that I ever kept company, or had any society, friendship, or conversation, with any jacobite. So averse have I been to the interest and the people, that I have studiously avoided their company on all occasions.

As nothing in the world has been more my aversion than the society of jacobites, so nothing can be a greater misfortune to me than to be accused and publicly reproached with what is, of all things in the world, most abhorred by me; and that which has made it the more afflicting is, that this charge arises from those very things which I did with the sincerest design to manifest the contrary.

But such is my present fate, and I am to submit to it; which I do with meekness and calmness, as to a judgment from heaven, and am practising that duty which I have studied long ago, of forgiving my enemies, and praying for them that despitefully use me.

Having given this brief history of the pardon, &c., I hope the impartial part of the world will grant me, that being thus graciously delivered a second time from the cruelty of my implacable enemies, and the ruin of a cruel and unjust persecution, and that by the mere clemency and goodness, my obligation to her majesty's goodness was far from being made less than it was before.

I have now run through the history of my obligation to her majesty, and to the person of my benefactor aforesaid. I shall state everything that followed this with all the clearness I can, and leave myself liable to as little cavil as I may; for I see myself assaulted by a sort of people who will do me no justice. I hear a great noise made of punishing those that are guilty, but, as I said before, not one word of clearing those that are innocent; and I must say, in this part they treat me, not only as I were no Christian, but as if they themselves were not Christians. They will neither prove the charge nor hear the defence, which is the unjustest thing in the world.

I foresee what will be alleged to the clause of my obligation, &c., to great persons, and I resolve to give my adversaries all the advantage they can desire by acknowledging beforehand, that no obligation to the queen, or to any benefactor, can justify any man's acting against the interest of his country, against his principles, his conscience, and his former profession.

I think this will anticipate all that can be said upon that head, and it will then remain to tell the fact, as I am not chargeable with it; which I shall do as clearly as possible in a few words.

It is none of my work to enter into the conduct of the queen or of the ministry in this case; the question is not what they have done, but what I have done; and though I am very far from thinking of them as some other people think, yet, for the sake of the present argument, I am to give them all up, and suppose, though not granting, that all which is suggested of them by the worst temper, the most censorious writer, the most scandalous pamphlet or lampoon should be true; and I'll go through some of the particulars, as I meet with them in public.

Ist. That they made a scandalous peace, unjustly broke the alliance, betrayed the confederates, and sold us all to the French.

God forbid it should be all truth, in the manner that we see it in print; but that I say is none of my business. But what hand had I in all this? I never wrote one word for the peace before it was made, or to justify it after it was made; let them produce it if they can. Nay, in a Review upon that subject while it was making, I printed it in plainer words than other men durst speak it at that time, that I did not like the peace, nor did I like any peace that was making since that of the partition, and that the protestant interest was not taken care of either in that or the treaty of Gertrudenburgh before it.

It is true that I did say, that since the peace was made, and we could not help it, that it was our business and our duty to make the best of it, to make the utmost advantage of it by commerce, navigation, and all kind of improvement that we could, and this I say still; and I must think it is more our duty to do so than the exclamations against the thing itself, which it is not in our power to retrieve. This is all that the worst enemy I have can charge me with. After the peace was made, and the Dutch and the emperor stood out, I gave my opinion of what I foresaw would necessarily be the consequence of that difference, viz., that it would inevitably involve these nations in a war with one or other of them; any one who was master of common sense in the public affairs might see that the standing out of the Dutch could have no other event. For if the confederates had conquered the French, they would certainly have fallen upon us by way of resentment, and there was no doubt but the same councils that led us to make a peace would oblige us to maintain it, by preventing too great impressions upon the French.

On the other hand, I alleged, that should the French prevail against the Dutch, unless he stopped at such limitations of conquest as the treaty obliged him to do, we must have been under the same necessity to renew the war against France; and for this reason, seeing we had made a peace, we were obliged to bring the rest of the confederates into it, and to bring the French to give them all such terms as they ought to be satisfied with.

This way of arguing was either so little understood, or so much maligned, that I suffered innumerable reproaches in print for having written for a war with the Dutch, which was neither in the expression, nor ever in my imagination; but I pass by these injuries as small and trifling compared to others I suffer under.

However, one thing I must say of the peace, let it be good or ill in itself, I cannot but think we have all reason to rejoice in behalf of his present majesty, that at his accession to the crown he found the nation in peace, and had the hands of the king of France tied up by a peace so as not to be able, without the most infamous breach of articles, to offer the least disturbance to his taking a quiet and leisurely possession, or so much as to countenance those that would.

Not but that I believe, if the war had been at the height, we should have been able to have preserved the crown for his present majesty, its only rightful lord; but I will not say it should have been so easy, so bloodless, so undisputed as now; and all the difference must be acknowledged to the peace, and this is all the good I ever yet said of it.

I come next to the general clamour of the ministry being for the pretender. I must speak my sentiments solemnly and plainly, as I always did in that matter, viz., that if it was so, I did not see it, nor did I ever see reason to believe it; this I am sure of, that if it was so, I never took one step in that kind of service, nor did I ever hear one word spoken by any one of the ministry that I had the honour to know or converse with, that favoured the pretender; but have had the honour to hear them all protest that there was no design to oppose the succession of Hanover in the least.

It may be objected to me, that they might be in the interest of the pretender for all that; it is true they might, but that is nothing to me. I am not vindicating their conduct, but my own; as I never was employed in anything that way, so I do still protest I do not believe it was ever in their design, and I have many reasons to confirm my thoughts in that case, which are not material to the present case. But be that as it will, it is enough to me that I acted nothing in any such interest, neither did I ever sin against the protestant succession of Hanover in thought, word, or deed; and if the ministry did, I did not see it, or so much as suspect them of it.

It was a disaster to the ministry, to be driven to the necessity of taking that set of men by the hand, who nobody can deny, were in that interest; but as the former ministry answered, when they were charged with a design to overthrow the church, because they favoured, joined with, and were united to the dissenters; I say they answered, that they made use of the dissenters, but granted them nothing (which, by the way, was too true;) so these gentlemen answer, that it is true they made use of jacobites, but did nothing for them.

But this by the by. Necessity is pleaded by both parties for doing things which neither side can justify. I wish both sides would for ever avoid the necessity of doing evil; for certainly it is the worst plea in the world, and generally made use of for the worst things.

I have often lamented the disaster which I saw employing jacobites was to the late ministry, and certainly it gave the greatest handle to the enemies of the ministry to fix that universal reproach upon them of being in the interest of the pretender. But there was no medium. The whigs refused to show them a safe retreat, or to give them the least opportunity to take any other measures, but at the risk of their own destruction; and they ventured upon that course in hopes of being able to stand alone at last without help of either the one or the other; in which they were no doubt, mistaken.

However, in this part, as I was always assured, and have good reason still to believe, that her majesty was steady in the interest of the house of Hanover, and as nothing was ever offered to me, or required of me, to the prejudice of that interest, on what ground can I be reproached with the secret reserved designs of any, if they had such designs, as I still verily believe they had not?

I see there are some men who would fain persuade the world, that every man that was in the interest of the late ministry, or employed by the late government, or that served the late queen, was for the pretender.

God forbid this should be true; and I think there needs very little to be said in answer to it. I can answer for myself, that it is notoriously false; and I think the easy and uninterrupted accession of his majesty to the crown contradicts it. I see no end which such a suggestion aims at, but to leave an odium upon all that had any duty or regard to her late majesty.

A subject is not always master of his sovereign's measures, nor always to examine what persons or parties the prince he serves employs, so be it that they break not in upon the constitution; that they govern according to law, and that he is employed in no illegal act, or have nothing desired of him inconsistent with the liberties and laws of his country. If this be not right, then a servant of the king's is in a worse case than a servant to any private person.

In all these things I have not erred; neither have I acted or done anything in the whole course of my life, either in the service of her majesty or of her ministry, that any one can say has the least deviation from the strictest regard to the protestant succession, and to the laws and liberties of my country.

I never saw an arbitrary action offered at, a law dispensed with, justice denied, or oppression set up, either by queen or ministry, in any branch of the administration, wherein I had the least concern.

If I have sinned against the whigs, it has been all negatively, viz., that I have not joined in the loud exclamations against the queen and against the ministry, and against their measures; and if this be my crime, my plea is twofold.

I. I did not really see cause for carrying their complaints to that violent degree.

2. Where I did see what, as before, I lamented and was sorry for, and could not join with or approve,—as joining with jacobites, the peace, &c.,—my obligation is my plea for my silence.

I have all the good thoughts of the person, and good wishes for the prosperity of my benefactor, that charity and that gratitude can inspire me with. I ever believed him to have the true interest of the protestant religion and of his country in his view; and if it should be otherwise, I should be very sorry. And I must repeat it again, that he always left me so entirely to my own judgment, in everything I did, that he never prescribed to me what I should write, or should not write, in my life; neither did he ever concern himself to dictate to or restrain me in any kind; nor did he see any one tract that I ever wrote before it was printed; so that all the notion of my writing by his direction is as much a slander upon him as it is possible anything of that kind can be; and if I have written anything which is offensive, unjust, or untrue, I must do that justice as to declare, he has no hand in it; the crime is my own.

As the reproach of his directing me to write is a slander upon the person I am speaking of, so that of my receiving pensions and payments from him for writing, is a slander upon me; and I speak it with the greatest sincerity, seriousness, and solemnity that it is possible for a Christian man to speak, that except the appointment I mentioned before, which her majesty was pleased to make me formerly, and which I received during the time of my lord Godolphin's ministry, I have not received of the late lord treasurer, or of any one else by his order, knowledge, or direction, one farthing, or the value of a farthing, during his whole administration; nor has all the interest I have been supposed to have in his lordship been able to procure me the arrears due to me in the time of the other ministry. So help me God.

I am under no necessity of making this declaration. The services I did, and for which her majesty was pleased to make me a small allowance, are known to the greatest men in the present administration; and some of them were then of the opinion, and I hope are so still, that I was not unworthy of her majesty's favour. The effect of those services, however small, is enjoyed by those great persons and by the whole nation to this day; and I had the honour once to be told, that they should never be forgotten. It is a misfortune that no man can avoid, to forfeit for his deference to the person and services of his queen, to whom he was inexpressibly obliged; and if I am fallen under the displeasure of the present government for anything I ever did in obedience to her majesty in the past, I may say it is my disaster; but I can never say it is my fault.

This brings me again to that other oppression which, as I said, I suffer under, and which, I think, is of a kind that no man ever suffered under so much as myself; and this is to have every libel, every pamphlet, be it ever so foolish, so malicious, so unmannerly, or so dangerous, be laid at my door, and be called publicly by my name. It has been in vain for me to struggle with this injury; it has been in vain for me to protest, to declare solemnly, nay, if I would have sworn that I had no hand in such a book or paper, never saw it, never read it, and the like, it was the same thing.

My name has been hackneyed about the street by the hawkers, and about the coffeehouses by the politicians, at such a rate as no patience could bear. One man will swear to the style; another to this or that expression; another to the way of printing; and all so positive that it is to no purpose to oppose it.

I published once, to stop this way of using me, that I would print nothing but what I set my name to, and held it for a year or two; but it was all one; I had the same treatment. I now have resolved for some time to write nothing at all, and yet I find it the same thing; two books lately published being called mine, for no other reason that I know of than that at the request of the printer, I revised two sheets of them at the press, and that they seemed to be written in favour of a certain person; which person, also, as I have been assured, had no hand in them, or any knowledge of them, till they were published in print.

This is a flail which I have no fence against, but to complain of the injustice of it, and that is but *the shortest way* to be treated with more injustice.

There is a mighty charge against me for being author and publisher of a paper called the 'Mercator.' I will state the fact first, and then speak to the subject.

It is true, that being desired to give my opinion in the affair of the commerce with France, I did, as I often had done in print many years before, declare that it was my opinion we ought to have an open trade with France, because I did believe we might have the advantage by such a trade; and of this opinion I am still. What part I had in the Mercator is well known; and could men answer with argument, and not with personal abuse, I would at any time defend every part of the Mercator which was of my doing. But to say the Mercator was mine, is false; I neither was the author of it, had the property of it, the printing of it, or the profit by it. I had never any payment or reward for writing any part of it, nor had I the power to put what I would into it. Yet the whole clamour fell upon me, because they knew not who else to load with it. And when they came to answer, the method was instead of argument, to threaten and reflect upon me, reproach me with private circumstances and misfortunes, and give language which no Christian ought to give, and which no gentleman ought to take.

I thought any Englishman had the liberty to speak his opinion in such things, for this had nothing to do with the public. The press was open to me as well as to others; and how or when I lost my English liberty of speaking my mind, I know not; neither how my speaking my opinion without fee or reward, could authorise them to call me villain, rascal, traitor, and such opprobrious names.

It was ever my opinion, and is so still, that were our wool kept from France, and our manufactures spread in France upon reasonable duties, all the improvements which the French have made in the woollen manufactures would decay, and in the end be little worth; and consequently, the hurt they could do us by them would be of little moment.

It was my opinion, and is so still, that the ninth article of the treaty of commerce was calculated for the advantage of our trade, let who will make it. That is nothing to me. My reasons are because it tied up the French to open the door to our manufactures at a certain duty of importation there, and left the parliament of Britain at liberty to shut theirs out by as high duties as they pleased here, there being no limitation upon us as to duties on French goods; but that other nations should pay the same.

While the French were thus bound, and the British free, I always thought we must be in a condition to trade to advantage, or it must be our own fault. This was my opinion, and is so still; and I would venture to maintain it against any man upon a public stage, before a jury of fifty merchants, and venture my life upon the cause, if I were assured of fair play in the dispute. But that it was my opinion that we might carry on a trade with France to our great advantage, and that we ought for that reason to trade with them, appears in the third, fourth, fifth, and sixth volumes of the Review, above nine years before the Mercator was thought of. It was not thought criminal to say so then; how it come to be villanous to say so now, God knows; I can give no account of it. I am still of the same opinion, and shall never be brought to say otherwise, unless I see the state of trade so altered as to alter my opinion; and if ever I do I shall be able to give good reasons for it.

The answer to these things, whether mine or no, was all pointed at me, and the arguments were generally in the terms villain, rascal, miscreant, liar, bankrupt, fellow, hireling, turncoat, &c. What the arguments were bettered by these methods, I leave others to judge of. Also, most of those things in the Mercator, for which I had such usage, were such as I was not the author of.

I do grant, had all the books which had been called by my name been written by me, I must of necessity have exasperated every side; and perhaps have deserved it; but I have the greatest injustice imaginable in this treatment, as I have in the perverting the design of what I have really written.

To sum up, therefore, my complaint in a few words:—

I was, from my first entering into the knowledge of public matters, and have ever been to this day, a sincere lover of the constitution of my country; zealous for liberty and the protestant interest; but a constant follower of moderate principles, a vigorous opposer of hot measures in all parties. I never once changed my opinion, my principles, or my party: and let what will be said of changing sides, this I maintain, that I never once deviated from the revolution principles, nor from the doctrine of liberty and property on which it was founded.

I own I could never be convinced of the great danger of the pretender in the time of the late ministry, nor can I be now convinced of the great danger of the church under this ministry. I believe the cry of the one was politically made use of then to serve other designs, and I plainly see the like use made of the other now. I spoke my mind freely then, and I have done the like now, in a small tract to that purpose not yet made public; and which if I live to publish I will publicly own, as I purpose to do everything I write, that my friends may know when I am abused, and they imposed on.

It has been the disaster of all parties in this nation to be very hot in their turn; and as often as they have been so I have differed with them, and ever must and shall do so. I will repeat some of the occasions on the whigs' side, because from that quarter the accusation of my turning about comes.

The first time I had the misfortune to differ with my friends was about the year 1683, when the Turks were besieging Vienna, and the whigs in England, generally speaking, were for the Turks taking it, which I, having read the history of the cruelty and perfidious dealings of the Turks in their wars, and how they had rooted out the name of the Christian religion in above threescore and ten kingdoms, could by no means agree with. And though then but a young man, and a younger author, I opposed it, and wrote against it, which was taken very unkindly indeed.

The next time I differed with my friends was when king James was wheedling the dissenters to take off the penal laws and test, which I could by no means come into. And, as in the first, I used to say, I had rather the popish house of Austria should ruin the protestants in Hungaria, than the infidel house of Ottoman should ruin both protestants and papists by overrunning Germany; so, in the other, I told the dissenters I had rather the church of England should pull our clothes off by fines and forfeitures, than the papists should fall both upon the church and the dissenters, and pull our skins off by fire and fagot.

The next difference I had with good men was about the scandalous practice of occasional conformity, in which I had the misfortune to make many honest men angry, rather because I had the better of the argument, than because they disliked what I said.

And now I have lived to see the dissenters themselves very quiet, if not very well pleased with an act of parliament to prevent it. Their friends indeed laid it on; they would be friends indeed if they would talk of taking it off again.

Again, I had a breach with honest men for their maltreating king William; of which I say nothing, because I think they are now opening their eyes, and making what amends they can to his memory.

The fifth difference I had with them was about the treaty of Partition, in which many honest men are mistaken, and in which I told them plainly then that they would at last end the war upon worse terms; and so it is my opinion they would have done, though, the treaty of Gertrudenburgh had taken place.

The sixth time I differed with them was when the old whigs fell upon the modern whigs, and when the duke of Marlborough and my lord Godolphin were used by the Observator in a manner worse, I must confess, for the time it lasted, than ever they were used since; nay, though it were by Abel and the Examiner; but the success failed. In this dispute my lord Godolphin did me the honour to tell me, I had served him and his grace also both faithfully and successfully. But his lordship is dead, and I have now no testimony of it but what is to be found in the Observator, where I am plentifully abused for being an enemy to my country, by acting in the interest of my lord Godolphin and the duke of Marlborough. What weathercock can turn with such tempers as these!

I am now on the seventh breach with them, and my crime now is, that I will not believe and say the same things of the queen and the late treasurer which I could not believe before of my lord Godolphin and the duke of Marlborough, and which in truth I cannot believe, and therefore could not say it of either of them; and which, if I had believed, yet I ought not to have been the man that should have said it for the reasons aforesaid.

In such turns of tempers and times, a man must be tenfold a vicar of Bray, or it is impossible but he must one time or other be out with everybody. This is my present condition, and for this I am reviled with having abandoned my principles, turned jacobite, and what not. God judge between me and these men. Would they come to any particulars with me, what real guilt I may have I would freely acknowledge; and if they would produce any evidence of the bribes, the pensions, and the rewards I have taken, I would declare honestly whether they were true or no. If they would give a list of the books which they charge me with, and the reasons why they lay them at my door, I would acknowledge my mistake, own what I have done, and let them know what I have not done. But these men neither show mercy, nor leave place for repentance; in which they act not only unlike their master, but contrary to his express commands.

It is true, good men have been used thus in former times; and all the comfort I have is, that these men have not the last judgment in their hands: if they had, dreadful would be the case of those who oppose them. But that day will show many men and things also in a different state from what they may now appear in. Some that now appear clear and fair will then be seen to be black and foul, and some that are now thought black and foul will then be approved and accepted; and thither I cheerfully appeal, concluding this part in the words of the prophet, *I heard the defaming of many; fear on every side; report, say they, and we will report it; all my familiars watched for my halting, saying, peradventure he will be enticed, and we shall prevail against him, and we shall take our revenge on him.* Jer. xx. 10.

Mr. Poole's Annotations has the following remarks on these lines; which, I think, are so much to that part of my case which is to follow, that I do not omit them. The words are these:—

"The prophet," says he, "here rendereth a reason why he thought of giving over his work as a prophet; his ears were continually filled with the obloquies and reproaches of such as reproached him; and besides, he was afraid on all hands, there were so many traps laid for him, so many devices devised against him. They did not only take advantage against him, but sought advantages, and invited others to raise stories of him; not only strangers, but those that he might have expected the greatest kindness from; those that pretended most courteously; 'They watch,' says he, 'for opportunities to do me justice, and lay in wait for my halting, desiring nothing more than that I might be enticed to speak, or do something which they might find matter of a colourable accusation, that so they might satisfy their malice upon me.' This hath always been the genius of wicked men. Job and David both made complaints much like this." These are Mr. Poole's words.

And this leads me to several particulars, in which my case may, without any arrogance, be likened to that of the sacred prophet, excepting the vast disparity of the persons.

No sooner was the queen dead, and the king, as right required, proclaimed, but the rage of men increased upon me to that degree, that the threats and insults I received were such as I am not able to express. If I offered to say a word in favour of the present settlement, it was called fawning, and turning round again; on the other hand, though I have meddled neither one way nor the other, nor written one book since the queen's death, yet a great many things are called by my name, and I bear every day the reproaches which all the answerers of those books cast, as well upon the subjects as the authors. I have not seen or spoken to my lord of Oxford but once since the king's landing, nor received the least message, order, or writing from his lordship, or any other way corresponded with him, yet he bears the reproach of my writing in his defence, and I the rage of men for doing it. I cannot say it is no affliction to me to be thus used, though my being entirely clear of the facts is a true support to me.

I am unconcerned at the rage and clamour of party men; but I cannot be unconcerned to hear men, who I think are good men and good Christians, prepossessed and mistaken about me. However, I cannot doubt but some time or other it will please God to open such men's eyes. A constant, steady adhering to personal virtue and to public peace, which, I thank God, I can appeal to him has always been my practice, will at last restore me to the opinion of sober and impartial men, and that is all I desire. What it will do with those who are resolutely partial and unjust, I cannot say, neither is that much my concern. But I cannot forbear giving one example of the hard treatment I receive, which has happened even while I am writing this tract. I have six children; I have educated them as well as my circumstances will permit, and so as I hope shall recommend them to better usage than their father meets with in this world.

I am not indebted one shilling in the world for any part of their education, or for anything else belonging to their bringing up; yet the author of the Flying Post published lately that I never paid for the education of any of my children. If any man in Britain has a shilling to demand of me for any part of their education, or anything belonging to them, let them come for it.

But these men care not what injurious things they write, nor what they say, whether truth or not, if it may but raise a reproach on me, though it were to be my ruin. I may well appeal to the honour and justice of my worst enemies in such cases as this:

Conscia mens recti fama mendacia ridet.

CONCLUSION BY THE PUBLISHER.

While this was at the press, and the copy thus far finished, the author was seized with a violent fit of an apoplexy, whereby he was disabled finishing what he designed in his further defence; and continuing now for above six weeks in a weak and languishing condition, neither able to go on nor likely to recover, at least in any short time, his friends thought it not fit to delay the publication of this any longer. If he recovers he may be able to finish what he began; if not, it is the opinion of most that know him that the treatment which he here complains of, and some others that he would have spoken of, have been the apparent cause of his disaster.

Atalantis Major.

Printed in *Olreeky*, the Chief City of
the North Part of *Atalantis Major.*

Anno Mundi 1711.

There having been a large Account given to the World of several
remarkable Adventures which happened lately in the famous *Atalantis*,
an Island, which the ingenious Authors found placed in the
Mediterranean Sea; the Success of which Accounts, but especially the
Usefulness of the Relation, to the Ends for which they were designed,
having been very remarkable, I thought it could not be unacceptable to
the World, (especially to those who *have been Already so delighted*
with News from that Island) to give a particular Historical Narration
of some remarkable Transactions which happened in the Great Island,
called, *Atalantis Major*, a famous well known Island, tho' much farther
North, lying in the *Ducaledonian* Ocean, which Island it was my good
Fortune to winter at, the last time I returned North about from *China*,
by the Streights of *Nassau* and *Wygates*, and the Eastern Coast of
Grand Tartary.

I have nothing to do to enquire, whether our late Authors mistook
or not, in placing the Island *Atalantis* in the *Mediterranean* Sea, or,
whether they might find some small Island of that Name among the
infinite Crowd of Islands of the *Egean* Sea: But as the mighty
Transactions of which my History shall be the faithful Relator, are of
too great Consequence in the World to be brought forth on so mean a
Stage; so the Place, and the mighty People, and by whom this
Revolution of Affairs have been mannaged, are all suitable to the
Greatness and Glory of the Actions themselves.

As Geographers have no doubt given a full Description of this
famous Island, and allowed it due Place in the Globes, where it stands
noted for the biggest of the Kind in the Northern World, I need spend
none of your Time in the Description of the Place, excepting such as
shall fall naturally in my Way, as I come to treat of the People, and
historically of their Behaviour.

The Island is possest by a brave, generous, powerful and wealthy
Nation, truly Great in their natural Gallantry of Spirit, terrible in the
Field, rich in the Product of their Lands, more in their general

Commerce, most of all in their Manufactures, Industry and Application: They have some few Errors in their Conduct, which seems owing to the Climate, which is cold and moist, or to their Diet, which is strong and luxurious, and particularly to their way of Living, which in Eating and Drinking, is high, to an Excess.

This makes them Cholerick, Envious, and above all Contentious, so that the Nation is ever divided into Parties and Factions: They pursue their Feuds with the most eagerness imaginable in their Turns, commit all Kinds of Errors even on both Sides alternately, as they get uppermost.

This occasions much Heat, tho' the Country is Cold, little Charity, and above all, (which the Climate has the blame off) they are by their own Confession, of short Memories, partly as to Injuries, but especially as to Kindnesses, Services and inherent Merit. Hence, Gratitude is not the national Virtue, nor is encouraging Virtue any Branch of the Manufacture of the Place; long Services often meet here with unjust Censures; overgrown Merit with necessary Contempt: He must be a bold Man that dares oblige them; he is sure to provoke them by it to use him very severely.

If they are reduc'd to any extreme Distress, he must be weary of his Life that Attempts to rescue them from the Danger; he is as sure to Die for it as they are sure to be Unjust: It is Natural to the Blood of the Race, if they are obliged beyond the Power of Payment, they presently hate, because they scorn to be in Debt. Hence also Benefactors are the most abhorr'd People in the World, they Walk always alone, for every Man keeps at a distance from them.

If a Man happens to be bound Apprentice to his own generous Spirit, and resolves to do them good, he must do it to God, to do it to them is to work to the Devil; he must be sure to run the Gauntlet, and bear the Lashes of Ten thousand Tongues, the Reproach of all those he serves, and will Die unpitied.

If ever they do relent, if ever they acknowledge Services, 'tis always after the Man is dead, that he may not upbraid them with it. An eminent great Man among them, and rich to a Prodigy, had been almost drowned, but was taken up in the Interval by a poor Man; when he came to himself, he gave the poor Man Six-pence, but could never abide the sight of him after: The poor Man afterwards had the Dissaster of being drowned himself, and then the rich Man bewail'd that he had not made him a better Return, wherefore, in abundant Gratitude, he settled upon the Widow and her Six Children, a noble Pension of 20 *s. per Annum*.

It was a saying of One of their great and wise Men, of a poor Servant that had saved his Life; he saved my Life, *said he*, and therefore I hate to see him, for it is an intolerable Life to have always a Creditor in my Sight that I cannot ballance Accounts with.

But all this is by the By. The Inhabitants of this Great Island are, those things excepted, a Noble, Gallant, Ancient, Wealthy People; and a Stranger may very well winter among them. I could say more in their Praise but the ensuing History calls me off from that Subject.

There happen'd in that famous Island, when I was last there, an Occasion upon some State Affairs to assemble an extraordinary Council of the Nobility, to consult together with the Sovereign; whole Hereditary Councellors they were by the Constitution of the Place: These were not chosen by the Inhabitants, as in such Cases among us our Parliament Men are chosen; but were by Birth and Blood, or by Dignities, High-Offices, *&c.* entitled to sit in the aforesaid Council, except one Part of the Island, who had by some former Constitution been a several distinct Government, and had a certain Number of Nobility of their own. This Part having by some ancient Treaty been join'd to the other, their whole Nobility were not intituled to the Right of sitting in Council as above; but they usually met by themselves upon such Occasions, and chose a certain Number to represent the whole Body. This Number was, as near as I can remember, Sixteen or thereabouts, not reckoning some who were singled out by the Sovereign to be advanc'd by new Titles, to be Members of the Great Body of the Hereditary Nobility; a Favour, which by the Stipulations of the said Agreement, was reserv'd to the Sovereign of that whole Island.

Now there happening, as I have noted, an Occasion to assemble this Great Council; the Nobility of that Part of the Island which were thus particularly constituted, behoved to meet, *as said is*, to elect the Number that were to represent them in the great Assembly; and the History of that Meeting having so many strange Circumstances in it, and making so much Noise in that Country, it cannot but be useful for us to be inform'd of it.

The Nobility of that Island, as I find it too much the Fate of all the Nobility in the World, were unhappily divided into Factions and separate Interests, and therefore before I proceed to the Relation, it will be necessary to give you a brief Account of these several Divisions, and as to the Characters of the Persons, it will necessarily fall into the Course of the Story.

The Divisions and Animosities which, as I say, were among the Nobility, were very unhappily occasion'd upon two several Foundations, and therefore consisted of two several Kinds.

This Island, it seems, was govern'd by a very glorious Queen, who however she was of the ancient Royal Blood of that Country, was yet for Reasons more especially respecting the Safety of the Country, plac'd upon the Throne by the Suffrage of the Nobility and People, without Regard to her Father or his Male Children, who for like Reasons of Safety they had Depos'd and render'd incapable: There being, it seems a Power reserv'd by the Constitution of that Place, to the said Nobility and People so to do a thing so like what we call in *England* Parliamentary Limitation, that it gives me great Reason to think the Power of Parliaments limiting the Crown is a natural Principle, and founded upon meer Original Light, since it should be so exactly establish'd in a Country so remote and so entirely excluded from Correspondence with *Europe*, as this of the Island of *Atalantis*.

The Queen of this Island, by the Assistance of exquisite Councellors, Punctual Management, and a mild merciful Administration, had obtain'd the entire Affection of Her Subjects at Home, and as long as she continued the Administration in those Hands she preserv'd that Affection very entire to herself; She had also, by the Conduct of eminent and most glorious Commanders, rendered her self Victorious abroad, in a long, terrible and expensive War, against the barbarous *Tartarian* Emperor, whose growing Greatness, had forced her Predecessor, in Conjunction with several neighbouring Nations, to have recourse to Arms, to keep up a Ballance of Power in that Part of the World, as long as those fortunate Generals commanded, her Affairs were blest by Sea and Land; till the *Barbarians* began to stoop their Pride, to be humbled, and they sought Peace, made great Offers of restoring the Kingdoms they had usurped, and of establishing a lasting Tranquillity in those Parts of the World.

How the Face of Affairs there altered, how some Factions prevailing at Home, made a Breach in all this blessed Harmony, how the faithful Councellors at Home were dismiss'd and disgrac'd, the victorious Generals Abroad ill used and ungratefully treated, by which the Publick Credit sunk at Home, the great Confederates of this glorious Queen were discouraged and allarmed, the *Barbarians* encouraged to hold out, carry on the War, and reject the Terms of

Peace, they would before have complied with: These are Things perhaps my stay in that Place not permitting me to get a full Account of, much less see the Issue of, I shall for the present omit, perhaps my next Voyage may more fully quallifie me to inform you.

My present Relation refers more especially to the Affair of the Election of those representing Nobles, which, as before, the Northern Part of the Island, by a late Treaty of Coalition, were obliged to send up as often as the Soveraign of the Country thought fit to Summon her Hereditary Council to meet, which Summons was generally once in Three Years.

To let you into the Nature of the unhappy Strife which is the Subject of my present Relation, it may be necessary to descend to a Historical Relation of some Facts for a few Years past, and to give the Characters of some Persons who have the principal Conduct in the present Affairs.

There had been a Contention in the last Election in the same Place, (we shall go no further back) of something of the like Nature with this; wherein the same Heat was unhappily breaking out against the Friends and Favourites of the great Queen of the Island, as had now come to a full height; it is too true, That the Factions which then agitated the Nobility being between the Court-Party then so called, and a flying Squadron of Noblemen, who were of the same general Denomination with themselves, that Breach tended so much to the dividing their Interest, that they could never effectually joyn it again, they made that Seperation of Affection then which they could never unite, let in those Enemies then which they could never get removed again, brought those Charges and Accusations against one another then which their Enemies have since made use off, and which they cannot now deny but are fatal to them.

The Parties are so naturally resembling our unhappy Divisions in *Britain*, have been so exactly pursued by our Methods, are so properly adapted to Persons as well as Things, so alike in Temper, Manners, Management and Design, to our Parties, of *Tory, Whig, High Church, Low Church, Old Whig, New Whig, High Flyer, Dissenter, Jacobite, Court, Country, Revolution, Union,* and the like. That to give the more lively Representation of them to your Minds, and to avoid the barbarous Words used in the Country, where the Language is altogether unknown to us, and unlike ours, I shall even call them by the same Names, giving a brief Description as I go on, and always desiring you to add a Subintelligitur for the word *Atalantick* to them all; as the

Atalantick Whigs, Atalantick Tories, Atalantick High Church, and so of all the rest: And whenever you meet with the Names or Distinctions of *Whig, Tory, High Church, Low Church*, &c. in this Discourse, the Author provides against any other Suggestion or Meaning, than that of the *Whigs, Tories, High Church, Low Church, Old Whig, New Whig, High Flyers, Dissenters, Jacobites*, &c. who are Inhabitants of the famous Island of *Atalantis Major*, situate beyond the North Cape, between the Degrees of 42 and 80 of Northern Latitude, as you sail from *China* into *Europe*, by the Streights of *Nassau*, the Island of *Nova Zembla*, (if it be an Island) and the like, being what we call the North-East Passages: And you cannot blame me for being thus Particular in this early Protestation, if you consider how ready the Men of this Age are to Censure, Condemn and Reproach, the Meaning of Authors, whether they themseves have any meaning or no. If any Man shall presume to say, there is no such Place, I may as readily answer their Presumption, by another less Criminal, *viz.* That they never have past that Way to *China*, and consequently cannot demonstrate the Truth of what they say.

Having thus premised what I think necessary, to fence this Work against the Malice of the Times, I am next to tell you, That I shall confine this Part of my Account to the Transactions of the Northern Part of this great Island, and therein to what happened in this Case of the Election of their Noble Councellors only; yet I must Hint a little at what had been transacting in the Southern Parts of the Island; and this is absolutely necessary, in order to make the other Accounts intelligible.

In order to this, you are to understand, That the Southern Part of the Island was the most remarkable of any, as to the Policy of their Government, and the Character of the People; and excepting *Englishmen* and *Polanders*, there is not such another Nation in the World: Here they reckoned about Fifty three several Sects, Divisions, and espoused Opinions in Religion, upon most of the Heads whereof the People actually seperated from one another; such as, (I.) *Churchmen*, and among them *High Church, Low Church, Non Jurors, Prelatists, Socinians, Arians, Arminians, Deists, Atheists, Immoralists, Flyers, Soul-Sleepers, Prophets*, &c. (2.) *Presbyterians*, and under that head all kind of Dissenters, *Cameronians, Independants, Anabaptists, Baptists, Seventh-Day-Men, Sabatarians, Donatists, Gnosticks, Antiprelatists, Muggletonians*, and various undistinguishable *Quakers* both wet and dry, *Sweet Singers, Family of Love, Christian Jews, Jewish Christians*, and the like. In the State, the Divisions were no less Fatal, or

the variety greater in Proportion, these we may, as I said before, call by
the Names which the like Factions are distinguish'd by here; such as
Tory, Whig, Low Church, Hot Whig, Old Whig, Modern Whig,
High Flyer, High Church, High Tory, a *Gillicranky,* a *Tantivy,*
Tackers, Non Jurors, Assassinators, Junto's, Squadroni, Court, Country,
Revolutionists, Non Resisters, Passive Obedience Men, and the like.

You may understand, that the Queen of the Island had thought fit
to change Hands in the Administration just before I came there, and
tho' it was given out that the change would not be from what we call
here a Whig to a Tory Ministry, in effect it past for no other, especially
for that the Whigs were generally laid by in every publick Matter, and
the Tories, or at least such as had appear'd with them were all taken in.

Among the Persons turn'd out of Employ, or very much envy'd in
it, we find two great Personages, Men of the greatest Eminency in their
Station that the Age had produc'd in that Island, their Country had no
Error to find in their Conduct except it were that it was so much in
debt to their Services, that they could not be capable of rewarding it,
therefore like the corrupted Nature of the whole Race of Man, they
hate the Men, as a late Author says, because they hate to be in debt
beyond the Power of Payment.

One of these presided over the Treasure, the other over the Army,
and except what may have happen'd since those days, their very Enemies
had not been able to assign any Reason from their own Behaviour, why
they dismist them. Of these more in the Process of the Story.

For the present it shall suffice to tell you, without other Preamble,
both these were by the Artifice of their Enemies, dispossess'd of the
Queen of the Island's Favour, and that with them fell the Juncto's and
Squadrons of their Friends in most Part of the Southern *Atalantis.*

In the North Part of the Island the Divisions of the Court had not
extended so far, at least they had not been push'd so vigorously, the
great Officers kept their Posts, whether Civil or Military, not the least
Alteration was made, except of a few inferiour Officers, and those but
casually; all seem'd to stand at a Stay till the Election of the noble
Councellors aforesaid, and till the sitting of the great Council, as above.

There were some of the Nobility of these Northern Parts that had
very much the Favour of their Prince, and by whom she had always
been directed in those things that related to that Part of Her
Dominions, These were,

I. The Duke *de Sanquarius,* a Northern Prince of great
Reputation who had the principal Trust in the Management of the late

Coalition, which, as is noted already, had formerly been made between this Northern Part of the Island and the Southern. This Prince was a Person of great Prudence and Policy, perfect Master of the Interest, Temper and Constitution of the Country and People; great and as a Master of his own Passions, that had an Insight into Persons as well as things, and was, without Dispute, the best qualify'd to manage that uneasy People, of any Man in that Part of the Island: He had a leading Interest among them, and us'd it with such Temper and such Clearness of Judgment, as seldom failed to bring to pass whatever he undertook. He was Viceroy in the great Meeting of the States of that Country, several times; in which he behav'd to the Satisfaction of his Sovereign and the general Good, even to the Confession of his Enemies, after the separate Government of that Part of the Island ceas'd he was receiv'd very graciously by the Queen, and made principal Secretary of State.

2. The Earl of *Stairdale* was another, a Nobleman of extraordinary Merit, distinguish'd for a thousand good Qualities; affable, generous, exceeding curteous, steddy in a sound Principle, wise above his Age, brave above his Neighbours. His Family had been famous for the Gown, he was like to make it more so by the Sword: He had at this time a very honourable Command in the Armies of *Atalantis Major*, and being the same thing as we call a Lieutenant General, was employed against the *Tartarians*.

3. The Earl of *Crawlinfordsay* a Nobleman of a most ancient Race, being the first of his Degree in the whole *Atalantis Major*, an honest, bold, gallant Person; he had so much Goodness in his Temper, Courage in his Heart, and Honesty in his Face, that made all Men love him; he was true to his Sovereign, and tho' his Fortunes too depended upon the *Court*, being Captain of the Queen's Guards, yet so true to his Honour, that he scorn'd to sacrifice his Principle to his Interest; had too much Courage to be bully'd, and too much Honesty to be brib'd; too much Wit to be wheedl'd and too much Warmth to forbear telling it in the Teeth of those that try'd all those ways to bring him into their Party.

4. The Prince of *Greeniccio* of the ancient Blood of *Agyllius*. This was a young Nobleman of great Hopes, and from whom great things were expected, an account of the very Race he was descended from. Had he inherited the Principles of his Family as he did the Honour and Estate, he must have been the Head of that very Party he now acted against, being the same for whose Cause two of his greatest Ancestors at least had both ventured and lost their Lives, but Grace not going by

Generation, nor Vertue by Inheritance any more in that Country than in ours. He neither own'd their Cause or imitated their Vertue, but gave himself up first to all Manner of Vice, and then with his Morals abandoned his Principles, flew in the Face of his Grandfathers injured *Grave*, join'd with his Murtherers, and the abhorr'd Betrayers of his Country, and plac'd himself at the Head of that very Party who had trampled on the Blood of his Family as well as Nation. He was in Temper brave but rash, had more Courage than Generosity, more Passion than Prudence, and more Regard to his Resentment than to his Honour; he was proud without Merit, ambitious without Prospect, revengeful without Injury; he would resent without Affront, and quarrel without Cause, would embroil himself without Reason, and come out of it without Honour: His Courage was rather in his Blood than in his Head, and as his Actions run often before his Thoughts, so his Thoughts often run before his Reason; yet he was pushing and that supply'd very much his Want of Policy; but he discover'd the Errors of his Judgment by the Warmth of his Behaviour in every thing he did he sought no Disguise, every Man knew him better than himself, and he never could be in a Plot because he conceal'd nothing.

He was a General in the Armys of *Atalantis Major* and excepting the chief Command of an Army, was very well fitted for the Field: He had behav'd himself very well on several Occasions against the *Tartarians*, and unless his ill Fate should place him above being commanded, he might in time be a great Man; at present, having all the Fire of a General without the Flegm, his great Misfortune and the only Thing that can ruin him is, That he thinks himself qualifyed to Command, and cannot bear the Lustre of their Merit that excel him.

5. The E. of *Marereskine.* This was a Nobleman whose Character is not so easy to describe; he appear'd in the Service of the Queen of the Island, but was suspected to lean to the *Tartars,* whose Interest he was known formerly to espouse; He was proud, peevish, subtle and diligent, affected more the Statesman than the Soldier, and therefore aim'd at the Place the Duke *de Sanquharius* enjoy'd of Secretary of State, but had not yet had his Ambition gratifyed.

You are to note also that the Queen of the Island had for several Years committed the Administration of her Affairs to two extraordinary Persons, Natives of the South Parts of the Island. The Prince *de Heymuthius* and the E. of *Dolphinus,* their Characters may be confin'd to this: In short, the first commanded all the Armies of *Atalantis Major,* and was Captain General and Commander in Chief;

the other, High Keeper of the Treasury of the Island, the greatest General and the greatest Minister of State the Island ever knew, who had raised the Glory of their Mistress, and the Honour of their Country, to the greatest Pitch the Age has ever seen; whose Merit I can no more describe than the Nation can requite.

Tho' these Characters seem to take up too much room in this Tract, yet it could not be avoided, it being impossible to let you into a true Notion of the Farce that was acted afterwards if the Actors had not been thus described.

Greeniccio was a Peer of the whole Island, and therefore had no Vote in the Northern Election, being one of the Hereditary Council aforesaid; but taking upon him the absolute Direction of the Affair, tho' he had really, as above, nothing to do with it, he rendred himself at the City Reeky, the Capital of that Part of the Kingdom a few Days before the Election.

Marereskine, who had really a Voice in the Election, was there before him, and had busily embark'd *Bellcampo*, Lord of the Isles, and Brother to *Greeniccio*, to make Parties, and prepare Parties, sollicite Votes, get Proxies, and the like, about the Countries.

This *Bellcampo*, Lord of the Isles, was an insinuating self-interested Man, had little Fortune of his own, but resolved to raise himself which side soever got upmost: He run with every Stream, kept fair with every Side, spoke smoothly to all, meant Service to none, his dear Self excepted. By this means he got up from one Step to another to some good Employments, which his Interest and Diligence procured for him rather than his Sincerity; for he was first made a Peer on the Side he now acted against, and now a Judge acting against the Side made him a Peer, and the like.

These were the Instruments of the Fate of North *Atalantis*; *Marereskine* acted one Part, *Greeniccio* another: And here it is, as I said before, that the differing Parties, appeared so like our *Whig* and *Tory*, *Episcopal* and *Presbyterian*, that I cannot better describe them to you than by the same Names, only with this Difference, That all the *Tories* and *Episcopal* People in North *Atalantis* were *Tartarians* profestly, and boldly owned themselves for the *Tartarian* Emperor.

And now the two last mentioned Engines, having acted covertly for some time, which they had the better opportunity to do, because they had both appeared among the other Party, *which now I'll call Whigs*; before, the first of these carried it stiff and forward when he talked with the great Officers, or such Lords as had some Dependance upon the Court: He told them of what the Queen expected from them, what was their Duty to do, that they would find it their Interest to do so and so, that they might consider in Time what they had to do, and the like: When he talk'd with any of the *Whig* Lords, for there was a Squadron of them left, that had a great sway yet in the Country, then he would talk of him, and Party and Queen, as one Knot, in the plural Number, most haughtily, thus: We are resolved to do so and so, and we must have none but such or such.

The *Lord of the Isles*, at the same time acted his usual Flattery on both Sides, insinuating to the *Whigs*, that they were in No Danger; that there was not the least Design against them or their Liberties; that the Queen was resolved to change Hands, but would not change Principles; that their Church should not be touched, that their Priviledges should not in the least be infringed, and that they need not fear. One time, this Politick Peer, as he would be thought, was very handsomely met with, the Story is this, whether designedly or no it matters not. He was one Day in Company with some of the North *Atalantis* Ministers, for there just as here, they have one Church established in the North, and another in the South of the Island; He used all his Art in persuading the Ministers that they should be easie, that they should fear nothing, that there was no Design to give them the least Disturbance; that this was a Politick Turn, not a Religious, and that they should do well to be satisfied, and to satisfie their People that they were in no Danger, and should fear nothing. One of the Ministers, who had heard him very patiently, but saw easily through all his cunning; returns, Thus my Lord, shall I tell your Lordship a Story, and then he goes on with it. We had in former times, one *John* —— who had the Honour to be his Majesty's Hangman in this City. This good Man had a most gentle easie Way of executing his Office; for when the poor People came into his Hands, and were to Die by his Operations, as many honest Men did in those cruel Days, (this by the way was home to his Lordship, for that this very *John* cut off his Lordships Grandfather's Head) all the while he was a fitting Things for the Execution of his Office, he would smile upon them, talk kindly to them, bid them not be afraid, Come, come, fear nothing, trust God, and the like: Then bringing them to the foot of the Ladder, he would still say, Be not afraid, come, come, fear nothing, step up one step, do not fear, trust in God, and so to another step and another; and just thus he carried 'em on, till at last, with the very Words in his Mouth, Fear nothing, he turn'd them off.

The honest Minister made no Application of the Story, much less took Notice, how his Lordship's own Grandfather not only fell by the same Hangman, but by the same Party that he then espoused: But he had too much Sense, and was too closely touch'd with the Story, not to make the Application himself; so he left the Ministers, giving no Reply at all to the Story.

This Story grew so popular, especially being printed by the Reviewer of that Country, that the Lord of the Isles could make nothing of his Design whenever he talk'd of the good Design of the Party; he was only laugh'd at, and bid remember his Grandfathers Hangman; so he became useless.

The Prince *Greeniccio* and the Earl of *Marereskine* then took upon them the Manegement of the whole Affair. They took publick Apartments in the Town, kept an affected State, called themselves the Queen's Managers, and had a Court as great as if they had been really so; they received the Visits of the Nobility with an Air of Majesty, and affected Gravity; and under this assumed Authority they took upon them to Closet the Noblemen when they came to pay their Respects to them; not to ask who they would give their Votes for, or to sollicit them to Vote for this or that, but in a Style haughty and insolent, especially to the Men of the greatest Character and Merit.

Greeniccio had several Ruffles with some of the Nobility, of which it may not be amiss to give some Account, because it may be for the Advantage of our Nobility to know, how Persons of like Quality in that Country can submit to be treated.

Bradalbino, a Nobleman of great Age and Authority in that Island, expected to be One of the Sixteen, and was told he was in the List; when he comes to Discourse with the Prince *de Greeniccio*, he tells him, Very plainly, That he thought it would be much for the Publick Good to put in Two or Three Lords, such as *Leslynus*, and one of the Family of *Boiilio*, being Men he thought could not properly be left out, and that if they were in, he would come into all the rest: The Prince, in a kind of Passion swore, By G——d, not of them; and but for naming them, laid aside *Bradalbino* himself.

Another Lord being an Officer in the Army, having the Court List proposed to him, answered, My Lord you kno' *Leslynus* is my General and Commander in Chief, and he could not as he commanded under him but Vote for his General, &c. *Greeniccio* in a fury returns, God d——n your General, what do you tell us of Commander in Chief? If that be all, we shall soon get you another Commander in Chief; you shall Vote for none such as he.

Another Lord expostulated with him a little to admit such and such with the Men he proposed; he answers, My Lord, I am no Hypocrite, I am above-board; this is the List we will have; the Q....n approves of it, and I will have no other; and swearing again, By-G——d, says he, 'Tis indifferent to me, keep out but the Men we are against; but I will have no *Go....phin* Men, no *Ma....bro'* Men, no Squadron Men, in short, no *Whigs* of any Denomination; as for the rest, it is indifferent, any but them. How, my Lord, says this Nobleman, What will you take *Tartarians*, (that is, as our *Jacobites*) rather than the honest Gentlemen that have been so true to the *Atalantic* Interest: I care not what they are, says the Prince, so they be none of these.

Among the Noblemen that he used with the most rudeness, was the Earl of *Crawlindford.* Whether he thought to Insult this faithful Nobleman, because he knew his Fortunes were low, and that he depended on the Court; or whether he took this Advantage to use him Ill on Account of an old Ruffle, in which he having challenged the Earl to Fight; and the Earl appearing ready to defend his Honour with his Sword; the Prince ashamed of the needless Quarrel, had declin'd it again, and came off but, so, so; choosing to risk his Honour rather than his Life; what was the Reason, Authors do not agree about; But the Prince used him most scandalously. The Earl prest him hard, and told him, How he had on all Occasions shewn himself faithful to the Queen, and to the *Atalantic* Interest, that he had gone into all such Measures as were for the Service of both, that he thought he had some Claim to be trusted in the Service of his Country.

The Prince told him plainly, He might set his Heart at rest, for he should not be one. He ask'd him, What Reason was assigned, what Objections were against him. The Prince, with much more Plainness than Prudence replies, They knew he was under Obligations to the President of the Treasure, and the great Commander of the Army; and he did not know but they might come to bring a Charge or Impeachment against them in the great *Atalantic* Council; and he would have no Body chosen but such as would give their Words they would come into such Measures. The Earl told him, If any thing could be offered to prove them Guilty, or any Crimes were made appear, he scorned to be so much obliged to any Man as not to dare to do Justice; and that he would readily join in an Impeachment, if there was Reason sufficient to Charge them; and to refuse him otherwise, implied, they wanted Crime and just Ground to form the Impeachment upon, and therefore must choose such a Set of Men as would Impeach innocent Men blindfold, to please a Party. The Prince told him, That the Resolution was to Impeach them, and he would have none chosen that would not agree to it. What, right or wrong, my Lord! says the Earl; to which the Prince, not suddenly replying, the Earl went on, Let what will come of it, and tho' I should lose all, nay, tho' I were to beg my Bread, I'll never submit to such base Terms, and so defied him. The Prince told him, It should be the worse for him; and there they parted.

There was a short Dispute between the Prince and the Earl of *Stairdale*; but the Earl had so much more Honesty than the Party, and so much more Sense and Wit than the Prince, that indeed he cared not much to talk to him, but left him to *Mareskine*. He was too hard for them both, and having baffled them in Discourse, he was no more to be Bullied by them, than he was to be Wheedled; he told 'em plainly, They were betraying their Country, selling and sacrificing the Priviledges of the Nobility, making themselves Tools to a Party, and giving themselves up in a base Manner to the Pleasure of a few Men, who, when they had got their Will would contemn them, would love the Folly, but P....s upon the Fools; and as to their List, he scorn'd to come into it, or into any of their menacing Measures. This put a short end to their Attempts upon him; and indeed, had the other Lords been advised by this gallant Gentleman, they had broke all their Schemes; but they were not all united in their Resolutions, or equally determined in their Measures.

Thus they went on, *Mareskine* mannag'd the most mildly; yet he told the Nobility of his Acquaintance: That the List was determined, that the Q....n expected they should Vote them all: that they would have no Mixtures: that her Majesty would have nothing to do with the *Whig* Lords, but there was other Work to do now than usual: Discoursing with some of the Lords, who were G———als in the Army, he told them plainly, They had resolved to Impeach the great Commander; and that it could not be expected, those who had Commands under him, and were Awed by him, should do Justice in that Case. They had often the Question put to them, What it was the great Commander, or the Keeper of the Treasure, had done, that they were to be Impeach'd for: But they could never be brought to offer the least tollerable Reason, except that the Prince *Greeniccio* let fall in his Passion sometimes, of which he had no manner of Government, That he had used him ill abroad.

Some, who had more nicely enquired into the Particulars of the ill Usage which was the Cause of this Resentment, have given the oddest contradicting Accounts of it that any History can Parallel: As first, That the great Commander had restrained the rashness of this young Hotspur General, who being but a Boy in Experience, compared to the Commander, was always for pushing into the Heart of *Tartary* with the Army; not considering, That to run up a Hundred Mile into the Country, and leave the Enemies Towns untaken, and their Armies in a Condition to Recruit, cut off their Convoys and Communication, and make their Subsistence impracticable, was the ready way to destroy them, as has been seen by a woful Example in *Spain*. But the General was wiser, and regarded more the Safety of the Army, and the Honour of his Mistress; and therefore, by the unanimous Approbation of all the allied Generals, (for it was not his own single Opinion) and according to the just Rules of War, went on gradually to take their fortified Towns, and ruin their Defences on the Frontiers, that at last, he might have a sure and easie Conquest of the rest: This was one Pretence. The second was just the Reverse of this: For at a great Battle with the *Tartarians*, the Commander having resolved to attack the Enemy in their advantageous Camp, and having drawn up in Battalia his whole Army, he gives the Post of Honour to the Prince, appointing him, with a select Body of the best Troops in the Army, to fall on upon the Right, and Charge the Enemy, while other Generals did the like, and with equal Hazard and more real Danger, on the Left. There was not a Gentleman in the Enemies Army but would have taken this as the greatest Testimony of his General's Esteem, and would have thought any Man in the Army his mortal Enemy that should have gone about to have deprived him of it. Nor was there any Man in the *Attalantick* Army, who did not take it as an Evidence of the great Opinion the Commander had of the Prince's Courage; and all the World talked of it as the greatest Honour could possibly be done the Prince.

Had not the Commander taken all needful Care to have him well back'd, had he not given him the best Troops in the Army to act under him, had he not plac'd a great Body of Horse to support him, had he not equally prest the Enemy in other Places, to prevent their doubling their Strength in that Part; had he done any Thing but what a Man of Honour would have thought himself obliged by, there might have been some Reason to Object: But to call giving a General a Post of Honour sacrificing him, because it was attended with Danger, is referr'd to the Determination of the Soldierly Part of Mankind. And as it would be laught at in *Tartary*, in *France*, and in *Britain*, where such Things are very seldom heard of; so I can assure the Reader, it was sufficiently laugh'd at in *Attalantis Major*, and the Prince of *Greeniccio* is become most intollerably ridiculous by the taking Notice of it.

Hence all Men in the Island of *Atalantick Major* conclude, he has Rashness without Courage, Fury without Honour, Passion without Judgment, and less regard to his Character than to his Resentment.

Nor has the Vanity of this Prince appeared less in his not sticking openly to discover, That he aims at the Command in general; that he thinks himself equally qualified for a Post of so great Trust, and that regard is not had to his Merit that he is so long suffered to Serve under another; at the same time not enquiring, whether the Allies of the Queen would have equal Confidence in him, as in the great Commander, on whose Judgment, all the Princes and States of the North have so much Dependance, to whom they have so chearfully committed their Troops, and under whose Conduct they have had such wonderful Success against the *Tartarian* Emperor: But it never was this Prince's Talent to think too much, his Heat was always too volatile, and his Head too light for his Hands.

We have brought him now to the Conclusion of the Affair: Having gone through his Catechizing of the Nobility, in which indeed they of his own Party appeared of a Temper patient and debased, below the true Spirit of Noblemen; (at least, God be praised, below the ancient Temper and Gallantry of the Nobility of *Great Britain*) Having come now to the Day for the Choice, which was the 10th Day of their Sixth Month, but as I suppose *November*: There appeared at the Place 33 Noblemen, besides the 16 which were chosen, and who every one Voted for themselves and for one another; so that of about 130 Noblemen, which they say are in the North Part of *Attalantis Major*, only 49 appeared.

There was a great Meeting of the honest Part of the Nobility, at another Place, to consult what was proper to be done in this new-fashion'd Way of Proceeding: Some proposed to go down in a Body to the Place where the rest were met, and protest against the Illegality of the Choice; that to impose a List upon the Nobility was not agreeable to the Nature of a free Choice; and that therefore they should protest, That whoever were returned by Virtue of that Meeting, were not legally Chosen, and had no right to Sit in the great Council of the Nobility.

This was sound Advice: But unhappily it was not resolved upon; and some they say slipt out of the Meeting for fear of Resentment, and went down and voted, and came up again *incognito*.

The rest resolved to send Two of their Number down to the Meeting, and offer their Service to Vote with them, provided they would declare their Measures: and that those that might be chosen would declare themselves for the true *Atalantick* Succession, against a pretending Claimant, who was then sheltred among the *Tartarians*: But they could receive no Satisfaction even to this so reasonable Request. But the Prince of *Greeniccio*, who had no right to Vote himself, yet run up and down, as a Broker, or a Party-Sollicitor, whispering and prompting, from one to another, to Influence and Settle them, (for some began to waver.) This Prince, I say, giving an answer, insolent and haughty, *like himself.* The Noble Persons that went, came away, and contented themselves, with telling them, they would having nothing to do with them. Thus, being but a Rump of the Nobility, they gave up their Liberties, Voted as they were commanded to do, signed a Roll of Names, and this they called a Choice.

The Number of the dissenting Nobility were about Twenty six, whereof Five did at last comply with their List, as they thought, being in publick Commands, supposing it might give a Handle to their Enemies, to misrepresent them to their Soveraign; but they nevertheless, upon all Occasions, testified their Dislike and Abhorrence of the Method, and of the Conduct of those concern'd in it.

Among those said Dissenters, were Two Dukes, One Marquis, Sixteen Earls, and Six Lords, besides many others, who were Absent.

We might be large in describing, and giving Characters of these dissenting Nobility. Among them we could not escape the Prince *de Rosymonte*, a Person, for Blood and Birth, eminent in that Country, more for his own excellent and inimitable Virtues, Grave, Sober, Judicious, even from his Youth, of whom one of the *Atalantick* Poets gave this bright Character.

Grave without Age, without Experience wise.

He was President of the Royal Council of that Country even while he was very young, an Honour the greatest of the Nobility were well pleased to see him adorned with, and made no Scruple to sit below him: His distinguish'd Modesty and Humility in all his publick Appearances, recommends him to the Affections of the whole Country; and tho' the Fortunes of his Family have suffered by the Disasters of the Times, yet he supports a handsome Figure suitable to the Dignity of his Character, Rich without Gaiety, Great without Affectation, Plentiful without Profusion, letting the World see he knows how and when, and to what Pitch to appear that when he pleases to be at Large, he can do it like a wise Man, or Retrench, he can do it like a Prince. It might be said, as a finishing stroke to his Character, he is just the Reverse of *Greeniccio*, for he is Fire without Thunder, Brave without Fury, Great without Pride, Gay without Vanity, Wise without Affectation, knows how to Obey and how to Command; he knows great Things enough to manage them, and is so Master of himself, as not to let them manage him; he knows how to be a Courtier without Ambition, and to Merit Favour rather than to seek it; he scorns to push his Fortunes over the Belly of his Principles, ever Faithful to himself, and by consequence to all that Trust him; he has too great a Value for Merit to envy it even in his Enemy, and too low Thoughts of the Pride and Conceit of Men without Merit, to approve of it even in his Friends.

This Noble Person appears at the Head of the dissenting Nobility: Nor does it lessen his Zeal for the Principles of Liberty, or the present Establishment of Religion in his Country; that some of his Ancestors, otherwise Noble, Brave and Great, appear'd on the other side; since the Liberties of his Country are the Center of his Actions, and the Prosperity of all Men the mark he aims at.

It may be a Character to the rest of the dissenting Lords, to say of them in general, That they were such as took a particular Pleasure in being Patrons of Virtue as well as Patrons of Liberty: That they were Men generally speaking distinguish'd for their constant Loyalty to their Prince, but ever with a view to the Fundamental Laws: That they had always Wisdom enough to know their Countries Rights, and Courage enough to defend them; Men of Honour, Men of Prudence, Men of Resolution: In short, They were Men admirably suited to the Character of their Leader; as he on the other hand, thought it his Honour to be at the Head of so illustrious a Body of Men, equally valuable for their Virtue, Capacities, Wisdom and Integrity.

It cannot be forgotten; That as these Noble Persons were Zealous for the Liberties of their Country, so truly they were Men that had the greatest Interest in it, having separately considered the best Estates of the whole Nobility, of that Country and joined together, were able to Buy twice their Number in the whole Assembly. It is true, that Estate is not any just Addition to the Character of a Person; but it will for ever remain a Truth; And all Nations will shew a regard to it, *viz.* that those may be supposed to be the most proper Persons to be trusted with the Conservation of the Liberties of their Country, who have by their Birth and Inheritance the largest Shares in the Possession of it.

This is illustrated by the Practice of that happy Country we live in, where this Story may perhaps be read, and where very lately, a Law has been made, to unquallifie all such to represent their Country in the Legislation and Power of raising Taxes, who are not possessed of such or such a Porportion in the Lands of their Country, as may suppose them Persons made naturally anxious for the Welfare of the whole, in regard to the Preservation of their Property. Unhappy *Atalantis!* Had such a Law pass'd for the Qualification of those Noblemen, who should be elected to the great Royal Council of thy Country; and should the Nobility so to be chosen have been limited to but one hundred *Perialo's* (a Gold Coin in that Country amounting by Estimation to about 2000 *l.* a Year Sterling) of yearly Estate in Lands, how few of the Sixteen now chosen could have shewn themselves in that august Meeting.

On the contrary, several of those now sent up, were not able to put themselves into a Posture to undertake the Journey, till they had sold the Magazines of Corn which they had laid up for the Year's Subsistance of their Families, or mortgaged their small Estates to borrow Money for the Expence.

Nor is it doubted in the least, but when those poor Noblemen come to find some of their *Tartarian* Expectations frustrated, with which it is manifest they were very Big when they went up; they will sorely regret the Misfortune of their Election; since they must be thereby so reduced, as almost to want Subsistance for their Families; and as for the Debts contracted, it is impossible some of them should ever Pay them.

It has been a too unhappy Truth in other Places as well as in *Atalantis Major,* That in such popular Elections, whether of Noblemen or others, Men are deluded with the Notion, that to be chosen by their Country to these great Councils of the Nation, must so recommend them, or make them so necessary to the State, to the Government, or the Ministers of State, that they cannot fail to make their Fortunes and raise Estates by their very Appearance: But this is so constantly found to fail, and so many have been almost ruin'd by the Expences they have been at to make a Figure as they call it, and to appear at Court like themselves on such Occasions, that it seems wonderful that Persons of Quality, who know their own Circumstances, and whose Fortunes, through the Disasters of their Families, may not be equal to their Dignity, should on so vain a Presumption push themselves upon the necessity of compleating their own Ruin, beggering their Families, and leaving their Posterity an Estate in Titles and Coronets, Things without the Support of competent Estates the most despicable in the World.

It might be very useful to our Readers, and perhaps something instructing might be gathered from it, with respect to the Affairs of *Europe* at this Time, to give some Account here of the Success of these strange Proceedings; what Figure these People made, when they came to Court, how they behav'd themselves when they came into the great Council, how they were made Tools there to the Politicians of those Times, even to act against their Interest, their Country, their own Designs.

In doing this, it would appear, How some of the Sixteen, more particularly known to be in the *Tartarian* Interest, and who had all along declared themselves for the Person and Title of the pretending Prince, who, as is noted before, put in a Claim to the Succession of the Throne: How these, I say, went up to the great Council, wheedled by the Subtilties of *Greeniccio*, and his Agents, to believe seriously that they went up directly to declare his Title; that they should be the Men that should have the Honour to declare his Right in the great Council of the Nobility; and that he should for the future own his Restoration, his Glory, and his Crown, to their Loyalty and steddy acting for him. This, they did not doubt, should tend not to their Honour only, but to the raising their decay'd Fortunes, for they were miserably Poor; since he could do no less than confer the greatest Trusts upon Persons who had with so much Fidelity acted for his Glory and Interest.

It would also to the eternal Shame and Disappointment of the *Atalantic Jacobites*, (if I may so call them) necessarily follow, that the History of their Conduct should come in at the same time to be considered, *viz.* How just the contrary to all this, and against the very Nature of the Thing they were obliged, even among the very first of their Transactings in their Publick Station, as Members of the great Council aforesaid, to appear in a Publick Address to the Soveraign of the Country, in which they were brought in recognizing Her just Title to Reign, (which they in their Hearts abhorr'd) promising to Stand by and Defend that Title with all their Might, (which they had hoped to see overthrown) engaging to assist Her to the utmost, against that very pretending Claimant as above, (who they Reverence as their lawful Prince) and to carry on the War with Vigour against the *Tartarian*

Emperor (that very Prince on whose Power they depended for the carrying on their Designs).

Had any *British*-Man of Sense, that understands the Language of the Countenance, but seen the Astonishment, the Chagrin, the Vexation and Anguish of Soul, that appear'd on the Faces of these *Atalantic* Noblemen, at this surprizing Event; how they gnashed their Teeth for Anger, and curst the Hour that ever they were Members of this grand Council; how they Bann'd, (an *Atalantis* Word used there, for what we call Swearing and Damning in our Country;) how they raged at *Greenwiccio*, and the *Lord of the Isles*, who they said had Betray'd them; and how strangely they look'd, upon the solemn Occasion of presenting this Address to their Soveraign: I say, could their Countenances but have been read by any in our Country, they would have taken them for Furies rather than Men, or for Men under some Frenzy, ridden with the Night-Mare, or scared with some Apparition.

It was not less odd, to see the Conduct of *Greeniccio*; for tho' he had not less Mischief in his Heart, yet it was of another Kind; and tho' he had not the same View of the Succession, nor perhaps was directly in the *Tartarian* Interest, and therefore shew'd no Pity, or Sympathy with the Mortifications of the other, yet he met with Disappointments equally perplexing, and which made him heartily repent the length he had gone; but as it was in his Nature to be rash, it was impossible to prevent his being disappointed almost in every Thing he went about: For it is in *Atalantis Major* just as it is in other Parts of the World, *viz.* That rash headstrong unthinking Tempers, generally precipitate themselves into innumerable Mischiefs, which Prudence and Patience would evite and prevent; and also, that these furious rash People, as they are hot and impatient under those Mischiefs when they are surprised with them, so they are not always the best able to extricate and deliver themselves.

This will necessarily lead us to a long History of the Disappointments he met with:

I. In his Project of charging and impeaching his General, and the great Testador, or —— of the Nations Treasure, which he could never, either bring Crime enough to justifie, or Friends enough to joyn in, and make it terrible.

2. How he was disappointed in his ambitious Views of being made General against the *Tartarians*; whereas, he had on the contrary, the Mortification, to see the great Commander continu'd, with an

addition of Generallissimo to his Titles of Command; and himself, like what we used to call in *England*, being *Kick'd up Stairs*, sent out of the Way with a Feather in his Cap, and the Title of General, to carry on a remote Unfortunate, and never-to-be Successful War in *Japan*, and the Lord knows where, among Barbarians and Savages.

This was not all; When upon his embracing this Title, which his Temper (naturally Ambitious) jumpt at, and eagerly closed with, he began to choose Officers, name Regiments, and draw out Forces to form the Army he was to Command, he found the new Generalissimo had supplanted him there too; for he had not only prevailed with the Queen of the Country, not to draw away any of the old Troops then establish'd for the *Tartarian* War, of which this *Gew-Gaw-General* fancied to himself he should form his Army: But the Generalissimo obtain'd, That the best Troops which were remaining in *Atalantis Major*, should be sent over to strengthen the Army against the *Tartars*: So that this new General was likely to go away to *Japan* without any Army, but such Troops as her *Atalantic* Majesty and Her Allies had hired from the *Emperor of China*, and such other People; and he had none but Strangers, Barbarians and Mercenaries to Command.

It is true, That his Design of drawing off the Troops from the *Tartarian* War, to carry on a *Wild-Goose War* in the remotest Parts of *Japan*, was like the rest of his Schemes, so inconsistent, so destructive to the general Design of the War, and would in all its probable Circumstances be so dangerous to the true Interest of *Atalantis Major*, That notwithstanding some had persuaded the Government to a *New Scheme*, and that the War was to be pushed on *ESPECIALLY* in *Japan* (a Thing which perhaps some encouraged at first, on purpose to draw him in to accept of that Command, which many of inferiour Rank to him had declin'd) yet when they came to look nearer into the Thing, and to see the fatal Prospect of weakning the Forces on the *Tartarian* side, while the *Emperor of Tartary* at the same Time was vigilant and forward in encreasing his Preparations, they soon found the Representations of the Generalissimo had such Weight in them, and were founded so much upon their general Good, that they thought fit to alter their Measures.

How *Greeniccio* was thus disappointed; how he resented it; how to Pacifie him, an Appearance of drawing some Troops together was made; how he was at last sent away with a whole Ship load of fine Promises; as he on the contrary loaded the same Ship back with a full

Freight of Schemes, Projects and Rhodomontadoes; how he went; what he did, and what he did not; how *Tinker* like, he mended the Work of those that went before, and left it for others to mend after him; these are Things I may give you a farther Account of when I return from my next Progress to that glorious Country of *Atalantis Major.*

AUGUSTA TRIUMPHANS:

OR, THE

WAY

TO MAKE

LONDON

THE MOST FLOURISHING

City in the Universe

A man who has the public good in view, ought not in the least to be alarmed at the tribute of ridicule which scoffers constantly pay to projecting heads. It is the business of a writer, who means well, to go directly forward, without regard to criticism, but to offer his thoughts as they occur; and if in twenty schemes he hits but on one to the purpose, he ought to be excused failing in the nineteen for the twentieth sake. It is a kind of good action to mean well, and the intention ought to palliate the failure; but the English, of all people in the world, show least mercy to schemists, for they treat them in the vilest manner; whereas other nations give them fair play for their lives, which is the reason why we are esteemed so bad at invention.

I have but a short time to live, nor would I waste my remaining thread of life in vain, but having often lamented sundry public abuses, and many schemes having occurred to my fancy, which to me carried an air of benefit, I was resolved to commit them to paper before my departure, and leave, at least, a testimony of my good will to my fellow-creatures.

But of all my reflections, none was more constantly my companion than a deep sorrow for the present decay of learning among us, and the manifest corruption of education; we have been a brave and learned people, and are insensibly dwindling into an effeminate, superficial race. Our young gentlemen are sent to the universities, it is true, but not under restraint or correction as formerly; not to study, but to drink; not for furniture for the head, but a feather for the cap, merely to say they have been at Oxford or Cambridge, as if the air of those places inspired knowledge without application. It is true we ought to have those places in reverence for the many learned men they have sent us; but why must we go so far for knowledge? Why should a young gentleman be sent raw from the nursery to live on his own hands, to be liable to a thousand temptations, and run the risk of being snapped up by sharping jilts, with which both universities abound, who make our youth of fortune their prey, and have brought misery into too many good families? Not only the hazard of their healths from debauches of both kinds, but the waste of their precious time renders the sending them so far off very hazardous. Why should such a metropolis as London be without an university? Would it not save considerably the expense we are at in sending our young gentlemen so far from London? Would it not add to the lustre of our state, and cultivate politeness among us? What benefits may we not in time expect from so glorious a design? Will not London become the scene of science? And what reason have we but to hope we may vie with any neighbouring nations? Not that I would have Oxford or Cambridge neglected, for the good they have done. Besides, there are too many fine endowments to be sunk; we may have universities at those places and at London too, without prejudice. Knowledge will never hurt us, and whoever lives to see an university here, will find it give quite another turn to the genius and spirit of our youth in general.

How many gentlemen pass their lives in a shameful indolence, who might employ themselves to the purpose, were such a design set on foot? Learning would flourish, art revive, and not only those who studied would benefit by it, but the blessing would be conveyed to others by conversation.

And in order to this so laudable design, small expense is required; the sole charge being the hire of a convenient hall or house, which, if they please, they may call a college. But I see no necessity the pupils have to lie or diet there; that may be done more reasonably and conveniently at home, under the eye of their friends; their only necessary business at college being to attend their tutors at stated hours; and, bed and board excepted, to conform themselves to college laws, and perform the same exercises as if they were actually at Oxford or Cambridge.

Let the best of tutors be provided, and professors in all faculties encouraged; this will do a double good, not only to the instructed, but to the instructors. What a fine provision may here be made for numbers of ingenious gentlemen now unpreferred? And to what a height may even a small beginning grow in time?

As London is so extensive, so its university may be composed of many colleges, quartered at convenient distances: for example, one at Westminster, one at St. James's, one near Ormond-street, that part of the town abounding in gentry; one in the centre of the Inns of Court, another near the Royal Exchange, and more if occasion and encouragement permit.

The same offices and regulations may be constituted, cooks, butlers, bed-makers, &c., excepted, as at other universities. As for endowment, there is no need, the whole may be done by subscription, and that an easy one, considering that nothing but instructions are paid for.

In a word, an academical education is so much wanted in London, that everybody of ability and figure will readily come into it; and I dare engage, the place need but be chosen, and tutors approved of, to complete the design at once.

It may be objected, that there is a kind of university at Gresham college, where professors in all sciences are maintained, and obliged to read lectures every day, or at least as often as demanded. The design is most laudable, but it smells too much of the *sine cure*; they only read in term time, and then their lectures are so hurried over, the audience is little the better. They cannot be turned out, it is a good settlement for life, and they are very easy in their studies when once fixed. Whereas were the professorship during good behaviour, there would be a study to maintain their posts, and their pupils would reap the benefit.

Upon second thought, I think colleges for university education might be formed at Westminster, Eton, the Charter-house, St. Paul's, Merchant Tailors, and other public schools, where youth might begin and end their studies; but this may be further considered of.

I had almost forgot the most material point, which is, that his majesty's sanction must first be obtained, and the university proposed have power to confer degrees, &c., and other academical privileges.

As I am quick to conceive, I am eager to have done, unwilling to overwork a subject; I had rather leave part to the conception of the readers, than to tire them or myself with protracting a theme, as if, like a chancery man or a hackney author, I wrote by the sheet for hire. So let us have done with this topic, and proceed to another, which is:—

A proposal to prevent murder, dishonour, and other abuses, by erecting an hospital for foundlings.

It is needless to run into a declamation on this head, since not a sessions passes but we see one or more merciless mothers tried for the murder of their bastard children; and, to the shame of good government, generally escape the vengeance due to shedders of innocent blood. For it is a common practice now among them to hire a set of old beldams, or pretended midwives, who make it their trade to bring them off for three or four guineas, having got the ready rote of swearing the child was not at its full growth, for which they have a hidden reserve; that is to say, the child was not at man's or woman's growth. Thus do these impious wretches cheat the world, and damn their own souls by a double meaning, which too often imposes on a cautious, merciful, and credulous jury, and gives wicked murderers means to escape and commit fresh sins, to which their acquitters, no doubt, are accessory.

I wonder so many men of sense as have been on the jury have been so often imposed upon by the stale pretence of a scrap or two of child-bed linen being found in the murderer's box, &c.; when, alas! perhaps, it was never put there till after the murder was committed; or if it was, but with a view of saving themselves by that devilish precaution; for so many have been acquitted on that pretence, that it is but too common a thing to provide child-bed linen beforehand for a poor innocent babe they are determined to murder.

But, alas! what are the exploded murders to those which escape the eye of the magistrate, and die in silence? Add to this, procured abortions and other indirect means which wicked wretches make use of to screen themselves from the censure of the world, which they dread more than the displeasure of their Maker.

Those who cannot be so hardhearted to murder their own offspring themselves, take a slower, though as sure, a way, and get it done by others, by dropping their children, and leaving them to be starved by parish nurses.

Thus is God robbed of a creature, in whom he had breathed the breath of life, and on whom he had stamped his image; the world of an inhabitant, who might have been of use; the king of a subject; and future generations of an issue not to be accounted for, had this infant lived to have been a parent.

It is therefore the height of charity and humanity to provide against this barbarity, to prevent this crying sin, and extract good, even out of evil, by saving these innocent babes from slaughter, and bringing them up in the nurture and fear of the Lord; to be of benefit to themselves and mankind in general.

And what nearer, what better way can we have, than to erect and to endow a proper hospital or house to receive them, where we may see them tenderly brought up, as so many living monuments of our charity; every one of them being a convincing proof of a Christian saved, and a murder prevented?

Nor will this be attended with so much charge as is imagined, for we find in many parishes, that parents have redemanded their children, on increase of circumstances, and paid all costs, with a handsome present in the bargain; and many times when a clandestine marriage is cleared up and openly avowed, they would purchase the first-fruits of their loves at any rate. Oftentimes a couple may have no more children, and an infant thus saved may arrive to inherit a good estate, and become a benefactor where it was once an object of charity.

But let us suppose the worst, and imagine the infant begot in sin and without the sanction of wedlock; is it therefore to be murdered, starved, or neglected, because its parents were wicked? Hard fate of innocent children to suffer for their parents' faults! Where God has thought fit to give his image and life, there is nourishment demanded; that calls aloud for our Christian and human assistance, and best shows our nobleness of soul, when we generously assist those who cannot help themselves.

If the fault devolved on the children, our church would deny them baptism, burial, and other Christian rites; but our religion carries more charity with it, they are not denied even to partake of our blessed sacraments, and are excluded no one branch or benefit accruing from Christianity; if so, how unjust are those who arraign them for their parents' faults, and how barbarous are those parents, who, though able, make no provision for them, because they are not legitimate. My child, is my child, let it be begot in sin or wedlock, and all the duties of a parent are incumbent on me so long as it lives; if it survives me, I ought to make a provision for it, according to my ability; and though I do not set it on a footing with my legitimate children, I ought in conscience to provide against want and shame, or I am answerable for every sin or extravagance my child is forced or led into, for want of my giving an allowance to prevent it.

We have an instance very fresh in every one's memory, of an ingenious, nay a sober young nobleman, for such I must call him, whose either father was a peer, and his mother a peeress. This unhappy gentleman, tossed from father to father, at last found none, and himself a vagabond forced to every shift; he in a manner starved for many years, yet was guilty of no capital crime, till that unhappy accident occurred, which God has given him grace and sense enough to repent. However, I cannot but think his hard-hearted mother will bear her portion of the guilt, till washed away by a severe repentance.

What a figure might this man have made in life, had due care been taken? If his peerage had not been adjusted, he might at least have been a fine gentleman; nay, probably have filled some handsome post in the government with applause, and called as much for respect as he does now for pity.

Nor is this gentleman the only person begot and neglected by noble, or rather ignoble parents; we have but too many now living, who owe their birth to the best of our peerage, and yet know not where to eat. Hard fate, when the child would be glad of the scraps which the servants throw away! But Heaven generally rewards them accordingly, for many noble families are become extinct, and large estates alienated into other houses, while their own issue want bread.

And now, methinks, I hear some over-squeamish ladies cry, What would this fellow be at? would not he set up a nursery for lewdness, and encourage fornication? who would be afraid of sinning, if they can so easily get rid of their bastards? we shall soon be overrun with foundlings when there is such encouragement given to whoredom. To which I answer, that I am as much against bastards being begot, as I am for their being murdered; but when a child is once begot, it cannot be unbegotten; and when once born, it must be kept; the fault, as I said before, is in the parents, not the child; and we ought to show our charity towards it as a fellow-creature and Christian, without any regard to its legitimacy or otherwise.

The only way to put a stop to this growing evil, would be to oblige all housekeepers not to admit a man and woman as lodgers till they were certified of their being lawfully married; for now-a-days nothing is more common than for a whoremonger and a strumpet to pretend marriage, till they have left a child or two on the parish, and then shift to another part of the town.

If there were no receivers, there would be no thieves; if there were no bawdyhouses, there would be no whores; and though persons letting lodgings be not actual procurers, yet, if they connive at the embraces of a couple, whose marriage is doubtful, they are no better than bawds, and their houses no more than brothels.

Now should anybody ask how shall this hospital be built? how endowed? to which I answer, follow the steps of the Venetians, the

Hamburghers, and other foreign states, &c., who have for ages past prosecuted this glorious design, and found their account therein. As for building a house, I am utterly against it, especially in the infancy of the affair: let a place convenient be hired. Why should such a considerable sum be sunk in building as has in late public structures, which have swallowed up part of the profits and dividend, if not the capital, of unwary stockmongers?

To my great joy I find my project already anticipated, and a noble subscription carrying on for this purpose; to promote which I exhort all persons of compassion and generosity, and I shall think myself happy, if what I have said on this head may anyways contribute to further the same.

Having said all I think material on this subject, I beg pardon for leaving my reader so abruptly, and crave leave to proceed to another article, viz.:—

A proposal to prevent the expensive importation of foreign musicians, &c., by forming an academy of our own.

It will no doubt be asked what have I to do with music? to which I answer, I have been a lover of the science from my infancy, and in my younger days was accounted no despicable performer on the viol and lute, then much in vogue. I esteem it the most innocent amusement in life; it generally relaxes, after too great a hurry of spirits, and composes the mind into a sedateness prone to everything that is generous and good; and when the more necessary parts of education are finished, it is a most genteel and commendable accomplishment; it saves a great deal of drinking and debauchery in our sex, and helps the ladies off with many an idle hour, which sometimes might probably be worse employed otherwise.

Our quality, gentry, and better sort of traders must have diversions; and if those that are commendable be denied, they will take to worse; now what can be more commendable than music, one of the seven liberal sciences, and no mean branch of the mathematics?

Were it for no other reason I should esteem it, because it was the favourite diversion of his late majesty, of glorious memory; who was as wise a prince as ever filled the British throne. Nor is it less esteemed by their present majesties, whose souls are formed for harmony, and who have not disdained to make it a part in the education of their sacred race.

Our nobility and gentry have shown their love to the science, by supporting at such prodigious expense the Italian opera, improperly called an academy; but they have at the same time shown no small partiality in discouraging anything English, and overloading the town with such heaps of foreign musicians.

An academy, rightly understood, is a place for the propagation of science, by training up persons thereto from younger to riper years, under the instruction and inspection of proper artists; how can the Italian opera properly be called an academy, when none are admitted but such as are, at least are thought, or ought to be, adepts in music? If that be an academy, so are the theatres of Drury-lane, and Lincolns-inn Fields; nay, Punch's opera may pass for a lower kind of academy. Would it not be a glorious thing to have an opera of our own, in our own most noble tongue, in which the composer, singers, and orchestra, should be of our own growth? Not that we ought to disclaim all obligations to Italy, the mother of music, the nurse of Corelli, Handel, Bononcini, Geminiani; but then we ought not to be so stupidly partial to imagine ourselves too brutal a part of mankind to make any progress in the science? By the same reason that we love it, we may excel in it; love begets application, and application perfection. We have already had a Purcel, and no doubt there are now many latent geniuses, who only want proper instruction, application, and encouragement, to become great ornaments of the science, and make England emulate even Rome itself.

What a number of excellent performers on all instruments have sprung up in England within these few years? That this is owing to the opera I will not deny, and so far the opera is an academy, as it refines the taste and inspires emulation.

But though we are happy in instrumental performers, we frequently send to Italy for singers, and that at no small expense; to remedy which I humbly propose that the governors of Christ's Hospital will show their public spirit, by forming an academy of music on their foundation, after this or the like manner.

That out of their great number of children, thirty boys be selected of good ears and propensity to music.

That these boys be divided into three classes, viz., six for wind instruments, such as the hautboy, bassoon, and German flute.

That sixteen others be selected for string instruments, or at least the most useful, viz., the violin and bass-violin.

That the remaining eight be particularly chosen for voice, and organ, or harpsichord. That all in due time be taught composition. The boys thus chosen, three masters should be elected, each most excellent in his way; that is to say, one for the wind instrument, another for the stringed, and a third for the voice and organ, &c.

Handsome salaries should be allowed these masters, to engage their constant attendance every day from eight till twelve in the morning; and I think 100*l.* per annum for each would be sufficient, which will be a trifle to so wealthy a body. The multiplicity of holidays should be abridged, and only a few kept; there cannot be too few, considering what a hinderance they are to juvenile studies. It is a vulgar error that has too long prevailed all over England to the great detriment of learning, and many boys have been made blockheads in complaisance to kings and saints dead for many ages past.

The morning employed in music, the boys should go in the afternoon, or so many hours, to the reading and writing school, and in the evening should practice, at least two hours before bed-time, and two before the master comes in the morning. This course held for seven or eight years, will make them fine proficients; but that they should not go too raw or young out of the academy, it is proper, that at the stated age of apprenticeship, they be bound to the hospital, to engage their greater application, and make them thorough masters, before they launch out into the world; for one great hinderance to many performers is, that they begin to teach too soon, and obstruct their genius.

What will not such a design produce in a few years? Will they not be able to perform a concert, choir, or opera, or all three, among themselves, and overpay the charge, as shall hereafter be specified?

For example, we will suppose such a design to be continued for ten years, we shall find an orchestra of forty hands, and a choir or opera of twenty voices, or admitting that of those twenty only five prove capital singers, it will answer the intent.

For the greater variety they may, if they think fit, take in two or more of their girls, where they find a promising genius, but this may be further considered of.

Now, when they are enabled to exhibit an opera, will they not gain considerably when their voices and hands cost them only a college subsistence? and it is but reasonable the profits accruing from operas, concerts, or otherwise, should go to the hospital, to make good all former and future expenses, and enable them to extend the design to a greater length and grandeur; so that instead of 1,500*l.* per annum, the price of one Italian singer, we shall for 300*l.* once in ten years, have sixty English musicians regularly educated, and enabled to live by their science.

There ought, moreover, to be annual probations, and proper prizes or premiums allotted, to excite emulation in the youths, and give life to their studies.

They have already a music school, as they call it, but the allowance is too poor for this design, and the attendance too small, it must be every day, or not at all.

This will be an academy indeed, and in process of time they will have even their masters among themselves; and what is the charge, compared with the profits, or their abilities?

One thing I had like to have forgot, which is, that with permission of the right reverend the lords spiritual, some performance in music, suitable to the solemnity of the day, be exhibited every Sunday after divine service. Sacred poesy, and rhetoric may be likewise introduced to make it an entertainment suitable to a Christian and polite audience; and indeed we seem to want some such commendable employment for the better sort; for we see the public walks and taverns crowded, and rather than be idle, they will go to Newport market.

That such an entertainment would be much preferable to drinking, gaming, or profane discourse, none can deny; and till it is proved to be prejudicial, I shall always imagine it necessary. The hall at the hospital will contain few less than seven hundred people, conveniently seated, which at so small a price as one shilling per head, will amount to 35*l.* per week; and if the performance deserve it, as no doubt it will in time, they may make it half a crown, or more, which must considerably increase the income of the hospital.

When they are able to make an opera, the profits will be yet more considerable, nor will they reap much less from what the youths bring in during their apprenticeship, when employed at concerts, theatres, or other public entertainments.

Having advanced what I think proper on this head, or at least enough for a hint, I proceed to offer,

That many youths and servants may be saved from destruction were the streets cleared of shameless and impudent strumpets, gaming tables totally suppressed, and a stop put to sabbath debauches.

The corruption of our children and servants is of importance sufficient to require our utmost precaution; and moreover, women servants (commonly called maid-servants) are such necessary creatures, that it is by no means below us to make them beneficial rather than prejudicial to us.

I shall not run into a description of their abuses; we know enough of those already. Our business now is to make them useful, first by ascertaining their wages at a proper standard.

Secondly, by obliging them to continue longer in service, not to stroll about from place to place, and throw themselves on the town on every dislike.

Thirdly, to prevent their being harboured by wicked persons, when out of place; or living too long on their own hands.

As for their wages, they have topped upon us already, and doubled them in spite of our teeth; but as they have had wit enough to get them, so will they, I doubt not, have the same sense to keep them, and much good may it do those indolent over-secure persons, who have given them this advantage. However, if they are honest and diligent, I would have them encouraged, and handsome wages allowed them; because, by this means, we provide for the children of the inferior class of people, who otherwise could not maintain themselves; nay, sometimes tradesmen, &c., reduced, are glad when their children cease to hang upon them, by getting into service, and by that means not only maintaining themselves, but being of use in other families. But then there ought to be some medium, some limitation to their wages, or they may extort more than can well be afforded.

Nothing calls for more redress than their quitting service for every idle disgust, leaving a master or mistress at a nonplus, and all under plea of a foolish old custom, called warning, nowhere practised but in London; for in other places they are hired by the year, or by the statute as they call it, which settles them in a place, at least for some time; whereas, when they are not limited, it encourages a roving temper, and makes them never easy.

If you turn them away without warning, they will make you pay a month's wages, be the provocation or offence never so great; but if they leave you, though never so abruptly, or unprovided, help yourselves how you can, there is no redress; though I think there ought, in all conscience, to be as much law for the master as for the servant.

No servant should quit a place where they are well fed and paid, without assigning a good reason before a magistrate. On the other hand, they should receive no abuse which should not be redressed; for we ought to treat them as servants, not slaves; and a medium ought to be observed on both sides. But if they are not restrained from quitting service on every vagary, they will throw themselves on the town, and not only ruin themselves, but others; for example, a girl quits a place and turns whore; if there is not a bastard to be murdered, or left to the parish, there is one or more unwary youths drawn in to support her in lewdness and idleness; in order to which, they rob their parents and masters, nay, sometimes, anybody else, to support their strumpets; so that many thieves owe their ruin and shameful deaths to harlots; not to mention the communication of loathsome distempers, and innumerable other evils, to which they give birth.

How many youths, of all ranks, are daily ruined? and how justly may be dreaded the loss of as many more, if a speedy stop be not put to this growing evil? Generations to come will curse the neglect of the present, and every sin committed for the future may be passed to our account, if we do not use our endeavours to the contrary.

And unless we prevent our maid-servants from being harboured by wicked persons when out of place, or living too long on their own hands, our streets will swarm with impudent shameless strumpets; the good will be molested; those prone to evil will be made yet more wicked, by having temptations thrown in their way; and, to crown all, we shall have scarce a servant left, but our wives, &c., must do the household-work themselves.

If this be not worthy the consideration of a legislature, I would fain know what is. Is it not time to limit their wages, when they are grown so wanton they know not what to ask? Is it not time to fix them, when they stroll from place to place, and we are hardly sure of a servant a month together? Is it not time to prevent the increase of harlots, by making it penal for servants to be harboured in idleness, and tempted to theft, whoredom, murder, &c., by living too long out of place? and I am sure it is high time to begin the work, by clearing the public streets of night-walkers, who are grown to such a pitch of impudence that peace and common decency are manifestly broken in our public streets. I wonder this has so long escaped the eye of the magistrate, especially when there are already in force laws sufficient to restrain this tide of uncleanness, which will one day overflow us.

The lewdest people upon earth, ourselves excepted, are not guilty of such open violations of the laws of decency. Go all the world over, and you will see no such impudence as in the streets of London, which makes many foreigners give our women in general a bad character, from the vile specimens they meet with from one end of the town to the other. Our sessions' papers are full of the trials of impudent sluts, who first decoy men and then rob them; a meanness the courtesans of Rome and Venice abhor.

How many honest women, those of the inferior sort especially, get loathsome distempers from their husband's commerce with these creatures, which distempers are often entailed on posterity; nor have we an hospital separated for that purpose, which does not contain too many instances of honest poor wretches made miserable by villains of husbands.

And now I have mentioned the villany of some husbands in the lower state of life, give me leave to propose, or at least to wish, that they were restrained from abusing their wives at that barbarous rate, which is now practised by butchers, carmen, and such inferior sort of fellows, who are public nuisances to civil neighbourhoods, and yet nobody cares to interpose, because the riot is between a man and his wife.

I see no reason why every profligate fellow shall have the liberty to disturb a whole neighbourhood, and abuse a poor honest creature at a most inhuman rate, and is not to be called to account because it is his wife; this sort of barbarity was never so notorious and so much encouraged as at present, for every vagabond thinks he may cripple his wife at pleasure; and it is enough to pierce a heart of stone to see how barbarously some poor creatures are beaten and abused by merciless dogs of husbands.

It gives an ill example to the growing generation, and this evil will gain ground on us if not prevented; it may be answered, the law has already provided redress, and a woman abused may swear the peace against her husband, but what woman cares to do that? It is revenging herself on herself, and not without considerable charge and trouble.

There ought to be a shorter way, and when a man has beaten his wife, which by the by is a most unmanly action, and great sign of cowardice, it behoves every neighbour who has the least humanity or compassion, to complain to the next justice of the peace, who should be empowered to set him in the stocks for the first offence; to have him well scourged at the whipping-post for the second; and if he persisted in his barbarous abuse of the holy marriage state, to send him to the house of correction till he should learn to use more mercy to his yoke-fellow.

How hard is it for a poor industrious woman to be up early and late, to sit in a cold shop, stall, or market, all weathers, to carry heavy loads from one end of the town to the other, or to work from morning till night, and even then dread going home for fear of being murdered? Some may think this too low a topic for me to expatiate upon, to which I answer, that it is a charitable and Christian one, and therefore not in the least beneath the consideration of any man who had a woman for his mother.

The mention of this leads me to exclaim against the vile practice now so much in vogue among the better sort as they are called, but the worst sort in fact; namely, the sending their wives to madhouses, at every whim or dislike, that they may be more secure and undisturbed in their debaucheries; which wicked custom is got to such a head, that the number of private madhouses in and about London are considerably increased within these few years.

This is the height of barbarity and injustice in a Christian country, it is a clandestine inquisition, nay worse.

How many ladies and gentlewomen are hurried away to these houses, which ought to be suppressed, or at least subject to daily examination, as hereafter shall be proposed?

How many, I say, of beauty, virtue, and fortune, are suddenly torn from their dear innocent babes, from the arms of an unworthy man, whom they love, perhaps, but too well, and who in return for that love, nay probably an ample fortune and a lovely offspring besides, grows weary of the pure streams of chaste love, and thirsting after the puddles of lawless lust, buries his virtuous wife alive, that he may have the greater freedom with his mistresses?

If they are not mad when they go into these cursed houses, they are soon made so by the barbarous usage they there suffer; and any woman of spirit, who has the least love for her husband, or concern for her family, cannot sit down tamely under a confinement and separation the most unaccountable and unreasonable.

Is it not enough to make any one mad to be suddenly clapped up, stripped, whipped, ill-fed, and worse used? To have no reason assigned for such treatment, no crime alleged, or accusers to confront? And what is worse, no soul to appeal to but merciless creatures, who answer but in laughter, surliness, contradiction, and too often stripes?

All conveniences for writing are denied, no messenger to be had to carry a letter to any relation or friend; and if this tyrannical inquisition, joined with the reasonable reflections a woman of any common understanding must necessarily make, be not sufficient to drive any soul stark staring mad, though before they were never so much in their right senses, I have no more to say.

When by this means a wicked husband has driven a poor creature mad, and robbed an injured wife of her reason, for it is much easier to create than to cure madness, then has the villain a handle for his roguery; then, perhaps, he will admit her distressed relations to see her, when it is too late to cure the madness he so artfully and barbarously has procured.

But this is not all: sometimes more dismal effects attend this inquisition, for death is but too often the cure of their madness and end of their sorrows; some with ill usage, some with grief, and many with both, are barbarously cut off in the prime of their years and flower of their health, who otherwise might have been mothers of a numerous issue, and survived many years. This is murder in the deepest sense, and much more cruel than dagger or poison, because more lingering; they die by piecemeal, and in all the agonies and terrors of a distracted mind.

Nay, it is murder upon murder, for the issue that might have been begot is to be accounted for to God and the public. Now, if this kind of murder is connived at, we shall no doubt have enough, nay, too much of it; for if a man is weary of his wife, has spent her fortune, and wants another, it is but sending her to a madhouse and the business is done at once.

How many have already been murdered after this manner is best known to just Heaven, and those unjust husbands and their damned accomplices, who, though now secure in their guilt, will one day find it is murder of the blackest dye, has the least claim to mercy, and calls aloud for the severest vengeance.

How many are yet to be sacrificed, unless a speedy stop be put to this most accursed practice, I tremble to think; our legislature cannot take this cause too soon in hand. This surely cannot be below their notice, and it will be an easy matter at once to suppress all these pretended madhouses. Indulge, gentle reader, for once the doting of an old man, and give him leave to lay down his little system without arraigning him of arrogance or ambition to be a lawgiver. In my humble opinion, all private madhouses should be suppressed at once, and it should be no less than felony to confine any person under pretence of madness without due authority.

For the cure of those who are really lunatic, licensed madhouses should be constituted in convenient parts of the town, which houses should be subject to proper visitation and inspection, nor should any person be sent to a madhouse without due reason, inquiry, and authority.

It may be objected, by persons determined to contradict every thing and approve nothing, that the abuses complained of are not so numerous or heinous as I would insinuate. Why are not facts advanced, they will be apt to say, to give a face of truth to these assertions? But I have two reasons to the contrary; the first is, the more you convince them, the more angry you make them, for they are never better pleased than when they have an opportunity of finding fault; therefore, to curry favour with the fault-finders, I have left them a loophole: the second and real is, because I do not care to bring an old house over my head by mentioning particular names or special cases, thereby drawing myself into vexatious prosecutions and suits at law from litigious wretches, who would be galled to find their villanies made public, and stick at no expense or foul play to revenge themselves. Not but I could bring many instances, particularly of an unhappy widow, put in by a villain of a husband, and now continued in for the sake of her jointure by her unnatural son, far from common honesty or humanity. Of another, whose husband keeps his mistress in black velvet, and is seen with her every night at the opera or play, while his poor wife (by much the finer woman, and of an understanding far superior to her thick-skulled tyrant,) is kept mean in diet and apparel; nay, ill-used into the bargain, notwithstanding her fortune supplies all the villain's extravagances, and he has not a shilling but what came from her: but a beggar when once set on horseback proves always the most unmerciful rider.

I cannot leave this subject without inserting one particular case.

A lady of known beauty, virtue, and fortune, nay more, of wisdom, not flashy wit, was, in the prime of her youth and beauty, and when her senses were perfectly sound, carried by her husband in his coach as to the opera; but the coachman had other instructions, and drove directly to a madhouse, where the poor innocent lady was no sooner introduced, under pretence of calling by the way to see some pictures he had a mind to buy, but the key was turned upon her, and she left a prisoner by her faithless husband, who while his injured wife was confined and used with the utmost barbarity, he, like a profligate wretch, ran through her fortune with strumpets, and then basely, under pretence of giving her liberty, extorted her to make over her jointure, which she had no sooner done but he laughed in her face, and left her to be as ill-used as ever. This he soon ran through, and (happily for the lady) died by the justice of heaven in a salivation his debauches had obliged him to undergo.

During her confinement, the villain of the madhouse frequently attempted her chastity; and the more she repulsed him the worse he treated her, till at last he drove her mad in good earnest. Her distressed brother, who is fond of her to the last degree, now confines her in part of his own house, treating her with great tenderness, but has the mortification to be assured by the ablest physicians that his poor sister is irrecoverably distracted.

Numberless are the instances I could produce, but they would be accounted fictitious, because I do not name the particular persons, for the reasons before assigned; but the sufferings of these poor ladies are not fictitious, nor are the villany of the madhouses, or the unnatural, though fashionable barbarity of husbands, chimeras, but too solid grievances, and manifest violations of the laws of God and man.

Most gracious and august queen Caroline! ornament of your sex, and pride of the British nation! the best of mothers, the best of wives, the best of women! Begin this auspicious reign with an action worthy your illustrious self, rescue your injured sex from this tyranny, nor let it be in the power of every brutal husband to cage and confine his wife at pleasure, a practice scarce heard of till of late years. Nip it in the bud, most gracious queen, and draw on yourself the blessings of numberless of the fair sex, now groaning under the severest and most unjust bondage. Restore them to their families; let them, by your means, enjoy light and liberty; that while they fondly embrace, and with tears of joy weep over their dear children, so long withheld from them, they may invoke accumulated blessings from heaven upon your royal head!

And you, ye fair illustrious circle! who adorn the British court! and every day surround our gracious queen: let generous pity inspire your souls, and move you to intercede with your noble consorts for redress in this injurious affair. Who can deny when you become suitors? and who knows but at your request a bill may be brought into the house to regulate these abuses? The cause is a noble and a common one, and ought to be espoused by every lady who would claim the least title to virtue or compassion. I am sure no honest member in either honourable house will be against so reasonable a bill; the business is for some public-spirited patriot to break the ice by bringing it into the house, and I dare lay my life it passes.

I must beg my reader's indulgence, being the most immethodical writer imaginable. It is true I lay down a scheme, but fancy is so fertile I often start fresh hints, and cannot but pursue them; pardon therefore, kind reader, my digressive way of writing, and let the subject, not the style or method, engage thy attention.

Return we, therefore, to complain of destructive gaming-houses, the bane of our youth, and ruin of our children and servants.

This is the most unprofitable evil upon earth, for it only tends to alienate the proper current of specie, to maintain a pack of idle sharping rascals, and beggar unwary gentlemen and traders.

I take the itch of gaming to be the most pernicious of vices, it is a kind of avaricious madness; and if people have not sense to command themselves by reason, they ought to be restrained by law; nor suffered to ruin themselves and families, to enrich a crew of sharpers.

There is no playing on the square with these villains; they are sure to cheat you, either by sleight of hand, confederacy, or false dice, &c.; they have so much the odds of their infatuated bubbles, that they might safely play a guinea to a shilling, and yet be sure of winning. This is but genteel pocket picking, or felony with another name, and yet, so fond are we of it, that from the footboy to the lord, all must have a touch of gaming; and there are sharpers of different stations and denominations, from Southwark-fair to the groom porters. Shame, that gentlemen should suffer every scoundrel to mix with them for gaming sake! And equal shame, that honest laborious tradesmen should be obstructed in crossing the public streets, by the gilt chariots of vagabond gamesters; who now infest the land, and brave even our nobility and gentry with their own money.

But the most barbarous part of this hellish trade is what they call setting of young gentlemen, apprentices, and others; this ought to be deemed felony without benefit of clergy; for it is the worst of thievery. Under pretence of taking a bottle, or spending an evening gaily, they draw their cull to the tavern, where they sit not long before the devil's bones or books are found accidentally on purpose, by the help of which they strip my gentleman in an instant, and then generously lend him his own money, to lose afresh, and create a debt which is but too often more justly paid than those more justly due.

If we look into some late bankruptcies we shall find some noted gamesters the principal creditors; I think, in such cases it would be but justice to make void the gamester's debt, and subject his estate to make good the deficiencies of the bankrupt's effects. If traders have no more wit, the public should have pity on them; and make it as penal to lose as to win; and, in truth, if cards, dice, &c., were totally suppressed, industry and arts would increase the more; gaming may make a man crafty, but not polite; one may understand cards and dice perfectly well, and be a blockhead in everything else.

I am sorry to see it so prevalent in the city among the trading part of mankind, who have introduced it into their clubs, and play so high of late that many bankrupts have been made by this pernicious practice.

It is the bane of all conversation; and those who can't sit an hour without gaming, should never go into a club to spoil company. In a word, it is mere madness, and a most stupid thing to hazard one's fortune, and perplex one's mind; nay, to sit up whole nights, poring over toys of pipped ivory and painted pasteboard, making ourselves worse than little children, whose innocent sports we so much ridicule.

To sum up all, I think it would be a noble retribution, to subject gamesters' estates to the use and support of the poor widows and orphans of their unfortunate bubbles.

Sunday debauches are abuses that call loud for amendment; it is in this pernicious soil the seeds of ruin are first sown. Instead of a day of rest, we make it a day of labour, by toiling in the devil's vineyard; and but too many surfeit themselves with the fruits of gluttony, drunkenness, and uncleanness.

Not that I am so superciliously strict, to have the sabbath kept as rigidly here as in Scotland, but then there ought to be a medium between the severity of a fast, and the riot of Saturnalia. Instead of a decent and cheerful solemnity, our taverns and publichouses have more business that day than all the week beside. Our apprentices plume themselves; nay, some scruple not to put on their swords and tie wigs, or toupees, and the loose end of the town is their rendezvous, Sunday being market-day all round the hundreds of Drury.

While we want servants to do our work, those hundreds, as they call them, are crowded with numbers of idle impudent sluts, who love sporting more than spinning, and inveigle our youth to their ruin; nay, many old lechers, beasts as they are! steal from their families, and seek these harlots' lurking holes, to practise their unaccountable schemes of new invented lewdnesses; some half hang themselves, others are whipped, some lie under a table and gnaw the bones that are thrown them, while others stand slaving among a parcel of drabs at a washing tub. Strange that the inclination should not die with the power, but that old fools should make themselves the prey and ridicule of a pack of strumpets!

Some heedless youths are wheedled into marriage, which makes them and their unhappy parents miserable all their lives; others are drawn into extravagancies, and but too often run into their master's cash, and for fear of a discovery, make away with themselves, or at least run away and leave their distracted parents in a thousand tears; not to mention the frustration of their fortune, and the miseries that attend a vagabond life. Thus honest parents lose their children, and traders their apprentices, and all from a liberty we have of late given our youth of rambling abroad on Sundays; for many, nowadays will lie out all night, or stay out so late to give no small disturbance in sober families. It therefore behoves every master of a family to have his servants under his eye; and if the going to church, meeting, or whatever place of worship suited their religion, were more enforced, it would be so much the better.

In short, the luxury of the age will be the ruin of the nation, if not prevented. We leave trade to game in stocks; we live above ourselves, and barter our ready money for trifles; tea and wine are all we seem anxious for, and God has given the blessings of life to an ungrateful people, who despise their own productions. Our very plough-fellows drink wine nowadays; our farmers, graziers, and butchers, are above malt liquors; and the wholesome breakfast of water-gruel and milk potage is changed for coffee and tea. This is the reason provisions and corn, &c., are so dear; we all work for vintners, and raise our prices one upon another to such a degree, it will be an impossibility to live, and we shall, of course, become our own devourers.

We strain at a gnat and swallow a camel; and, in this instance, the publichouses are kept open to furnish our luxury, while we deny ourselves other necessaries of life, out of a scruple of conscience. For example; in extreme hot weather, when meat will not keep from Saturday to Sunday, we throw, or cause to be thrown away, vast quantities of tainted meat, and have generally stinking dinners, because the butchers dare not sell a joint of meat on a Sunday morning. Now, though I would not have the Sabbath so far violated as to have it a market-day, yet, rather than abuse God's mercies by throwing away creatures given for our use, nay, for our own healths and cleanliness sake, I would have the same indulgence in extreme hot weather, as there is for milk and mackerel; that is to say, that meat might be killed in the cool of the morning, viz., one or two of the clock, and sold till nine, and no longer; nor should villanous informers have power to molest them in this innocent and reasonable amendment of a ridiculous vulgar error.

I cannot forbear taking notice of the extravagant use, or rather abuse, of that nauseous liquor called Geneva, among our lower sort. Those who deny that an inferior class of people are most necessary in a body politic, contradict reason and experience itself, since they are most useful when industrious, and as pernicious when lazy. By their industry our manufactures, trade, and commerce are carried on; the merchant in his counting-house, and the captain in his cabin, would find but little employment were it not that many hands carried on the different branches of the concern they superintended.

But now, so far are our common people infatuated with Geneva, that half the work is not done now as formerly. It debilitates and enervates them, and they are not near so strong and healthy as formerly. This accursed liquor is in itself so diuretic, it overstrains the parts of generation, and makes our common people incapable of getting such lusty children as they used to do. Add to this, that the women, by drinking it, spoil their milk, and by giving it to young children, as they foolishly do, spoil the stomach, and hinder digestion; so that in less than an age, we may expect a fine spindle-shanked generation.

There is not in nature so unhealthy a liquor as Geneva, especially as commonly sold; it curdles the blood, it stupefies the senses, it weakens the nerves, it spoils the eyesight, and entirely ruins the stomach; nay, some stomachs have been rendered so cold by the use of Geneva, that lamp spirits have not been a dram warm enough for them. Surely they will come to drink aquafortis at last!

On the contrary, our own malt liquors, especially common draught beer, is most wholesome and nourishing, and has brought up better generations than the present: it is strengthening, cooling, and balsamic; it helps digestion, and carries nourishment with it; and, in spite of the whims of some physicians, is most pertinent to a human, especially a good wholesome English, constitution. Nay, the honest part of the faculty deny not the use of small beer, well brewed, even in fevers. I, myself, have found great benefit by it; and if it be good in its kind, it is the finest jalap upon earth.

If this abuse of Geneva be not stopped, we may go whoop for husbandmen, labourers, &c. Trade must consequently stand still, and the credit of the nation sink; nor is the abatement of the excise, though very considerable, and most worthy notice, any ways comparable to the corruption of manners, the destruction of health, and all the train of evils we are threatened with from pernicious Geneva.

An effectual method to prevent street robberies.

The principal encouragements and opportunity given to street robbers is, that our streets are so poorly watched; the watchmen, for the most part, being decrepit, superannuated wretches, with one foot in the grave and the other ready to follow; so feeble that a puff of breath can blow them down. Poor crazy mortals! much fitter for an almshouse than a watchhouse. A city watched and guarded by such animals is wretchedly watched indeed.

Nay, so little terror do our watchmen carry with them, that hardy thieves make a mere jest of them, and sometimes oblige even the very watchman who should apprehend them to light them in their roguery. And what can a poor creature do, in terror of his life, surrounded by a pack of ruffians, and no assistance near?

Add to this, that our rogues are grown more wicked than ever, and vice in all kinds is so much winked at, that robbery is accounted a petty crime. We take pains to puff them up in their villany, and thieves are set out in so amiable a light in the Beggar's Opera, that it has taught them to value themselves on their profession rather than be ashamed of it.

There was some cessation of street robberies, from the time of Bunworth and Blewitt's execution, until the introduction of this pious opera. Now we find the Cartouchian villanies revived, and London, that used to be the most safe and peaceful city in the universe, is now a scene of rapine and danger. If some of Cartouch's gang be not come over to instruct our thieves, and propagate their schemes, we have, doubtless, a Cartouch of our own, and a gang which, if not suppressed, may be full as pernicious as ever Cartouch's was, and London will be as dangerous as Paris, if due care be not taken.

We ought to begin our endeavours to suppress these villanies, first by heavenly, and then by earthly means.

By heavenly means, in enforcing and encouraging a reformation of manners, by suppressing of vice and immorality, and punishing profaneness and licentiousness. Our youth are corrupted by filthy, lewd ballads, sung and sold publicly in our streets; nay, unlicensed and unstamped, notwithstanding acts of parliament to the contrary.

Coachmen, carmen, &c., are indulged in swearing after the most blasphemous, shocking, and unaccountable rate that ever was known. New oaths and blasphemies are daily uttered and invented; and rather than not exercise this hellish talent, they will vent their curses on their very horses; and, oh stupid! damn the blood of a post, rather than want something to curse.

Our common women, too, have learned this vice; and not only strumpets, but labouring women, who keep our markets, and vend things about street, swear and curse at a most hideous rate. Their children learn it from their parents, and those of the middle, or even the better sort of people, if they pass through the streets to school, or to play, catch the infection, and carry home such words as must consequently be very shocking to sober parents.

Our youth, in general, have too much liberty; the Sabbath is not kept with due solemnity; masters and mistresses of families are too remiss in the care of the souls committed to their charge. Family prayer is neglected; and, to the shame of scoffers be it spoken, too much ridiculed. All ages and sexes, if in health, should be obliged to attend public worship, according to their respective opinions. Were it only to keep youth out of harm's way it would do well. But it is to be hoped, if their parents, masters, or mistresses, should oblige their attendance at public devotion, they would edify by what they should hear, and many wicked acts would be stifled in their infancy, and checked even in the intention, by good and useful doctrine.

Our common people make it a day of debauch, and get so drunk on a Sunday they cannot work for a day or two following. Nay, since the use of Geneva has become so common, many get so often drunk they cannot work at all, but run from one irregularity to another, till at last they become arrant rogues. And this is the foundation of all our present complaints.

We will suppose a man able to maintain himself and family by his trade, and at the same time to be a Geneva drinker. This fellow first makes himself incapable of working by being continually drunk; this runs him behindhand, and he either pawns or neglects his work, for which reason nobody will employ him. At last, fear of arrests, his own hunger, the cries of his family for bread, his natural desire to support an irregular life, and a propense hatred to labour, turn but too many an honest tradesman into an arrant desperate rogue. And these are commonly the means that furnish us with thieves and villains in general.

Thus is a man, that might be useful in a body politic, rendered obnoxious to the same: and if this trade of wickedness goes on, they will grow and increase upon us, insomuch that we shall not dare to stir out of our habitations; nay, it will be well if they arrive not to the impudence of plundering our houses at noonday.

Where is the courage of the English nation, that a gentleman, with six or seven servants, shall be robbed by one single highwayman? Yet we have lately had instances of this; and for this we may thank our effeminacy, our toupee wigs, and powdered pates, our tea, and other scandalous fopperies; and, above all, the disuse of noble and manly sports, so necessary to a brave people, once in vogue, but now totally lost among us.

Let not the reader think I run from my subject if I search the bottom of the distemper before I propose a cure, which having done, though indeed but slightly, for this is an argument could be carried to a much greater length, I proceed next to propose earthly means in the manner following.

Let the watch be composed of stout able-bodied men, and of those at least treble the number now subsisting, that is to say, a watchman to every forty houses, twenty on one side of the way, and twenty on the other; for it is observable that a man cannot well see distinctly beyond the extent of twenty houses in a row; if it is a single row, and no opposite houses, the charge must be greater and their safety less. This man should be elected and paid by the housekeepers themselves, to prevent misapplication and abuse, so much complained of in the distribution of public money.

He should be allowed ten shillings per annum by each housekeeper, which at forty houses, as above specified, amounts to 20*l.* per annum, almost treble to what is at present allowed; and yet most housekeepers are charged at least 2s. 6d. a quarter to the watch, whose beat is, generally speaking, little less than the compass of half a mile.

This salary is something of encouragement, and a pretty settlement to a poor man, who with frugality may live decently thereon, and by due rest be enabled to give vigilant attendance.

If a housekeeper break, or a house is empty, the poor watchman ought not to suffer, the deficiency should be made up by the housekeepers remaining.

Or, indeed, all housekeepers might be excused, if a tax of only one shilling per annum were levied on every bachelor within the bills of mortality, and above the age of one-and-twenty, who is not a housekeeper: for these young sparks are a kind of unprofitable gentry to the state; they claim public safety and advantages, and yet pay nothing to the public; nay, indeed, they in a manner live upon the public, for (on a Sunday especially) at least a million of these gentlemen quarter themselves upon the married men, and rob many families of part of a week's provision, more particularly when they play a good knife and fork, and are of the family of the Tuckers.

I beg pardon for this whimsical proposal, which, ludicrous as it seems, has something in it; and may be improved. Return we, in the mean time, to our subject.

The watch thus stationed, strengthened, and encouraged, let every watchman be armed with firearms and sword; and let no watchman stand above twenty doors distant from his fellow.

Let each watchman be provided with a bugle-horn, to sound an alarm, or in time of danger; and let it be made penal, if not felony, for any but a watchman to sound a horn in and about the city, from the time of their going on, to that of their going off.

An objection will be here made on account of the postboys, to obviate which, I had thoughts of a bell, but that would be too ponderous and troublesome for a watchman to carry, besides his arms and lantern. As to a fixed bell, if the watchman is at another part of his walk, how can he give notice? Besides, rogues may play tricks with the bell; whereas a horn is portable, always ready, and most alarming.

Let the postboys therefore use some other signal, since this is most convenient to this more material purpose. They may carry a bell in a holster with ease, and give notice by that, as well as those who collect the letters.

That the watchmen may see from one end of their walks to the other, let a convenient number of lamps be set up, and those not of the convex kind, which blind the eyes, and are of no manner of use; they dazzle, but give no distinct light: and further, rather than prevent robberies, many, deceived and blinded by these *ignes fatui*, have been run over by coaches, carts, &c. People stumble more upon one another, even under these very lamps, than in the dark. In short, they are most unprofitable lights, and in my opinion, rather abuses than benefits.

Besides, I see no reason why every ten housekeepers cannot find a lamp among themselves, and let their watchman dress it, rather than fatten a crew of directors; but we are so fond of companies, it is a wonder we have not our shoes blacked by one, and a set of directors made rich at the expense of our very black-guards. Convenient turnpikes and stoppages may be made to prevent escapes, and it will be proper for a watchman to be placed at one of these, fixed at the end of a lane, court, alley, or other thoroughfare, which may happen in any part of his beat, and so as not to obstruct his view to both ends thereof, or being able to give notice, as aforesaid; for the watch ought to be in view, as well as in the hearing of each other, or they may be overpowered, and much danger may happen.

The streets thus guarded and illuminated, what remains but that the money allotted by the government be instantly paid on conviction of every offender; for delays in this case are of dangerous consequence, and nobody will venture their lives in hopes of a reward, if it be not duly and timely paid. If there is reason of complaint on this head, it ought to be looked into by those at the helm; for nothing can be more vile than for underlings to abuse the benevolence of the public, or their superiors, by sinking, abridging, or delaying public or private benefits. And it is by no means below the dignity or care, even of the greatest, to see the disposal of their own bounty and charity; for it loses but too often by the carriage: and where a nobleman or other generous person has ordered five guineas to be given, it is well if the proper object has had even one.

Something allowed by the Chamber of London to every person apprehending a robber, would have a good effect, especially if it be not told over a gridiron, but paid without delay or abatement. And what if the fewer custards are eat, so it augment the public safety.

Some of our common soldiery are, and I hope unjustly, suspected. This may be easily confuted, if strict orders are enforced, that none but commission or warrant officers shall be out of their quarters after ten at night. But if we consider, that neither Blewit, Bunworth, or their gangs, were soldiers, and that of those who have been executed for ten years past, not one in ten were soldiers, but, on the contrary, seamen discharged and thrown on the public without present subsistence, which makes them desperate; but I hope the act now depending for the encouragement of seamen, &c., will sufficiently remove that obstacle also. This, I hope, will stop the mouths of censorious persons, who unjustly arraign our soldiery for the vices of others. However, to make all easy, I believe the generality of them will gladly submit to the restraint proposed, merely to show their innocence.

Mean time, would his most sacred majesty let them partake of his bounty, as the officers, &c., have done, and raise their pay, were it but one penny *per diem*, it would be a most royal bounty, would considerably contribute to their support, and put them above any sordid views: and there was never more occasion than now, when provisions of all kinds are so excessive dear.

Having offered my little mite to the public, I beg they will excuse the deficiency of my style, and multitude of my errors, for my intention's sake. I write without prospect of gain; if I am censured, it is what I can but expect; but if among all my schemes one proves of service, my desires and labours are amply answered.

Omissions

In my scheme for an university in London I proposed only a hall or public room; on recollection I find it should be a large house or inn, in the nature of a college, with store of convenient rooms for gentlemen, not only to study separately, but wherein to lodge their books, for it would be most inconvenient to lug them backwards and forwards. They may indeed breakfast, sup, and sleep at home, but it will be highly necessary they should dine in commons, or at least near the college; not that I would have cooks, butlers, caterers, manciples, and the whole train of college cannibals retained; but for fear they should stay too long at home, or be hindered from returning to study in due time, some proper place or person might be pitched upon to keep an ordinary, at a prefixed price and hour, and for the students only.

My reasons are these:—

First, A young gentleman may live too far from college.

Second, The college hours for dinner may not agree with those of the family.

Third, Company may drop in and detain him.

These being, I think, the only material objections could be offered, I hope I have amply provided against them, and rendered my project more perfect and unexceptionable.

One omission I made in the discourse on madhouses, &c., is, that maiden ladies as well as widows and wives are liable to the inquisition there complained of, and I am informed a good estate is lately come to a worthless family by the death, or rather murder, of an innocent young creature, who being left very rich, chose to live with her friends; but well had it been for her had she taken up her abode among strangers, for they staved off all proposals for marriage a considerable time, and when at last they found the lady would not be hindered from altering her condition, she was hurried away to a madhouse, where she miserably ended her days, while they rioted in the pillage of her fortune. Thus neither maid, wife, or widow, are safe while these accursed madhouses are suffered; nay, I see no reason, if the age improves in wickedness, as in all probability it may, but the men, *per contra*, may take their turns. Younger brothers, &c., may clap up their elders, and jump into their estates, for there are no questions asked at these madhouses, but who is the paymaster, and how much; give them but their price, mad or not mad, it is no matter whom they confine; so that if any person lives longer than his relations think convenient, they know their remedy; it is but sending them to a madhouse and the estate is their own.

Having answered all that I think liable to objection, and recollected what I had omitted, I desire to stand or fall by the judgment of the serious part of mankind; wherein they shall correct me I will kiss the rod and suffer with patience; but if a pack of hackney scribblers shall attack me only by way of a get-penny, I shall not be provoked to answer them, be they never so scurrilous, lest I be accounted as one of them.

TO LIEUTENANT-COLONEL SAMUEL ROBINSON.

Sir,

I shall congratulate you on your election into the chamberlainship of the city of London, or otherwise, as you shall acquit yourself in answering candidly and impartially to the following queries.

I. whether there is not money sufficient in the chamber of London to pay off the orphan's fund? Or if not a sufficient sum, what sum it is, and what is the deficiency? How long it has lain there, and what interest has been made upon it?

II. If there are not considerable arrears due from many wards, and what those arrears are?

III. Who are these poor orphans we pay so much money to? and whether they are not some of the richest men in the city of London, who have got the stock into their own hands, and find it so snug a fund they do not care to get out of it.

IV. If it would not be much better to gather in the arrears, join them to the money in the office, and collect the overplus at once, rather than suffer the tax to become eternal, and to pay so much interest.

This is but a reasonable request; and if colonel Robinson is the honest gentleman fame reports him to be, he will make no scruple to give a ready answer. And indeed it will be but a handsome return made to his fellow citizens for their choice of him, to begin his office with such an act of justice, honesty, and public satisfaction, for many people do not know what is meant by the orphan's tax; they pay it with remorse, and think themselves aggrieved. Even those who know the reason of the fund think it has been continued long enough, wish it were once paid off, suspect some secret in the affair, and give their tongues the liberty all losers claim; Our fathers, say they, have eaten sour grapes, and our teeth are set on edge, we are visited for their transgressions, and may be to the world's end, unless we shall find an honest chamberlain who will unveil this cloudy affair, and gives us a prospect of relief.

Thus, sir, it lies at your door to gain the applause of the whole city, a few misers excepted, by a generous and gentlemanlike discovery of this affair. And you are thus publicly called upon, that your discovery may be as public and beneficial to all. If you comply, I shall think you an honest man, above a fellow feeling, or being biassed, and most worthy your office; if not, give me leave to think, the citizens of London have made but an indifferent choice.

I am,

Sir,

Yours, as you prove yourself,

Andrew Moreton.

Sept. 23,

1728.

AN HUMBLE PROPOSAL

TO THE

PEOPLE OF ENGLAND,

For the Increase of their

TRADE,

And Encouragement of their

MANUFACTURES;

Whether
The present uncertainty of Affairs
issues in
Peace or War.

By the Author of the Complete Tradesman.

PREFACE

TO THE
PEOPLE OF ENGLAND.

It deserves some notice, that just at, or soon after writing these sheets, we have an old dispute warmly revived among us, upon the question of our trade being declined, or not declined. I have nothing to do with the parties, nor with the reason of their strife upon that subject; I think they are wrong on both sides, and yet it is hardly worth while to set them to rights, their quarrel being quite of another nature, and the good of our trade little or nothing concerned in it.

Nor do they seem to desire to be set right, but rather to want an occasion to keep up a strife which perhaps serves some other of their wicked purposes, better than peace would do; and indeed, those who seek to quarrel, who can reconcile?

I meddle not with the question, I say, whether trade be declined or not; but I may easily show the people of England, that if they please to concern themselves a little for its prosperity, it will prosper; and on the contrary, if they will sink it and discourage it, it is evidently in their power, and it will sink and decline accordingly.

You have here some popular mistakes with respect to our woollen manufacture fairly stated, our national indolence in that very particular reproved, and the consequence laid before you; if you will not make use of the hints here given, the fault is nobody's but your own.

Never had any nation the power of improving their trade, and of advancing their own manufactures, so entirely in their own hands as we have at this time, and have had for many years past, without troubling the legislature about it at all: and though it is of the last importance to the whole nation, and, I may say, to almost every individual in it; nay, and that it is evident you all know it to be so; yet how next to impossible is it to persuade any one person to set a foot forward towards so great and so good a work; and how much labour has been spent in vain to rouse us up to it?

The following sheets are as one alarm more given to the lethargic age, if possible, to open their eyes to their own prosperity; the author sums up his introduction to it in this short positive assertion, which he is ready to make good, viz., That if the trade of England is not in a flourishing and thriving condition, the fault and only occasion of it is all our own, and is wholly in our own power to mend, whenever we please.

SEASONABLE PROPOSAL, &c.

As by my title I profess to be addressing myself to Englishmen, I think I need not tell them that they live by trade; that their commerce has raised them from what they were to what they are, and may, if cultivated and improved, raise them yet further to what they never were; and this in few words is an index of my present work.

It is worth an Englishman's remark, that we were esteemed as a growing thriving nation in trade as far back as in the reigns of the two last Henries; manufactures were planted, navigation increased, the people began to apply, and trade bringing in wealth, they were greatly encouraged; yet in king Henry VIII.'s reign, and even towards the latter end of it, too, we find several acts of parliament passed for regulating the price of provisions, and particularly that beef and pork should not be sold in the market for more than a halfpenny per pound avoirdupoise, and mutton and veal at three farthings.

As the trading men to whom I write may make some estimate of things by calculating one thing by another, so this leads them to other heads of trade to calculate from; as, first, the value of money, which bore some proportion, though I think not a full and just equality to the provisions, as follows:—silver was at 2s. 4d. per ounce, and gold at 2l. 5s. to 2l. 10s. per ounce; something less in the silver, and more in the gold than half of the present value.

As for the rate of lands and houses, they bore a yet greater distance in value from what they produce now; so that indeed it bears no proportion, for we find the rent of lands so raised, and their value so improved, that there are many examples where the lands, valued even in queen Elizabeth's days at 20l. to 25l. per annum, are now worth from 200l. to 300l. per annum, and in some places much more.

It is true, this advance is to be accounted for by the improvement made of the soil, by manuring, cultivating, and enclosing; by stocks of cattle, by labour, and by the arts of husbandry, which are also improved; and so this part is not so immediately within my present design; it is a large subject, and merits to be spoken of at large by itself; because as the improvement of land has been extraordinary great, and the landed interest is prodigiously increased by it, so it is capable of much more and greater improvement than has been made for above a hundred years past. But this I say is not my present design; it is too great an article to be couched in a few words.

Yet it requires this notice here; viz., that trade has been a principal agent even in the improvement of our land; as it has furnished the money to the husbandman to stock his land, and to employ servants and labourers in the working part; and as it has found him a market for the consumption of the produce of his land, and at an advanced price too, by which he has received a good return to enable him to go on.

The short inference from these premises is this: as by trade the whole kingdom is thus advanced in wealth, and the value of lands, and of the produce of lands, and of labour, is so remarkably increased, why should we not go on with vigour and spirit in trade, and by all proper and possible methods and endeavours, increase and cultivate our commerce; that we may still increase and improve in wealth, in value of lands, in stock, and in all the arts of trade, such as manufactures, navigation, fishery, husbandry, and, in short, study an improvement of trade in all its branches.

No doubt it would be our wisdom to do thus; and nothing of the kind can be more surprising than that it should not be our practice; and thus I am brought down to the case before me.

If it should be objected that the remark is needless, that we are an industrious and laborious people, that we are the best manufacturers in the world, thoroughly versed in all the methods and arts for that purpose; and that our trade is improved to the utmost in all places, and all cases possible; if it should, I say, be thus argued, for I know some have such a taint of our national vanity that they do talk at this rate,—

My answer is short, and direct in the negative; and I do affirm that we are not that industrious, applying, improving people that we pretend to be, and that we ought to be, and might be. That we are the best manufacturers I deny; and yet at the same time I grant that we make the best manufactures in the world; but the reason of that is greatly owing not to our own skill exceeding others, so much as to our being furnished from the bounty of Heaven with the best materials and best conveniencies for the work, of any nation in the world, shall take notice in its place.

But not to dwell upon our capacities for improving in trade, I might clear all that part without giving up the least article of my complaint; for it is not our capacity to improve that I call in question, but our application to the right methods; nay, I must add, that while I call upon your diligence, and press you to application, I am supposed to grant your capacities; otherwise I was calling upon you to no purpose, and pressing you to do what at the same time I allowed you had no power to perform.

Without complimenting your national vanity, therefore, I am to grant you have not only the means of improvement in your hands, but the capacity of improving also; and on this account I must add, are the more inexcusable if the thing is not in practice.

Indeed it is something wonderful, and not easy to be accounted for, that a whole nation should, as if they were in a lethargic dream, shut their eyes to the apparent advantages of their commerce; and this just now, when their circumstances seem so evidently to stand in need of encouragement, and that they are more than ordinarily at a kind of stop in their usual progression of trade.

It is debated much among men of business, whether trade is at this time in a prosperous and thriving condition, or in a languishing and declining state; or, in a word, whether we are going backwards or forward. I shall not meddle with that debate here, having no occasion to take up the little space allowed me in anything remote from my design. But I will propose it as I really believe it to be: namely, that we are rather in a state of balance between both, a middle between the extremes; I hope we are not much declined, and I fear we are not much advanced. But I must add, that if we do not immediately set about some new methods for altering this depending condition, we shall soon decline; and on the contrary, if we should exert ourselves, we have before us infinite advantages of improving and advancing our commerce, and that to a great degree.

This is stating it to the meanest understanding; there is no mystery at all in the thing; if you will apply, you will rise; if you will remain indolent and inactive, you will sink and starve. Trade in England, at this time, is like a ship at sea, that has sprung a leak in sight of the shore, or within a few days' sail of it; if the crew will ply their pump and work hard, they may not only keep her above water, but will bring her safe into port; whereas if they neglect the pump, or do not exert their strength, the water grows upon them and they are in apparent danger of sinking before they reach the shore.

Or, if you will have a coarser comparison, take the pump room in the rasp-house, or house of correction, at Amsterdam; where the slothful person is put into a good, dry, and wholesome room, with a pump at one side and a spring or water-pipe at the other; if he pleases to work, he may live and keep the water down, but if he sleeps he drowns.

The moral is exactly the same in both cases, and suits with the present circumstances of our trade in England most exactly, only with this difference to the advantage of the latter; namely, that the application which I call upon the people of England to exert themselves in, is not a mere labour of the hand; I do not tax the poor with mere sloth and negligence, idly lying still when they should work, that is not our grievance at present; for though there may be too much of that sort too, among a few of the drunken, loitering part of mankind, and they suffer for it sufficiently in their poverty, yet that, I say, is not the point, idleness is not here a national crime, the English are not naturally a slothful, indolent, or lazy people.

But it is an application proper to the method of business which is wanting among us, and in this we shall find room for reproof on one hand, and direction on the other; and our reader, I dare say, will acknowledge there is reason for both.

It must in the first place be acknowledged, that England has indeed the greatest encouragement for their industry of any nation in Europe; and as therefore their want of improving those advantages and encouragements, lays them more open to our just reproof, than other nation's would be, or can be who want them, so it moves me with the more importunity to press home the argument, which reason and the nature of the thing furnishes, to persuade them. Reason dictates that no occasion should be let slip by which England above all nations in the world should improve the advantages they have in their hands; not only because they have them, but because their people so universally depend upon them. The manufactures are their bread, the life, the comfort of their poor, and the soul of their trade; nature dictates, that as they are given them to improve, and that by industry and application they are capable of being improved; so they ought to starve if they do not improve them to the utmost.

Let us see in a few words what nature and providence has done for us; nay, what they have done for us exclusive of the rest of the world. The bounty of Heaven has stored us with the principles of commerce, fruitful of a vast variety of things essential to trade, and which call upon us as it were in the voice of nature, bidding us work, and with annexed encouragement to do so from the visible apparent success of industry. Here the voice of the world is plain, like the answer of an oracle; thus, dig and find, plough and reap, fish and take, spin and live; in a word, trade and thrive; and this with such extraordinary circumstances, that it is as if there was a bar upon the neighbouring nations, and it had been spoken from Heaven thus: These are for you only, and not for any other nation; you, my favourites, of England; you, singled out to be great, opulent, powerful, above all your neighbours, and to be made so by your own industry and my bounty.

To explain this, allow me a small digression, to run over the detail of Heaven's bounty, and see what God and nature has done for us beyond what it has done for other nations; nature, as I have said, will dictate to us what Heaven expects from us, for the improving the blessings bestowed, and for making ourselves that rich and powerful people which he has determined us to be.

Our country is furnished, I say, with the principles of commerce in a very extraordinary manner; that is to say, so as no other country in Europe, or perhaps in the world, is supplied with.

I. With the product of the earth. This is of two kinds: I. That of the inside or bowels of the earth, the same of which, as above, the voice of Heaven to us, is, dig and find, under which article is principally our lead, and tin-coal; I name these only, because of these this island seems to have an exclusive grant; there being none, or but very small quantities of them, found in any other nation; and it is upon exclusive benefits that I am chiefly speaking. 2. We have besides these, iron, copper, *lapis calaminaris*, vulgarly called callamy, with several other minerals, which may be said to be in common to us and the rest of the world, of which the particulars at large, and the places where they are found, may be fully seen in a late tract, of which I shall have frequently occasion to speak in this work, entitled, A Plan of the Commerce of Great Britain, to which I refer, as indeed to a general index of the trade and produce of this whole island.

II. The product of the surface, which I include in that part, plough and reap; and though this is not indeed an exclusive product, yet I may observe that the extraordinary increase which our lands, under an excellent cultivation, generally yield, as well in corn and cattle, is an uncommon argument for the industry of the husbandmen; and I might enter into a comparison with advantage, against almost any countries in Europe, by comparing the quantity produced on both sides, with the quantity of land which produce those quantities.

You may find some calculations of the produce of our own country in the book above mentioned, viz., The Plan of the Commerce of Great Britain, where the consumption of malt in England is calculated by the value of the duties of excise, and where it appears that there is annually consumed in England, besides what is exported to foreign countries, forty millions of bushels of malt, besides also all the barley, the meal of which is made into bread, which is a very great quantity; most of the northern counties in England feeding very much upon barley bread; and besides all the barley either exported or used at home in the corn unmalted; all which put together, I am assured, amounts to no less than ten millions of bushels more.

The quantity of barley only is so exceeding great, that I am told it bears, in proportion to the land it grows on, an equality to as much land in France, as all the sowed land in the whole kingdom of England; or take it thus, that fifty millions of bushels of barley growing in France, would take up as much ground as all the lands which are at any time sowed in England with any corn, whether barley, oats, or wheat.

N. B. I do not say all the arable lands of England, because we know there are a very great number of acres of land which every year lie fallow (though in tillage) and unsowed, according to the usage of our husbandry; so they cannot be reckoned to produce any corn at all, otherwise the quantity might be much greater.

This is a testimony of the fertility of our soil; and on the other hand, the fertility is a testimony of the diligence and application of our people, and the success which attends that diligence.

We are told that in some parts of England, especially in the counties of Essex, Hertford, Cambridge, Bedford, Bucks, Oxford, Northampton, Lincoln, and Nottingham, it is very frequent to have the lands produce from seven to ten quarters of barley upon an acre, which is a produce not heard of in the most fruitful of all those we call corn countries abroad, much less in France. On the contrary, if they have a great produce of corn, it is because they have a vast extent of land for it to grow upon, and which land they either have no other use for, or it may be is fit for no other use; whereas our corn grounds are far from being the richest or the best of our lands, the prime of our land being laid up, as the ploughmen call it, to feed upon, that is, to keep dairies of cows, as in Essex, Suffolk, and the fens; or for grazing grounds, for fatting the large mutton and beef, for which England is so particularly famed. These grazing countries are chiefly in Sussex, and in the marshes of Romney, and other parts in Kent; also in the rich vales of Aylesbury, and others in Bucks and Berkshire, the isle of Ely, the bank of Trent, the counties of Lincoln, Leicester and Stafford, Warwick and Chester, as also in the county of Somerset, Lancaster, north riding of Yorkshire, and bank of Tees, in the bishoprick of Durham.

When this product of England is considered, the diligence and success of our husbandry in England will be found to be beyond that of the most industrious people in Europe. But I must not dwell here, my view lies another way; nor do the people of England want so much to be called upon to improve in husbandry, as they do in manufactures and other things; not but that even in this, the lands not yet cultivated do call aloud upon us too; but I say it is not the present case.

I come in the next article to that yet louder call of the oracle, as above, namely, fish and take. Indeed this is an improvement not fully preserved, or a produce not sufficiently improved; the advantages nature offers here cannot be said to be fully accepted of and embraced.

This is a large field, and much remains to be said and done too in it, for the increase of wealth, and the employment of our people; and though I am not of the opinion which some have carried to an unaccountable length in this case, viz., that we should set up the fishery by companies and societies, which has been often attempted, and has proved abortive and ill-grounded; or that we ought by force, or are able by all our advantages to beat out the Dutch from it; yet we might certainly very much enlarge and increase our own share in it; take greater quantities than we do; cure and pack them better than we do; come sooner to market with them than we do; and consume greater quantities at home than we do; the consequence of which would be that we should breed up and employ more seamen, build and fit out more fishing-vessels and ships for merchandise than we do now, and which we are unaccountably blameable that we do not.

And here I must observe, that the increasing the fishery would even contribute to our vending as well as catching a greater quantity of fish, and to take off the disadvantage which we now lie under with the Dutch, by the consequence of trade in the fishery itself. The case is this: the chief market for white herring, which is the fishery I am speaking of, is the port of Dantzic and Konigsberg, from which ports the whole kingdom of Poland, and great duchy of Lithuania, are supplied with fish by the navigation of the great river of the Vistula, and the smaller rivers of the Pragel and Niemen, &c.

The return brought from thence is in canvass, oak, and spruce, plank and timber, sturgeon, some hemp and flax, pot ashes, &c., but chiefly corn.

Here the Dutch have an infinite advantage of us, which is never to be surmounted or overcome, and for which reason it is impossible for us ever to beat them out of this trade; viz., the Dutch send yearly a very great number of ships to Dantzic, &c., to fetch corn; some say they send a thousand sail every year; and I believe they do send so many ships, or those ships going so many times, or making so many voyages in the year as amounts to the same number of freights, and so is the same thing.

All these ships going for corn for the Dutch, have their chief supply of corn from that country; it follows, then, that their herrings are carried for nothing, seeing the ships which carry them must go light if they did not carry the fish; whereas, on the other hand, our fish must pay freight in whatever vessel it may go.

When our ships, then, from Scotland, for there the fishery chiefly lies, and from thence the trade must take its rise; I say, when they have carried their fish to the ports above-named, of Dantzic and Konigsberg, how must they come back, and with what shall they be loaded?

The only answer that can be given is, that they must bring back the goods mentioned before, or, in shorter terms, naval stores, though indeed not much of naval stores neither, except timber and plank, for the hemp and tar, which are the main articles, are fetched further; viz., from Riga, Revel, Narva, and Petersburg. But suppose after delivering their fish, some of the ships should go to those ports to seek freight, and load naval stores there, which is the utmost help in the trade that can be expected.

The next question is, whither shall they carry them, and for whose account shall they be loaden? To go for Scotland, would not be an answer; for Scotland, having but a few ships, could not take off any quantity proportioned to such a commerce; for if we were to push the Dutch out of the trade, we must be supposed to employ two or three hundred sail of ships at least, to carry herrings to Dantzic, &c.

To say they might take freight at London, and load for England, would be no answer neither; for besides that even England itself would not take off a quantity of those goods equal to the number of ships which would want freight, so if England did, yet those ships would still have one dead freight, for they would be left to go light home at last, to Scotland, otherwise how shall they be at hand to load next year? And even that one dead freight would abate the profit of the voyage; and so still the Dutch would have the advantage.

Upon the whole, take it how and which way we will, it will for ever be true, that though our fish were every way equal to the Dutch, which yet we cannot affirm, and though it came as soon to market, and carried as good a price there, all which I fear must a little fall short, yet it would still be true that the Dutch would gain and we should lose.

There is yet another addition to the advantage of Holland, viz., in the return of money; that whereas when our fish shall be sold, we shall want to remit back the produce in money; that is to say, so much of it as cannot be brought back in goods. And the difference in the exchange must be against us; but it is in favour of the Dutch; for if they did not send their herrings and other fish to Dantzic, they must remit money to pay for their corn; and even as it is, they are obliged to send other goods, such as whale oil, the produce of their Greenland fishery, English manufactures, and the like; whereas the Scots' merchants, having no market for corn, and not a demand for a sufficient value in naval stores, &c., viz. the product of the country, must bring the overplus by exchange to their loss, the exchange running the other way.

It is true, this is a digression; but it is needful to show how weak those notions are, which prompt us to believe we are able to beat the Dutch out of the fishing trade by increasing our number of busses, and taking a larger quantity of fish.

But this brings me back to the first argument; if you can find a way to enlarge your shipping in the fishery, and send greater quantities of fish to market, and yet sell them to advantage, you would by consequence enlarge your demand for naval stores, and so be able to bring more ships home loaden from thence; that is to say, to dispose of more of their freight at home; and indeed nothing else can do it.

N. B. This very difference in the trade is the reason why a greater quantity of English manufactures are not sent from hence to Dantzic, as was formerly done; viz., not that the consumption of those goods is lessened in Poland, or that less woollen manufactures are demanded at Dantzic or at Konigsberg; but it is that the Dutch carry our manufactures from their own country; this they can do to advantage; besides their costing nothing freight, as above, though they are sold to little or no profit, because they want the value there to pay for their corn, and must otherwise remit money to loss for the payment.

As these things are not touched at before in any discourses on this subject, but we are daily filled with clamours and complaints at the indolence and negligence of our Scots and northern Britons, for not outworking the Dutch in their fishing trade, I think it is not foreign to the purpose to have thus stated the case, and to have shown that it is not indeed a neglect in our management, that the Dutch thrive in the fishing trade, and we sit still, as they call it, and look on, which really is not so in fact, but that the nature of the thing gives the advantage to the

Dutch, and throws the trade into their hands, in a manner that no industry or application of ours could or can prevent.

Having thus vindicated our people where they are really not deserving blame, let us look forward from hence and see with the same justice where they are in another case likewise less to blame than is generally imagined; namely, in the white fishing, or the taking of cod-fish in these northern seas, which is also represented as if it was so plentiful of fish that any quantity might be taken and cured, and so the French, the Scots, and the Portuguese, might be supplied from hence much cheaper and more to advantage than by going so long a voyage as to the banks of Newfoundland.

This also is a mistake, and the contrary is evident; that there is a good white fishing upon the coast, as well of the north part of the British coast as on the east side of Scotland, is very true; the Scots, to give them their due, do cure a tolerable quantity of fish, even in or near the frith of Edinburgh; also there is a good fishery for cod on the west side, and among the islands of the Leuze, and the other parts called the western islands of Scotland; but the mistake lies in the quantity, which is not sufficient to supply the demand in those ports mentioned above, nor is it such as makes it by far so easy to load a ship as at Newfoundland, where it is done in the one-fifth part of the time, and consequently so much cheaper; and the author of this has found this to be so by experience.

Yet it cannot be said with justice that the Scots' fishermen are negligent, and do not improve this fishing to advantage, for that really they do kill and cure as many as can be easily done to make them come within a price, and more cannot be done; that is to say, it would be to no purpose to do it; for it will for ever be true in trade, that what cannot be done to advantage, may be said not to be possible to be done; because gain is the end of commerce, and the merchant cannot do what he cannot get by.

It may be true that in the herring fishery the consumption might be increased at home, and in some places also abroad, and so far that fishery is not so fully pursued; but I do not see that the increase of it can be very considerable, there being already a prodigious quantity cured more than ever in Ireland on every side of that kingdom, and also on the west of England; but if it may be increased, so much the more will be the advantage of the commerce; of which by itself.

But from this I come to the main article of the British trade, I mean our wool, or, as it is generally expressed, the woollen manufacture, and this is what I mean, when I said as above, spin and live.

In this likewise I must take the liberty to say, and insist upon it, that the English people cannot be said to be idle or slothful, or to neglect the advantages which are put into their hands of the greatest manufactures in Europe, if not in the whole world.

On the other hand, the people of England have run up their manufactures to such a prodigy of magnitude, that though it is extended into almost every part of the known world, I mean, the world as it is known in trade; yet even that whole world is scarce equal to its consumption, and is hardly able to take off the quantity; the negligence therefore of the English people is not so much liable to reproof in this part, as some pretend to tell us; the trade of our woollen manufacture being evidently increased within these few years past, far beyond what it ever was before.

I know abundance of our people talk very dismal things of the decay of our woollen manufacture, and that it is declined much they insist upon it; being prohibited in many places and countries abroad, of their setting up other manufactures of their own in the room of it, of their pretending to mimick and imitate it, and supply themselves with the produce of their own land, and the labour of their own people, and indeed France has for many years gone some length in this method of erecting woollen manufactures in the room of ours, and making their own productions serve instead of our completely finished manufacture: but all these imitations are weak and unperforming, and show abundantly how little reason we have to apprehend their endeavours, or that they will be able to supplant our manufacture there or any where else; for that even in France itself, where the imitation of our manufactures is carried on to the utmost perfection; yet they are obliged to take off great quantities of our finest and best goods; and such is the necessity of their affairs, that they to this day run them in, that is, import them clandestinely at the greatest risk, in spite of the strictest prohibition, and of the severest penalties, death and the galleys excepted; a certain token that their imitation of our manufactures is so far from pleasing and supplying other parts of the world, that they are not sufficient to supply, or good enough to please themselves.

I must confess the imitating our manufactures has been carried further in France than in any other part of the world, and yet we do not see they have been able so to affect the consumption as to have any visible influence upon our trade; or, that we abate the quantity which we usually made, but that if they have checked the export at all, we have still found other channels of trade which have fully carried off our quantity, and shall still do so, though other nations were able to imitate us to, and this is very particularly stated and explained by the author of the book above mentioned, called the Plan of the English Commerce, where the extending our manufactures is handled more at large than I have room for in the narrow compass of this tract, and therefore I again refer my reader thither, as to the fountain head.

But I go on to touch the heads of things. The French do imitate our manufactures in a better manner, and in greater quantity than other nations; and why do we not prevent them? It is a terrible satire upon our vigilance, or upon the method of our custom-house men, that we do not prevent it; seeing the French themselves will not stick to acknowledge, that without a supply of our wool, which is evident they have now with very small difficulty from Ireland, they could do little in it, and indeed nothing at all to the purpose.

On the other hand, it is not so with France in regard to their silk manufactures, in which although we have not the principles of the work, I mean the silk growing within our dominions, but are obliged to bring it from Italy, yet we have so effectually shut out the French silk manufactures from our market, that in a word we have no occasion at all for them; nay, if you will believe some of our manufacturers, the French buy some of our wrought silks and carry them into France; but whether the particular be so in fact or no, this I can take upon me from good evidence to affirm, that whereas we usually imported in the ordinary course of trade, at least a million to twelve hundred thousand pounds' value a year in wrought silks from France; now we import so little as is not worth naming; and yet it is allowed that we do not wear less silk, or silks of a meaner value, than we usually did before, so that all the difference is clear gain on the English side in the balance of trade.

The contemplation of this very article furnishes a most eminent encouragement to our people, to increase and improve their trade; and especially to gain upon the rest of Europe, in making all the most useful manufactures of other nations their own.

Nor would this increase of our trade be a small article in the balance of business, when we come to calculate the improvement we have made in that particular article, by encroaching upon our neighbours, more than they have been able to make upon us; and this also you will find laid down at large in the account of the improvement of our manufactures in general, calculated in the piece above mentioned, chap. v. p. 164.

If then the encroachments of France upon our woollen manufactures are so small, as very little to influence our trade, or lessen the quantity made here, and would be less if due care was taken to keep our wool out of their hands; and that at the same time we have encroached upon their trade in the silk manufactures only, besides others, such as paper, glass, linen, hats, &c., to the value of twelve hundred thousand pounds a year, then France has got little by prohibiting the English manufactures, and perhaps had much better have let it alone.

However, I must not omit here what is so natural a consequence from these premises, viz., that here lies the first branch of our Humble Proposal to the People of England for Increase of their Commerce, and Improvement of their Manufactures; namely, that they would keep their wool at home.

I know it will be asked immediately how shall it be done? and the answer indeed requires more time and room to debate it, than can be allowed me here. But the general answer must be given; certainly it is practicable to be done, and I am sure it is absolutely necessary. I shall say more to it presently.

But I go on with the discourse of the woollen manufactures in general; nothing is more certain, than that it is the greatest and most extensive branch of our whole trade, and, as the piece above mentioned says positively, is really the greatest manufacture in the world. Vide Plan, chap. v. p. 172. 179.

Nor can the stop of its vent, in this or that part of the world, greatly affect it; if foreign trade abates its demand in one place, it increases it in another; and it certainly goes on increasing prodigiously every year, in direct confutation of the phlegmatic assertions of those, who, with as much malice as ignorance, endeavour to run it down, and depreciate its worth as well as credit, by their ill-grounded calculations.

We might call for evidence in this cause the vast increase of our exportation in the woollen manufactures only to Portugal; which, for above twenty-five years past, has risen from a very moderate trade to such a magnitude, that we now export more woollen goods in particular yearly to Portugal, than both Spain and Portugal took off before, notwithstanding Spain has been represented as so extraordinary a branch of trade. The occasion of this increase is fully explained, by the said Plan of the English Commerce, to be owing to the increase of the Portuguese colonies in the Brazils, and in the kingdoms of Congo and Angola on the west side of Africa; and of Melinda and the coast of Zanguebar on the east side; in all which the Portuguese have so civilized the natives and black inhabitants of the country, as to bring them, where they went even stark naked before, to clothe decently and modestly now, and to delight to do so, in such a degree as they will hardly ever be brought to go unclothed again; and all these nations are clothed more or less with our English woollen manufactures, and the same in proportion in their East India factories.

The like growth and increase of our own colonies, is another article to confirm this argument, viz., that the consumption of our manufactures is increased: it is evident that the number of our people, inhabitants of those colonies, visibly increases every day; so must by a natural consequence the consumption of the cloths they wear.

And this increase is so great, and is so demonstrably growing every day greater, that it is more than equal to all the decrease occasioned by the check or prohibitions put upon our manufactures, whether by the imitation of the French or any other European nation.

I might dwell upon this article, and extend the observation to the East Indies, where a remarkable difference is evident between the present and the past times; for whereas a few years past the quantity of European goods, whether of English or other manufactures, was very small, and indeed not worth naming; on the contrary, now the number of European inhabitants in the several factories of the English, Dutch, and Portuguese, is so much increased, and the people who are subject to them also, and who they bring in daily to clothe after the European fashion, especially at Batavia, at Fort St. George, at Surat, Goa, and other principal factories, that the demand for our manufactures is grown very considerable, and daily increasing. This also the said Plan of the Commerce insists much on, and explains in a more particular manner.

But to proceed: not only our English colonies and factories are increased, as also the Portuguese in the Brazils, and in the south part of Africa; not only the factories of the English and Dutch in the East Indies are increased, and the number of Europeans there being increased call for a greater quantity of European goods than ever; but even the Spaniards, and their colonies in the West Indies, I mean in New Spain, and other dominions of the Spaniards in America, are increased in people, and that not so much the Spaniards themselves, though they too are more numerous than ever, but the civilized free Indians, as they are called, are exceedingly multiplied.

These are Indians in blood, but being native subjects of Spain, know no other nation, nor do they speak any other language than Spanish, being born and educated among them. They are tradesmen, handicrafts, and bred to all kinds of business, and even merchants too, as the Spaniards are, and some of them exceeding rich; of these they tell us there are thirty thousand families in the city of Lima only, and doubtless the numbers of these increase daily.

As all these go clothed like Spaniards, as well themselves as their wives, children, and servants, of which they have likewise a great many, so it necessarily follows that they greatly increase the consumption of European goods, and that the demand of English manufactures in particular increases in proportion, these manufactures being more than two-thirds of the ordinary habit or dress of those people, as it is also of the furniture of their houses; all which they take from their first patrons, the Spaniards.

It will seem a very natural inquiry here, how I can pretend to charge the English nation with indolence or negligence in their labouring or working their woollen manufactures; when it is apparent they work up all the wool which their whole nation produces, that the whole growth and produce of their sheep is wrought up by them, and that they buy a prodigious quantity from Ireland and Scotland, and work up all that too, and that with this they make such an infinite quantity of goods, that they, as it were, glut and gorge the whole world with their manufactures.

My answer is positive and direct, viz., that notwithstanding all this, they are chargeable with an unaccountable, unjustifiable, and, I had almost said, a most scandalous indolence and neglect, and that in respect to this woollen manufacture in particular; a neglect so gross, that by it they suffer a manifest injury in trade. This neglect consists of three heads:

1. They do not work up all the wool which they might come at, and which they ought to work up, and about which they have still spare hands enough to set to work.

2. They with difficulty sell off or consume the quantity of goods they make; whereas they might otherwise vend a much greater quantity, both abroad and at home.

3. They do not sufficiently apply themselves to the improving and enlarging their colonies abroad, which, as they are already increased, and

have increased the consumption of the manufactures, so they are capable of being much further improved, and would thereby still further improve and increase the manufactures. By so much as they do not work up the wool, by so much they neglect the advantage put into their hands; for the wool of Great Britain and Ireland is certainly a singular and exclusive gift from Heaven, for the advantage of this great and opulent nation. If Heaven has given the wool, and we do not improve the gift by manufacturing it all up, so far we are to be reproached with indolence and neglect; and no wonder if the wool goes from Ireland to France by whole shiploads at a time; for what must the poor Irish do with their wool? If they manufacture it we will not let them trade with those manufactures, or export them beyond sea. Our reasons for that prohibition are indeed very good, though too long to debate in this place: but no reason can be alleged that can in any sense of the thing be justifiable, why we should not either give leave to export the manufactures, or take the wool.

But to speak of the reason to ourselves, for the other is a reason to them (I mean the Irish). The reason to ourselves is this: we ought to take the wool ourselves, that the French might not have it to erect and imitate our own manufactures in France, and so supplant our trade.

Certainly, if we could take the whole quantity of the Irish wool off their hands, we might with ease prevent it being carried to France; for much of it goes that way, merely because they cannot get money for it at home.

This I charge therefore as a neglect, and an evident proof of indolence; namely, that we do not take effectual care to secure all the wool in Ireland; give the Irish money for it at a reasonable market price, and then cause it to be brought to England as to the general market.

I know it will be objected, that England does already take off as much as they can, and as much as they want; and to bring over more than they can use, will sink the market, and be an injury to ourselves; but I am prepared to answer this directly and effectually, and you shall have a full reply to it immediately.

But, in the mean time, this is a proof of the first proposition; namely, that we do not work up all our own wool, for the Irish wool is, and ought to be, esteemed as our own, in the present debate about trade; for that it is carried away from our own dominions, and is made use of by those that rival our manufactures to the ruin of our own trade.

That the Irish are prohibited exporting their wool, is true; but it seems a little severe to prohibit them exporting their wool, and their manufactures too, and then not to buy the wool of them neither.

It is alleged by some, that we do take off all the wool they bring us, and that we could and would take it all, if they would bring it all. To this I answer; if the Irish people do not bring it all to us, it is either that it is too far for the poor people who own the wool to bring it to the south and east coast of Ireland, there being no markets in the west and north-west parts of that island, where they could sell it; and the farmers and sheep-breeders are no merchants, nor have they carriage for so long a journey; but either the public ought to appoint proper places whether it shall be carried, and where they would receive money for it at a certain rate; or erect markets where those who deal in wool might come to buy, and where those who have it to sell would find buyers.

No doubt but the want of buyers is the reason why so much of the Irish wool is carried over to France; besides, if markets were appointed where the poor farmers could always find buyers at one price or another, there would be then no pretence for them to carry it away in the dark, and by stealth, to the sea side, as is now the case; and the justice of prohibitions and seizures would be more easily to be defended; indeed there would be no excuse for the running it off, nor would there want any excuse for seizing it, if they attempted to run it off.

But I am called upon to answer the objection mentioned above; namely, that the manufactures in England do indeed already take off a very great quantity of the Irish wool, as much as they have occasion for; nay, they condescend so far to the Irish, as to allow them to manufacture a great deal of that wool which they take off; that is to say, to spin it into yarn, of which yarn so great a quantity is brought into England yearly, as they assure us amounts to sixty thousand packs of wool; as may be seen by a fair calculation in the book above mentioned, called the Plan; in a word, that the English are not in a condition to take off any more. Now this is that which leads me directly to the question in hand; whether the English are able to take off any more of the Irish wool and yarn, or no. I do not affirm, that, as the trade in England is now carried on, they are able, perhaps they are not; but I insist, that if we were thoroughly resolved in England to take such wise measures as we ought to take, and as we are well able to do, for the improvement and increase of our manufactures, we might and should be able to take off, and work up the whole growth of the wool of Ireland; and this I shall presently demonstrate, as I think, past doubt.

But before I come to the scheme for the performance of this, give me leave to lay down some particulars of the advantage this would be to our country, and to our commerce, supposing the thing could be brought to pass; and then I shall show how easily it might be brought to pass.

I. By taking off this great quantity of wool and yarn, supposing one half of the quantity to be spun, many thousands of the poor people of Ireland who are now in a starving condition for want of employment, would be set immediately to work, and be put in a condition to get their bread; so that it would be a present advantage to the Irish themselves, and that far greater than it can be now, their wool which goes away to France being all carried off unwrought.

2. Due care being then taken to prevent any exportation of wool to France, as, I take it for granted, might be done with much more ease when the Irish had encouragement to sell their wool at home, we should soon find a difference in the expense of wool, by the French being disabled from imitating our manufactures abroad, and the consumption of our own would naturally increase in proportion. First, they would not be able to thrust their manufactures into foreign markets as they now do, by which the sale of our manufactures must necessarily be abated; and, secondly, they would want supplies at home, and consequently our manufactures would be more called for, even in France itself, and that in spite of penalties and prohibitions.

Thus by our taking off the Irish wool, we should in time prevent its exportation to France; and by preventing its going to France, we should disable the French, and increase the consumption of our own manufactures in all the ports whither they now send them, and even in France itself.

I have met with some people who have made calculations of the quantity of wool which is sent annually from Ireland to France, and they have done it by calculating, first how many packs of wool the whole kingdom of Ireland may produce; and this they do again from the number of sheep which they say are fed in Ireland in the whole. How right this calculation may be I will not determine.

First, they tell us, there are fed in Ireland thirty millions of sheep, and as all these sheep are supposed be sheared once every year, they must produce exactly thirty millions of fleeces, allowing the fell wool in proportion to the number of sheep killed.

It is observable, by a very critical account of the wool produced annually in Romney marsh, in the county of Kent, and published in the said Plan of the English Commerce, that the fleeces of wool of those large sheep, generally weigh above four pounds and a half each. It is computed thus; first he tells us that Romney marsh contains 47,110 acres of land, that they feed 141,330 sheep, whose wool being shorn, makes up 2,523 packs of wool, the sum of which is, that every acre feeds three sheep, every sheep yields one fleece, and 56 fleeces make one pack of wool, all which comes out to 2,523 packs of wool, twenty-three fleeces over, every pack weighing two hundred and forty pounds of wool. Vide Plan, &c. p. 259.

I need not observe here, that the sheep in Ireland are not near so large as the sheep in Romney marsh, these last being generally the largest breed of sheep in England, except a few on the bank of the river Tees in the bishoprick of Durham. Now if these large sheep yield fleeces of four pounds and a half of wool, we may be supposed to allow the Irish sheep, take them one with another, to yield three pounds of wool to a fleece, or to a sheep, out of which must be deducted the fell wool, most of which is of a shorter growth, and therefore cannot be reckoned so much by at least a pound to a sheep. Begin then to account for the wool, and we may make some calculation from thence of the number of sheep.

1. If of the Romney marsh fleeces, weighing four pounds and a half each, fifty-six fleeces make one pack of wool; then seventy fleeces Irish wool, weighing three pounds each fleece, make a pack.

2. If we import from Ireland one hundred thousand packs of wool, as well in the fleece as in the yarn, then we import the wool of seven millions of sheep fed in Ireland every year.

Come we next to the gross quantity of wool; as the Irish make all their own manufactures, that is to say, all the woollen manufactures, needful for their own use, such as for wearing apparel, house furniture, &c., we cannot suppose but that they use much more than the quantity exported to England, besides that, it is too well known, that notwithstanding the prohibition of exportation, they do daily ship off great quantities of woollen goods, not only to the West Indies, but also to France, to Spain, and Italy; and we have had frequent complaints of our merchants from Lisbon and Oporto, of the great quantity of Irish woollen manufactures that are brought thither, as well broadcloth as serges, druggets, duroys, frieze, long-ells, and all the other sorts of goods which are usually exported from England; add these clandestine exportations to the necessary clothing, furniture, and equipages, of that whole nation, in which are reckoned two millions and a half of people, and we cannot suppose they make use of less than two hundred thousand packs of wool yearly among themselves, which is the wool of fourteen millions of sheep more.

We must, then, allow all the rest of the wool to be run or smuggled, call it what you please, to France, which must be at least a hundred to a hundred and twenty thousand packs more: for it seems the Irish tell us that they feed thirty millions of sheep in the whole kingdom of Ireland.

If, then, they run over to France a hundred thousand packs of wool yearly, which I take to be the least, all this amounts to twenty-eight millions of fleeces together; the other two millions of fleeces may justly be deducted for the difference between the quantity of wool taken from the sheep that are killed, which we call fell wool, and the fleece wool shorn.

Upon the foot of this calculation, there are a hundred thousand packs of wool produced in Ireland every year, which we ought to take off, and which, for want of our taking it off, is carried away to France, where it is wholly employed to mimick our manufactures and abuse our trade; lessening thereby the demand of our own goods abroad, and even in France itself. This, therefore, is a just reproach to our nation, and they are certainly guilty of a great neglect in not taking off that wool, and more effectually preventing it being carried away to France.

It must be confessed, that unless we do find some way to take off this wool from the Irish, we cannot so reasonably blame them for selling it to the French, or to anybody else that will buy, for what else can they do with it, seeing you shut up all their ports against the manufacturers; at least you shut them up as far as you are able; and if you will neither let them manufacture it, for not letting them transport the manufacture when made is in effect forbidding to make them; I say, if you will neither let them manufacture their wool nor take it off their hands, what must they do with it?

But I come next to the grand objection; namely, that we cannot take it off, that we do take off as much as we can use, and a very great quantity it is too; that we are not able to take more, that is to say, we know not what to do with it if we take it; that we cannot manufacture it, or if we do, we cannot sell the goods; and so, according to the known rule in trade, that what cannot be done with profit or without loss, we may say of it that it cannot be done; so in the sense of trade, we cannot take their wool off, and if they must run it over to France, they must, we cannot help it.

This, I say, is a very great mistake; and I do affirm, that as we ought to take off the whole quantity of the Irish wool, so we may and are able to do it. That our manufacture is capable of being so increased, and the consumption of it increased also, as well at home as abroad; that it would in the ordinary course of trade call for all the wool of Ireland, if it were much more than it is, and employ it profitably; besides employing many thousands of poor people more than are now employed, and who indeed want employment.

Upon this foundation, and to bring this to be true, as I shall presently make appear, I must add, that a just reproach lies upon us for indolence, and an unaccountable neglect of our national interests, in not sufficiently exerting ourselves to improve our trade and increase our manufactures; which is the title, as it is the true design, of this whole work.

The affirming, as above, that we are able to increase our manufacture, and by that increase to take off more wool, may, perhaps, be thought an arrogance too great to be justified, and would be a begging the question in an egregious manner, if I were not in a condition to prove what I say; I shall therefore apply myself directly to evidence, and to put it out of doubt:—

By increasing our manufacture, I am content to be understood to mean the increasing the consumption, otherwise, to increase quantity only, would be to ruin the manufacturers, not improve the trade. This increasing the consumption is to be considered under two generals.
1. The consumption at home.
2. The exportation, or consumption abroad.

I begin with the last; namely, the consumption abroad. This is too wide a field to enter upon in particular here, I refer it to be treated at large by itself; but as far as it serves to prove what I have affirmed above, namely, that the consumption of our manufactures may be improved abroad, so far it is needful to speak of it here; I shall confine it to the English colonies and factories abroad.

It is evident, that by the increase of our colonies, the consumption of our manufactures has been exceedingly increased; not only experience proves it, but the nature of the thing makes it impossible to be otherwise; the island of St. Christopher, is a demonstration beyond all argument; that island is increased in its product and people, by the French giving it up to us at the treaty of Utrecht. Its product of sugar is almost equal to that of Barbadoes, and will in a very few years exceed it; the exports from hence to that island are increased in proportion; why then do we not increase our possessions, plant new colonies, and better people our old ones? Both might be done to infinite advantage, as might be made out, had we room for it, past contradiction.

We talk of, and expect a war with Spain; were the advantages which new settlements in the abandoned countries of America, as well the island as the continent considered, we should all wish for such a war, that the English might by their superiority at sea, get and maintain a firm footing, as well on the continent as the islands of America: there the Spainards, like the fable of the dog in the manger, neither improve it themselves, nor will admit others to improve; I mean in all the south continent of America, from Buenos Ayres to port St. Julien, a country fruitful, a climate healthful, able to maintain plentifully any numbers, even to millions of people, with an uninterrupted communication within the land, as far as to the golden mountain of the Andes or Cordilleras, where the Chilians, unsubdued by any European power, a docible, civilized people, but abhorring the Spaniards, would not fail to establish a commerce infinitely profitable, exchanging gold for all your English manufactures, to an inexpressible advantage.

Among the islands, why should not we, as well as the French, plant upon the fruitful countries of Cuba and Hispaniola, as rich and capable of raising sugars, cocoa, ginger, pimento, indigo, cotton, and all the other productions usual in that latitude, as either the Barbadoes or Jamaica.

Our factories, for they cannot yet be called colonies, on the coast of Africa, offer us the like advantages. Why are they not turned into populous and powerful colonies, as they might be? Why not encouraged from hence? And why is not their trade espoused and protected as our other colonies and factories? but left to be ravaged by the naked and contemptible negroes; plundered, and their trade ravished by the more unjust and more merciless interlopers, who, instead of thieves, for they are no better, would be called separate traders only, though they break in by violence and fraud upon the property of an established company, and rob them of their commerce, even under the protection of their own forts and castles, which these paid nothing towards the cost of.

Why does not England enlarge and encourage the commerce of the coast of Guinea? plant and fortify, and establish such possessions there as other nations, the Portuguese for example, in the opposite coast on the same latitude? Is it not all owing to the most unaccountable indolence and neglect? What hinders but that we might ere now have had strong towns and an inhabited district round them, and a hundred thousand Christians dwelling at large in that country, as the Portuguese have now at Melinda, in the same latitude, on the eastern coast?

And what hinders, but that same indolence and neglect, that they have not there growing at this time, the coffee of Mocha, as the Dutch have at Batavia; the tea of China, the cocoa of the Caraccas, the spices of the Moluccas, and all the other productions of the remotest Indies, which grow now in the same latitude, and which cost us so much treasure yearly to purchase, and which, as has been tried, would prosper here as well as in the countries from which we fetch them?

What a consumption of English manufacture would follow such a plantation? and what an increase of trade would necessarily attend an increase of people there?

I have not room to enlarge here upon these heads; they are fully stated in the said Plan of English Commerce, and in several other tracts of trade lately published by the same author, and to that I refer. See the Plan, chap. iii. page 335. and chap. v. page 363.

I come next to the consumption at home, and here indeed the proof lies heavy upon ourselves; nothing but an unaccountable supreme negligence of our own apparent advantages can be the cause of the whole grievance; such a negligence, as I think, no nation but the English are, or can be guilty of; I mean no nation that has the like advantage of a manufacture, and that has a hundred thousand packs of wool every year unwrought up, and a million of people unemployed.

N. B. All our manufactures, whether of wool, silk, or thread, and all other wares, hard or soft, though we have a very great variety, yet do not employ all our people, by a great many; nay, we have some whole counties into which the woollen, or silk, or linen manufacture, may be said never to have set their feet, I mean as to the working part; or so little as not to be worth naming; such in particular as Cambridge, Huntingdon, Hertford, Bedford; the first three are of late indeed come into the spinning part a little, but it is but very little; the like may be said of the counties of Cheshire, Stafford, Derby, and Lincoln, in all which very little, if any, manufactures are carried on; neither are the counties of Kent, Sussex, Surry, or Hampshire, employed in any of the woollen manufactures worth mentioning; the last indeed on the side about Alton and Alresford, may be said to do a little; and the first just at Canterbury and Cranbrook. But what is all they do compared to the extent of four counties so populous that it is thought there are near a million of people in them?

Seeing then, I say, there are yet so many people want employ, and so much wool unwrought up, and which for want of being thus wrought up, is carried away by a clandestine, smuggling, pernicious trade, to employ our enemies in trade, the French, and to endanger our manufactures at foreign markets, how great is our negligence, and how much to the reproach of our country is it, that we do not improve this trade, and increase the consumption of the manufactures as we ought to do? I mean the consumption at home, for of the foreign consumption I have spoken already.

It seems to follow here as a natural inquiry, after what has been said, that we should ask, How is this to be done, and by what method can the people of England increase the home consumption of their woollen manufactures?

I cannot give a more direct answer to this question, or introduce what follows in a better manner, than in the very words of the author of the book so often mentioned above, as follows, speaking of this very thing, thus:—

"The next branch of complaint," says this author, "is, that the consumption of our woollen manufacture is lessened at home.

"This, indeed," continues he, "though least regarded, has the most truth and reason in it, and merits to be more particularly inquired into; but supposing the fact to be true, let me ask the complainer this question, viz., why do we not mend it? and that without laws, without teazing the parliament and our sovereign, for what they find difficult enough to effect even by law? The remedy is our own, and in our own power. I say, why do not the people of Great Britain, by general custom and by universal consent, increase the consumption of their own manufacture by rejecting the trifles and toys of foreigners?

"Why do we not appear dressed in the growth of our own country, and made fine by the labour of our own hands?" Vide Plan of the English Commerce, p. 252.

And again, p. 254; "We must turn the complaints of the people upon themselves, and entreat them to encourage the manufactures of England by a more general use and wearing of them. This alone would increase the consumption, as that alone would increase the manufacture itself."

I cannot put this into a plainer or better way of arguing, or in words more intelligible to every capacity.

Did ever any nation but ours complain of the declining of their trade and at the same time discourage it among themselves? Complain that foreigners prohibit our manufactures, and at the same time prohibit it themselves? for refusing to wear it is the worst and severest way of prohibiting it.

We do indeed put a prohibition upon our trade when we stop up the stream, and dam up the channel of its consumption, by putting a slight upon the wearing it, and, as it were, voting it out of fashion; for if you once vote your goods out of wear, you vote them out of the market, and you had as good vote them contraband.

With what an impetuous gust of the fancy did we run into the product of the East Indies for some years ago? How did we patiently look on and see the looms empty, the workmen fled, the wives and children starve and beg, the parishes loaded, and the poor's rates rise to a surprising height, while the ladies flourished in fine Massulapatam, chints, Indian damasks, China atlasses, and an innumerable number of rich silks, the product of the coast of Malabar, Coromandel, and the Bay of Bengal, and the poorer sort with calicoes? And with what infinite difficulty was a remedy obtained, and with what regret did the ladies part with that foreign pageantry, and stoop to wear the richest silks of their own manufacture, though these were the life of their country's prosperity, and those the ruin of it?

When this was the case, how fared our trade? The state of it was thus, in a few words:—

The poor, as above, wanted bread; the wool lay on hand, sunk in price, and wanted a market; the manufacturers wanted orders, and when they made goods, knew not where to sell them; all was melancholy and dismal on that side; nothing but the East India trade could be said to thrive; their ships went out full of money and came home full of poison; for it was all poison to our trade. The immense sums of ready money that went abroad to India impoverished our trade, and indeed bid fair to starve it, and, in a word, to beggar the nation.

At home we were so far from working up the whole quantity or growth of our wool, that three or four years' growth lay on hand in the poor tenants' houses, for want of which they could not pay their rent.

The wool from Scotland, which comes all to us now, went another way, viz., to France, for the Union was not then made, and yet we had too much at home. Nor was the quantity brought from Ireland half so much as it is now.

Was all this difference from our own wearing, or not wearing the produce of our own manufacture? How unaccountably stupid then are we to run still retrograde to the public good of our country, and ruin our own commerce, by rejecting our own manufacture, setting our people to furnish other nations with cloths, and recommending the manufacture to other countries, and rejecting them ourselves?

If the difference was small, and the clothing of our own people was a thing of small moment, that it made no impression on the commerce, or the manufacture in general, it might be said to be too little to take notice of.

If our consumption at home is thus considerable, and the clothing of our own people does consume the wool of many millions of sheep; if the silk trade employs many thousands of families; if there is an absolute necessity of working up if possible all the growth of our wool, as well of Ireland as of England, or that else it would be run over to France, to the encouragement of rival manufactures, and the ruin of our own; in a word, if our own people, falling into a general use of our own manufacture, would effectually do this, and their continuing to neglect it would effectually throw our manufacture into convulsions, and stagnate the whole trade of the kingdom; if our wearing foreign silk manufactures did annually carry out 1,200,000*l.* sterling per annum for silks, to France and Italy, and above 600,000*l.* per annum for the like to India, all in spices, to the impoverishing our trade, by emptying us of all our ready money, as well as starving our poor for want of employment.

Again, if these grievances were very much abated, and indeed almost remedied by the several acts of parliament, first to prohibit East India silks, then to lay high duties, equal to prohibition, upon French silks; and, in the last place, an act to prohibit the use and wearing of printed calicoes; I say, if these acts have gone so far in the retrieving the dying condition of our woollen manufacture, and encouraging the silk manufacture; that in the first, we have wrought up all the English growth of wool, and that of Scotland too, which was never done before; and in the last have improved so remarkably in the silk manufacture, that all that vast sum of 1,800,000*l.* per annum, expended before in French and Indian silks, is now turned into the pockets of our own poor, and kept all at home, and the silks become a mere English manufacture as was before a foreign.

If all this is true, as it is most certainly, what witchcraft must it be that has seized upon the fancy of this nation? What spirit of blindness and infatuation must have possessed us? that we are in all haste running back into the old, stupid, and dull unthinking state, and growing fond of anything, nay of everything that is injurious to our own commerce, and be it as ruinous as it will to our own poor, and to our own manufactures; nay, though we see our trade sick and languishing, and our poor starving before our eyes; and know that we ourselves are the only cause of it, are yet so obstinately and unalterable averse to our own manufacture, and fond of novelties and trifles, that we will not wear our own goods, but will at any hazard make use of things foreign to us, the labour and advantage of strangers, pagans, negroes, or any kind of people, rather than our own.

Unhappy temper, unknown in any nation but ours! The wiser pagans and Mahometans, natives of India, Persia, China, Japan, Siam, Pegu, act otherwise; wherever we find any people in these parts, we find them clothed with their own manufacture, whether of silk, cotton, herba, or of whatever other materials they were made; nor to this day have our nicest or finest manufactures, though perfectly new to them, (and novelties we see take with us to a frenzy and distraction) touched their fancies, or so much as tempted them to wear them; all our endeavours to persuade them have been in vain; but with us, any new fancy, any far-fetched novelty, however antick, however extravagant in price, nay the dearer the more prevailing, presently touches our wandering fancy, and makes us cast off our finest and most agreeable produce, the fruit of our own industry, and the labour of our own poor, making a mode of the foreign gewgaw, let it be as wild and barbarous as it will.

But I meet with an objection in my way here, which is insisted upon with the utmost warmth; namely:—

Objection: you seem to acknowledge that the prohibition of India silks and the duties upon French silks, have effectually answered the end as to silks; and that the late act against the use and wearing of printed or painted calicoes has likewise had its effect on the woollen manufacture. There is nothing now left to support your complaint but the printed linen; which, though it is become a general wear, yet is our own product and growth, and the labour of our own poor; for the Scots and Irish, by whom the linen is manufactured, are our own subjects, and ought as much to be in our concern as any of the rest, and that linen is as much our own manufacture as the silk and the wool.

Nothing could, in my opinion, be more surprising of its kind, than to hear with what warmth this very argument was urged to the parliament, and to the public, by not the Scots and Irish only, but even by some of our own people, possessed and persuaded by the other, at the time the act against the printed calicoes was depending before the parliament; as if an upstart, and in itself trifling manufacture, however increased by the corruption of our people's humour and fancy, could be an equivalent to the grand manufacture of wool in England, which is the fund of our whole commerce, and has been the spring and fountain of our wealth and prosperity for above three hundred years; a manufacture which employs millions of our people, which has raised the wealth of the whole nation from what it then was to what it now is; a manufacture that has made us the greatest trading nation in the world, and upon which all our wealth and commerce still depends.

I insist upon it that no novelty is to be encouraged among us to the prejudice of this chief and main support of our country, let it be of what kind it will; nor is it at all to the purpose to say such or such a novelty is made at home, and is the work of our own people; it is to say nothing at all, for we ought no more to set up particular manufactures to the prejudice of the woollen trade in general, which is the grand product of the whole nation, and on which our whole prosperity depends, than we would spread an universal infection among us, on pretence that the vegetable or plant from whence the destructive effluvia proceeded, was the growth of our own land; or than we should publish the Alcoran and the most heretical, blasphemous, or immodest books, to taint the morals and principles of the people, on pretence that the paper and print were our own manufactures.

I am for encouraging all manufactures that can be invented and set up among us, and that may tend to the employment of the poor and improvement of our produce; such things having a national tendency to raising the rent of our lands, assisting the consumption of our growth, and, in a word, increasing trade in general; I say I am for encouraging new manufactures of all sorts, with this one exception only, namely, that they do not interfere with, and tend to the prejudice of the woollen manufacture, which is the main and essential manufacture of England.

But the woollen manufacture is the life and blood of the whole nation, the soul of our trade, the top of all manufactures, and nothing can be erected that either rivals it or any way lessens it or interferes with it, without wounding us in the more noble and vital part, and, in effect, endangering the whole.

To set up a manufacture of painted linen, which, touching the particular pride and gay humour of the ordinary sort of people, intercepts the woollen manufacture, which they would otherwise be clothed with, is so far wounding and supplanting the woollen manufacture for a paltry trifle, and though it is indeed in itself but a trifle, yet as the poorer sort of people, the servants, and the wives and children of the farmers and country people, and of the labouring poor, who wear this new fangle, are a vast multitude, the wound strikes deeper into the quantity than most people imagine, makes a large abatement of the consumption of wool, lessening the labour of the poor manufacturers very considerably; and on this account, I say, it ought not to be encouraged, though it be our own manufacture.

Do we not, from this very principle, prohibit the planting tobacco in England, though our own land would produce it? Do we not know there are coals in Blackheath, Muzzle-hill, and other places, but that we must not work them that we may not hurt the navigation? The reason is exactly the same here.

This consideration is so pungent in itself, and so naturally touches every Englishman that has the good of his country at heart, that one would think there should be no occasion for an act of parliament to oblige them to it; but they should be moved by a mere concern of mind, and generous endeavour for the public prosperity, not to fall in with or encourage any new project, any new custom or fashion, without first inquiring particularly whether it would not be injurious to the prosperity of the main and grand article of the English Commerce, the woollen manufacture.

Were this public spirit among us, we need fear no upstart manufacture breaking in upon us, whether printed linen or anything else; for no people of sense, having the good of their country at heart, would touch it, much less make it a general fashion. But, as the Plan of English Commerce observes, our people, the ladies especially, have such a passion for the fashion, that they have been the greatest enemies to our woollen manufacture; and I must add that this passion for the fashion of printed linens at this time is a greater blow to the woollen manufacture of England than all the prohibitions in Germany and Italy, of which we may have formed such frightful ideas in our minds; or even than all the imitation of our manufactures abroad, whether in France, or any other part of Europe.

And yet, to conclude all,

How easy, how very easy is it for us to prevent it; which, by the way, deserves a whole book by itself.

FINIS.

The Fortunes & Misfortunes of the Famous Moll Flanders &c.

Who was Born in Newgate, and during a Life of continu'd
Variety for Threescore Years, besides her Childhood, was Twelve Year
a Whore, five times a Wife (whereof once to her own Brother), Twelve
Year a Thief, Eight Year a Transported Felon in Virginia, at last grew
Rich, liv'd Honest, and dies a Penitent. Written from her own
Memorandums ...

by
Daniel Defoe

THE AUTHOR'S PREFACE

The world is so taken up of late with novels and romances, that it will be hard for a private history to be taken for genuine, where the names and other circumstances of the person are concealed, and on this account we must be content to leave the reader to pass his own opinion upon the ensuing sheet, and take it just as he pleases.

The author is here supposed to be writing her own history, and in the very beginning of her account she gives the reasons why she thinks fit to conceal her true name, after which there is no occasion to say any more about that.

It is true that the original of this story is put into new words, and the style of the famous lady we here speak of is a little altered; particularly she is made to tell her own tale in modester words that she told it at first, the copy which came first to hand having been written in language more like one still in Newgate than one grown penitent and humble, as she afterwards pretends to be.

The pen employed in finishing her story, and making it what you now see it to be, has had no little difficulty to put it into a dress fit to be seen, and to make it speak language fit to be read. When a woman debauched from her youth, nay, even being the offspring of debauchery and vice, comes to give an account of all her vicious practices, and even to descend to the particular occasions and circumstances by which she ran through in threescore years, an author must be hard put to it wrap it up so clean as not to give room, especially for vicious readers, to turn it to his disadvantage.

All possible care, however, has been taken to give no lewd ideas, no immodest turns in the new dressing up of this story; no, not to the worst parts of her expressions. To this purpose some of the vicious part of her life, which could not be modestly told, is quite left out, and several other parts are very much shortened. What is left 'tis hoped will not offend the chastest reader or the modest hearer; and as the best use is made even of the worst story, the moral 'tis hoped will keep the reader serious, even where the story might incline him to be otherwise. To give the history of a wicked life repented of, necessarily requires that the wicked part should be make as wicked as the real history of it will bear, to illustrate and give a beauty to the penitent part, which is certainly the best and brightest, if related with equal spirit and life.

It is suggested there cannot be the same life, the same brightness and beauty, in relating the penitent part as is in the criminal part. If there is any truth in that suggestion, I must be allowed to say 'tis because there is not the same taste and relish in the reading, and indeed it is to true that the difference lies not in the real worth of the subject so much as in the gust and palate of the reader.

But as this work is chiefly recommended to those who know how to read it, and how to make the good uses of it which the story all along recommends to them, so it is to be hoped that such readers will be more leased with the moral than the fable, with the application than with the relation, and with the end of the writer than with the life of the person written of.

There is in this story abundance of delightful incidents, and all of them usefully applied. There is an agreeable turn artfully given them in the relating, that naturally instructs the reader, either one way or other. The first part of her lewd life with the young gentleman at Colchester has so many happy turns given it to expose the crime, and warn all whose circumstances are adapted to it, of the ruinous end of such things, and the foolish, thoughtless, and abhorred conduct of both the parties, that it abundantly atones for all the lively description she gives of her folly and wickedness.

The repentance of her lover at the Bath, and how brought by the just alarm of his fit of sickness to abandon her; the just caution given there against even the lawful intimacies of the dearest friends, and how unable they are to preserve the most solemn resolutions of virtue without divine assistance; these are parts which, to a just discernment, will appear to have more real beauty in them all the amorous chain of story which introduces it.

In a word, as the whole relation is carefully garbled of all the levity and looseness that was in it, so it all applied, and with the utmost care, to virtuous and religious uses. None can, without being guilty of manifest injustice, cast any reproach upon it, or upon our design in publishing it.

The advocates for the stage have, in all ages, made this the great argument to persuade people that their plays are useful, and that they ought to be allowed in the most civilised and in the most religious government; namely, that they are applied to virtuous purposes, and that by the most lively representations, they fail not to recommend virtue and generous principles, and to discourage and expose all sorts of vice and corruption of manners; and were it true that they did so, and that they constantly adhered to that rule, as the test of their acting on the theatre, much might be said in their favour.

Throughout the infinite variety of this book, this fundamental is most strictly adhered to; there is not a wicked action in any part of it, but is first and last rendered unhappy and unfortunate; there is not a superlative villain brought upon the stage, but either he is brought to an unhappy end, or brought to be a penitent; there is not an ill thing mentioned but it is condemned, even in the relation, nor a virtuous, just thing but it carries its praise along with it. What can more exactly answer the rule laid down, to recommend even those representations of things which have so many other just objections leaving against them? namely, of example, of bad company, obscene language, and the like.

Upon this foundation this book is recommended to the reader as a work from every part of which something may be learned, and some just and religious inference is drawn, by which the reader will have something of instruction, if he pleases to make use of it.

All the exploits of this lady of fame, in her depredations upon mankind, stand as so many warnings to honest people to beware of them, intimating to them by what methods innocent people are drawn in, plundered and robbed, and by consequence how to avoid them. Her robbing a little innocent child, dressed fine by the vanity of the mother, to go to the dancing-school, is a good memento to such people hereafter, as is likewise her picking the gold watch from the young lady's side in the Park.

Her getting a parcel from a hare-brained wench at the coaches in St. John Street; her booty made at the fire, and again at Harwich, all give us excellent warnings in such cases to be more present to ourselves in sudden surprises of every sort.

Her application to a sober life and industrious management at last in Virginia, with her transported spouse, is a story fruitful of instruction to all the unfortunate creatures who are obliged to seek their re-establishment abroad, whether by the misery of transportation or other disaster; letting them know that diligence and application have their due encouragement, even in the remotest parts of the world, and that no case can be so low, so despicable, or so empty of prospect, but that an unwearied industry will go a great way to deliver us from it, will in time raise the meanest creature to appear again the world, and give him a new case for his life.

There are a few of the serious inferences which we are led by the hand to in this book, and these are fully sufficient to justify any man in recommending it to the world, and much more to justify the publication of it.

There are two of the most beautiful parts still behind, which this story gives some idea of, and lets us into the parts of them, but they are either of them too long to be brought into the same volume, and indeed are, as I may call them, whole volumes of themselves, viz.: I. The life of her governess, as she calls her, who had run through, it seems, in a few years, all the eminent degrees of a gentlewoman, a whore, and a bawd; a midwife and a midwife-keeper, as they are called; a pawnbroker, a childtaker, a receiver of thieves, and of thieves' purchase, that is to say, of stolen goods; and in a word, herself a thief, a breeder up of thieves and the like, and yet at last a penitent.

The second is the life of her transported husband, a highwayman, who it seems, lived a twelve years' life of successful villainy upon the road, and even at last came off so well as to be a volunteer transport, not a convict; and in whose life there is an incredible variety.

But, as I have said, these are things too long to bring in here, so neither can I make a promise of the coming out by themselves.

We cannot say, indeed, that this history is carried on quite to the end of the life of this famous Moll Flanders, as she calls herself, for nobody can write their own life to the full end of it, unless they can write it after they are dead. But her husband's life, being written by a third hand, gives a full account of them both, how long they lived together in that country, and how they both came to England again, after about eight years, in which time they were grown very rich, and where she lived, it seems, to be very old, but was not so extraordinary a penitent as she was at first; it seems only that indeed she always spoke with abhorrence of her former life, and of every part of it.

In her last scene, at Maryland and Virginia, many pleasant things happened, which makes that part of her life very agreeable, but they are not told with the same elegancy as those accounted for by herself; so it is still to the more advantage that we break off here.

MOLL FLANDERS

My true name is so well known in the records or registers at Newgate, and in the Old Bailey, and there are some things of such consequence still depending there, relating to my particular conduct, that it is not be expected I should set my name or the account of my family to this work; perhaps, after my death, it may be better known; at present it would not be proper, no not though a general pardon should be issued, even without exceptions and reserve of persons or crimes.

It is enough to tell you, that as some of my worst comrades, who are out of the way of doing me harm (having gone out of the world by the steps and the string, as I often expected to go), knew me by the name of Moll Flanders, so you may give me leave to speak of myself under that name till I dare own who I have been, as well as who I am.

I have been told that in one of neighbour nations, whether it be in France or where else I know not, they have an order from the king, that when any criminal is condemned, either to die, or to the galleys, or to be transported, if they leave any children, as such are generally unprovided for, by the poverty or forfeiture of their parents, so they are immediately taken into the care of the Government, and put into a hospital called the House of Orphans, where they are bred up, clothed, fed, taught, and when fit to go out, are placed out to trades or to services, so as to be well able to provide for themselves by an honest, industrious behaviour.

Had this been the custom in our country, I had not been left a poor desolate girl without friends, without clothes, without help or helper in the world, as was my fate; and by which I was not only exposed to very great distresses, even before I was capable either of understanding my case or how to amend it, but brought into a course of life which was not only scandalous in itself, but which in its ordinary course tended to the swift destruction both of soul and body.

But the case was otherwise here. My mother was convicted of felony for a certain petty theft scarce worth naming, viz. having an opportunity of borrowing three pieces of fine holland of a certain draper in Cheapside. The circumstances are too long to repeat, and I have heard them related so many ways, that I can scarce be certain which is the right account.

However it was, this they all agree in, that my mother pleaded her belly, and being found quick with child, she was respited for about seven months; in which time having brought me into the world, and being about again, she was called down, as they term it, to her former judgment, but obtained the favour of being transported to the plantations, and left me about half a year old; and in bad hands, you may be sure.

This is too near the first hours of my life for me to relate anything of myself but by hearsay; it is enough to mention, that as I was born in such an unhappy place, I had no parish to have recourse to for my nourishment in my infancy; nor can I give the least account how I was kept alive, other than that, as I have been told, some relation of my mother's took me away for a while as a nurse, but at whose expense, or by whose direction, I know nothing at all of it.

The first account that I can recollect, or could ever learn of myself, was that I had wandered among a crew of those people they call gypsies, or Egyptians; but I believe it was but a very little while that I had been among them, for I had not had my skin discoloured or blackened, as they do very young to all the children they carry about with them; nor can I tell how I came among them, or how I got from them.

It was at Colchester, in Essex, that those people left me; and I have a notion in my head that I left them there (that is, that I hid myself and would not go any farther with them), but I am not able to be particular in that account; only this I remember, that being taken up by some of the parish officers of Colchester, I gave an account that I came into the town with the gypsies, but that I would not go any farther with them, and that so they had left me, but whither they were gone that I knew not, nor could they expect it of me; for though they send round the country to inquire after them, it seems they could not be found.

I was now in a way to be provided for; for though I was not a parish charge upon this or that part of the town by law, yet as my case came to be known, and that I was too young to do any work, being not above three years old, compassion moved the magistrates of the town to order some care to be taken of me, and I became one of their own as much as if I had been born in the place.

In the provision they made for me, it was my good hap to be put to nurse, as they call it, to a woman who was indeed poor but had been in better circumstances, and who got a little livelihood by taking such as I was supposed to be, and keeping them with all necessaries, till they were at a certain age, in which it might be supposed they might go to service or get their own bread.

This woman had also had a little school, which she kept to teach children to read and to work; and having, as I have said, lived before that in good fashion, she bred up the children she took with a great deal of art, as well as with a great deal of care.

But that which was worth all the rest, she bred them up very religiously, being herself a very sober, pious woman, very house-wifely and clean, and very mannerly, and with good behaviour. So that in a word, expecting a plain diet, coarse lodging, and mean clothes, we were brought up as mannerly and as genteelly as if we had been at the dancing-school.

I was continued here till I was eight years old, when I was terrified with news that the magistrates (as I think they called them) had ordered that I should go to service. I was able to do but very little service wherever I was to go, except it was to run of errands and be a drudge to some cookmaid, and this they told me of often, which put me into a great fright; for I had a thorough aversion to going to service, as they called it (that is, to be a servant), though I was so young; and I told my nurse, as we called her, that I believed I could get my living without going to service, if she pleased to let me; for she had taught me to work with my needle, and spin worsted, which is the chief trade of that city, and I told her that if she would keep me, I would work for her, and I would work very hard.

I talked to her almost every day of working hard; and, in short, I did nothing but work and cry all day, which grieved the good, kind woman so much, that at last she began to be concerned for me, for she loved me very well.

One day after this, as she came into the room where all we poor children were at work, she sat down just over against me, not in her usual place as mistress, but as if she set herself on purpose to observe me and see me work. I was doing something she had set me to; as I remember, it was marking some shirts which she had taken to make, and after a while she began to talk to me. 'Thou foolish child,' says she, 'thou art always crying (for I was crying then); 'prithee, what dost cry for?' 'Because they will take me away,' says I, 'and put me to service, and I can't work housework.' 'Well, child,' says she, 'but though you can't work housework, as you call it, you will learn it in time, and they won't put you to hard things at first.' 'Yes, they will,' says I, 'and if I can't do it they will beat me, and the maids will beat me to make me do great work, and I am but a little girl and I can't do it'; and then I cried again, till I could not speak any more to her.

This moved my good motherly nurse, so that she from that time resolved I should not go to service yet; so she bid me not cry, and she would speak to Mr. Mayor, and I should not go to service till I was bigger.

Well, this did not satisfy me, for to think of going to service was such a frightful thing to me, that if she had assured me I should not have gone till I was twenty years old, it would have been the same to me; I should have cried, I believe, all the time, with the very apprehension of its being to be so at last.

When she saw that I was not pacified yet, she began to be angry with me. 'And what would you have?' says she; 'don't I tell you that you shall not go to service till your are bigger?' 'Ay,' said I, 'but then I must go at last.' 'Why, what?' said she; 'is the girl mad? What would you be—a gentlewoman?' 'Yes,' says I, and cried heartily till I roared out again.

This set the old gentlewoman a-laughing at me, as you may be sure it would. 'Well, madam, forsooth,' says she, gibing at me, 'you would be a gentlewoman; and pray how will you come to be a gentlewoman? What! will you do it by your fingers' end?'

'Yes,' says I again, very innocently.

'Why, what can you earn?' says she; 'what can you get at your work?'

'Threepence,' said I, 'when I spin, and fourpence when I work plain work.'

'Alas! poor gentlewoman,' said she again, laughing, 'what will that do for thee?'

'It will keep me,' says I, 'if you will let me live with you.' And this I said in such a poor petitioning tone, that it made the poor woman's heart yearn to me, as she told me afterwards.

'But,' says she, 'that will not keep you and buy you clothes too; and who must buy the little gentlewoman clothes?' says she, and smiled all the while at me.

'I will work harder, then,' says I, 'and you shall have it all.'

'Poor child! it won't keep you,' says she; 'it will hardly keep you in victuals.'

'Then I will have no victuals,' says I, again very innocently; 'let me but live with you.'

'Why, can you live without victuals?' says she.

'Yes,' again says I, very much like a child, you may be sure, and still I cried heartily.

I had no policy in all this; you may easily see it was all nature; but it was joined with so much innocence and so much passion that, in short, it set the good motherly creature a-weeping too, and she cried at last as fast as I did, and then took me and led me out of the teaching-room. 'Come,' says she, 'you shan't go to service; you shall live with me'; and this pacified me for the present.

Some time after this, she going to wait on the Mayor, and talking of such things as belonged to her business, at last my story came up, and my good nurse told Mr. Mayor the whole tale. He was so pleased with it, that he would call his lady and his two daughters to hear it, and it made mirth enough among them, you may be sure.

However, not a week had passed over, but on a sudden comes Mrs. Mayoress and her two daughters to the house to see my old nurse, and to see her school and the children. When they had looked about them a little, 'Well, Mrs. ———,' says the Mayoress to my nurse, 'and pray which is the little lass that intends to be a gentlewoman?' I heard her, and I was terribly frighted at first, though I did not know why neither; but Mrs. Mayoress comes up to me. 'Well, miss,' says she, 'and what are you at work upon?' The word miss was a language that had hardly been heard of in our school, and I wondered what sad name it was she called me. However, I stood up, made a curtsy, and she took my work out of my hand, looked on it, and said it was very well; then she took up one of the hands. 'Nay,' says she, 'the child may come to be a gentlewoman for aught anybody knows; she has a gentlewoman's hand,' says she. This pleased me mightily, you may be sure; but Mrs. Mayoress did not stop there, but giving me my work again, she put her hand in her pocket, gave me a shilling, and bid me mind my work, and learn to work well, and I might be a gentlewoman for aught she knew.

Now all this while my good old nurse, Mrs. Mayoress, and all the rest of them did not understand me at all, for they meant one sort of thing by the word gentlewoman, and I meant quite another; for alas! all I understood by being a gentlewoman was to be able to work for myself, and get enough to keep me without that terrible bugbear going to service, whereas they meant to live great, rich and high, and I know not what.

Well, after Mrs. Mayoress was gone, her two daughters came in, and they called for the gentlewoman too, and they talked a long while to me, and I answered them in my innocent way; but always, if they asked me whether I resolved to be a gentlewoman, I answered Yes. At last one of them asked me what a gentlewoman was? That puzzled me much; but, however, I explained myself negatively, that it was one that did not go to service, to do housework. They were pleased to be familiar with me, and like my little prattle to them, which, it seems, was agreeable enough to them, and they gave me money too.

As for my money, I gave it all to my mistress-nurse, as I called her, and told her she should have all I got for myself when I was a gentlewoman, as well as now. By this and some other of my talk, my old tutoress began to understand me about what I meant by being a gentlewoman, and that I understood by it no more than to be able to get my bread by my own work; and at last she asked me whether it was not so.

I told her, yes, and insisted on it, that to do so was to be a gentlewoman; 'for,' says I, 'there is such a one,' naming a woman that mended lace and washed the ladies' laced-heads; 'she,' says I, 'is a gentlewoman, and they call her madam.'

'Poor child,' says my good old nurse, 'you may soon be such a gentlewoman as that, for she is a person of ill fame, and has had two or three bastards.'

I did not understand anything of that; but I answered, 'I am sure they call her madam, and she does not go to service nor do housework'; and therefore I insisted that she was a gentlewoman, and I would be such a gentlewoman as that.

The ladies were told all this again, to be sure, and they made themselves merry with it, and every now and then the young ladies, Mr. Mayor's daughters, would come and see me, and ask where the little gentlewoman was, which made me not a little proud of myself.

This held a great while, and I was often visited by these young ladies, and sometimes they brought others with them; so that I was known by it almost all over the town.

I was now about ten years old, and began to look a little womanish, for I was mighty grave and humble, very mannerly, and as I had often heard the ladies say I was pretty, and would be a very handsome woman, so you may be sure that hearing them say so made me not a little proud. However, that pride had no ill effect upon me yet; only, as they often gave me money, and I gave it to my old nurse, she, honest woman, was so just to me as to lay it all out again for me, and gave me head-dresses, and linen, and gloves, and ribbons, and I went very neat, and always clean; for that I would do, and if I had rags on, I would always be clean, or else I would dabble them in water myself; but, I say, my good nurse, when I had money given me, very honestly laid it out for me, and would always tell the ladies this or that was bought with their money; and this made them oftentimes give me more, till at last I was indeed called upon by the magistrates, as I understood it, to go out to service; but then I was come to be so good a workwoman myself, and the ladies were so kind to me, that it was plain I could maintain myself—that is to say, I could earn as much for my nurse as she was able by it to keep me—so she told them that if they would give her leave, she would keep the gentlewoman, as she called me, to be her assistant and teach the children, which I was very well able to do; for I was very nimble at my work, and had a good hand with my needle, though I was yet very young.

But the kindness of the ladies of the town did not end here, for when they came to understand that I was no more maintained by the public allowance as before, they gave me money oftener than formerly; and as I grew up they brought me work to do for them, such as linen to make, and laces to mend, and heads to dress up, and not only paid me for doing them, but even taught me how to do them; so that now I was a gentlewoman indeed, as I understood that word, I not only found myself clothes and paid my nurse for my keeping, but got money in my pocket too beforehand.

The ladies also gave me clothes frequently of their own or their children's; some stockings, some petticoats, some gowns, some one thing, some another, and these my old woman managed for me like a mere mother, and kept them for me, obliged me to mend them, and turn them and twist them to the best advantage, for she was a rare housewife.

At last one of the ladies took so much fancy to me that she would have me home to her house, for a month, she said, to be among her daughters.

Now, though this was exceeding kind in her, yet, as my old good woman said to her, unless she resolved to keep me for good and all, she would do the little gentlewoman more harm than good. 'Well,' says the lady, 'that's true; and therefore I'll only take her home for a week, then, that I may see how my daughters and she agree together, and how I like her temper, and then I'll tell you more; and in the meantime, if anybody comes to see her as they used to do, you may only tell them you have sent her out to my house.'

This was prudently managed enough, and I went to the lady's house; but I was so pleased there with the young ladies, and they so pleased with me, that I had enough to do to come away, and they were as unwilling to part with me.

However, I did come away, and lived almost a year more with my honest old woman, and began now to be very helpful to her; for I was almost fourteen years old, was tall of my age, and looked a little womanish; but I had such a taste of genteel living at the lady's house that I was not so easy in my old quarters as I used to be, and I thought it was fine to be a gentlewoman indeed, for I had quite other notions of a gentlewoman now than I had before; and as I thought, I say, that it was fine to be a gentlewoman, so I loved to be among gentlewomen, and therefore I longed to be there again.

About the time that I was fourteen years and a quarter old, my good nurse, mother I rather to call her, fell sick and died. I was then in a sad condition indeed, for as there is no great bustle in putting an end to a poor body's family when once they are carried to the grave, so the poor good woman being buried, the parish children she kept were immediately removed by the church-wardens; the school was at an end, and the children of it had no more to do but just stay at home till they were sent somewhere else; and as for what she left, her daughter, a married woman with six or seven children, came and swept it all away at once, and removing the goods, they had no more to say to me than to jest with me, and tell me that the little gentlewoman might set up for herself if she pleased.

I was frighted out of my wits almost, and knew not what to do, for I was, as it were, turned out of doors to the wide world, and that which was still worse, the old honest woman had two-and-twenty shillings of mine in her hand, which was all the estate the little gentlewoman had in the world; and when I asked the daughter for it, she huffed me and laughed at me, and told me she had nothing to do with it.

It was true the good, poor woman had told her daughter of it, and that it lay in such a place, that it was the child's money, and had called once or twice for me to give it me, but I was, unhappily, out of the way somewhere or other, and when I came back she was past being in a condition to speak of it. However, the daughter was so honest afterwards as to give it me, though at first she used me cruelly about it.

Now was I a poor gentlewoman indeed, and I was just that very night to be turned into the wide world; for the daughter removed all the goods, and I had not so much as a lodging to go to, or a bit of bread to eat. But it seems some of the neighbours, who had known my circumstances, took so much compassion of me as to acquaint the lady in whose family I had been a week, as I mentioned above; and immediately she sent her maid to fetch me away, and two of her daughters came with the maid though unsent. So I went with them, bag and baggage, and with a glad heart, you may be sure. The fright of my condition had made such an impression upon me, that I did not want now to be a gentlewoman, but was very willing to be a servant, and that any kind of servant they thought fit to have me be.

But my new generous mistress, for she exceeded the good woman I was with before, in everything, as well as in the matter of estate; I say, in everything except honesty; and for that, though this was a lady most exactly just, yet I must not forget to say on all occasions, that the first, though poor, was as uprightly honest as it was possible for any one to be.

I was no sooner carried away, as I have said, by this good gentlewoman, but the first lady, that is to say, the Mayoress that was, sent her two daughters to take care of me; and another family which had taken notice of me when I was the little gentlewoman, and had given me work to do, sent for me after her, so that I was mightily made of, as we say; nay, and they were not a little angry, especially madam the Mayoress, that her friend had taken me away from her, as she called it; for, as she said, I was hers by right, she having been the first that took any notice of me. But they that had me would not part with me; and as for me, though I should have been very well treated with any of the others, yet I could not be better than where I was.

Here I continued till I was between seventeen and eighteen years old, and here I had all the advantages for my education that could be imagined; the lady had masters home to the house to teach her daughters to dance, and to speak French, and to write, and other to teach them music; and I was always with them, I learned as fast as they; and though the masters were not appointed to teach me, yet I learned by imitation and inquiry all that they learned by instruction and direction; so that, in short, I learned to dance and speak French as well as any of them, and to sing much better, for I had a better voice than any of them. I could not so readily come at playing on the harpsichord or spinet, because I had no instrument of my own to practice on, and could only come at theirs in the intervals when they left it, which was uncertain; but yet I learned tolerably well too, and the young ladies at length got two instruments, that is to say, a harpsichord and a spinet too, and then they taught me themselves. But as to dancing, they could hardly help my learning country-dances, because they always wanted me to make up even number; and, on the other hand, they were as heartily willing to learn me everything that they had been taught themselves, as I could be to take the learning.

By this means I had, as I have said above, all the advantages of education that I could have had if I had been as much a gentlewoman as they were with whom I lived; and in some things I had the advantage of my ladies, though they were my superiors; but they were all the gifts of nature, and which all their fortunes could not furnish. First, I was apparently handsomer than any of them; secondly, I was better shaped; and, thirdly, I sang better, by which I mean I had a better voice; in all which you will, I hope, allow me to say, I do not speak my own conceit of myself, but the opinion of all that knew the family.

I had with all these the common vanity of my sex, viz. that being really taken for very handsome, or, if you please, for a great beauty, I very well knew it, and had as good an opinion of myself as anybody else could have of me; and particularly I loved to hear anybody speak of it, which could not but happen to me sometimes, and was a great satisfaction to me.

Thus far I have had a smooth story to tell of myself, and in all this part of my life I not only had the reputation of living in a very good family, and a family noted and respected everywhere for virtue and sobriety, and for every valuable thing; but I had the character too of a very sober, modest, and virtuous young woman, and such I had always been; neither had I yet any occasion to think of anything else, or to know what a temptation to wickedness meant.

But that which I was too vain of was my ruin, or rather my vanity was the cause of it. The lady in the house where I was had two sons, young gentlemen of very promising parts and of extraordinary behaviour, and it was my misfortune to be very well with them both, but they managed themselves with me in a quite different manner.

The eldest, a gay gentleman that knew the town as well as the country, and though he had levity enough to do an ill-natured thing, yet had too much judgment of things to pay too dear for his pleasures; he began with the unhappy snare to all women, viz. taking notice upon all occasions how pretty I was, as he called it, how agreeable, how well-carriaged, and the like; and this he contrived so subtly, as if he had known as well how to catch a woman in his net as a partridge when he went a-setting; for he would contrive to be talking this to his sisters when, though I was not by, yet when he knew I was not far off but that

I should be sure to hear him. His sisters would return softly to him, 'Hush, brother, she will hear you; she is but in the next room.' Then he would put it off and talk softlier, as if he had not know it, and begin to acknowledge he was wrong; and then, as if he had forgot himself, he would speak aloud again, and I, that was so well pleased to hear it, was sure to listen for it upon all occasions.

After he had thus baited his hook, and found easily enough the method how to lay it in my way, he played an opener game; and one day, going by his sister's chamber when I was there, doing something about dressing her, he comes in with an air of gaiety. 'Oh, Mrs. Betty,' said he to me, 'how do you do, Mrs. Betty? Don't your cheeks burn, Mrs. Betty?' I made a curtsy and blushed, but said nothing. 'What makes you talk so, brother?' says the lady. 'Why,' says he, 'we have been talking of her below-stairs this half-hour.' 'Well,' says his sister, 'you can say no harm of her, that I am sure, so 'tis no matter what you have been talking about.' 'Nay,' says he, "tis so far from talking harm of her, that we have been talking a great deal of good, and a great many fine things have been said of Mrs. Betty, I assure you; and particularly, that she is the handsomest young woman in Colchester; and, in short, they begin to toast her health in the town.'

'I wonder at you, brother,' says the sister. 'Betty wants but one thing, but she had as good want everything, for the market is against our sex just now; and if a young woman have beauty, birth, breeding, wit, sense, manners, modesty, and all these to an extreme, yet if she have not money, she's nobody, she had as good want them all for nothing but money now recommends a woman; the men play the game all into their own hands.'

Her younger brother, who was by, cried, 'Hold, sister, you run too fast; I am an exception to your rule. I assure you, if I find a woman so accomplished as you talk of, I say, I assure you, I would not trouble myself about the money.'

'Oh,' says the sister, 'but you will take care not to fancy one, then, without the money.'

'You don't know that neither,' says the brother.

'But why, sister,' says the elder brother, 'why do you exclaim so at the men for aiming so much at the fortune? You are none of them that want a fortune, whatever else you want.'

'I understand you, brother,' replies the lady very smartly; 'you suppose I have the money, and want the beauty; but as times go now, the first will do without the last, so I have the better of my neighbours.'

'Well,' says the younger brother, 'but your neighbours, as you call them, may be even with you, for beauty will steal a husband sometimes in spite of money, and when the maid chances to be handsomer than the mistress, she oftentimes makes as good a market, and rides in a coach before her.'

I thought it was time for me to withdraw and leave them, and I did so, but not so far but that I heard all their discourse, in which I heard abundance of the fine things said of myself, which served to prompt my vanity, but, as I soon found, was not the way to increase my interest in the family, for the sister and the younger brother fell grievously out about it; and as he said some very disobliging things to her upon my account, so I could easily see that she resented them by her future conduct to me, which indeed was very unjust to me, for I had never had the least thought of what she suspected as to her younger brother; indeed, the elder brother, in his distant, remote way, had said a great many things as in jest, which I had the folly to believe were in earnest, or to flatter myself with the hopes of what I ought to have supposed he never intended, and perhaps never thought of.

It happened one day that he came running upstairs, towards the room where his sisters used to sit and work, as he often used to do; and calling to them before he came in, as was his way too, I, being there alone, stepped to the door, and said, 'Sir, the ladies are not here, they are walked down the garden.' As I stepped forward to say this, towards the door, he was just got to the door, and clasping me in his arms, as if it had been by chance, 'Oh, Mrs. Betty,' says he, 'are you here? That's better still; I want to speak with you more than I do with them'; and then, having me in his arms, he kissed me three or four times.

I struggled to get away, and yet did it but faintly neither, and he held me fast, and still kissed me, till he was almost out of breath, and then, sitting down, says, 'Dear Betty, I am in love with you.'

His words, I must confess, fired my blood; all my spirits flew about my heart and put me into disorder enough, which he might easily have seen in my face. He repeated it afterwards several times, that he was in love with me, and my heart spoke as plain as a voice, that I liked it; nay, whenever he said, 'I am in love with you,' my blushes plainly replied, 'Would you were, sir.'

However, nothing else passed at that time; it was but a surprise, and when he was gone I soon recovered myself again. He had stayed longer with me, but he happened to look out at the window and see his sisters coming up the garden, so he took his leave, kissed me again, told me he was very serious, and I should hear more of him very quickly, and away he went, leaving me infinitely pleased, though surprised; and had there not been one misfortune in it, I had been in the right, but the mistake lay here, that Mrs. Betty was in earnest and the gentleman was not.

From this time my head ran upon strange things, and I may truly say I was not myself; to have such a gentleman talk to me of being in love with me, and of my being such a charming creature, as he told me I was; these were things I knew not how to bear, my vanity was elevated to the last degree. It is true I had my head full of pride, but, knowing nothing of the wickedness of the times, I had not one thought of my own safety or of my virtue about me; and had my young master offered it at first sight, he might have taken any liberty he thought fit with me; but he did not see his advantage, which was my happiness for that time.

After this attack it was not long but he found an opportunity to catch me again, and almost in the same posture; indeed, it had more of design in it on his part, though not on my part. It was thus: the young ladies were all gone a-visiting with their mother; his brother was out of town; and as for his father, he had been in London for a week before. He had so well watched me that he knew where I was, though I did not so much as know that he was in the house; and he briskly comes up the stairs and, seeing me at work, comes into the room to me directly, and began just as he did before, with taking me in his arms, and kissing me for almost a quarter of an hour together.

It was his younger sister's chamber that I was in, and as there was nobody in the house but the maids below-stairs, he was, it may be, the ruder; in short, he began to be in earnest with me indeed. Perhaps he found me a little too easy, for God knows I made no resistance to him while he only held me in his arms and kissed me; indeed, I was too well pleased with it to resist him much.

However, as it were, tired with that kind of work, we sat down, and there he talked with me a great while; he said he was charmed with me, and that he could not rest night or day till he had told me how he was in love with me, and, if I was able to love him again, and would make him happy, I should be the saving of his life, and many such fine things. I said little to him again, but easily discovered that I was a fool, and that I did not in the least perceive what he meant.

Then he walked about the room, and taking me by the hand, I walked with him; and by and by, taking his advantage, he threw me down upon the bed, and kissed me there most violently; but, to give him his due, offered no manner of rudeness to me, only kissed a great while. After this he thought he had heard somebody come upstairs, so got off from the bed, lifted me up, professing a great deal of love for me, but told me it was all an honest affection, and that he meant no ill to me; and with that he put five guineas into my hand, and went away downstairs.

I was more confounded with the money than I was before with the love, and began to be so elevated that I scarce knew the ground I stood on. I am the more particular in this part, that if my story comes to be read by any innocent young body, they may learn from it to guard themselves against the mischiefs which attend an early knowledge of their own beauty. If a young woman once thinks herself handsome, she never doubts the truth of any man that tells her he is in love with her; for if she believes herself charming enough to captivate him, 'tis natural to expect the effects of it.

This young gentleman had fired his inclination as much as he had my vanity, and, as if he had found that he had an opportunity and was sorry he did not take hold of it, he comes up again in half an hour or thereabouts, and falls to work with me again as before, only with a little less introduction.

And first, when he entered the room, he turned about and shut the door. 'Mrs. Betty,' said he, 'I fancied before somebody was coming upstairs, but it was not so; however,' adds he, 'if they find me in the room with you, they shan't catch me a-kissing of you.' I told him I did not know who should be coming upstairs, for I believed there was nobody in the house but the cook and the other maid, and they never came up those stairs. 'Well, my dear,' says he, "tis good to be sure, however'; and so he sits down, and we began to talk. And now, though I was still all on fire with his first visit, and said little, he did as it were put words in my mouth, telling me how passionately he loved me, and that though he could not mention such a thing till he came to this estate, yet he was resolved to make me happy then, and himself too; that is to say, to marry me, and abundance of such fine things, which I, poor fool, did not understand the drift of, but acted as if there was no such thing as any kind of love but that which tended to matrimony; and if he had spoke of that, I had no room, as well as no power, to have said no; but we were not come that length yet.

We had not sat long, but he got up, and, stopping my very breath with kisses, threw me upon the bed again; but then being both well warmed, he went farther with me than decency permits me to mention, nor had it been in my power to have denied him at that moment, had he offered much more than he did.

However, though he took these freedoms with me, it did not go to that which they call the last favour, which, to do him justice, he did not attempt; and he made that self-denial of his a plea for all his freedoms with me upon other occasions after this. When this was over, he stayed but a little while, but he put almost a handful of gold in my hand, and left me, making a thousand protestations of his passion for me, and of his loving me above all the women in the world.

It will not be strange if I now began to think, but alas! it was but with very little solid reflection. I had a most unbounded stock of vanity and pride, and but a very little stock of virtue. I did indeed case sometimes with myself what young master aimed at, but thought of nothing but the fine words and the gold; whether he intended to marry me, or not to marry me, seemed a matter of no great consequence to me; nor did my thoughts so much as suggest to me the necessity of making any capitulation for myself, till he came to make a kind of formal proposal to me, as you shall hear presently.

Thus I gave up myself to a readiness of being ruined without the least concern and am a fair memento to all young women whose vanity prevails over their virtue. Nothing was ever so stupid on both sides. Had I acted as became me, and resisted as virtue and honour require, this gentleman had either desisted his attacks, finding no room to expect the accomplishment of his design, or had made fair and honourable proposals of marriage; in which case, whoever had blamed him, nobody could have blamed me. In short, if he had known me, and how easy the trifle he aimed at was to be had, he would have troubled his head no farther, but have given me four or five guineas, and have lain with me the next time he had come at me. And if I had known his thoughts, and how hard he thought I would be to be gained, I might have made my own terms with him; and if I had not capitulated for an immediate marriage, I might for a maintenance till marriage, and might have had what I would; for he was already rich to excess, besides what he had in expectation; but I seemed wholly to have abandoned all such thoughts as these, and was taken up only with the pride of my beauty, and of being beloved by such a gentleman. As for the gold, I spent whole hours in looking upon it; I told the guineas over and over a thousand times a day. Never poor vain creature was so wrapt up with every part of the story as I was, not considering what was before me, and how near my ruin was at the door; indeed, I think I rather wished for that ruin than studied to avoid it.

In the meantime, however, I was cunning enough not to give the least room to any in the family to suspect me, or to imagine that I had the least correspondence with this young gentleman. I scarce ever looked towards him in public, or answered if he spoke to me when anybody was near us; but for all that, we had every now and then a little encounter, where we had room for a word or two, an now and then a kiss, but no fair opportunity for the mischief intended; and especially considering that he made more circumlocution than, if he had known by thoughts, he had occasion for; and the work appearing difficult to him, he really made it so.

But as the devil is an unwearied tempter, so he never fails to find opportunity for that wickedness he invites to. It was one evening that I was in the garden, with his two younger sisters and himself, and all very innocently merry, when he found means to convey a note into my hand, by which he directed me to understand that he would to-morrow desire me publicly to go of an errand for him into the town, and that I should see him somewhere by the way.

Accordingly, after dinner, he very gravely says to me, his sisters being all by, 'Mrs. Betty, I must ask a favour of you.' 'What's that?' says his second sister. 'Nay, sister,' says he very gravely, 'if you can't spare Mrs. Betty to-day, any other time will do.' Yes, they said, they could spare her well enough, and the sister begged pardon for asking, which they did but of mere course, without any meaning. 'Well, but, brother,' says the eldest sister, 'you must tell Mrs. Betty what it is; if it be any private business that we must not hear, you may call her out. There she is.' 'Why, sister,' says the gentleman very gravely, 'what do you mean? I only desire her to go into the High Street' (and then he pulls out a turnover), 'to such a shop'; and then he tells them a long story of two fine neckcloths he had bid money for, and he wanted to have me go and make an errand to buy a neck to the turnover that he showed, to see if they would take my money for the neckcloths; to bid a shilling more, and haggle with them; and then he made more errands, and so continued to have such petty business to do, that I should be sure to stay a good while.

When he had given me my errands, he told them a long story of a visit he was going to make to a family they all knew, and where was to be such-and-such gentlemen, and how merry they were to be, and very formally asks his sisters to go with him, and they as formally excused themselves, because of company that they had notice was to come and visit them that afternoon; which, by the way, he had contrived on purpose.

He had scarce done speaking to them, and giving me my errand, but his man came up to tell him that Sir W—— H——'s coach stopped at the door; so he runs down, and comes up again immediately. 'Alas!' says he aloud, 'there's all my mirth spoiled at once; sir W—— has sent his coach for me, and desires to speak with me upon some earnest business.' It seems this Sir W—— was a gentleman who lived about three miles out of town, to whom he had spoken on purpose the day before, to lend him his chariot for a particular occasion, and had appointed it to call for him, as it did, about three o'clock.

Immediately he calls for his best wig, hat, and sword, and ordering his man to go to the other place to make his excuse— that was to say, he made an excuse to send his man away—he prepares to go into the coach. As he was going, he stopped a while, and speaks mighty earnestly to me about his business, and finds an opportunity to say very softly to me, 'Come away, my dear, as soon as ever you can.' I said nothing, but made a curtsy, as if I had done so to what he said in public. In about a quarter of an hour I went out too; I had no dress other than before, except that I had a hood, a mask, a fan, and a pair of gloves in my pocket; so that there was not the least suspicion in the house. He waited for me in the coach in a back-lane, which he knew I must pass by, and had directed the coachman whither to go, which was to a certain place, called Mile End, where lived a confidant of his, where we went in, and where was all the convenience in the world to be as wicked as we pleased.

When we were together he began to talk very gravely to me, and to tell me he did not bring me there to betray me; that his passion for me would not suffer him to abuse me; that he resolved to marry me as soon as he came to his estate; that in the meantime, if I would grant his request, he would maintain me very honourably; and made me a thousand protestations of his sincerity and of his affection to me; and that he would never abandon me, and as I may say, made a thousand more preambles than he need to have done.

However, as he pressed me to speak, I told him I had no reason to question the sincerity of his love to me after so many protestations, but—and there I stopped, as if I left him to guess the rest. 'But what, my dear?' says he. 'I guess what you mean: what if you should be with child? Is not that it? Why, then,' says he, 'I'll take care of you and provide for you, and the child too; and that you may see I am not in jest,' says he, 'here's an earnest for you,' and with that he pulls out a silk purse, with an hundred guineas in it, and gave it me. 'And I'll give you such another,' says he, 'every year till I marry you.'

My colour came and went, at the sight of the purse and with the fire of his proposal together, so that I could not say a word, and he easily perceived it; so putting the purse into my bosom, I made no more resistance to him, but let him do just what he pleased, and as often as he pleased; and thus I finished my own destruction at once, for from this day, being forsaken of my virtue and my modesty, I had nothing of value left to recommend me, either to God's blessing or man's assistance.

But things did not end here. I went back to the town, did the business he publicly directed me to, and was at home before anybody thought me long. As for my gentleman, he stayed out, as he told me he would, till late at night, and there was not the least suspicion in the family either on his account or on mine.

We had, after this, frequent opportunities to repeat our crime — chiefly by his contrivance—especially at home, when his mother and the young ladies went abroad a-visiting, which he watched so narrowly as never to miss; knowing always beforehand when they went out, and then failed not to catch me all alone, and securely enough; so that we took our fill of our wicked pleasure for near half a year; and yet, which was the most to my satisfaction, I was not with child.

But before this half-year was expired, his younger brother, of whom I have made some mention in the beginning of the story, falls to work with me; and he, finding me alone in the garden one evening, begins a story of the same kind to me, made good honest professions of being in love with me, and in short, proposes fairly and honourably to marry me, and that before he made any other offer to me at all.

I was now confounded, and driven to such an extremity as the like was never known; at least not to me. I resisted the proposal with obstinacy; and now I began to arm myself with arguments. I laid before him the inequality of the match; the treatment I should meet with in the family; the ingratitude it would be to his good father and mother, who had taken me into their house upon such generous principles, and when I was in such a low condition; and, in short, I said everything to dissuade him from his design that I could imagine, except telling him the truth, which would indeed have put an end to it all, but that I durst not think of mentioning.

But here happened a circumstance that I did not expect indeed, which put me to my shifts; for this young gentleman, as he was plain and honest, so he pretended to nothing with me but what was so too; and, knowing his own innocence, he was not so careful to make his having a kindness for Mrs. Betty a secret I the house, as his brother was. And though he did not let them know that he had talked to me about it, yet he said enough to let his sisters perceive he loved me, and his mother saw it too, which, though they took no notice of it to me, yet they did to him, an immediately I found their carriage to me altered, more than ever before.

I saw the cloud, though I did not foresee the storm. It was easy, I say, to see that their carriage to me was altered, and that it grew worse and worse every day; till at last I got information among the servants that I should, in a very little while, be desired to remove.

I was not alarmed at the news, having a full satisfaction that I should be otherwise provided for; and especially considering that I had reason every day to expect I should be with child, and that then I should be obliged to remove without any pretences for it.

After some time the younger gentleman took an opportunity to tell me that the kindness he had for me had got vent in the family. He did not charge me with it, he said, for he know well enough which way it came out. He told me his plain way of talking had been the occasion of it, for that he did not make his respect for me so much a secret as he might have done, and the reason was, that he was at a point, that if I would consent to have him, he would tell them all openly that he loved me, and that he intended to marry me; that it was true his father and mother might resent it, and be unkind, but that he was now in a way to live, being bred to the law, and he did not fear maintaining me agreeable to what I should expect; and that, in short, as he believed I would not be ashamed of him, so he was resolved not to be ashamed of me, and that he scorned to be afraid to own me now, whom he resolved to own after I was his wife, and therefore I had nothing to do but to give him my hand, and he would answer for all the rest.

I was now in a dreadful condition indeed, and now I repented heartily my easiness with the eldest brother; not from any reflection of conscience, but from a view of the happiness I might have enjoyed, and had now made impossible; for though I had no great scruples of conscience, as I have said, to struggle with, yet I could not think of being a whore to one brother and a wife to the other. But then it came into my thoughts that the first brother had promised to made me his wife when he came to his estate; but I presently remembered what I had often thought of, that he had never spoken a word of having me for a wife after he had conquered me for a mistress; and indeed, till now, though I said I thought of it often, yet it gave me no disturbance at all, for as he did not seem in the least to lessen his affection to me, so neither did he lessen his bounty, though he had the discretion himself to desire me not to lay out a penny of what he gave me in clothes, or to make the least show extraordinary, because it would necessarily give jealousy in the family, since everybody know I could come at such things no manner of ordinary way, but by some private friendship, which they would presently have suspected.

But I was now in a great strait, and knew not what to do. The main difficulty was this: the younger brother not only laid close siege to me, but suffered it to be seen. He would come into his sister's room, and his mother's room, and sit down, and talk a thousand kind things of me, and to me, even before their faces, and when they were all there. This grew so public that the whole house talked of it, and his mother reproved him for it, and their carriage to me appeared quite altered. In short, his mother had let fall some speeches, as if she intended to put me out of the family; that is, in English, to turn me out of doors. Now I was sure this could not be a secret to his brother, only that he might not think, as indeed nobody else yet did, that the youngest brother had made any proposal to me about it; but as I easily could see that it would go farther, so I saw likewise there was an absolute necessity to speak of it to him, or that he would speak of it to me, and which to do first I knew not; that is, whether I should break it to him or let it alone till he should break it to me.

Upon serious consideration, for indeed now I began to consider things very seriously, and never till now; I say, upon serious consideration, I resolved to tell him of it first; and it was not long before I had an opportunity, for the very next day his brother went to London upon some business, and the family being out a-visiting, just as it had happened before, and as indeed was often the case, he came according to his custom, to spend an hour or two with Mrs. Betty.

When he came had had sat down a while, he easily perceived there was an alteration in my countenance, that I was not so free and pleasant with him as I used to be, and particularly, that I had been a-crying; he was not long before he took notice of it, and asked me in very kind terms what was the matter, and if anything troubled me. I would have put it off if I could, but it was not to be concealed; so after suffering many importunities to draw that out of me which I longed as much as possible to disclose, I told him that it was true something did trouble me, and something of such a nature that I could not conceal from him, and yet that I could not tell how to tell him of it neither; that it was a thing that not only surprised me, but greatly perplexed me, and that I knew not what course to take, unless he would direct me. He told me with great tenderness, that let it be what it would, I should not let it trouble me, for he would protect me from all the world.

I then began at a distance, and told him I was afraid the ladies had got some secret information of our correspondence; for that it was easy to see that their conduct was very much changed towards me for a great while, and that now it was come to that pass that they frequently found fault with me, and sometimes fell quite out with me, though I never gave them the least occasion; that whereas I used always to lie with the eldest sister, I was lately put to lie by myself, or with one of the maids; and that I had overheard them several times talking very unkindly about me; but that which confirmed it all was, that one of the servants had told me that she had heard I was to be turned out, and that it was not safe for the family that I should be any longer in the house.

He smiled when he herd all this, and I asked him how he could make so light of it, when he must needs know that if there was any discovery I was undone for ever, and that even it would hurt him, though not ruin him as it would me. I upbraided him, that he was like all the rest of the sex, that, when they had the character and honour of a woman at their mercy, oftentimes made it their jest, and at least looked upon it as a trifle, and counted the ruin of those they had had their will of as a thing of no value.

He saw me warm and serious, and he changed his style immediately; he told me he was sorry I should have such a thought of him; that he had never given me the least occasion for it, but had been as tender of my reputation as he could be of his own; that he was sure our correspondence had been managed with so much address, that not one creature in the family had so much as a suspicion of it; that if he smiled when I told him my thoughts, it was at the assurance he lately received, that our understanding one another was not so much as known or guessed at; and that when he had told me how much reason he had to be easy, I should smile as he did, for he was very certain it would give me a full satisfaction.

'This is a mystery I cannot understand,' says I, 'or how it should be to my satisfaction that I am to be turned out of doors; for if our correspondence is not discovered, I know not what else I have done to change the countenances of the whole family to me, or to have them treat me as they do now, who formerly used me with so much tenderness, as if I had been one of their own children.'

'Why, look you, child,' says he, 'that they are uneasy about you, that is true; but that they have the least suspicion of the case as it is, and as it respects you and I, is so far from being true, that they suspect my brother Robin; and, in short, they are fully persuaded he makes love to you; nay, the fool has put it into their heads too himself, for he is continually bantering them about it, and making a jest of himself. I confess I think he is wrong to do so, because he cannot but see it vexes them, and makes them unkind to you; but 'tis a satisfaction to me, because of the assurance it gives me, that they do not suspect me in the least, and I hope this will be to your satisfaction too.'

'So it is,' says I, 'one way; but this does not reach my case at all, nor is this the chief thing that troubles me, though I have been concerned about that too.' 'What is it, then?' says he. With which I fell to tears, and could say nothing to him at all. He strove to pacify me all he could, but began at last to be very pressing upon me to tell what it was. At last I answered that I thought I ought to tell him too, and that he had some right to know it; besides, that I wanted his direction in the case, for I was in such perplexity that I knew not what course to take, and then I related the whole affair to him. I told him how imprudently his brother had managed himself, in making himself so public; for that if he had kept it a secret, as such a thing out to have been, I could but have denied him positively, without giving any reason for it, and he would in time have ceased his solicitations; but that he had the vanity, first, to depend upon it that I would not deny him, and then had taken the freedom to tell his resolution of having me to the whole house.

I told him how far I had resisted him, and told him how sincere and honourable his offers were. 'But,' says I, 'my case will be doubly hard; for as they carry it ill to me now, because he desires to have me, they'll carry it worse when they shall find I have denied him; and they will presently say, there's something else in it, and then out it comes that I am married already to somebody else, or that I would never refuse a match so much above me as this was.'

This discourse surprised him indeed very much. He told me that it was a critical point indeed for me to manage, and he did not see which way I should get out of it; but he would consider it, and let me know next time we met, what resolution he was come to about it; and in the meantime desired I would not give my consent to his brother, nor yet give him a flat denial, but that I would hold him in suspense a while.

I seemed to start at his saying I should not give him my consent. I told him he knew very well I had no consent to give; that he had engaged himself to marry me, and that my consent was the same time engaged to him; that he had all along told me I was his wife, and I looked upon myself as effectually so as if the ceremony had passed; and that it was from his own mouth that I did so, he having all along persuaded me to call myself his wife.

'Well, my dear,' says he, 'don't be concerned at that now; if I am not your husband, I'll be as good as a husband to you; and do not let those things trouble you now, but let me look a little farther into this affair, and I shall be able to say more next time we meet.'

He pacified me as well as he could with this, but I found he was very thoughtful, and that though he was very kind to me and kissed me a thousand times, and more I believe, and gave me money too, yet he offered no more all the while we were together, which was above two hours, and which I much wondered at indeed at that time, considering how it used to be, and what opportunity we had.

His brother did not come from London for five or six days, and it was two days more before he got an opportunity to talk with him; but then getting him by himself he began to talk very close to him about it, and the same evening got an opportunity (for we had a long conference together) to repeat all their discourse to me, which, as near as I can remember, was to the purpose following. He told him he heard strange news of him since he went, viz. that he made love to Mrs. Betty. 'Well, says his brother a little angrily, 'and so I do. And what then? What has anybody to do with that?' 'Nay,' says his brother, 'don't be angry, Robin; I don't pretend to have anything to do with it; nor do I pretend to be angry with you about it. But I find they do concern themselves about it, and that they have used the poor girl ill about it, which I should take as done to myself.' 'Whom do you mean by THEY?' says Robin. 'I mean my mother and the girls,' says the elder brother. 'But hark ye,' says his brother, 'are you in earnest? Do you really love this girl? You may be free with me, you know.' 'Why, then,' says Robin, 'I will be free with you; I do love her above all the women in the world, and I will have her, let them say and do what they will. I believe the girl will not deny me.'

It struck me to the heart when he told me this, for though it was most rational to think I would not deny him, yet I knew in my own conscience I must deny him, and I saw my ruin in my being obliged to do so; but I knew it was my business to talk otherwise then, so I interrupted him in his story thus.

'Ay!' said I, 'does he think I cannot deny him? But he shall find I can deny him, for all that.'

'Well, my dear,' says he, 'but let me give you the whole story as it went on between us, and then say what you will.'

Then he went on and told me that he replied thus: 'But, brother, you know she has nothing, and you may have several ladies with good fortunes.'

"'Tis no matter for that,' said Robin; 'I love the girl, and I will never please my pocket in marrying, and not please my fancy.' 'And so, my dear,' adds he, 'there is no opposing him.'

'Yes, yes,' says I, 'you shall see I can oppose him; I have learnt to say No, now though I had not learnt it before; if the best lord in the land offered me marriage now, I could very cheerfully say No to him.'

'Well, but, my dear,' says he, 'what can you say to him? You know, as you said when we talked of it before, he well ask you many questions about it, and all the house will wonder what the meaning of it should be.'

'Why,' says I, smiling, 'I can stop all their mouths at one clap by telling him, and them too, that I am married already to his elder brother.'

He smiled a little too at the word, but I could see it startled him, and he could not hide the disorder it put him into. However, he returned, 'Why, though that may be true in some sense, yet I suppose you are but in jest when you talk of giving such an answer as that; it may not be convenient on many accounts.'

'No, no,' says I pleasantly, 'I am not so fond of letting the secret come out without your consent.'

'But what, then, can you say to him, or to them,' says he, 'when they find you positive against a match which would be apparently so much to your advantage?'

'Why,' says I, 'should I be at a loss? First of all, I am not obliged to give me any reason at all; on the other hand, I may tell them I am married already, and stop there, and that will be a full stop too to him, for he can have no reason to ask one question after it.'

'Ay,' says he; 'but the whole house will tease you about that, even to father and mother, and if you deny them positively, they will be disobliged at you, and suspicious besides.'

'Why,' says I, 'what can I do? What would have me do? I was in straight enough before, and as I told you, I was in perplexity before, and acquainted you with the circumstances, that I might have your advice.'

'My dear,' says he, 'I have been considering very much upon it, you may be sure, and though it is a piece of advice that has a great many mortifications in it to me, and may at first seem strange to you, yet, all things considered, I see no better way for you than to let him go on; and if you find him hearty and in earnest, marry him.'

I gave him a look full of horror at those words, and, turning pale as death, was at the very point of sinking down out of the chair I sat in; when, giving a start, 'My dear,' says he aloud, 'what's the matter with you? Where are you a-going?' and a great many such things; and with jogging and called to me, fetched me a little to myself, though it was a good while before I fully recovered my senses, and was not able to speak for several minutes more.

When I was fully recovered he began again. 'My dear,' says he, 'what made you so surprised at what I said? I would have you consider seriously of it? You may see plainly how the family stand in this case, and they would be stark mad if it was my case, as it is my brother's; and for aught I see, it would be my ruin and yours too.'

'Ay!' says I, still speaking angrily; 'are all your protestations and vows to be shaken by the dislike of the family? Did I not always object that to you, and you made light thing of it, as what you were above, and would value; and is it come to this now?' said I. 'Is this your faith and honour, your love, and the solidity of your promises?'

He continued perfectly calm, notwithstanding all my reproaches, and I was not sparing of them at all; but he replied at last, 'My dear, I have not broken one promise with you yet; I did tell you I would marry you when I was come to my estate; but you see my father is a hale, healthy man, and may live these thirty years still, and not be older than several are round us in town; and you never proposed my marrying you sooner, because you knew it might be my ruin; and as to all the rest, I have not failed you in anything, you have wanted for nothing.'

I could not deny a word of this, and had nothing to say to it in general. 'But why, then,' says I, 'can you persuade me to such a horrid step as leaving you, since you have not left me? Will you allow no affection, no love on my side, where there has been so much on your side? Have I made you no returns? Have I given no testimony of my sincerity and of my passion? Are the sacrifices I have made of honour and modesty to you no proof of my being tied to you in bonds too strong to be broken?'

'But here, my dear,' says he, 'you may come into a safe station, and appear with honour and with splendour at once, and the remembrance of what we have done may be wrapt up in an eternal silence, as if it had never happened; you shall always have my respect, and my sincere affection, only then it shall be honest, and perfectly just to my brother; you shall be my dear sister, as now you are my dear——' and there he stopped.

'Your dear whore,' says I, 'you would have said if you had gone on, and you might as well have said it; but I understand you. However, I desire you to remember the long discourses you have had with me, and the many hours' pains you have taken to persuade me to believe myself an honest woman; that I was your wife intentionally, though not in the eyes of the world, and that it was as effectual a marriage that had passed between us as is we had been publicly wedded by the parson of the parish. You know and cannot but remember that these have been your own words to me.'

I found this was a little too close upon him, but I made it up in what follows. He stood stock-still for a while and said nothing, and I went on thus: 'You cannot,' says I, 'without the highest injustice, believe that I yielded upon all these persuasions without a love not to be questioned, not to be shaken again by anything that could happen afterward. If you have such dishonourable thoughts of me, I must ask you what foundation in any of my behaviour have I given for such a suggestion?

'If, then, I have yielded to the importunities of my affection, and if I have been persuaded to believe that I am really, and in the essence of the thing, your wife, shall I now give the lie to all those arguments and call myself your whore, or mistress, which is the same thing? And will you transfer me to your brother? Can you transfer my affection? Can you bid me cease loving you, and bid me love him? It is in my power, think you, to make such a change at demand? No, sir,' said I, 'depend upon it 'tis impossible, and whatever the change of your side may be, I will ever be true; and I had much rather, since it is come that unhappy length, be your whore than your brother's wife.'

He appeared pleased and touched with the impression of this last discourse, and told me that he stood where he did before; that he had not been unfaithful to me in any one promise he had ever made yet, but that there were so many terrible things presented themselves to his view in the affair before me, and that on my account in particular, that he had thought of the other as a remedy so effectual as nothing could come up to it. That he thought this would not be entire parting us, but we might love as friends all our days, and perhaps with more satisfaction than we should in the station we were now in, as things might happen; that he durst say, I could not apprehend anything from him as to betraying a secret, which could not but be the destruction of us both, if it came out; that he had but one question to ask of me that could lie in the way of it, and if that question was answered in the negative, he could not but think still it was the only step I could take.

I guessed at his question presently, namely, whether I was sure I was not with child? As to that, I told him he need not be concerned about it, for I was not with child. 'Why, then, my dear,' says he, 'we have no time to talk further now. Consider of it, and think closely about it; I cannot but be of the opinion still, that it will be the best course you can take.' And with this he took his leave, and the more hastily too, his mother and sisters ringing at the gate, just at the moment that he had risen up to go.

He left me in the utmost confusion of thought; and he easily perceived it the next day, and all the rest of the week, for it was but Tuesday evening when we talked; but he had no opportunity to come at me all that week, till the Sunday after, when I, being indisposed, did not go to church, and he, making some excuse for the like, stayed at home.

And now he had me an hour and a half again by myself, and we fell into the same arguments all over again, or at least so near the same, as it would be to no purpose to repeat them. At last I asked him warmly, what opinion he must have of my modesty, that he could suppose I should so much as entertain a thought of lying with two brothers, and assured him it could never be. I added, if he was to tell me that he would never see me more, than which nothing but death could be more terrible, yet I could never entertain a thought so dishonourable to myself, and so base to him; and therefore, I entreated him, if he had one grain of respect or affection left for me, that he would speak no more of it to me, or that he would pull his sword out and kill me. He appeared surprised at my obstinacy, as he called it; told me I was unkind to myself, and unkind to him in it; that it was a crisis unlooked for upon us both, and impossible for either of us to foresee, but that he did not see any other way to save us both from ruin, and therefore he thought it the more unkind; but that if he must say no more of it to me, he added with an unusual coldness, that he did not know anything else we had to talk of; and so he rose up to take his leave. I rose up too, as if with the same indifference; but when he came to give me as it were a parting kiss, I burst out into such a passion of crying, that though I would have spoke, I could not, and only pressing his hand, seemed to give him the adieu, but cried vehemently.

He was sensibly moved with this; so he sat down again, and said a great many kind things to me, to abate the excess of my passion, but still urged the necessity of what he had proposed; all the while insisting, that if I did refuse, he would notwithstanding provide for me; but letting me plainly see that he would decline me in the main point—nay, even as a mistress; making it a point of honour not to lie with the woman that, for aught he knew, might come to be his brother's wife.

The bare loss of him as a gallant was not so much my affliction as the loss of his person, whom indeed I loved to distraction; and the loss of all the expectations I had, and which I always had built my hopes upon, of having him one day for my husband. These things oppressed my mind so much, that, in short, I fell very ill; the agonies of my mind, in a word, threw me into a high fever, and long it was, that none in the family expected my life.

I was reduced very low indeed, and was often delirious and light-headed; but nothing lay so near me as the fear that, when I was light-headed, I should say something or other to his prejudice. I was distressed in my mind also to see him, and so he was to see me, for he really loved me most passionately; but it could not be; there was not the least room to desire it on one side or other, or so much as to make it decent.

It was near five weeks that I kept my bed and though the violence of my fever abated in three weeks, yet it several times returned; and the physicians said two or three times, they could do no more for me, but that they must leave nature and the distemper to fight it out, only strengthening the first with cordials to maintain the struggle. After the end of five weeks I grew better, but was so weak, so altered, so melancholy, and recovered so slowly, that they physicians apprehended I should go into a consumption; and which vexed me most, they gave it as their opinion that my mind was oppressed, that something troubled me, and, in short, that I was in love. Upon this, the whole house was set upon me to examine me, and to press me to tell whether I was in love or not, and with whom; but as I well might, I denied my being in love at all.

They had on this occasion a squabble one day about me at table, that had like to have put the whole family in an uproar, and for some time did so. They happened to be all at table but the father; as for me, I was ill, and in my chamber. At the beginning of the talk, which was just as they had finished their dinner, the old gentlewoman, who had sent me somewhat to eat, called her maid to go up and ask me if I would have any more; but the maid brought down word I had not eaten half what she had sent me already.

'Alas, says the old lady, 'that poor girl! I am afraid she will never be well.'

'Well!' says the elder brother, 'how should Mrs. Betty be well? They say she is in love.'

'I believe nothing of it,' says the old gentlewoman.

'I don't know,' says the eldest sister, 'what to say to it; they have made such a rout about her being so handsome, and so charming, and I know not what, and that in her hearing too, that has turned the creature's head, I believe, and who knows what possessions may follow such doings? For my part, I don't know what to make of it.'

'Why, sister, you must acknowledge she is very handsome,' says the elder brother.

'Ay, and a great deal handsomer than you, sister,' says Robin, 'and that's your mortification.'

'Well, well, that is not the question,' says his sister; 'that girl is well enough, and she knows it well enough; she need not be told of it to make her vain.'

'We are not talking of her being vain,' says the elder brother, 'but of her being in love; it may be she is in love with herself; it seems my sisters think so.'

'I would she was in love with me,' says Robin; 'I'd quickly put her out of her pain.'

'What d'ye mean by that, son,' says the old lady; 'how can you talk so?'

'Why, madam,' says Robin, again, very honestly, 'do you think I'd let the poor girl die for love, and of one that is near at hand to be had, too?'

'Fie, brother!', says the second sister, 'how can you talk so? Would you take a creature that has not a groat in the world?'

'Prithee, child,' says Robin, 'beauty's a portion, and good-humour with it is a double portion; I wish thou hadst half her stock of both for thy portion.' So there was her mouth stopped.

'I find,' says the eldest sister, 'if Betty is not in love, my brother is. I wonder he has not broke his mind to Betty; I warrant she won't say No.'

'They that yield when they're asked,' says Robin, 'are one step before them that were never asked to yield, sister, and two steps before them that yield before they are asked; and that's an answer to you, sister.'

This fired the sister, and she flew into a passion, and said, things were come to that pass that it was time the wench, meaning me, was out of the family; and but that she was not fit to be turned out, she hoped her father and mother would consider of it as soon as she could be removed.

Robin replied, that was business for the master and mistress of the family, who where not to be taught by one that had so little judgment as his eldest sister.

It ran up a great deal farther; the sister scolded, Robin rallied and bantered, but poor Betty lost ground by it extremely in the family. I heard of it, and I cried heartily, and the old lady came up to me, somebody having told her that I was so much concerned about it. I complained to her, that it was very hard the doctors should pass such a censure upon me, for which they had no ground; and that it was still harder, considering the circumstances I was under in the family; that I hoped I had done nothing to lessen her esteem for me, or given any occasion for the bickering between her sons and daughters, and I had more need to think of a coffin than of being in love, and begged she would not let me suffer in her opinion for anybody's mistakes but my own.

She was sensible of the justice of what I said, but told me, since there had been such a clamour among them, and that her younger son talked after such a rattling way as he did, she desired I would be so faithful to her as to answer her but one question sincerely. I told her I would, with all my heart, and with the utmost plainness and sincerity. Why, then, the question was, whether there way anything between her son Robert and me. I told her with all the protestations of sincerity that I was able to make, and as I might well, do, that there was not, nor every had been; I told her that Mr. Robert had rattled and jested, as she knew it was his way, and that I took it always, as I supposed he meant it, to be a wild airy way of discourse that had no signification in it; and again assured her, that there was not the least tittle of what she understood by it between us; and that those who had suggested it had done me a great deal of wrong, and Mr. Robert no service at all.

The old lady was fully satisfied, and kissed me, spoke cheerfully to me, and bid me take care of my health and want for nothing, and so took her leave. But when she came down she found the brother and all his sisters together by the ears; they were angry, even to passion, at his upbraiding them with their being homely, and having never had any sweethearts, never having been asked the question, and their being so forward as almost to ask first. He rallied them upon the subject of Mrs. Betty; how pretty, how good-humoured, how she sung better then they did, and danced better, and how much handsomer she was; and in doing this he omitted no ill-natured thing that could vex them, and indeed, pushed too hard upon them. The old lady came down in the height of it, and to put a stop it to, told them all the discourse she had had with me, and how I answered, that there was nothing between Mr. Robert and I.

'She's wrong there,' says Robin, 'for if there was not a great deal between us, we should be closer together than we are. I told her I loved her hugely,' says he, 'but I could never make the jade believe I was in earnest.' 'I do not know how you should,' says his mother; 'nobody in their senses could believe you were in earnest, to talk so to a poor girl, whose circumstances you know so well.

'But prithee, son,' adds she, 'since you tell me that you could not make her believe you were in earnest, what must we believe about it? For you ramble so in your discourse, that nobody knows whether you are in earnest or in jest; but as I find the girl, by your own confession, has answered truly, I wish you would do so too, and tell me seriously, so that I may depend upon it. Is there anything in it or no? Are you in earnest or no? Are you distracted, indeed, or are you not? 'Tis a weighty question, and I wish you would make us easy about it.'

'By my faith, madam,' says Robin, "tis in vain to mince the matter or tell any more lies about it; I am in earnest, as much as a man is that's going to be hanged. If Mrs. Betty would say she loved me, and that she would marry me, I'd have her tomorrow morning fasting, and say, 'To have and to hold,' instead of eating my breakfast.'

'Well,' says the mother, 'then there's one son lost'; and she said it in a very mournful tone, as one greatly concerned at it.

'I hope not, madam,' says Robin; 'no man is lost when a good wife has found him.'

'Why, but, child,' says the old lady, 'she is a beggar.'

'Why, then, madam, she has the more need of charity,' says Robin; 'I'll take her off the hands of the parish, and she and I'll beg together.'

'It's bad jesting with such things,' says the mother.

'I don't jest, madam,' says Robin. 'We'll come and beg your pardon, madam; and your blessing, madam, and my father's.'

'This is all out of the way, son,' says the mother. 'If you are in earnest you are undone.'

'I am afraid not,' says he, 'for I am really afraid she won't have me; after all my sister's huffing and blustering, I believe I shall never be able to persuade her to it.'

'That's a fine tale, indeed; she is not so far out of her senses neither. Mrs. Betty is no fool,' says the younger sister. 'Do you think she has learnt to say No, any more than other people?'

'No, Mrs. Mirth-wit,' says Robin, 'Mrs. Betty's no fool; but Mrs. Betty may be engaged some other way, and what then?'

'Nay,' says the eldest sister, 'we can say nothing to that. Who must it be to, then? She is never out of the doors; it must be between you.'

'I have nothing to say to that,' says Robin. 'I have been examined enough; there's my brother. If it must be between us, go to work with him.'

This stung the elder brother to the quick, and he concluded that Robin had discovered something. However, he kept himself from appearing disturbed. 'Prithee,' says he, 'don't go to shame your stories off upon me; I tell you, I deal in no such ware; I have nothing to say to Mrs. Betty, nor to any of the Mrs. Bettys in the parish'; and with that he rose up and brushed off.

'No,' says the eldest sister, 'I dare answer for my brother; he knows the world better.'

Thus the discourse ended, but it left the elder brother quite confounded. He concluded his brother had made a full discovery, and he began to doubt whether I had been concerned in it or not; but with all his management he could not bring it about to get at me. At last he was so perplexed that he was quite desperate, and resolved he would come into my chamber and see me, whatever came of it. In order to do this, he contrived it so, that one day after dinner, watching his eldest sister till he could see her go upstairs, he runs after her. 'Hark ye, sister,' says he, 'where is this sick woman? May not a body see her?' 'Yes,' says the sister, 'I believe you may; but let me go first a little, and I'll tell you.' So she ran up to the door and gave me notice, and presently called to him again. 'Brother,' says she, 'you may come if you please.' So in he came, just in the same kind of rant. 'Well,' says he at the door as he came in, 'where is this sick body that's in love? How do ye do, Mrs. Betty?' I would have got up out of my chair, but was so weak I could not for a good while; and he saw it, and his sister to, and she said, 'Come, do not strive to stand up; my brother desires no ceremony, especially now you are so weak.' 'No, no, Mrs. Betty, pray sit still,' says he, and so sits himself down in a chair over against me, and appeared as if he was mighty merry.

He talked a lot of rambling stuff to his sister and to me, sometimes of one thing, sometimes of another, on purpose to amuse his sister, and every now and then would turn it upon the old story, directing it to me. 'Poor Mrs. Betty,' says he, 'it is a sad thing to be in love; why, it has reduced you sadly.' At last I spoke a little. 'I am glad to see you so merry, sir,' says I; 'but I think the doctor might have found something better to do than to make his game at his patients. If I had been ill of no other distemper, I know the proverb too well to have let him come to me.' 'What proverb?' says he, 'Oh! I remember it now. What—

"Where love is the case,
The doctor's an ass."

Is not that it, Mrs. Betty?' I smiled and said nothing. 'Nay,' says he, 'I think the effect has proved it to be love, for it seems the doctor has been able to do you but little service; you mend very slowly, they say. I doubt there's somewhat in it, Mrs. Betty; I doubt you are sick of the incurables, and that is love.' I smiled and said, 'No, indeed, sir, that's none of my distemper.'

We had a deal of such discourse, and sometimes others that signified as little. By and by he asked me to sing them a song, at which I smiled, and said my singing days were over. At last he asked me if he should play upon his flute to me; his sister said she believe it would hurt me, and that my head could not bear it. I bowed, and said, No, it would not hurt me. 'And, pray, madam.' said I, 'do not hinder it; I love the music of the flute very much.' Then his sister said, 'Well, do, then, brother.' With that he pulled out the key of his closet. 'Dear sister,' says he, 'I am very lazy; do step to my closet and fetch my flute; it lies in such a drawer,' naming a place where he was sure it was not, that she might be a little while a-looking for it.

As soon as she was gone, he related the whole story to me of the discourse his brother had about me, and of his pushing it at him, and his concern about it, which was the reason of his contriving this visit to me. I assured him I had never opened my mouth either to his brother or to anybody else. I told him the dreadful exigence I was in; that my love to him, and his offering to have me forget that affection and remove it to another, had thrown me down; and that I had a thousand times wished I might die rather than recover, and to have the same circumstances to struggle with as I had before, and that his backwardness to life had been the great reason of the slowness of my recovering. I added that I foresaw that as soon as I was well, I must quit the family, and that as for marrying his brother, I abhorred the thoughts of it after what had been my case with him, and that he might depend upon it I would never see his brother again upon that subject; that if he would break all his vows and oaths and engagements with me, be that between his conscience and his honour and himself; but he should never be able to say that I, whom he had persuaded to call myself his wife, and who had given him the liberty to use me as a wife, was not as faithful to him as a wife ought to be, whatever he might be to me.

He was going to reply, and had said that he was sorry I could not be persuaded, and was a-going to say more, but he heard his sister a-coming, and so did I; and yet I forced out these few words as a reply, that I could never be persuaded to love one brother and marry another. He shook his head and said, 'Then I am ruined,' meaning himself; and that moment his sister entered the room and told him she could not find the flute. 'Well,' says he merrily, 'this laziness won't do'; so he gets up and goes himself to go to look for it, but comes back without it too; not but that he could have found it, but because his mind was a little disturbed, and he had no mind to play; and, besides, the errand he sent his sister on was answered another way; for he only wanted an opportunity to speak to me, which he gained, though not much to his satisfaction.

I had, however, a great deal of satisfaction in having spoken my mind to him with freedom, and with such an honest plainness, as I have related; and though it did not at all work the way I desired, that is to say, to oblige the person to me the more, yet it took from him all possibility of quitting me but by a downright breach of honour, and giving up all the faith of a gentleman to me, which he had so often engaged by, never to abandon me, but to make me his wife as soon as he came to his estate.

It was not many weeks after this before I was about the house again, and began to grow well; but I continued melancholy, silent, dull, and retired, which amazed the whole family, except he that knew the reason of it; yet it was a great while before he took any notice of it, and I, as backward to speak as he, carried respectfully to him, but never offered to speak a word to him that was particular of any kind whatsoever; and this continued for sixteen or seventeen weeks; so that, as I expected every day to be dismissed the family, on account of what distaste they had taken another way, in which I had no guilt, so I expected to hear no more of this gentleman, after all his solemn vows and protestations, but to be ruined and abandoned.

At last I broke the way myself in the family for my removing; for being talking seriously with the old lady one day, about my own circumstances in the world, and how my distemper had left a heaviness upon my spirits, that I was not the same thing I was before, the old lady said, 'I am afraid, Betty, what I have said to you about my son has had some influence upon you, and that you are melancholy on his account; pray, will you let me know how the matter stands with you both, if it may not be improper? For, as for Robin, he does nothing but rally and banter when I speak of it to him.' 'Why, truly, madam,' said I 'that matter stands as I wish it did not, and I shall be very sincere with you in it, whatever befalls me for it. Mr. Robert has several times proposed marriage to me, which is what I had no reason to expect, my poor circumstances considered; but I have always resisted him, and that perhaps in terms more positive than became me, considering the regard that I ought to have for every branch of your family; but,' said I, 'madam, I could never so far forget my obligation to you and all your house, to offer to consent to a thing which I know must needs be disobliging to you, and this I have made my argument to him, and have positively told him that I would never entertain a thought of that kind unless I had your consent, and his father's also, to whom I was bound by so many invincible obligations.'

'And is this possible, Mrs. Betty?' says the old lady. 'Then you have been much juster to us than we have been to you; for we have all looked upon you as a kind of snare to my son, and I had a proposal to make to you for your removing, for fear of it; but I had not yet mentioned it to you, because I thought you were not thorough well, and I was afraid of grieving you too much, lest it should throw you down again; for we have all a respect for you still, though not so much as to have it be the ruin of my son; but if it be as you say, we have all wronged you very much.'

'As to the truth of what I say, madam,' said I, 'refer you to your son himself; if he will do me any justice, he must tell you the story just as I have told it.'

Away goes the old lady to her daughters and tells them the whole story, just as I had told it her; and they were surprised at it, you may be sure, as I believed they would be. One said she could never have thought it; another said Robin was a fool; a third said she would not believe a word of it, and she would warrant that Robin would tell the story another way. But the old gentlewoman, who was resolved to go to the bottom of it before I could have the least opportunity of acquainting her son with what had passed, resolved too that she would talk with her son immediately, and to that purpose sent for him, for he was gone but to a lawyer's house in the town, upon some petty business of his own, and upon her sending he returned immediately.

Upon his coming up to them, for they were all still together, 'Sit down, Robin,' says the old lady, 'I must have some talk with you.' 'With all my heart, madam,' says Robin, looking very merry. 'I hope it is about a good wife, for I am at a great loss in that affair.' 'How can that be?' says his mother; 'did not you say you resolved to have Mrs. Betty?' 'Ay, madam,' says Robin, 'but there is one has forbid the banns.' 'Forbid, the banns!' says his mother; 'who can that be?' 'Even Mrs. Betty herself,' says Robin. 'How so?' says his mother. 'Have you asked her the question, then?' 'Yes, indeed, madam,' says Robin. 'I have attacked her in form five times since she was sick, and am beaten off; the jade is so stout she won't capitulate nor yield upon any terms, except such as I cannot effectually grant.' 'Explain yourself,' says the mother, 'for I am surprised; I do not understand you. I hope you are not in earnest.'

'Why, madam,' says he, 'the case is plain enough upon me, it explains itself; she won't have me, she says; is not that plain enough? I think 'tis plain, and pretty rough too.' 'Well, but,' says the mother, 'you talk of conditions that you cannot grant; what does she want—a settlement? Her jointure ought to be according to her portion; but what fortune does she bring you?' 'Nay, as to fortune,' says Robin, 'she is rich enough; I am satisfied in that point; but 'tis I that am not able to come up to her terms, and she is positive she will not have me without.'

Here the sisters put in. 'Madam,' says the second sister, "tis impossible to be serious with him; he will never give a direct answer to anything; you had better let him alone, and talk no more of it to him; you know how to dispose of her out of his way if you thought there was anything in it.' Robin was a little warmed with his sister's rudeness, but he was even with her, and yet with good manners too. 'There are two sorts of people, madam,' says he, turning to his mother, 'that there is no contending with; that is, a wise body and a fool; 'tis a little hard I should engage with both of them together.'

The younger sister then put in. 'We must be fools indeed,' says she, 'in my brother's opinion, that he should think we can believe he has seriously asked Mrs. Betty to marry him, and that she has refused him.'

'Answer, and answer not, say Solomon,' replied her brother. 'When your brother had said to your mother that he had asked her no less than five times, and that it was so, that she positively denied him, methinks a younger sister need not question the truth of it when her mother did not.' 'My mother, you see, did not understand it,' says the second sister. 'There's some difference,' says Robin, 'between desiring me to explain it, and telling me she did not believe it.'

'Well, but, son,' says the old lady, 'if you are disposed to let us into the mystery of it, what were these hard conditions?' 'Yes, madam,' says Robin, 'I had done it before now, if the teasers here had not worried my by way of interruption. The conditions are, that I bring my father and you to consent to it, and without that she protests she will never see me more upon that head; and to these conditions, as I said, I suppose I shall never be able to grant. I hope my warm sisters will be answered now, and blush a little; if not, I have no more to say till I hear further.'

This answer was surprising to them all, though less to the mother, because of what I had said to her. As to the daughters, they stood mute a great while; but the mother said with some passion, 'Well, I had heard this before, but I could not believe it; but if it is so, they we have all done Betty wrong, and she has behaved better than I ever expected.' 'Nay,' says the eldest sister, 'if it be so, she has acted handsomely indeed.' 'I confess,' says the mother, 'it was none of her fault, if he was fool enough to take a fancy to her; but to give such an answer to him, shows more respect to your father and me than I can tell how to express; I shall value the girl the better for it as long as I know her.' 'But I shall not,' says Robin, 'unless you will give your consent.' 'I'll consider of that a while,' says the mother; 'I assure you, if there were not some other objections in the way, this conduct of hers would go a great way to bring me to consent.' 'I wish it would go quite through it,' says Robin; 'if you had a much thought about making me easy as you have about making me rich, you would soon consent to it.'

'Why, Robin,' says the mother again, 'are you really in earnest? Would you so fain have her as you pretend?' 'Really, madam,' says Robin, 'I think 'tis hard you should question me upon that head after all I have said. I won't say that I will have her; how can I resolve that point, when you see I cannot have her without your consent? Besides, I am not bound to marry at all. But this I will say, I am in earnest in, that I will never have anybody else if I can help it; so you may determine for me. Betty or nobody is the word, and the question which of the two shall be in your breast to decide, madam, provided only, that my good-humoured sisters here may have no vote in it.'

All this was dreadful to me, for the mother began to yield, and Robin pressed her home on it. On the other hand, she advised with the eldest son, and he used all the arguments in the world to persuade her to consent; alleging his brother's passionate love for me, and my generous regard to the family, in refusing my own advantages upon such a nice point of honour, and a thousand such things. And as to the father, he was a man in a hurry of public affairs and getting money, seldom at home, thoughtful of the main chance, but left all those things to his wife.

You may easily believe, that when the plot was thus, as they thought, broke out, and that every one thought they knew how things were carried, it was not so difficult or so dangerous for the elder brother, whom nobody suspected of anything, to have a freer access to me than before; nay, the mother, which was just as he wished, proposed it to him to talk with Mrs. Betty. 'For it may be, son,' said she, 'you may see farther into the thing than I, and see if you think she has been so positive as Robin says she has been, or no.' This was as well as he could wish, and he, as it were, yielding to talk with me at his mother's request, she brought me to him into her own chamber, told me her son had some business with me at her request, and desired me to be very sincere with him, and then she left us together, and he went and shut the door after her.

He came back to me and took me in his arms, and kissed me very tenderly; but told me he had a long discourse to hold with me, and it was not come to that crisis, that I should make myself happy or miserable as long as I lived; that the thing was now gone so far, that if I could not comply with his desire, we would both be ruined. Then he told the whole story between Robin, as he called him, and his mother and sisters and himself, as it is above. 'And now, dear child,' says he, 'consider what it will be to marry a gentleman of a good family, in good circumstances, and with the consent of the whole house, and to enjoy all that he world can give you; and what, on the other hand, to be sunk into the dark circumstances of a woman that has lost her reputation; and that though I shall be a private friend to you while I live, yet as I shall be suspected always, so you will be afraid to see me, and I shall be afraid to own you.'

He gave me no time to reply, but went on with me thus: 'What has happened between us, child, so long as we both agree to do so, may be buried and forgotten. I shall always be your sincere friend, without any inclination to nearer intimacy, when you become my sister; and we shall have all the honest part of conversation without any reproaches between us of having done amiss. I beg of you to consider it, and to not stand in the way of your own safety and prosperity; and to satisfy you that I am sincere,' added he, 'I here offer you #500 in money, to make you some amends for the freedoms I have taken with you, which we shall look upon as some of the follies of our lives, which 'tis hoped we may repent of.'

He spoke this in so much more moving terms than it is possible for me to express, and with so much greater force of argument than I can repeat, that I only recommend it to those who read the story, to suppose, that as he held me above an hour and a half in that discourse, so he answered all my objections, and fortified his discourse with all the arguments that human wit and art could devise.

I cannot say, however, that anything he said made impression enough upon me so as to give me any thought of the matter, till he told me at last very plainly, that if I refused, he was sorry to add that he could never go on with me in that station as we stood before; that though he loved me as well as ever, and that I was as agreeable to him as ever, yet sense of virtue had not so far forsaken him as to suffer him to lie with a woman that his brother courted to make his wife; and if he took his leave of me, with a denial in this affair, whatever he might do for me in the point of support, grounded on his first engagement of maintaining me, yet he would not have me be surprised that he was obliged to tell me he could not allow himself to see me any more; and that, indeed, I could not expect it of him.

I received this last part with some token of surprise and disorder, and had much ado to avoid sinking down, for indeed I loved him to an extravagance not easy to imagine; but he perceived my disorder. He entreated me to consider seriously of it; assured me that it was the only way to preserve our mutual affection; that in this station we might love as friends, with the utmost passion, and with a love of relation untainted, free from our just reproaches, and free from other people's suspicions; that he should ever acknowledge his happiness owing to me; that he would be debtor to me as long as he lived, and would be paying that debt as long as he had breath. Thus he wrought me up, in short, to a kind of hesitation in the matter; having the dangers on one side represented in lively figures, and indeed, heightened by my imagination of being turned out to the wide world a mere cast-off whore, for it was no less, and perhaps exposed as such, with little to provide for myself, with no friend, no acquaintance in the whole world, out of that town, and there I could not pretend to stay. All this terrified me to the last degree, and he took care upon all occasions to lay it home to me in the worst colours that it could be possible to be drawn in. On the other hand, he failed not to set forth the easy, prosperous life which I was going to live.

He answered all that I could object from affection, and from former engagements, with telling me the necessity that was before us of taking other measures now; and as to his promises of marriage, the nature of things, he said, had put an end to that, by the probability of my being his brother's wife, before the time to which his promises all referred.

Thus, in a word, I may say, he reasoned me out of my reason; he conquered all my arguments, and I began to see a danger that I was in, which I had not considered of before, and that was, of being dropped by both of them and left alone in the world to shift for myself.

This, and his persuasion, at length prevailed with me to consent, though with so much reluctance, that it was easy to see I should go to church like a bear to the stake. I had some little apprehensions about me, too, lest my new spouse, who, by the way, I had not the least affection for, should be skillful enough to challenge me on another account, upon our first coming to bed together. But whether he did it with design or not, I know not, but his elder brother took care to make him very much fuddled before he went to bed, so that I had the satisfaction of a drunken bedfellow the first night. How he did it I know not, but I concluded that he certainly contrived it, that his brother might be able to make no judgment of the difference between a maid and a married woman; nor did he ever entertain any notions of it, or disturb his thoughts about it.

I should go back a little here to where I left off. The elder brother having thus managed me, his next business was to manage his mother, and he never left till he had brought her to acquiesce and be passive in the thing, even without acquainting the father, other than by post letters; so that she consented to our marrying privately, and leaving her to mange the father afterwards.

Then he cajoled with his brother, and persuaded him what service he had done him, and how he had brought his mother to consent, which, though true, was not indeed done to serve him, but to serve himself; but thus diligently did he cheat him, and had the thanks of a faithful friend for shifting off his whore into his brother's arms for a wife. So certainly does interest banish all manner of affection, and so naturally do men give up honour and justice, humanity, and even Christianity, to secure themselves.

I must now come back to brother Robin, as we always called him, who having got his mother's consent, as above, came big with the news to me, and told me the whole story of it, with a sincerity so visible, that I must confess it grieved me that I must be the instrument to abuse so honest a gentleman. But there was no remedy; he would have me, and I was not obliged to tell him that I was his brother's whore, though I had no other way to put him off; so I came gradually into it, to his satisfaction, and behold we were married.

Modesty forbids me to reveal the secrets of the marriage-bed, but nothing could have happened more suitable to my circumstances than that, as above, my husband was so fuddled when he came to bed, that he could not remember in the morning whether he had had any conversation with me or no, and I was obliged to tell him he had, though in reality he had not, that I might be sure he could make to inquiry about anything else.

It concerns the story in hand very little to enter into the further particulars of the family, or of myself, for the five years that I lived with this husband, only to observe that I had two children by him, and that at the end of five years he died. He had been really a very good husband to me, and we lived very agreeably together; but as he had not received much from them, and had in the little time he lived acquired no great matters, so my circumstances were not great, nor was I much mended by the match. Indeed, I had preserved the elder brother's bonds to me, to pay #500, which he offered me for my consent to marry his brother; and this, with what I had saved of the money he formerly gave me, about as much more by my husband, left me a widow with about #1200 in my pocket.

My two children were, indeed, taken happily off my hands by my husband's father and mother, and that, by the way, was all they got by Mrs. Betty.

I confess I was not suitably affected with the loss of my husband, nor indeed can I say that I ever loved him as I ought to have done, or as was proportionable to the good usage I had from him, for he was a tender, kind, good-humoured man as any woman could desire; but his brother being so always in my sight, at least while we were in the country, was a continual snare to me, and I never was in bed with my husband but I wished myself in the arms of his brother; and though his brother never offered me the least kindness that way after our marriage, but carried it just as a brother out to do, yet it was impossible for me to do so to him; in short, I committed adultery and incest with him every day in my desires, which, without doubt, was as effectually criminal in the nature of the guilt as if I had actually done it.

Before my husband died his elder brother was married, and we, being then removed to London, were written to by the old lady to come and be at the wedding. My husband went, but I pretended indisposition, and that I could not possibly travel, so I stayed behind; for, in short, I could not bear the sight of his being given to another woman, though I knew I was never to have him myself.

I was now, as above, left loose to the world, and being still young and handsome, as everybody said of me, and I assure you I thought myself so, and with a tolerable fortune in my pocket, I put no small value upon myself. I was courted by several very considerable tradesmen, and particularly very warmly by one, a linen-draper, at whose house, after my husband's death, I took a lodging, his sister being my acquaintance. Here I had all the liberty and all the opportunity to be gay and appear in company that I could desire, my landlord's sister being one of the maddest, gayest things alive, and not so much mistress of her virtue as I thought as first she had been. She brought me into a world of wild company, and even brought home several persons, such as she liked well enough to gratify, to see her pretty widow, so she was pleased to call me, and that name I got in a little time in public. Now, as fame and fools make an assembly, I was here wonderfully caressed, had abundance of admirers, and such as called themselves lovers; but I found not one fair proposal among them all. As for their common design, that I understood too well to be drawn into any more snares of that kind. The case was altered with me: I had money in my pocket, and had nothing to say to them. I had been tricked once by that cheat called love, but the game was over; I was resolved now to be married or nothing, and to be well married or not at all.

I loved the company, indeed, of men of mirth and wit, men of gallantry and figure, and was often entertained with such, as I was also with others; but I found by just observation, that the brightest men came upon the dullest errand—that is to say, the dullest as to what I aimed at. On the other hand, those who came with the best proposals were the dullest and most disagreeable part of the world. I was not averse to a tradesman, but then I would have a tradesman, forsooth, that was something of a gentleman too; that when my husband had a mind to carry me to the court, or to the play, he might become a sword, and look as like a gentleman as another man; and not be one that had the mark of his apron-strings upon his coat, or the mark of his hat upon his periwig; that should look as if he was set on to his sword, when his sword was put on to him, and that carried his trade in his countenance.

Well, at last I found this amphibious creature, this land-water thing called a gentleman-tradesman; and as a just plague upon my folly, I was catched in the very snare which, as I might say, I laid for myself. I said for myself, for I was not trepanned, I confess, but I betrayed myself.

This was a draper, too, for though my comrade would have brought me to a bargain with her brother, yet when it came to the point, it was, it seems, for a mistress, not a wife; and I kept true to this notion, that a woman should never be kept for a mistress that had money to keep herself.

Thus my pride, not my principle, my money, not my virtue, kept me honest; though, as it proved, I found I had much better have been sold by my she-comrade to her brother, than have sold myself as I did to a tradesman that was rake, gentleman, shopkeeper, and beggar, all together.

But I was hurried on (by my fancy to a gentleman) to ruin myself in the grossest manner that every woman did; for my new husband coming to a lump of money at once, fell into such a profusion of expense, that all I had, and all he had before, if he had anything worth mentioning, would not have held it out above one year.

He was very fond of me for about a quarter of a year, and what I got by that was, that I had the pleasure of seeing a great deal of my money spent upon myself, and, as I may say, had some of the spending it too. 'Come, my dear,' says he to me one day, 'shall we go and take a turn into the country for about a week?' 'Ay, my dear,' says I, 'whither would you go?' 'I care not whither,' says he, 'but I have a mind to look like quality for a week. We'll go to Oxford,' says he. 'How,' says I, 'shall we go? I am no horsewoman, and 'tis too far for a coach.' 'Too far!' says he; 'no place is too far for a coach-and-six. If I carry you out, you shall travel like a duchess.' 'Hum,' says I, 'my dear, 'tis a frolic; but if you have a mind to it, I don't care.' Well, the time was appointed, we had a rich coach, very good horses, a coachman, postillion, and two footmen in very good liveries; a gentleman on horseback, and a page with a feather in his hat upon another horse. The servants all called him my lord, and the inn-keepers, you may be sure, did the like, and I was her honour the Countess, and thus we traveled to Oxford, and a very pleasant journey we had; for, give him his due, not a beggar alive knew better how to be a lord than my husband. We saw all the rarities at Oxford, talked with two or three Fellows of colleges about putting out a young nephew, that was left to his lordship's care, to the University, and of their being his tutors. We diverted ourselves with bantering several other poor scholars, with hopes of being at least his lordship's chaplains and putting on a scarf; and thus having lived like quality indeed, as to expense, we went away for Northampton, and, in a word, in about twelve days' ramble came home again, to the tune of about #93 expense.

Vanity is the perfection of a fop. My husband had this excellence, that he valued nothing of expense; and as his history, you may be sure, has very little weight in it, 'tis enough to tell you that in about two years and a quarter he broke, and was not so happy to get over into the Mint, but got into a sponging-house, being arrested in an action too heavy from him to give bail to, so he sent for me to come to him.

It was no surprise to me, for I had foreseen some time that all was going to wreck, and had been taking care to reserve something if I could, though it was not much, for myself. But when he sent for me, he behaved much better than I expected, and told me plainly he had played the fool, and suffered himself to be surprised, which he might have prevented; that now he foresaw he could not stand it, and therefore he would have me go home, and in the night take away everything I had in the house of any value, and secure it; and after that, he told me that if I could get away one hundred or two hundred pounds in goods out of the shop, I should do it; 'only,' says he, 'let me know nothing of it, neither what you take nor whither you carry it; for as for me,' says he, 'I am resolved to get out of this house and be gone; and if you never hear of me more, my dear,' says he, 'I wish you well; I am only sorry for the injury I have done you.' He said some very handsome things to me indeed at parting; for I told you he was a gentleman, and that was all the benefit I had of his being so; that he used me very handsomely and with good manners upon all occasions, even to the last, only spent all I had, and left me to rob the creditors for something to subsist on.

However, I did as he bade me, that you may be sure; and having thus taken my leave of him, I never saw him more, for he found means to break out of the bailiff's house that night or the next, and go over into France, and for the rest of the creditors scrambled for it as well as they could. How, I knew not, for I could come at no knowledge of anything, more than this, that he came home about three o'clock in the morning, caused the rest of his goods to be removed into the Mint, and the shop to be shut up; and having raised what money he could get together, he got over, as I said, to France, from whence I had one or two letters from him, and no more. I did not see him when he came home, for he having given me such instructions as above, and I having made the best of my time, I had no more business back again at the house, not knowing but I might have been stopped there by the creditors; for a commission of bankrupt being soon after issued, they might have stopped me by orders from the commissioners. But my husband, having so dexterously got out of the bailiff's house by letting himself down in a most desperate manner from almost the top of the house to the top of another building, and leaping from thence, which was almost two storeys, and which was enough indeed to have broken his neck, he came home and got away his goods before the creditors could come to seize; that is to say, before they could get out the commission, and be ready to send their officers to take possession.

My husband was so civil to me, for still I say he was much of a gentleman, that in the first letter he wrote me from France, he let me know where he had pawned twenty pieces of fine holland for #30, which were really worth #90, and enclosed me the token and an order for the taking them up, paying the money, which I did, and made in time above #100 of them, having leisure to cut them and sell them, some and some, to private families, as opportunity offered.

However, with all this, and all that I had secured before, I found, upon casting things up, my case was very much altered, any my fortune much lessened; for, including the hollands and a parcel of fine muslins, which I carried off before, and some plate, and other things, I found I could hardly muster up #500; and my condition was very odd, for though I had no child (I had had one by my gentleman draper, but it was buried), yet I was a widow bewitched; I had a husband and no husband, and I could not pretend to marry again, though I knew well enough my husband would never see England any more, if he lived fifty years. Thus, I say, I was limited from marriage, what offer might soever be made me; and I had not one friend to advise with in the condition I was in, least not one I durst trust the secret of my circumstances to, for if the commissioners were to have been informed where I was, I should have been fetched up and examined upon oath, and all I have saved be taken away from me.

Upon these apprehensions, the first thing I did was to go quite out of my knowledge, and go by another name. This I did effectually, for I went into the Mint too, took lodgings in a very private place, dressed up in the habit of a widow, and called myself Mrs. Flanders.

Here, however, I concealed myself, and though my new acquaintances knew nothing of me, yet I soon got a great deal of company about me; and whether it be that women are scarce among the sorts of people that generally are to be found there, or that some consolations in the miseries of the place are more requisite than on other occasions, I soon found an agreeable woman was exceedingly valuable among the sons of affliction there, and that those that wanted money to pay half a crown on the pound to their creditors, and that run in debt at the sign of the Bull for their dinners, would yet find money for a supper, if they liked the woman.

However, I kept myself safe yet, though I began, like my Lord Rochester's mistress, that loved his company, but would not admit him farther, to have the scandal of a whore, without the joy; and upon this score, tired with the place, and indeed with the company too, I began to think of removing.

It was indeed a subject of strange reflection to me to see men who were overwhelmed in perplexed circumstances, who were reduced some degrees below being ruined, whose families were objects of their own terror and other people's charity, yet while a penny lasted, nay, even beyond it, endeavouring to drown themselves, labouring to forget former things, which now it was the proper time to remember, making more work for repentance, and sinning on, as a remedy for sin past.

But it is none of my talent to preach; these men were too wicked, even for me. There was something horrid and absurd in their way of sinning, for it was all a force even upon themselves; they did not only act against conscience, but against nature; they put a rape upon their temper to drown the reflections, which their circumstances continually gave them; and nothing was more easy than to see how sighs would interrupt their songs, and paleness and anguish sit upon their brows, in spite of the forced smiles they put on; nay, sometimes it would break out at their very mouths when they had parted with their money for a lewd treat or a wicked embrace. I have heard them, turning about, fetch a deep sigh, and cry, 'What a dog am I! Well, Betty, my dear, I'll drink thy health, though'; meaning the honest wife, that perhaps had not a half-crown for herself and three or four children. The next morning they are at their penitentials again; and perhaps the poor weeping wife comes over to him, either brings him some account of what his creditors are doing, and how she and the children are turned out of doors, or some other dreadful news; and this adds to his self-reproaches; but when he has thought and pored on it till he is almost mad, having no principles to support him, nothing within him or above him to comfort him, but finding it all darkness on every side, he flies to the same relief again, viz. to drink it away, debauch it away, and falling into company of men in just the same condition with himself, he repeats the crime, and thus he goes every day one step onward of his way to destruction.

I was not wicked enough for such fellows as these yet. On the contrary, I began to consider here very seriously what I had to do; how things stood with me, and what course I ought to take. I knew I had no friends, no, not one friend or relation in the world; and that little I had left apparently wasted, which when it was gone, I saw nothing but misery and starving was before me. Upon these considerations, I say, and filled with horror at the place I was in, and the dreadful objects which I had always before me, I resolved to be gone.

I had made an acquaintance with a very sober, good sort of a woman, who was a widow too, like me, but in better circumstances. Her husband had been a captain of a merchant ship, and having had the misfortune to be cast away coming home on a voyage from the West Indies, which would have been very profitable if he had come safe, was so reduced by the loss, that though he had saved his life then, it broke his heart, and killed him afterwards; and his widow, being pursued by the creditors, was forced to take shelter in the Mint. She soon made things up with the help of friends, and was at liberty again; and finding that I rather was there to be concealed, than by any particular prosecutions and finding also that I agreed with her, or rather she with me, in a just abhorrence of the place and of the company, she invited to go home with her till I could put myself in some posture of settling in the world to my mind; withal telling me, that it was ten to one but some good captain of a ship might take a fancy to me, and court me, in that part of the town where she lived.

I accepted her offer, and was with her half a year, and should have been longer, but in that interval what she proposed to me happened to herself, and she married very much to her advantage. But whose fortune soever was upon the increase, mine seemed to be upon the wane, and I found nothing present, except two or three boatswains, or such fellows, but as for the commanders, they were generally of two sorts: I. Such as, having good business, that is to say, a good ship, resolved not to marry but with advantage, that is, with a good fortune; 2. Such as, being out of employ, wanted a wife to help them to a ship; I mean (I) a wife who, having some money, could enable them to hold, as they call it, a good part of a ship themselves, so to encourage owners to come in; or (2) a wife who, if she had not money, had friends who were concerned in shipping, and so could help to put the young man into a good ship, which to them is as good as a portion; and neither of these was my case, so I looked like one that was to lie on hand.

This knowledge I soon learned by experience, viz. that the state of things was altered as to matrimony, and that I was not to expect at London what I had found in the country: that marriages were here the consequences of politic schemes for forming interests, and carrying on business, and that Love had no share, or but very little, in the matter.

That as my sister-in-law at Colchester had said, beauty, wit, manners, sense, good humour, good behaviour, education, virtue, piety, or any other qualification, whether of body or mind, had no power to recommend; that money only made a woman agreeable; that men chose mistresses indeed by the gust of their affection, and it was requisite to a whore to be handsome, well-shaped, have a good mien and a graceful behaviour; but that for a wife, no deformity would shock the fancy, no ill qualities the judgment; the money was the thing; the portion was neither crooked nor monstrous, but the money was always agreeable, whatever the wife was.

On the other hand, as the market ran very unhappily on the men's side, I found the women had lost the privilege of saying No; that it was a favour now for a woman to have the Question asked, and if any young lady had so much arrogance as to counterfeit a negative, she never had the opportunity given her of denying twice, much less of recovering that false step, and accepting what she had but seemed to decline. The men had such choice everywhere, that the case of the women was very unhappy; for they seemed to ply at every door, and if the man was by great chance refused at one house, he was sure to be received at the next.

Besides this, I observed that the men made no scruple to set themselves out, and to go a-fortunehunting, as they call it, when they had really no fortune themselves to demand it, or merit to deserve it; and that they carried it so high, that a woman was scarce allowed to inquire after the character or estate of the person that pretended to her. This I had an example of, in a young lady in the next house to me, and with whom I had contracted an intimacy; she was courted by a young captain, and though she had near #2000 to her fortune, she did but inquire of some of his neighbours about his character, his morals, or substance, and he took occasion at the next visit to let her know, truly, that he took it very ill, and that he should not give her the trouble of his visits any more. I heard of it, and I had begun my acquaintance with her, I went to see her upon it. She entered into a close conversation with me about it, and unbosomed herself very freely. I perceived presently that though she thought herself very ill used, yet she had no power to resent it, and was exceedingly piqued that she had lost him, and particularly that another of less fortune had gained him.

I fortified her mind against such a meanness, as I called it; I told her, that as low as I was in the world, I would have despised a man that should think I ought to take him upon his own recommendation only, without having the liberty to inform myself of his fortune and of his character; also I told her, that as she had a good fortune, she had no need to stoop to the disaster of the time; that it was enough that the men could insult us that had but little money to recommend us, but if she suffered such an affront to pass upon her without resenting it, she would be rendered low-prized upon all occasions, and would be the contempt of all the women in that part of the town; that a woman can never want an opportunity to be revenged of a man that has used her ill, and that there were ways enough to humble such a fellow as that, or else certainly women were the most unhappy creatures in the world.

I found she was very well pleased with the discourse, and she told me seriously that she would be very glad to make him sensible of her just resentment, and either to bring him on again, or have the satisfaction of her revenge being as public as possible.

I told her, that if she would take my advice, I would tell her how she should obtain her wishes in both those things, and that I would engage I would bring the man to her door again, and make him beg to be let in. She smiled at that, and soon let me see, that if he came to her door, her resentment was not so great as to give her leave to let him stand long there.

However, she listened very willingly to my offer of advice; so I told her that the first thing she ought to do was a piece of justice to herself, namely, that whereas she had been told by several people that he had reported among the ladies that he had left her, and pretended to give the advantage of the negative to himself, she should take care to have it well spread among the women—which she could not fail of an opportunity to do in a neighbourhood so addicted to family news as that she live in was—that she had inquired into his circumstances, and found he was not the man as to estate he pretended to be. 'Let them be told, madam,' said I, 'that you had been well informed that he was not the man that you expected, and that you thought it was not safe to meddle with him; that you heard he was of an ill temper, and that he boasted how he had used the women ill upon many occasions, and that particularly he was debauched in his morals', etc. The last of which, indeed, had some truth in it; but at the same time I did not find that she seemed to like him much the worse for that part.

As I had put this into her head, she came most readily into it. Immediately she went to work to find instruments, and she had very little difficulty in the search, for telling her story in general to a couple of gossips in the neighbourhood, it was the chat of the tea-table all over that part of the town, and I met with it wherever I visited; also, as it was known that I was acquainted with the young lady herself, my opinion was asked very often, and I confirmed it with all the necessary aggravations, and set out his character in the blackest colours; but then as a piece of secret intelligence, I added, as what the other gossips knew nothing of, viz. that I had heard he was in very bad circumstances; that he was under a necessity of a fortune to support his interest with the owners of the ship he commanded; that his own part was not paid for, and if it was not paid quickly, his owners would put him out of the ship, and his chief mate was likely to command it, who offered to buy that part which the captain had promised to take.

I added, for I confess I was heartily piqued at the rogue, as I called him, that I had heard a rumour, too, that he had a wife alive at Plymouth, and another in the West Indies, a thing which they all knew was not very uncommon for such kind of gentlemen.

This worked as we both desire it, for presently the young lady next door, who had a father and mother that governed both her and her fortune, was shut up, and her father forbid him the house. Also in one place more where he went, the woman had the courage, however strange it was, to say No; and he could try nowhere but he was reproached with his pride, and that he pretended not to give the women leave to inquire into his character, and the like.

Well, by this time he began to be sensible of his mistake; and having alarmed all the women on that side of the water, he went over to Ratcliff, and got access to some of the ladies there; but though the young women there too were, according to the fate of the day, pretty willing to be asked, yet such was his ill-luck, that his character followed him over the water and his good name was much the same there as it was on our side; so that though he might have had wives enough, yet it did not happen among the women that had good fortunes, which was what he wanted.

But this was not all; she very ingeniously managed another thing herself, for she got a young gentleman, who as a relation, and was indeed a married man, to come and visit her two or three times a week in a very fine chariot and good liveries, and her two agents, and I also, presently spread a report all over, that this gentleman came to court her; that he was a gentleman of a #1000 a year, and that he was fallen in love with her, and that she was going to her aunt's in the city, because it was inconvenient for the gentleman to come to her with his coach in Redriff, the streets being so narrow and difficult.

This took immediately. The captain was laughed at in all companies, and was ready to hang himself. He tried all the ways possible to come at her again, and wrote the most passionate letters to her in the world, excusing his former rashness; and in short, by great application, obtained leave to wait on her again, as he said, to clear his reputation.

At this meeting she had her full revenge of him; for she told him she wondered what he took her to be, that she should admit any man to a treaty of so much consequence as that to marriage, without inquiring very well into his circumstances; that if he thought she was to be huffed into wedlock, and that she was in the same circumstances which her neighbours might be in, viz. to take up with the first good Christian that came, he was mistaken; that, in a word, his character was really bad, or he was very ill beholden to his neighbours; and that unless he could clear up some points, in which she had justly been prejudiced, she had no more to say to him, but to do herself justice, and give him the satisfaction of knowing that she was not afraid to say No, either to him or any man else.

With that she told him what she had heard, or rather raised herself by my means, of his character; his not having paid for the part he pretended to own of the ship he commanded; of the resolution of his owners to put him out of the command, and to put his mate in his stead; and of the scandal raised on his morals; his having been reproached with such-and-such women, and having a wife at Plymouth and in the West Indies, and the like; and she asked him whether he could deny that she had good reason, if these things were not cleared up, to refuse him, and in the meantime to insist upon having satisfaction in points to significant as they were.

He was so confounded at her discourse that he could not answer a word, and she almost began to believe that all was true, by his disorder, though at the same time she knew that she had been the raiser of all those reports herself.

After some time he recovered himself a little, and from that time became the most humble, the most modest, and most importunate man alive in his courtship.

She carried her jest on a great way. She asked him, if he thought she was so at her last shift that she could or ought to bear such treatment, and if he did not see that she did not want those who thought it worth their while to come farther to her than he did; meaning the gentleman whom she had brought to visit her by way of sham.

She brought him by these tricks to submit to all possible measures to satisfy her, as well of his circumstances as of his behaviour. He brought her undeniable evidence of his having paid for his part of the ship; he brought her certificates from his owners, that the report of their intending to remove him from the command of the ship and put his chief mate in was false and groundless; in short, he was quite the reverse of what he was before.

Thus I convinced her, that if the men made their advantage of our sex in the affair of marriage, upon the supposition of there being such choice to be had, and of the women being so easy, it was only owing to this, that the women wanted courage to maintain their ground and to play their part; and that, according to my Lord Rochester,

'A woman's ne'er so ruined but she can Revenge herself on her undoer, Man.'

After these things this young lady played her part so well, that though she resolved to have him, and that indeed having him was the main bent of her design, yet she made his obtaining her be to him the most difficult thing in the world; and this she did, not by a haughty reserved carriage, but by a just policy, turning the tables upon him, and playing back upon him his own game; for as he pretended, by a kind of lofty carriage, to place himself above the occasion of a character, and to make inquiring into his character a kind of an affront to him, she broke with him upon that subject, and at the same time that she make him submit to all possible inquiry after his affairs, she apparently shut the door against his looking into her own.

It was enough to him to obtain her for a wife. As to what she had, she told him plainly, that as he knew her circumstances, it was but just she should know his; and though at the same time he had only known her circumstances by common fame, yet he had made so many protestations of his passion for her, that he could ask no more but her hand to his grand request, and the like ramble according to the custom of lovers. In short, he left himself no room to ask any more questions about her estate, and she took the advantage of it like a prudent woman, for she placed part of her fortune so in trustees, without letting him know anything of it, that it was quite out of his reach, and made him be very well content with the rest.

It is true she was pretty well besides, that is to say, she had about #1400 in money, which she gave him; and the other, after some time, she brought to light as a perquisite to herself, which he was to accept as a mighty favour, seeing though it was not to be his, it might ease him in the article of her particular expenses; and I must add, that by this conduct the gentleman himself became not only the more humble in his applications to her to obtain her, but also was much the more an obliging husband to her when he had her. I cannot but remind the ladies here how much they place themselves below the common station of a wife, which, if I may be allowed not to be partial, is low enough already; I say, they place themselves below their common station, and prepare their own mortifications, by their submitting so to be insulted by the men beforehand, which I confess I see no necessity of.

This relation may serve, therefore, to let the ladies see that the advantage is not so much on the other side as the men think it is; and though it may be true that the men have but too much choice among us, and that some women may be found who will dishonour themselves, be cheap, and easy to come at, and will scarce wait to be asked, yet if they will have women, as I may say, worth having, they may find them as uncomeatable as ever and that those that are otherwise are a sort of people that have such deficiencies, when had, as rather recommend the ladies that are difficult than encourage the men to go on with their easy courtship, and expect wives equally valuable that will come at first call.

Nothing is more certain than that the ladies always gain of the men by keeping their ground, and letting their pretended lovers see they can resent being slighted, and that they are not afraid of saying No. They, I observe, insult us mightily with telling us of the number of women; that the wars, and the sea, and trade, and other incidents have carried the men so much away, that there is no proportion between the numbers of the sexes, and therefore the women have the disadvantage; but I am far from granting that the number of women is so great, or the number of men so small; but if they will have me tell the truth, the disadvantage of the women is a terrible scandal upon the men, and it lies here, and here only; namely, that the age is so wicked, and the sex so debauched, that, in short, the number of such men as an honest woman ought to meddle with is small indeed, and it is but here and there that a man is to be found who is fit for a woman to venture upon.

But the consequence even of that too amounts to no more than this, that women ought to be the more nice; for how do we know the just character of the man that makes the offer? To say that the woman should be the more easy on this occasion, is to say we should be the forwarder to venture because of the greatness of the danger, which, in my way of reasoning, is very absurd.

On the contrary, the women have ten thousand times the more reason to be wary and backward, by how much the hazard of being betrayed is the greater; and would the ladies consider this, and act the wary part, they would discover every cheat that offered; for, in short, the lives of very few men nowadays will bear a character; and if the ladies do but make a little inquiry, they will soon be able to distinguish the men and deliver themselves. As for women that do not think their own safety worth their thought, that, impatient of their perfect state, resolve, as they call it, to take the first good Christian that comes, that run into matrimony as a horse rushes into the battle, I can say nothing to them but this, that they are a sort of ladies that are to be prayed for among the rest of distempered people, and to me they look like people that venture their whole estates in a lottery where there is a hundred thousand blanks to one prize.

No man of common-sense will value a woman the less for not giving up herself at the first attack, or for accepting his proposal without inquiring into his person or character; on the contrary, he must think her the weakest of all creatures in the world, as the rate of men now goes. In short, he must have a very contemptible opinion of her capacities, nay, every of her understanding, that, having but one case of her life, shall call that life away at once, and make matrimony, like death, be a leap in the dark.

I would fain have the conduct of my sex a little regulated in this particular, which is the thing in which, of all the parts of life, I think at this time we suffer most in; 'tis nothing but lack of courage, the fear of not being married at all, and of that frightful state of life called an old maid, of which I have a story to tell by itself. This, I say, is the woman's snare; but would the ladies once but get above that fear and manage rightly, they would more certainly avoid it by standing their ground, in a case so absolutely necessary to their felicity, that by exposing themselves as they do; and if they did not marry so soon as they may do otherwise, they would make themselves amends by marrying safer. She is always married too soon who gets a bad husband, and she is never married too late who gets a good one; in a word, there is no woman, deformity or lost reputation excepted, but if she manages well, may be married safely one time or other; but if she precipitates herself, it is ten thousand to one but she is undone.

But I come now to my own case, in which there was at this time no little nicety. The circumstances I was in made the offer of a good husband the most necessary thing in the world to me, but I found soon that to be made cheap and easy was not the way. It soon began to be found that the widow had no fortune, and to say this was to say all that was ill of me, for I began to be dropped in all the discourses of matrimony. Being well-bred, handsome, witty, modest, and agreeable; all which I had allowed to my character—whether justly or no is not the purpose—I say, all these would not do without the dross, which way now become more valuable than virtue itself. In short, the widow, they said, had no money.

I resolved, therefore, as to the state of my present circumstances, that it was absolutely necessary to change my station, and make a new appearance in some other place where I was not known, and even to pass by another name if I found occasion.

I communicated my thoughts to my intimate friend, the captain's lady, whom I had so faithfully served in her case with the captain, and who was as ready to serve me in the same kind as I could desire. I made no scruple to lay my circumstances open to her; my stock was but low, for I had made but about #540 at the close of my last affair, and I had wasted some of that; however, I had about #460 left, a great many very rich clothes, a gold watch, and some jewels, though of no extraordinary value, and about #30 or #40 left in linen not disposed of.

My dear and faithful friend, the captain's wife, was so sensible of the service I had done her in the affair above, that she was not only a steady friend to me, but, knowing my circumstances, she frequently made me presents as money came into her hands, such as fully amounted to a maintenance, so that I spent none of my own; and at last she made this unhappy proposal to me, viz. that as we had observed, as above, how the men made no scruple to set themselves out as persons meriting a woman of fortune, when they had really no fortune of their own, it was but just to deal with them in their own way and, if it was possible, to deceive the deceiver.

The captain's lady, in short, put this project into my head, and told me if I would be ruled by her I should certainly get a husband of fortune, without leaving him any room to reproach me with want of my own. I told her, as I had reason to do, that I would give up myself wholly to her directions, and that I would have neither tongue to speak nor feet to step in that affair but as she should direct me, depending that she would extricate me out of every difficulty she brought me into, which she said she would answer for.

The first step she put me upon was to call her cousin, and to to a relation's house of hers in the country, where she directed me, and where she brought her husband to visit me; and calling me cousin, she worked matters so about, that her husband and she together invited me most passionately to come to town and be with them, for they now live in a quite different place from where they were before. In the next place, she tells her husband that I had at least #1500 fortune, and that after some of my relations I was like to have a great deal more.

It was enough to tell her husband this; there needed nothing on my side. I was but to sit still and wait the event, for it presently went all over the neighbourhood that the young widow at Captain ———'s was a fortune, that she had at least #1500, and perhaps a great deal more, and that the captain said so; and if the captain was asked at any time about me, he made no scruple to affirm it, though he knew not one word of the matter, other than that his wife had told him so; and in this he thought no harm, for he really believed it to be so, because he had it from his wife: so slender a foundation will those fellows build upon, if they do but think there is a fortune in the game. With the reputation of this fortune, I presently found myself blessed with admirers enough, and that I had my choice of men, as scarce as they said they were, which, by the way, confirms what I was saying before. This being my case, I, who had a subtle game to play, had nothing now to do but to single out from them all the properest man that might be for my purpose; that is to say, the man who was most likely to depend upon the hearsay of a fortune, and not inquire too far into the particulars; and unless I did this I did nothing, for my case would not bear much inquiry.

I picked out my man without much difficulty, by the judgment I made of his way of courting me. I had let him run on with his protestations and oaths that he loved me above all the world; that if I would make him happy, that was enough; all which I knew was upon supposition, nay, it was upon a full satisfaction, that I was very rich, though I never told him a word of it myself.

This was my man; but I was to try him to the bottom, and indeed in that consisted my safety; for if he baulked, I knew I was undone, as surely as he was undone if he took me; and if I did not make some scruple about his fortune, it was the way to lead him to raise some about mine; and first, therefore, I pretended on all occasions to doubt his sincerity, and told him, perhaps he only courted me for my fortune. He stopped my mouth in that part with the thunder of his protestations, as above, but still I pretended to doubt.

One morning he pulls off his diamond ring, and writes upon the glass of the sash in my chamber this line—

'You I love, and you alone.'

I read it, and asked him to lend me his ring, with which I wrote under it, thus—

'And so in love says every one.'

He takes his ring again, and writes another line thus—

'Virtue alone is an estate.'

I borrowed it again, and I wrote under it—

'But money's virtue, gold is fate.'

He coloured as red as fire to see me turn so quick upon him, and in a kind of a rage told me he would conquer me, and writes again thus—

'I scorn your gold, and yet I love.'

I ventured all upon the last cast of poetry, as you'll see, for I wrote boldly under his last—

'I'm poor: let's see how kind you'll prove.'

This was a sad truth to me; whether he believed me or no, I could not tell; I supposed then that he did not. However, he flew to me, took me in his arms, and, kissing me very eagerly, and with the greatest passion imaginable, he held me fast till he called for a pen and ink, and then told me he could not wait the tedious writing on the glass, but, pulling out a piece of paper, he began and wrote again—

'Be mine, with all your poverty.'

I took his pen, and followed him immediately, thus—

'Yet secretly you hope I lie.'

He told me that was unkind, because it was not just, and that I put him upon contradicting me, which did not consist with good manners, any more than with his affection; and therefore, since I had insensibly drawn him into this poetical scribble, he begged I would not oblige him to break it off; so he writes again—

'Let love alone be our debate.'

I wrote again—

'She loves enough that does not hate.'

This he took for a favour, and so laid down the cudgels, that is to say, the pen; I say, he took if for a favour, and a mighty one it was, if he had known all. However, he took it as I meant it, that is, to let him think I was inclined to go on with him, as indeed I had all the reason in the world to do, for he was the best-humoured, merry sort of a fellow that I ever met with, and I often reflected on myself how doubly criminal it was to deceive such a man; but that necessity, which pressed me to a settlement suitable to my condition, was my authority for it; and certainly his affection to me, and the goodness of his temper, however they might argue against using him ill, yet they strongly argued to me that he would better take the disappointment than some fiery-tempered wretch, who might have nothing to recommend him but those passions which would serve only to make a woman miserable all her days.

Besides, though I jested with him (as he supposed it) so often about my poverty, yet, when he found it to be true, he had foreclosed all manner of objection, seeing, whether he was in jest or in earnest, he had declared he took me without any regard to my portion, and, whether I was in jest or in earnest, I had declared myself to be very poor; so that, in a word, I had him fast both ways; and though he might say afterwards he was cheated, yet he could never say that I had cheated him.

He pursued me close after this, and as I saw there was no need to fear losing him, I played the indifferent part with him longer than prudence might otherwise have dictated to me. But I considered how much this caution and indifference would give me the advantage over him, when I should come to be under the necessity of owning my own circumstances to him; and I managed it the more warily, because I found he inferred from thence, as indeed he ought to do, that I either had the more money or the more judgment, and would not venture at all.

I took the freedom one day, after we had talked pretty close to the subject, to tell him that it was true I had received the compliment of a lover from him, namely, that he would take me without inquiring into my fortune, and I would make him a suitable return in this, viz. that I would make as little inquiry into his as consisted with reason, but I hoped he would allow me to ask a few questions, which he would answer or not as he thought fit; and that I would not be offended if he did not answer me at all; one of these questions related to our manner of living, and the place where, because I had heard he had a great plantation in Virginia, and that he had talked of going to live there, and I told him I did not care to be transported.

He began from this discourse to let me voluntarily into all his affairs, and to tell me in a frank, open way all his circumstances, by which I found he was very well to pass in the world; but that great part of his estate consisted of three plantations, which he had in Virginia, which brought him in a very good income, generally speaking, to the tune of #300, a year, but that if he was to live upon them, would bring him in four times as much. 'Very well,' thought I; 'you shall carry me thither as soon as you please, though I won't tell you so beforehand.'

I jested with him extremely about the figure he would make in Virginia; but I found he would do anything I desired, though he did not seem glad to have me undervalue his plantations, so I turned my tale. I told him I had good reason not to go there to live, because if his plantations were worth so much there, I had not a fortune suitable to a gentleman of #1200 a year, as he said his estate would be.

He replied generously, he did not ask what my fortune was; he had told me from the beginning he would not, and he would be as good as his word; but whatever it was, he assured me he would never desire me to go to Virginia with him, or go thither himself without me, unless I was perfectly willing, and made it my choice.

All this, you may be sure, was as I wished, and indeed nothing could have happened more perfectly agreeable. I carried it on as far as this with a sort of indifferency that he often wondered at, more than at first, but which was the only support of his courtship; and I mention it the rather to intimate again to the ladies that nothing but want of courage for such an indifferency makes our sex so cheap, and prepares them to be ill-used as they are; would they venture the loss of a pretending fop now and then, who carries it high upon the point of his own merit, they would certainly be less slighted, and courted more. Had I discovered really and truly what my great fortune was, and that in all I had not full #500 when he expected #1500, yet I had hooked him so fast, and played him so long, that I was satisfied he would have had me in my worst circumstances; and indeed it was less a surprise to him when he learned the truth than it would have been, because having not the least blame to lay on me, who had carried it with an air of indifference to the last, he would not say one word, except that indeed he thought it had been more, but that if it had been less he did not repent his bargain; only that he should not be able to maintain me so well as he intended.

In short, we were married, and very happily married on my side, I assure you, as to the man; for he was the best-humoured man that every woman had, but his circumstances were not so good as I imagined, as, on the other hand, he had not bettered himself by marrying so much as he expected.

When we were married, I was shrewdly put to it to bring him that little stock I had, and to let him see it was no more; but there was a necessity for it, so I took my opportunity one day when we were alone, to enter into a short dialogue with him about it. 'My dear,' said I, 'we have been married a fortnight; is it not time to let you know whether you have got a wife with something or with nothing?' 'Your own time for that, my dear,' says he; 'I am satisfied that I have got the wife I love; I have not troubled you much,' says he, 'with my inquiry after it.'

'That's true,' says I, 'but I have a great difficulty upon me about it, which I scarce know how to manage.'

'What's that, m' dear?' says he.

'Why,' says I, "tis a little hard upon me, and 'tis harder upon you. I am told that Captain ———' (meaning my friend's husband) 'has told you I had a great deal more money than I ever pretended to have, and I am sure I never employed him to do so.'

'Well,' says he, 'Captain ——— may have told me so, but what then? If you have not so much, that may lie at his door, but you never told me what you had, so I have no reason to blame you if you have nothing at all.'

'That's is so just,' said I, 'and so generous, that it makes my having but a little a double affliction to me.'

'The less you have, my dear,' says he, 'the worse for us both; but I hope your affliction you speak of is not caused for fear I should be unkind to you, for want of a portion. No, no, if you have nothing, tell me plainly, and at once; I may perhaps tell the captain he has cheated me, but I can never say you have cheated me, for did you not give it under your hand that you were poor? and so I ought to expect you to be.'

'Well,' said I, 'my dear, I am glad I have not been concerned in deceiving you before marriage. If I deceive you since, 'tis ne'er the worse; that I am poor is too true, but not so poor as to have nothing neither'; so I pulled out some bank bills, and gave him about #160. 'There's something, my dear,' said I, 'and not quite all neither.'

I had brought him so near to expecting nothing, by what I had said before, that the money, though the sum was small in itself, was doubly welcome to him; he owned it was more than he looked for, and that he did not question by my discourse to him, but that my fine clothes, gold watch, and a diamond ring or two, had been all my fortune.

I let him please himself with that #160 two or three days, and then, having been abroad that day, and as if I had been to fetch it, I brought him #100 more home in gold, and told him there was a little more portion for him; and, in short, in about a week more I brought him #180 more, and about #60 in linen, which I made him believe I had been obliged to take with the #100 which I gave him in gold, as a composition for a debt of #600, being little more than five shillings in the pound, and overvalued too.

'And now, my dear,' says I to him, 'I am very sorry to tell you, that there is all, and that I have given you my whole fortune.' I added, that if the person who had my #600 had not abused me, I had been worth #1000 to him, but that as it was, I had been faithful to him, and reserved nothing to myself, but if it had been more he should have had it.

He was so obliged by the manner, and so pleased with the sum, for he had been in a terrible fright lest it had been nothing at all, that he accepted it very thankfully. And thus I got over the fraud of passing for a fortune without money, and cheating a man into marrying me on pretence of a fortune; which, by the way, I take to be one of the most dangerous steps a woman can take, and in which she runs the most hazard of being ill-used afterwards.

My husband, to give him his due, was a man of infinite good nature, but he was no fool; and finding his income not suited to the manner of living which he had intended, if I had brought him what he expected, and being under a disappointment in his return of his plantations in Virginia, he discovered many times his inclination of going over to Virginia, to live upon his own; and often would be magnifying the way of living there, how cheap, how plentiful, how pleasant, and the like.

I began presently to understand this meaning, and I took him up very plainly one morning, and told him that I did so; that I found his estate turned to no account at this distance, compared to what it would do if he lived upon the spot, and that I found he had a mind to go and live there; and I added, that I was sensible he had been disappointed in a wife, and that finding his expectations not answered that way, I could do no less, to make him amends, than tell him that I was very willing to go over to Virginia with him and live there.

He said a thousand kind things to me upon the subject of my making such a proposal to him. He told me, that however he was disappointed in his expectations of a fortune, he was not disappointed in a wife, and that I was all to him that a wife could be, and he was more than satisfied on the whole when the particulars were put together, but that this offer was so kind, that it was more than he could express.

To bring the story short, we agreed to go. He told me that he had a very good house there, that it was well furnished, that his mother was alive and lived in it, and one sister, which was all the relations he had; that as soon as he came there, his mother would remove to another house, which was her own for life, and his after her decease; so that I should have all the house to myself; and I found all this to be exactly as he had said.

To make this part of the story short, we put on board the ship which we went in, a large quantity of good furniture for our house, with stores of linen and other necessaries, and a good cargo for sale, and away we went.

To give an account of the manner of our voyage, which was long and full of dangers, is out of my way; I kept no journal, neither did my husband. All that I can say is, that after a terrible passage, frighted twice with dreadful storms, and once with what was still more terrible, I mean a pirate who came on board and took away almost all our provisions; and which would have been beyond all to me, they had once taken my husband to go along with them, but by entreaties were prevailed with to leave him;—I say, after all these terrible things, we arrived in York River in Virginia, and coming to our plantation, we were received with all the demonstrations of tenderness and affection, by my husband's mother, that were possible to be expressed.

We lived here all together, my mother-in-law, at my entreaty, continuing in the house, for she was too kind a mother to be parted with; my husband likewise continued the same as at first, and I thought myself the happiest creature alive, when an odd and surprising event put an end to all that felicity in a moment, and rendered my condition the most uncomfortable, if not the most miserable, in the world.

My mother was a mighty cheerful, good-humoured old woman — I may call her old woman, for her son was above thirty; I say she was very pleasant, good company, and used to entertain me, in particular, with abundance of stories to divert me, as well of the country we were in as of the people.

Among the rest, she often told me how the greatest part of the inhabitants of the colony came thither in very indifferent circumstances from England; that, generally speaking, they were of two sorts; either, first, such as were brought over by masters of ships to be sold as servants. 'Such as we call them, my dear,' says she, 'but they are more properly called slaves.' Or, secondly, such as are transported from Newgate and other prisons, after having been found guilty of felony and other crimes punishable with death.

'When they come here,' says she, 'we make no difference; the planters buy them, and they work together in the field till their time is out. When 'tis expired,' said she, 'they have encouragement given them to plant for themselves; for they have a certain number of acres of land allotted them by the country, and they go to work to clear and cure the land, and then to plant it with tobacco and corn for their own use; and as the tradesmen and merchants will trust them with tools and clothes and other necessaries, upon the credit of their crop before it is grown, so they again plant every year a little more than the year before, and so buy whatever they want with the crop that is before them.

'Hence, child,' says she, 'man a Newgate-bird becomes a great man, and we have,' continued she, 'several justices of the peace, officers of the trained bands, and magistrates of the towns they live in, that have been burnt in the hand.'

She was going on with that part of the story, when her own part in it interrupted her, and with a great deal of good-humoured confidence she told me she was one of the second sort of inhabitants herself; that she came away openly, having ventured too far in a particular case, so that she was become a criminal. 'And here's the mark of it, child,' says she; and, pulling off her glove, 'look ye here,' says she, turning up the palm of her hand, and showed me a very fine white arm and hand, but branded in the inside of the hand, as in such cases it must be.

This story was very moving to me, but my mother, smiling, said, 'You need not think a thing strange, daughter, for as I told you, some of the best men in this country are burnt in the hand, and they are not ashamed to own it. There's Major ———,' says she, 'he was an eminent pickpocket; there's Justice Ba———r, was a shoplifter, and both of them were burnt in the hand; and I could name you several such as they are.'

We had frequent discourses of this kind, and abundance of instances she gave me of the like. After some time, as she was telling some stories of one that was transported but a few weeks ago, I began in an intimate kind of way to ask her to tell me something of her own story, which she did with the utmost plainness and sincerity; how she had fallen into very ill company in London in her young days, occasioned by her mother sending her frequently to carry victuals and other relief to a kinswoman of hers who was a prisoner in Newgate, and who lay in a miserable starving condition, was afterwards condemned to be hanged, but having got respite by pleading her belly, dies afterwards in the prison.

Here my mother-in-law ran out in a long account of the wicked practices in that dreadful place, and how it ruined more young people that all the town besides. 'And child,' says my mother, 'perhaps you may know little of it, or, it may be, have heard nothing about it; but depend upon it,' says she, 'we all know here that there are more thieves and rogues made by that one prison of Newgate than by all the clubs and societies of villains in the nation; 'tis that cursed place,' says my mother, 'that half peopled this colony.'

Here she went on with her own story so long, and in so particular a manner, that I began to be very uneasy; but coming to one particular that required telling her name, I thought I should have sunk down in the place. She perceived I was out of order, and asked me if I was not well, and what ailed me. I told her I was so affected with the melancholy story she had told, and the terrible things she had gone through, that it had overcome me, and I begged of her to talk no more of it. 'Why, my dear,' says she very kindly, 'what need these things trouble you? These passages were long before your time, and they give me no trouble at all now; nay, I look back on them with a particular satisfaction, as they have been a means to bring me to this place.' Then she went on to tell me how she very luckily fell into a good family, where, behaving herself well, and her mistress dying, her master married her, by whom she had my husband and his sister, and that by her diligence and good management after her husband's death, she had improved the plantations to such a degree as they then were, so that most of the estate was of her getting, not her husband's, for she had been a widow upwards of sixteen years.

I heard this part of they story with very little attention, because I wanted much to retire and give vent to my passions, which I did soon after; and let any one judge what must be the anguish of my mind, when I came to reflect that this was certainly no more or less than my own mother, and I had now had two children, and was big with another by my own brother, and lay with him still every night.

I was now the most unhappy of all women in the world. Oh! had the story never been told me, all had been well; it had been no crime to have lain with my husband, since as to his being my relation I had known nothing of it.

I had now such a load on my mind that it kept me perpetually waking; to reveal it, which would have been some ease to me, I could not find would be to any purpose, and yet to conceal it would be next to impossible; nay, I did not doubt but I should talk of it in my sleep, and tell my husband of it whether I would or no. If I discovered it, the least thing I could expect was to lose my husband, for he was too nice and too honest a man to have continued my husband after he had known I had been his sister; so that I was perplexed to the last degree.

I leave it to any man to judge what difficulties presented to my view. I was away from my native country, at a distance prodigious, and the return to me unpassable. I lived very well, but in a circumstance insufferable in itself. If I had discovered myself to my mother, it might be difficult to convince her of the particulars, and I had no way to prove them. On the other hand, if she had questioned or doubted me, I had been undone, for the bare suggestion would have immediately separated me from my husband, without gaining my mother or him, who would have been neither a husband nor a brother; so that between the surprise on one hand, and the uncertainty on the other, I had been sure to be undone.

In the meantime, as I was but too sure of the fact, I lived therefore in open avowed incest and whoredom, and all under the appearance of an honest wife; and though I was not much touched with the crime of it, yet the action had something in it shocking to nature, and made my husband, as he thought himself, even nauseous to me.

However, upon the most sedate consideration, I resolved that it was absolutely necessary to conceal it all and not make the least discovery of it either to mother or husband; and thus I lived with the greatest pressure imaginable for three years more, but had no more children.

During this time my mother used to be frequently telling me old stories of her former adventures, which, however, were no ways pleasant to me; for by it, though she did not tell it me in plain terms, yet I could easily understand, joined with what I had heard myself, of my first tutors, that in her younger days she had been both whore and thief; but I verily believed she had lived to repent sincerely of both, and that she was then a very pious, sober, and religious woman.

Well, let her life have been what it would then, it was certain that my life was very uneasy to me; for I lived, as I have said, but in the worst sort of whoredom, and as I could expect no good of it, so really no good issue came of it, and all my seeming prosperity wore off, and ended in misery and destruction. It was some time, indeed, before it came to this, for, but I know not by what ill fate guided, everything went wrong with us afterwards, and that which was worse, my husband grew strangely altered, forward, jealous, and unkind, and I was as impatient of bearing his carriage, as the carriage was unreasonable and unjust. These things proceeded so far, that we came at last to be in such ill terms with one another, that I claimed a promise of him, which he entered willingly into with me when I consented to come from England with him, viz. that if I found the country not to agree with me, or that I did not like to live there, I should come away to England again when I pleased, giving him a year's warning to settle his affairs.

I say, I now claimed this promise of him, and I must confess I did it not in the most obliging terms that could be in the world neither; but I insisted that he treated me ill, that I was remote from my friends, and could do myself no justice, and that he was jealous without cause, my conversation having been unblamable, and he having no pretense for it, and that to remove to England would take away all occasion from him.

I insisted so peremptorily upon it, that he could not avoid coming to a point, either to keep his word with me or to break it; and this, notwithstanding he used all the skill he was master of, and employed his mother and other agents to prevail with me to alter my resolutions; indeed, the bottom of the thing lay at my heart, and that made all his endeavours fruitless, for my heart was alienated from him as a husband. I loathed the thoughts of bedding with him, and used a thousand pretenses of illness and humour to prevent his touching me, fearing nothing more than to be with child by him, which to be sure would have prevented, or at least delayed, my going over to England.

However, at last I put him so out of humour, that he took up a rash and fatal resolution; in short, I should not go to England; and though he had promised me, yet it was an unreasonable thing for me to desire it; that it would be ruinous to his affairs, would unhinge his whole family, and be next to an undoing him in the world; that therefore I ought not to desire it of him, and that no wife in the world that valued her family and her husband's prosperity would insist upon such a thing.

This plunged me again, for when I considered the thing calmly, and took my husband as he really was, a diligent, careful man in the main work of laying up an estate for his children, and that he knew nothing of the dreadful circumstances that he was in, I could not but confess to myself that my proposal was very unreasonable, and what no wife that had the good of her family at heart would have desired.

But my discontents were of another nature; I looked upon him no longer as a husband, but as a near relation, the son of my own mother, and I resolved somehow or other to be clear of him, but which way I did not know, nor did it seem possible.

It is said by the ill-natured world, of our sex, that if we are set on a thing, it is impossible to turn us from our resolutions; in short, I never ceased poring upon the means to bring to pass my voyage, and came that length with my husband at last, as to propose going without him. This provoked him to the last degree, and he called me not only an unkind wife, but an unnatural mother, and asked me how I could entertain such a thought without horror, as that of leaving my two children (for one was dead) without a mother, and to be brought up by strangers, and never to see them more. It was true, had things been right, I should not have done it, but now it was my real desire never to see them, or him either, any more; and as to the charge of unnatural, I could easily answer it to myself, while I knew that the whole relation was unnatural in the highest degree in the world.

However, it was plain there was no bringing my husband to anything; he would neither go with me nor let me go without him, and it was quite out of my power to stir without his consent, as any one that knows the constitution of the country I was in, knows very well.

We had many family quarrels about it, and they began in time to grow up to a dangerous height; for as I was quite estranged form my husband (as he was called) in affection, so I took no heed to my words, but sometimes gave him language that was provoking; and, in short, strove all I could to bring him to a parting with me, which was what above all things in the world I desired most.

He took my carriage very ill, and indeed he might well do so, for at last I refused to bed with him, and carrying on the breach upon all occasions to extremity, he told me once he thought I was mad, and if I did not alter my conduct, he would put me under cure; that is to say, into a madhouse. I told him he should find I was far enough from mad, and that it was not in his power, or any other villain's, to murder me. I confess at the same time I was heartily frighted at his thoughts of putting me into a madhouse, which would at once have destroyed all the possibility of breaking the truth out, whatever the occasion might be; for that then no one would have given credit to a word of it.

This therefore brought me to a resolution, whatever came of it, to lay open my whole case; but which way to do it, or to whom, was an inextricable difficulty, and took me many months to resolve. In the meantime, another quarrel with my husband happened, which came up to such a mad extreme as almost pushed me on to tell it him all to his face; but though I kept it in so as not to come to the particulars, I spoke so much as put him into the utmost confusion, and in the end brought out the whole story.

He began with a calm expostulation upon my being so resolute to go to England; I defended it, and one hard word bringing on another, as is usual in all family strife, he told me I did not treat him as if he was my husband, or talk of my children as if I was a mother; and, in short, that I did not deserve to be used as a wife; that he had used all the fair means possible with me; that he had argued with all the kindness and calmness that a husband or a Christian ought to do, and that I made him such a vile return, that I treated him rather like a dog than a man, and rather like the most contemptible stranger than a husband; that he was very loth to use violence with me, but that, in short, he saw a necessity of it now, and that for the future he should be obliged to take such measures as should reduce me to my duty.

My blood was now fired to the utmost, though I knew what he had said was very true, and nothing could appear more provoked. I told him, for his fair means and his foul, they were equally contemned by me; that for my going to England, I was resolved on it, come what would; and that as to treating him not like a husband, and not showing myself a mother to my children, there might be something more in it than he understood at present; but, for his further consideration, I thought fit to tell him thus much, that he neither was my lawful husband, nor they lawful children, and that I had reason to regard neither of them more than I did.

I confess I was moved to pity him when I spoke it, for he turned pale as death, and stood mute as one thunderstruck, and once or twice I thought he would have fainted; in short, it put him in a fit something like an apoplex; he trembled, a sweat or dew ran off his face, and yet he was cold as a clod, so that I was forced to run and fetch something for him to keep life in him. When he recovered of that, he grew sick and vomited, and in a little after was put to bed, and the next morning was, as he had been indeed all night, in a violent fever.

However, it went off again, and he recovered, though but slowly, and when he came to be a little better, he told me I had given him a mortal wound with my tongue, and he had only one thing to ask before he desired an explanation. I interrupted him, and told him I was sorry I had gone so far, since I saw what disorder it put him into, but I desired him not to talk to me of explanations, for that would but make things worse.

This heightened his impatience, and, indeed, perplexed him beyond all bearing; for now he began to suspect that there was some mystery yet unfolded, but could not make the least guess at the real particulars of it; all that ran in his brain was, that I had another husband alive, which I could not say in fact might not be true, but I assured him, however, there was not the least of that in it; and indeed, as to my other husband, he was effectually dead in law to me, and had told me I should look on him as such, so I had not the least uneasiness on that score.

But now I found the thing too far gone to conceal it much longer, and my husband himself gave me an opportunity to ease myself of the secret, much to my satisfaction. He had laboured with me three or four weeks, but to no purpose, only to tell him whether I had spoken these words only as the effect of my passion, to put him in a passion, or whether there was anything of truth in the bottom of them. But I continued inflexible, and would explain nothing, unless he would first consent to my going to England, which he would never do, he said, while he lived; on the other hand, I said it was in my power to make him willing when I pleased—nay, to make him entreat me to go; and this increased his curiosity, and made him importunate to the highest degree, but it was all to no purpose.

At length he tells all this story to his mother, and sets her upon me to get the main secret out of me, and she used her utmost skill with me indeed; but I put her to a full stop at once by telling her that the reason and mystery of the whole matter lay in herself, and that it was my respect to her that had made me conceal it; and that, in short, I could go no farther, and therefore conjured her not to insist upon it.

She was struck dumb at this suggestion, and could not tell what to say or to think; but, laying aside the supposition as a policy of mine, continued her importunity on account of her son, and, if possible, to make up the breach between us two. As to that, I told her that it was indeed a good design in her, but that it was impossible to be done; and that if I should reveal to her the truth of what she desired, she would grant it to be impossible, and cease to desire it. At last I seemed to be prevailed on by her importunity, and told her I dared trust her with a secret of the greatest importance, and she would soon see that this was so, and that I would consent to lodge it in her breast, if she would engage solemnly not to acquaint her son with it without my consent.

She was long in promising this part, but rather than not come at the main secret, she agreed to that too, and after a great many other preliminaries, I began, and told her the whole story. First I told her how much she was concerned in all the unhappy breach which had happened between her son and me, by telling me her own story and her London name; and that the surprise she saw I was in was upon that occasion. The I told her my own story, and my name, and assured her, by such other tokens as she could not deny, that I was no other, nor more or less, than her own child, her daughter, born of her body in Newgate; the same that had saved her from the gallows by being in her belly, and the same that she left in such-and-such hands when she was transported.

It is impossible to express the astonishment she was in; she was not inclined to believe the story, or to remember the particulars, for she immediately foresaw the confusion that must follow in the family upon it. But everything concurred so exactly with the stories she had told me of herself, and which, if she had not told me, she would perhaps have been content to have denied, that she had stopped her own mouth, and she had nothing to do but to take me about the neck and kiss me, and cry most vehemently over me, without speaking one word for a long time together. At last she broke out: 'Unhappy child!' says she, 'what miserable chance could bring thee hither? and in the arms of my own son, too! Dreadful girl,' says she, 'why, we are all undone! Married to thy own brother! Three children, and two alive, all of the same flesh and blood! My son and my daughter lying together as husband and wife! All confusion and distraction for ever! Miserable family! what will become of us? What is to be said? What is to be done?' And thus she ran on for a great while; nor had I any power to speak, or if I had, did I know what to say, for every word wounded me to the soul. With this kind of amazement on our thoughts we parted for the first time, though my mother was more surprised than I was, because it was more news to her than to me. However, she promised again to me at parting, that she would say nothing of it to her son, till we had talked of it again.

It was not long, you may be sure, before we had a second conference upon the same subject; when, as if she had been willing to forget the story she had told me of herself, or to suppose that I had forgot some of the particulars, she began to tell them with alterations and omissions; but I refreshed her memory and set her to rights in many things which I supposed she had forgot, and then came in so opportunely with the whole history, that it was impossible for her to go from it; and then she fell into her rhapsodies again, and exclamations at the severity of her misfortunes. When these things were a little over with her, we fell into a close debate about what should be first done before we gave an account of the matter to my husband. But to what purpose could be all our consultations? We could neither of us see our way through it, nor see how it could be safe to open such a scene to him. It was impossible to make any judgment, or give any guess at what temper he would receive it in, or what measures he would take upon it; and if he should have so little government of himself as to make it public, we easily foresaw that it would be the ruin of the whole family, and expose my mother and me to the last degree; and if at last he should take the advantage the law would give him, he might put me away with disdain and leave me to sue for the little portion that I had, and perhaps waste it all in the suit, and then be a beggar; the children would be ruined too, having no legal claim to any of his effects; and thus I should see him, perhaps, in the arms of another wife in a few months, and be myself the most miserable creature alive.

My mother was as sensible of this as I; and, upon the whole, we knew not what to do. After some time we came to more sober resolutions, but then it was with this misfortune too, that my mother's opinion and mine were quite different from one another, and indeed inconsistent with one another; for my mother's opinion was, that I should bury the whole thing entirely, and continue to live with him as my husband till some other event should make the discovery of it more convenient; and that in the meantime she would endeavour to reconcile us together again, and restore our mutual comfort and family peace; that we might lie as we used to do together, and so let the whole matter remain a secret as close as death. 'For, child,' says she, 'we are both undone if it comes out.'

To encourage me to this, she promised to make me easy in my circumstances, as far as she was able, and to leave me what she could at her death, secured for me separately from my husband; so that if it should come out afterwards, I should not be left destitute, but be able to stand on my own feet and procure justice from him.

This proposal did not agree at all with my judgment of the thing, though it was very fair and kind in my mother; but my thoughts ran quite another way.

As to keeping the thing in our own breasts, and letting it all remain as it was, I told her it was impossible; and I asked her how she could think I could bear the thoughts of lying with my own brother. In the next place, I told her that her being alive was the only support of the discovery, and that while she owned me for her child, and saw reason to be satisfied that I was so, nobody else would doubt it; but that if she should die before the discovery, I should be taken for an impudent creature that had forged such a thing to go away from my husband, or should be counted crazed and distracted. Then I told her how he had threatened already to put me into a madhouse, and what concern I had been in about it, and how that was the thing that drove me to the necessity of discovering it to her as I had done.

From all which I told her, that I had, on the most serious reflections I was able to make in the case, come to this resolution, which I hoped she would like, as a medium between both, viz. that she should use her endeavours with her son to give me leave to go to England, as I had desired, and to furnish me with a sufficient sum of money, either in goods along with me, or in bills for my support there, all along suggesting that he might one time or other think it proper to come over to me.

That when I was gone, she should then, in cold blood, and after first obliging him in the solemnest manner possible to secrecy, discover the case to him, doing it gradually, and as her own discretion should guide her, so that he might not be surprised with it, and fly out into any passions and excesses on my account, or on hers; and that she should concern herself to prevent his slighting the children, or marrying again, unless he had a certain account of my being dead.

This was my scheme, and my reasons were good; I was really alienated from him in the consequences of these things; indeed, I mortally hated him as a husband, and it was impossible to remove that riveted aversion I had to him. At the same time, it being an unlawful, incestuous living, added to that aversion, and though I had no great concern about it in point of conscience, yet everything added to make cohabiting with him the most nauseous thing to me in the world; and I think verily it was come to such a height, that I could almost as willingly have embraced a dog as have let him offer anything of that kind to me, for which reason I could not bear the thoughts of coming between the sheets with him. I cannot say that I was right in point of policy in carrying it such a length, while at the same time I did not resolve to discover the thing to him; but I am giving an account of what was, not of what ought or ought not to be.

In their directly opposite opinion to one another my mother and I continued a long time, and it was impossible to reconcile our judgments; many disputes we had about it, but we could never either of us yield our own, or bring over the other.

I insisted on my aversion to lying with my own brother, and she insisted upon its being impossible to bring him to consent to my going from him to England; and in this uncertainty we continued, not differing so as to quarrel, or anything like it, but so as not to be able to resolve what we should do to make up that terrible breach that was before us.

At last I resolved on a desperate course, and told my mother my resolution, viz. that, in short, I would tell him of it myself. My mother was frighted to the last degree at the very thoughts of it; but I bid her be easy, told her I would do it gradually and softly, and with all the art and good-humour I was mistress of, and time it also as well as I could, taking him in good-humour too. I told her I did not question but, if I could be hypocrite enough to feign more affection to him than I really had, I should succeed in all my design, and we might part by consent, and with a good agreement, for I might live him well enough for a brother, though I could not for a husband.

All this while he lay at my mother to find out, if possible, what was the meaning of that dreadful expression of mine, as he called it, which I mentioned before: namely, that I was not his lawful wife, nor my children his legal children. My mother put him off, told him she could bring me to no explanations, but found there was something that disturbed me very much, and she hoped she should get it out of me in time, and in the meantime recommended to him earnestly to use me more tenderly, and win me with his usual good carriage; told him of his terrifying and affrighting me with his threats of sending me to a madhouse, and the like, and advised him not to make a woman desperate on any account whatever.

He promised her to soften his behaviour, and bid her assure me that he loved me as well as ever, and that he had so such design as that of sending me to a madhouse, whatever he might say in his passion; also he desired my mother to use the same persuasions to me too, that our affections might be renewed, and we might lie together in a good understanding as we used to do.

I found the effects of this treaty presently. My husband's conduct was immediately altered, and he was quite another man to me; nothing could be kinder and more obliging than he was to me upon all occasions; and I could do no less than make some return to it, which I did as well as I could, but it was but in an awkward manner at best, for nothing was more frightful to me than his caresses, and the apprehensions of being with child again by him was ready to throw me into fits; and this made me see that there was an absolute necessity of breaking the case to him without any more delay, which, however, I did with all the caution and reserve imaginable.

He had continued his altered carriage to me near a month, and we began to live a new kind of life with one another; and could I have satisfied myself to have gone on with it, I believe it might have continued as long as we had continued alive together. One evening, as we were sitting and talking very friendly together under a little awning, which served as an arbour at the entrance from our house into the garden, he was in a very pleasant, agreeable humour, and said abundance of kind things to me relating to the pleasure of our present good agreement, and the disorders of our past breach, and what a satisfaction it was to him that we had room to hope we should never have any more of it.

I fetched a deep sigh, and told him there was nobody in the world could be more delighted than I was in the good agreement we had always kept up, or more afflicted with the breach of it, and should be so still; but I was sorry to tell him that there was an unhappy circumstance in our case, which lay too close to my heart, and which I knew not how to break to him, that rendered my part of it very miserable, and took from me all the comfort of the rest.

He importuned me to tell him what it was. I told him I could not tell how to do it; that while it was concealed from him I alone was unhappy, but if he knew it also, we should be both so; and that, therefore, to keep him in the dark about it was the kindest thing that I could do, and it was on that account alone that I kept a secret from him, the very keeping of which, I thought, would first or last be my destruction.

It is impossible to express his surprise at this relation, and the double importunity which he used with me to discover it to him. He told me I could not be called kind to him, nay, I could not be faithful to him if I concealed it from him. I told him I thought so too, and yet I could not do it. He went back to what I had said before to him, and told me he hoped it did not relate to what I had said in my passion, and that he had resolved to forget all that as the effect of a rash, provoked spirit. I told him I wished I could forget it all too, but that it was not to be done, the impression was too deep, and I could not do it: it was impossible.

He then told me he was resolved not to differ with me in anything, and that therefore he would importune me no more about it, resolving to acquiesce in whatever I did or said; only begged I should then agree, that whatever it was, it should no more interrupt our quiet and our mutual kindness.

This was the most provoking thing he could have said to me, for I really wanted his further importunities, that I might be prevailed with to bring out that which indeed it was like death to me to conceal; so I answered him plainly that I could not say I was glad not to be importuned, thought I could not tell how to comply. 'But come, my dear,' said I, 'what conditions will you make with me upon the opening this affair to you?'

'Any conditions in the world,' said he, 'that you can in reason desire of me.' 'Well,' said I, 'come, give it me under your hand, that if you do not find I am in any fault, or that I am willingly concerned in the causes of the misfortune that is to follow, you will not blame me, use me the worse, do my any injury, or make me be the sufferer for that which is not my fault.'

'That,' says he, 'is the most reasonable demand in the world: not to blame you for that which is not your fault. Give me a pen and ink,' says he; so I ran in and fetched a pen, ink, and paper, and he wrote the condition down in the very words I had proposed it, and signed it with his name. 'Well,' says he, 'what is next, my dear?'

'Why,' says I, 'the next is, that you will not blame me for not discovering the secret of it to you before I knew it.'

'Very just again,' says he; 'with all my heart'; so he wrote down that also, and signed it.

'Well, my dear,' says I, 'then I have but one condition more to make with you, and that is, that as there is nobody concerned in it but you and I, you shall not discover it to any person in the world, except your own mother; and that in all the measures you shall take upon the discovery, as I am equally concerned in it with you, though as innocent as yourself, you shall do nothing in a passion, nothing to my prejudice or to your mother's prejudice, without my knowledge and consent.'

This a little amazed him, and he wrote down the words distinctly, but read them over and over before he signed them, hesitating at them several times, and repeating them: 'My mother's prejudice! and your prejudice! What mysterious thing can this be?' However, at last he signed it.

'Well, says I, 'my dear, I'll ask you no more under your hand; but as you are to hear the most unexpected and surprising thing that perhaps ever befell any family in the world, I beg you to promise me you will receive it with composure and a presence of mind suitable to a man of sense.'

'I'll do my utmost,' says he, 'upon condition you will keep me no longer in suspense, for you terrify me with all these preliminaries.'

'Well, then,' says I, 'it is this: as I told you before in a heat, that I was not your lawful wife, and that our children were not legal children, so I must let you know now in calmness and in kindness, but with affliction enough, that I am your own sister, and you my own brother, and that we are both the children of our mother now alive, and in the house, who is convinced of the truth of it, in a manner not to be denied or contradicted.'

I saw him turn pale and look wild; and I said, 'Now remember your promise, and receive it with presence of mind; for who could have said more to prepare you for it than I have done?' However, I called a servant, and got him a little glass of rum (which is the usual dram of that country), for he was just fainting away. When he was a little recovered, I said to him, 'This story, you may be sure, requires a long explanation, and therefore, have patience and compose your mind to hear it out, and I'll make it as short as I can'; and with this, I told him what I thought was needful of the fact, and particularly how my mother came to discover it to me, as above. 'And now, my dear,' says I, 'you will see reason for my capitulations, and that I neither have been the cause of this matter, nor could be so, and that I could know nothing of it before now.'

'I am fully satisfied of that,' says he, 'but 'tis a dreadful surprise to me; however, I know a remedy for it all, and a remedy that shall put an end to your difficulties, without your going to England.' 'That would be strange,' said I, 'as all the rest.' 'No, no,' says he, 'I'll make it easy; there's nobody in the way of it but myself.' He looked a little disordered when he said this, but I did not apprehend anything from it at that time, believing, as it used to be said, that they who do those things never talk of them, or that they who talk of such things never do them.

But things were not come to their height with him, and I observed he became pensive and melancholy; and in a word, as I thought, a little distempered in his head. I endeavoured to talk him into temper, and to reason him into a kind of scheme for our government in the affair, and sometimes he would be well, and talk with some courage about it; but the weight of it lay too heavy upon his thoughts, and, in short, it went so far that he made attempts upon himself, and in one of them had actually strangled himself and had not his mother come into the room in the very moment, he had died; but with the help of a Negro servant she cut him down and recovered him.

Things were now come to a lamentable height in the family. My pity for him now began to revive that affection which at first I really had for him, and I endeavoured sincerely, by all the kind carriage I could, to make up the breach; but, in short, it had gotten too great a head, it preyed upon his spirits, and it threw him into a long, lingering consumption, though it happened not to be mortal. In this distress I did not know what to do, as his life was apparently declining, and I might perhaps have married again there, very much to my advantage; it had been certainly my business to have stayed in the country, but my mind was restless too, and uneasy; I hankered after coming to England, and nothing would satisfy me without it.

In short, by an unwearied importunity, my husband, who was apparently decaying, as I observed, was at last prevailed with; and so my own fate pushing me on, the way was made clear for me, and my mother concurring, I obtained a very good cargo for my coming to England.

When I parted with my brother (for such I am now to call him), we agreed that after I arrived he should pretend to have an account that I was dead in England, and so might marry again when he would. He promised, and engaged to me to correspond with me as a sister, and to assist and support me as long as I lived; and that if he died before me, he would leave sufficient to his mother to take care of me still, in the name of a sister, and he was in some respects careful of me, when he heard of me; but it was so oddly managed that I felt the disappointments very sensibly afterwards, as you shall hear in its time.

I came away for England in the month of August, after I had been eight years in that country; and now a new scene of misfortunes attended me, which perhaps few women have gone through the life of.

We had an indifferent good voyage till we came just upon the coast of England, and where we arrived in two-and-thirty days, but were then ruffled with two or three storms, one of which drove us away to the coast of Ireland, and we put in at Kinsdale. We remained there about thirteen days, got some refreshment on shore, and put to sea again, though we met with very bad weather again, in which the ship sprung her mainmast, as they called it, for I knew not what they meant. But we got at last into Milford Haven, in Wales, where, though it was remote from our port, yet having my foot safe upon the firm ground of my native country, the isle of Britain, I resolved to venture it no more upon the waters, which had been so terrible to me; so getting my clothes and money on shore, with my bills of loading and other papers, I resolved to come for London, and leave the ship to get to her port as she could; the port whither she was bound was to Bristol, where my brother's chief correspondent lived.

I got to London in about three weeks, where I heard a little while after that the ship was arrived in Bristol, but at the same time had the misfortune to know that by the violent weather she had been in, and the breaking of her mainmast, she had great damage on board, and that a great part of her cargo was spoiled.

I had now a new scene of life upon my hands, and a dreadful appearance it had. I was come away with a kind of final farewell. What I brought with me was indeed considerable, had it come safe, and by the help of it, I might have married again tolerably well; but as it was, I was reduced to between two or three hundred pounds in the whole, and this without any hope of recruit. I was entirely without friends, nay, even so much as without acquaintance, for I found it was absolutely necessary not to revive former acquaintances; and as for my subtle friend that set me up formerly for a fortune, she was dead, and her husband also; as I was informed, upon sending a person unknown to inquire.

The looking after my cargo of goods soon after obliged me to take a journey to Bristol, and during my attendance upon that affair I took the diversion of going to the Bath, for as I was still far from being old, so my humour, which was always gay, continued so to an extreme; and being now, as it were, a woman of fortune though I was a woman without a fortune, I expected something or other might happen in my way that might mend my circumstances, as had been my case before.

The Bath is a place of gallantry enough; expensive, and full of snares. I went thither, indeed, in the view of taking anything that might offer, but I must do myself justice, as to protest I knew nothing amiss; I meant nothing but in an honest way, nor had I any thoughts about me at first that looked the way which afterwards I suffered them to be guided.

Here I stayed the whole latter season, as it is called there, and contracted some unhappy acquaintances, which rather prompted the follies I fell afterwards into than fortified me against them. I lived pleasantly enough, kept good company, that is to say, gay, fine company; but had the discouragement to find this way of living sunk me exceedingly, and that as I had no settled income, so spending upon the main stock was but a certain kind of bleeding to death; and this gave me many sad reflections in the interval of my other thoughts. However, I shook them off, and still flattered myself that something or other might offer for my advantage.

But I was in the wrong place for it. I was not now at Redriff, where, if I had set myself tolerably up, some honest sea captain or other might have talked with me upon the honourable terms of matrimony; but I was at the Bath, where men find a mistress sometimes, but very rarely look for a wife; and consequently all the particular acquaintances a woman can expect to make there must have some tendency that way.

I had spent the first season well enough; for though I had contracted some acquaintance with a gentleman who came to the Bath for his diversion, yet I had entered into no felonious treaty, as it might be called. I had resisted some casual offers of gallantry, and had managed that way well enough. I was not wicked enough to come into the crime for the mere vice of it, and I had no extraordinary offers made me that tempted me with the main thing which I wanted.

However, I went this length the first season, viz. I contracted an acquaintance with a woman in whose house I lodged, who, though she did not keep an ill house, as we call it, yet had none of the best principles in herself. I had on all occasions behaved myself so well as not to get the least slur upon my reputation on any account whatever, and all the men that I had conversed with were of so good reputation that I had not given the least reflection by conversing with them; nor did any of them seem to think there was room for a wicked correspondence, if they had any of them offered it; yet there was one gentleman, as above, who always singled me out for the diversion of my company, as he called it, which, as he was pleased to say, was very agreeable to him, but at that time there was no more in it.

I had many melancholy hours at the Bath after the company was gone; for though I went to Bristol sometime for the disposing my effects, and for recruits of money, yet I chose to come back to Bath for my residence, because being on good terms with the woman in whose house I lodged in the summer, I found that during the winter I lived rather cheaper there than I could do anywhere else. Here, I say, I passed the winter as heavily as I had passed the autumn cheerfully; but having contracted a nearer intimacy with the said woman in whose house I lodged, I could not avoid communicating to her something of what lay hardest upon my mind and particularly the narrowness of my circumstances, and the loss of my fortune by the damage of my goods at sea. I told her also, that I had a mother and a brother in Virginia in good circumstances; and as I had really written back to my mother in particular to represent my condition, and the great loss I had received, which indeed came to almost #500, so I did not fail to let my new friend know that I expected a supply from thence, and so indeed I did; and as the ships went from Bristol to York River, in Virginia, and back again generally in less time from London, and that my brother corresponded chiefly at Bristol, I thought it was much better for me to wait here for my returns than to go to London, where also I had not the least acquaintance.

My new friend appeared sensibly affected with my condition, and indeed was so very kind as to reduce the rate of my living with her to so low a price during the winter, that she convinced me she got nothing by me; and as for lodging, during the winter I paid nothing at all.

When the spring season came on, she continued to be as kind to me as she could, and I lodged with her for a time, till it was found necessary to do otherwise. She had some persons of character that frequently lodged in her house, and in particular the gentleman who, as I said, singled me out for his companion the winter before; and he came down again with another gentleman in his company and two servants, and lodged in the same house. I suspected that my landlady had invited him thither, letting him know that I was still with her; but she denied it, and protested to me that she did not, and he said the same.

In a word, this gentleman came down and continued to single me out for his peculiar confidence as well as conversation. He was a complete gentleman, that must be confessed, and his company was very agreeable to me, as mine, if I might believe him, was to him. He made no professions to be but of an extraordinary respect, and he had such an opinion of my virtue, that, as he often professed, he believed if he should offer anything else, I should reject him with contempt. He soon understood from me that I was a widow; that I had arrived at Bristol from Virginia by the last ships; and that I waited at Bath till the next Virginia fleet should arrive, by which I expected considerable effects. I understood by him, and by others of him, that he had a wife, but that the lady was distempered in her head, and was under the conduct of her own relations, which he consented to, to avoid any reflections that might (as was not unusual in such cases) be cast on him for mismanaging her cure; and in the meantime he came to the Bath to divert his thoughts from the disturbance of such a melancholy circumstance as that was.

My landlady, who of her own accord encouraged the correspondence on all occasions, gave me an advantageous character of him, as a man of honour and of virtue, as well as of great estate. And indeed I had a great deal of reason to say so of him too; for though we lodged both on a floor, and he had frequently come into my chamber, even when I was in bed, and I also into his when he was in bed, yet he never offered anything to me further than a kiss, or so much as solicited me to anything till long after, as you shall hear.

I frequently took notice to my landlady of his exceeding modesty, and she again used to tell me, she believed it was so from the beginning; however, she used to tell me that she thought I ought to expect some gratification from him for my company, for indeed he did, as it were, engross me, and I was seldom from him. I told her I had not given him the least occasion to think I wanted it, or that I would accept of it from him. She told me she would take that part upon her, and she did so, and managed it so dexterously, that the first time we were together alone, after she had talked with him, he began to inquire a little into my circumstances, as how I had subsisted myself since I came on shore, and whether I did not want money. I stood off very boldly. I told him that though my cargo of tobacco was damaged, yet that it was not quite lost; that the merchant I had been consigned to had so honestly managed for me that I had not wanted, and that I hoped, with frugal management, I should make it hold out till more would come, which I expected by the next fleet; that in the meantime I had retrenched my expenses, and whereas I kept a maid last season, now I lived without; and whereas I had a chamber and a dining-room then on the first floor, as he knew, I now had but one room, two pair of stairs, and the like. 'But I live,' said I, 'as well satisfied now as I did then'; adding, that his company had been a means to make me live much more cheerfully than otherwise I should have done, for which I was much obliged to him; and so I put off all room for any offer for the present. However, it was not long before he attacked me again, and told me he found that I was backward to trust him with the secret of my circumstances, which he was sorry for; assuring me that he inquired into it with no design to satisfy his own curiosity, but merely to assist me, if there was any occasion; but since I would not own myself to stand in need of any assistance, he had but one thing more to desire of me, and that was, that I would promise him that when I was any way straitened, or like to be so, I would frankly tell him of it, and that I would make use of him with the same freedom that he made the offer; adding, that I should always find I had a true friend, though perhaps I was afraid to trust him.

I omitted nothing that was fit to be said by one infinitely obliged, to let him know that I had a due sense of his kindness; and indeed from that time I did not appear so much reserved to him as I had done before, though still within the bounds of the strictest virtue on both sides; but how free soever our conversation was, I could not arrive to that sort of freedom which he desired, viz. to tell him I wanted money, though I was secretly very glad of his offer.

Some weeks passed after this, and still I never asked him for money; when my landlady, a cunning creature, who had often pressed me to it, but found that I could not do it, makes a story of her own inventing, and comes in bluntly to me when we were together. 'Oh, widow!' says she, 'I have bad news to tell you this morning.' 'What is that?' said I; 'are the Virginia ships taken by the French?'—for that was my fear. 'No, no,' says she, 'but the man you sent to Bristol yesterday for money is come back, and says he has brought none.'

Now I could by no means like her project; I though it looked too much like prompting him, which indeed he did not want, and I clearly saw that I should lose nothing by being backward to ask, so I took her up short. 'I can't image why he should say so to you,' said I, 'for I assure you he brought me all the money I sent him for, and here it is,' said I (pulling out my purse with about twelve guineas in it); and added, 'I intend you shall have most of it by and by.'

He seemed distasted a little at her talking as she did at first, as well as I, taking it, as I fancied he would, as something forward of her; but when he saw me give such an answer, he came immediately to himself again. The next morning we talked of it again, when I found he was fully satisfied, and, smiling, said he hoped I would not want money and not tell him of it, and that I had promised him otherwise. I told him I had been very much dissatisfied at my landlady's talking so publicly the day before of what she had nothing to do with; but I supposed she wanted what I owed her, which was about eight guineas, which I had resolved to give her, and had accordingly given it her the same night she talked so foolishly.

He was in a might good humour when he heard me say I had paid her, and it went off into some other discourse at that time. But the next morning, he having heard me up about my room before him, he called to me, and I answering, he asked me to come into his chamber. He was in bed when I came in, and he made me come and sit down on his bedside, for he said he had something to say to me which was of some moment. After some very kind expressions, he asked me if I would be very honest to him, and give a sincere answer to one thing he would desire of me. After some little cavil at the word 'sincere,' and asking him if I had ever given him any answers which were not sincere, I promised him I would. Why, then, his request was, he said, to let him see my purse. I immediately put my hand into my pocket, and, laughing to him, pulled it out, and there was in it three guineas and a half. Then he asked me if there was all the money I had. I told him No, laughing again, not by a great deal.

Well, then, he said, he would have me promise to go and fetch him all the money I had, every farthing. I told him I would, and I went into my chamber and fetched him a little private drawer, where I had about six guineas more, and some silver, and threw it all down upon the bed, and told him there was all my wealth, honestly to a shilling. He looked a little at it, but did not tell it, and huddled it all into the drawer again, and then reaching his pocket, pulled out a key, and bade me open a little walnut-tree box he had upon the table, and bring him such a drawer, which I did. In which drawer there was a great deal of money in gold, I believe near two hundred guineas, but I knew not how much. He took the drawer, and taking my hand, made me put it in and take a whole handful. I was backward at that, but he held my hand hard in his hand, and put it into the drawer, and made me take out as many guineas almost as I could well take up at once.

When I had done so, he made me put them into my lap, and took my little drawer, and poured out all my money among his, and bade me get me gone, and carry it all home into my own chamber.

I relate this story the more particularly because of the good-humour there was in it, and to show the temper with which we conversed. It was not long after this but he began every day to find fault with my clothes, with my laces and headdresses, and, in a word, pressed me to buy better; which, by the way, I was willing enough to do, though I did not seem to be so, for I loved nothing in the world better than fine clothes. I told him I must housewife the money he had lent me, or else I should not be able to pay him again. He then told me, in a few words, that as he had a sincere respect for me, and knew my circumstances, he had not lent me that money, but given it me, and that he thought I had merited it from him by giving him my company so entirely as I had done. After this he made me take a maid, and keep house, and his friend that come with him to Bath being gone, he obliged me to diet him, which I did very willingly, believing, as it appeared, that I should lose nothing by it, nor did the woman of the house fail to find her account in it too.

We had lived thus near three months, when the company beginning to wear away at the Bath, he talked of going away, and fain he would have me to go to London with him. I was not very easy in that proposal, not knowing what posture I was to live in there, or how he might use me. But while this was in debate he fell very sick; he had gone out to a place in Somersetshire, called Shepton, where he had some business and was there taken very ill, and so ill that he could not travel; so he sent his man back to Bath, to beg me that I would hire a coach and come over to him. Before he went, he had left all his money and other things of value with me, and what to do with them I did not know, but I secured them as well as I could, and locked up the lodgings and went to him, where I found him very ill indeed; however, I persuaded him to be carried in a litter to the Bath, where there was more help and better advice to be had.

He consented, and I brought him to the Bath, which was about fifteen miles, as I remember. Here he continued very ill of a fever, and kept his bed five weeks, all which time I nursed him and tended him myself, as much and as carefully as if I had been his wife; indeed, if I had been his wife I could not have done more. I sat up with him so much and so often, that at last, indeed, he would not let me sit up any longer, and then I got a pallet-bed into his room, and lay in it just at his bed's feet.

I was indeed sensibly affected with his condition, and with the apprehension of losing such a friend as he was, and was like to be to me, and I used to sit and cry by him many hours together. However, at last he grew better, and gave hopes that he would recover, as indeed he did, though very slowly.

Were it otherwise than what I am going to say, I should not be backward to disclose it, as it is apparent I have done in other cases in this account; but I affirm, that through all this conversation, abating the freedom of coming into the chamber when I or he was in bed, and abating the necessary offices of attending him night and day when he was sick, there had not passed the least immodest word or action between us. Oh that it had been so to the last!

After some time he gathered strength and grew well apace, and I would have removed my pallet-bed, but he would not let me, till he was able to venture himself without anybody to sit up with him, and then I removed to my own chamber.

He took many occasions to express his sense of my tenderness and concern for him; and when he grew quite well, he made me a present of fifty guineas for my care and, as he called it, for hazarding my life to save his.

And now he made deep protestations of a sincere inviolable affection for me, but all along attested it to be with the utmost reserve for my virtue and his own. I told him I was fully satisfied of it. He carried it that length that he protested to me, that if he was naked in bed with me, he would as sacredly preserve my virtue as he would defend it if I was assaulted by a ravisher. I believed him, and told him I did so; but this did not satisfy him, he would, he said, wait for some opportunity to give me an undoubted testimony of it.

It was a great while after this that I had occasion, on my own business, to go to Bristol, upon which he hired me a coach, and would go with me, and did so; and now indeed our intimacy increased. From Bristol he carried me to Gloucester, which was merely a journey of pleasure, to take the air; and here it was our hap to have no lodging in the inn but in one large chamber with two beds in it. The master of the house going up with us to show his rooms, and coming into that room, said very frankly to him, 'Sir, it is none of my business to inquire whether the lady be your spouse or no, but if not, you may lie as honestly in these two beds as if you were in two chambers,' and with that he pulls a great curtain which drew quite across the room and effectually divided the beds. 'Well,' says my friend, very readily, 'these beds will do, and as for the rest, we are too near akin to lie together, though we may lodge near one another'; and this put an honest face on the thing too. When we came to go to bed, he decently went out of the room till I was in bed, and then went to bed in the bed on his own side of the room, but lay there talking to me a great while.

At last, repeating his usual saying, that he could lie naked in the bed with me and not offer me the least injury, he starts out of his bed. 'And now, my dear,' says he, 'you shall see how just I will be to you, and that I can keep my word,' and away he comes to my bed.

I resisted a little, but I must confess I should not have resisted him much if he had not made those promises at all; so after a little struggle, as I said, I lay still and let him come to bed. When he was there he took me in his arms, and so I lay all night with him, but he had no more to do with me, or offered anything to me, other than embracing me, as I say, in his arms, no, not the whole night, but rose up and dressed him in the morning, and left me as innocent for him as I was the day I was born.

This was a surprising thing to me, and perhaps may be so to others, who know how the laws of nature work; for he was a strong, vigorous, brisk person; nor did he act thus on a principle of religion at all, but of mere affection; insisting on it, that though I was to him to most agreeable woman in the world, yet, because he loved me, he could not injure me.

I own it was a noble principle, but as it was what I never understood before, so it was to me perfectly amazing. We traveled the rest of the journey as we did before, and came back to the Bath, where, as he had opportunity to come to me when he would, he often repeated the moderation, and I frequently lay with him, and he with me, and although all the familiarities between man and wife were common to us, yet he never once offered to go any farther, and he valued himself much upon it. I do not say that I was so wholly pleased with it as he thought I was, for I own much wickeder than he, as you shall hear presently.

We lived thus near two years, only with this exception, that he went three times to London in that time, and once he continued there four months; but, to do him justice, he always supplied me with money to subsist me very handsomely.

Had we continued thus, I confess we had had much to boast of; but as wise men say, it is ill venturing too near the brink of a command, so we found it; and here again I must do him the justice to own that the first breach was not on his part. It was one night that we were in bed together warm and merry, and having drunk, I think, a little more wine that night, both of us, than usual, although not in the least to disorder either of us, when, after some other follies which I cannot name, and being clasped close in his arms, I told him (I repeat it with shame and horror of soul) that I could find in my heart to discharge him of his engagement for one night and no more.

He took me at my word immediately, and after that there was no resisting him; neither indeed had I any mind to resist him any more, let what would come of it.

Thus the government of our virtue was broken, and I exchanged the place of friend for that unmusical, harsh-sounding title of whore. In the morning we were both at our penitentials; I cried very heartily, he expressed himself very sorry; but that was all either of us could do at that time, and the way being thus cleared, and the bars of virtue and conscience thus removed, we had the less difficult afterwards to struggle with.

It was but a dull kind of conversation that we had together for all the rest of that week; I looked on him with blushes, and every now and then started that melancholy objection, 'What if I should be with child now? What will become of me then?' He encouraged me by telling me, that as long as I was true to him, he would be so to me; and since it was gone such a length (which indeed he never intended), yet if I was with child, he would take care of that, and of me too. This hardened us both. I assured him if I was with child, I would die for want of a midwife rather than name him as the father of it; and he assured me I should never want if I should be with child. These mutual assurances hardened us in the thing, and after this we repeated the crime as often as we pleased, till at length, as I had feared, so it came to pass, and I was indeed with child.

After I was sure it was so, and I had satisfied him of it too, we began to think of taking measures for the managing it, and I proposed trusting the secret to my landlady, and asking her advice, which he agreed to. My landlady, a woman (as I found) used to such things, made light of it; she said she knew it would come to that at last, and made us very merry about it. As I said above, we found her an experienced old lady at such work; she undertook everything, engaged to procure a midwife and a nurse, to satisfy all inquiries, and bring us off with reputation, and she did so very dexterously indeed.

When I grew near my time she desired my gentleman to go away to London, or make as if he did so. When he was gone, she acquainted the parish officers that there was a lady ready to lie in at her house, but that she knew her husband very well, and gave them, as she pretended, an account of his name, which she called Sir Walter Cleve; telling them he was a very worthy gentleman, and that she would answer for all inquiries, and the like. This satisfied the parish officers presently, and I lay in with as much credit as I could have done if I had really been my Lady Cleve, and was assisted in my travail by three or four of the best citizens' wives of Bath who lived in the neighbourhood, which, however, made me a little the more expensive to him. I often expressed my concern to him about it, but he bid me not be concerned at it.

As he had furnished me very sufficiently with money for the extraordinary expenses of my lying in, I had everything very handsome about me, but did not affect to be gay or extravagant neither; besides, knowing my own circumstances, and knowing the world as I had done, and that such kind of things do not often last long, I took care to lay up as much money as I could for a wet day, as I called it; making him believe it was all spent upon the extraordinary appearance of things in my lying in.

By this means, and including what he had given me as above, I had at the end of my lying in about two hundred guineas by me, including also what was left of my own.

I was brought to bed of a fine boy indeed, and a charming child it was; and when he heard of it he wrote me a very kind, obliging letter about it, and then told me, he thought it would look better for me to come away for London as soon as I was up and well; that he had provided apartments for me at Hammersmith, as if I came thither only from London; and that after a little while I should go back to the Bath, and he would go with me.

I liked this offer very well, and accordingly hired a coach on purpose, and taking my child, and a wet-nurse to tend and suckle it, and a maid-servant with me, away I went for London.

He met me at Reading in his own chariot, and taking me into that, left the servant and the child in the hired coach, and so he brought me to my new lodgings at Hammersmith; with which I had abundance of reason to be very well pleased, for they were very handsome rooms, and I was very well accommodated.

And now I was indeed in the height of what I might call my prosperity, and I wanted nothing but to be a wife, which, however, could not be in this case, there was no room for it; and therefore on all occasions I studied to save what I could, as I have said above, against a time of scarcity, knowing well enough that such things as these do not always continue; that men that keep mistresses often change them, grow weary of them, or jealous of them, or something or other happens to make them withdraw their bounty; and sometimes the ladies that are thus well used are not careful by a prudent conduct to preserve the esteem of their persons, or the nice article of their fidelity, and then they are justly cast off with contempt.

But I was secured in this point, for as I had no inclination to change, so I had no manner of acquaintance in the whole house, and so no temptation to look any farther. I kept no company but in the family when I lodged, and with the clergyman's lady at next door; so that when he was absent I visited nobody, nor did he ever find me out of my chamber or parlour whenever he came down; if I went anywhere to take the air, it was always with him.

The living in this manner with him, and his with me, was certainly the most undesigned thing in the world; he often protested to me, that when he became first acquainted with me, and even to the very night when we first broke in upon our rules, he never had the least design of lying with me; that he always had a sincere affection for me, but not the least real inclination to do what he had done. I assured him I never suspected him; that if I had I should not so easily have yielded to the freedom which brought it on, but that it was all a surprise, and was owing to the accident of our having yielded too far to our mutual inclinations that night; and indeed I have often observed since, and leave it as a caution to the readers of this story, that we ought to be cautious of gratifying our inclinations in loose and lewd freedoms, lest we find our resolutions of virtue fail us in the junction when their assistance should be most necessary.

It is true, and I have confessed it before, that from the first hour I began to converse with him, I resolved to let him lie with me, if he offered it; but it was because I wanted his help and assistance, and I knew no other way of securing him than that. But when were that night together, and, as I have said, had gone such a length, I found my weakness; the inclination was not to be resisted, but I was obliged to yield up all even before he asked it.

However, he was so just to me that he never upbraided me with that; nor did he ever express the least dislike of my conduct on any other occasion, but always protested he was as much delighted with my company as he was the first hour we came together: I mean, came together as bedfellows.

It is true that he had no wife, that is to say, she was as no wife to him, and so I was in no danger that way, but the just reflections of conscience oftentimes snatch a man, especially a man of sense, from the arms of a mistress, as it did him at last, though on another occasion.

On the other hand, though I was not without secret reproaches of my own conscience for the life I led, and that even in the greatest height of the satisfaction I ever took, yet I had the terrible prospect of poverty and starving, which lay on me as a frightful spectre, so that there was no looking behind me. But as poverty brought me into it, so fear of poverty kept me in it, and I frequently resolved to leave it quite off, if I could but come to lay up money enough to maintain me. But these were thoughts of no weight, and whenever he came to me they vanished; for his company was so delightful, that there was no being melancholy when he was there; the reflections were all the subject of those hours when I was alone.

I lived six years in this happy but unhappy condition, in which time I brought him three children, but only the first of them lived; and though I removed twice in those six years, yet I came back the sixth year to my first lodgings at Hammersmith. Here it was that I was one morning surprised with a kind but melancholy letter from my gentleman, intimating that he was very ill, and was afraid he should have another fit of sickness, but that his wife's relations being in the house with him, it would not be practicable to have me with him, which, however, he expressed his great dissatisfaction in, and that he wished I could be allowed to tend and nurse him as I did before.

I was very much concerned at this account, and was very impatient to know how it was with him. I waited a fortnight or thereabouts, and heard nothing, which surprised me, and I began to be very uneasy indeed. I think, I may say, that for the next fortnight I was near to distracted. It was my particular difficulty that I did not know directly where he was; for I understood at first he was in the lodgings of his wife's mother; but having removed myself to London, I soon found, by the help of the direction I had for writing my letters to him, how to inquire after him, and there I found that he was at a house in Bloomsbury, whither he had, a little before he fell sick, removed his whole family; and that his wife and wife's mother were in the same house, though the wife was not suffered to know that she was in the same house with her husband.

Here I also soon understood that he was at the last extremity, which made me almost at the last extremity too, to have a true account. One night I had the curiosity to disguise myself like a servant-maid, in a round cap and straw hat, and went to the door, as sent by a lady of his neighbourhood, where he lived before, and giving master and mistress's service, I said I was sent to know how Mr. —— did, and how he had rested that night. In delivering this message I got the opportunity I desired; for, speaking with one of the maids, I held a long gossip's tale with her, and had all the particulars of his illness, which I found was a pleurisy, attended with a cough and a fever. She told me also who was in the house, and how his wife was, who, by her relation, they were in some hopes might recover her understanding; but as to the gentleman himself, in short she told me the doctors said there was very little hopes of him, that in the morning they thought he had been dying, and that he was but little better then, for they did not expect that he could live over the next night.

This was heavy news for me, and I began now to see an end of my prosperity, and to see also that it was very well I had played to good housewife, and secured or saved something while he was alive, for that now I had no view of my own living before me.

It lay very heavy upon my mind, too, that I had a son, a fine lovely boy, about five years old, and no provision made for it, at least that I knew of. With these considerations, and a sad heart, I went home that evening, and began to cast with myself how I should live, and in what manner to bestow myself, for the residue of my life.

You may be sure I could not rest without inquiring again very quickly what was become of him; and not venturing to go myself, I sent several sham messengers, till after a fortnight's waiting longer, I found that there was hopes of his life, though he was still very ill; then I abated my sending any more to the house, and in some time after I learned in the neighbourhood that he was about house, and then that he was abroad again.

I made no doubt then but that I should soon hear of him, and began to comfort myself with my circumstances being, as I thought, recovered. I waited a week, and two weeks, and with much surprise and amazement I waited near two months and heard nothing, but that, being recovered, he was gone into the country for the air, and for the better recovery after his distemper. After this it was yet two months more, and then I understood he was come to his city house again, but still I heard nothing from him.

I had written several letters for him, and directed them as usual, and found two or three of them had been called for, but not the rest. I wrote again in a more pressing manner than ever, and in one of them let him know, that I must be forced to wait on him myself, representing my circumstances, the rent of lodgings to pay, and the provision for the child wanting, and my own deplorable condition, destitute of subsistence for his most solemn engagement to take care of and provide for me. I took a copy of this letter, and finding it lay at the house near a month and was not called for, I found means to have the copy of it put into his own hands at a coffee-house, where I had by inquiry found he used to go.

This letter forced an answer from him, by which, though I found I was to be abandoned, yet I found he had sent a letter to me some time before, desiring me to go down to the Bath again. Its contents I shall come to presently.

It is true that sick-beds are the time when such correspondences as this are looked on with different countenances, and seen with other eyes than we saw them with, or than they appeared with before. My lover had been at the gates of death, and at the very brink of eternity; and, it seems, had been struck with a due remorse, and with sad reflections upon his past life of gallantry and levity; and among the rest, criminal correspondence with me, which was neither more nor less than a long-continued life of adultery, and represented itself as it really was, not as it had been formerly thought by him to be, and he looked upon it now with a just and religious abhorrence.

I cannot but observe also, and leave it for the direction of my sex in such cases of pleasure, that whenever sincere repentance succeeds such a crime as this, there never fails to attend a hatred of the object; and the more the affection might seem to be before, the hatred will be the more in proportion. It will always be so, indeed it can be no otherwise; for there cannot be a true and sincere abhorrence of the offence, and the love to the cause of it remain; there will, with an abhorrence of the sin, be found a detestation of the fellow-sinner; you can expect no other.

I found it so here, though good manners and justice in this gentleman kept him from carrying it on to any extreme but the short history of his part in this affair was thus: he perceived by my last letter, and by all the rest, which he went for after, that I was not gone to Bath, that his first letter had not come to my hand; upon which he write me this following:—

'MADAM,—I am surprised that my letter, dated the 8th of last month, did not come to your hand; I give you my word it was delivered at your lodgings, and to the hands of your maid.

'I need not acquaint you with what has been my condition for some time past; and how, having been at the edge of the grave, I am, by the unexpected and undeserved mercy of Heaven, restored again. In the condition I have been in, it cannot be strange to you that our unhappy correspondence had not been the least of the burthens which lay upon my conscience. I need say no more; those things that must be repented of, must be also reformed.

I wish you would think of going back to the Bath. I enclose you here a bill for #50 for clearing yourself at your lodgings, and carrying you down, and hope it will be no surprise to you to add, that on this account only, and not for any offence given me on your side, I can see you no more. I will take due care of the child; leave him where he is, or take him with you, as you please. I wish you the like reflections, and that they may be to your advantage.—I am,' etc.

I was struck with this letter as with a thousand wounds, such as I cannot describe; the reproaches of my own conscience were such as I cannot express, for I was not blind to my own crime; and I reflected that I might with less offence have continued with my brother, and lived with him as a wife, since there was no crime in our marriage on that score, neither of us knowing it.

But I never once reflected that I was all this while a married woman, a wife to Mr. —— the linen-draper, who, though he had left me by the necessity of his circumstances, had no power to discharge me from the marriage contract which was between us, or to give me a legal liberty to marry again; so that I had been no less than a whore and an adulteress all this while. I then reproached myself with the liberties I had taken, and how I had been a snare to this gentleman, and that indeed I was principal in the crime; that now he was mercifully snatched out of the gulf by a convincing work upon his mind, but that I was left as if I was forsaken of God's grace, and abandoned by Heaven to a continuing in my wickedness.

Under these reflections I continued very pensive and sad for near month, and did not go down to the Bath, having no inclination to be with the woman whom I was with before; lest, as I thought, she should prompt me to some wicked course of life again, as she had done; and besides, I was very loth she should know I was cast off as above.

And now I was greatly perplexed about my little boy. It was death to me to part with the child, and yet when I considered the danger of being one time or other left with him to keep without a maintenance to support him, I then resolved to leave him where he was; but then I concluded also to be near him myself too, that I then might have the satisfaction of seeing him, without the care of providing for him.

I sent my gentleman a short letter, therefore, that I had obeyed his orders in all things but that of going back to the Bath, which I could not think of for many reasons; that however parting from him was a wound to me that I could never recover, yet that I was fully satisfied his reflections were just, and would be very far from desiring to obstruct his reformation or repentance.

Then I represented my own circumstances to him in the most moving terms that I was able. I told him that those unhappy distresses which first moved him to a generous and an honest friendship for me, would, I hope, move him to a little concern for me now, though the criminal part of our correspondence, which I believed neither of us intended to fall into at the time, was broken off; that I desired to repent as sincerely as he had done, but entreated him to put me in some condition that I might not be exposed to the temptations which the devil never fails to excite us to from the frightful prospect of poverty and distress; and if he had the least apprehensions of my being troublesome to him, I begged he would put me in a posture to go back to my mother in Virginia, from when he knew I came, and that would put an end to all his fears on that account. I concluded, that if he would send me #50 more to facilitate my going away, I would send him back a general release, and would promise never to disturb him more with any importunities; unless it was to hear of the well-doing of the child, whom, if I found my mother living and my circumstances able, I would send for to come over to me, and take him also effectually off his hands.

This was indeed all a cheat thus far, viz. that I had no intention to go to Virginia, as the account of my former affairs there may convince anybody of; but the business was to get this last #50 of him, if possible, knowing well enough it would be the last penny I was ever to expect.

However, the argument I used, namely, of giving him a general release, and never troubling him any more, prevailed effectually with him, and he sent me a bill for the money by a person who brought with him a general release for me to sign, and which I frankly signed, and received the money; and thus, though full sore against my will, a final end was put to this affair.

And here I cannot but reflect upon the unhappy consequence of too great freedoms between persons stated as we were, upon the pretence of innocent intentions, love of friendship, and the like; for the flesh has generally so great a share in those friendships, that is great odds but inclination prevails at last over the most solemn resolutions; and that vice breaks in at the breaches of decency, which really innocent friendship ought to preserve with the greatest strictness. But I leave the readers of these things to their own just reflections, which they will be more able to make effectual than I, who so soon forgot myself, and am therefore but a very indifferent monitor.

I was now a single person again, as I may call myself; I was loosed from all the obligations either of wedlock or mistress-ship in the world, except my husband the linen-draper, whom, I having not now heard from in almost fifteen years, nobody could blame me for thinking myself entirely freed from; seeing also he had at his going away told me, that if I did not hear frequently from him, I should conclude he was dead, and I might freely marry again to whom I pleased.

I now began to cast up my accounts. I had by many letters and much importunity, and with the intercession of my mother too, had a second return of some goods from my brother (as I now call him) in Virginia, to make up the damage of the cargo I brought away with me, and this too was upon the condition of my sealing a general release to him, and to send it him by his correspondent at Bristol, which, though I thought hard of, yet I was obliged to promise to do. However, I managed so well in this case, that I got my goods away before the release was signed, and then I always found something or other to say to evade the thing, and to put off the signing it at all; till at length I pretended I must write to my brother, and have his answer, before I could do it.

Including this recruit, and before I got the last #50, I found my strength to amount, put all together, to about #400, so that with that I had about #450. I had saved above #100 more, but I met with a disaster with that, which was this—that a goldsmith in whose hands I had trusted it, broke, so I lost #70 of my money, the man's composition not making above #30 out of his #100. I had a little plate, but not much, and was well enough stocked with clothes and linen.

With this stock I had the world to begin again; but you are to consider that I was not now the same woman as when I lived at Redriff; for, first of all, I was near twenty years older, and did not look the better for my age, nor for my rambles to Virginia and back again; and though I omitted nothing that might set me out to advantage, except painting, for that I never stooped to, and had pride enough to think I did not want it, yet there would always be some difference seen between five-and-twenty and two-and-forty.

I cast about innumerable ways for my future state of life, and began to consider very seriously what I should do, but nothing offered. I took care to make the world take me for something more than I was, and had it given out that I was a fortune, and that my estate was in my own hands; the last of which was very true, the first of it was as above. I had no acquaintance, which was one of my worst misfortunes, and the consequence of that was, I had no adviser, at least who could assist and advise together; and above all, I had nobody to whom I could in confidence commit the secret of my circumstances to, and could depend upon for their secrecy and fidelity; and I found by experience, that to be friendless is the worst condition, next to being in want that a woman can be reduced to: I say a woman, because 'tis evident men can be their own advisers, and their own directors, and know how to work themselves out of difficulties and into business better than women; but if a woman has no friend to communicate her affairs to, and to advise and assist her, 'tis ten to one but she is undone; nay, and the more money she has, the more danger she is in of being wronged and deceived; and this was my case in the affair of the #100 which I left in the hands of the goldsmith, as above, whose credit, it seems, was upon the ebb before, but I, that had no knowledge of things and nobody to consult with, knew nothing of it, and so lost my money.

In the next place, when a woman is thus left desolate and void of counsel, she is just like a bag of money or a jewel dropped on the highway, which is a prey to the next comer; if a man of virtue and upright principles happens to find it, he will have it cried, and the owner may come to hear of it again; but how many times shall such a thing fall into hands that will make no scruple of seizing it for their own, to once that it shall come into good hands?

This was evidently my case, for I was now a loose, unguided creature, and had no help, no assistance, no guide for my conduct; I knew what I aimed at and what I wanted, but knew nothing how to pursue the end by direct means. I wanted to be placed in a settle state of living, and had I happened to meet with a sober, good husband, I should have been as faithful and true a wife to him as virtue itself could have formed. If I had been otherwise, the vice came in always at the door of necessity, not at the door of inclination; and I understood too well, by the want of it, what the value of a settled life was, to do anything to forfeit the felicity of it; nay, I should have made the better wife for all the difficulties I had passed through, by a great deal; nor did I in any of the time that I had been a wife give my husbands the least uneasiness on account of my behaviour.

But all this was nothing; I found no encouraging prospect. I waited; I lived regularly, and with as much frugality as became my circumstances, but nothing offered, nothing presented, and the main stock wasted apace. What to do I knew not; the terror of approaching poverty lay hard upon my spirits. I had some money, but where to place it I knew not, nor would the interest of it maintain me, at least not in London.

At length a new scene opened. There was in the house where I lodged a north-country woman that went for a gentlewoman, and nothing was more frequent in her discourse than her account of the cheapness of provisions, and the easy way of living in her country; how plentiful and how cheap everything was, what good company they kept, and the like; till at last I told her she almost tempted me to go and live in her country; for I that was a widow, though I had sufficient to live on, yet had no way of increasing it; and that I found I could not live here under #100 a year, unless I kept no company, no servant, made no appearance, and buried myself in privacy, as if I was obliged to it by necessity.

I should have observed, that she was always made to believe, as everybody else was, that I was a great fortune, or at least that I had three or four thousand pounds, if not more, and all in my own hands; and she was mighty sweet upon me when she thought me inclined in the least to go into her country. She said she had a sister lived near Liverpool, that her brother was a considerable gentleman there, and had a great estate also in Ireland; that she would go down there in about two months, and if I would give her my company thither, I should be as welcome as herself for a month or more as I pleased, till I should see how I liked the country; and if I thought fit to live there, she would undertake they would take care, though they did not entertain lodgers themselves, they would recommend me to some agreeable family, where I should be placed to my content.

If this woman had known my real circumstances, she would never have laid so many snares, and taken so many weary steps to catch a poor desolate creature that was good for little when it was caught; and indeed I, whose case was almost desperate, and thought I could not be much worse, was not very anxious about what might befall me, provided they did me no personal injury; so I suffered myself, though not without a great deal of invitation and great professions of sincere friendship and real kindness—I say, I suffered myself to be prevailed upon to go with her, and accordingly I packed up my baggage, and put myself in a posture for a journey, though I did not absolutely know whither I was to go.

And now I found myself in great distress; what little I had in the world was all in money, except as before, a little plate, some linen, and my clothes; as for my household stuff, I had little or none, for I had lived always in lodgings; but I had not one friend in the world with whom to trust that little I had, or to direct me how to dispose of it, and this perplexed me night and day. I thought of the bank, and of the other companies in London, but I had no friend to commit the management of it to, and keep and carry about with me bank bills, tallies, orders, and such things, I looked upon at as unsafe; that if they were lost, my money was lost, and then I was undone; and, on the other hand, I might be robbed and perhaps murdered in a strange place for them. This perplexed me strangely, and what to do I knew not.

It came in my thoughts one morning that I would go to the bank myself, where I had often been to receive the interest of some bills I had, which had interest payable on them, and where I had found a clerk, to whom I applied myself, very honest and just to me, and particularly so fair one time that when I had mistold my money, and taken less than my due, and was coming away, he set me to rights and gave me the rest, which he might have put into his own pocket.

I went to him and represented my case very plainly, and asked if he would trouble himself to be my adviser, who was a poor friendless widow, and knew not what to do. He told me, if I desired his opinion of anything within the reach of his business, he would do his endeavour that I should not be wronged, but that he would also help me to a good sober person who was a grave man of his acquaintance, who was a clerk in such business too, though not in their house, whose judgment was good, and whose honesty I might depend upon. 'For,' added he, 'I will answer for him, and for every step he takes; if he wrongs you, madam, of one farthing, it shall lie at my door, I will make it good; and he delights to assist people in such cases—he does it as an act of charity.'

I was a little at a stand in this discourse; but after some pause I told him I had rather have depended upon him, because I had found him honest, but if that could not be, I would take his recommendation sooner than any one's else. 'I dare say, madam,' says he, 'that you will be as well satisfied with my friend as with me, and he is thoroughly able to assist you, which I am not.' It seems he had his hands full of the business of the bank, and had engaged to meddle with no other business that that of his office, which I heard afterwards, but did not understand then. He added, that his friend should take nothing of me for his advice or assistance, and this indeed encouraged me very much.

He appointed the same evening, after the bank was shut and business over, for me to meet him and his friend. And indeed as soon as I saw his friend, and he began but to talk of the affair, I was fully satisfied that I had a very honest man to deal with; his countenance spoke it, and his character, as I heard afterwards, was everywhere so good, that I had no room for any more doubts upon me.

After the first meeting, in which I only said what I had said before, we parted, and he appointed me to come the next day to him, telling me I might in the meantime satisfy myself of him by inquiry, which, however, I knew not how well to do, having no acquaintance myself.

Accordingly I met him the next day, when I entered more freely with him into my case. I told him my circumstances at large: that I was a widow come over from America, perfectly desolate and friendless; that I had a little money, and but a little, and was almost distracted for fear of losing it, having no friend in the world to trust with the management of it; that I was going into the north of England to live cheap, that my stock might not waste; that I would willingly lodge my money in the bank, but that I durst not carry the bills about me, and the like, as above; and how to correspond about it, or with whom, I knew not.

He told me I might lodge the money in the bank as an account, and its being entered into the books would entitle me to the money at any time, and if I was in the north I might draw bills on the cashier and receive it when I would; but that then it would be esteemed as running cash, and the bank would give no interest for it; that I might buy stock with it, and so it would lie in store for me, but that then if I wanted to dispose if it, I must come up to town on purpose to transfer it, and even it would be with some difficulty I should receive the half-yearly dividend, unless I was here in person, or had some friend I could trust with having the stock in his name to do it for me, and that would have the same difficulty in it as before; and with that he looked hard at me and smiled a little. At last, says he, 'Why do you not get a head steward, madam, that may take you and your money together into keeping, and then you would have the trouble taken off your hands?' 'Ay, sir, and the money too, it may be,' said I; 'for truly I find the hazard that way is as much as 'tis t'other way'; but I remember I said secretly to myself, 'I wish you would ask me the question fairly, I would consider very seriously on it before I said No.'

He went on a good way with me, and I thought once or twice he was in earnest, but to my real affliction, I found at last he had a wife; but when he owned he had a wife he shook his head, and said with some concern, that indeed he had a wife, and no wife. I began to think he had been in the condition of my late lover, and that his wife had been distempered or lunatic, or some such thing. However, we had not much more discourse at that time, but he told me he was in too much hurry of business then, but that if I would come home to his house after their business was over, he would by that time consider what might be done for me, to put my affairs in a posture of security. I told him I would come, and desired to know where he lived. He gave me a direction in writing, and when he gave it me he read it to me, and said, 'There 'tis, madam, if you dare trust yourself with me.' 'Yes, sir,' said I, 'I believe I may venture to trust you with myself, for you have a wife, you say, and I don't want a husband; besides, I dare trust you with my money, which is all I have in the world, and if that were gone, I may trust myself anywhere.'

He said some things in jest that were very handsome and mannerly, and would have pleased me very well if they had been in earnest; but that passed over, I took the directions, and appointed to attend him at his house at seven o'clock the same evening.

When I came he made several proposals for my placing my money in the bank, in order to my having interest for it; but still some difficulty or other came in the way, which he objected as not safe; and I found such a sincere disinterested honesty in him, that I began to muse with myself, that I had certainly found the honest man I wanted, and that I could never put myself into better hands; so I told him with a great deal of frankness that I had never met with a man or woman yet that I could trust, or in whom I could think myself safe, but that I saw he was so disinterestedly concerned for my safety, that I said I would freely trust him with the management of that little I had, if he would accept to be steward for a poor widow that could give him no salary.

He smiled and, standing up, with great respect saluted me. He told me he could not but take it very kindly that I had so good an opinion of him; that he would not deceive me, that he would do anything in his power to serve me, and expect no salary; but that he could not by any means accept of a trust, that it might bring him to be suspected of self-interest, and that if I should die he might have disputes with my executors, which he should be very loth to encumber himself with.

I told him if those were all his objections I would soon remove them, and convince him that there was not the least room for any difficulty; for that, first, as for suspecting him, if ever I should do it, now is the time to suspect him, and not put the trust into his hands, and whenever I did suspect him, he could but throw it up then and refuse to go any further. Then, as to executors, I assured him I had no heirs, nor any relations in England, and I should alter my condition before I died, and then his trust and trouble should cease together, which, however, I had no prospect of yet; but I told him if I died as I was, it should be all his own, and he would deserve it by being so faithful to me as I was satisfied he would be.

He changed his countenance at this discourse, and asked me how I came to have so much good-will for him; and, looking very much pleased, said he might very lawfully wish he was a single man for my sake. I smiled, and told him as he was not, my offer could have no design upon him in it, and to wish, as he did, was not to be allowed, 'twas criminal to his wife.

He told me I was wrong. 'For,' says he, 'madam, as I said before, I have a wife and no wife, and 'twould be no sin to me to wish her hanged, if that were all.' 'I know nothing of your circumstances that way, sir,' said I; 'but it cannot be innocent to wish your wife dead.' 'I tell you,' says he again, 'she is a wife and no wife; you don't know what I am, or what she is.'

'That's true,' said I; 'sir, I do not know what you are, but I believe you to be an honest man, and that's the cause of all my confidence in you.'

'Well, well,' says he, 'and so I am, I hope, too. But I am something else too, madam; for,' says he, 'to be plain with you, I am a cuckold, and she is a whore.' He spoke it in a kind of jest, but it was with such an awkward smile, that I perceived it was what struck very close to him, and he looked dismally when he said it.

'That alters the case indeed, sir,' said I, 'as to that part you were speaking of; but a cuckold, you know, may be an honest man; it does not alter that case at all. Besides, I think,' said I, 'since your wife is so dishonest to you, you are too honest to her to own her for your wife; but that,' said I, 'is what I have nothing to do with.'

'Nay,' says he, 'I do not think to clear my hands of her; for, to be plain with you, madam,' added he, 'I am no contended cuckold neither: on the other hand, I assure you it provokes me the highest degree, but I can't help myself; she that will be a whore, will be a whore.'

I waived the discourse and began to talk of my business; but I found he could not have done with it, so I let him alone, and he went on to tell me all the circumstances of his case, too long to relate here; particularly, that having been out of England some time before he came to the post he was in, she had had two children in the meantime by an officer of the army; and that when he came to England and, upon her submission, took her again, and maintained her very well, yet she ran away from him with a linen-draper's apprentice, robbed him of what she could come at, and continued to live from him still. 'So that, madam,' says he, 'she is a whore not by necessity, which is the common bait of your sex, but by inclination, and for the sake of the vice.'

Well, I pitied him, and wished him well rid of her, and still would have talked of my business, but it would not do. At last he looks steadily at me. 'Look you, madam,' says he, 'you came to ask advice of me, and I will serve you as faithfully as if you were my own sister; but I must turn the tables, since you oblige me to do it, and are so friendly to me, and I think I must ask advice of you. Tell me, what must a poor abused fellow do with a whore? What can I do to do myself justice upon her?'

'Alas! sir,' says I, ''tis a case too nice for me to advise in, but it seems she has run away from you, so you are rid of her fairly; what can you desire more?' 'Ay, she is gone indeed,' said he, 'but I am not clear of her for all that.'

'That's true,' says I; 'she may indeed run you into debt, but the law has furnished you with methods to prevent that also; you may cry her down, as they call it.'

'No, no,' says he, 'that is not the case neither; I have taken care of all that; 'tis not that part that I speak of, but I would be rid of her so that I might marry again.'

'Well, sir,' says I, 'then you must divorce her. If you can prove what you say, you may certainly get that done, and then, I suppose, you are free.'

'That's very tedious and expensive,' says he.

'Why,' says I, 'if you can get any woman you like to take your word, I suppose your wife would not dispute the liberty with you that she takes herself.'

'Ay,' says he, 'but 'twould be hard to bring an honest woman to do that; and for the other sort,' says he, 'I have had enough of her to meddle with any more whores.'

It occurred to me presently, 'I would have taken your word with all my heart, if you had but asked me the question'; but that was to myself. To him I replied, 'Why, you shut the door against any honest woman accepting you, for you condemn all that should venture upon you at once, and conclude, that really a woman that takes you now can't be honest.'

'Why,' says he, 'I wish you would satisfy me that an honest woman would take me; I'd venture it'; and then turns short upon me, 'Will you take me, madam?'

'That's not a fair question,' says I, 'after what you have said; however, lest you should think I wait only for a recantation of it, I shall answer you plainly, No, not I; my business is of another kind with you, and I did not expect you would have turned my serious application to you, in my own distracted case, into a comedy.'

'Why, madam,' says he, 'my case is as distracted as yours can be, and I stand in as much need of advice as you do, for I think if I have not relief somewhere, I shall be made myself, and I know not what course to take, I protest to you.'

'Why, sir,' says I, ''tis easy to give advice in your case, much easier than it is in mine.' 'Speak then,' says he, 'I beg of you, for now you encourage me.'

'Why,' says I, 'if your case is so plain as you say it is, you may be legally divorced, and then you may find honest women enough to ask the question of fairly; the sex is not so scarce that you can want a wife.'

'Well, then,' said he, 'I am in earnest; I'll take your advice; but shall I ask you one question seriously beforehand?'

'Any question,' said I, 'but that you did before.'

'No, that answer will not do,' said he, 'for, in short, that is the question I shall ask.'

'You may ask what questions you please, but you have my answer to that already,' said I. 'Besides, sir,' said I, 'can you think so ill of me as that I would give any answer to such a question beforehand? Can any woman alive believe you in earnest, or think you design anything but to banter her?'

'Well, well,' says he, 'I do not banter you, I am in earnest; consider of it.'

'But, sir,' says I, a little gravely, 'I came to you about my own business; I beg of you to let me know, what you will advise me to do?'

'I will be prepared,' says he, 'against you come again.'

'Nay,' says I, 'you have forbid my coming any more.'

'Why so?' said he, and looked a little surprised.

'Because,' said I, 'you can't expect I should visit you on the account you talk of.'

'Well,' says he, 'you shall promise me to come again, however, and I will not say any more of it till I have gotten the divorce, but I desire you will prepare to be better conditioned when that's done, for you shall be the woman, or I will not be divorced at all; why, I owe it to your unlooked-for kindness, if it were to nothing else, but I have other reasons too.'

He could not have said anything in the world that pleased me better; however, I knew that the way to secure him was to stand off while the thing was so remote, as it appeared to be, and that it was time enough to accept of it when he was able to perform it; so I said very respectfully to him, it was time enough to consider of these things when he was in a condition to talk of them; in the meantime, I told him, I was going a great way from him, and he would find objects enough to please him better. We broke off here for the present, and he made me promise him to come again the next day, for his resolutions upon my own business, which after some pressing I did; though had he seen farther into me, I wanted no pressing on that account.

I came the next evening, accordingly, and brought my maid with me, to let him see that I kept a maid, but I sent her away as soon as I was gone in. He would have had me let the maid have stayed, but I would not, but ordered her aloud to come for me again about nine o'clock. But he forbade that, and told me he would see me safe home, which, by the way, I was not very well please with, supposing he might do that to know where I lived and inquire into my character and circumstances. However, I ventured that, for all that the people there or thereabout knew of me, was to my advantage; and all the character he had of me, after he had inquired, was that I was a woman of fortune, and that I was a very modest, sober body; which, whether true or not in the main, yet you may see how necessary it is for all women who expect anything in the world, to preserve the character of their virtue, even when perhaps they may have sacrificed the thing itself.

I found, and was not a little please with it, that he had provided a supper for me. I found also he lived very handsomely, and had a house very handsomely furnished; all of which I was rejoiced at indeed, for I looked upon it as all my own.

We had now a second conference upon the subject-matter of the last conference. He laid his business very home indeed; he protested his affection to me, and indeed I had no room to doubt it; he declared that it began from the first moment I talked with him, and long before I had mentioned leaving my effects with him. ''Tis no matter when it began,' thought I; 'if it will but hold, 'twill be well enough.' He then told me how much the offer I had made of trusting him with my effects, and leaving them to him, had engaged him. 'So I intended it should,' thought I, 'but then I thought you had been a single man too.' After we had supped, I observed he pressed me very hard to drink two or three glasses of wine, which, however, I declined, but drank one glass or two. He then told me he had a proposal to make to me, which I should promise him I would not take ill if I should not grant it. I told him I hoped he would make no dishonourable proposal to me, especially in his own house, and that if it was such, I desired he would not propose it, that I might not be obliged to offer any resentment to him that did not become the respect I professed for him, and the trust I had placed in him in coming to his house; and begged of him he would give me leave to go away, and accordingly began to put on my gloves and prepare to be gone, though at the same time I no more intended it than he intended to let me.

Well, he importuned me not to talk of going; he assured me he had no dishonourable thing in his thoughts about me, and was very far from offering anything to me that was dishonourable, and if I thought so, he would choose to say no more of it.

That part I did not relish at all. I told him I was ready to hear anything that he had to say, depending that he would say nothing unworthy of himself, or unfit for me to hear. Upon this, he told me his proposal was this: that I would marry him, though he had not yet obtained the divorce from the whore his wife; and to satisfy me that he meant honourably, he would promise not to desire me to live with him, or go to bed with him till the divorce was obtained. My heart said yes to this offer at first word, but it was necessary to play the hypocrite a little more with him; so I seemed to decline the motion with some warmth, and besides a little condemning the thing as unfair, told him that such a proposal could be of no signification, but to entangle us both in great difficulties; for if he should not at last obtain the divorce, yet we could not dissolve the marriage, neither could we proceed in it; so that if he was disappointed in the divorce, I left him to consider what a condition we should both be in.

In short, I carried on the argument against this so far, that I convinced him it was not a proposal that had any sense in it. Well, then he went from it to another, and that was, that I would sign and seal a contract with him, conditioning to marry him as soon as the divorce was obtained, and to be void if he could not obtain it.

I told him such a thing was more rational than the other; but as this was the first time that ever I could imagine him weak enough to be in earnest in this affair, I did not use to say Yes at first asking; I would consider of it.

I played with this lover as an angler does with a trout. I found I had him fast on the hook, so I jested with his new proposal, and put him off. I told him he knew little of me, and bade him inquire about me; I let him also go home with me to my lodging, though I would not ask him to go in, for I told him it was not decent.

In short, I ventured to avoid signing a contract of marriage, and the reason why I did it was because the lady that had invited me so earnestly to go with her into Lancashire insisted so positively upon it, and promised me such great fortunes, and such fine things there, that I was tempted to go and try. 'Perhaps,' said I, 'I may mend myself very much'; and then I made no scruple in my thoughts of quitting my honest citizen, whom I was not so much in love with as not to leave him for a richer.

In a word, I avoided a contract; but told him I would go into the north, that he should know where to write to me by the consequence of the business I had entrusted with him; that I would give him a sufficient pledge of my respect for him, for I would leave almost all I had in the world in his hands; and I would thus far give him my word, that as soon as he had sued out a divorce from his first wife, he would send me an account of it, I would come up to London, and that then we would talk seriously of the matter.

It was a base design I went with, that I must confess, though I was invited thither with a design much worse than mine was, as the sequel will discover. Well, I went with my friend, as I called her, into Lancashire. All the way we went she caressed me with the utmost appearance of a sincere, undissembled affection; treated me, except my coach-hire, all the way; and her brother brought a gentleman's coach to Warrington to receive us, and we were carried from thence to Liverpool with as much ceremony as I could desire. We were also entertained at a merchant's house in Liverpool three or four days very handsomely; I forbear to tell his name, because of what followed. Then she told me she would carry me to an uncle's house of hers, where we should be nobly entertained. She did so; her uncle, as she called him, sent a coach and four horses for us, and we were carried near forty miles I know not whither.

We came, however, to a gentleman's seat, where was a numerous family, a large park, extraordinary company indeed, and where she was called cousin. I told her if she had resolved to bring me into such company as this, she should have let me have prepared myself, and have furnished myself with better clothes. The ladies took notice of that, and told me very genteelly they did not value people in their country so much by their clothes as they did in London; that their cousin had fully informed them of my quality, and that I did not want clothes to set me off; in short, they entertained me, not like what I was, but like what they thought I had been, namely, a widow lady of a great fortune.

The first discovery I made here was, that the family were all Roman Catholics, and the cousin too, whom I called my friend; however, I must say that nobody in the world could behave better to me, and I had all the civility shown me that I could have had if I had been of their opinion. The truth is, I had not so much principle of any kind as to be nice in point of religion, and I presently learned to speak favourably of the Romish Church; particularly, I told them I saw little but the prejudice of education in all the difference that were among Christians about religion, and if it had so happened that my father had been a Roman Catholic, I doubted not but I should have been as well pleased with their religion as my own.

This obliged them in the highest degree, and as I was besieged day and night with good company and pleasant discourse, so I had two or three old ladies that lay at me upon the subject of religion too. I was so complaisant, that though I would not completely engage, yet I made no scruple to be present at their mass, and to conform to all their gestures as they showed me the pattern, but I would not come too cheap; so that I only in the main encouraged them to expect that I would turn Roman Catholic, if I was instructed in the Catholic doctrine as they called it, and so the matter rested.

I stayed here about six weeks; and then my conductor led me back to a country village, about six miles from Liverpool, where her brother (as she called him) came to visit me in his own chariot, and in a very good figure, with two footmen in a good livery; and the next thing was to make love to me. As it had happened to me, one would think I could not have been cheated, and indeed I thought so myself, having a safe card at home, which I resolved not to quit unless I could mend myself very much. However, in all appearance this brother was a match worth my listening to, and the least his estate was valued at was #1000 a year, but the sister said it was worth #1500 a year, and lay most of it in Ireland.

I that was a great fortune, and passed for such, was above being asked how much my estate was; and my false friend taking it upon a foolish hearsay, had raised it from #500 to #5000, and by the time she came into the country she called it #15,000. The Irishman, for such I understood him to be, was stark mad at this bait; in short, he courted me, made me presents, and ran in debt like a madman for the expenses of his equipage and of his courtship. He had, to give him his due, the appearance of an extraordinary fine gentleman; he was tall, well-shaped, and had an extraordinary address; talked as naturally of his park and his stables, of his horses, his gamekeepers, his woods, his tenants, and his servants, as if we had been in the mansion-house, and I had seen them all about me.

He never so much as asked me about my fortune or estate, but assured me that when we came to Dublin he would jointure me in #600 a year good land; and that we could enter into a deed of settlement or contract here for the performance of it.

This was such language indeed as I had not been used to, and I was here beaten out of all my measures; I had a she-devil in my bosom, every hour telling me how great her brother lived. One time she would come for my orders, how I would have my coaches painted, and how lined; and another time what clothes my page should wear; in short, my eyes were dazzled. I had now lost my power of saying No, and, to cut the story short, I consented to be married; but to be the more private, we were carried farther into the country, and married by a Romish clergyman, who I was assured would marry us as effectually as a Church of England parson.

I cannot say but I had some reflections in this affair upon the dishonourable forsaking my faithful citizen, who loved me sincerely, and who was endeavouring to quit himself of a scandalous whore by whom he had been indeed barbarously used, and promised himself infinite happiness in his new choice; which choice was now giving up herself to another in a manner almost as scandalous as hers could be.

But the glittering shoe of a great estate, and of fine things, which the deceived creature that was now my deceiver represented every hour to my imagination, hurried me away, and gave me no time to think of London, or of anything there, much less of the obligation I had to a person of infinitely more real merit than what was now before me.

But the thing was done; I was now in the arms of my new spouse, who appeared still the same as before; great even to magnificence, and nothing less than #1000 a year could support the ordinary equipage he appeared in.

After we had been married about a month, he began to talk of my going to West Chester in order to embark for Ireland. However, he did not hurry me, for we stayed near three weeks longer, and then he sent to Chester for a coach to meet us at the Black Rock, as they call it, over against Liverpool. Thither we went in a fine boat they call a pinnace, with six oars; his servants, and horses, and baggage going in the ferry-boat. He made his excuse to me that he had no acquaintance in Chester, but he would go before and get some handsome apartment for me at a private house. I asked him how long we should stay at Chester. He said, not at all, any longer than one night or two, but he would immediately hire a coach to go to Holyhead. Then I told him he should by no means give himself the trouble to get private lodgings for one night or two, for that Chester being a great place, I made no doubt but there would be very good inns and accommodation enough; so we lodged at an inn in the West Street, not far from the Cathedral; I forget what sign it was at.

Here my spouse, talking of my going to Ireland, asked me if I had no affairs to settle at London before we went off. I told him No, not of any great consequence, but what might be done as well by letter from

Dublin. 'Madam,' says he, very respectfully, 'I suppose the greatest part of your estate, which my sister tells me is most of it in money in the Bank of England, lies secure enough, but in case it required transferring, or any way altering its property, it might be necessary to go up to London and settle those things before we went over.'

I seemed to look strange at it, and told him I knew not what he meant; that I had no effects in the Bank of England that I knew of; and I hoped he could not say that I had ever told him I had. No, he said, I had not told him so, but his sister had said the greatest part of my estate lay there. 'And I only mentioned it, me dear,' said he, 'that if there was any occasion to settle it, or order anything about it, we might not be obliged to the hazard and trouble of another voyage back again'; for he added, that he did not care to venture me too much upon the sea.

I was surprised at this talk, and began to consider very seriously what the meaning of it must be; and it presently occurred to me that my friend, who called him brother, had represented me in colours which were not my due; and I thought, since it was come to that pitch, that I would know the bottom of it before I went out of England, and before I should put myself into I knew not whose hands in a strange country.

Upon this I called his sister into my chamber the next morning, and letting her know the discourse her brother and I had been upon the evening before, I conjured her to tell me what she had said to him, and upon what foot it was that she had made this marriage. She owned that she had told him that I was a great fortune, and said that she was told so at London. 'Told so!' says I warmly; 'did I ever tell you so?' No, she said, it was true I did not tell her so, but I had said several times that what I had was in my own disposal. 'I did so,' returned I very quickly and hastily, 'but I never told you I had anything called a fortune; no, not that I had #100, or the value of #100, in the world. Any how did it consist with my being a fortune,' said I, 'that I should come here into the north of England with you, only upon the account of living cheap?' At these words, which I spoke warm and high, my husband, her brother (as she called him), came into the room, and I desired him to come and sit down, for I had something of moment to say before them both, which it was absolutely necessary he should hear.

He looked a little disturbed at the assurance with which I seemed to speak it, and came and sat down by me, having first shut the door; upon which I began, for I was very much provoked, and turning myself to him, 'I am afraid,' says I, 'my dear' (for I spoke with kindness on his side), 'that you have a very great abuse put upon you, and an injury done you never to be repaired in your marrying me, which, however, as I have had no hand in it, I desire I may be fairly acquitted of it, and that the blame may lie where it ought to lie, and nowhere else, for I wash my hands of every part of it.'

'What injury can be done me, my dear,' says he, 'in marrying you. I hope it is to my honour and advantage every way.' 'I will soon explain it to you,' says I, 'and I fear you will have no reason to think yourself well used; but I will convince you, my dear,' says I again, 'that I have had no hand in it'; and there I stopped a while.

He looked now scared and wild, and began, I believe, to suspect what followed; however, looking towards me, and saying only, 'Go on,' he sat silent, as if to hear what I had more to say; so I went on. 'I asked you last night,' said I, speaking to him, 'if ever I made any boast to you of my estate, or ever told you I had any estate in the Bank of England or anywhere else, and you owned I had not, as is most true; and I desire you will tell me here, before your sister, if ever I gave you any reason from me to think so, or that ever we had any discourse about it'; and he owned again I had not, but said I had appeared always as a woman of fortune, and he depended on it that I was so, and hoped he was not deceived. 'I am not inquiring yet whether you have been deceived or not,' said I; 'I fear you have, and I too; but I am clearing myself from the unjust charge of being concerned in deceiving you.

'I have been now asking your sister if ever I told her of any fortune or estate I had, or gave her any particulars of it; and she owns I never did. Any pray, madam,' said I, turning myself to her, 'be so just to me, before your brother, to charge me, if you can, if ever I pretended to you that I had an estate; and why, if I had, should I come down into this country with you on purpose to spare that little I had, and live cheap?' She could not deny one word, but said she had been told in London that I had a very great fortune, and that it lay in the Bank of England.

'And now, dear sir,' said I, turning myself to my new spouse again, 'be so just to me as to tell me who has abused both you and me so much as to make you believe I was a fortune, and prompt you to court me to this marriage?' He could not speak a word, but pointed to her; and, after some more pause, flew out in the most furious passion that ever I saw a man in my life, cursing her, and calling her all the whores and hard names he could think of; and that she had ruined him, declaring that she had told him I had #15,000, and that she was to have #500 of him for procuring this match for him. He then added, directing his speech to me, that she was none of his sister, but had been his whore for two years before, that she had had #100 of him in part of this bargain, and that he was utterly undone if things were as I said; and in his raving he swore he would let her heart's blood out immediately, which frightened her and me too. She cried, said she had been told so in the house where I lodged. But this aggravated him more than before, that she should put so far upon him, and run things such a length upon no other authority than a hearsay; and then, turning to me again, said very honestly, he was afraid we were both undone. 'For, to be plain, my dear, I have no estate,' says he; 'what little I had, this devil has made me run out in waiting on you and putting me into this equipage.' She took the opportunity of his being earnest in talking with me, and got out of the room, and I never saw her more.

I was confounded now as much as he, and knew not what to say. I thought many ways that I had the worst of it, but his saying he was undone, and that he had no estate neither, put me into a mere distraction. 'Why,' says I to him, 'this has been a hellish juggle, for we are married here upon the foot of a double fraud; you are undone by the disappointment, it seems; and if I had had a fortune I had been cheated too, for you say you have nothing.'

'You would indeed have been cheated, my dear,' says he, 'but you would not have been undone, for #15,000 would have maintained us both very handsomely in this country; and I assure you,' added he, 'I had resolved to have dedicated every groat of it to you; I would not have wronged you of a shilling, and the rest I would have made up in my affection to you, and tenderness of you, as long as I lived.'

This was very honest indeed, and I really believe he spoke as he intended, and that he was a man that was as well qualified to make me happy, as to his temper and behaviour, as any man ever was; but his having no estate, and being run into debt on this ridiculous account in the country, made all the prospect dismal and dreadful, and I knew not what to say, or what to think of myself.

I told him it was very unhappy that so much love, and so much good nature as I discovered in him, should be thus precipitated into misery; that I saw nothing before us but ruin; for as to me, it was my unhappiness that what little I had was not able to relieve us week, and with that I pulled out a bank bill of #20 and eleven guineas, which I told him I had saved out of my little income, and that by the account that creature had given me of the way of living in that country, I expected it would maintain me three or four years; that if it was taken from me, I was left destitute, and he knew what the condition of a woman among strangers must be, if she had no money in her pocket; however, I told him, if he would take it, there it was.

He told me with a great concern, and I thought I saw tears stand in his eyes, that he would not touch it; that he abhorred the thoughts of stripping me and make me miserable; that, on the contrary, he had fifty guineas left, which was all he had in the world, and he pulled it out and threw it down on the table, bidding me take it, though he were to starve for want of it.

I returned, with the same concern for him, that I could not bear to hear him talk so; that, on the contrary, if he could propose any probable method of living, I would do anything that became me on my part, and that I would live as close and as narrow as he could desire.

He begged of me to talk no more at that rate, for it would make him distracted; he said he was bred a gentleman, though he was reduced to a low fortune, and that there was but one way left which he could think of, and that would not do, unless I could answer him one question, which, however, he said he would not press me to. I told him I would answer it honestly; whether it would be to his satisfaction or not, that I could not tell.

'Why, then, my dear, tell me plainly,' says he, 'will the little you have keep us together in any figure, or in any station or place, or will it not?'

It was my happiness hitherto that I had not discovered myself or my circumstances at all—no, not so much as my name; and seeing these was nothing to be expected from him, however good-humoured and however honest he seemed to be, but to live on what I knew would soon be wasted, I resolved to conceal everything but the bank bill and the eleven guineas which I had owned; and I would have been very glad to have lost that and have been set down where he took me up. I had indeed another bank bill about me of #30, which was the whole of what I brought with me, as well to subsist on in the country, as not knowing what might offer; because this creature, the go-between that had thus betrayed us both, had made me believe strange things of my marrying to my advantage in the country, and I was not willing to be without money, whatever might happen. This bill I concealed, and that made me the freer of the rest, in consideration of his circumstances, for I really pitied him heartily.

But to return to his question, I told him I never willingly deceived him, and I never would. I was very sorry to tell him that the little I had would not subsist us; that it was not sufficient to subsist me alone in the south country, and that this was the reason that made me put myself into the hands of that woman who called him brother, she having assured me that I might board very handsomely at a town called Manchester, where I had not yet been, for about #6 a year; and my whole income not being about #15 a year, I thought I might live easy upon it, and wait for better things.

He shook his head and remained silent, and a very melancholy evening we had; however, we supped together, and lay together that night, and when we had almost supped he looked a little better and more cheerful, and called for a bottle of wine. 'Come, my dear,' says he, 'though the case is bad, it is to no purpose to be dejected. Come, be as easy as you can; I will endeavour to find out some way or other to live; if you can but subsist yourself, that is better than nothing. I must try the world again; a man ought to think like a man; to be discouraged is to yield to the misfortune.' With this he filled a glass and drank to me, holding my hand and pressing it hard in his hand all the while the wine went down, and protesting afterwards his main concern was for me.

It was really a true, gallant spirit he was of, and it was the more grievous to me. 'Tis something of relief even to be undone by a man of honour, rather than by a scoundrel; but here the greatest disappointment was on his side, for he had really spent a great deal of money, deluded by this madam the procuress; and it was very remarkable on what poor terms he proceeded. First the baseness of the creature herself is to be observed, who, for the getting #100 herself, could be content to let him spend three or four more, though perhaps it was all he had in the world, and more than all; when she had not the least ground, more than a little tea-table chat, to say that I had any estate, or was a fortune, or the like. It is true the design of deluding a woman of fortune, if I had been so, was base enough; the putting the face of great things upon poor circumstances was a fraud, and bad enough; but the case a little differed too, and that in his favour, for he was not a rake that made a trade to delude women, and, as some have done, get six or seven fortunes after one another, and then rifle and run away from them; but he was really a gentleman, unfortunate and low, but had lived well; and though, if I had had a fortune, I should have been enraged at the slut for betraying me, yet really for the man, a fortune would not have been ill bestowed on him, for he was a lovely person indeed, of generous principles, good sense, and of abundance of good-humour.

We had a great deal of close conversation that night, for we neither of us slept much; he was as penitent for having put all those cheats upon me as if it had been felony, and that he was going to execution; he offered me again every shilling of the money he had about him, and said he would go into the army and seek the world for more.

I asked him why he would be so unkind to carry me into Ireland, when I might suppose he could not have subsisted me there. He took me in his arms. 'My dear,' said he, 'depend upon it, I never designed to go to Ireland at all, much less to have carried you thither, but came hither to be out of the observation of the people, who had heard what I pretended to, and withal, that nobody might ask me for money before I was furnished to supply them.'

'But where, then,' said I, 'were we to have gone next?'

'Why, my dear,' said he, 'I'll confess the whole scheme to you as I had laid it; I purposed here to ask you something about your estate, as you see I did, and when you, as I expected you would, had entered into some account with me of the particulars, I would have made an excuse to you to have put off our voyage to Ireland for some time, and to have gone first towards London.

'Then, my dear,' said he, 'I resolved to have confessed all the circumstances of my own affairs to you, and let you know I had indeed made use of these artifices to obtain your consent to marry me, but had now nothing to do but ask to your pardon, and to tell you how abundantly, as I have said above, I would endeavour to make you forget what was past, by the felicity of the days to come.'

'Truly,' said I to him, 'I find you would soon have conquered me; and it is my affliction now, that I am not in a condition to let you see how easily I should have been reconciled to you, and have passed by all the tricks you had put upon me, in recompense of so much good-humour. But, my dear,' said I, 'what can we do now? We are both undone, and what better are we for our being reconciled together, seeing we have nothing to live on?'

We proposed a great many things, but nothing could offer where there was nothing to begin with. He begged me at last to talk no more of it, for, he said, I would break his heart; so we talked of other things a little, till at last he took a husband's leave of me, and so we went to sleep.

He rose before me in the morning; and indeed, having lain awake almost all night, I was very sleepy, and lay till near eleven o'clock. In this time he took his horses and three servants, and all his linen and baggage, and away he went, leaving a short but moving letter for me on the table, as follows:—

'MY DEAR—I am a dog; I have abused you; but I have been drawn into do it by a base creature, contrary to my principle and the general practice of my life. Forgive me, my dear! I ask your pardon with the greatest sincerity; I am the most miserable of men, in having deluded you. I have been so happy to possess you, and now am so wretched as to be forced to fly from you. Forgive me, my dear; once more I say, forgive me! I am not able to see you ruined by me, and myself unable to support you. Our marriage is nothing; I shall never be able to see you again; I here discharge you from it; if you can marry to your advantage, do not decline it on my account; I here swear to you on my faith, and on the word of a man of honour, I will never disturb your repose if I should know of it, which, however, is not likely. On the other hand, if you should not marry, and if good fortune should befall me, it shall be all yours, wherever you are.

'I have put some of the stock of money I have left into your pocket; take places for yourself and your maid in the stage-coach, and go for London; I hope it will bear your charges thither, without breaking into your own. Again I sincerely ask your pardon, and will do so as often as I shall ever think of you. Adieu, my dear, for ever!—I am, your most affectionately, J.E.'

Nothing that ever befell me in my life sank so deep into my heart as this farewell. I reproached him a thousand times in my thoughts for leaving me, for I would have gone with him through the world, if I had begged my bread. I felt in my pocket, and there found ten guineas, his gold watch, and two little rings, one a small diamond ring worth only about #6, and the other a plain gold ring.

I sat me down and looked upon these things two hours together, and scarce spoke a word, till my maid interrupted me by telling me my dinner was ready. I ate but little, and after dinner I fell into a vehement fit of crying, every now and then calling him by his name, which was James. 'O Jemmy!' said I, 'come back, come back. I'll give you all I have; I'll beg, I'll starve with you.' And thus I ran raving about the room several times, and then sat down between whiles, and then walking about again, called upon him to come back, and then cried again; and thus I passed the afternoon, till about seven o'clock, when it was near dusk, in the evening, being August, when, to my unspeakable surprise, he comes back into the inn, but without a servant, and comes directly up into my chamber.

I was in the greatest confusion imaginable, and so was he too. I could not imagine what should be the occasion of it, and began to be at odds with myself whether to be glad or sorry; but my affection biassed all the rest, and it was impossible to conceal my joy, which was too great for smiles, for it burst out into tears. He was no sooner entered the room but he ran to me and took me in his arms, holding me fast, and almost stopping my breath with his kisses, but spoke not a word. At length I began. 'My dear,' said I, 'how could you go away from me?' to which he gave no answer, for it was impossible for him to speak.

When our ecstasies were a little over, he told me he was gone about fifteen miles, but it was not in his power to go any farther without coming back to see me again, and to take his leave of me once more.

I told him how I had passed my time, and how loud I had called him to come back again. He told me he heard me very plain upon Delamere Forest, at a place about twelve miles off. I smiled. 'Nay,' says he, 'do not think I am in jest, for if ever I heard your voice in my life, I heard you call me aloud, and sometimes I thought I saw you running after me.' 'Why,' said I, 'what did I say?'—for I had not named the words to him. 'You called aloud,' says he, 'and said, O Jemmy! O Jemmy! come back, come back.'

I laughed at him. 'My dear,' says he, 'do not laugh, for, depend upon it, I heard your voice as plain as you hear mine now; if you please, I'll go before a magistrate and make oath of it.' I then began to be amazed and surprised, and indeed frightened, and told him what I had really done, and how I had called after him, as above.

When we had amused ourselves a while about this, I said to him: 'Well, you shall go away from me no more; I'll go all over the world with you rather.' He told me it would be a very difficult thing for him to leave me, but since it must be, he hoped I would make it as easy to me as I could; but as for him, it would be his destruction that he foresaw.

However, he told me that he considered he had left me to travel to London alone, which was too long a journey; and that as he might as well go that way as any way else, he was resolved to see me safe thither, or near it; and if he did go away then without taking his leave, I should not take it ill of him; and this he made me promise.

He told me how he had dismissed his three servants, sold their horses, and sent the fellows away to seek their fortunes, and all in a little time, at a town on the road, I know not where. 'And,' says he, 'it cost me some tears all alone by myself, to think how much happier they were than their master, for they could go to the next gentleman's house to see for a service, whereas,' said he, 'I knew not wither to go, or what to do with myself.'

I told him I was so completely miserable in parting with him, that I could not be worse; and that now he was come again, I would not go from him, if he would take me with him, let him go whither he would, or do what he would. And in the meantime I agreed that we would go together to London; but I could not be brought to consent he should go away at last and not take his leave of me, as he proposed to do; but told him, jesting, that if he did, I would call him back again as loud as I did before. Then I pulled out his watch and gave it him back, and his two rings, and his ten guineas; but he would not take them, which made me very much suspect that he resolved to go off upon the road and leave me.

The truth is, the circumstances he was in, the passionate expressions of his letter, the kind, gentlemanly treatment I had from him in all the affair, with the concern he showed for me in it, his manner of parting with that large share which he gave me of his little stock left—all these had joined to make such impressions on me, that I really loved him most tenderly, and could not bear the thoughts of parting with him.

Two days after this we quitted Chester, I in the stage-coach, and he on horseback. I dismissed my maid at Chester. He was very much against my being without a maid, but she being a servant hired in the country, and I resolving to keep no servant at London, I told him it would have been barbarous to have taken the poor wench and have turned her away as soon as I came to town; and it would also have been a needless charge on the road, so I satisfied him, and he was easy enough on the score.

He came with me as far as Dunstable, within thirty miles of London, and then he told me fate and his own misfortunes obliged him to leave me, and that it was not convenient for him to go to London, for reasons which it was of no value to me to know, and I saw him preparing to go. The stage-coach we were in did not usually stop at Dunstable, but I desiring it but for a quart of an hour, they were content to stand at an inndoor a while, and we went into the house.

Being in the inn, I told him I had but one favour more to ask of him, and that was, that since he could not go any farther, he would give me leave to stay a week or two in the town with him, that we might in that time think of something to prevent such a ruinous thing to us both, as a final separation would be; and that I had something of moment to offer him, that I had never said yet, and which perhaps he might find practicable to our mutual advantage.

This was too reasonable a proposal to be denied, so he called the landlady of the house, and told her his wife was taken ill, and so ill that she could not think of going any farther in the stage-coach, which had tired her almost to death, and asked if she could not get us a lodging for two or three days in a private house, where I might rest me a little, for the journey had been too much for me. The landlady, a good sort of woman, well-bred and very obliging, came immediately to see me; told me she had two or three very good rooms in a part of the house quite out of the noise, and if I saw them, she did not doubt but I would like them, and I should have one of her maids, that should do nothing else but be appointed to wait on me. This was so very kind, that I could not but accept of it, and thank her; so I went to look on the rooms and liked them very well, and indeed they were extraordinarily furnished, and very pleasant lodgings; so we paid the stage-coach, took out our baggage, and resolved to stay here a while.

Here I told him I would live with him now till all my money was spent, but would not let him spend a shilling of his own. We had some kind squabble about that, but I told him it was the last time I was like to enjoy his company, and I desired he would let me be master in that thing only, and he should govern in everything else; so he acquiesced.

Here one evening, taking a walk into the fields, I told him I would now make the proposal to him I had told him of; accordingly I related to him how I had lived in Virginia, that I had a mother I believed was alive there still, though my husband was dead some years. I told him that had not my effects miscarried, which, by the way, I magnified pretty much, I might have been fortune good enough to him to have kept us from being parted in this manner. Then I entered into the manner of peoples going over to those countries to settle, how they had a quantity of land given them by the Constitution of the place; and if not, that it might be purchased at so easy a rate this it was not worth naming.

I then gave him a full and distinct account of the nature of planting; how with carrying over but two or three hundred pounds value in English goods, with some servants and tools, a man of application would presently lay a foundation for a family, and in a very few years be certain to raise an estate.

I let him into the nature of the product of the earth; how the ground was cured and prepared, and what the usual increase of it was; and demonstrated to him, that in a very few years, with such a beginning, we should be as certain of being rich as we were now certain of being poor.

He was surprised at my discourse; for we made it the whole subject of our conversation for near a week together, in which time I laid it down in black and white, as we say, that it was morally impossible, with a supposition of any reasonable good conduct, but that we must thrive there and do very well.

Then I told him what measures I would take to raise such a sum of #300 or thereabouts; and I argued with him how good a method it would be to put an end to our misfortunes and restore our circumstances in the world, to what we had both expected; and I added, that after seven years, if we lived, we might be in a posture to leave our plantations in good hands, and come over again and receive the income of it, and live here and enjoy it; and I gave him examples of some that had done so, and lived now in very good circumstances in London.

In short, I pressed him so to it, that he almost agreed to it, but still something or other broke it off again; till at last he turned the tables, and he began to talk almost to the same purpose of Ireland.

He told me that a man that could confine himself to country life, and that could find but stock to enter upon any land, should have farms there for #50 a year, as good as were here let for #200 a year; that the produce was such, and so rich the land, that if much was not laid up, we were sure to live as handsomely upon it as a gentleman of #3000 a year could do in England and that he had laid a scheme to leave me in London, and go over and try; and if he found he could lay a handsome foundation of living suitable to the respect he had for me, as he doubted not he should do, he would come over and fetch me.

I was dreadfully afraid that upon such a proposal he would have taken me at my word, viz. to sell my little income as I called it, and turn it into money, and let him carry it over into Ireland and try his experiment with it; but he was too just to desire it, or to have accepted it if I had offered it; and he anticipated me in that, for he added, that he would go and try his fortune that way, and if he found he could do anything at it to live, then, by adding mine to it when I went over, we should live like ourselves; but that he would not hazard a shilling of mine till he had made the experiment with a little, and he assured me that if he found nothing to be done in Ireland, he would then come to me and join in my project for Virginia.

He was so earnest upon his project being to be tried first, that I could not withstand him; however, he promised to let me hear from him in a very little time after his arriving there, to let me know whether his prospect answered his design, that if there was not a possibility of success, I might take the occasion to prepare for our other voyage, and then, he assured me, he would go with me to America with all his heart.

I could bring him to nothing further than this. However, those consultations entertained us near a month, during which I enjoyed his company, which indeed was the most entertaining that ever I met in my life before. In this time he let me into the whole story of his own life, which was indeed surprising, and full of an infinite variety sufficient to fill up a much brighter history, for its adventures and incidents, than any I ever say in print; but I shall have occasion to say more of him hereafter.

We parted at last, though with the utmost reluctance on my side; and indeed he took his leave very unwillingly too, but necessity obliged him, for his reasons were very good why he would not come to London, as I understood more fully some time afterwards.

I gave him a direction how to write to me, though still I reserved the grand secret, and never broke my resolution, which was not to let him ever know my true name, who I was, or where to be found; he likewise let me know how to write a letter to him, so that, he said, he would be sure to receive it.

I came to London the next day after we parted, but did not go directly to my old lodgings; but for another nameless reason took a private lodging in St. John's Street, or, as it is vulgarly called, St. Jones's, near Clerkenwell; and here, being perfectly alone, I had leisure to sit down and reflect seriously upon the last seven months' ramble I had made, for I had been abroad no less. The pleasant hours I had with my last husband I looked back on with an infinite deal of pleasure; but that pleasure was very much lessened when I found some time after that I was really with child.

This was a perplexing thing, because of the difficulty which was before me where I should get leave to lie in; it being one of the nicest things in the world at that time of day for a woman that was a stranger, and had no friends, to be entertained in that circumstance without security, which, by the way, I had not, neither could I procure any.

I had taken care all this while to preserve a correspondence with my honest friend at the bank, or rather he took care to correspond with me, for he wrote to me once a week; and though I had not spent my money so fast as to want any from him, yet I often wrote also to let him know I was alive. I had left directions in Lancashire, so that I had these letters, which he sent, conveyed to me; and during my recess at St. Jones's received a very obliging letter from him, assuring me that his process for a divorce from his wife went on with success, though he met with some difficulties in it that he did not expect.

I was not displeased with the news that his process was more tedious than he expected; for though I was in no condition to have him yet, not being so foolish to marry him when I knew myself to be with child by another man, as some I know have ventured to do, yet I was not willing to lose him, and, in a word, resolved to have him if he continued in the same mind, as soon as I was up again; for I saw apparently I should hear no more from my husband; and as he had all along pressed to marry, and had assured me he would not be at all disgusted at it, or ever offer to claim me again, so I made no scruple to resolve to do it if I could, and if my other friend stood to his bargain; and I had a great deal of reason to be assured that he would stand to it, by the letters he wrote to me, which were the kindest and most obliging that could be.

I now grew big, and the people where I lodged perceived it, and began to take notice of it to me, and, as far as civility would allow, intimated that I must think of removing. This put me to extreme perplexity, and I grew very melancholy, for indeed I knew not what course to take. I had money, but no friends, and was like to have a child upon my hands to keep, which was a difficulty I had never had upon me yet, as the particulars of my story hitherto make appear.

In the course of this affair I fell very ill, and my melancholy really increased my distemper; my illness proved at length to be only an ague, but my apprehensions were really that I should miscarry. I should not say apprehensions, for indeed I would have been glad to miscarry, but I could never be brought to entertain so much as a thought of endeavouring to miscarry, or of taking any thing to make me miscarry; I abhorred, I say, so much as the thought of it.

However, speaking of it in the house, the gentlewoman who kept the house proposed to me to send for a midwife. I scrupled it at first, but after some time consented to it, but told her I had no particular acquaintance with any midwife, and so left it to her.

It seems the mistress of the house was not so great a stranger to such cases as mine was as I thought at first she had been, as will appear presently, and she sent for a midwife of the right sort—that is to say, the right sort for me.

The woman appeared to be an experienced woman in her business, I mean as a midwife; but she had another calling too, in which she was as expert as most women if not more. My landlady had told her I was very melancholy, and that she believed that had done me harm; and once, before me, said to her, 'Mrs. B——' (meaning the midwife), 'I believe this lady's trouble is of a kind that is pretty much in your way, and therefore if you can do anything for her, pray do, for she is a very civil gentlewoman'; and so she went out of the room.

I really did not understand her, but my Mother Midnight began very seriously to explain what she mean, as soon as she was gone. 'Madam,' says she, 'you seem not to understand what your landlady means; and when you do understand it, you need not let her know at all that you do so.

'She means that you are under some circumstances that may render your lying in difficult to you, and that you are not willing to be exposed. I need say no more, but to tell you, that if you think fit to communicate so much of your case to me, if it be so, as is necessary, for I do not desire to pry into those things, I perhaps may be in a position to help you and to make you perfectly easy, and remove all your dull thoughts upon that subject.'

Every word this creature said was a cordial to me, and put new life and new spirit into my heart; my blood began to circulate immediately, and I was quite another body; I ate my victuals again, and grew better presently after it. She said a great deal more to the same purpose, and then, having pressed me to be free with her, and promised in the solemnest manner to be secret, she stopped a little, as if waiting to see what impression it made on me, and what I would say.

I was too sensible to the want I was in of such a woman, not to accept her offer; I told her my case was partly as she guessed, and partly not, for I was really married, and had a husband, though he was in such fine circumstances and so remote at that time, as that he could not appear publicly.

She took me short, and told me that was none of her business; all the ladies that came under her care were married women to her. 'Every woman,' she says, 'that is with child has a father for it,' and whether that father was a husband or no husband, was no business of hers; her business was to assist me in my present circumstances, whether I had a husband or no. 'For, madam,' says she, 'to have a husband that cannot appear, is to have no husband in the sense of the case; and, therefore, whether you are a wife or a mistress is all one to me.'

I found presently, that whether I was a whore or a wife, I was to pass for a whore here, so I let that go. I told her it was true, as she said, but that, however, if I must tell her my case, I must tell it her as it was; so I related it to her as short as I could, and I concluded it to her thus. 'I trouble you with all this, madam,' said I, 'not that, as you said before, it is much to the purpose in your affair, but this is to the purpose, namely, that I am not in any pain about being seen, or being public or concealed, for 'tis perfectly indifferent to me; but my difficulty is, that I have no acquaintance in this part of the nation.'

'I understand you, madam' says she; 'you have no security to bring to prevent the parish impertinences usual in such cases, and perhaps,' says she, 'do not know very well how to dispose of the child when it comes.' 'The last,' says I, 'is not so much my concern as the first.' 'Well, madam,' answered the midwife, 'dare you put yourself into my hands? I live in such a place; though I do not inquire after you, you may inquire after me. My name is B——; I live in such a street'—naming the street—'at the sign of the Cradle. My profession is a midwife, and I have many ladies that come to my house to lie in. I have given security to the parish in general terms to secure them from any charge from whatsoever shall come into the world under my roof. I have but one question to ask in the whole affair, madam,' says she, 'and if that be answered you shall be entirely easy for all the rest.'

I presently understood what she meant, and told her, 'Madam, I believe I understand you. I thank God, though I want friends in this part of the world, I do not want money, so far as may be necessary, though I do not abound in that neither': this I added because I would not make her expect great things. 'Well, madam,' says she, 'that is the thing indeed, without which nothing can be done in these cases; and yet,' says she, 'you shall see that I will not impose upon you, or offer anything that is unkind to you, and if you desire it, you shall know everything beforehand, that you may suit yourself to the occasion, and be neither costly or sparing as you see fit.'

I told her she seemed to be so perfectly sensible of my condition, that I had nothing to ask of her but this, that as I had told her that I had money sufficient, but not a great quantity, she would order it so that I might be at as little superfluous charge as possible.

She replied that she would bring in an account of the expenses of it in two or three shapes, and like a bill of fare, I should choose as I pleased; and I desired her to do so.

The next day she brought it, and the copy of her three bills was a follows:—

1. For three months' lodging in her house, including my diet, at 10s. a week . . . . 6#, 0s., 0d.

2. For a nurse for the month, and use of childbed linen . . . . 1#, 10s., 0d.

3. For a minister to christen the child, and to the godfathers and clerk . . . . 1#, 10s., 0d.

4. For a supper at the christening if I had five friends at it . . . . 1#, 0s., 0d.

For her fees as a midwife, and the taking off the trouble of the parish . . . . 3#, 3s., 0d.

To her maid servant attending . . . . 0#, 10s., 0d.

13#, 13s., 0d.

This was the first bill; the second was the same terms:—

1. For three months' lodging and diet, etc., at 20s. per week . . . . 13#, 0s., 0d.

2. For a nurse for the month, and the use of linen and lace . . . . 2#, 10s., 0d.

3. For the minister to christen the child, etc., as above . . . . 2#, 0s., 0d.

4. For supper and for sweetmeats . . . . 3#, 3s., 0d.

For her fees as above . . . . 5#, 5s., 0d.

For a servant-maid . . . . 1#, 0s., 0d.

26#, 18s., 0d.

This was the second-rate bill; the third, she said, was for a degree higher, and when the father or friends appeared:—

1. For three months' lodging and diet, having two
rooms and a garret for a servant . . . . . . 30#, 0s., 0d.,

2. For a nurse for the month, and the finest suit
of childbed linen . . . . 4#, 4s., 0d.

3. For the minister to christen the child, etc. 2#, 10s., 0d.

4. For a supper, the gentlemen to send in the
wine . . . . 6#, 0s., 0d.

For my fees, etc. . . . . 10#, 10s., 0d.

The maid, besides their own maid, only
. . . . 0#, 10s., 0d.

53#, 14s., 0d.

I looked upon all three bills, and smiled, and told her I did not see but that she was very reasonable in her demands, all things considered, and for that I did not doubt but her accommodations were good.

She told me I should be judge of that when I saw them. I told her I was sorry to tell her that I feared I must be her lowest-rated customer. 'And perhaps, madam,' said I, 'you will make me the less welcome upon that account.' 'No, not at all,' said she; 'for where I have one of the third sort I have two of the second, and four to one of the first, and I get as much by them in proportion as by any; but if you doubt my care of you, I will allow any friend you have to overlook and see if you are well waited on or no.'

Then she explained the particulars of her bill. 'In the first place, madam,' said she, 'I would have you observe that here is three months' keeping; you are but ten shillings a week; I undertake to say you will not complain of my table. I suppose,' says she, 'you do not live cheaper where you are now?' 'No, indeed,' said I, 'not so cheap, for I give six shillings per week for my chamber, and find my own diet as well as I can, which costs me a great deal more.'

'Then, madam,' says she, 'if the child should not live, or should be dead-born, as you know sometimes happens, then there is the minister's article saved; and if you have no friends to come to you, you may save the expense of a supper; so that take those articles out, madam,' says she, 'your lying in will not cost you above #5, 3s. in all more than your ordinary charge of living.'

This was the most reasonable thing that I ever heard of; so I smiled, and told her I would come and be her customer; but I told her also, that as I had two months and more to do, I might perhaps be obliged to stay longer with her than three months, and desired to know if she would not be obliged to remove me before it was proper. No, she said; her house was large, and besides, she never put anybody to remove, that had lain in, till they were willing to go; and if she had more ladies offered, she was not so ill-beloved among her neighbours but she could provide accommodations for twenty, if there was occasion.

I found she was an eminent lady in her way; and, in short, I agreed to put myself into her hands, and promised her. She then talked of other things, looked about into my accommodations where I was, found fault with my wanting attendance and conveniences, and that I should not be used so at her house. I told her I was shy of speaking, for the woman of the house looked stranger, or at least I thought so, since I had been ill, because I was with child; and I was afraid she would put some affront or other upon me, supposing that I had been able to give but a slight account of myself.

'Oh dear,' said she, 'her ladyship is no stranger to these things; she has tried to entertain ladies in your condition several times, but she could not secure the parish; and besides, she is not such a nice lady as you take her to be; however, since you are a-going, you shall not meddle with her, but I'll see you are a little better looked after while you are here than I think you are, and it shall not cost you the more neither.'

I did not understand her at all; however, I thanked her, and so we parted. The next morning she sent me a chicken roasted and hot, and a pint bottle of sherry, and ordered the maid to tell me that she was to wait on me every day as long as I stayed there.

This was surprisingly good and kind, and I accepted it very willingly. At night she sent to me again, to know if I wanted anything, and how I did, and to order the maid to come to her in the morning with my dinner. The maid had orders to make me some chocolate in the morning before she came away, and did so, and at noon she brought me the sweetbread of a breast of veal, whole, and a dish of soup for my dinner; and after this manner she nursed me up at a distance, so that I was mightily well pleased, and quickly well, for indeed my dejections before were the principal part of my illness.

I expected, as is usually the case among such people, that the servant she sent me would have been some imprudent brazen wench of Drury Lane breeding, and I was very uneasy at having her with me upon that account; so I would not let her lie in that house the first night by any means, but had my eyes about me as narrowly as if she had been a public thief.

My gentlewoman guessed presently what was the matter, and sent her back with a short note, that I might depend upon the honesty of her maid; that she would be answerable for her upon all accounts; and that she took no servants into her house without very good security for their fidelity. I was then perfectly easy; and indeed the maid's behaviour spoke for itself, for a modester, quieter, soberer girl never came into anybody's family, and I found her so afterwards.

As soon as I was well enough to go abroad, I went with the maid to see the house, and to see the apartment I was to have; and everything was so handsome and so clean and well, that, in short, I had nothing to say, but was wonderfully pleased and satisfied with what I had met with, which, considering the melancholy circumstances I was in, was far beyond what I looked for.

It might be expected that I should give some account of the nature of the wicked practices of this woman, in whose hands I was now fallen; but it would be too much encouragement to the vice, to let the world see what easy measures were here taken to rid the women's unwelcome burthen of a child clandestinely gotten. This grave matron had several sorts of practice, and this was one particular, that if a child was born, though not in her house (for she had occasion to be called to many private labours), she had people at hand, who for a piece of money would take the child off their hands, and off from the hands of the parish too; and those children, as she said, were honestly provided for and taken care of. What should become of them all, considering so many, as by her account she was concerned with, I cannot conceive.

I had many times discourses upon that subject with her; but she was full of this argument, that she save the life of many an innocent lamb, as she called them, which would otherwise perhaps have been murdered; and of many women who, made desperate by the misfortune, would otherwise be tempted to destroy their children, and bring themselves to the gallows. I granted her that this was true, and a very commendable thing, provided the poor children fell into good hands afterwards, and were not abused, starved, and neglected by the nurses that bred them up. She answered, that she always took care of that, and had no nurses in her business but what were very good, honest people, and such as might be depended upon.

I could say nothing to the contrary, and so was obliged to say, 'Madam, I do not question you do your part honestly, but what those people do afterwards is the main question'; and she stopped my mouth again with saying that she took the utmost care about it.

The only thing I found in all her conversation on these subjects that gave me any distaste, was, that one time in discouraging about my being far gone with child, and the time I expected to come, she said something that looked as if she could help me off with my burthen sooner, if I was willing; or, in English, that she could give me something to make me miscarry, if I had a desire to put an end to my troubles that way; but I soon let her see that I abhorred the thoughts of it; and, to do her justice, she put it off so cleverly, that I could not say she really intended it, or whether she only mentioned the practice as a horrible thing; for she couched her words so well, and took my meaning so quickly, that she gave her negative before I could explain myself.

To bring this part into as narrow a compass as possible, I quitted my lodging at St. Jones's and went to my new governess, for so they called her in the house, and there I was indeed treated with so much courtesy, so carefully looked to, so handsomely provided, and everything so well, that I was surprised at it, and could not at first see what advantage my governess made of it; but I found afterwards that she professed to make no profit of lodgers' diet, nor indeed could she get much by it, but that her profit lay in the other articles of her management, and she made enough that way, I assure you; for 'tis scarce credible what practice she had, as well abroad as at home, and yet all upon the private account, or, in plain English, the whoring account.

While I was in her house, which was near four months, she had no less than twelve ladies of pleasure brought to bed within the doors, and I think she had two-and-thirty, or thereabouts, under her conduct without doors, whereof one, as nice as she was with me, was lodged with my old landlady at St. Jones's.

This was a strange testimony of the growing vice of the age, and such a one, that as bad as I had been myself, it shocked my very senses. I began to nauseate the place I was in and, about all, the wicked practice; and yet I must say that I never saw, or do I believe there was to be seen, the least indecency in the house the whole time I was there.

Not a man was ever seen to come upstairs, except to visit the lying-in ladies within their month, nor then without the old lady with them, who made it a piece of honour of her management that no man should touch a woman, no, not his own wife, within the month; nor would she permit any man to lie in the house upon any pretence whatever, no, not though she was sure it was with his own wife; and her general saying for it was, that she cared not how many children were born in her house, but she would have none got there if she could help it.

It might perhaps be carried further than was needful, but it was an error of the right hand if it was an error, for by this she kept up the reputation, such as it was, of her business, and obtained this character, that though she did take care of the women when they were debauched, yet she was not instrumental to their being debauched at all; and yet it was a wicked trade she drove too.

While I was there, and before I was brought to bed, I received a letter from my trustee at the bank, full of kind, obliging things, and earnestly pressing me to return to London. It was near a fortnight old when it came to me, because it had been first sent into Lancashire, and then returned to me. He concludes with telling me that he had obtained a decree, I think he called it, against his wife, and that he would be ready to make good his engagement to me, if I would accept of him, adding a great many protestations of kindness and affection, such as he would have been far from offering if he had known the circumstances I had been in, and which as it was I had been very far from deserving.

I returned an answer to his letter, and dated it at Liverpool, but sent it by messenger, alleging that it came in cover to a friend in town. I gave him joy of his deliverance, but raised some scruples at the lawfulness of his marrying again, and told him I supposed he would consider very seriously upon that point before he resolved on it, the consequence being too great for a man of his judgment to venture rashly upon a thing of that nature; so concluded, wishing him very well in whatever he resolved, without letting him into anything of my own mind, or giving any answer to his proposal of my coming to London to him, but mentioned at a distance my intention to return the latter end of the year, this being dated in April.

I was brought to bed about the middle of May and had another brave boy, and myself in as good condition as usual on such occasions. My governess did her part as a midwife with the greatest art and dexterity imaginable, and far beyond all that ever I had had any experience of before.

Her care of me in my travail, and after in my lying in, was such, that if she had been my own mother it could not have been better. Let none be encouraged in their loose practices from this dexterous lady's management, for she is gone to her place, and I dare say has left nothing behind her that can or will come up on it.

I think I had been brought to bed about twenty-two days when I received another letter from my friend at the bank, with the surprising news that he had obtained a final sentence of divorce against his wife, and had served her with it on such a day, and that he had such an answer to give to all my scruples about his marrying again, as I could not expect, and as he had no desire of; for that his wife, who had been under some remorse before for her usage of him, as soon as she had the account that he had gained his point, had very unhappily destroyed herself that same evening.

He expressed himself very handsomely as to his being concerned at her disaster, but cleared himself of having any hand in it, and that he had only done himself justice in a case in which he was notoriously injured and abused. However, he said that he was extremely afflicted at it, and had no view of any satisfaction left in his world, but only in the hope that I would come and relieve him by my company; and then he pressed me violently indeed to give him some hopes that I would at least come up to town and let him see me, when he would further enter into discourse about it.

I was exceedingly surprised at the news, and began now seriously to reflect on my present circumstances, and the inexpressible misfortune it was to me to have a child upon my hands, and what to do in it I knew not. At last I opened my case at a distance to my governess. I appeared melancholy and uneasy for several days, and she lay at me continually to know what trouble me. I could not for my life tell her that I had an offer of marriage, after I had so often told her that I had a husband, so that I really knew not what to say to her. I owned I had something which very much troubled me, but at the same time told her I could not speak of it to any one alive.

She continued importuning me several days, but it was impossible, I told her, for me to commit the secret to anybody. This, instead of being an answer to her, increased her importunities; she urged her having been trusted with the greatest secrets of this nature, that it was her business to conceal everything, and that to discover things of that nature would be her ruin. She asked me if ever I had found her tattling to me of other people's affairs, and how could I suspect her? She told me, to unfold myself to her was telling it to nobody; that she was silent as death; that it must be a very strange case indeed that she could not help me out of; but to conceal it was to deprive myself of all possible help, or means of help, and to deprive her of the opportunity of serving me. In short, she had such a bewitching eloquence, and so great a power of persuasion that there was no concealing anything from her.

So I resolved to unbosom myself to her. I told her the history of my Lancashire marriage, and how both of us had been disappointed; how we came together, and how we parted; how he absolutely discharged me, as far as lay in him, free liberty to marry again, protesting that if he knew it he would never claim me, or disturb or expose me; that I thought I was free, but was dreadfully afraid to venture, for fear of the consequences that might follow in case of a discovery.

Then I told her what a good offer I had; showed her my friend's two last letters, inviting me to come to London, and let her see with what affection and earnestness they were written, but blotted out the name, and also the story about the disaster of his wife, only that she was dead.

She fell a-laughing at my scruples about marrying, and told me the other was no marriage, but a cheat on both sides; and that, as we were parted by mutual consent, the nature of the contract was destroyed, and the obligation was mutually discharged. She had arguments for this at the tip of her tongue; and, in short, reasoned me out of my reason; not but that it was too by the help of my own inclination.

But then came the great and main difficulty, and that was the child; this, she told me in so many words, must be removed, and that so as that it should never be possible for any one to discover it. I knew there was no marrying without entirely concealing that I had had a child, for he would soon have discovered by the age of it that it was born, nay, and gotten too, since my parley with him, and that would have destroyed all the affair.

But it touched my heart so forcibly to think of parting entirely with the child, and, for aught I knew, of having it murdered, or starved by neglect and ill-usage (which was much the same), that I could not think of it without horror. I wish all those women who consent to the disposing their children out of the way, as it is called, for decency sake, would consider that 'tis only a contrived method for murder; that is to say, a-killing their children with safety.

It is manifest to all that understand anything of children, that we are born into the world helpless, and incapable either to supply our own wants or so much as make them known; and that without help we must perish; and this help requires not only an assisting hand, whether of the mother or somebody else, but there are two things necessary in that assisting hand, that is, care and skill; without both which, half the children that are born would die, nay, though they were not to be denied food; and one half more of those that remained would be cripples or fools, lose their limbs, and perhaps their sense. I question not but that these are partly the reasons why affection was placed by nature in the hearts of mothers to their children; without which they would never be able to give themselves up, as 'tis necessary they should, to the care and waking pains needful to the support of their children.

Since this care is needful to the life of children, to neglect them is to murder them; again, to give them up to be managed by those people who have none of that needful affection placed by nature in them, is to neglect them in the highest degree; nay, in some it goes farther, and is a neglect in order to their being lost; so that 'tis even an intentional murder, whether the child lives or dies.

All those things represented themselves to my view, and that is the blackest and most frightful form: and as I was very free with my governess, whom I had now learned to call mother, I represented to her all the dark thoughts which I had upon me about it, and told her what distress I was in. She seemed graver by much at this part than at the other; but as she was hardened in these things beyond all possibility of being touched with the religious part, and the scruples about the murder, so she was equally impenetrable in that part which related to affection. She asked me if she had not been careful and tender to me in my lying in, as if I had been her own child. I told her I owned she had. 'Well, my dear,' says she, 'and when you are gone, what are you to me? And what would it be to me if you were to be hanged? Do you think there are not women who, as it is their trade and they get their bread by it, value themselves upon their being as careful of children as their own mothers can be, and understand it rather better? Yes, yes, child,' says she, 'fear it not; how were we nursed ourselves? Are you sure you was nursed up by your own mother? and yet you look fat and fair, child,' says the old beldam; and with that she stroked me over the face. 'Never be concerned, child,' says she, going on in her drolling way; 'I have no murderers about me; I employ the best and the honestest nurses that can be had, and have as few children miscarry under their hands as there would if they were all nursed by mothers; we want neither care nor skill.'

She touched me to the quick when she asked if I was sure that I was nursed by my own mother; on the contrary I was sure I was not; and I trembled, and looked pale at the very expression. 'Sure,' said I to myself, 'this creature cannot be a witch, or have any conversation with a spirit, that can inform her what was done with me before I was able to know it myself'; and I looked at her as if I had been frightened; but reflecting that it could not be possible for her to know anything about me, that disorder went off, and I began to be easy, but it was not presently.

She perceived the disorder I was in, but did not know the meaning of it; so she ran on in her wild talk upon the weakness of my supposing that children were murdered because they were not all nursed by the mother, and to persuade me that the children she disposed of were as well used as if the mothers had the nursing of them themselves.

'It may be true, mother,' says I, 'for aught I know, but my doubts are very strongly grounded indeed.' 'Come, then,' says she, 'let's hear some of them.' 'Why, first,' says I, 'you give a piece of money to these people to take the child off the parent's hands, and to take care of it as long as it lives. Now we know, mother,' said I, 'that those are poor people, and their gain consists in being quit of the charge as soon as they can; how can I doubt but that, as it is best for them to have the child die, they are not over solicitous about life?'

'This is all vapours and fancy,' says the old woman; 'I tell you their credit depends upon the child's life, and they are as careful as any mother of you all.'

'O mother,' says I, 'if I was but sure my little baby would be carefully looked to, and have justice done it, I should be happy indeed; but it is impossible I can be satisfied in that point unless I saw it, and to see it would be ruin and destruction to me, as now my case stands; so what to do I know not.'

'A fine story!' says the governess. 'You would see the child, and you would not see the child; you would be concealed and discovered both together. These are things impossible, my dear; so you must e'en do as other conscientious mothers have done before you, and be contented with things as they must be, though they are not as you wish them to be.'

I understood what she meant by conscientious mothers; she would have said conscientious whores, but she was not willing to disoblige me, for really in this case I was not a whore, because legally married, the force of former marriage excepted.

However, let me be what I would, I was not come up to that pitch of hardness common to the profession; I mean, to be unnatural, and regardless of the safety of my child; and I preserved this honest affection so long, that I was upon the point of giving up my friend at the bank, who lay so hard at me to come to him and marry him, that, in short, there was hardly any room to deny him.

At last my old governess came to me, with her usual assurance. 'Come, my dear,' says she, 'I have found out a way how you shall be at a certainty that your child shall be used well, and yet the people that take care of it shall never know you, or who the mother of the child is.'

'Oh mother,' says I, 'if you can do so, you will engage me to you for ever.' 'Well,' says she, 'are you willing to be a some small annual expense, more than what we usually give to the people we contract with?' 'Ay,' says I, 'with all my heart, provided I may be concealed.' 'As to that,' says the governess, 'you shall be secure, for the nurse shall never so much as dare to inquire about you, and you shall once or twice a year go with me and see your child, and see how 'tis used, and be satisfied that it is in good hands, nobody knowing who you are.'

'Why,' said I, 'do you think, mother, that when I come to see my child, I shall be able to conceal my being the mother of it? Do you think that possible?'

'Well, well,' says my governess, 'if you discover it, the nurse shall be never the wiser; for she shall be forbid to ask any questions about you, or to take any notice. If she offers it, she shall lose the money which you are suppose to give her, and the child shall be taken from her too.'

I was very well pleased with this. So the next week a countrywoman was brought from Hertford, or thereabouts, who was to take the child off our hands entirely for #10 in money. But if I would allow #5 a year more of her, she would be obliged to bring the child to my governess's house as often as we desired, or we should come down and look at it, and see how well she used it.

The woman was very wholesome-looking, a likely woman, a cottager's wife, but she had very good clothes and linen, and everything well about her; and with a heavy heart and many a tear, I let her have my child. I had been down at Hertford, and looked at her and at her dwelling, which I liked well enough; and I promised her great things if she would be kind to the child, so she knew at first word that I was the child's mother. But she seemed to be so much out of the way, and to have no room to inquire after me, that I thought I was safe enough. So, in short, I consented to let her have the child, and I gave her #10; that is to say, I gave it to my governess, who gave it the poor woman before my face, she agreeing never to return the child back to me, or to claim anything more for its keeping or bringing up; only that I promised, if she took a great deal of care of it, I would give her something more as often as I came to see it; so that I was not bound to pay the #5, only that I promised my governess I would do it. And thus my great care was over, after a manner, which though it did not at all satisfy my mind, yet was the most convenient for me, as my affairs then stood, of any that could be thought of at that time.

I then began to write to my friend at the bank in a more kindly style, and particularly about the beginning of July I sent him a letter, that I proposed to be in town some time in August. He returned me an answer in the most passionate terms imaginable, and desired me to let him have timely notice, and he would come and meet me, two day's journey. This puzzled me scurvily, and I did not know what answer to make of it. Once I resolved to take the stage-coach to West Chester, on purpose only to have the satisfaction of coming back, that he might see me really come in the same coach; for I had a jealous thought, though I had no ground for it at all, lest he should think I was not really in the country. And it was no ill-grounded thought as you shall hear presently.

I endeavoured to reason myself out of it, but it was in vain; the impression lay so strong on my mind, that it was not to be resisted. At last it came as an addition to my new design of going into the country, that it would be an excellent blind to my old governess, and would cover entirely all my other affairs, for she did not know in the least whether my new lover lived in London or in Lancashire; and when I told her my resolution, she was fully persuaded it was in Lancashire.

Having taken my measure for this journey I let her know it, and sent the maid that tended me, from the beginning, to take a place for me in the coach. She would have had me let the maid have waited on me down to the last stage, and come up again in the waggon, but I convinced her it would not be convenient. When I went away, she told me she would enter into no measures for correspondence, for she saw evidently that my affection to my child would cause me to write to her, and to visit her too when I came to town again. I assured her it would, and so took my leave, well satisfied to have been freed from such a house, however good my accommodations there had been, as I have related above.

I took the place in the coach not to its full extent, but to a place called Stone, in Cheshire, I think it is, where I not only had no manner of business, but not so much as the least acquaintance with any person in the town or near it. But I knew that with money in the pocket one is at home anywhere; so I lodged there two or three days, till, watching my opportunity, I found room in another stage-coach, and took passage back again for London, sending a letter to my gentleman that I should be such a certain day at Stony-Stratford, where the coachman told me he was to lodge.

It happened to be a chance coach that I had taken up, which, having been hired on purpose to carry some gentlemen to West Chester who were going for Ireland, was now returning, and did not tie itself to exact times or places as the stages did; so that, having been obliged to lie still on Sunday, he had time to get himself ready to come out, which otherwise he could not have done.

However, his warning was so short, that he could not reach to Stony-Stratford time enough to be with me at night, but he met me at a place called Brickhill the next morning, as we were just coming in to tow.

I confess I was very glad to see him, for I had thought myself a little disappointed over-night, seeing I had gone so far to contrive my coming on purpose. He pleased me doubly too by the figure he came in, for he brought a very handsome (gentleman's) coach and four horses, with a servant to attend him.

He took me out of the stage-coach immediately, which stopped at an inn in Brickhill; and putting into the same inn, he set up his own coach, and bespoke his dinner. I asked him what he meant by that, for I was for going forward with the journey. He said, No, I had need of a little rest upon the road, and that was a very good sort of a house, though it was but a little town; so we would go no farther that night, whatever came of it.

I did not press him much, for since he had come so to meet me, and put himself to so much expense, it was but reasonable I should oblige him a little too; so I was easy as to that point.

After dinner we walked to see the town, to see the church, and to view the fields, and the country, as is usual for strangers to do; and our landlord was our guide in going to see the church. I observed my gentleman inquired pretty much about the parson, and I took the hint immediately that he certainly would propose to be married; and though it was a sudden thought, it followed presently, that, in short, I would not refuse him; for, to be plain, with my circumstances I was in no condition now to say No; I had no reason now to run any more such hazards.

But while these thoughts ran round in my head, which was the work but of a few moments, I observed my landlord took him aside and whispered to him, though not very softly neither, for so much I overheard: 'Sir, if you shall have occasion———' the rest I could not hear, but it seems it was to this purpose: 'Sir, if you shall have occasion for a minister, I have a friend a little way off that will serve you, and be as private as you please.' My gentleman answered loud enough for me to hear, 'Very well, I believe I shall.'

I was no sooner come back to the inn but he fell upon me with irresistible words, that since he had had the good fortune to meet me, and everything concurred, it would be hastening his felicity if I would put an end to the matter just there. 'What do you mean?' says I, colouring a little. 'What, in an inn, and upon the road! Bless us all,' said I, as if I had been surprised, 'how can you talk so?' 'Oh, I can talk so very well,' says he, 'I came a-purpose to talk so, and I'll show you that I did'; and with that he pulls out a great bundle of papers. 'You fright me,' said I; 'what are all these?' 'Don't be frighted, my dear,' said he, and kissed me. This was the first time that he had been so free to call me 'my dear'; then he repeated it, 'Don't be frighted; you shall see what it is all'; then he laid them all abroad. There was first the deed or sentence of divorce from his wife, and the full evidence of her playing the whore; then there were the certificates of the minister and churchwardens of the parish where she lived, proving that she was buried, and intimating the manner of her death; the copy of the coroner's warrant for a jury to sit upon her, and the verdict of the jury, who brought it in Non compos mentis. All this was indeed to the purpose, and to give me satisfaction, though, by the way, I was not so scrupulous, had he known all, but that I might have taken him without it. However, I looked them all over as well as I could, and told him that this was all very clear indeed, but that he need not have given himself the trouble to have brought them out with him, for it was time enough. Well, he said, it might be time enough for me, but no time but the present time was time enough for him.

There were other papers rolled up, and I asked him what they were. 'Why, ay,' says he, 'that's the question I wanted to have you ask me'; so he unrolls them and takes out a little shagreen case, and gives me out of it a very fine diamond ring. I could not refuse it, if I had a mind to do so, for he put it upon my finger; so I made him a curtsy and accepted it. Then he takes out another ring: 'And this,' says he, 'is for another occasion,' so he puts that in his pocket. 'Well, but let me see it, though,' says I, and smiled; 'I guess what it is; I think you are mad.' 'I should have been mad if I had done less,' says he, and still he did not show me, and I had a great mind to see it; so I says, 'Well, but let me see it.' 'Hold,' says he, 'first look here'; then he took up the roll again and read it, and behold! it was a licence for us to be married. 'Why,' says I, 'are you distracted? Why, you were fully satisfied that I would comply and yield at first word, or resolved to take no denial.' 'The last is certainly the case,' said he. 'But you may be mistaken,' said I. 'No, no,' says he, 'how can you think so? I must not be denied, I can't be denied'; and with that he fell to kissing me so violently, I could not get rid of him.

There was a bed in the room, and we were walking to and again, eager in the discourse; at last he takes me by surprise in his arms, and threw me on the bed and himself with me, and holding me fast in his arms, but without the least offer of any indecency, courted me to consent with such repeated entreaties and arguments, protesting his affection, and vowing he would not let me go till I had promised him, that at last I said, 'Why, you resolve not to be denied, indeed, I can't be denied.' 'Well, well,' said I, and giving him a slight kiss, 'then you shan't be denied,' said I; 'let me get up.'

He was so transported with my consent, and the kind manner of it, that I began to think once he took it for a marriage, and would not stay for the form; but I wronged him, for he gave over kissing me, and then giving me two or three kisses again, thanked me for my kind yielding to him; and was so overcome with the satisfaction and joy of it, that I saw tears stand in his eyes.

I turned from him, for it filled my eyes with tears too, and I asked him leave to retire a little to my chamber. If ever I had a grain of true repentance for a vicious and abominable life for twenty-four years past, it was then. On, what a felicity is it to mankind, said I to myself, that they cannot see into the hearts of one another! How happy had it been for me if I had been wife to a man of so much honesty, and so much affection from the beginning!

Then it occurred to me, 'What an abominable creature am I! and how is this innocent gentleman going to be abused by me! How little does he think, that having divorced a whore, he is throwing himself into the arms of another! that he is going to marry one that has lain with two brothers, and has had three children by her own brother! one that was born in Newgate, whose mother was a whore, and is now a transported thief! one that has lain with thirteen men, and has had a child since he saw me! Poor gentleman!' said I, 'what is he going to do?' After this reproaching myself was over, it following thus: 'Well, if I must be his wife, if it please God to give me grace, I'll be a true wife to him, and love him suitably to the strange excess of his passion for me; I will make him amends if possible, by what he shall see, for the cheats and abuses I put upon him, which he does not see.'

He was impatient for my coming out of my chamber, but finding me long, he went downstairs and talked with my landlord about the parson.

My landlord, an officious though well-meaning fellow, had sent away for the neighbouring clergyman; and when my gentleman began to speak of it to him, and talk of sending for him, 'Sir,' says he to him, 'my friend is in the house'; so without any more words he brought them together. When he came to the minister, he asked him if he would venture to marry a couple of strangers that were both willing. The parson said that Mr. ——— had said something to him of it; that he hoped it was no clandestine business; that he seemed to be a grave gentleman, and he supposed madam was not a girl, so that the consent of friends should be wanted. 'To put you out of doubt of that,' says my gentleman, 'read this paper'; and out he pulls the license. 'I am satisfied,' says the minister; 'where is the lady?' 'You shall see her presently,' says my gentleman.

When he had said thus he comes upstairs, and I was by that time come out of my room; so he tells me the minister was below, and that he had talked with him, and that upon showing him the license, he was free to marry us with all his heart, 'but he asks to see you'; so he asked if I would let him come up.

"Tis time enough,' said I, 'in the morning, is it not?' 'Why,' said he, 'my dear, he seemed to scruple whether it was not some young girl stolen from her parents, and I assured him we were both of age to command our own consent; and that made him ask to see you.' 'Well,' said I, 'do as you please'; so up they brings the parson, and a merry, good sort of gentleman he was. He had been told, it seems, that we had met there by accident, that I came in the Chester coach, and my gentleman in his own coach to meet me; that we were to have met last night at Stony-Stratford, but that he could not reach so far. 'Well, sir,' says the parson, 'every ill turn has some good in it. The disappointment, sir,' says he to my gentleman, 'was yours, and the good turn is mine, for if you had met at Stony-Stratford I had not had the honour to marry you. Landlord, have you a Common Prayer Book?'

I started as if I had been frightened. 'Lord, sir,' says I, 'what do you mean? What, to marry in an inn, and at night too?' 'Madam,' says the minister, 'if you will have it be in the church, you shall; but I assure you your marriage will be as firm here as in the church; we are not tied by the canons to marry nowhere but in the church; and if you will have it in the church, it will be a public as a county fair; and as for the time of day, it does not at all weigh in this case; our princes are married in their chambers, and at eight or ten o'clock at night.'

I was a great while before I could be persuaded, and pretended not to be willing at all to be married but in the church. But it was all grimace; so I seemed at last to be prevailed on, and my landlord and his wife and daughter were called up. My landlord was father and clerk and all together, and we were married, and very merry we were; though I confess the self-reproaches which I had upon me before lay close to me, and extorted every now and then a deep sigh from me, which my bridegroom took notice of, and endeavoured to encourage me, thinking, poor man, that I had some little hesitations at the step I had taken so hastily.

We enjoyed ourselves that evening completely, and yet all was kept so private in the inn that not a servant in the house knew of it, for my landlady and her daughter waited on me, and would not let any of the maids come upstairs, except while we were at supper. My landlady's daughter I called my bridesmaid; and sending for a shopkeeper the next morning, I gave the young woman a good suit of knots, as good as the town would afford, and finding it was a lace-making town, I gave her mother a piece of bone-lace for a head.

One reason that my landlord was so close was, that he was unwilling the minister of the parish should hear of it; but for all that somebody heard of it, so at that we had the bells set a-ringing the next morning early, and the music, such as the town would afford, under our window; but my landlord brazened it out, that we were married before we came thither, only that, being his former guests, we would have our wedding-supper at his house.

We could not find in our hearts to stir the next day; for, in short, having been disturbed by the bells in the morning, and having perhaps not slept overmuch before, we were so sleepy afterwards that we lay in bed till almost twelve o'clock.

I begged my landlady that we might not have any more music in the town, nor ringing of bells, and she managed it so well that we were very quiet; but an odd passage interrupted all my mirth for a good while. The great room of the house looked into the street, and my new spouse being belowstairs, I had walked to the end of the room; and it being a pleasant, warm day, I had opened the window, and was standing at it for some air, when I saw three gentlemen come by on horseback and go into an inn just against us.

It was not to be concealed, nor was it so doubtful as to leave me any room to question it, but the second of the three was my Lancashire husband. I was frightened to death; I never was in such a consternation in my life; I though I should have sunk into the ground; my blood ran chill in my veins, and I trembled as if I had been in a cold fit of ague. I say, there was no room to question the truth of it; I knew his clothes, I knew his horse, and I knew his face.

The first sensible reflect I made was, that my husband was not by to see my disorder, and that I was very glad of it. The gentlemen had not been long in the house but they came to the window of their room, as is usual; but my window was shut, you may be sure. However, I could not keep from peeping at them, and there I saw him again, heard him call out to one of the servants of the house for something he wanted, and received all the terrifying confirmations of its being the same person that were possible to be had.

My next concern was to know, if possible, what was his business there; but that was impossible. Sometimes my imagination formed an idea of one frightful thing, sometimes of another; sometime I thought he had discovered me, and was come to upbraid me with ingratitude and breach of honour; and every moment I fancied he was coming up the stairs to insult me; and innumerable fancies came into my head of what was never in his head, nor ever could be, unless the devil had revealed it to him.

I remained in this fright nearly two hours, and scarce ever kept my eye from the window or door of the inn where they were. At last, hearing a great clatter in the passage of their inn, I ran to the window, and, to my great satisfaction, saw them all three go out again and travel on westward. Had they gone towards London, I should have been still in a fright, lest I should meet him on the road again, and that he should know me; but he went the contrary way, and so I was eased of that disorder.

We resolved to be going the next day, but about six o'clock at night we were alarmed with a great uproar in the street, and people riding as if they had been out of their wits; and what was it but a hue-and-cry after three highwaymen that had robbed two coaches and some other travellers near Dunstable Hill, and notice had, it seems, been given that they had been seen at Brickhill at such a house, meaning the house where those gentlemen had been.

The house was immediately beset and searched, but there were witnesses enough that the gentlemen had been gone over three hours. The crowd having gathered about, we had the news presently; and I was heartily concerned now another way. I presently told the people of the house, that I durst to say those were not the persons, for that I knew one of the gentlemen to be a very honest person, and of a good estate in Lancashire.

The constable who came with the hue-and-cry was immediately informed of this, and came over to me to be satisfied from my own mouth, and I assured him that I saw the three gentlemen as I was at the window; that I saw them afterwards at the windows of the room they dined in; that I saw them afterwards take horse, and I could assure him I knew one of them to be such a man, that he was a gentleman of a very good estate, and an undoubted character in Lancashire, from whence I was just now upon my journey.

The assurance with which I delivered this gave the mob gentry a check, and gave the constable such satisfaction, that he immediately sounded a retreat, told his people these were not the men, but that he had an account they were very honest gentlemen; and so they went all back again. What the truth of the matter was I knew not, but certain it was that the coaches were robbed at Dunstable Hill, and #560 in money taken; besides, some of the lace merchants that always travel that way had been visited too. As to the three gentlemen, that remains to be explained hereafter.

Well, this alarm stopped us another day, though my spouse was for travelling, and told me that it was always safest travelling after a robbery, for that the thieves were sure to be gone far enough off when they had alarmed the country; but I was afraid and uneasy, and indeed principally lest my old acquaintance should be upon the road still, and should chance to see me.

I never lived four pleasanter days together in my life. I was a mere bride all this while, and my new spouse strove to make me entirely easy in everything. Oh could this state of life have continued, how had all my past troubles been forgot, and my future sorrows avoided! But I had a past life of a most wretched kind to account for, some if it in this world as well as in another.

We came away the fifth day; and my landlord, because he saw me uneasy, mounted himself, his son, and three honest country fellows with good firearms, and, without telling us of it, followed the coach, and would see us safe into Dunstable. We could do no less than treat them very handsomely at Dunstable, which cost my spouse about ten or twelve shillings, and something he gave the men for their time too, but my landlord would take nothing for himself.

This was the most happy contrivance for me that could have fallen out; for had I come to London unmarried, I must either have come to him for the first night's entertainment, or have discovered to him that I had not one acquaintance in the whole city of London that could receive a poor bride for the first night's lodging with her spouse. But now, being an old married woman, I made no scruple of going directly home with him, and there I took possession at once of a house well furnished, and a husband in very good circumstances, so that I had a prospect of a very happy life, if I knew how to manage it; and I had leisure to consider of the real value of the life I was likely to live. How different it was to be from the loose ungoverned part I had acted before, and how much happier a life of virtue and sobriety is, than that which we call a life of pleasure.

Oh had this particular scene of life lasted, or had I learned from that time I enjoyed it, to have tasted the true sweetness of it, and had I not fallen into that poverty which is the sure bane of virtue, how happy had I been, not only here, but perhaps for ever! for while I lived thus, I was really a penitent for all my life past. I looked back on it with abhorrence, and might truly be said to hate myself for it. I often reflected how my lover at the Bath, struck at the hand of God, repented and abandoned me, and refused to see me any more, though he loved me to an extreme; but I, prompted by that worst of devils, poverty, returned to the vile practice, and made the advantage of what they call a handsome face to be the relief to my necessities, and beauty be a pimp to vice.

Now I seemed landed in a safe harbour, after the stormy voyage of life past was at an end, and I began to be thankful for my deliverance. I sat many an hour by myself, and wept over the remembrance of past follies, and the dreadful extravagances of a wicked life, and sometimes I flattered myself that I had sincerely repented.

But there are temptations which it is not in the power of human nature to resist, and few know what would be their case if driven to the same exigencies. As covetousness is the root of all evil, so poverty is, I believe, the worst of all snares. But I waive that discourse till I come to an experiment.

I lived with this husband with the utmost tranquillity; he was a quiet, sensible, sober man; virtuous, modest, sincere, and in his business diligent and just. His business was in a narrow compass, and his income sufficient to a plentiful way of living in the ordinary way. I do not say to keep an equipage, and make a figure, as the world calls it, nor did I expect it, or desire it; for as I abhorred the levity and extravagance of my former life, so I chose now to live retired, frugal, and within ourselves. I kept no company, made no visits; minded my family, and obliged my husband; and this kind of life became a pleasure to me.

We lived in an uninterrupted course of ease and content for five years, when a sudden blow from an almost invisible hand blasted all my happiness, and turned me out into the world in a condition the reverse of all that had been before it.

My husband having trusted one of his fellow-clerks with a sum of money, too much for our fortunes to bear the loss of, the clerk failed, and the loss fell very heavy on my husband, yet it was not so great neither but that, if he had had spirit and courage to have looked his misfortunes in the face, his credit was so good that, as I told him, he would easily recover it; for to sink under trouble is to double the weight, and he that will die in it, shall die in it.

It was in vain to speak comfortably to him; the wound had sunk too deep; it was a stab that touched the vitals; he grew melancholy and disconsolate, and from thence lethargic, and died. I foresaw the blow, and was extremely oppressed in my mind, for I saw evidently that if he died I was undone.

I had had two children by him and no more, for, to tell the truth, it began to be time for me to leave bearing children, for I was now eight-and-forty, and I suppose if he had lived I should have had no more.

I was now left in a dismal and disconsolate case indeed, and in several things worse than ever. First, it was past the flourishing time with me when I might expect to be courted for a mistress; that agreeable part had declined some time, and the ruins only appeared of what had been; and that which was worse than all this, that I was the most dejected, disconsolate creature alive. I that had encouraged my husband, and endeavoured to support his spirits under his trouble, could not support my own; I wanted that spirit in trouble which I told him was so necessary to him for bearing the burthen.

But my case was indeed deplorable, for I was left perfectly friendless and helpless, and the loss my husband had sustained had reduced his circumstances so low, that though indeed I was not in debt, yet I could easily foresee that what was left would not support me long; that while it wasted daily for subsistence, I had not way to increase it one shilling, so that it would be soon all spent, and then I saw nothing before me but the utmost distress; and this represented itself so lively to my thoughts, that it seemed as if it was come, before it was really very near; also my very apprehensions doubled the misery, for I fancied every sixpence that I paid for a loaf of bread was the last that I had in the world, and that to-morrow I was to fast, and be starved to death.

In this distress I had no assistant, no friend to comfort or advise me; I sat and cried and tormented myself night and day, wringing my hands, and sometimes raving like a distracted woman; and indeed I have often wondered it had not affected my reason, for I had the vapours to such a degree, that my understanding was sometimes quite lost in fancies and imaginations.

I lived two years in this dismal condition, wasting that little I had, weeping continually over my dismal circumstances, and, as it were, only bleeding to death, without the least hope or prospect of help from God or man; and now I had cried too long, and so often, that tears were, as I might say, exhausted, and I began to be desperate, for I grew poor apace.

For a little relief I had put off my house and took lodgings; and as I was reducing my living, so I sold off most of my goods, which put a little money in my pocket, and I lived near a year upon that, spending very sparingly, and eking things out to the utmost; but still when I looked before me, my very heart would sink within me at the inevitable approach of misery and want. Oh let none read this part without seriously reflecting on the circumstances of a desolate state, and how they would grapple with mere want of friends and want of bread; it will certainly make them think not of sparing what they have only, but of looking up to heaven for support, and of the wise man's prayer, 'Give me not poverty, lest I steal.'

Let them remember that a time of distress is a time of dreadful temptation, and all the strength to resist is taken away; poverty presses, the soul is made desperate by distress, and what can be done? It was one evening, when being brought, as I may say, to the last gasp, I think I may truly say I was distracted and raving, when prompted by I know not what spirit, and, as it were, doing I did not know what or why, I dressed me (for I had still pretty good clothes) and went out. I am very sure I had no manner of design in my head when I went out; I neither knew nor considered where to go, or on what business; but as the devil carried me out and laid his bait for me, so he brought me, to be sure, to the place, for I knew not whither I was going or what I did.

Wandering thus about, I knew not whither, I passed by an apothecary's shop in Leadenhall Street, when I saw lie on a stool just before the counter a little bundle wrapped in a white cloth; beyond it stood a maid-servant with her back to it, looking towards the top of the shop, where the apothecary's apprentice, as I suppose, was standing upon the counter, with his back also to the door, and a candle in his hand, looking and reaching up to the upper shelf for something he wanted, so that both were engaged mighty earnestly, and nobody else in the shop.

This was the bait; and the devil, who I said laid the snare, as readily prompted me as if he had spoke, for I remember, and shall never forget it, 'twas like a voice spoken to me over my shoulder, 'Take the bundle; be quick; do it this moment.' It was no sooner said but I stepped into the shop, and with my back to the wench, as if I had stood up for a cart that was going by, I put my hand behind me and took the bundle, and went off with it, the maid or the fellow not perceiving me, or any one else.

It is impossible to express the horror of my soul all the while I did it. When I went away I had no heart to run, or scarce to mend my pace. I crossed the street indeed, and went down the first turning I came to, and I think it was a street that went through into Fenchurch Street. From thence I crossed and turned through so many ways and turnings, that I could never tell which way it was, not where I went; for I felt not the ground I stepped on, and the farther I was out of danger, the faster I went, till, tired and out of breath, I was forced to sit down on a little bench at a door, and then I began to recover, and found I was got into Thames Street, near Billingsgate. I rested me a little and went on; my blood was all in a fire; my heart beat as if I was in a sudden fright. In short, I was under such a surprise that I still knew not wither I was going, or what to do.

After I had tired myself thus with walking a long way about, and so eagerly, I began to consider and make home to my lodging, where I came about nine o'clock at night.

When the bundle was made up for, or on what occasion laid where I found it, I knew not, but when I came to open it I found there was a suit of childbed-linen in it, very good and almost new, the lace very fine; there was a silver porringer of a pint, a small silver mug and six spoons, with some other linen, a good smock, and three silk handkerchiefs, and in the mug, wrapped up in a paper, 18s. 6d. in money.

All the while I was opening these things I was under such dreadful impressions of fear, and I such terror of mind, though I was perfectly safe, that I cannot express the manner of it. I sat me down, and cried most vehemently. 'Lord,' said I, 'what am I now? a thief! Why, I shall be taken next time, and be carried to Newgate and be tried for my life!' And with that I cried again a long time, and I am sure, as poor as I was, if I had durst for fear, I would certainly have carried the things back again; but that went off after a while. Well, I went to bed for that night, but slept little; the horror of the fact was upon my mind, and I knew not what I said or did all night, and all the next day. Then I was impatient to hear some news of the loss; and would fain know how it was, whether they were a poor body's goods, or a rich. 'Perhaps,' said I, 'it may be some poor widow like me, that had packed up these goods to go and sell them for a little bread for herself and a poor child, and are now starving and breaking their hearts for want of that little they would have fetched.' And this thought tormented me worse than all the rest, for three or four days' time.

But my own distresses silenced all these reflections, and the prospect of my own starving, which grew every day more frightful to me, hardened my heart by degrees. It was then particularly heavy upon my mind, that I had been reformed, and had, as I hoped, repented of all my past wickedness; that I had lived a sober, grave, retired life for several years, but now I should be driven by the dreadful necessity of my circumstances to the gates of destruction, soul and body; and two or three times I fell upon my knees, praying to God, as well as I could, for deliverance; but I cannot but say, my prayers had no hope in them. I knew not what to do; it was all fear without, and dark within; and I reflected on my past life as not sincerely repented of, that Heaven was now beginning to punish me on this side the grave, and would make me as miserable as I had been wicked.

Had I gone on here I had perhaps been a true penitent; but I had an evil counsellor within, and he was continually prompting me to relieve myself by the worst means; so one evening he tempted me again, by the same wicked impulse that had said 'Take that bundle,' to go out again and seek for what might happen.

I went out now by daylight, and wandered about I knew not whither, and in search of I knew not what, when the devil put a snare in my way of a dreadful nature indeed, and such a one as I have never had before or since. Going through Aldersgate Street, there was a pretty little child who had been at a dancing-school, and was going home, all alone; and my prompter, like a true devil, set me upon this innocent creature. I talked to it, and it prattled to me again, and I took it by the hand and led it along till I came to a paved alley that goes into Bartholomew Close, and I led it in there. The child said that was not its way home. I said, 'Yes, my dear, it is; I'll show you the way home.' The child had a little necklace on of gold beads, and I had my eye upon that, and in the dark of the alley I stooped, pretending to mend the child's clog that was loose, and took off her necklace, and the child never felt it, and so led the child on again. Here, I say, the devil put me upon killing the child in the dark alley, that it might not cry, but the very thought frighted me so that I was ready to drop down; but I turned the child about and bade it go back again, for that was not its way home. The child said, so she would, and I went through into Bartholomew Close, and then turned round to another passage that goes into St. John Street; then, crossing into Smithfield, went down Chick Lane and into Field Lane to Holborn Bridge, when, mixing with the crowd of people usually passing there, it was not possible to have been found out; and thus I enterprised my second sally into the world.

The thoughts of this booty put out all the thoughts of the first, and the reflections I had made wore quickly off; poverty, as I have said, hardened my heart, and my own necessities made me regardless of anything. The last affair left no great concern upon me, for as I did the poor child no harm, I only said to myself, I had given the parents a just reproof for their negligence in leaving the poor little lamb to come home by itself, and it would teach them to take more care of it another time.

This string of beads was worth about twelve or fourteen pounds. I suppose it might have been formerly the mother's, for it was too big for the child's wear, but that perhaps the vanity of the mother, to have her child look fine at the dancing-school, had made her let the child wear it; and no doubt the child had a maid sent to take care of it, but she, careless jade, was taken up perhaps with some fellow that had met her by the way, and so the poor baby wandered till it fell into my hands.

However, I did the child no harm; I did not so much as fright it, for I had a great many tender thoughts about me yet, and did nothing but what, as I may say, mere necessity drove me to.

I had a great many adventures after this, but I was young in the business, and did not know how to manage, otherwise than as the devil put things into my head; and indeed he was seldom backward to me. One adventure I had which was very lucky to me. I was going through Lombard Street in the dusk of the evening, just by the end of Three King court, when on a sudden comes a fellow running by me as swift as lightning, and throws a bundle that was in his hand, just behind me, as I stood up against the corner of the house at the turning into the alley. Just as he threw it in he said, 'God bless you, mistress, let it lie there a little,' and away he runs swift as the wind. After him comes two more, and immediately a young fellow without his hat, crying 'Stop thief!' and after him two or three more. They pursued the two last fellows so close, that they were forced to drop what they had got, and one of them was taken into the bargain, and other got off free.

I stood stock-still all this while, till they came back, dragging the poor fellow they had taken, and lugging the things they had found, extremely well satisfied that they had recovered the booty and taken the thief; and thus they passed by me, for I looked only like one who stood up while the crowd was gone.

Once or twice I asked what was the matter, but the people neglected answering me, and I was not very importunate; but after the crowd was wholly past, I took my opportunity to turn about and take up what was behind me and walk away. This, indeed, I did with less disturbance than I had done formerly, for these things I did not steal, but they were stolen to my hand. I got safe to my lodgings with this cargo, which was a piece of fine black lustring silk, and a piece of velvet; the latter was but part of a piece of about eleven yards; the former was a whole piece of near fifty yards. It seems it was a mercer's shop that they had rifled. I say rifled, because the goods were so considerable that they had lost; for the goods that they recovered were pretty many, and I believe came to about six or seven several pieces of silk. How they came to get so many I could not tell; but as I had only robbed the thief, I made no scruple at taking these goods, and being very glad of them too.

I had pretty good luck thus far, and I made several adventures more, though with but small purchase, yet with good success, but I went in daily dread that some mischief would befall me, and that I should certainly come to be hanged at last. The impression this made on me was too strong to be slighted, and it kept me from making attempts that, for ought I knew, might have been very safely performed; but one thing I cannot omit, which was a bait to me many a day. I walked frequently out into the villages round the town, to see if nothing would fall in my way there; and going by a house near Stepney, I saw on the window-board two rings, one a small diamond ring, and the other a gold ring, to be sure laid there by some thoughtless lady, that had more money then forecast, perhaps only till she washed her hands.

I walked several times by the window to observe if I could see whether there was anybody in the room or no, and I could see nobody, but still I was not sure. It came presently into my thoughts to rap at the glass, as if I wanted to speak with somebody, and if anybody was there they would be sure to come to the window, and then I would tell them to remove those rings, for that I had seen two suspicious fellows take notice of them. This was a ready thought. I rapped once or twice and nobody came, when, seeing the coast clear, I thrust hard against the square of the glass, and broke it with very little noise, and took out the two rings, and walked away with them very safe. The diamond ring was worth about #3, and the other about 9s.

I was now at a loss for a market for my goods, and especially for my two pieces of silk. I was very loth to dispose of them for a trifle, as the poor unhappy thieves in general do, who, after they have ventured their lives for perhaps a thing of value, are fain to sell it for a song when they have done; but I was resolved I would not do thus, whatever shift I made, unless I was driven to the last extremity. However, I did not well know what course to take. At last I resolved to go to my old governess, and acquaint myself with her again. I had punctually supplied the #5 a year to her for my little boy as long as I was able, but at last was obliged to put a stop to it. However, I had written a letter to her, wherein I had told her that my circumstances were reduced very low; that I had lost my husband, and that I was not able to do it any longer, and so begged that the poor child might not suffer too much for its mother's misfortunes.

I now made her a visit, and I found that she drove something of the old trade still, but that she was not in such flourishing circumstances as before; for she had been sued by a certain gentleman who had had his daughter stolen from him, and who, it seems, she had helped to convey away; and it was very narrowly that she escaped the gallows. The expense also had ravaged her, and she was become very poor; her house was but meanly furnished, and she was not in such repute for her practice as before; however, she stood upon her legs, as they say, and a she was a stirring, bustling woman, and had some stock left, she was turned pawnbroker, and lived pretty well.

She received me very civilly, and with her usual obliging manner told me she would not have the less respect for me for my being reduced; that she had taken care my boy was very well looked after, though I could not pay for him, and that the woman that had him was easy, so that I needed not to trouble myself about him till I might be better able to do it effectually.

I told her that I had not much money left, but that I had some things that were money's worth, if she could tell me how I might turn them into money. She asked me what it was I had. I pulled out the string of gold beads, and told her it was one of my husband's presents to me; then I showed her the two parcels of silk, which I told her I had from Ireland, and brought up to town with me; and the little diamond ring. As to the small parcel of plate and spoons, I had found means to dispose of them myself before; and as for the childbed-linen I had, she offered me to take it herself, believing it to have been my own. She told me that she was turned pawnbroker, and that she would sell those things for me as pawn to her; and so she sent presently for proper agents that bought them, being in her hands, without any scruple, and gave good prices too.

I now began to think this necessary woman might help me a little in my low condition to some business, for I would gladly have turned my hand to any honest employment if I could have got it. But here she was deficient; honest business did not come within her reach. If I had been younger, perhaps she might have helped me to a spark, but my thoughts were off that kind of livelihood, as being quite out of the way after fifty, which was my case, and so I told her.

She invited me at last to come, and be at her house till I could find something to do, and it should cost me very little, and this I gladly accepted of. And now living a little easier, I entered into some measures to have my little son by my last husband taken off; and this she made easy too, reserving a payment only of #5 a year, if I could pay it. This was such a help to me, that for a good while I left off the wicked trade that I had so newly taken up; and gladly I would have got my bread by the help of my needle if I could have got work, but that was very hard to do for one that had no manner of acquaintance in the world.

However, at last I got some quilting work for ladies' beds, petticoats, and the like; and this I liked very well, and worked very hard, and with this I began to live; but the diligent devil, who resolved I should continue in his service, continually prompted me to go out and take a walk, that is to say, to see if anything would offer in the old way.

One evening I blindly obeyed his summons, and fetched a long circuit through the streets, but met with no purchase, and came home very weary and empty; but not content with that, I went out the next evening too, when going by an alehouse I saw the door of a little room open, next the very street, and on the table a silver tankard, things much in use in public-houses at that time. It seems some company had been drinking there, and the careless boys had forgot to take it away.

I went into the box frankly, and setting the silver tankard on the corner of the bench, I sat down before it, and knocked with my foot; a boy came presently, and I bade him fetch me a pint of warm ale, for it was cold weather; the boy ran, and I heard him go down the cellar to draw the ale. While the boy was gone, another boy came into the room, and cried, 'D' ye call?' I spoke with a melancholy air, and said, 'No, child; the boy is gone for a pint of ale for me.'

While I sat here, I heard the woman in the bar say, 'Are they all gone in the five?' which was the box I sat in, and the boy said, 'Yes.' 'Who fetched the tankard away?' says the woman. 'I did,' says another boy; 'that's it,' pointing, it seems, to another tankard, which he had fetched from another box by mistake; or else it must be, that the rogue forgot that he had not brought it in, which certainly he had not.

I heard all this, much to my satisfaction, for I found plainly that the tankard was not missed, and yet they concluded it was fetched away; so I drank my ale, called to pay, and as I went away I said, 'Take care of your plate, child,' meaning a silver pint mug, which he brought me drink in. The boy said, 'Yes, madam, very welcome,' and away I came.

I came home to my governess, and now I thought it was a time to try her, that if I might be put to the necessity of being exposed, she might offer me some assistance. When I had been at home some time, and had an opportunity of talking to her, I told her I had a secret of the greatest consequence in the world to commit to her, if she had respect enough for me to keep it a secret. She told me she had kept one of my secrets faithfully; why should I doubt her keeping another? I told her the strangest thing in the world had befallen me, and that it had made a thief of me, even without any design, and so told her the whole story of the tankard. 'And have you brought it away with you, my dear?' says she. 'To be sure I have,' says I, and showed it her. 'But what shall I do now,' says I; 'must not carry it again?'

'Carry it again!' says she. 'Ay, if you are minded to be sent to Newgate for stealing it.' 'Why,' says I, 'they can't be so base to stop me, when I carry it to them again?' 'You don't know those sort of people, child,' says she; 'they'll not only carry you to Newgate, but hang you too, without any regard to the honesty of returning it; or bring in an account of all the other tankards they have lost, for you to pay for.' 'What must I do, then?' says I. 'Nay,' says she, 'as you have played the cunning part and stole it, you must e'en keep it; there's no going back now. Besides, child,' says she, 'don't you want it more than they do? I wish you could light of such a bargain once a week.'

This gave me a new notion of my governess, and that since she was turned pawnbroker, she had a sort of people about her that were none of the honest ones that I had met with there before.

I had not been long there but I discovered it more plainly than before, for every now and then I saw hilts of swords, spoons, forks, tankards, and all such kind of ware brought in, not to be pawned, but to be sold downright; and she bought everything that came without asking any questions, but had very good bargains, as I found by her discourse.

I found also that in following this trade she always melted down the plate she bought, that it might not be challenged; and she came to me and told me one morning that she was going to melt, and if I would, she would put my tankard in, that it might not be seen by anybody. I told her, with all my heart; so she weighed it, and allowed me the full value in silver again; but I found she did not do the same to the rest of her customers.

Some time after this, as I was at work, and very melancholy, she begins to ask me what the matter was, as she was used to do. I told her my heart was heavy; I had little work, and nothing to live on, and knew not what course to take. She laughed, and told me I must go out again and try my fortune; it might be that I might meet with another piece of plate. 'O mother!' says I, 'that is a trade I have no skill in, and if I should be taken I am undone at once.' Says she, 'I could help you to a schoolmistress that shall make you as dexterous as herself.' I trembled at that proposal, for hitherto I had had no confederates, nor any acquaintance among that tribe. But she conquered all my modesty, and all my fears; and in a little time, by the help of this confederate, I grew as impudent a thief, and as dexterous as ever Moll Cutpurse was, though, if fame does not belie her, not half so handsome.

The comrade she helped me to dealt in three sorts of craft, viz. shoplifting, stealing of shop-books and pocket-books, and taking off gold watches from the ladies' sides; and this last she did so dexterously that no woman ever arrived to the performance of that art so as to do it like her. I liked the first and the last of these things very well, and I attended her some time in the practice, just as a deputy attends a midwife, without any pay.

At length she put me to practice. She had shown me her art, and I had several times unhooked a watch from her own side with great dexterity. At last she showed me a prize, and this was a young lady big with child, who had a charming watch. The thing was to be done as she came out of church. She goes on one side of the lady, and pretends, just as she came to the steps, to fall, and fell against the lady with so much violence as put her into a great fright, and both cried out terribly. In the very moment that she jostled the lady, I had hold of the watch, and holding it the right way, the start she gave drew the hook out, and she never felt it. I made off immediately, and left my schoolmistress to come out of her pretended fright gradually, and the lady too; and presently the watch was missed. 'Ay,' says my comrade, 'then it was those rogues that thrust me down, I warrant ye; I wonder the gentlewoman did not miss her watch before, then we might have taken them.'

She humoured the thing so well that nobody suspected her, and I was got home a full hour before her. This was my first adventure in company. The watch was indeed a very fine one, and had a great many trinkets about it, and my governess allowed us #20 for it, of which I had half. And thus I was entered a complete thief, hardened to the pitch above all the reflections of conscience or modesty, and to a degree which I must acknowledge I never thought possible in me.

Thus the devil, who began, by the help of an irresistible poverty, to push me into this wickedness, brought me on to a height beyond the common rate, even when my necessities were not so great, or the prospect of my misery so terrifying; for I had now got into a little vein of work, and as I was not at a loss to handle my needle, it was very probable, as acquaintance came in, I might have got my bread honestly enough.

I must say, that if such a prospect of work had presented itself at first, when I began to feel the approach of my miserable circumstances—I say, had such a prospect of getting my bread by working presented itself then, I had never fallen into this wicked trade, or into such a wicked gang as I was now embarked with; but practice had hardened me, and I grew audacious to the last degree; and the more so because I had carried it on so long, and had never been taken; for, in a word, my new partner in wickedness and I went on together so long, without being ever detected, that we not only grew bold, but we grew rich, and we had at one time one-and-twenty gold watches in our hands.

I remember that one day being a little more serious than ordinary, and finding I had so good a stock beforehand as I had, for I had near #200 in money for my share, it came strongly into my mind, no doubt from some kind spirit, if such there be, that at first poverty excited me, and my distresses drove me to these dreadful shifts; so seeing those distresses were now relieved, and I could also get something towards a maintenance by working, and had so good a bank to support me, why should I now not leave off, as they say, while I was well? that I could not expect to go always free; and if I was once surprised, and miscarried, I was undone.

This was doubtless the happy minute, when, if I had hearkened to the blessed hint, from whatsoever had it came, I had still a cast for an easy life. But my fate was otherwise determined; the busy devil that so industriously drew me in had too fast hold of me to let me go back; but as poverty brought me into the mire, so avarice kept me in, till there was no going back. As to the arguments which my reason dictated for persuading me to lay down, avarice stepped in and said, 'Go on, go on; you have had very good luck; go on till you have gotten four or five hundred pounds, and they you shall leave off, and then you may live easy without working at all.'

Thus I, that was once in the devil's clutches, was held fast there as with a charm, and had no power to go without the circle, till I was engulfed in labyrinths of trouble too great to get out at all.

However, these thoughts left some impression upon me, and made me act with some more caution than before, and more than my directors used for themselves. My comrade, as I called her, but rather she should have been called my teacher, with another of her scholars, was the first in the misfortune; for, happening to be upon the hunt for purchase, they made an attempt upon a linen-draper in Cheapside, but were snapped by a hawk's-eyed journeyman, and seized with two pieces of cambric, which were taken also upon them.

This was enough to lodge them both in Newgate, where they had the misfortune to have some of their former sins brought to remembrance. Two other indictments being brought against them, and the facts being proved upon them, they were both condemned to die. They both pleaded their bellies, and were both voted quick with child; though my tutoress was no more with child than I was.

I went frequently to see them, and condole with them, expecting that it would be my turn next; but the place gave me so much horror, reflecting that it was the place of my unhappy birth, and of my mother's misfortunes, and that I could not bear it, so I was forced to leave off going to see them.

And oh! could I have but taken warning by their disasters, I had been happy still, for I was yet free, and had nothing brought against me; but it could not be, my measure was not yet filled up.

My comrade, having the brand of an old offender, was executed; the young offender was spared, having obtained a reprieve, but lay starving a long while in prison, till at last she got her name into what they call a circuit pardon, and so came off.

This terrible example of my comrade frighted me heartily, and for a good while I made no excursions; but one night, in the neighbourhood of my governess's house, they cried 'Fire.' My governess looked out, for we were all up, and cried immediately that such a gentlewoman's house was all of a light fire atop, and so indeed it was. Here she gives me a job. 'Now, child,' says she, 'there is a rare opportunity, for the fire being so near that you may go to it before the street is blocked up with the crowd.' She presently gave me my cue. 'Go, child,' says she, 'to the house, and run in and tell the lady, or anybody you see, that you come to help them, and that you came from such a gentlewoman (that is, one of her acquaintance farther up the street).' She gave me the like cue to the next house, naming another name that was also an acquaintance of the gentlewoman of the house.

Away I went, and, coming to the house, I found them all in confusion, you may be sure. I ran in, and finding one of the maids, 'Lord! sweetheart,' says I, 'how came this dismal accident? Where is your mistress? Any how does she do? Is she safe? And where are the children? I come from Madam —— to help you.' Away runs the maid. 'Madam, madam,' says she, screaming as loud as she could yell, 'here is a gentlewoman come from Madam —— to help us.' The poor woman, half out of her wits, with a bundle under her arm, an two little children, comes toward me. 'Lord! madam,' says I, 'let me carry the poor children to Madam ——,' she desires you to send them; she'll take care of the poor lambs;' and immediately I takes one of them out of her hand, and she lifts the other up into my arms. 'Ay, do, for God's sake,' says she, 'carry them to her. Oh! thank her for her kindness.' 'Have you anything else to secure, madam?' says I; 'she will take care of it.' 'Oh dear! ay,' says she, 'God bless her, and thank her. Take this bundle of plate and carry it to her too. Oh, she is a good woman. Oh Lord! we are utterly ruined, utterly undone!' And away she runs from me out of her wits, and the maids after her; and away comes I with the two children and the bundle.

I was no sooner got into the street but I saw another woman come to me. 'Oh!' says she, 'mistress,' in a piteous tone, 'you will let fall the child. Come, this is a sad time; let me help you'; and immediately lays hold of my bundle to carry it for me. 'No,' says I; 'if you will help me, take the child by the hand, and lead it for me but to the upper end of the street; I'll go with you and satisfy you for your pains.'

She could not avoid going, after what I said; but the creature, in short, was one of the same business with me, and wanted nothing but the bundle; however, she went with me to the door, for she could not help it. When we were come there I whispered her, 'Go, child,' said I, 'I understand your trade; you may meet with purchase enough.'

She understood me and walked off. I thundered at the door with the children, and as the people were raised before by the noise of the fire, I was soon let in, and I said, 'Is madam awake? Pray tell her Mrs. —— desires the favour of her to take the two children in; poor lady, she will be undone, their house is all of a flame,' They took the children in very civilly, pitied the family in distress, and away came I with my bundle. One of the maids asked me if I was not to leave the bundle too. I said, 'No, sweetheart, 'tis to go to another place; it does not belong to them.'

I was a great way out of the hurry now, and so I went on, clear of anybody's inquiry, and brought the bundle of plate, which was very considerable, straight home, and gave it to my old governess. She told me she would not look into it, but bade me go out again to look for more.

She gave me the like cue to the gentlewoman of the next house to that which was on fire, and I did my endeavour to go, but by this time the alarm of fire was so great, and so many engines playing, and the street so thronged with people, that I could not get near the house whatever I would do; so I came back again to my governess's, and taking the bundle up into my chamber, I began to examine it. It is with horror that I tell what a treasure I found there; 'tis enough to say, that besides most of the family plate, which was considerable, I found a gold chain, an old-fashioned thing, the locket of which was broken, so that I suppose it had not been used some years, but the gold was not the worse for that; also a little box of burying-rings, the lady's wedding-ring, and some broken bits of old lockets of gold, a gold watch, and a purse with about #24 value in old pieces of gold coin, and several other things of value.

This was the greatest and the worst prize that ever I was concerned in; for indeed, though, as I have said above, I was hardened now beyond the power of all reflection in other cases, yet it really touched me to the very soul when I looked into this treasure, to think of the poor disconsolate gentlewoman who had lost so much by the fire besides; and who would think, to be sure, that she had saved her plate and best things; how she would be surprised and afflicted when she should find that she had been deceived, and should find that the person that took her children and her goods, had not come, as was pretended, from the gentlewoman in the next street, but that the children had been put upon her without her own knowledge.

I say, I confess the inhumanity of this action moved me very much, and made me relent exceedingly, and tears stood in my eyes upon that subject; but with all my sense of its being cruel and inhuman, I could never find in my heart to make any restitution. The reflection wore off, and I began quickly to forget the circumstances that attended the taking them.

Nor was this all; for though by this job I was become considerably richer than before, yet the resolution I had formerly taken, of leaving off this horrid trade when I had gotten a little more, did not return, but I must still get farther, and more; and the avarice joined so with the success, that I had no more thought of coming to a timely alteration of life, though without it I could expect no safety, no tranquillity in the possession of what I had so wickedly gained; but a little more, and a little more, was the case still.

At length, yielding to the importunities of my crime, I cast off all remorse and repentance, and all the reflections on that head turned to no more than this, that I might perhaps come to have one booty more that might complete my desires; but though I certainly had that one booty, yet every hit looked towards another, and was so encouraging to me to go on with the trade, that I had no gust to the thought of laying it down.

In this condition, hardened by success, and resolving to go on, I fell into the snare in which I was appointed to meet with my last reward for this kind of life. But even this was not yet, for I met with several successful adventures more in this way of being undone.

I remained still with my governess, who was for a while really concerned for the misfortune of my comrade that had been hanged, and who, it seems, knew enough of my governess to have sent her the same way, and which made her very uneasy; indeed, she was in a very great fright.

It is true that when she was gone, and had not opened mouth to tell what she knew, my governess was easy as to that point, and perhaps glad she was hanged, for it was in her power to have obtained a pardon at the expense of her friends; but on the other hand, the loss of her, and the sense of her kindness in not making her market of what she knew, moved my governess to mourn very sincerely for her. I comforted her as well as I could, and she in return hardened me to merit more completely the same fate.

However, as I have said, it made me the more wary, and particularly I was very shy of shoplifting, especially among the mercers and drapers, who are a set of fellows that have their eyes very much about them. I made a venture or two among the lace folks and the milliners, and particularly at one shop where I got notice of two young women who were newly set up, and had not been bred to the trade. There I think I carried off a piece of bone-lace, worth six or seven pounds, and a paper of thread. But this was but once; it was a trick that would not serve again.

It was always reckoned a safe job when we heard of a new shop, and especially when the people were such as were not bred to shops. Such may depend upon it that they will be visited once or twice at their beginning, and they must be very sharp indeed if they can prevent it.

I made another adventure or two, but they were but trifles too, though sufficient to live on. After this nothing considerable offering for a good while, I began to think that I must give over the trade in earnest; but my governess, who was not willing to lose me, and expected great things of me, brought me one day into company with a young woman and a fellow that went for her husband, though as it appeared afterwards, she was not his wife, but they were partners, it seems, in the trade they carried on, and partners in something else. In short, they robbed together, lay together, were taken together, and at last were hanged together.

I came into a kind of league with these two by the help of my governess, and they carried me out into three or four adventures, where I rather saw them commit some coarse and unhandy robberies, in which nothing but a great stock of impudence on their side, and gross negligence on the people's side who were robbed, could have made them successful. So I resolved from that time forward to be very cautious how I adventured upon anything with them; and indeed, when two or three unlucky projects were proposed by them, I declined the offer, and persuaded them against it. One time they particularly proposed robbing a watchmaker of three gold watches, which they had eyed in the daytime, and found the place where he laid them. One of them had so many keys of all kinds, that he made no question to open the place where the watchmaker had laid them; and so we made a kind of an appointment; but when I came to look narrowly into the thing, I found they proposed breaking open the house, and this, as a thing out of my way, I would not embark in, so they went without me. They did get into the house by main force, and broke up the locked place where the watches were, but found but one of the gold watches, and a silver one, which they took, and got out of the house again very clear. But the family, being alarmed, cried out 'Thieves,' and the man was pursued and taken; the young woman had got off too, but unhappily was stopped at a distance, and the watches found upon her. And thus I had a second escape, for they were convicted, and both hanged, being old offenders, though but young people. As I said before that they robbed together and lay together, so now they hanged together, and there ended my new partnership.

I began now to be very wary, having so narrowly escaped a scouring, and having such an example before me; but I had a new tempter, who prompted me every day—I mean my governess; and now a prize presented, which as it came by her management, so she expected a good share of the booty. There was a good quantity of Flanders lace lodged in a private house, where she had gotten intelligence of it, and Flanders lace being prohibited, it was a good booty to any custom-house officer that could come at it. I had a full account from my governess, as well of the quantity as of the very place where it was concealed, and I went to a custom-house officer, and told him I had such a discovery to make to him of such a quantity of lace, if he would assure me that I should have my due share of the reward. This was so just an offer, that nothing could be fairer; so he agreed, and taking a constable and me with him, we beset the house. As I told him I could go directly to the place, he left it to me; and the hole being very dark, I squeezed myself into it, with a candle in my hand, and so reached the pieces out to him, taking care as I gave him some so to secure as much about myself as I could conveniently dispose of. There was near #300 worth of lace in the hole, and I secured about #50 worth of it to myself. The people of the house were not owners of the lace, but a merchant who had entrusted them with it; so that they were not so surprised as I thought they would be.

I left the officer overjoyed with his prize, and fully satisfied with what he had got, and appointed to meet him at a house of his own directing, where I came after I had disposed of the cargo I had about me, of which he had not the least suspicion. When I came to him he began to capitulate with me, believing I did not understand the right I had to a share in the prize, and would fain have put me off with #20, but I let him know that I was not so ignorant as he supposed I was; and yet I was glad, too, that he offered to bring me to a certainty.

I asked #100, and he rose up to #30; I fell to #80, and he rose again to #40; in a word, he offered #50, and I consented, only demanding a piece of lace, which I though came to about #8 or #9, as if it had been for my own wear, and he agreed to it. So I got #50 in money paid me that same night, and made an end of the bargain; nor did he ever know who I was, or where to inquire for me, so that if it had been discovered that part of the goods were embezzled, he could have made no challenge upon me for it.

I very punctually divided this spoil with my governess, and I passed with her from this time for a very dexterous manager in the nicest cases. I found that this last was the best and easiest sort of work that was in my way, and I made it my business to inquire out prohibited goods, and after buying some, usually betrayed them, but none of these discoveries amounted to anything considerable, not like that I related just now; but I was willing to act safe, and was still cautious of running the great risks which I found others did, and in which they miscarried every day.

The next thing of moment was an attempt at a gentlewoman's good watch. It happened in a crowd, at a meeting-house, where I was in very great danger of being taken. I had full hold of her watch, but giving a great jostle, as if somebody had thrust me against her, and in the juncture giving the watch a fair pull, I found it would not come, so I let it go that moment, and cried out as if I had been killed, that somebody had trod upon my foot, and that there were certainly pickpockets there, for somebody or other had given a pull at my watch; for you are to observe that on these adventures we always went very well dressed, and I had very good clothes on, and a gold watch by my side, as like a lady as other fold.

I had no sooner said so, but the other gentlewoman cried out 'A pickpocket' too, for somebody, she said, had tried to pull her watch away.

When I touched her watch I was close to her, but when I cried out I stopped as it were short, and the crowd bearing her forward a little, she made a noise too, but it was at some distance from me, so that she did not in the least suspect me; but when she cried out 'A pickpocket,' somebody cried, 'Ay, and here has been another! this gentlewoman has been attempted too.'

At that very instance, a little farther in the crowd, and very luckily too, they cried out 'A pickpocket,' again, and really seized a young fellow in the very act. This, though unhappy for the wretch, was very opportunely for my case, though I had carried it off handsomely enough before; but now it was out of doubt, and all the loose part of the crowd ran that way, and the poor boy was delivered up to the rage of the street, which is a cruelty I need not describe, and which, however, they are always glad of, rather than to be sent to Newgate, where they lie often a long time, till they are almost perished, and sometimes they are hanged, and the best they can look for, if they are convicted, is to be transported.

This was a narrow escape to me, and I was so frighted that I ventured no more at gold watches a great while. There was indeed a great many concurring circumstances in this adventure which assisted to my escape; but the chief was, that the woman whose watch I had pulled at was a fool; that is to say, she was ignorant of the nature of the attempt, which one would have thought she should not have been, seeing she was wise enough to fasten her watch so that it could not be slipped up. But she was in such a fright that she had no thought about her proper for the discovery; for she, when she felt the pull, screamed out, and pushed herself forward, and put all the people about her into disorder, but said not a word of her watch, or of a pickpocket, for a least two minutes' time, which was time enough for me, and to spare.

For as I had cried out behind her, as I have said, and bore myself back in the crowd as she bore forward, there were several people, at least seven or eight, the throng being still moving on, that were got between me and her in that time, and then I crying out 'A pickpocket,' rather sooner than she, or at least as soon, she might as well be the person suspected as I, and the people were confused in their inquiry; whereas, had she with a presence of mind needful on such an occasion, as soon as she felt the pull, not screamed out as she did, but turned immediately round and seized the next body that was behind her, she had infallibly taken me.

This is a direction not of the kindest sort to the fraternity, but 'tis certainly a key to the clue of a pickpocket's motions, and whoever can follow it will as certainly catch the thief as he will be sure to miss if he does not.

I had another adventure, which puts this matter out of doubt, and which may be an instruction for posterity in the case of a pickpocket. My good old governess, to give a short touch at her history, though she had left off the trade, was, as I may say, born a pickpocket, and, as I understood afterwards, had run through all the several degrees of that art, and yet had never been taken but once, when she was so grossly detected, that she was convicted and ordered to be transported; but being a woman of a rare tongue, and withal having money in her pocket, she found means, the ship putting into Ireland for provisions, to get on shore there, where she lived and practised her old trade for some years; when falling into another sort of bad company, she turned midwife and procuress, and played a hundred pranks there, which she gave me a little history of in confidence between us as we grew more intimate; and it was to this wicked creature that I owed all the art and dexterity I arrived to, in which there were few that ever went beyond me, or that practised so long without any misfortune.

It was after those adventures in Ireland, and when she was pretty well known in that country, that she left Dublin and came over to England, where, the time of her transportation being not expired, she left her former trade, for fear of falling into bad hands again, for then she was sure to have gone to wreck. Here she set up the same trade she had followed in Ireland, in which she soon, by her admirable management and good tongue, arrived to the height which I have already described, and indeed began to be rich, though her trade fell off again afterwards, as I have hinted before.

I mentioned thus much of the history of this woman here, the better to account for the concern she had in the wicked life I was now leading, into all the particulars of which she led me, as it were, by the hand, and gave me such directions, and I so well followed them, that I grew the greatest artist of my time and worked myself out of every danger with such dexterity, that when several more of my comrades ran themselves into Newgate presently, and by that time they had been half a year at the trade, I had now practised upwards of five years, and the people at Newgate did not so much as know me; they had heard much of me indeed, and often expected me there, but I always got off, though many times in the extremest danger.

One of the greatest dangers I was now in, was that I was too well known among the trade, and some of them, whose hatred was owing rather to envy than any injury I had done them, began to be angry that I should always escape when they were always catched and hurried to Newgate. These were they that gave me the name of Moll Flanders; for it was no more of affinity with my real name or with any of the name I had ever gone by, than black is of kin to white, except that once, as before, I called myself Mrs. Flanders; when I sheltered myself in the Mint; but that these rogues never knew, nor could I ever learn how they came to give me the name, or what the occasion of it was.

I was soon informed that some of these who were gotten fast into Newgate had vowed to impeach me; and as I knew that two or three of them were but too able to do it, I was under a great concern about it, and kept within doors for a good while. But my governess—whom I always made partner in my success, and who now played a sure game with me, for that she had a share of the gain and no share in the hazard—I say, my governess was something impatient of my leading such a useless, unprofitable life, as she called it; and she laid a new contrivance for my going abroad, and this was to dress me up in men's clothes, and so put me into a new kind of practice.

I was tall and personable, but a little too smooth-faced for a man; however, I seldom went abroad but in the night, it did well enough; but it was a long time before I could behave in my new clothes—I mean, as to my craft. It was impossible to be so nimble, so ready, so dexterous at these things in a dress so contrary to nature; and I did everything clumsily, so I had neither the success nor the easiness of escape that I had before, and I resolved to leave it off; but that resolution was confirmed soon after by the following accident.

As my governess disguised me like a man, so she joined me with a man, a young fellow that was nimble enough at his business, and for about three weeks we did very well together. Our principal trade was watching shopkeepers' counters, and slipping off any kind of goods we could see carelessly laid anywhere, and we made several good bargains, as we called them, at this work. And as we kept always together, so we grew very intimate, yet he never knew that I was not a man, nay, though I several times went home with him to his lodgings, according as our business directed, and four or five times lay with him all night. But our design lay another way, and it was absolutely necessary to me to conceal my sex from him, as appeared afterwards. The circumstances of our living, coming in late, and having such and such business to do as required that nobody should be trusted with the coming into our lodgings, were such as made it impossible to me to refuse lying with him, unless I would have owned my sex; and as it was, I effectually concealed myself. But his ill, and my good fortune, soon put an end to this life, which I must own I was sick of too, on several other accounts. We had made several prizes in this new way of business, but the last would be extraordinary. There was a shop in a certain street which had a warehouse behind it that looked into another street, the house making the corner of the turning.

Through the window of the warehouse we saw, lying on the counter or showboard, which was just before it, five pieces of silks, besides other stuffs, and though it was almost dark, yet the people, being busy in the fore-shop with customers, had not had time to shut up those windows, or else had forgot it.

This the young fellow was so overjoyed with, that he could not restrain himself. It lay all within his reach he said, and he swore violently to me that he would have it, if he broke down the house for it. I dissuaded him a little, but saw there was no remedy; so he ran rashly upon it, slipped out a square of the sash window dexterously enough, and without noise, and got out four pieces of the silks, and came with them towards me, but was immediately pursued with a terrible clutter and noise. We were standing together indeed, but I had not taken any of the goods out of his hand, when I said to him hastily, 'You are undone, fly, for God's sake!' He ran like lightning, and I too, but the pursuit was hotter after him because he had the goods, than after me. He dropped two of the pieces, which stopped them a little, but the crowd increased and pursued us both. They took him soon after with the other two pieces upon him, and then the rest followed me. I ran for it and got into my governess's house whither some quick-eyed people followed me to warmly as to fix me there. They did not immediately knock, at the door, by which I got time to throw off my disguise and dress me in my own clothes; besides, when they came there, my governess, who had her tale ready, kept her door shut, and called out to them and told them there was no man come in there. The people affirmed there did a man come in there, and swore they would break open the door.

My governess, not at all surprised, spoke calmly to them, told them they should very freely come and search her house, if they should bring a constable, and let in none but such as the constable would admit, for it was unreasonable to let in a whole crowd. This they could not refuse, though they were a crowd. So a constable was fetched immediately, and she very freely opened the door; the constable kept the door, and the men he appointed searched the house, my governess going with them from room to room. When she came to my room she called to me, and said aloud, 'Cousin, pray open the door; here's some gentlemen that must come and look into your room.'

I had a little girl with me, which was my governess's grandchild, as she called her; and I bade her open the door, and there sat I at work with a great litter of things about me, as if I had been at work all day, being myself quite undressed, with only night-clothes on my head, and a loose morning-gown wrapped about me. My governess made a kind of excuse for their disturbing me, telling me partly the occasion of it, and that she had no remedy but to open the doors to them, and let them satisfy themselves, for all she could say to them would not satisfy them. I sat still, and bid them search the room if they pleased, for if there was anybody in the house, I was sure they were not in my room; and as for the rest of the house, I had nothing to say to that, I did not understand what they looked for.

Everything looked so innocent and to honest about me, that they treated me civiller than I expected, but it was not till they had searched the room to a nicety, even under the bed, in the bed, and everywhere else where it was possible anything could be hid. When they had done this, and could find nothing, they asked my pardon for troubling me, and went down.

When they had thus searched the house from bottom to top, and then top to bottom, and could find nothing, they appeased the mob pretty well; but they carried my governess before the justice. Two men swore that they saw the man whom they pursued go into her house. My governess rattled and made a great noise that her house should be insulted, and that she should be used thus for nothing; that if a man did come in, he might go out again presently for aught she knew, for she was ready to make oath that no man had been within her doors all that day as she knew of (and that was very true indeed); that is might be indeed that as she was abovestairs, any fellow in a fright might find the door open and run in for shelter when he was pursued, but that she knew nothing of it; and if it had been so, he certainly went out again, perhaps at the other door, for she had another door into an alley, and so had made his escape and cheated them all.

This was indeed probable enough, and the justice satisfied himself with giving her an oath that she had not received or admitted any man into her house to conceal him, or protect or hide him from justice. This oath she might justly take, and did so, and so she was dismissed.

It is easy to judge what a fright I was in upon this occasion, and it was impossible for my governess ever to bring me to dress in that disguise again; for, as I told her, I should certainly betray myself.

My poor partner in this mischief was now in a bad case, for he was carried away before my Lord Mayor, and by his worship committed to Newgate, and the people that took him were so willing, as well as able, to prosecute him, that they offered themselves to enter into recognisances to appear at the sessions and pursue the charge against him.

However, he got his indictment deferred, upon promise to discover his accomplices, and particularly the man that was concerned with him in his robbery; and he failed not to do his endeavour, for he gave in my name, whom he called Gabriel Spencer, which was the name I went by to him; and here appeared the wisdom of my concealing my name and sex from him, which, if he had ever known I had been undone.

He did all he could to discover this Gabriel Spencer; he described me, he discovered the place where he said I lodged, and, in a word, all the particulars that he could of my dwelling; but having concealed the main circumstances of my sex from him, I had a vast advantage, and he never could hear of me. He brought two or three families into trouble by his endeavouring to find me out, but they knew nothing of me, any more than that I had a fellow with me that they had seen, but knew nothing of. And as for my governess, though she was the means of his coming to me, yet it was done at second-hand, and he knew nothing of her.

This turned to his disadvantage; for having promised discoveries, but not being able to make it good, it was looked upon as trifling with the justice of the city, and he was the more fiercely pursued by the shopkeepers who took him.

I was, however, terribly uneasy all this while, and that I might be quite out of the way, I went away from my governess's for a while; but not knowing wither to wander, I took a maid-servant with me, and took the stage-coach to Dunstable, to my old landlord and landlady, where I had lived so handsomely with my Lancashire husband. Here I told her a formal story, that I expected my husband every day from Ireland, and that I had sent a letter to him that I would meet him at Dunstable at her house, and that he would certainly land, if the wind was fair, in a few days, so that I was come to spend a few days with them till he should come, for he was either come post, or in the West Chester coach, I knew not which; but whichsoever it was, he would be sure to come to that house to meet me.

My landlady was mighty glad to see me, and my landlord made such a stir with me, that if I had been a princess I could not have been better used, and here I might have been welcome a month or two if I had thought fit.

But my business was of another nature. I was very uneasy (though so well disguised that it was scarce possible to detect me) lest this fellow should somehow or other find me out; and though he could not charge me with this robbery, having persuaded him not to venture, and having also done nothing in it myself but run away, yet he might have charged me with other things, and have bought his own life at the expense of mine.

This filled me with horrible apprehensions. I had no recourse, no friend, no confidante but my old governess, and I knew no remedy but to put my life in her hands, and so I did, for I let her know where to send to me, and had several letters from her while I stayed here. Some of them almost scared me out my wits but at last she sent me the joyful news that he was hanged, which was the best news to me that I had heard a great while.

I had stayed here five weeks, and lived very comfortably indeed (the secret anxiety of my mind excepted); but when I received this letter I looked pleasantly again, and told my landlady that I had received a letter from my spouse in Ireland, that I had the good news of his being very well, but had the bad news that his business would not permit him to come away so soon as he expected, and so I was like to go back again without him.

My landlady complimented me upon the good news however, that I had heard he was well. 'For I have observed, madam,' says she, 'you hadn't been so pleasant as you used to be; you have been over head and ears in care for him, I dare say,' says the good woman; ''tis easy to be seen there's an alteration in you for the better,' says she. 'Well, I am sorry the esquire can't come yet,' says my landlord; 'I should have been heartily glad to have seen him. But I hope, when you have certain news of his coming, you'll take a step hither again, madam,' says he; 'you shall be very welcome whenever you please to come.'

With all these fine compliments we parted, and I came merry enough to London, and found my governess as well pleased as I was. And now she told me she would never recommend any partner to me again, for she always found, she said, that I had the best luck when I ventured by myself. And so indeed I had, for I was seldom in any danger when I was by myself, or if I was, I got out of it with more dexterity than when I was entangled with the dull measures of other people, who had perhaps less forecast, and were more rash and impatient than I; for though I had as much courage to venture as any of them, yet I used more caution before I undertook a thing, and had more presence of mind when I was to bring myself off.

I have often wondered even at my own hardiness another way, that when all my companions were surprised and fell so suddenly into the hand of justice, and that I so narrowly escaped, yet I could not all this while enter into one serious resolution to leave off this trade, and especially considering that I was now very far from being poor; that the temptation of necessity, which is generally the introduction of all such wickedness, was now removed; for I had near #500 by me in ready money, on which I might have lived very well, if I had thought fit to have retired; but I say, I had not so much as the least inclination to leave off; no, not so much as I had before when I had but #200 beforehand, and when I had no such frightful examples before my eyes as these were. From hence 'tis evident to me, that when once we are hardened in crime, no fear can affect us, no example give us any warning.

I had indeed one comrade whose fate went very near me for a good while, though I wore it off too in time. That case was indeed very unhappy. I had made a prize of a piece of very good damask in a mercer's shop, and went clear off myself, but had conveyed the piece to this companion of mine when we went out of the shop, and she went one way and I went another. We had not been long out of the shop but the mercer missed his piece of stuff, and sent his messengers, one one way and one another, and they presently seized her that had the piece, with the damask upon her. As for me, I had very luckily stepped into a house where there was a lace chamber, up one pair of stairs, and had the satisfaction, or the terror indeed, of looking out of the window upon the noise they made, and seeing the poor creature dragged away in triumph to the justice, who immediately committed her to Newgate.

I was careful to attempt nothing in the lace chamber, but tumbled their goods pretty much to spend time; then bought a few yards of edging and paid for it, and came away very sad-hearted indeed for the poor woman, who was in tribulation for what I only had stolen.

Here again my old caution stood me in good stead; namely, that though I often robbed with these people, yet I never let them know who I was, or where I lodged, nor could they ever find out my lodging, though they often endeavoured to watch me to it. They all knew me by the name of Moll Flanders, though even some of them rather believed I was she than knew me to be so. My name was public among them indeed, but how to find me out they knew not, nor so much as how to guess at my quarters, whether they were at the east end of the town or the west; and this wariness was my safety upon all these occasions.

I kept close a great while upon the occasion of this woman's disaster. I knew that if I should do anything that should miscarry, and should be carried to prison, she would be there and ready to witness against me, and perhaps save her life at my expense. I considered that I began to be very well known by name at the Old Bailey, though they did not know my face, and that if I should fall into their hands, I should be treated as an old offender; and for this reason I was resolved to see what this poor creature's fate should be before I stirred abroad, though several times in her distress I conveyed money to her for her relief.

At length she came to her trial. She pleaded she did not steal the thing, but that one Mrs. Flanders, as she heard her called (for she did not know her), gave the bundle to her after they came out of the shop, and bade her carry it home to her lodging. They asked her where this Mrs. Flanders was, but she could not produce her, neither could she give the least account of me; and the mercer's men swearing positively that she was in the shop when the goods were stolen, that they immediately missed them, and pursued her, and found them upon her, thereupon the jury brought her in guilty; but the Court, considering that she was really not the person that stole the goods, an inferior assistant, and that it was very possible she could not find out this Mrs. Flanders, meaning me, though it would save her life, which indeed was true—I say, considering all this, they allowed her to be transported, which was the utmost favour she could obtain, only that the Court told her that if she could in the meantime produce the said Mrs. Flanders, they would intercede for her pardon; that is to say, if she could find me out, and hand me, she should not be transported. This I took care to make impossible to her, and so she was shipped off in pursuance of her sentence a little while after.

I must repeat it again, that the fate of this poor woman troubled me exceedingly, and I began to be very pensive, knowing that I was really the instrument of her disaster; but the preservation of my own life, which was so evidently in danger, took off all my tenderness; and seeing that she was not put to death, I was very easy at her transportation, because she was then out of the way of doing me any mischief, whatever should happen.

The disaster of this woman was some months before that of the last-recited story, and was indeed partly occasion of my governess proposing to dress me up in men's clothes, that I might go about unobserved, as indeed I did; but I was soon tired of that disguise, as I have said, for indeed it exposed me to too many difficulties.

I was now easy as to all fear of witnesses against me, for all those that had either been concerned with me, or that knew me by the name of Moll Flanders, were either hanged or transported; and if I should have had the misfortune to be taken, I might call myself anything else, as well as Moll Flanders, and no old sins could be placed into my account; so I began to run a-tick again with the more freedom, and several successful adventures I made, though not such as I had made before.

We had at that time another fire happened not a great way off from the place where my governess lived, and I made an attempt there, as before, but as I was not soon enough before the crowd of people came in, and could not get to the house I aimed at, instead of a prize, I got a mischief, which had almost put a period to my life and all my wicked doings together; for the fire being very furious, and the people in a great fright in removing their goods, and throwing them out of window, a wench from out of a window threw a feather-bed just upon me. It is true, the bed being soft, it broke no bones; but as the weight was great, and made greater by the fall, it beat me down, and laid me dead for a while. Nor did the people concern themselves much to deliver me from it, or to recover me at all; but I lay like one dead and neglected a good while, till somebody going to remove the bed out of the way, helped me up. It was indeed a wonder the people in the house had not thrown other goods out after it, and which might have fallen upon it, and then I had been inevitably killed; but I was reserved for further afflictions.

This accident, however, spoiled my market for that time, and I came home to my governess very much hurt and bruised, and frighted to the last degree, and it was a good while before she could set me upon my feet again.

It was now a merry time of the year, and Bartholomew Fair was begun. I had never made any walks that way, nor was the common part of the fair of much advantage to me; but I took a turn this year into the cloisters, and among the rest I fell into one of the raffling shops. It was a thing of no great consequence to me, nor did I expect to make much of it; but there came a gentleman extremely well dressed and very rich, and as 'tis frequent to talk to everybody in those shops, he singled me out, and was very particular with me. First he told me he would put in for me to raffle, and did so; and some small matter coming to his lot, he presented it to me (I think it was a feather muff); then he continued to keep talking to me with a more than common appearance of respect, but still very civil, and much like a gentleman.

He held me in talk so long, till at last he drew me out of the raffling place to the shop-door, and then to a walk in the cloister, still talking of a thousand things cursorily without anything to the purpose. At last he told me that, without compliment, he was charmed with my company, and asked me if I durst trust myself in a coach with him; he told me he was a man of honour, and would not offer anything to me unbecoming him as such. I seemed to decline it a while, but suffered myself to be importuned a little, and then yielded.

I was at a loss in my thoughts to conclude at first what this gentleman designed; but I found afterwards he had had some drink in his head, and that he was not very unwilling to have some more. He carried me in the coach to the Spring Garden, at Knightsbridge, where we walked in the gardens, and he treated me very handsomely; but I found he drank very freely. He pressed me also to drink, but I declined it.

Hitherto he kept his word with me, and offered me nothing amiss. We came away in the coach again, and he brought me into the streets, and by this time it was near ten o'clock at night, and he stopped the coach at a house where, it seems, he was acquainted, and where they made no scruple to show us upstairs into a room with a bed in it. At first I seemed to be unwilling to go up, but after a few words I yielded to that too, being willing to see the end of it, and in hope to make something of it at last. As for the bed, etc., I was not much concerned about that part.

Here he began to be a little freer with me than he had promised; and I by little and little yielded to everything, so that, in a word, he did what he pleased with me; I need say no more. All this while he drank freely too, and about one in the morning we went into the coach again. The air and the shaking of the coach made the drink he had get more up in his head than it was before, and he grew uneasy in the coach, and was for acting over again what he had been doing before; but as I thought my game now secure, I resisted him, and brought him to be a little still, which had not lasted five minutes but he fell fast asleep.

I took this opportunity to search him to a nicety. I took a gold watch, with a silk purse of gold, his fine full-bottom periwig and silver-fringed gloves, his sword and fine snuff-box, and gently opening the coach door, stood ready to jump out while the coach was going on; but the coach stopped in the narrow street beyond Temple Bar to let another coach pass, I got softly out, fastened the door again, and gave my gentleman and the coach the slip both together, and never heard more of them.

This was an adventure indeed unlooked for, and perfectly undesigned by me; though I was not so past the merry part of life, as to forget how to behave, when a fop so blinded by his appetite should not know an old woman from a young. I did not indeed look so old as I was by ten or twelve years; yet I was not a young wench of seventeen, and it was easy enough to be distinguished. There is nothing so absurd, so surfeiting, so ridiculous, as a man heated by wine in his head, and wicked gust in his inclination together; he is in the possession of two devils at once, and can no more govern himself by his reason than a mill can grind without water; his vice tramples upon all that was in him that had any good in it, if any such thing there was; nay, his very sense is blinded by its own rage, and he acts absurdities even in his views; such a drinking more, when he is drunk already; picking up a common woman, without regard to what she is or who she is, whether sound or rotten, clean or unclean, whether ugly or handsome, whether old or young, and so blinded as not really to distinguish. Such a man is worse than a lunatic; prompted by his vicious, corrupted head, he no more knows what he is doing than this wretch of mine knew when I picked his pocket of his watch and his purse of gold.

These are the men of whom Solomon says, 'They go like an ox to the slaughter, till a dart strikes through their liver'; an admirable description, by the way, of the foul disease, which is a poisonous deadly contagion mingling with the blood, whose centre or foundation is in the liver; from whence, by the swift circulation of the whole mass, that dreadful nauseous plague strikes immediately through his liver, and his spirits are infected, his vitals stabbed through as with a dart.

It is true this poor unguarded wretch was in no danger from me, though I was greatly apprehensive at first of what danger I might be in from him; but he was really to be pitied in one respect, that he seemed to be a good sort of man in himself; a gentleman that had no harm in his design; a man of sense, and of a fine behaviour, a comely handsome person, a sober solid countenance, a charming beautiful face, and everything that could be agreeable; only had unhappily had some drink the night before, had not been in bed, as he told me when we were together; was hot, and his blood fired with wine, and in that condition his reason, as it were asleep, had given him up.

As for me, my business was his money, and what I could make of him; and after that, if I could have found out any way to have done it, I would have sent him safe home to his house and to his family, for 'twas ten to one but he had an honest, virtuous wife and innocent children, that were anxious for his safety, and would have been glad to have gotten him home, and have taken care of him till he was restored to himself. And then with what shame and regret would he look back upon himself! how would he reproach himself with associating himself with a whore! picked up in the worst of all holes, the cloister, among the dirt and filth of all the town! how would he be trembling for fear he had got the pox, for fear a dart had struck through his liver, and hate himself every time he looked back upon the madness and brutality of his debauch! how would he, if he had any principles of honour, as I verily believe he had—I say, how would he abhor the thought of giving any ill distemper, if he had it, as for aught he knew he might, to his modest and virtuous wife, and thereby sowing the contagion in the life-blood of his posterity.

Would such gentlemen but consider the contemptible thoughts which the very women they are concerned with, in such cases as these, have of them, it would be a surfeit to them. As I said above, they value not the pleasure, they are raised by no inclination to the man, the passive jade thinks of no pleasure but the money; and when he is, as it were, drunk in the ecstasies of his wicked pleasure, her hands are in his pockets searching for what she can find there, and of which he can no more be sensible in the moment of his folly that he can forethink of it when he goes about it.

I knew a woman that was so dexterous with a fellow, who indeed deserved no better usage, that while he was busy with her another way, conveyed his purse with twenty guineas in it out of his fob-pocket, where he had put it for fear of her, and put another purse with gilded counters in it into the room of it. After he had done, he says to her, 'Now han't you picked my pocket?' She jested with him, and told him she supposed he had not much to lose; he put his hand to his fob, and with his fingers felt that his purse was there, which fully satisfied him, and so she brought off his money. And this was a trade with her; she kept a sham gold watch, that is, a watch of silver gilt, and a purse of counters in her pocket to be ready on all such occasions, and I doubt not practiced it with success.

I came home with this last booty to my governess, and really when I told her the story, it so affected her that she was hardly able to forbear tears, to know how such a gentleman ran a daily risk of being undone every time a glass of wine got into his head.

But as to the purchase I got, and how entirely I stripped him, she told me it pleased her wonderfully. 'Nay child,' says she, 'the usage may, for aught I know, do more to reform him than all the sermons that ever he will hear in his life.' And if the remainder of the story be true, so it did.

I found the next day she was wonderful inquisitive about this gentleman; the description I had given her of him, his dress, his person, his face, everything concurred to make her think of a gentleman whose character she knew, and family too. She mused a while, and I going still on with the particulars, she starts up; says she, 'I'll lay #100 I know the gentleman.'

'I am sorry you do,' says I, 'for I would not have him exposed on any account in the world; he has had injury enough already by me, and I would not be instrumental to do him any more.' 'No, no,' says she, 'I will do him no injury, I assure you, but you may let me satisfy my curiosity a little, for if it is he, I warrant you I find it out.' I was a little startled at that, and told her, with an apparent concern in my face, that by the same rule he might find me out, and then I was undone. She returned warmly, 'Why, do you think I will betray you, child? No, no,' says she, 'not for all he is worth in the world. I have kept your counsel in worse things than these; sure you may trust me in this.' So I said no more at that time.

She laid her scheme another way, and without acquainting me of it, but she was resolved to find it out if possible. So she goes to a certain friend of hers who was acquainted in the family that she guessed at, and told her friend she had some extraordinary business with such a gentleman (who, by the way, was no less than a baronet, and of a very good family), and that she knew not how to come at him without somebody to introduce her. Her friend promised her very readily to do it, and accordingly goes to the house to see if the gentleman was in town.

The next day she come to my governess and tells her that Sir —— was at home, but that he had met with a disaster and was very ill, and there was no speaking with him. 'What disaster?' says my governess hastily, as if she was surprised at it. 'Why,' says her friend, 'he had been at Hampstead to visit a gentleman of his acquaintance, and as he came back again he was set upon and robbed; and having got a little drink too, as they suppose, the rogues abused him, and he is very ill.' 'Robbed!' says my governess, 'and what did they take from him?' 'Why,' says her friend, 'they took his gold watch and his gold snuff-box, his fine periwig, and what money he had in his pocket, which was considerable, to be sure, for Sir —— never goes without a purse of guineas about him.'

'Pshaw!' says my old governess, jeering, 'I warrant you he has got drunk now and got a whore, and she has picked his pocket, and so he comes home to his wife and tells her he has been robbed. That's an old sham; a thousand such tricks are put upon the poor women every day.'

'Fie!' says her friend, 'I find you don't know Sir ——; why he is as civil a gentleman, there is not a finer man, nor a soberer, graver, modester person in the whole city; he abhors such things; there's nobody that knows him will think such a thing of him.' 'Well, well,' says my governess, 'that's none of my business; if it was, I warrant I should find there was something of that kind in it; your modest men in common opinion are sometimes no better than other people, only they keep a better character, or, if you please, are the better hypocrites.'

'No, no,' says her friend, 'I can assure you Sir —— is no hypocrite, he is really an honest, sober gentleman, and he has certainly been robbed.' 'Nay,' says my governess, 'it may be he has; it is no business of mine, I tell you; I only want to speak with him; my business is of another nature.' 'But,' says her friend, 'let your business be of what nature it will, you cannot see him yet, for he is not fit to be seen, for he is very ill, and bruised very much,' 'Ay,' says my governess, 'nay, then he has fallen into bad hands, to be sure,' And then she asked gravely, 'Pray, where is he bruised?' 'Why, in the head,' says her friend, 'and one of his hands, and his face, for they used him barbarously.' 'Poor gentleman,' says my governess, 'I must wait, then, till he recovers'; and adds, 'I hope it will not be long, for I want very much to speak with him.'

Away she comes to me and tells me this story. 'I have found out your fine gentleman, and a fine gentleman he was,' says she; 'but, mercy on him, he is in a sad pickle now. I wonder what the d——l you have done to him; why, you have almost killed him.' I looked at her with disorder enough. 'I killed him!' says I; 'you must mistake the person; I am sure I did nothing to him; he was very well when I left him,' said I, 'only drunk and fast asleep.' 'I know nothing of that,' says she, 'but he is in a sad pickle now'; and so she told me all that her friend had said to her. 'Well, then,' says I, 'he fell into bad hands after I left him, for I am sure I left him safe enough.'

About ten days after, or a little more, my governess goes again to her friend, to introduce her to this gentleman; she had inquired other ways in the meantime, and found that he was about again, if not abroad again, so she got leave to speak with him.

She was a woman of a admirable address, and wanted nobody to introduce her; she told her tale much better than I shall be able to tell it for her, for she was a mistress of her tongue, as I have said already. She told him that she came, though a stranger, with a single design of doing him a service and he should find she had no other end in it; that as she came purely on so friendly an account, she begged promise from him, that if he did not accept what she should officiously propose he would not take it ill that she meddled with what was not her business. She assured him that as what she had to say was a secret that belonged to him only, so whether he accepted her offer or not, it should remain a secret to all the world, unless he exposed it himself; nor should his refusing her service in it make her so little show her respect as to do him the least injury, so that he should be entirely at liberty to act as he thought fit.

He looked very shy at first, and said he knew nothing that related to him that required much secrecy; that he had never done any man any wrong, and cared not what anybody might say of him; that it was no part of his character to be unjust to anybody, nor could he imagine in what any man could render him any service; but that if it was so disinterested a service as she said, he could not take it ill from any one that they should endeavour to serve him; and so, as it were, left her a liberty either to tell him or not to tell, as she thought fit.

She found him so perfectly indifferent, that she was almost afraid to enter into the point with him; but, however, after some other circumlocutions she told him that by a strange and unaccountable accident she came to have a particular knowledge of the late unhappy adventure he had fallen into, and that in such a manner, that there was nobody in the world but herself and him that were acquainted with it, no, not the very person that was with him.

He looked a little angrily at first. 'What adventure?' said he. 'Why,' said she, 'of your being robbed coming from Knightbr——; Hampstead, sir, I should say,' says she. 'Be not surprised, sir,' says she, 'that I am able to tell you every step you took that day from the cloister in Smithfield to the Spring Garden at Knightsbridge, and thence to the —— in the Strand, and how you were left asleep in the coach afterwards. I say, let not this surprise you, for, sir, I do not come to make a booty of you, I ask nothing of you, and I assure you the woman that was with you knows nothing who you are, and never shall; and yet perhaps I may serve you further still, for I did not come barely to let you know that I was informed of these things, as if I wanted a bribe to conceal them; assure yourself, sir,' said she, 'that whatever you think fit to do or say to me, it shall be all a secret as it is, as much as if I were in my grave.'

He was astonished at her discourse, and said gravely to her, 'Madam, you are a stranger to me, but it is very unfortunate that you should be let into the secret of the worst action of my life, and a thing that I am so justly ashamed of, that the only satisfaction of it to me was, that I thought it was known only to God and my own conscience.' 'Pray, sir,' says she, 'do not reckon the discovery of it to me to be any part of your misfortune. It was a thing, I believe, you were surprised into, and perhaps the woman used some art to prompt you to it; however, you will never find any just cause,' said she, 'to repent that I came to hear of it; nor can your own mouth be more silent in it that I have been, and ever shall be.'

'Well,' says he, 'but let me do some justice to the woman too; whoever she is, I do assure you she prompted me to nothing, she rather declined me. It was my own folly and madness that brought me into it all, ay, and brought her into it too; I must give her her due so far. As to what she took from me, I could expect no less from her in the condition I was in, and to this hour I know not whether she robbed me or the coachman; if she did it, I forgive her, and I think all gentlemen that do so should be used in the same manner; but I am more concerned for some other things that I am for all that she took from me.'

My governess now began to come into the whole matter, and he opened himself freely to her. First she said to him, in answer to what he had said about me, 'I am glad, sir, you are so just to the person that you were with; I assure you she is a gentlewoman, and no woman of the town; and however you prevailed with her so far as you did, I am sure 'tis not her practice. You ran a great venture indeed, sir; but if that be any part of your care, I am persuaded you may be perfectly easy, for I dare assure you no man has touched her, before you, since her husband, and he has been dead now almost eight years.'

It appeared that this was his grievance, and that he was in a very great fright about it; however, when my governess said this to him, he appeared very well pleased, and said, 'Well, madam, to be plain with you, if I was satisfied of that, I should not so much value what I lost; for, as to that, the temptation was great, and perhaps she was poor and wanted it.' 'If she had not been poor, sir ———,' says my governess, 'I assure you she would never have yielded to you; and as her poverty first prevailed with her to let you do as you did, so the same poverty prevailed with her to pay herself at last, when she saw you were in such a condition, that if she had not done it, perhaps the next coachman might have done it.'

'Well,' says he, 'much good may it do her. I say again, all the gentlemen that do so ought to be used in the same manner, and then they would be cautious of themselves. I have no more concern about it, but on the score which you hinted at before, madam.' Here he entered into some freedoms with her on the subject of what passed between us, which are not so proper for a woman to write, and the great terror that was upon his mind with relation to his wife, for fear he should have received any injury from me, and should communicate if farther; and asked her at last if she could not procure him an opportunity to speak with me. My governess gave him further assurances of my being a woman clear from any such thing, and that he was as entirely safe in that respect as he was with his own lady; but as for seeing me, she said it might be of dangerous consequence; but, however, that she would talk with me, and let him know my answer, using at the same time some arguments to persuade him not to desire it, and that it could be of no service to him, seeing she hoped he had no desire to renew a correspondence with me, and that on my account it was a kind of putting my life in his hands.

He told her he had a great desire to see me, that he would give her any assurances that were in his power, not to take any advantages of me, and that in the first place he would give me a general release from all demands of any kind. She insisted how it might tend to a further divulging the secret, and might in the end be injurious to him, entreating him not to press for it; so at length he desisted.

They had some discourse upon the subject of the things he had lost, and he seemed to be very desirous of his gold watch, and told her if she could procure that for him, he would willingly give as much for it as it was worth. She told him she would endeavour to procure it for him, and leave the valuing it to himself.

Accordingly the next day she carried the watch, and he gave her thirty guineas for it, which was more than I should have been able to make of it, though it seems it cost much more. He spoke something of his periwig, which it seems cost him threescore guineas, and his snuff-box, and in a few days more she carried them too; which obliged him very much, and he gave her thirty more. The next day I sent him his fine sword and cane gratis, and demanded nothing of him, but I had no mind to see him, unless it had been so that he might be satisfied I knew who he was, which he was not willing to.

Then he entered into a long talk with her of the manner how she came to know all this matter. She formed a long tale of that part; how she had it from one that I had told the whole story to, and that was to help me dispose of the goods; and this confidante brought the things to her, she being by profession a pawnbroker; and she hearing of his worship's disaster, guessed at the thing in general; that having gotten the things into her hands, she had resolved to come and try as she had done. She then gave him repeated assurances that it should never go out of her mouth, and though she knew the woman very well, yet she had not let her know, meaning me, anything of it; that is to say, who the person was, which, by the way, was false; but, however, it was not to his damage, for I never opened my mouth of it to anybody.

I had a great many thoughts in my head about my seeing him again, and was often sorry that I had refused it. I was persuaded that if I had seen him, and let him know that I knew him, I should have made some advantage of him, and perhaps have had some maintenance from him; and though it was a life wicked enough, yet it was not so full of danger as this I was engaged in. However, those thoughts wore off, and I declined seeing him again, for that time; but my governess saw him often, and he was very kind to her, giving her something almost every time he saw her. One time in particular she found him very merry, and as she thought he had some wine in his head, and he pressed her again very earnestly to let him see that woman that, as he said, had bewitched him so that night, my governess, who was from the beginning for my seeing him, told him he was so desirous of it that she could almost yield of it, if she could prevail upon me; adding that if he would please to come to her house in the evening, she would endeavour it, upon his repeated assurances of forgetting what was past.

Accordingly she came to me, and told me all the discourse; in short, she soon biassed me to consent, in a case which I had some regret in my mind for declining before; so I prepared to see him. I dressed me to all the advantage possible, I assure you, and for the first time used a little art; I say for the first time, for I had never yielded to the baseness of paint before, having always had vanity enough to believe I had no need of it.

At the hour appointed he came; and as she observed before, so it was plain still, that he had been drinking, though very far from what we call being in drink. He appeared exceeding pleased to see me, and entered into a long discourse with me upon the old affair. I begged his pardon very often for my share of it, protested I had not any such design when first I met him, that I had not gone out with him but that I took him for a very civil gentleman, and that he made me so many promises of offering no uncivility to me.

He alleged the wine he drank, and that he scarce knew what he did, and that if it had not been so, I should never have let him take the freedom with me that he had done. He protested to me that he never touched any woman but me since he was married to his wife, and it was a surprise upon him; complimented me upon being so particularly agreeable to him, and the like; and talked so much of that kind, till I found he had talked himself almost into a temper to do the same thing over again. But I took him up short. I protested I had never suffered any man to touch me since my husband died, which was near eight years. He said he believed it to be so truly; and added that madam had intimated as much to him, and that it was his opinion of that part which made his desire to see me again; and that since he had once broke in upon his virtue with me, and found no ill consequences, he could be safe in venturing there again; and so, in short, it went on to what I expected, and to what will not bear relating.

My old governess had foreseen it, as well as I, and therefore led him into a room which had not a bed in it, and yet had a chamber within it which had a bed, whither we withdrew for the rest of the night; and, in short, after some time being together, he went to bed, and lay there all night. I withdrew, but came again undressed in the morning, before it was day, and lay with him the rest of the time.

Thus, you see, having committed a crime once is a sad handle to the committing of it again; whereas all the regret and reflections wear off when the temptation renews itself. Had I not yielded to see him again, the corrupt desire in him had worn off, and 'tis very probable he had never fallen into it with anybody else, as I really believe he had not done before.

When he went away, I told him I hoped he was satisfied he had not been robbed again. He told me he was satisfied in that point, and could trust me again, and putting his hand in his pocket, gave me five guineas, which was the first money I had gained that way for many years.

I had several visits of the like kind from him, but he never came into a settled way of maintenance, which was what I would have best pleased with. Once, indeed, he asked me how I did to live. I answered him pretty quick, that I assured him I had never taken that course that I took with him, but that indeed I worked at my needle, and could just maintain myself; that sometime it was as much as I was able to do, and I shifted hard enough.

He seemed to reflect upon himself that he should be the first person to lead me into that, which he assured me he never intended to do himself; and it touched him a little, he said, that he should be the cause of his own sin and mine too. He would often make just reflections also upon the crime itself, and upon the particular circumstances of it with respect to himself; how wine introduced the inclinations how the devil led him to the place, and found out an object to tempt him, and he made the moral always himself.

When these thoughts were upon him he would go away, and perhaps not come again in a month's time or longer; but then as the serious part wore off, the lewd part would wear in, and then he came prepared for the wicked part. Thus we lived for some time; thought he did not keep, as they call it, yet he never failed doing things that were handsome, and sufficient to maintain me without working, and, which was better, without following my old trade.

But this affair had its end too; for after about a year, I found that he did not come so often as usual, and at last he left if off altogether without any dislike to bidding adieu; and so there was an end of that short scene of life, which added no great store to me, only to make more work for repentance.

However, during this interval I confined myself pretty much at home; at least, being thus provided for, I made no adventures, no, not for a quarter of a year after he left me; but then finding the fund fail, and being loth to spend upon the main stock, I began to think of my old trade, and to look abroad into the street again; and my first step was lucky enough.

I had dressed myself up in a very mean habit, for as I had several shapes to appear in, I was now in an ordinary stuff-gown, a blue apron, and a straw hat and I placed myself at the door of the Three Cups Inn in St. John Street. There were several carriers used the inn, and the stage-coaches for Barnet, for Totteridge, and other towns that way stood always in the street in the evening, when they prepared to set out, so that I was ready for anything that offered, for either one or other. The meaning was this; people come frequently with bundles and small parcels to those inns, and call for such carriers or coaches as they want, to carry them into the country; and there generally attend women, porters' wives or daughters, ready to take in such things for their respective people that employ them.

It happened very oddly that I was standing at the inn gate, and a woman that had stood there before, and which was the porter's wife belonging to the Barnet stage-coach, having observed me, asked if I waited for any of the coaches. I told her Yes, I waited for my mistress, that was coming to go to Barnet. She asked me who was my mistress, and I told her any madam's name that came next me; but as it seemed, I happened upon a name, a family of which name lived at Hadley, just beyond Barnet.

I said no more to her, or she to me, a good while; but by and by, somebody calling her at a door a little way off, she desired me that if anybody called for the Barnet coach, I would step and call her at the house, which it seems was an alehouse. I said Yes, very readily, and away she went.

She was no sooner gone but comes a wench and a child, puffing and sweating, and asks for the Barnet coach. I answered presently,

'Here.' 'Do you belong to the Barnet coach?' says she. 'Yes, sweetheart,' said I; 'what do ye want?' 'I want room for two passengers,' says she. 'Where are they, sweetheart?' said I. 'Here's this girl, pray let her go into the coach,' says she, 'and I'll go and fetch my mistress.' 'Make haste, then, sweetheart,' says I, 'for we may be full else.' The maid had a great bundle under her arm; so she put the child into the coach, and I said, 'You had best put your bundle into the coach too.' 'No,' says she, 'I am afraid somebody should slip it away from the child.' 'Give to me, then,' said I, 'and I'll take care of it.' 'Do, then,' says she, 'and be sure you take of it.' 'I'll answer for it,' said I, 'if it were for #20 value.' 'There, take it, then,' says she, and away she goes.

As soon as I had got the bundle, and the maid was out of sight, I goes on towards the alehouse, where the porter's wife was, so that if I had met her, I had then only been going to give her the bundle, and to call her to her business, as if I was going away, and could stay no longer; but as I did not meet her, I walked away, and turning into Charterhouse Lane, then crossed into Batholomew Close, so into Little Britain, and through the Bluecoat Hospital, into Newgate Street.

To prevent my being known, I pulled off my blue apron, and wrapped the bundle in it, which before was made up in a piece of painted calico, and very remarkable; I also wrapped up my straw hat in it, and so put the bundle upon my head; and it was very well that I did thus, for coming through the Bluecoat Hospital, who should I meet but the wench that had given me the bundle to hold. It seems she was going with her mistress, whom she had been gone to fetch, to the Barnet coaches.

I saw she was in haste, and I had no business to stop her; so away she went, and I brought my bundle safe home to my governess. There was no money, nor plate, or jewels in the bundle, but a very good suit of Indian damask, a gown and a petticoat, a laced-head and ruffles of very good Flanders lace, and some linen and other things, such as I knew very well the value of.

This was not indeed my own invention, but was given me by one that had practised it with success, and my governess liked it extremely; and indeed I tried it again several times, though never twice near the same place; for the next time I tried it in White Chapel, just by the corner of Petticoat Lane, where the coaches stand that go out to Stratford and Bow, and that side of the country, and another time at the Flying Horse, without Bishopgate, where the Cheston coaches then lay; and I had always the good luck to come off with some booty.

Another time I placed myself at a warehouse by the waterside, where the coasting vessels from the north come, such as from Newcastle-upon-Tyne, Sunderland, and other places. Here, the warehouses being shut, comes a young fellow with a letter; and he wanted a box and a hamper that was come from Newcastle-upon-Tyne. I asked him if he had the marks of it; so he shows me the letter, by virtue of which he was to ask for it, and which gave an account of the contents, the box being full of linen, and the hamper full of glass ware. I read the letter, and took care to see the name, and the marks, the name of the person that sent the goods, the name of the person that they were sent to; then I bade the messenger come in the morning, for that the warehouse-keeper would not be there any more that night.

Away went I, and getting materials in a public house, I wrote a letter from Mr. John Richardson of Newcastle to his dear cousin Jemmy Cole, in London, with an account that he sent by such a vessel (for I remembered all the particulars to a title), so many pieces of huckaback linen, so many ells of Dutch holland and the like, in a box, and a hamper of flint glasses from Mr. Henzill's glasshouse; and that the box was marked I. C. No. I, and the hamper was directed by a label on the cording.

About an hour after, I came to the warehouse, found the warehouse-keeper, and had the goods delivered me without any scruple; the value of the linen being about #22.

I could fill up this whole discourse with the variety of such adventures, which daily invention directed to, and which I managed with the utmost dexterity, and always with success.

At length—as when does the pitcher come safe home that goes so very often to the well?—I fell into some small broils, which though they could not affect me fatally, yet made me known, which was the worst thing next to being found guilty that could befall me.

I had taken up the disguise of a widow's dress; it was without any real design in view, but only waiting for anything that might offer, as I often did. It happened that while I was going along the street in Covent Garden, there was a great cry of 'Stop thief! Stop thief!' some artists had, it seems, put a trick upon a shopkeeper, and being pursued, some of them fled one way, and some another; and one of them was, they said, dressed up in widow's weeds, upon which the mob gathered about me, and some said I was the person, others said no. Immediately came the mercer's journeyman, and he swore aloud I was the person, and so seized on me. However, when I was brought back by the mob to the mercer's shop, the master of the house said freely that I was not the woman that was in his shop, and would have let me go immediately; but another fellow said gravely, 'Pray stay till Mr. ———' (meaning the journeyman) 'comes back, for he knows her.' So they kept me by force near half an hour. They had called a constable, and he stood in the shop as my jailer; and in talking with the constable I inquired where he lived, and what trade he was; the man not apprehending in the least what happened afterwards, readily told me his name, and trade, and where he lived; and told me as a jest, that I might be sure to hear of his name when I came to the Old Bailey.

Some of the servants likewise used me saucily, and had much ado to keep their hands off me; the master indeed was civiller to me than they, but he would not yet let me go, though he owned he could not say I was in his shop before.

I began to be a little surly with him, and told him I hoped he would not take it ill if I made myself amends upon him in a more legal way another time; and desired I might send for friends to see me have right done me. No, he said, he could give no such liberty; I might ask it when I came before the justice of peace; and seeing I threatened him, he would take care of me in the meantime, and would lodge me safe in Newgate. I told him it was his time now, but it would be mine by and by, and governed my passion as well as I was able. However, I spoke to the constable to call me a porter, which he did, and then I called for pen, ink, and paper, but they would let me have none. I asked the porter his name, and where he lived, and the poor man told it me very willingly. I bade him observe and remember how I was treated there; that he saw I was detained there by force. I told him I should want his evidence in another place, and it should not be the worse for him to speak. The porter said he would serve me with all his heart. 'But, madam,' says he, 'let me hear them refuse to let you go, then I may be able to speak the plainer.'

With that I spoke aloud to the master of the shop, and said, 'Sir, you know in your own conscience that I am not the person you look for, and that I was not in your shop before, therefore I demand that you detain me here no longer, or tell me the reason of your stopping me.' The fellow grew surlier upon this than before, and said he would do neither till he thought fit. 'Very well,' said I to the constable and to the porter; 'you will be pleased to remember this, gentlemen, another time.' The porter said, 'Yes, madam'; and the constable began not to like it, and would have persuaded the mercer to dismiss him, and let me go, since, as he said, he owned I was not the person. 'Good, sir,' says the mercer to him tauntingly, 'are you a justice of peace or a constable? I charged you with her; pray do you do your duty.' The constable told him, a little moved, but very handsomely, 'I know my duty, and what I am, sir; I doubt you hardly know what you are doing.' They had some other hard words, and in the meantime the journeyman, impudent and unmanly to the last degree, used me barbarously, and one of them, the same that first seized upon me, pretended he would search me, and began to lay hands on me. I spit in his face, called out to the constable, and bade him to take notice of my usage. 'And pray, Mr. Constable,' said I, 'ask that villain's name,' pointing to the man. The constable reproved him decently, told him that he did not know what he did, for he knew that his master acknowledged I was not the person that was in his shop; 'and,' says the constable, 'I am afraid your master is bringing himself, and me too, into trouble, if this gentlewoman comes to prove who she is, and where she was, and it appears that she is not the woman you pretend to.' 'Damn her,' says the fellow again, with a impudent, hardened face, 'she is the lady, you may depend upon it; I'll swear she is the same body that was in the shop, and that I gave the pieces of satin that is lost into her own hand. You shall hear more of it when Mr. William and Mr. Anthony (those were other journeymen) come back; they will know her again as well as I.'

Just as the insolent rogue was talking thus to the constable, comes back Mr. William and Mr. Anthony, as he called them, and a great rabble with them, bringing along with them the true widow that I was pretended to be; and they came sweating and blowing into the shop, and with a great deal of triumph, dragging the poor creature in the most butcherly manner up towards their master, who was in the back shop, and cried out aloud, 'Here's the widow, sir; we have catcher her at last.' 'What do ye mean by that?' says the master. 'Why, we have her already; there she sits,' says he, 'and Mr. ———,' says he, 'can swear this is she.' The other man, whom they called Mr. Anthony, replied, 'Mr. ——— may say what he will, and swear what he will, but this is the woman, and there's the remnant of satin she stole; I took it out of her clothes with my own hand.'

I sat still now, and began to take a better heart, but smiled and said nothing; the master looked pale; the constable turned about and looked at me. 'Let 'em alone, Mr. Constable,' said I; 'let 'em go on.' The case was plain and could not be denied, so the constable was charged with the right thief, and the mercer told me very civilly he was sorry for the mistake, and hoped I would not take it ill; that they had so many things of this nature put upon them every day, that they could not be blamed for being very sharp in doing themselves justice. 'Not take it ill, sir!' said I; 'how can I take it well! If you had dismissed me when your insolent fellow seized on me it the street, and brought me to you, and when you yourself acknowledged I was not the person, I would have put it by, and not taken it ill, because of the many ill things I believe you have put upon you daily; but your treatment of me since has been insufferable, and especially that of your servant; I must and will have reparation for that.'

Then he began to parley with me, said he would make me any reasonable satisfaction, and would fain have had me tell him what it was I expected. I told him that I should not be my own judge, the law should decide it for me; and as I was to be carried before a magistrate, I should let him hear there what I had to say. He told me there was no occasion to go before the justice now, I was at liberty to go where I pleased; and so, calling to the constable, told him he might let me go, for I was discharged. The constable said calmly to him, 'sir, you asked me just now if I knew whether I was a constable or justice, and bade me do my duty, and charged me with this gentlewoman as a prisoner. Now, sir, I find you do not understand what is my duty, for you would make me a justice indeed; but I must tell you it is not in my power. I may keep a prisoner when I am charged with him, but 'tis the law and the magistrate alone that can discharge that prisoner; therefore 'tis a mistake, sir; I must carry her before a justice now, whether you think well of it or not.' The mercer was very high with the constable at first; but the constable happening to be not a hired officer, but a good, substantial kind of man (I think he was a corn-handler), and a man of good sense, stood to his business, would not discharge me without going to a justice of the peace; and I insisted upon it too. When the mercer saw that, 'Well,' says he to the constable, 'you may carry her where you please; I have nothing to say to her.' 'But, sir,' says the constable, 'you will go with us, I hope, for 'tis you that charged me with her.' 'No, not I,' says the mercer; 'I tell you I have nothing to say to her.' 'But pray, sir, do,' says the constable; 'I desire it of you for your own sake, for the justice can do nothing without you.' 'Prithee, fellow,' says the mercer, 'go about your business; I tell you I have nothing to say to the gentlewoman. I charge you in the king's name to dismiss her.' 'Sir,' says the constable, 'I find you don't know what it is to be constable; I beg of you don't oblige me to be rude to you.' 'I think I need not; you are rude enough already,' says the mercer. 'No, sir,' says the constable, 'I am not rude; you have broken the peace in bringing an honest woman out of the street, when she was about her lawful occasion, confining her in your shop, and ill-using her here by your servants; and now can you say I am rude to you? I think I am civil to you in not commanding or charging you in the king's name to go with me, and charging every man I see that passes your door to aid and assist me in carrying you by force; this you cannot but know I have power to do, and yet I forbear it, and once more entreat you to go with me.' Well, he would not for all this, and gave the constable ill language. However, the constable kept his temper, and would not be provoked; and then I put in and said, 'Come, Mr. Constable, let him alone; I shall find ways enough to fetch him before a magistrate, I don't fear that; but there's the fellow,' says I, 'he was the man that seized on me as I was innocently going along the street, and you are a witness of the violence with me since; give me leave to charge you with him, and carry him before the justice.' 'Yes, madam,' says the constable; and turning to the fellow 'Come, young gentleman,' says he to the journeyman, 'you must go along with us; I hope you are not above the constable's power, though your master is.'

The fellow looked like a condemned thief, and hung back, then looked at his master, as if he could help him; and he, like a fool, encourage the fellow to be rude, and he truly resisted the constable, and pushed him back with a good force when he went to lay hold on him, at which the constable knocked him down, and called out for help; and immediately the shop was filled with people, and the constable seized the master and man, and all his servants.

This first ill consequence of this fray was, that the woman they had taken, who was really the thief, made off, and got clear away in the crowd; and two other that they had stopped also; whether they were really guilty or not, that I can say nothing to.

By this time some of his neighbours having come in, and, upon inquiry, seeing how things went, had endeavoured to bring the hot-brained mercer to his senses, and he began to be convinced that he was in the wrong; and so at length we went all very quietly before the justice, with a mob of about five hundred people at our heels; and all the way I went I could hear the people ask what was the matter, and other reply and say, a mercer had stopped a gentlewoman instead of a thief, and had afterwards taken the thief, and now the gentlewoman had taken the mercer, and was carrying him before the justice. This pleased the people strangely, and made the crowd increase, and they cried out as they went, 'Which is the rogue? which is the mercer?' and especially the women. Then when they saw him they cried out, 'That's he, that's he'; and every now and then came a good dab of dirt at him; and thus we marched a good while, till the mercer thought fit to desire the constable to call a coach to protect himself from the rabble; so we rode the rest of the way, the constable and I, and the mercer and his man.

When we came to the justice, which was an ancient gentleman in Bloomsbury, the constable giving first a summary account of the matter, the justice bade me speak, and tell what I had to say. And first he asked my name, which I was very loth to give, but there was no remedy, so I told him my name was Mary Flanders, that I was a widow, my husband being a sea captain, died on a voyage to Virginia; and some other circumstances I told which he could never contradict, and that I lodged at present in town with such a person, naming my governess; but that I was preparing to go over to America, where my husband's effects lay, and that I was going that day to buy some clothes to put myself into second mourning, but had not yet been in any shop, when that fellow, pointing to the mercer's journeyman, came rushing upon me with such fury as very much frighted me, and carried me back to his master's shop, where, though his master acknowledged I was not the person, yet he would not dismiss me, but charged a constable with me.

Then I proceeded to tell how the journeyman treated me; how they would not suffer me to send for any of my friends; how afterwards they found the real thief, and took the very goods they had lost upon her, and all the particulars as before.

Then the constable related his case: his dialogue with the mercer about discharging me, and at last his servant's refusing to go with him, when he had charged him with him, and his master encouraging him to do so, and at last his striking the constable, and the like, all as I have told it already.

The justice then heard the mercer and his man. The mercer indeed made a long harangue of the great loss they have daily by lifters and thieves; that it was easy for them to mistake, and that when he found it he would have dismissed me, etc., as above. As to the journeyman, he had very little to say, but that he pretended other of the servants told him that I was really the person.

Upon the whole, the justice first of all told me very courteously I was discharged; that he was very sorry that the mercer's man should in his eager pursuit have so little discretion as to take up an innocent person for a guilty person; that if he had not been so unjust as to detain me afterward, he believed I would have forgiven the first affront; that, however, it was not in his power to award me any reparation for anything, other than by openly reproving them, which he should do; but he supposed I would apply to such methods as the law directed; in the meantime he would bind him over.

But as to the breach of the peace committed by the journeyman, he told me he should give me some satisfaction for that, for he should commit him to Newgate for assaulting the constable, and for assaulting me also.

Accordingly he sent the fellow to Newgate for that assault, and his master gave bail, and so we came away; but I had the satisfaction of seeing the mob wait upon them both, as they came out, hallooing and throwing stones and dirt at the coaches they rode in; and so I came home to my governess.

After this hustle, coming home and telling my governess the story, she falls a-laughing at me. 'Why are you merry?' says I; 'the story has not so much laughing room in it as you imagine; I am sure I have had a great deal of hurry and fright too, with a pack of ugly rogues.' 'Laugh!' says my governess; 'I laugh, child, to see what a lucky creature you are; why, this job will be the best bargain to you that ever you made in your life, if you manage it well. I warrant you,' says she, 'you shall make the mercer pay you #500 for damages, besides what you shall get out of the journeyman.'

I had other thoughts of the matter than she had; and especially, because I had given in my name to the justice of peace; and I knew that my name was so well known among the people at Hick's Hall, the Old Bailey, and such places, that if this cause came to be tried openly, and my name came to be inquired into, no court would give much damages, for the reputation of a person of such a character. However, I was obliged to begin a prosecution in form, and accordingly my governess found me out a very creditable sort of a man to manage it, being an attorney of very good business, and of a good reputation, and she was certainly in the right of this; for had she employed a pettifogging hedge solicitor, or a man not known, and not in good reputation, I should have brought it to but little.

I met this attorney, and gave him all the particulars at large, as they are recited above; and he assured me it was a case, as he said, that would very well support itself, and that he did not question but that a jury would give very considerable damages on such an occasion; so taking his full instructions he began the prosecution, and the mercer being arrested, gave bail. A few days after his giving bail, he comes with his attorney to my attorney, to let him know that he desired to accommodate the matter; that it was all carried on in the heat of an unhappy passion; that his client, meaning me, had a sharp provoking tongue, that I used them ill, gibing at them, and jeering them, even while they believed me to be the very person, and that I had provoked them, and the like.

My attorney managed as well on my side; made them believe was a widow of fortune, that I was able to do myself justice, and had great friends to stand by me too, who had all made me promise to sue to the utmost, and that if it cost me a thousand pounds I would be sure to have satisfaction, for that the affronts I had received were insufferable.

However, they brought my attorney to this, that he promised he would not blow the coals, that if I inclined to accommodation, he would not hinder me, and that he would rather persuade me to peace than to war; for which they told him he should be no loser; all which he told me very honestly, and told me that if they offered him any bribe, I should certainly know it; but upon the whole he told me very honestly that if I would take his opinion, he would advise me to make it up with them, for that as they were in a great fright, and were desirous above all things to make it up, and knew that, let it be what it would, they would be allotted to bear all the costs of the suit; he believed they would give me freely more than any jury or court of justice would give upon a trial. I asked him what he thought they would be brought to. He told me he could not tell as to that, but he would tell me more when I saw him again.

Some time after this, they came again to know if he had talked with me. He told them he had; that he found me not so averse to an accommodation as some of my friends were, who resented the disgrace offered me, and set me on; that they blowed the coals in secret, prompting me to revenge, or do myself justice, as they called it; so that he could not tell what to say to it; he told them he would do his endeavour to persuade me, but he ought to be able to tell me what proposal they made. They pretended they could not make any proposal, because it might be made use of against them; and he told them, that by the same rule he could not make any offers, for that might be pleaded in abatement of what damages a jury might be inclined to give. However, after some discourse and mutual promises that no advantage should be taken on either side, by what was transacted then or at any other of those meetings, they came to a kind of a treaty; but so remote, and so wide from one another, that nothing could be expected from it; for my attorney demanded #500 and charges, and they offered #50 without charges; so they broke off, and the mercer proposed to have a meeting with me myself; and my attorney agreed to that very readily.

My attorney gave me notice to come to this meeting in good clothes, and with some state, that the mercer might see I was something more than I seemed to be that time they had me. Accordingly I came in a new suit of second mourning, according to what I had said at the justice's. I set myself out, too, as well as a widow's dress in second mourning would admit; my governess also furnished me with a good pearl necklace, that shut in behind with a locket of diamonds, which she had in pawn; and I had a very good figure; and as I stayed till I was sure they were come, I came in a coach to the door, with my maid with me.

When I came into the room the mercer was surprised. He stood up and made his bow, which I took a little notice of, and but a little, and went and sat down where my own attorney had pointed to me to sit, for it was his house. After a little while the mercer said, he did not know me again, and began to make some compliments his way. I told him, I believed he did not know me at first, and that if he had, I believed he would not have treated me as he did.

He told me he was very sorry for what had happened, and that it was to testify the willingness he had to make all possible reparation that he had appointed this meeting; that he hoped I would not carry things to extremity, which might be not only too great a loss to him, but might be the ruin of his business and shop, in which case I might have the satisfaction of repaying an injury with an injury ten times greater; but that I would then get nothing, whereas he was willing to do me any justice that was in his power, without putting himself or me to the trouble or charge of a suit at law.

I told him I was glad to hear him talk so much more like a man of sense than he did before; that it was true, acknowledgment in most cases of affronts was counted reparation sufficient; but this had gone too far to be made up so; that I was not revengeful, nor did I seek his ruin, or any man's else, but that all my friends were unanimous not to let me so far neglect my character as to adjust a thing of this kind without a sufficient reparation of honour; that to be taken up for a thief was such an indignity as could not be put up; that my character was above being treated so by any that knew me, but because in my condition of a widow I had been for some time careless of myself, and negligent of myself, I might be taken for such a creature, but that for the particular usage I had from him afterwards,—and then I repeated all as before; it was so provoking I had scarce patience to repeat it.

Well, he acknowledged all, and was might humble indeed; he made proposals very handsome; he came up to #100 and to pay all the law charges, and added that he would make me a present of a very good suit of clothes. I came down to #300, and I demanded that I should publish an advertisement of the particulars in the common newspapers.

This was a clause he never could comply with. However, at last he came up, by good management of my attorney, to #150 and a suit of black silk clothes; and there I agree, and as it were, at my attorney's request, complied with it, he paying my attorney's bill and charges, and gave us a good supper into the bargain.

When I came to receive the money, I brought my governess with me, dressed like an old duchess, and a gentleman very well dressed, who we pretended courted me, but I called him cousin, and the lawyer was only to hint privately to him that his gentleman courted the widow.

He treated us handsomely indeed, and paid the money cheerfully enough; so that it cost him #200 in all, or rather more. At our last meeting, when all was agreed, the case of the journeyman came up, and the mercer begged very hard for him; told me he was a man that had kept a shop of his own, and been in good business, had a wife, and several children, and was very poor; that he had nothing to make satisfaction with, but he should come to beg my pardon on his knees, if I desired it, as openly as I pleased. I had no spleen at the saucy rogue, nor were his submissions anything to me, since there was nothing to be got by him, so I thought it was as good to throw that in generously as not; so I told him I did not desire the ruin of any man, and therefore at his request I would forgive the wretch; it was below me to seek any revenge.

When we were at supper he brought the poor fellow in to make acknowledgment, which he would have done with as much mean humility as his offence was with insulting haughtiness and pride, in which he was an instance of a complete baseness of spirit, impious, cruel, and relentless when uppermost and in prosperity, abject and low-spirited when down in affliction. However, I abated his cringes, told him I forgave him, and desired he might withdraw, as if I did not care for the sight of him, though I had forgiven him.

I was now in good circumstances indeed, if I could have known my time for leaving off, and my governess often said I was the richest of the trade in England; and so I believe I was, for I had #700 by me in money, besides clothes, rings, some plate, and two gold watches, and all of them stolen, for I had innumerable jobs besides these I have mentioned. Oh! had I even now had the grace of repentance, I had still leisure to have looked back upon my follies, and have made some reparation; but the satisfaction I was to make for the public mischiefs I had done was yet left behind; and I could not forbear going abroad again, as I called it now, than any more I could when my extremity really drove me out for bread.

It was not long after the affair with the mercer was made up, that I went out in an equipage quite different from any I had ever appeared in before. I dressed myself like a beggar woman, in the coarsest and most despicable rags I could get, and I walked about peering and peeping into every door and window I came near; and indeed I was in such a plight now that I knew as ill how to behave in as ever I did in any. I naturally abhorred dirt and rags; I had been bred up tight and cleanly, and could be no other, whatever condition I was in; so that this was the most uneasy disguise to me that ever I put on. I said presently to myself that this would not do, for this was a dress that everybody was shy and afraid of; and I thought everybody looked at me, as if they were afraid I should come near them, lest I should take something from them, or afraid to come near me, lest they should get something from me. I wandered about all the evening the first time I went out, and made nothing of it, but came home again wet, draggled, and tired. However, I went out again the next night, and then I met with a little adventure, which had like to have cost me dear. As I was standing near a tavern door, there comes a gentleman on horseback, and lights at the door, and wanting to go into the tavern, he calls one of the drawers to hold his horse. He stayed pretty long in the tavern, and the drawer heard his master call, and thought he would be angry with him. Seeing me stand by him, he called to me, 'Here, woman,' says he, 'hold this horse a while, till I go in; if the gentleman comes, he'll give you something.' 'Yes,' says I, and takes the horse, and walks off with him very soberly, and carried him to my governess.

This had been a booty to those that had understood it; but never was poor thief more at a loss to know what to do with anything that was stolen; for when I came home, my governess was quite confounded, and what to do with the creature, we neither of us knew. To send him to a stable was doing nothing, for it was certain that public notice would be given in the Gazette, and the horse described, so that we durst not go to fetch it again.

All the remedy we had for this unlucky adventure was to go and set up the horse at an inn, and send a note by a porter to the tavern, that the gentleman's horse that was lost such a time was left at such an inn, and that he might be had there; that the poor woman that held him, having led him about the street, not being able to lead him back again, had left him there. We might have waited till the owner had published and offered a reward, but we did not care to venture the receiving the reward.

So this was a robbery and no robbery, for little was lost by it, and nothing was got by it, and I was quite sick of going out in a beggar's dress; it did not answer at all, and besides, I thought it was ominous and threatening.

While I was in this disguise, I fell in with a parcel of folks of a worse kind than any I ever sorted with, and I saw a little into their ways too. These were coiners of money, and they made some very good offers to me, as to profit; but the part they would have had me have embarked in was the most dangerous part. I mean that of the very working the die, as they call it, which, had I been taken, had been certain death, and that at a stake—I say, to be burnt to death at a stake; so that though I was to appearance but a beggar, and they promised mountains of gold and silver to me to engage, yet it would not do. It is true, if I had been really a beggar, or had been desperate as when I began, I might perhaps have closed with it; for what care they to die that can't tell how to live? But at present this was not my condition, at least I was for no such terrible risks as those; besides, the very thoughts of being burnt at a stake struck terror into my very soul, chilled my blood, and gave me the vapours to such a degree, as I could not think of it without trembling.

This put an end to my disguise too, for as I did not like the proposal, so I did not tell them so, but seemed to relish it, and promised to meet again. But I durst see them no more; for if I had seen them, and not complied, though I had declined it with the greatest assurance of secrecy in the world, they would have gone near to have murdered me, to make sure work, and make themselves easy, as they call it. What kind of easiness that is, they may best judge that understand how easy men are that can murder people to prevent danger.

This and horse-stealing were things quite out of my way, and I might easily resolve I would have to more to say to them; my business seemed to lie another way, and though it had hazard enough in it too, yet it was more suitable to me, and what had more of art in it, and more room to escape, and more chances for a-coming off if a surprise should happen.

I had several proposals made also to me about that time, to come into a gang of house-breakers; but that was a thing I had no mind to venture at neither, any more than I had at the coining trade. I offered to go along with two men and a woman, that made it their business to get into houses by stratagem, and with them I was willing enough to venture. But there were three of them already, and they did not care to part, nor I to have too many in a gang, so I did not close with them, but declined them, and they paid dear for their next attempt.

But at length I met with a woman that had often told me what adventures she had made, and with success, at the waterside, and I closed with her, and we drove on our business pretty well. One day we came among some Dutch people at St. Catherine's, where we went on pretence to buy goods that were privately got on shore. I was two or three times in a house where we saw a good quantity of prohibited goods, and my companion once brought away three pieces of Dutch black silk that turned to good account, and I had my share of it; but in all the journeys I made by myself, I could not get an opportunity to do anything, so I laid it aside, for I had been so often, that they began to suspect something, and were so shy, that I saw nothing was to be done.

This baulked me a little, and I resolved to push at something or other, for I was not used to come back so often without purchase; so the next day I dressed myself up fine, and took a walk to the other end of the town. I passed through the Exchange in the Strand, but had no notion of finding anything to do there, when on a sudden I saw a great cluttering in the place, and all the people, shopkeepers as well as others, standing up and staring; and what should it be but some great duchess come into the Exchange, and they said the queen was coming. I set myself close up to a shop-side with my back to the counter, as if to let the crowd pass by, when keeping my eye upon a parcel of lace which the shopkeeper was showing to some ladies that stood by me, the shopkeeper and her maid were so taken up with looking to see who was coming, and what shop they would go to, that I found means to slip a paper of lace into my pocket and come clear off with it; so the lady-milliner paid dear enough for her gaping after the queen.

I went off from the shop, as if driven along by the throng, and mingling myself with the crowd, went out at the other door of the

Exchange, and so got away before they missed their lace; and because I would not be followed, I called a coach and shut myself up in it. I had scarce shut the coach doors up, but I saw the milliner's maid and five or six more come running out into the street, and crying out as if they were frightened. They did not cry 'Stop thief!' because nobody ran away, but I could hear the word 'robbed,' and 'lace,' two or three times, and saw the wench wringing her hands, and run staring to and again, like one scared. The coachman that had taken me up was getting up into the box, but was not quite up, so that the horse had not begun to move; so that I was terrible uneasy, and I took the packet of lace and laid it ready to have dropped it out at the flap of the coach, which opens before, just behind the coachman; but to my great satisfaction, in less than a minute the coach began to move, that is to say, as soon as the coachman had got up and spoken to his horses; so he drove away without any interruption, and I brought off my purchase, which was work near #20.

The next day I dressed up again, but in quite different clothes, and walked the same way again, but nothing offered till I came into St. James's Park, where I saw abundance of fine ladies in the Park, walking in the Mall, and among the rest there was a little miss, a young lady of about twelve or thirteen years old, and she had a sister, as I suppose it was, with her, that might be about nine years old. I observed the biggest had a fine gold watch on, and a good necklace of pearl, and they had a footman in livery with them; but as it is not usual for the footman to go behind the ladies in the Mall, so I observed the footman stopped at their going into the Mall, and the biggest of the sisters spoke to him, which I perceived was to bid him be just there when they came back.

When I heard her dismiss the footman, I stepped up to him and asked him, what little lady that was? and held a little chat with him about what a pretty child it was with her, and how genteel and well-carriaged the lady, the eldest, would be: how womanish, and how grave; and the fool of a fellow told me presently who she was; that she was Sir Thomas ———'s eldest daughter, of Essex, and that she was a great fortune; that her mother was not come to town yet; but she was with Sir William ———'s lady, of Suffolk, at her lodging in Suffolk Street, and a great deal more; that they had a maid and a woman to wait on them, besides Sir Thomas's coach, the coachman, and himself; and that young lady was governess to the whole family, as well here as at home too; and, in short, told me abundance of things enough for my business.

I was very well dressed, and had my gold watch as well as she; so I left the footman, and I puts myself in a rank with this young lady, having stayed till she had taken one double turn in the Mall, and was going forward again; by and by I saluted her by her name, with the title of Lady Betty. I asked her when she heard from her father; when my lady her mother would be in town, and how she did.

I talked so familiarly to her of her whole family that she could not suspect but that I knew them all intimately. I asked her why she would come abroad without Mrs. Chime with her (that was the name of her woman) to take of Mrs. Judith, that was her sister. Then I entered into a long chat with her about her sister, what a fine little lady she was, and asked her if she had learned French, and a thousand such little things to entertain her, when on a sudden we saw the guards come, and the crowd ran to see the king go by to the Parliament House.

The ladies ran all to the side of the Mall, and I helped my lady to stand upon the edge of the boards on the side of the Mall, that she might be high enough to see; and took the little one and lifted her quite up; during which, I took care to convey the gold watch so clean away from the Lady Betty, that she never felt it, nor missed it, till all the crowd was gone, and she was gotten into the middle of the Mall among the other ladies.

I took my leave of her in the very crowd, and said to her, as if in haste, 'Dear Lady Betty, take care of your little sister.' And so the crowd did as it were thrust me away from her, and that I was obliged unwillingly to take my leave.

The hurry in such cases is immediately over, and the place clear as soon as the king is gone by; but as there is always a great running and clutter just as the king passes, so having dropped the two little ladies, and done my business with them without any miscarriage, I kept hurrying on among the crowd, as if I ran to see the king, and so I got before the crowd and kept so till I came to the end of the Mall, when the king going on towards the Horse Guards, I went forward to the passage, which went then through against the lower end of the Haymarket, and there I bestowed a coach upon myself, and made off, and I confess I have not yet been so good as my word, viz. to go and visit my Lady Betty.

I was once of the mind to venture staying with Lady Betty till she missed the watch, and so have made a great outcry about it with her, and have got her into the coach, and put myself in the coach with her, and have gone home with her; for she appeared so fond of me, and so perfectly deceived by my so readily talking to her of all her relations and family, that I thought it was very easy to push the thing farther, and to have got at least the necklace of pearl; but when I considered that though the child would not perhaps have suspected me, other people might, and that if I was searched I should be discovered, I thought it was best to go off with what I had got, and be satisfied.

I came accidentally afterwards to hear, that when the young lady missed her watch, she made a great outcry in the Park, and sent her footman up and down to see if he could find me out, she having described me so perfectly that he knew presently that it was the same person that had stood and talked so long with him, and asked him so many questions about them; but I gone far enough out of their reach before she could come at her footman to tell him the story.

I made another adventure after this, of a nature different from all I had been concerned in yet, and this was at a gaming-house near Covent Garden.

I saw several people go in and out; and I stood in the passage a good while with another woman with me, and seeing a gentleman go up that seemed to be of more than ordinary fashion, I said to him, 'Sir, pray don't they give women leave to go up?' 'Yes, madam,' says he, 'and to play too, if they please.' 'I mean so, sir,' said I. And with that he said he would introduce me if I had a mind; so I followed him to the door, and he looking in, 'There, madam,' says he, 'are the gamesters, if you have a mind to venture.' I looked in and said to my comrade aloud, 'Here's nothing but men; I won't venture among them.' At which one of the gentlemen cried out, 'You need not be afraid, madam, here's none but fair gamesters; you are very welcome to come and set what you please.' so I went a little nearer and looked on, and some of them brought me a chair, and I sat down and saw the box and dice go round apace; then I said to my comrade, 'The gentlemen play too high for us; come, let us go.'

The people were all very civil, and one gentleman in particular encouraged me, and said, 'Come, madam, if you please to venture, if you dare trust me, I'll answer for it you shall have nothing put upon you here.' 'No, sir,' said I, smiling, 'I hope the gentlemen would not cheat a woman.' But still I declined venturing, though I pulled out a purse with money in it, that they might see I did not want money.

After I had sat a while, one gentleman said to me, jeering, 'Come, madam, I see you are afraid to venture for yourself; I always had good luck with the ladies, you shall set for me, if you won't set for yourself.' I told him, 'sir, I should be very loth to lose your money,' though I added, 'I am pretty lucky too; but the gentlemen play so high, that I dare not indeed venture my own.'

'Well, well,' says he, 'there's ten guineas, madam; set them for me.' so I took his money and set, himself looking on. I ran out nine of the guineas by one and two at a time, and then the box coming to the next man to me, my gentleman gave me ten guineas more, and made me set five of them at once, and the gentleman who had the box threw out, so there was five guineas of his money again. He was encouraged at this, and made me take the box, which was a bold venture. However, I held the box so long that I had gained him his whole money, and had a good handful of guineas in my lap, and which was the better luck, when I threw out, I threw but at one or two of those that had set me, and so went off easy.

When I was come this length, I offered the gentleman all the gold, for it was his own; and so would have had him play for himself, pretending I did not understand the game well enough. He laughed, and said if I had but good luck, it was no matter whether I understood the game or no; but I should not leave off. However, he took out the fifteen guineas that he had put in at first, and bade me play with the rest. I would have told them to see how much I had got, but he said, 'No, no, don't tell them, I believe you are very honest, and 'tis bad luck to tell them'; so I played on.

I understood the game well enough, though I pretended I did not, and played cautiously. It was to keep a good stock in my lap, out of which I every now and then conveyed some into my pocket, but in such a manner, and at such convenient times, as I was sure he could not see it.

I played a great while, and had very good luck for him; but the last time I held the box, they set me high, and I threw boldly at all; I held the box till I gained near fourscore guineas, but lost above half of it back in the last throw; so I got up, for I was afraid I should lose it all back again, and said to him, 'Pray come, sir, now, and take it and play for yourself; I think I have done pretty well for you.' He would have had me play on, but it grew late, and I desired to be excused. When I gave it up to him, I told him I hoped he would give me leave to tell it now, that I might see what I had gained, and how lucky I had been for him; when I told them, there were threescore and three guineas. 'Ay,' says I, 'if it had not been for that unlucky throw, I had got you a hundred guineas.' So I gave him all the money, but he would not take it till I had put my hand into it, and taken some for myself, and bid me please myself. I refused it, and was positive I would not take it myself; if he had a mind to anything of that kind, it should be all his own doings.

The rest of the gentlemen seeing us striving cried, 'Give it her all'; but I absolutely refused that. Then one of them said, 'D—n ye, jack, halve it with her; don't you know you should be always upon even terms with the ladies.' So, in short, he divided it with me, and I brought away thirty guineas, besides about forty-three which I had stole privately, which I was sorry for afterward, because he was so generous.

Thus I brought home seventy-three guineas, and let my old governess see what good luck I had at play. However, it was her advice that I should not venture again, and I took her counsel, for I never went there any more; for I knew as well as she, if the itch of play came in, I might soon lose that, and all the rest of what I had got.

Fortune had smiled upon me to that degree, and I had thriven so much, and my governess too, for she always had a share with me, that really the old gentlewoman began to talk of leaving off while we were well, and being satisfied with what we had got; but, I know not what fate guided me, I was as backward to it now as she was when I proposed it to her before, and so in an ill hour we gave over the thoughts of it for the present, and, in a word, I grew more hardened and audacious than ever, and the success I had made my name as famous as any thief of my sort ever had been at Newgate, and in the Old Bailey.

I had sometime taken the liberty to play the same game over again, which is not according to practice, which however succeeded not amiss; but generally I took up new figures, and contrived to appear in new shapes every time I went abroad.

It was not a rumbling time of the year, and the gentlemen being most of them gone out of town, Tunbridge, and Epsom, and such places were full of people. But the city was thin, and I thought our trade felt it a little, as well as other; so that at the latter end of the year I joined myself with a gang who usually go every year to Stourbridge Fair, and from thence to Bury Fair, in Suffolk. We promised ourselves great things there, but when I came to see how things were, I was weary of it presently; for except mere picking of pockets, there was little worth meddling with; neither, if a booty had been made, was it so easy carrying it off, nor was there such a variety of occasion for business in our way, as in London; all that I made of the whole journey was a gold watch at Bury Fair, and a small parcel of linen at Cambridge, which gave me an occasion to take leave of the place. It was on old bite, and I thought might do with a country shopkeeper, though in London it would not.

I bought at a linen-draper's shop, not in the fair, but in the town of Cambridge, as much fine holland and other things as came to about seven pounds; when I had done, I bade them be sent to such an inn, where I had purposely taken up my being the same morning, as if I was to lodge there that night.

I ordered the draper to send them home to me, about such an hour, to the inn where I lay, and I would pay him his money. At the time appointed the draper sends the goods, and I placed one of our gang at the chamber door, and when the innkeeper's maid brought the messenger to the door, who was a young fellow, an apprentice, almost a man, she tells him her mistress was asleep, but if he would leave the things and call in about an hour, I should be awake, and he might have the money. He left the parcel very readily, and goes his way, and in about half an hour my maid and I walked off, and that very evening I hired a horse, and a man to ride before me, and went to Newmarket, and from thence got my passage in a coach that was not quite full to St. Edmund's Bury, where, as I told you, I could make but little of my trade, only at a little country opera-house made a shift to carry off a gold watch from a lady's side, who was not only intolerably merry, but, as I thought, a little fuddled, which made my work much easier.

I made off with this little booty to Ipswich, and from thence to Harwich, where I went into an inn, as if I had newly arrived from Holland, not doubting but I should make some purchase among the foreigners that came on shore there; but I found them generally empty of things of value, except what was in their portmanteaux and Dutch hampers, which were generally guarded by footmen; however, I fairly got one of their portmanteaux one evening out of the chamber where the gentleman lay, the footman being fast asleep on the bed, and I suppose very drunk.

The room in which I lodged lay next to the Dutchman's, and having dragged the heavy thing with much ado out of the chamber into mine, I went out into the street, to see if I could find any possibility of carrying it off. I walked about a great while, but could see no probability either of getting out the thing, or of conveying away the goods that were in it if I had opened it, the town being so small, and I a perfect stranger in it; so I was returning with a resolution to carry it back again, and leave it where I found it. Just in that very moment I heard a man make a noise to some people to make haste, for the boat was going to put off, and the tide would be spent. I called to the fellow, 'What boat is it, friend,' says I, 'that you belong to?' 'The Ipswich wherry, madam,' says he. 'When do you go off?' says I. 'This moment, madam,' says he; 'do you want to go thither?' 'Yes,' said I, 'if you can stay till I fetch my things.' 'Where are your things, madam?' says he. 'At such an inn,' said I. 'Well, I'll go with you, madam,' says he, very civilly, 'and bring them for you.' 'Come away, then,' says I, and takes him with me.

The people of the inn were in a great hurry, the packet-boat from Holland being just come in, and two coaches just come also with passengers from London, for another packet-boat that was going off for Holland, which coaches were to go back next day with the passengers that were just landed. In this hurry it was not much minded that I came to the bar and paid my reckoning, telling my landlady I had gotten my passage by sea in a wherry.

These wherries are large vessels, with good accommodation for carrying passengers from Harwich to London; and though they are called wherries, which is a word used in the Thames for a small boat rowed with one or two men, yet these are vessels able to carry twenty passengers, and ten or fifteen tons of goods, and fitted to bear the sea. All this I had found out by inquiring the night before into the several ways of going to London.

My landlady was very courteous, took my money for my reckoning, but was called away, all the house being in a hurry. So I left her, took the fellow up to my chamber, gave him the trunk, or portmanteau, for it was like a trunk, and wrapped it about with an old apron, and he went directly to his boat with it, and I after him, nobody asking us the least question about it; as for the drunken Dutch footman he was still asleep, and his master with other foreign gentlemen at supper, and very merry below, so I went clean off with it to Ipswich; and going in the night, the people of the house knew nothing but that I was gone to London by the Harwich wherry, as I had told my landlady.

I was plagued at Ipswich with the custom-house officers, who stopped my trunk, as I called it, and would open and search it. I was willing, I told them, they should search it, but husband had the key, and he was not yet come from Harwich; this I said, that if upon searching it they should find all the things be such as properly belonged to a man rather than a woman, it should not seem strange to them. However, they being positive to open the trunk I consented to have it be broken open, that is to say, to have the lock taken off, which was not difficult.

They found nothing for their turn, for the trunk had been searched before, but they discovered several things very much to my satisfaction, as particularly a parcel of money in French pistols, and some Dutch ducatoons or rix-dollars, and the rest was chiefly two periwigs, wearing-linen, and razors, wash-balls, perfumes, and other useful things necessary for a gentleman, which all passed for my husband's, and so I was quit to them.

It was now very early in the morning, and not light, and I knew not well what course to take; for I made no doubt but I should be pursued in the morning, and perhaps be taken with the things about me; so I resolved upon taking new measures. I went publicly to an inn in the town with my trunk, as I called it, and having taken the substance out, I did not think the lumber of it worth my concern; however, I gave it the landlady of the house with a charge to take great care of it, and lay it up safe till I should come again, and away I walked in to the street.

When I was got into the town a great way from the inn, I met with an ancient woman who had just opened her door, and I fell into chat with her, and asked her a great many wild questions of things all remote to my purpose and design; but in my discourse I found by her how the town was situated, that I was in a street that went out towards Hadley, but that such a street went towards the water-side, such a street towards Colchester, and so the London road lay there.

I had soon my ends of this old woman, for I only wanted to know which was the London road, and away I walked as fast as I could; not that I intended to go on foot, either to London or to Colchester, but I wanted to get quietly away from Ipswich.

I walked about two or three miles, and then I met a plain countryman, who was busy about some husbandry work, I did not know what, and I asked him a great many questions first, not much to the purpose, but at last told him I was going for London, and the coach was full, and I could not get a passage, and asked him if he could tell me where to hire a horse that would carry double, and an honest man to ride before me to Colchester, that so I might get a place there in the coaches. The honest clown looked earnestly at me, and said nothing for above half a minute, when, scratching his poll, 'A horse, say you and to Colchester, to carry double? why yes, mistress, alack-a-day, you may have horses enough for money.' 'Well, friend,' says I, 'that I take for granted; I don't expect it without money.' 'Why, but, mistress,' says he, 'how much are you willing to give?' 'Nay,' says I again, 'friend, I don't know what your rates are in the country here, for I am a stranger; but if you can get one for me, get it as cheap as you can, and I'll give you somewhat for your pains.'

'Why, that's honestly said too,' says the countryman. 'Not so honest, neither,' said I to myself, 'if thou knewest all.' 'Why, mistress,' says he, 'I have a horse that will carry double, and I don't much care if I go myself with you,' and the like. 'Will you?' says I; 'well, I believe you are an honest man; if you will, I shall be glad of it; I'll pay you in reason.' 'Why, look ye, mistress,' says he, 'I won't be out of reason with you, then; if I carry you to Colchester, it will be worth five shillings for myself and my horse, for I shall hardly come back to-night.'

In short, I hired the honest man and his horse; but when we came to a town upon the road (I do not remember the name of it, but it stands upon a river), I pretended myself very ill, and I could go no farther that night but if he would stay there with me, because I was a stranger, I would pay him for himself and his horse with all my heart.

This I did because I knew the Dutch gentlemen and their servants would be upon the road that day, either in the stagecoaches or riding post, and I did not know but the drunken fellow, or somebody else that might have seen me at Harwich, might see me again, and so I thought that in one day's stop they would be all gone by.

We lay all that night there, and the next morning it was not very early when I set out, so that it was near ten o'clock by the time I got to Colchester. It was no little pleasure that I saw the town where I had so many pleasant days, and I made many inquiries after the good old friends I had once had there, but could make little out; they were all dead or removed. The young ladies had been all married or gone to London; the old gentleman and the old lady that had been my early benefactress all dead; and which troubled me most, the young gentleman my first lover, and afterwards my brother-in-law, was dead; but two sons, men grown, were left of him, but they too were transplanted to London.

I dismissed my old man here, and stayed incognito for three or four days in Colchester, and then took a passage in a waggon, because I would not venture being seen in the Harwich coaches. But I needed not have used so much caution, for there was nobody in Harwich but the woman of the house could have known me; nor was it rational to think that she, considering the hurry she was in, and that she never saw me but once, and that by candlelight, should have ever discovered me.

I was now returned to London, and though by the accident of the last adventure I got something considerable, yet I was not fond of any more country rambles, nor should I have ventured abroad again if I had carried the trade on to the end of my days. I gave my governess a history of my travels; she liked the Harwich journey well enough, and in discoursing of these things between ourselves she observed, that a thief being a creature that watches the advantages of other people's mistakes, 'tis impossible but that to one that is vigilant and industrious many opportunities must happen, and therefore she thought that one so exquisitely keen in the trade as I was, would scarce fail of something extraordinary wherever I went.

On the other hand, every branch of my story, if duly considered, may be useful to honest people, and afford a due caution to people of some sort or other to guard against the like surprises, and to have their eyes about them when they have to do with strangers of any kind, for 'tis very seldom that some snare or other is not in their way. The moral, indeed, of all my history is left to be gathered by the senses and judgment of the reader; I am not qualified to preach to them. Let the experience of one creature completely wicked, and completely miserable, be a storehouse of useful warning to those that read.

I am drawing now towards a new variety of the scenes of life. Upon my return, being hardened by along race of crime, and success unparalleled, at least in the reach of my own knowledge, I had, as I have said, no thoughts of laying down a trade which, if I was to judge by the example of other, must, however, end at last in misery and sorrow.

It was on the Christmas day following, in the evening, that, to finish a long train of wickedness, I went abroad to see what might offer in my way; when going by a working silversmith's in Foster Lane, I saw a tempting bait indeed, and not be resisted by one of my occupation, for the shop had nobody in it, as I could see, and a great deal of loose plate lay in the window, and at the seat of the man, who usually, as I suppose, worked at one side of the shop.

I went boldly in, and was just going to lay my hand upon a piece of plate, and might have done it, and carried it clear off, for any care that the men who belonged to the shop had taken of it; but an officious fellow in a house, not a shop, on the other side of the way, seeing me go in, and observing that there was nobody in the shop, comes running over the street, and into the shop, and without asking me what I was, or who, seizes upon me, an cries out for the people of the house.

I had not, as I said above, touched anything in the shop, and seeing a glimpse of somebody running over to the shop, I had so much presence of mind as to knock very hard with my foot on the floor of the house, and was just calling out too, when the fellow laid hands on me.

However, as I had always most courage when I was in most danger, so when the fellow laid hands on me, I stood very high upon it, that I came in to buy half a dozen of silver spoons; and to my good fortune, it was a silversmith's that sold plate, as well as worked plate for other shops. The fellow laughed at that part, and put such a value upon the service that he had done his neighbour, that he would have it be that I came not to buy, but to steal; and raising a great crowd. I said to the master of the shop, who by this time was fetched home from some neighbouring place, that it was in vain to make noise, and enter into talk there of the case; the fellow had insisted that I came to steal, and he must prove it, and I desired we might go before a magistrate without any more words; for I began to see I should be too hard for the man that had seized me.

The master and mistress of the shop were really not so violent as the man from t'other side of the way; and the man said, 'Mistress, you might come into the shop with a good design for aught I know, but it seemed a dangerous thing for you to come into such a shop as mine is, when you see nobody there; and I cannot do justice to my neighbour, who was so kind to me, as not to acknowledge he had reason on his side; though, upon the whole, I do not find you attempted to take anything, and I really know not what to do in it.' I pressed him to go before a magistrate with me, and if anything could be proved on me that was like a design of robbery, I should willingly submit, but if not, I expected reparation.

Just while we were in this debate, and a crowd of people gathered about the door, came by Sir T. B., an alderman of the city, and justice of the peace, and the goldsmith hearing of it, goes out, and entreated his worship to come in and decide the case.

Give the goldsmith his due, he told his story with a great deal of justice and moderation, and the fellow that had come over, and seized upon me, told his with as much heat and foolish passion, which did me good still, rather than harm. It came then to my turn to speak, and I told his worship that I was a stranger in London, being newly come out of the north; that I lodged in such a place, that I was passing this street, and went into the goldsmith's shop to buy half a dozen of spoons. By great luck I had an old silver spoon in my pocket, which I pulled out, and told him I had carried that spoon to match it with half a dozen of new ones, that it might match some I had in the country.

That seeing nobody I the shop, I knocked with my foot very hard to make the people hear, and had also called aloud with my voice; 'tis true, there was loose plate in the shop, but that nobody could say I had touched any of it, or gone near it; that a fellow came running into the shop out of the street, and laid hands on me in a furious manner, in the very moments while I was calling for the people of the house; that if he had really had a mind to have done his neighbour any service, he should have stood at a distance, and silently watched to see whether I had touched anything or no, and then have clapped in upon me, and taken me in the fact. 'That is very true,' says Mr. Alderman, and turning to the fellow that stopped me, he asked him if it was true that I knocked with my foot? He said, yes, I had knocked, but that might be because of his coming. 'Nay,' says the alderman, taking him short, 'now you contradict yourself, for just now you said she was in the shop with her back to you, and did not see you till you came upon her.' Now it was true that my back was partly to the street, but yet as my business was of a kind that required me to have my eyes every way, so I really had a glance of him running over, as I said before, though he did not perceive it.

After a full hearing, the alderman gave it as his opinion that his neighbour was under a mistake, and that I was innocent, and the goldsmith acquiesced in it too, and his wife, and so I was dismissed; but as I was going to depart, Mr. Alderman said, 'But hold, madam, if you were designing to buy spoons, I hope you will not let my friend here lose his customer by the mistake.' I readily answered, 'No, sir, I'll buy the spoons still, if he can match my odd spoon, which I brought for a pattern'; and the goldsmith showed me some of the very same fashion. So he weighed the spoons, and they came to five-and-thirty shillings, so I pulls out my purse to pay him, in which I had near twenty guineas, for I never went without such a sum about me, whatever might happen, and I found it of use at other times as well as now.

When Mr. Alderman saw my money, he said, 'Well, madam, now I am satisfied you were wronged, and it was for this reason that I moved you should buy the spoons, and stayed till you had bought them, for if you had not had money to pay for them, I should have suspected that you did not come into the shop with an intent to buy, for indeed the sort of people who come upon these designs that you have been charged with, are seldom troubled with much gold in their pockets, as I see you are.'

I smiled, and told his worship, that then I owed something of his favour to my money, but I hoped he saw reason also in the justice he had done me before. He said, yes, he had, but this had confirmed his opinion, and he was fully satisfied now of my having been injured. So I came off with flying colours, though from an affair in which I was at the very brink of destruction.

It was but three days after this, that not at all made cautious by my former danger, as I used to be, and still pursuing the art which I had so long been employed in, I ventured into a house where I saw the doors open, and furnished myself, as I though verily without being perceived, with two pieces of flowered silks, such as they call brocaded silk, very rich. It was not a mercer's shop, nor a warehouse of a mercer, but looked like a private dwelling-house, and was, it seems, inhabited by a man that sold goods for the weavers to the mercers, like a broker or factor.

That I may make short of this black part of this story, I was attacked by two wenches that came open-mouthed at me just as I was going out at the door, and one of them pulled me back into the room, while the other shut the door upon me. I would have given them good words, but there was no room for it, two fiery dragons could not have been more furious than they were; they tore my clothes, bullied and roared as if they would have murdered me; the mistress of the house came next, and then the master, and all outrageous, for a while especially.

I gave the master very good words, told him the door was open, and things were a temptation to me, that I was poor and distressed, and poverty was when many could not resist, and begged him with tears to have pity on me. The mistress of the house was moved with compassion, and inclined to have let me go, and had almost persuaded her husband to it also, but the saucy wenches were run, even before they were sent, and had fetched a constable, and then the master said he could not go back, I must go before a justice, and answered his wife that he might come into trouble himself if he should let me go.

The sight of the constable, indeed, struck me with terror, and I thought I should have sunk into the ground. I fell into faintings, and indeed the people themselves thought I would have died, when the woman argued again for me, and entreated her husband, seeing they had lost nothing, to let me go. I offered him to pay for the two pieces, whatever the value was, though I had not got them, and argued that as he had his goods, and had really lost nothing, it would be cruel to pursue me to death, and have my blood for the bare attempt of taking them. I put the constable in mind that I had broke no doors, nor carried anything away; and when I came to the justice, and pleaded there that I had neither broken anything to get in, nor carried anything out, the justice was inclined to have released me; but the first saucy jade that stopped me, affirming that I was going out with the goods, but that she stopped me and pulled me back as I was upon the threshold, the justice upon that point committed me, and I was carried to Newgate. That horrid place! my very blood chills at the mention of its name; the place where so many of my comrades had been locked up, and from whence they went to the fatal tree; the place where my mother suffered so deeply, where I was brought into the world, and from whence I expected no redemption but by an infamous death: to conclude, the place that had so long expected me, and which with so much art and success I had so long avoided.

I was not fixed indeed; 'tis impossible to describe the terror of my mind, when I was first brought in, and when I looked around upon all the horrors of that dismal place. I looked on myself as lost, and that I had nothing to think of but of going out of the world, and that with the utmost infamy: the hellish noise, the roaring, swearing, and clamour, the stench and nastiness, and all the dreadful crowd of afflicting things that I saw there, joined together to make the place seem an emblem of hell itself, and a kind of an entrance into it.

Now I reproached myself with the many hints I had had, as I have mentioned above, from my own reason, from the sense of my good circumstances, and of the many dangers I had escaped, to leave off while I was well, and how I had withstood them all, and hardened my thoughts against all fear. It seemed to me that I was hurried on by an inevitable and unseen fate to this day of misery, and that now I was to expiate all my offences at the gallows; that I was now to give satisfaction to justice with my blood, and that I was come to the last hour of my life and of my wickedness together. These things poured themselves in upon my thoughts in a confused manner, and left me overwhelmed with melancholy and despair.

Them I repented heartily of all my life past, but that repentance yielded me no satisfaction, no peace, no, not in the least, because, as I said to myself, it was repenting after the power of further sinning was taken away. I seemed not to mourn that I had committed such crimes, and for the fact as it was an offence against God and my neighbour, but I mourned that I was to be punished for it. I was a penitent, as I thought, not that I had sinned, but that I was to suffer, and this took away all the comfort, and even the hope of my repentance in my own thoughts.

I got no sleep for several nights or days after I came into that wretched place, and glad I would have been for some time to have died there, though I did not consider dying as it ought to be considered neither; indeed, nothing could be filled with more horror to my imagination than the very place, nothing was more odious to me than the company that was there. Oh! if I had but been sent to any place in the world, and not to Newgate, I should have thought myself happy.

In the next place, how did the hardened wretches that were there before me triumph over me! What! Mrs. Flanders come to Newgate at last? What! Mrs. Mary, Mrs. Molly, and after that plain Moll Flanders? They thought the devil had helped me, they said, that I had reigned so long; they expected me there many years ago, and was I come at last? Then they flouted me with my dejections, welcomed me to the place, wished me joy, bid me have a good heart, not to be cast down, things might not be so bad as I feared, and the like; then called for brandy, and drank to me, but put it all up to my score, for they told me I was but just come to the college, as they called it, and sure I had money in my pocket, though they had none.

I asked one of this crew how long she had been there. She said four months. I asked her how the place looked to her when she first came into it. 'Just as it did now to you,' says she, dreadful and frightful'; that she thought she was in hell; 'and I believe so still,' adds she, 'but it is natural to me now, I don't disturb myself about it.' 'I suppose,' says I, 'you are in no danger of what is to follow?' 'Nay,' says she, 'for you are mistaken there, I assure you, for I am under sentence, only I pleaded my belly, but I am no more with child than the judge that tried me, and I expect to be called down next sessions.' This 'calling down' is calling down to their former judgment, when a woman has been respited for her belly, but proves not to be with child, or if she has been with child, and has been brought to bed. 'Well,' says I, 'are you thus easy?' 'Ay,' says she, 'I can't help myself; what signifies being sad? If I am hanged, there's an end of me,' says she; and away she turns dancing, and sings as she goes the following piece of Newgate wit ———
'If I swing by the string
I shall hear the bell ring
And then there's an end of poor Jenny.'

I mention this because it would be worth the observation of any prisoner, who shall hereafter fall into the same misfortune, and come to that dreadful place of Newgate, how time, necessity, and conversing with the wretches that are there familiarizes the place to them; how at last they become reconciled to that which at first was the greatest dread upon their spirits in the world, and are as impudently cheerful and merry in their misery as they were when out of it.

I cannot say, as some do, this devil is not so black as he is painted; for indeed no colours can represent the place to the life, not any soul conceive aright of it but those who have been suffers there. But how hell should become by degree so natural, and not only tolerable, but even agreeable, is a thing unintelligible but by those who have experienced it, as I have.

The same night that I was sent to Newgate, I sent the news of it to my old governess, who was surprised at it, you may be sure, and spent the night almost as ill out of Newgate, as I did in it.

The next morning she came to see me; she did what she could to comfort me, but she saw that was to no purpose; however, as she said, to sink under the weight was but to increase the weight; she immediately applied herself to all the proper methods to prevent the effects of it, which we feared, and first she found out the two fiery jades that had surprised me. She tampered with them, offered them money, and, in a word, tried all imaginable ways to prevent a prosecution; she offered one of the wenches #100 to go away from her mistress, and not to appear against me, but she was so resolute, that though she was but a servant maid at #3 a year wages or thereabouts, she refused it, and would have refused it, as my governess said she believed, if she had offered her #500. Then she attacked the other maid; she was not so hard-hearted in appearance as the other, and sometimes seemed inclined to be merciful; but the first wench kept her up, and changed her mind, and would not so much as let my governess talk with her, but threatened to have her up for tampering with the evidence.

Then she applied to the master, that is to say, the man whose goods had been stolen, and particularly to his wife, who, as I told you, was inclined at first to have some compassion for me; she found the woman the same still, but the man alleged he was bound by the justice that committed me, to prosecute, and that he should forfeit his recognisance.

My governess offered to find friends that should get his recognisances off of the file, as they call it, and that he should not suffer; but it was not possible to convince him that could be done, or that he could be safe any way in the world but by appearing against me; so I was to have three witnesses of fact against me, the master and his two maids; that is to say, I was as certain to be cast for my life as I was certain that I was alive, and I had nothing to do but to think of dying, and prepare for it. I had but a sad foundation to build upon, as I said before, for all my repentance appeared to me to be only the effect of my fear of death, not a sincere regret for the wicked life that I had lived, and which had brought this misery upon me, for the offending my Creator, who was now suddenly to be my judge.

I lived many days here under the utmost horror of soul; I had death, as it were, in view, and thought of nothing night and day, but of gibbets and halters, evil spirits and devils; it is not to be expressed by words how I was harassed, between the dreadful apprehensions of death and the terror of my conscience reproaching me with my past horrible life.

The ordinary of Newgate came to me, and talked a little in his way, but all his divinity ran upon confessing my crime, as he called it (though he knew not what I was in for), making a full discovery, and the like, without which he told me God would never forgive me; and he said so little to the purpose, that I had no manner of consolation from him; and then to observe the poor creature preaching confession and repentance to me in the morning, and find him drunk with brandy and spirits by noon, this had something in it so shocking, that I began to nauseate the man more than his work, and his work too by degrees, for the sake of the man; so that I desired him to trouble me no more.

I know not how it was, but by the indefatigable application of my diligent governess I had no bill preferred against me the first sessions, I mean to the grand jury, at Guildhall; so I had another month or five weeks before me, and without doubt this ought to have been accepted by me, as so much time given me for reflection upon what was past, and preparation for what was to come; or, in a word, I ought to have esteemed it as a space given me for repentance, and have employed it as such, but it was not in me. I was sorry (as before) for being in Newgate, but had very few signs of repentance about me.

On the contrary, like the waters in the cavities and hollows of mountains, which petrify and turn into stone whatever they are suffered to drop on, so the continual conversing with such a crew of hell-hounds as I was, had the same common operation upon me as upon other people. I degenerated into stone; I turned first stupid and senseless, then brutish and thoughtless, and at last raving mad as any of them were; and, in short, I became as naturally pleased and easy with the place, as if indeed I had been born there.

It is scarce possible to imagine that our natures should be capable of so much degeneracy, as to make that pleasant and agreeable that in itself is the most complete misery. Here was a circumstance that I think it is scarce possible to mention a worse: I was as exquisitely miserable as, speaking of common cases, it was possible for any one to be that had life and health, and money to help them, as I had.

I had weight of guilt upon me enough to sink any creature who had the least power of reflection left, and had any sense upon them of the happiness of this life, of the misery of another; then I had at first remorse indeed, but no repentance; I had now neither remorse nor repentance. I had a crime charged on me, the punishment of which was death by our law; the proof so evident, that there was no room for me so much as to plead not guilty. I had the name of an old offender, so that I had nothing to expect but death in a few weeks' time, neither had I myself any thoughts of escaping; and yet a certain strange lethargy of soul possessed me. I had no trouble, no apprehensions, no sorrow about me, the first surprise was gone; I was, I may well say, I know not how; my senses, my reason, nay, my conscience, were all asleep; my course of life for forty years had been a horrid complication of wickedness, whoredom, adultery, incest, lying, theft; and, in a word, everything but murder and treason had been my practice from the age of eighteen, or thereabouts, to three-score; and now I was engulfed in the misery of punishment, and had an infamous death just at the door, and yet I had no sense of my condition, no thought of heaven or hell at least, that went any farther than a bare flying touch, like the stitch or pain that gives a hint and goes off. I neither had a heart to ask God's mercy, nor indeed to think of it. And in this, I think, I have given a brief description of the completest misery on earth.

All my terrifying thoughts were past, the horrors of the place were become familiar, and I felt no more uneasiness at the noise and clamours of the prison, than they did who made that noise; in a word, I was become a mere Newgate-bird, as wicked and as outrageous as any of them; nay, I scarce retained the habit and custom of good breeding and manners, which all along till now ran through my conversation; so thorough a degeneracy had possessed me, that I was no more the same thing that I had been, than if I had never been otherwise than what I was now.

In the middle of this hardened part of my life I had another sudden surprise, which called me back a little to that thing called sorrow, which indeed I began to be past the sense of before. They told me one night that there was brought into the prison late the night before three highwaymen, who had committed robbery somewhere on the road to Windsor, Hounslow Heath, I think it was, and were pursued to Uxbridge by the country, and were taken there after a gallant resistance, in which I know not how many of the country people were wounded, and some killed.

It is not to be wondered that we prisoners were all desirous enough to see these brave, topping gentlemen, that were talked up to be such as their fellows had not been known, and especially because it was said they would in the morning be removed into the press-yard, having given money to the head master of the prison, to be allowed the liberty of that better part of the prison. So we that were women placed ourselves in the way, that we would be sure to see them; but nothing could express the amazement and surprise I was in, when the very first man that came out I knew to be my Lancashire husband, the same who lived so well at Dunstable, and the same who I afterwards saw at Brickhill, when I was married to my last husband, as has been related.

I was struck dumb at the sight, and knew neither what to say nor what to do; he did not know me, and that was all the present relief I had. I quitted my company, and retired as much as that dreadful place suffers anybody to retire, and I cried vehemently for a great while. 'Dreadful creature that I am,' said I, 'how may poor people have I made miserable? How many desperate wretches have I sent to the devil?' He had told me at Chester he was ruined by that match, and that his fortunes were made desperate on my account; for that thinking I had been a fortune, he was run into debt more than he was able to pay, and that he knew not what course to take; that he would go into the army and carry a musket, or buy a horse and take a tour, as he called it; and though I never told him that I was a fortune, and so did not actually deceive him myself, yet I did encourage the having it thought that I was so, and by that means I was the occasion originally of his mischief.

The surprise of the thing only struck deeper into my thoughts, any gave me stronger reflections than all that had befallen me before. I grieved day and night for him, and the more for that they told me he was the captain of the gang, and that he had committed so many robberies, that Hind, or Whitney, or the Golden Farmer were fools to him; that he would surely be hanged if there were no more men left in the country he was born in; and that there would abundance of people come in against him.

I was overwhelmed with grief for him; my own case gave me no disturbance compared to this, and I loaded myself with reproaches on his account. I bewailed his misfortunes, and the ruin he was now come to, at such a rate, that I relished nothing now as I did before, and the first reflections I made upon the horrid, detestable life I had lived began to return upon me, and as these things returned, my abhorrence of the place I was in, and of the way of living in it, returned also; in a word, I was perfectly changed, and become another body.

While I was under these influences of sorrow for him, came notice to me that the next sessions approaching there would be a bill preferred to the grand jury against me, and that I should be certainly tried for my life at the Old Bailey. My temper was touched before, the hardened, wretched boldness of spirit which I had acquired abated, and conscious in the prison, guilt began to flow in upon my mind. In short, I began to think, and to think is one real advance from hell to heaven. All that hellish, hardened state and temper of soul, which I have said so much of before, is but a deprivation of thought; he that is restored to his power of thinking, is restored to himself.

As soon as I began, I say, to think, the first think that occurred to me broke out thus: 'Lord! what will become of me? I shall certainly die! I shall be cast, to be sure, and there is nothing beyond that but death! I have no friends; what shall I do? I shall be certainly cast! Lord, have mercy upon me! What will become of me?' This was a sad thought, you will say, to be the first, after so long a time, that had started into my soul of that kind, and yet even this was nothing but fright at what was to come; there was not a word of sincere repentance in it all. However, I was indeed dreadfully dejected, and disconsolate to the last degree; and as I had no friend in the world to communicate my distressed thoughts to, it lay so heavy upon me, that it threw me into fits and swoonings several times a day. I sent for my old governess, and she, give her her due, acted the part of a true friend. She left no stone unturned to prevent the grand jury finding the bill. She sought out one or two of the jurymen, talked with them, and endeavoured to possess them with favourable dispositions, on account that nothing was taken away, and no house broken, etc.; but all would not do, they were over-ruled by the rest; the two wenches swore home to the fact, and the jury found the bill against me for robbery and house-breaking, that is, for felony and burglary.

I sunk down when they brought me news of it, and after I came to myself again, I thought I should have died with the weight of it. My governess acted a true mother to me; she pitied me, she cried with me, and for me, but she could not help me; and to add to the terror of it, 'twas the discourse all over the house that I should die for it. I could hear them talk it among themselves very often, and see them shake their heads and say they were sorry for it, and the like, as is usual in the place. But still nobody came to tell me their thoughts, till at last one of the keepers came to me privately, and said with a sigh, 'Well, Mrs. Flanders, you will be tried on Friday' (this was but a Wednesday); 'what do you intend to do?' I turned as white as a clout, and said, 'God knows what I shall do; for my part, I know not what to do.' 'Why,' says he, 'I won't flatter you, I would have you prepare for death, for I doubt you will be cast; and as they say you are an old offender, I doubt you will find but little mercy. They say,' added he, 'your case is very plain, and that the witnesses swear so home against you, there will be no standing it.'

This was a stab into the very vitals of one under such a burthen as I was oppressed with before, and I could not speak to him a word, good or bad, for a great while; but at last I burst out into tears, and said to him, 'Lord! Mr. ———, what must I do?' 'Do!' says he, 'send for the ordinary; send for a minister and talk with him; for, indeed, Mrs. Flanders, unless you have very good friends, you are no woman for this world.'

This was plain dealing indeed, but it was very harsh to me, at least I thought it so. He left me in the greatest confusion imaginable, and all that night I lay awake. And now I began to say my prayers, which I had scarce done before since my last husband's death, or from a little while after. And truly I may well call it saying my prayers, for I was in such a confusion, and had such horror upon my mind, that though I cried, and repeated several times the ordinary expression of 'Lord, have mercy upon me!' I never brought myself to any sense of my being a miserable sinner, as indeed I was, and of confessing my sins to God, and begging pardon for the sake of Jesus Christ. I was overwhelmed with the sense of my condition, being tried for my life, and being sure to be condemned, and then I was as sure to be executed, and on this account I cried out all night, 'Lord, what will become of me? Lord! what shall I do? Lord! I shall be hanged! Lord, have mercy upon me!' and the like.

My poor afflicted governess was now as much concerned as I, and a great deal more truly penitent, though she had no prospect of being brought to trial and sentence. Not but that she deserved it as much as I, and so she said herself; but she had not done anything herself for many years, other than receiving what I and others stole, and encouraging us to steal it. But she cried, and took on like a distracted body, wringing her hands, and crying out that she was undone, that she believed there was a curse from heaven upon her, that she should be damned, that she had been the destruction of all her friends, that she had brought such a one, and such a one, and such a one to the gallows; and there she reckoned up ten or eleven people, some of which I have given account of, that came to untimely ends; and that now she was the occasion of my ruin, for she had persuaded me to go on, when I would have left off. I interrupted her there. 'No, mother, no,' said I, 'don't speak of that, for you would have had me left off when I got the mercer's money again, and when I came home from Harwich, and I would not hearken to you; therefore you have not been to blame; it is I only have ruined myself, I have brought myself to this misery'; and thus we spent many hours together.

Well, there was no remedy; the prosecution went on, and on the Thursday I was carried down to the sessions-house, where I was arraigned, as they called it, and the next day I was appointed to be tried. At the arraignment I pleaded 'Not guilty,' and well I might, for I was indicted for felony and burglary; that is, for feloniously stealing two pieces of brocaded silk, value #46, the goods of Anthony Johnson, and for breaking open his doors; whereas I knew very well they could not pretend to prove I had broken up the doors, or so much as lifted up a latch.

On the Friday I was brought to my trial. I had exhausted my spirits with crying for two or three days before, so that I slept better the Thursday night than I expected, and had more courage for my trial than indeed I thought possible for me to have.

When the trial began, the indictment was read, I would have spoke, but they told me the witnesses must be heard first, and then I should have time to be heard. The witnesses were the two wenches, a couple of hard-mouthed jades indeed, for though the thing was truth in the main, yet they aggravated it to the utmost extremity, and swore I had the goods wholly in my possession, that I had hid them among my clothes, that I was going off with them, that I had one foot over the threshold when they discovered themselves, and then I put t' other over, so that I was quite out of the house in the street with the goods before they took hold of me, and then they seized me, and brought me back again, and they took the goods upon me. The fact in general was all true, but I believe, and insisted upon it, that they stopped me before I had set my foot clear of the threshold of the house. But that did not argue much, for certain it was that I had taken the goods, and I was bringing them away, if I had not been taken.

But I pleaded that I had stole nothing, they had lost nothing, that the door was open, and I went in, seeing the goods lie there, and with design to buy. If, seeing nobody in the house, I had taken any of them up in my hand it could not be concluded that I intended to steal them, for that I never carried them farther than the door to look on them with the better light.

The Court would not allow that by any means, and made a kind of a jest of my intending to buy the goods, that being no shop for the selling of anything, and as to carrying them to the door to look at them, the maids made their impudent mocks upon that, and spent their wit upon it very much; told the Court I had looked at them sufficiently, and approved them very well, for I had packed them up under my clothes, and was a-going with them.

In short, I was found guilty of felony, but acquitted of the burglary, which was but small comfort to me, the first bringing me to a sentence of death, and the last would have done no more. The next day I was carried down to receive the dreadful sentence, and when they came to ask me what I had to say why sentence should not pass, I stood mute a while, but somebody that stood behind me prompted me aloud to speak to the judges, for that they could represent things favourably for me. This encouraged me to speak, and I told them I had nothing to say to stop the sentence, but that I had much to say to bespeak the mercy of the Court; that I hoped they would allow something in such a case for the circumstances of it; that I had broken no doors, had carried nothing off; that nobody had lost anything; that the person whose goods they were was pleased to say he desired mercy might be shown (which indeed he very honestly did); that, at the worst, it was the first offence, and that I had never been before any court of justice before; and, in a word, I spoke with more courage that I thought I could have done, and in such a moving tone, and though with tears, yet not so many tears as to obstruct my speech, that I could see it moved others to tears that heard me.

The judges sat grave and mute, gave me an easy hearing, and time to say all that I would, but, saying neither Yes nor No to it, pronounced the sentence of death upon me, a sentence that was to me like death itself, which, after it was read, confounded me. I had no more spirit left in me, I had no tongue to speak, or eyes to look up either to God or man.

My poor governess was utterly disconsolate, and she that was my comforter before, wanted comfort now herself; and sometimes mourning, sometimes raging, was as much out of herself, as to all outward appearance, as any mad woman in Bedlam. Nor was she only disconsolate as to me, but she was struck with horror at the sense of her own wicked life, and began to look back upon it with a taste quite different from mine, for she was penitent to the highest degree for her sins, as well as sorrowful for the misfortune. She sent for a minister, too, a serious, pious, good man, and applied herself with such earnestness, by his assistance, to the work of a sincere repentance, that I believe, and so did the minister too, that she was a true penitent; and, which is still more, she was not only so for the occasion, and at that juncture, but she continued so, as I was informed, to the day of her death.

It is rather to be thought of than expressed what was now my condition. I had nothing before me but present death; and as I had no friends to assist me, or to stir for me, I expected nothing but to find my name in the dead warrant, which was to come down for the execution, the Friday afterwards, of five more and myself.

In the meantime my poor distressed governess sent me a minister, who at her request first, and at my own afterwards, came to visit me. He exhorted me seriously to repent of all my sins, and to dally no longer with my soul; not flattering myself with hopes of life, which, he said, he was informed there was no room to expect, but unfeignedly to look up to God with my whole soul, and to cry for pardon in the name of Jesus Christ. He backed his discourses with proper quotations of Scripture, encouraging the greatest sinner to repent, and turn from their evil way, and when he had done, he kneeled down and prayed with me.

It was now that, for the first time, I felt any real signs of repentance. I now began to look back upon my past life with abhorrence, and having a kind of view into the other side of time, and things of life, as I believe they do with everybody at such a time, began to look with a different aspect, and quite another shape, than they did before. The greatest and best things, the views of felicity, the joy, the griefs of life, were quite other things; and I had nothing in my thoughts but what was so infinitely superior to what I had known in life, that it appeared to me to be the greatest stupidity in nature to lay any weight upon anything, though the most valuable in this world.

The word eternity represented itself with all its incomprehensible additions, and I had such extended notions of it, that I know not how to express them. Among the rest, how vile, how gross, how absurd did every pleasant thing look!—I mean, that we had counted pleasant before—especially when I reflected that these sordid trifles were the things for which we forfeited eternal felicity.

With these reflections came, of mere course, severe reproaches of my own mind for my wretched behaviour in my past life; that I had forfeited all hope of any happiness in the eternity that I was just going to enter into, and on the contrary was entitled to all that was miserable, or had been conceived of misery; and all this with the frightful addition of its being also eternal.

I am not capable of reading lectures of instruction to anybody, but I relate this in the very manner in which things then appeared to me, as far as I am able, but infinitely short of the lively impressions which they made on my soul at that time; indeed, those impressions are not to be explained by words, or if they are, I am not mistress of words enough to express them. It must be the work of every sober reader to make just reflections on them, as their own circumstances may direct; and, without question, this is what every one at some time or other may feel something of; I mean, a clearer sight into things to come than they had here, and a dark view of their own concern in them.

But I go back to my own case. The minister pressed me to tell him, as far as I though convenient, in what state I found myself as to the sight I had of things beyond life. He told me he did not come as ordinary of the place, whose business it is to extort confessions from prisoners, for private ends, or for the further detecting of other offenders; that his business was to move me to such freedom of discourse as might serve to disburthen my own mind, and furnish him to administer comfort to me as far as was in his power; and assured me, that whatever I said to him should remain with him, and be as much a secret as if it was known only to God and myself; and that he desired to know nothing of me, but as above to qualify him to apply proper advice and assistance to me, and to pray to God for me.

This honest, friendly way of treating me unlocked all the sluices of my passions. He broke into my very soul by it; and I unravelled all the wickedness of my life to him. In a word, I gave him an abridgment of this whole history; I gave him a picture of my conduct for fifty years in miniature.

I hid nothing from him, and he in return exhorted me to sincere repentance, explained to me what he meant by repentance, and then drew out such a scheme of infinite mercy, proclaimed from heaven to sinners of the greatest magnitude, that he left me nothing to say, that looked like despair, or doubting of being accepted; and in this condition he left me the first night.

He visited me again the next morning, and went on with his method of explaining the terms of divine mercy, which according to him consisted of nothing more, or more difficult, than that of being sincerely desirous of it, and willing to accept it; only a sincere regret for, and hatred of, those things I had done, which rendered me so just an object of divine vengeance. I am not able to repeat the excellent discourses of this extraordinary man; 'tis all that I am able to do, to say that he revived my heart, and brought me into such a condition that I never knew anything of in my life before. I was covered with shame and tears for things past, and yet had at the same time a secret surprising joy at the prospect of being a true penitent, and obtaining the comfort of a penitent—I mean, the hope of being forgiven; and so swift did thoughts circulate, and so high did the impressions they had made upon me run, that I thought I could freely have gone out that minute to execution, without any uneasiness at all, casting my soul entirely into the arms of infinite mercy as a penitent.

The good gentleman was so moved also in my behalf with a view of the influence which he saw these things had on me, that he blessed God he had come to visit me, and resolved not to leave me till the last moment; that is, not to leave visiting me.

It was no less than twelve days after our receiving sentence before any were ordered for execution, and then upon a Wednesday the dead warrant, as they call it, came down, and I found my name was among them. A terrible blow this was to my new resolutions; indeed my heart sank within me, and I swooned away twice, one after another, but spoke not a word. The good minister was sorely afflicted for me, and did what he could to comfort me with the same arguments, and the same moving eloquence that he did before, and left me not that evening so long as the prisonkeepers would suffer him to stay in the prison, unless he would be locked up with me all night, which he was not willing to be.

I wondered much that I did not see him all the next day, it being the day before the time appointed for execution; and I was greatly discouraged, and dejected in my mind, and indeed almost sank for want of the comfort which he had so often, and with such success, yielded me on his former visits. I waited with great impatience, and under the greatest oppressions of spirits imaginable, till about four o'clock he came to my apartment; for I had obtained the favour, by the help of money, nothing being to be done in that place without it, not to be kept in the condemned hole, as they call it, among the rest of the prisoners who were to die, but to have a little dirty chamber to myself.

My heart leaped within me for joy when I heard his voice at the door, even before I saw him; but let any one judge what kind of motion I found in my soul, when after having made a short excuse for his not coming, he showed me that his time had been employed on my account; that he had obtained a favourable report from the Recorder to the Secretary of State in my particular case, and, in short, that he had brought me a reprieve.

He used all the caution that he was able in letting me know a thing which it would have been a double cruelty to have concealed; and yet it was too much for me; for as grief had overset me before, so did joy overset me now, and I fell into a much more dangerous swooning than I did at first, and it was not without a great difficulty that I was recovered at all.

The good man having made a very Christian exhortation to me, not to let the joy of my reprieve put the remembrance of my past sorrow out of my mind, and having told me that he must leave me, to go and enter the reprieve in the books, and show it to the sheriffs, stood up just before his going away, and in a very earnest manner prayed to God for me, that my repentance might be made unfeigned and sincere; and that my coming back, as it were, into life again, might not be a returning to the follies of life which I had made such solemn resolutions to forsake, and to repent of them. I joined heartily in the petition, and must needs say I had deeper impressions upon my mind all that night, of the mercy of God in sparing my life, and a greater detestation of my past sins, from a sense of the goodness which I had tasted in this case, than I had in all my sorrow before.

This may be thought inconsistent in itself, and wide from the business of this book; particularly, I reflect that many of those who may be pleased and diverted with the relation of the wild and wicked part of my story may not relish this, which is really the best part of my life, the most advantageous to myself, and the most instructive to others. Such, however, will, I hope, allow me the liberty to make my story complete. It would be a severe satire on such to say they do not relish the repentance as much as they do the crime; and that they had rather the history were a complete tragedy, as it was very likely to have been.

But I go on with my relation. The next morning there was a sad scene indeed in the prison. The first thing I was saluted with in the morning was the tolling of the great bell at St. Sepulchre's, as they call it, which ushered in the day. As soon as it began to toll, a dismal groaning and crying was heard from the condemned hole, where there lay six poor souls who were to be executed that day, some from one crime, some for another, and two of them for murder.

This was followed by a confused clamour in the house, among the several sorts of prisoners, expressing their awkward sorrows for the poor creatures that were to die, but in a manner extremely differing one from another. Some cried for them; some huzzaed, and wished them a good journey; some damned and cursed those that had brought them to it—that is, meaning the evidence, or prosecutors—many pitying them, and some few, but very few, praying for them.

There was hardly room for so much composure of mind as was required for me to bless the merciful Providence that had, as it were, snatched me out of the jaws of this destruction. I remained, as it were, dumb and silent, overcome with the sense of it, and not able to express what I had in my heart; for the passions on such occasions as these are certainly so agitated as not to be able presently to regulate their own motions.

All the while the poor condemned creatures were preparing to their death, and the ordinary, as they call him, was busy with them, disposing them to submit to their sentence—I say, all this while I was seized with a fit of trembling, as much as I could have been if I had been in the same condition, as to be sure the day before I expected to be; I was so violently agitated by this surprising fit, that I shook as if it had been in the cold fit of an ague, so that I could not speak or look but like one distracted. As soon as they were all put into carts and gone, which, however, I had not courage enough to see—I say, as soon as they were gone, I fell into a fit of crying involuntarily, and without design, but as a mere distemper, and yet so violent, and it held me so long, that I knew not what course to take, nor could I stop, or put a check to it, no, not with all the strength and courage I had.

This fit of crying held me near two hours, and, as I believe, held me till they were all out of the world, and then a most humble, penitent, serious kind of joy succeeded; a real transport it was, or passion of joy and thankfulness, but still unable to give vent to it by words, and in this I continued most part of the day.

In the evening the good minister visited me again, and then fell to his usual good discourses. He congratulated my having a space yet allowed me for repentance, whereas the state of those six poor creatures was determined, and they were now past the offers of salvation; he earnestly pressed me to retain the same sentiments of the things of life that I had when I had a view of eternity; and at the end of all told me I should not conclude that all was over, that a reprieve was not a pardon, that he could not yet answer for the effects of it; however, I had this mercy, that I had more time given me, and that it was my business to improve that time.

This discourse, though very seasonable, left a kind of sadness on my heart, as if I might expect the affair would have a tragical issue still, which, however, he had no certainty of; and I did not indeed, at that time, question him about it, he having said that he would do his utmost to bring it to a good end, and that he hoped he might, but he would not have me be secure; and the consequence proved that he had reason for what he said.

It was about a fortnight after this that I had some just apprehensions that I should be included in the next dead warrant at the ensuing sessions; and it was not without great difficulty, and at last a humble petition for transportation, that I avoided it, so ill was I beholding to fame, and so prevailing was the fatal report of being an old offender; though in that they did not do me strict justice, for I was not in the sense of the law an old offender, whatever I was in the eye of the judge, for I had never been before them in a judicial way before; so the judges could not charge me with being an old offender, but the Recorder was pleased to represent my case as he thought fit.

I had now a certainty of life indeed, but with the hard conditions of being ordered for transportation, which indeed was hard condition in itself, but not when comparatively considered; and therefore I shall make no comments upon the sentence, nor upon the choice I was put to. We shall all choose anything rather than death, especially when 'tis attended with an uncomfortable prospect beyond it, which was my case.

The good minister, whose interest, though a stranger to me, had obtained me the reprieve, mourned sincerely for this part. He was in hopes, he said, that I should have ended my days under the influence of good instruction, that I should not have been turned loose again among such a wretched crew as they generally are, who are thus sent abroad, where, as he said, I must have more than ordinary secret assistance from the grace of God, if I did not turn as wicked again as ever.

I have not for a good while mentioned my governess, who had during most, if not all, of this part been dangerously sick, and being in as near a view of death by her disease as I was by my sentence, was a great penitent—I say, I have not mentioned her, nor indeed did I see her in all this time; but being now recovering, and just able to come abroad, she came to see me.

I told her my condition, and what a different flux and reflux of tears and hopes I had been agitated with; I told her what I had escaped, and upon what terms; and she was present when the minister expressed his fears of my relapsing into wickedness upon my falling into the wretched companies that are generally transported. Indeed I had a melancholy reflection upon it in my own mind, for I knew what a dreadful gang was always sent away together, and I said to my governess that the good minister's fears were not without cause. 'Well, well,' says she, 'but I hope you will not be tempted with such a horrid example as that.' And as soon as the minister was gone, she told me she would not have me discouraged, for perhaps ways and means might be found out to dispose of me in a particular way, by myself, of which she would talk further to me afterward.

I looked earnestly at her, and I thought she looked more cheerful than she usually had done, and I entertained immediately a thousand notions of being delivered, but could not for my life image the methods, or think of one that was in the least feasible; but I was too much concerned in it to let her go from me without explaining herself, which, though she was very loth to do, yet my importunity prevailed, and, while I was still pressing, she answered me in a few words, thus: 'Why, you have money, have you not? Did you ever know one in your life that was transported and had a hundred pounds in his pocket, I'll warrant you, child?' says she.

I understood her presently, but told her I would leave all that to her, but I saw no room to hope for anything but a strict execution of the order, and as it was a severity that was esteemed a mercy, there was no doubt but it would be strictly observed. She said no more but this: 'We will try what can be done,' and so we parted for that night.

I lay in the prison near fifteen weeks after this order for transportation was signed. What the reason of it was, I know not, but at the end of this time I was put on board of a ship in the Thames, and with me a gang of thirteen as hardened vile creatures as ever Newgate produced in my time; and it would really well take up a history longer than mine to describe the degrees of impudence and audacious villainy that those thirteen were arrived to, and the manner of their behaviour in the voyage; of which I have a very diverting account by me, which the captain of the ship who carried them over gave me the minutes of, and which he caused his mate to write down at large.

It may perhaps be thought trifling to enter here into a relation of all the little incidents which attended me in this interval of my circumstances; I mean, between the final order of my transportation and the time of my going on board the ship; and I am too near the end of my story to allow room for it; but something relating to me and my Lancashire husband I must not omit.

He had, as I have observed already, been carried from the master's side of the ordinary prison into the press-yard, with three of his comrades, for they found another to add to them after some time; here, for what reason I knew not, they were kept in custody without being brought to trial almost three months. It seems they found means to bribe or buy off some of those who were expected to come in against them, and they wanted evidence for some time to convict them. After some puzzle on this account, at first they made a shift to get proof enough against two of them to carry them off; but the other two, of which my Lancashire husband was one, lay still in suspense. They had, I think, one positive evidence against each of them, but the law strictly obliging them to have two witnesses, they could make nothing of it. Yet it seems they were resolved not to part with the men neither, not doubting but a further evidence would at last come in; and in order to this, I think publication was made, that such prisoners being taken, any one that had been robbed by them might come to the prison and see them.

I took this opportunity to satisfy my curiosity, pretending that I had been robbed in the Dunstable coach, and that I would go to see the two highwaymen. But when I came into the press-yard, I so disguised myself, and muffled my face up so, that he could see little of me, and consequently knew nothing of who I was; and when I came back, I said publicly that I knew them very well.

Immediately it was rumoured all over the prison that Moll Flanders would turn evidence against one of the highwaymen, and that I was to come off by it from the sentence of transportation.

They heard of it, and immediately my husband desired to see this Mrs. Flanders that knew him so well, and was to be an evidence against him; and accordingly I had leave given to go to him. I dressed myself up as well as the best clothes that I suffered myself ever to appear in there would allow me, and went to the press-yard, but had for some time a hood over my face. He said little to me at first, but asked me if I knew him. I told him, Yes, very well; but as I concealed my face, so I counterfeited my voice, that he had not the least guess at who I was. He asked me where I had seen him. I told him between Dunstable and Brickhill; but turning to the keeper that stood by, I asked if I might not be admitted to talk with him alone. He said Yes, yes, as much as I pleased, and so very civilly withdrew.

As soon as he was gone, I had shut the door, I threw off my hood, and bursting out into tears, 'My dear,' says I, 'do you not know me?' He turned pale, and stood speechless, like one thunderstruck, and, not able to conquer the surprise, said no more but this, 'Let me sit down'; and sitting down by a table, he laid his elbow upon the table, and leaning his head on his hand, fixed his eyes on the ground as one stupid. I cried so vehemently, on the other hand, that it was a good while ere I could speak any more; but after I had given some vent to my passion by tears, I repeated the same words, 'My dear, do you not know me?' At which he answered, Yes, and said no more a good while.

After some time continuing in the surprise, as above, he cast up his eyes towards me and said, 'How could you be so cruel?' I did not readily understand what he meant; and I answered, 'How can you call me cruel? What have I been cruel to you in?' 'To come to me,' says he, 'in such a place as this, is it not to insult me? I have not robbed you, at least not on the highway.'

I perceived by this that he knew nothing of the miserable circumstances I was in, and thought that, having got some intelligence of his being there, I had come to upbraid him with his leaving me. But I had too much to say to him to be affronted, and told him in few words, that I was far from coming to insult him, but at best I came to condole mutually; that he would be easily satisfied that I had no such view, when I should tell him that my condition was worse than his, and that many ways. He looked a little concerned at the general expression of my condition being worse than his, but, with a kind smile, looked a little wildly, and said, 'How can that be? When you see me fettered, and in Newgate, and two of my companions executed already, can you can your condition is worse than mine?'

'Come, my dear,' says I, 'we have a long piece of work to do, if I should be to relate, or you to hear, my unfortunate history; but if you are disposed to hear it, you will soon conclude with me that my condition is worse than yours.' 'How is that possible,' says he again, 'when I expect to be cast for my life the very next sessions?' 'Yes, says I, ''tis very possible, when I shall tell you that I have been cast for my life three sessions ago, and am under sentence of death; is not my case worse than yours?'

Then indeed, he stood silent again, like one struck dumb, and after a while he starts up. 'Unhappy couple!' says he. 'How can this be possible?' I took him by the hand. 'Come, my dear,' said I, 'sit down, and let us compare our sorrows. I am a prisoner in this very house, and in much worse circumstances than you, and you will be satisfied I do not come to insult you, when I tell you the particulars.' Any with this we sat down together, and I told him so much of my story as I thought was convenient, bringing it at last to my being reduced to great poverty, and representing myself as fallen into some company that led me to relieve my distresses by way that I had been utterly unacquainted with, and that they making an attempt at a tradesman's house, I was seized upon for having been but just at the door, the maid-servant pulling me in; that I neither had broke any lock nor taken anything away, and that notwithstanding that, I was brought in guilty and sentenced to die; but that the judges, having been made sensible of the hardship of my circumstances, had obtained leave to remit the sentence upon my consenting to be transported.

I told him I fared the worse for being taken in the prison for one Moll Flanders, who was a famous successful thief, that all of them had heard of, but none of them had ever seen; but that, as he knew well, was none of my name. But I placed all to the account of my ill fortune, and that under this name I was dealt with as an old offender, though this was the first thing they had ever known of me. I gave him a long particular of things that had befallen me since I saw him, but I told him if I had seen him since he might think I had, and then gave him an account how I had seen him at Brickhill; how furiously he was pursued, and how, by giving an account that I knew him, and that he was a very honest gentleman, one Mr. ———, the hue-and-cry was stopped, and the high constable went back again.

He listened most attentively to all my story, and smiled at most of the particulars, being all of them petty matters, and infinitely below what he had been at the head of; but when I came to the story of Brickhill, he was surprised. 'And was it you, my dear,' said he, 'that gave the check to the mob that was at our heels there, at Brickhill?' 'Yes,' said

I, 'it was I indeed.' And then I told him the particulars which I had observed him there. 'Why, then,' said he, 'it was you that saved my life at that time, and I am glad I owe my life to you, for I will pay the debt to you now, and I'll deliver you from the present condition you are in, or I will die in the attempt.'

I told him, by no means; it was a risk too great, not worth his running the hazard of, and for a life not worth his saving. 'Twas no matter for that, he said, it was a life worth all the world to him; a life that had given him a new life; 'for,' says he, 'I was never in real danger of being taken, but that time, till the last minute when I was taken.' Indeed, he told me his danger then lay in his believing he had not been pursued that way; for they had gone from Hockey quite another way, and had come over the enclosed country into Brickhill, not by the road, and were sure they had not been seen by anybody.

Here he gave me a long history of his life, which indeed would make a very strange history, and be infinitely diverting. He told me he took to the road about twelve years before he married me; that the woman which called him brother was not really his sister, or any kin to him, but one that belonged to their gang, and who, keeping correspondence with him, lived always in town, having good store of acquaintance; that she gave them a perfect intelligence of persons going out of town, and that they had made several good booties by her correspondence; that she thought she had fixed a fortune for him when she brought me to him, but happened to be disappointed, which he really could not blame her for; that if it had been his good luck that I had had the estate, which she was informed I had, he had resolved to leave off the road and live a retired, sober live but never to appear in public till some general pardon had been passed, or till he could, for money, have got his name into some particular pardon, that so he might have been perfectly easy; but that, as it had proved otherwise, he was obliged to put off his equipage and take up the old trade again.

He gave me a long account of some of his adventures, and particularly one when he robbed the West Chester coaches near Lichfield, when he got a very great booty; and after that, how he robbed five graziers, in the west, going to Burford Fair in Wiltshire to buy sheep. He told me he got so much money on those two occasions, that if he had known where to have found me, he would certainly have embraced my proposal of going with me to Virginia, or to have settled in a plantation on some other parts of the English colonies in America.

He told me he wrote two or three letters to me, directed according to my order, but heard nothing from me. This I indeed knew to be true, but the letters coming to my hand in the time of my latter husband, I could do nothing in it, and therefore chose to give no answer, that so he might rather believe they had miscarried.

Being thus disappointed, he said, he carried on the old trade ever since, though when he had gotten so much money, he said, he did not run such desperate risks as he did before. Then he gave me some account of several hard and desperate encounters which he had with gentlemen on the road, who parted too hardly with their money, and showed me some wounds he had received; and he had one or two very terrible wounds indeed, as particularly one by a pistol bullet, which broke his arm, and another with a sword, which ran him quite through the body, but that missing his vitals, he was cured again; one of his comrades having kept with him so faithfully, and so friendly, as that he assisted him in riding near eighty miles before his arm was set, and then got a surgeon in a considerable city, remote from that place where it was done, pretending they were gentlemen travelling towards Carlisle and that they had been attacked on the road by highwaymen, and that one of them had shot him into the arm and broke the bone.

This, he said, his friend managed so well, that they were not suspected at all, but lay still till he was perfectly cured. He gave me so many distinct accounts of his adventures, that it is with great reluctance that I decline the relating them; but I consider that this is my own story, not his.

I then inquired into the circumstances of his present case at that time, and what it was he expected when he came to be tried. He told me that they had no evidence against him, or but very little; for that of three robberies, which they were all charged with, it was his good fortune that he was but in one of them, and that there was but one witness to be had for that fact, which was not sufficient, but that it was expected some others would come in against him; that he thought indeed, when he first saw me, that I had been one that came of that errand; but that if somebody came in against him, he hoped he should be cleared; that he had had some intimation, that if he would submit to transport himself, he might be admitted to it without a trial, but that he could not think of it with any temper, and thought he could much easier submit to be hanged.

I blamed him for that, and told him I blamed him on two accounts; first, because if he was transported, there might be a hundred ways for him that was a gentleman, and a bold enterprising man, to find his way back again, and perhaps some ways and means to come back before he went. He smiled at that part, and said he should like the last the best of the two, for he had a kind of horror upon his mind at his being sent over to the plantations, as Romans sent condemned slaves to work in the mines; that he thought the passage into another state, let it be what it would, much more tolerable at the gallows, and that this was the general notion of all the gentlemen who were driven by the exigence of their fortunes to take the road; that at the place of execution there was at least an end of all the miseries of the present state, and as for what was to follow, a man was, in his opinion, as likely to repent sincerely in the last fortnight of his life, under the pressures and agonies of a jail and the condemned hole, as he would ever be in the woods and wilderness of America; that servitude and hard labour were things gentlemen could never stoop to; that it was but the way to force them to be their own executioners afterwards, which was much worse; and that therefore he could not have any patience when he did but think of being transported.

I used the utmost of my endeavour to persuade him, and joined that known woman's rhetoric to it—I mean, that of tears. I told him the infamy of a public execution was certainly a greater pressure upon the spirits of a gentleman than any of the mortifications that he could meet with abroad could be; that he had at least in the other a chance for his life, whereas here he had none at all; that it was the easiest thing in the world for him to manage the captain of a ship, who were, generally speaking, men of good-humour and some gallantry; and a small matter of conduct, especially if there was any money to be had, would make way for him to buy himself off when he came to Virginia.

He looked wistfully at me, and I thought I guessed at what he meant, that is to say, that he had no money; but I was mistaken, his meaning was another way. 'You hinted just now, my dear,' said he, 'that there might be a way of coming back before I went, by which I understood you that it might be possible to buy it off here. I had rather give #200 to prevent going, than #100 to be set at liberty when I came there.' 'That is, my dear,' said I, 'because you do not know the place so well as I do.' 'That may be,' said he; 'and yet I believe, as well as you know it, you would do the same, unless it is because, as you told me, you have a mother there.'

I told him, as to my mother, it was next to impossible but that she must be dead many years before; and as for any other relations that I might have there, I knew them not now; that since the misfortunes I had been under had reduced me to the condition I had been in for some years, I had not kept up any correspondence with them; and that he would easily believe, I should find but a cold reception from them if I should be put to make my first visit in the condition of a transported felon; that therefore, if I went thither, I resolved not to see them; but that I had many views in going there, if it should be my fate, which took off all the uneasy part of it; and if he found himself obliged to go also, I should easily instruct him how to manage himself, so as never to go a servant at all, especially since I found he was not destitute of money, which was the only friend in such a condition.

He smiled, and said he did not tell me he had money. I took him up short, and told him I hoped he did not understand by my speaking, that I should expect any supply from him if he had money; that, on the other hand, though I had not a great deal, yet I did not want, and while I had any I would rather add to him than weaken him in that article, seeing, whatever he had, I knew in the case of transportation he would have occasion of it all.

He expressed himself in a most tender manner upon that head. He told me what money he had was not a great deal, but that he would never hide any of it from me if I wanted it, and that he assured me he did not speak with any such apprehensions; that he was only intent upon what I had hinted to him before he went; that here he knew what to do with himself, but that there he should be the most ignorant, helpless wretch alive.

I told him he frighted and terrified himself with that which had no terror in it; that if he had money, as I was glad to hear he had, he might not only avoid the servitude supposed to be the consequence of transportation, but begin the world upon a new foundation, and that such a one as he could not fail of success in, with the common application usual in such cases; that he could not but call to mind that is was what I had recommended to him many years before and had proposed it for our mutual subsistence and restoring our fortunes in the world; and I would tell him now, that to convince him both of the certainty of it and of my being fully acquainted with the method, and also fully satisfied in the probability of success, he should first see me deliver myself from the necessity of going over at all, and then that I would go with him freely, and of my own choice, and perhaps carry enough with me to satisfy him that I did not offer it for want of being able to live without assistance from him, but that I thought our mutual misfortunes had been such as were sufficient to reconcile us both to quitting this part of the world, and living where nobody could upbraid us with what was past, or we be in any dread of a prison, and without agonies of a condemned hole to drive us to it; this where we should look back on all our past disasters with infinite satisfaction, when we should consider that our enemies should entirely forget us, and that we should live as new people in a new world, nobody having anything to say to us, or we to them.

I pressed this home to him with so many arguments, and answered all his own passionate objections so effectually that he embraced me, and told me I treated him with such sincerity and affection as overcame him; that he would take my advice, and would strive to submit to his fate in hope of having the comfort of my assistance, and of so faithful a counsellor and such a companion in his misery. But still he put me in mind of what I had mentioned before, namely, that there might be some way to get off before he went, and that it might be possible to avoid going at all, which he said would be much better. I told him he should see, and be fully satisfied, that I would do my utmost in that part too, and if it did not succeed, yet that I would make good the rest.

We parted after this long conference with such testimonies of kindness and affection as I thought were equal, if not superior, to that at our parting at Dunstable; and now I saw more plainly than before, the reason why he declined coming at that time any farther with me toward London than Dunstable, and why, when we parted there, he told me it was not convenient for him to come part of the way to London to bring me going, as he would otherwise have done. I have observed that the account of his life would have made a much more pleasing history than this of mine; and, indeed, nothing in it was more strange than this part, viz. that he carried on that desperate trade full five-and-twenty years and had never been taken, the success he had met with had been so very uncommon, and such that sometimes he had lived handsomely, and retired in place for a year or two at a time, keeping himself and a man-servant to wait on him, and had often sat in the coffee-houses and heard the very people whom he had robbed give accounts of their being robbed, and of the place and circumstances, so that he could easily remember that it was the same.

In this manner, it seems, he lived near Liverpool at the time he unluckily married me for a fortune. Had I been the fortune he expected, I verily believe, as he said, that he would have taken up and lived honestly all his days.

He had with the rest of his misfortunes the good luck not to be actually upon the spot when the robbery was done which he was committed for, and so none of the persons robbed could swear to him, or had anything to charge upon him. But it seems as he was taken with the gang, one hard-mouthed countryman swore home to him, and they were like to have others come in according to the publication they had made; so that they expected more evidence against him, and for that reason he was kept in hold.

However, the offer which was made to him of admitting him to transportation was made, as I understood, upon the intercession of some great person who pressed him hard to accept of it before a trial; and indeed, as he knew there were several that might come in against him, I thought his friend was in the right, and I lay at him night and day to delay it no longer.

At last, with much difficulty, he gave his consent; and as he was not therefore admitted to transportation in court, and on his petition, as I was, so he found himself under a difficulty to avoid embarking himself as I had said he might have done; his great friend, who was his intercessor for the favour of that grant, having given security for him that he should transport himself, and not return within the term.

This hardship broke all my measures, for the steps I took afterwards for my own deliverance were hereby rendered wholly ineffectual, unless I would abandon him, and leave him to go to America by himself; than which he protested he would much rather venture, although he were certain to go directly to the gallows.

I must now return to my case. The time of my being transported according to my sentence was near at hand; my governess, who continued my fast friend, had tried to obtain a pardon, but it could not be done unless with an expense too heavy for my purse, considering that to be left naked and empty, unless I had resolved to return to my old trade again, had been worse than my transportation, because there I knew I could live, here I could not. The good minister stood very hard on another account to prevent my being transported also; but he was answered, that indeed my life had been given me at his first solicitations, and therefore he ought to ask no more. He was sensibly grieved at my going, because, as he said, he feared I should lose the good impressions which a prospect of death had at first made on me, and which were since increased by his instructions; and the pious gentleman was exceedingly concerned about me on that account.

On the other hand, I really was not so solicitous about it as I was before, but I industriously concealed my reasons for it from the minister, and to the last he did not know but that I went with the utmost reluctance and affliction.

It was in the month of February that I was, with seven other convicts, as they called us, delivered to a merchant that traded to Virginia, on board a ship, riding, as they called it, in Deptford Reach. The officer of the prison delivered us on board, and the master of the vessel gave a discharge for us.

We were for that night clapped under hatches, and kept so close that I thought I should have been suffocated for want of air; and the next morning the ship weighed, and fell down the river to a place they call Bugby's Hole, which was done, as they told us, by the agreement of the merchant, that all opportunity of escape should be taken from us. However, when the ship came thither and cast anchor, we were allowed more liberty, and particularly were permitted to come up on the deck, but not up on the quarter-deck, that being kept particularly for the captain and for passengers.

When by the noise of the men over my head, and the motion of the ship, I perceived that they were under sail, I was at first greatly surprised, fearing we should go away directly, and that our friends would not be admitted to see us any more; but I was easy soon after, when I found they had come to an anchor again, and soon after that we had notice given by some of the men where we were, that the next morning we should have the liberty to come up on deck, and to have our friends come and see us if we had any.

All that night I lay upon the hard boards of the deck, as the passengers did, but we had afterwards the liberty of little cabins for such of us as had any bedding to lay in them, and room to stow any box or trunk for clothes and linen, if we had it (which might well be put in), for some of them had neither shirt nor shift or a rag of linen or woollen, but what was on their backs, or a farthing of money to help themselves; and yet I did not find but they fared well enough in the ship, especially the women, who got money from the seamen for washing their clothes, sufficient to purchase any common things that they wanted.

When the next morning we had the liberty to come up on the deck, I asked one of the officers of the ship, whether I might not have the liberty to send a letter on shore, to let my friends know where the ship lay, and to get some necessary things sent to me. This was, it seems, the boatswain, a very civil, courteous sort of man, who told me I should have that, or any other liberty that I desired, that he could allow me with safety. I told him I desired no other; and he answered that the ship's boat would go up to London the next tide, and he would order my letter to be carried.

Accordingly, when the boat went off, the boatswain came to me and told me the boat was going off, and that he went in it himself, and asked me if my letter was ready he would take care of it. I had prepared myself, you may be sure, pen, ink, and paper beforehand, and I had gotten a letter ready directed to my governess, and enclosed another for my fellow-prisoner, which, however, I did not let her know was my husband, not to the last. In that to my governess, I let her know where the ship lay, and pressed her earnestly to send me what things I knew she had got ready for me for my voyage.

When I gave the boatswain the letter, I gave him a shilling with it, which I told him was for the charge of a messenger or porter, which I entreated him to send with the letter as soon as he came on shore, that if possible I might have an answer brought back by the same hand, that I might know what was become of my things; 'for sir,' says I, 'if the ship should go away before I have them on board, I am undone.'

I took care, when I gave him the shilling, to let him see that I had a little better furniture about me than the ordinary prisoners, for he saw that I had a purse, and in it a pretty deal of money; and I found that the very sight of it immediately furnished me with very different treatment from what I should otherwise have met with in the ship; for though he was very courteous indeed before, in a kind of natural compassion to me, as a woman in distress, yet he was more than ordinarily so afterwards, and procured me to be better treated in the ship than, I say, I might otherwise have been; as shall appear in its place.

He very honestly had my letter delivered to my governess's own hands, and brought me back an answer from her in writing; and when he gave me the answer, gave me the shilling again. 'There,' says he, 'there's your shilling again too, for I delivered the letter myself.' I could not tell what to say, I was so surprised at the thing; but after some pause, I said, 'Sir, you are too kind; it had been but reasonable that you had paid yourself coach-hire, then.'

'No, no,' says he, 'I am overpaid. What is the gentlewoman? Your sister.'

'No, sir,' says I, 'she is no relation to me, but she is a dear friend, and all the friends I have in the world.' 'Well,' says he, 'there are few such friends in the world. Why, she cried after you like a child,' 'Ay,' says I again, 'she would give a hundred pounds, I believe, to deliver me from this dreadful condition I am in.'

'Would she so?' says he. 'For half the money I believe I could put you in a way how to deliver yourself.' But this he spoke softly, that nobody could hear.

'Alas! sir,' said I, 'but then that must be such a deliverance as, if I should be taken again, would cost me my life.' 'Nay,' said he, 'if you were once out of the ship, you must look to yourself afterwards; that I can say nothing to.' So we dropped the discourse for that time.

In the meantime, my governess, faithful to the last moment, conveyed my letter to the prison to my husband, and got an answer to it, and the next day came down herself to the ship, bringing me, in the first place, a sea-bed as they call it, and all its furniture, such as was convenient, but not to let the people think it was extraordinary. She brought with her a sea-chest—that is, a chest, such as are made for seamen, with all the conveniences in it, and filled with everything almost that I could want; and in one of the corners of the chest, where there was a private drawer, was my bank of money—this is to say, so much of it as I had resolved to carry with me; for I ordered a part of my stock to be left behind me, to be sent afterwards in such goods as I should want when I came to settle; for money in that country is not of much use where all things are brought for tobacco, much more is it a great loss to carry it from hence.

But my case was particular; it was by no means proper to me to go thither without money or goods, and for a poor convict, that was to be sold as soon as I came on shore, to carry with me a cargo of goods would be to have notice taken of it, and perhaps to have them seized by the public; so I took part of my stock with me thus, and left the other part with my governess.

My governess brought me a great many other things, but it was not proper for me to look too well provided in the ship, at least till I knew what kind of a captain we should have. When she came into the ship, I thought she would have died indeed; her heart sank at the sight of me, and at the thoughts of parting with me in that condition, and she cried so intolerably, I could not for a long time have any talk with her.

I took that time to read my fellow-prisoner's letter, which, however, greatly perplexed me. He told me was determined to go, but found it would be impossible for him to be discharged time enough for going in the same ship, and which was more than all, he began to question whether they would give him leave to go in what ship he pleased, though he did voluntarily transport himself; but that they would see him put on board such a ship as they should direct, and that he would be charged upon the captain as other convict prisoners were; so that he began to be in despair of seeing me till he came to Virginia, which made him almost desperate; seeing that, on the other hand, if I should not be there, if any accident of the sea or of mortality should take me away, he should be the most undone creature there in the world.

This was very perplexing, and I knew not what course to take. I told my governess the story of the boatswain, and she was mighty eager with me treat with him; but I had no mind to it, till I heard whether my husband, or fellow-prisoner, so she called him, could be at liberty to go with me or no. At last I was forced to let her into the whole matter, except only that of his being my husband. I told her I had made a positive bargain or agreement with him to go, if he could get the liberty of going in the same ship, and that I found he had money.

Then I read a long lecture to her of what I proposed to do when we came there, how we could plant, settle, and, in short, grow rich without any more adventures; and, as a great secret, I told her that we were to marry as soon as he came on board.

She soon agreed cheerfully to my going when she heard this, and she made it her business from that time to get him out of the prison in time, so that he might go in the same ship with me, which at last was brought to pass, though with great difficulty, and not without all the forms of a transported prisoner-convict, which he really was not yet, for he had not been tried, and which was a great mortification to him. As our fate was now determined, and we were both on board, actually bound to Virginia, in the despicable quality of transported convicts destined to be sold for slaves, I for five years, and he under bonds and security not to return to England any more, as long as he lived, he was very much dejected and cast down; the mortification of being brought on board, as he was, like a prisoner, piqued him very much, since it was first told him he should transport himself, and so that he might go as a gentleman at liberty. It is true he was not ordered to be sold when he came there, as we were, and for that reason he was obliged to pay for his passage to the captain, which we were not; as to the rest, he was as much at a loss as a child what to do with himself, or with what he had, but by directions.

Our first business was to compare our stock. He was very honest to me, and told me his stock was pretty good when he came into the prison, but the living there as he did in a figure like a gentleman, and, which was ten times as much, the making of friends, and soliciting his case, had been very expensive; and, in a word, all his stock that he had left was #108, which he had about him all in gold.

I gave him an account of my stock as faithfully, that is to say, of what I had taken to carry with me, for I was resolved, whatever should happen, to keep what I had left with my governess in reserve; that in case I should die, what I had with me was enough to give him, and that which was left in my governess's hands would be her own, which she had well deserved of me indeed.

My stock which I had with me was #246 some odd shillings; so that we had #354 between us, but a worse gotten estate was scarce ever put together to being the world with.

Our greatest misfortune as to our stock was that it was all in money, which every one knows is an unprofitable cargo to be carried to the plantations. I believe his was really all he had left in the world, as he told me it was; but I, who had between #700 and #800 in bank when this disaster befell me, and who had one of the faithfullest friends in the world to manage it for me, considering she was a woman of manner of religious principles, had still #300 left in her hand, which I reserved as above; besides, some very valuable things, as particularly two gold watches, some small pieces of plate, and some rings—all stolen goods. The plate, rings, and watches were put in my chest with the money, and with this fortune, and in the sixty-first year of my age, I launched out into a new world, as I may call it, in the condition (as to what appeared) only of a poor, naked convict, ordered to be transported in respite from the gallows. My clothes were poor and mean, but not ragged or dirty, and none knew in the whole ship that I had anything of value about me.

However, as I had a great many very good clothes and linen in abundance, which I had ordered to be packed up in two great boxes, I had them shipped on board, not as my goods, but as consigned to my real name in Virginia; and had the bills of loading signed by a captain in my pocket; and in these boxes was my plate and watches, and everything of value except my money, which I kept by itself in a private drawer in my chest, which could not be found, or opened, if found, with splitting the chest to pieces.

In this condition I lay for three weeks in the ship, not knowing whether I should have my husband with me or no, and therefore not resolving how or in what manner to receive the honest boatswain's proposal, which indeed he thought a little strange at first.

At the end of this time, behold my husband came on board. He looked with a dejected, angry countenance, his great heart was swelled with rage and disdain; to be dragged along with three keepers of Newgate, and put on board like a convict, when he had not so much as been brought to a trial. He made loud complaints of it by his friends, for it seems he had some interest; but his friends got some check in their application, and were told he had had favour enough, and that they had received such an account of him, since the last grant of his transportation, that he ought to think himself very well treated that he was not prosecuted anew. This answer quieted him at once, for he knew too much what might have happened, and what he had room to expect; and now he saw the goodness of the advice to him, which prevailed with him to accept of the offer of a voluntary transportation. And after this his chagrin at these hell-hounds, as he called them, was a little over, he looked a little composed, began to be cheerful, and as I was telling him how glad I was to have him once more out of their hands, he took me in his arms, and acknowledged with great tenderness that I had given him the best advice possible. 'My dear,' says he, 'thou has twice saved my life; from henceforward it shall be all employed for you, and I'll always take your advice.'

The ship began now to fill; several passengers came on board, who were embarked on no criminal account, and these had accommodations assigned them in the great cabin, and other parts of the ship, whereas we, as convicts, were thrust down below, I know not where. But when my husband came on board, I spoke to the boatswain, who had so early given me hints of his friendship in carrying my letter. I told him he had befriended me in many things, and I had not made any suitable return to him, and with that I put a guinea into his hand. I told him that my husband was now come on board; that though we were both under the present misfortune, yet we had been persons of a different character from the wretched crew that we came with, and desired to know of him, whether the captain might not be moved to admit us to some conveniences in the ship, for which we would make him what satisfaction he pleased, and that we would gratify him for his pains in procuring this for us. He took the guinea, as I could see, with great satisfaction, and assured me of his assistance.

Then he told us he did not doubt but that the captain, who was one of the best-humoured gentlemen in the world, would be easily brought to accommodate us as well as we could desire, and, to make me easy, told me he would go up the next tide on purpose to speak to the captain about it. The next morning, happening to sleep a little longer than ordinary, when I got up, and began to look abroad, I saw the boatswain among the men in his ordinary business. I was a little melancholy at seeing him there, and going forward to speak to him, he saw me, and came towards me, but not giving him time to speak first, I said, smiling, 'I doubt, sir, you have forgot us, for I see you are very busy.' He returned presently, 'Come along with me, and you shall see.' So he took me into the great cabin, and there sat a good sort of a gentlemanly man for a seaman, writing, and with a great many papers before him.

'Here,' says the boatswain to him that was a-writing, 'is the gentlewoman that the captain spoke to you of'; and turning to me, he said, 'I have been so far from forgetting your business, that I have been up at the captain's house, and have represented faithfully to the captain what you said, relating to you being furnished with better conveniences for yourself and your husband; and the captain has sent this gentleman, who is made of the ship, down with me, on purpose to show you everything, and to accommodate you fully to your content, and bid me assure you that you shall not be treated like what you were at first expected to be, but with the same respect as other passengers are treated.'

The mate then spoke to me, and, not giving me time to thank the boatswain for his kindness, confirmed what the boatswain had said, and added that it was the captain's delight to show himself kind and charitable, especially to those that were under any misfortunes, and with that he showed me several cabins built up, some in the great cabin, and some partitioned off, out of the steerage, but opening into the great cabin on purpose for the accommodation of passengers, and gave me leave to choose where I would. However, I chose a cabin which opened into the steerage, in which was very good conveniences to set our chest and boxes, and a table to eat on.

The mate then told me that the boatswain had given so good a character of me and my husband, as to our civil behaviour, that he had orders to tell me we should eat with him, if we thought fit, during the whole voyage, on the common terms of passengers; that we might lay in some fresh provisions, if we pleased; or if not, he should lay in his usual store, and we should have share with him. This was very reviving news to me, after so many hardships and afflictions as I had gone through of late. I thanked him, and told him the captain should make his own terms with us, and asked him leave to go and tell my husband of it, who was not very well, and was not yet out of his cabin. Accordingly I went, and my husband, whose spirits were still so much sunk with the indignity (as he understood it) offered him, that he was scare yet himself, was so revived with the account that I gave him of the reception we were like to have in the ship, that he was quite another man, and new vigour and courage appeared in his very countenance. So true is it, that the greatest of spirits, when overwhelmed by their afflictions, are subject to the greatest dejections, and are the most apt to despair and give themselves up.

After some little pause to recover himself, my husband came up with me, and gave the mate thanks for the kindness, which he had expressed to us, and sent suitable acknowledgment by him to the captain, offering to pay him by advance, whatever he demanded for our passage, and for the conveniences he had helped us to. The mate told him that the captain would be on board in the afternoon, and that he would leave all that till he came. Accordingly, in the afternoon the captain came, and we found him the same courteous, obliging man that the boatswain had represented him to be; and he was so well pleased with my husband's conversation, that, in short, he would not let us keep the cabin we had chosen, but gave us one that, as I said before, opened into the great cabin.

Nor were his conditions exorbitant, or the man craving and eager to make a prey of us, but for fifteen guineas we had our whole passage and provisions and cabin, ate at the captain's table, and were very handsomely entertained.

The captain lay himself in the other part of the great cabin, having let his round house, as they call it, to a rich planter who went over with his wife and three children, who ate by themselves. He had some other ordinary passengers, who quartered in the steerage, and as for our old fraternity, they were kept under the hatches while the ship lay there, and came very little on the deck.

I could not refrain acquainting my governess with what had happened; it was but just that she, who was so really concerned for me, should have part in my good fortune. Besides, I wanted her assistance to supply me with several necessaries, which before I was shy of letting anybody see me have, that it might not be public; but now I had a cabin and room to set things in, I ordered abundance of good things for our comfort in the voyage, as brandy, sugar, lemons, etc., to make punch, and treat our benefactor, the captain; and abundance of things for eating and drinking in the voyage; also a larger bed, and bedding proportioned to it; so that, in a word, we resolved to want for nothing in the voyage.

All this while I had provided nothing for our assistance when we should come to the place and begin to call ourselves planters; and I was far from being ignorant of what was needful on that occasion; particularly all sorts of tools for the planter's work, and for building; and all kinds of furniture for our dwelling, which, if to be bought in the country, must necessarily cost double the price.

So I discoursed that point with my governess, and she went and waited upon the captain, and told him that she hoped ways might be found out for her two unfortunate cousins, as she called us, to obtain our freedom when we came into the country, and so entered into a discourse with him about the means and terms also, of which I shall say more in its place; and after thus sounding the captain, she let him know, though we were unhappy in the circumstances that occasioned our going, yet that we were not unfurnished to set ourselves to work in the country, and we resolved to settle and live there as planters, if we might be put in a way how to do it. The captain readily offered his assistance, told her the method of entering upon such business, and how easy, nay, how certain it was for industrious people to recover their fortunes in such a manner. 'Madam,' says he, "tis no reproach to any many in that country to have been sent over in worse circumstances than I perceive your cousins are in, provided they do but apply with diligence and good judgment to the business of that place when they come there.'

She then inquired of him what things it was necessary we should carry over with us, and he, like a very honest as well as knowing man, told her thus: 'Madam, your cousins in the first place must procure somebody to buy them as servants, in conformity to the conditions of their transportation, and then, in the name of that person, they may go about what they will; they may either purchase some plantations already begun, or they may purchase land of the Government of the country, and begin where they please, and both will be done reasonably.' She bespoke his favour in the first article, which he promised to her to take upon himself, and indeed faithfully performed it, and as to the rest, he promised to recommend us to such as should give us the best advice, and not to impose upon us, which was as much as could be desired.

She then asked him if it would not be necessary to furnish us with a stock of tools and materials for the business of planting, and he said, 'Yes, by all means.' And then she begged his assistance in it. She told him she would furnish us with everything that was convenient whatever it cost her. He accordingly gave her a long particular of things necessary for a planter, which, by his account, came to about fourscore or a hundred pounds. And, in short, she went about as dexterously to buy them, as if she had been an old Virginia merchant; only that she bought, by my direction, above twice as much of everything as he had given her a list of.

These she put on board in her own name, took his bills of loading for them, and endorsed those bills of loading to my husband, insuring the cargo afterwards in her own name, by our order; so that we were provided for all events, and for all disasters.

I should have told you that my husband gave her all his whole stock of #108, which, as I have said, he had about him in gold, to lay out thus, and I gave her a good sum besides; so that I did not break into the stock which I had left in her hands at all, but after we had sorted out our whole cargo, we had yet near #200 in money, which was more than enough for our purpose.

In this condition, very cheerful, and indeed joyful at being so happily accommodated as we were, we set sail from Bugby's Hole to Gravesend, where the ship lay about ten more days, and where the captain came on board for good and all. Here the captain offered us a civility, which indeed we had no reason to expect, namely, to let us go on shore and refresh ourselves, upon giving our words in a solemn manner that we would not go from him, and that we would return peaceably on board again. This was such an evidence of his confidence in us, that it overcame my husband, who, in a mere principle of gratitude, told him, as he could not be in any capacity to make a suitable return for such a favour, so he could not think of accepting of it, nor could he be easy that the captain should run such a risk. After some mutual civilities, I gave my husband a purse, in which was eighty guineas, and he put in into the captain's hand. 'There, captain,' says he, 'there's part of a pledge for our fidelity; if we deal dishonestly with you on any account, 'tis your own.' And on this we went on shore.

Indeed, the captain had assurance enough of our resolutions to go, for that having made such provision to settle there, it did not seem rational that we would choose to remain here at the expense and peril of life, for such it must have been if we had been taken again. In a word, we went all on shore with the captain, and supped together in Gravesend, where we were very merry, stayed all night, lay at the house where we supped, and came all very honestly on board again with him in the morning. Here we bought ten dozen bottles of good beer, some wine, some fowls, and such things as we thought might be acceptable on board.

My governess was with us all this while, and went with us round into the Downs, as did also the captain's wife, with whom she went back. I was never so sorrowful at parting with my own mother as I was at parting with her, and I never saw her more. We had a fair easterly wind sprung up the third day after we came to the Downs, and we sailed from thence the 10th of April. Nor did we touch any more at any place, till, being driven on the coast of Ireland by a very hard gale of wind, the ship came to an anchor in a little bay, near the mouth of a river, whose name I remember not, but they said the river came down from Limerick, and that it was the largest river in Ireland.

Here, being detained by bad weather for some time, the captain, who continued the same kind, good-humoured man as at first, took us two on shore with him again. He did it now in kindness to my husband indeed, who bore the sea very ill, and was very sick, especially when it blew so hard. Here we bought in again a store of fresh provisions, especially beef, pork, mutton, and fowls, and the captain stayed to pickle up five or six barrels of beef to lengthen out the ship's store. We were here not above five days, when the weather turning mild, and a fair wind, we set sail again, and in two-and-forty days came safe to the coast of Virginia.

When we drew near to the shore, the captain called me to him, and told me that he found by my discourse I had some relations in the place, and that I had been there before, and so he supposed I understood the custom in their disposing the convict prisoners when they arrived. I told him I did not, and that as to what relations I had in the place, he might be sure I would make myself known to none of them while I was in the circumstances of a prisoner, and that as to the rest, we left ourselves entirely to him to assist us, as he was pleased to promise us he would do. He told me I must get somebody in the place to come and buy us as servants, and who must answer for us to the governor of the country, if he demanded us. I told him we should do as he should direct; so he brought a planter to treat with him, as it were, for the purchase of these two servants, my husband and me, and there we were formally sold to him, and went ashore with him. The captain went with us, and carried us to a certain house, whether it was to be called a tavern or not I know not, but we had a bowl of punch there made of rum, etc., and were very merry. After some time the planter gave us a certificate of discharge, and an acknowledgment of having served him faithfully, and we were free from him the next morning, to go wither we would.

For this piece of service the captain demanded of us six thousand weight of tabacco, which he said he was accountable for to his freighter, and which we immediately bought for him, and made him a present of twenty guineas besides, with which he was abundantly satisfied.

It is not proper to enter here into the particulars of what part of the colony of Virginia we settled in, for divers reasons; it may suffice to mention that we went into the great river Potomac, the ship being bound thither; and there we intended to have settled first, though afterwards we altered our minds.

The first thing I did of moment after having gotten all our goods on shore, and placed them in a storehouse, or warehouse, which, with a lodging, we hired at the small place or village where we landed—I say, the first thing was to inquire after my mother, and after my brother (that fatal person whom I married as a husband, as I have related at large). A little inquiry furnished me with information that Mrs. ——, that is, my mother, was dead; that my brother (or husband) was alive, which I confess I was not very glad to hear; but which was worse, I found he was removed from the plantation where he lived formerly, and where I lived with him, and lived with one of his sons in a plantation just by the place where we landed, and where we had hired a warehouse.

I was a little surprised at first, but as I ventured to satisfy myself that he could not know me, I was not only perfectly easy, but had a great mind to see him, if it was possible to so do without his seeing me. In order to that I found out by inquiry the plantation where he lived, and with a woman of that place whom I got to help me, like what we call a chairwoman, I rambled about towards the place as if I had only a mind to see the country and look about me. At last I came so near that I saw the dwellinghouse. I asked the woman whose plantation that was; she said it belonged to such a man, and looking out a little to our right hands, 'there,' says she, is the gentleman that owns the plantation, and his father with him.' 'What are their Christian names?' said I. 'I know not,' says she, 'what the old gentleman's name is, but the son's name is Humphrey; and I believe,' says she, 'the father's is so too.' You may guess, if you can, what a confused mixture of joy and fight possessed my thoughts upon this occasion, for I immediately knew that this was nobody else but my own son, by that father she showed me, who was my own brother. I had no mask, but I ruffled my hood so about my face, that I depended upon it that after above twenty years' absence, and withal not expecting anything of me in that part of the world, he would not be able to know anything of me. But I need not have used all that caution, for the old gentleman was grown dim-sighted by some distemper which had fallen upon his eyes, and could but just see well enough to walk about, and not run against a tree or into a ditch. The woman that was with me had told me that by a mere accident, knowing nothing of what importance it was to me. As they drew near to us, I said, 'Does he know you, Mrs. Owen?' (so they called the woman). 'Yes,' said she, 'if he hears me speak, he will know me; but he can't see well enough to know me or anybody else'; and so she told me the story of his sight, as I have related. This made me secure, and so I threw open my hoods again, and let them pass by me. It was a wretched thing for a mother thus to see her own son, a handsome, comely young gentleman in flourishing circumstances, and durst not make herself known to him, and durst not take any notice of him. Let any mother of children that reads this consider it, and but think with what anguish of mind I restrained myself; what yearnings of soul I had in me to embrace him, and weep over him; and how I thought all my entrails turned within me, that my very bowels moved, and I knew not what to do, as I now know not how to express those agonies! When he went from me I stood gazing and trembling, and looking after him as long as I could see him; then sitting down to rest me, but turned from her, and lying on my face, wept, and kissed the ground that he had set his foot on.

I could not conceal my disorder so much from the woman but that she perceived it, and thought I was not well, which I was obliged to pretend was true; upon which she pressed me to rise, the ground being damp and dangerous, which I did accordingly, and walked away.

As I was going back again, and still talking of this gentleman and his son, a new occasion of melancholy offered itself thus. The woman began, as if she would tell me a story to divert me: 'There goes,' says she, 'a very odd tale among the neighbours where this gentleman formerly live.' 'What was that?' said I. 'Why,' says she, 'that old gentleman going to England, when he was a young man, fell in love with a young lady there, one of the finest women that ever was seen, and married her, and brought her over hither to his mother who was then living. He lived here several years with her,' continued she, 'and had several children by her, of which the young gentleman that was with him now was one; but after some time, the old gentlewoman, his mother, talking to her of something relating to herself when she was in England, and of her circumstances in England, which were bad enough, the daughter-in-law began to be very much surprised and uneasy; and, in short, examining further into things, it appeared past all contradiction that the old gentlewoman was her own mother, and that consequently that son was his wife's own brother, which struck the whole family with horror, and put them into such confusion that it had almost ruined them all. The young woman would not live with him; the son, her brother and husband, for a time went distracted; and at last the young woman went away for England, and has never been heard of since.'

It is easy to believe that I was strangely affected with this story, but 'tis impossible to describe the nature of my disturbance. I seemed astonished at the story, and asked her a thousand questions about the particulars, which I found she was thoroughly acquainted with. At last I began to inquire into the circumstances of the family, how the old gentlewoman, I mean my mother, died, and how she left what she had; for my mother had promised me very solemnly, that when she died she would do something for me, and leave it so, as that, if I was living, I should one way or other come at it, without its being in the power of her son, my brother and husband, to prevent it. She told me she did not know exactly how it was ordered, but she had been told that my mother had left a sum of money, and had tied her plantation for the payment of it, to be made good to the daughter, if ever she could be heard of, either in England or elsewhere; and that the trust was left with this son, who was the person that we saw with his father.

This was news too good for me to make light of, and, you may be sure, filled my heart with a thousand thoughts, what course I should take, how, and when, and in what manner I should make myself known, or whether I should ever make myself know or no.

Here was a perplexity that I had not indeed skill to manage myself in, neither knew I what course to take. It lay heavy upon my mind night and day. I could neither sleep nor converse, so that my husband perceived it, and wondered what ailed me, strove to divert me, but it was all to no purpose. He pressed me to tell him what it was troubled me, but I put it off, till at last, importuning me continually, I was forced to form a story, which yet had a plain truth to lay it upon too. I told him I was troubled because I found we must shift our quarters and alter our scheme of settling, for that I found I should be known if I stayed in that part of the country; for that my mother being dead, several of my relations were come into that part where we then was, and that I must either discover myself to them, which in our present circumstances was not proper on many accounts, or remove; and which to do I knew not, and that this it was that made me so melancholy and so thoughtful.

He joined with me in this, that it was by no means proper for me to make myself known to anybody in the circumstances in which we then were; and therefore he told me he would be willing to remove to any other part of the country, or even to any other country if I thought fit. But now I had another difficulty, which was, that if I removed to any other colony, I put myself out of the way of ever making a due search after those effects which my mother had left. Again I could never so much as think of breaking the secret of my former marriage to my new husband; it was not a story, as I thought, that would bear telling, nor could I tell what might be the consequences of it; and it was impossible to search into the bottom of the thing without making it public all over the country, as well who I was, as what I now was also.

In this perplexity I continued a great while, and this made my spouse very uneasy; for he found me perplexed, and yet thought I was not open with him, and did not let him into every part of my grievance; and he would often say, he wondered what he had done that I would not trust him with whatever it was, especially if it was grievous and afflicting. The truth is, he ought to have been trusted with everything, for no man in the world could deserve better of a wife; but this was a thing I knew not how to open to him, and yet having nobody to disclose any part of it to, the burthen was too heavy for my mind; for let them say what they please of our sex not being able to keep a secret, my life is a plain conviction to me of the contrary; but be it our sex, or the man's sex, a secret of moment should always have a confidant, a bosom friend, to whom we may communicate the joy of it, or the grief of it, be it which it will, or it will be a double weight upon the spirits, and perhaps become even insupportable in itself; and this I appeal to all human testimony for the truth of.

And this is the cause why many times men as well as women, and men of the greatest and best qualities other ways, yet have found themselves weak in this part, and have not been able to bear the weight of a secret joy or of a secret sorrow, but have been obliged to disclose it, even for the mere giving vent to themselves, and to unbend the mind oppressed with the load and weights which attended it. Nor was this any token of folly or thoughtlessness at all, but a natural consequence of the thing; and such people, had they struggled longer with the oppression, would certainly have told it in their sleep, and disclosed the secret, let it have been of what fatal nature soever, without regard to the person to whom it might be exposed. This necessity of nature is a thing which works sometimes with such vehemence in the minds of those who are guilty of any atrocious villainy, such as secret murder in particular, that they have been obliged to discover it, though the consequence would necessarily be their own destruction. Now, though it may be true that the divine justice ought to have the glory of all those discoveries and confessions, yet 'tis as certain that Providence, which ordinarily works by the hands of nature, makes use here of the same natural causes to produce those extraordinary effects.

I could give several remarkable instances of this in my long conversation with crime and with criminals. I knew one fellow that, while I was in prison in Newgate, was one of those they called then night-fliers. I know not what other word they may have understood it by since, but he was one who by connivance was admitted to go abroad every evening, when he played his pranks, and furnished those honest people they call thief-catchers with business to find out the next day, and restore for a reward what they had stolen the evening before. This fellow was as sure to tell in his sleep all that he had done, and every step he had taken, what he had stolen, and where, as sure as if he had engaged to tell it waking, and that there was no harm or danger in it, and therefore he was obliged, after he had been out, to lock himself up, or be locked up by some of the keepers that had him in fee, that nobody should hear him; but, on the other hand, if he had told all the particulars, and given a full account of his rambles and success, to any comrade, any brother thief, or to his employers, as I may justly call them, then all was well with him, and he slept as quietly as other people.

As the publishing this account of my life is for the sake of the just moral of very part of it, and for instruction, caution, warning, and improvement to every reader, so this will not pass, I hope, for an unnecessary digression concerning some people being obliged to disclose the greatest secrets either of their own or other people's affairs.

Under the certain oppression of this weight upon my mind, I laboured in the case I have been naming; and the only relief I found for it was to let my husband into so much of it as I thought would convince him of the necessity there was for us to think of settling in some other part of the world; and the next consideration before us was, which part of the English settlements we should go to. My husband was a perfect stranger to the country, and had not yet so much as a geographical knowledge of the situation of the several places; and I, that, till I wrote this, did not know what the word geographical signified, had only a general knowledge from long conversation with people that came from or went to several places; but this I knew, that Maryland, Pennsylvania, East and West Jersey, New York, and New England lay all north of Virginia, and that they were consequently all colder climates, to which for that very reason, I had an aversion. For that as I naturally loved warm weather, so now I grew into years I had a stronger inclination to shun a cold climate. I therefore considered of going to Caroline, which is the only southern colony of the English on the continent of America, and hither I proposed to go; and the rather because I might with great ease come from thence at any time, when it might be proper to inquire after my mother's effects, and to make myself known enough to demand them.

With this resolution I proposed to my husband our going away from where we was, and carrying all our effects with us to Caroline, where we resolved to settle; for my husband readily agreed to the first part, viz. that was not at all proper to stay where we was, since I had assured him we should be known there, and the rest I effectually concealed from him.

But now I found a new difficulty upon me. The main affair grew heavy upon my mind still, and I could not think of going out of the country without somehow or other making inquiry into the grand affair of what my mother had done for me; nor could I with any patience bear the thought of going away, and not make myself known to my old husband (brother), or to my child, his son; only I would fain have had this done without my new husband having any knowledge of it, or they having any knowledge of him, or that I had such a thing as a husband.

I cast about innumerable ways in my thoughts how this might be done. I would gladly have sent my husband away to Caroline with all our goods, and have come after myself, but this was impracticable; he would never stir without me, being himself perfectly unacquainted with the country, and with the methods of settling there or anywhere else. Then I thought we would both go first with part of our goods, and that when we were settled I should come back to Virginia and fetch the remainder; but even then I knew he would never part with me, and be left there to go on alone. The case was plain; he was bred a gentleman, and by consequence was not only unacquainted, but indolent, and when we did settle, would much rather go out into the woods with his gun, which they call there hunting, and which is the ordinary work of the Indians, and which they do as servants; I say, he would rather do that than attend the natural business of his plantation.

These were therefore difficulties insurmountable, and such as I knew not what to do in. I had such strong impressions on my mind about discovering myself to my brother, formerly my husband, that I could not withstand them; and the rather, because it ran constantly in my thoughts, that if I did not do it while he lived, I might in vain endeavour to convince my son afterward that I was really the same person, and that I was his mother, and so might both lose the assistance and comfort of the relation, and the benefit of whatever it was my mother had left me; and yet, on the other hand, I could never think it proper to discover myself to them in the circumstances I was in, as well relating to the having a husband with me as to my being brought over by a legal transportation as a criminal; on both which accounts it was absolutely necessary to me to remove from the place where I was, and come again to him, as from another place and in another figure.

Upon those considerations, I went on with telling my husband the absolute necessity there was of our not settling in Potomac River, at least that we should be presently made public there; whereas if we went to any other place in the world, we should come in with as much reputation as any family that came to plant; that, as it was always agreeable to the inhabitants to have families come among them to plant, who brought substance with them, either to purchase plantations or begin new ones, so we should be sure of a kind, agreeable reception, and that without any possibility of a discovery of our circumstances.

I told him in general, too, that as I had several relations in the place where we were, and that I durst not now let myself be known to them, because they would soon come into a knowledge of the occasion and reason of my coming over, which would be to expose myself to the last degree, so I had reason to believe that my mother, who died here, had left me something, and perhaps considerable, which it might be very well worth my while to inquire after; but that this too could not be done without exposing us publicly, unless we went from hence; and then, wherever we settled, I might come, as it were, to visit and to see my brother and nephews, make myself known to them, claim and inquire after what was my due, be received with respect, and at the same time have justice done me with cheerfulness and good will; whereas, if I did it now, I could expect nothing but with trouble, such as exacting it by force, receiving it with curses and reluctance, and with all kinds of affronts, which he would not perhaps bear to see; that in case of being obliged to legal proofs of being really her daughter, I might be at loss, be obliged to have recourse to England, and it may be to fail at last, and so lose it, whatever it might be. With these arguments, and having thus acquainted my husband with the whole secret so far as was needful of him, we resolved to go and seek a settlement in some other colony, and at first thoughts, Caroline was the place we pitched upon.

In order to this we began to make inquiry for vessels going to Carolina, and in a very little while got information, that on the other side the bay, as they call it, namely, in Maryland, there was a ship which came from Carolina, laden with rice and other goods, and was going back again thither, and from thence to Jamaica, with provisions. On this news we hired a sloop to take in our goods, and taking, as it were, a final farewell of Potomac River, we went with all our cargo over to Maryland.

This was a long and unpleasant voyage, and my spouse said it was worse to him than all the voyage from England, because the weather was but indifferent, the water rough, and the vessel small and inconvenient. In the next place, we were full a hundred miles up Potomac River, in a part which they call Westmoreland County, and as that river is by far the greatest in Virginia, and I have heard say it is the greatest river in the world that falls into another river, and not directly into the sea, so we had base weather in it, and were frequently in great danger; for though we were in the middle, we could not see land on either side for many leagues together. Then we had the great river or bay of Chesapeake to cross, which is where the river Potomac falls into it, near thirty miles broad, and we entered more great vast waters whose names I know not, so that our voyage was full two hundred miles, in a poor, sorry sloop, with all our treasure, and if any accident had happened to us, we might at last have been very miserable; supposing we had lost our goods and saved our lives only, and had then been left naked and destitute, and in a wild, strange place not having one friend or acquaintance in all that part of the world. The very thought of it gives me some horror, even since the danger is past.

Well, we came to the place in five days' sailing; I think they call it Philip's Point; and behold, when we came thither, the ship bound to Carolina was loaded and gone away but three days before. This was a disappointment; but, however, I, that was to be discouraged with nothing, told my husband that since we could not get passage to

Caroline, and that the country we was in was very fertile and good, we would, if he liked of it, see if we could find out anything for our tune where we was, and that if he liked things we would settle here.

We immediately went on shore, but found no conveniences just at that place, either for our being on shore or preserving our goods on shore, but was directed by a very honest Quaker, whom we found there, to go to a place about sixty miles east; that is to say, nearer the mouth of the bay, where he said he lived, and where we should be accommodated, either to plant, or to wait for any other place to plant in that might be more convenient; and he invited us with so much kindness and simple honesty, that we agreed to go, and the Quaker himself went with us.

Here we bought us two servants, viz. an English woman-servant just come on shore from a ship of Liverpool, and a Negro man-servant, things absolutely necessary for all people that pretended to settle in that country. This honest Quaker was very helpful to us, and when we came to the place that he proposed to us, found us out a convenient storehouse for our goods, and lodging for ourselves and our servants; and about two months or thereabouts afterwards, by his direction, we took up a large piece of land from the governor of that country, in order to form our plantation, and so we laid the thoughts of going to Caroline wholly aside, having been very well received here, and accommodated with a convenient lodging till we could prepare things, and have land enough cleared, and timber and materials provided for building us a house, all which we managed by the direction of the Quaker; so that in one year's time we had nearly fifty acres of land cleared, part of it enclosed, and some of it planted with tabacco, though not much; besides, we had garden ground and corn sufficient to help supply our servants with roots and herbs and bread.

And now I persuaded my husband to let me go over the bay again, and inquire after my friends. He was the willinger to consent to it now, because he had business upon his hands sufficient to employ him, besides his gun to divert him, which they call hunting there, and which he greatly delighted in; and indeed we used to look at one another, sometimes with a great deal of pleasure, reflecting how much better that was, not than Newgate only, but than the most prosperous of our circumstances in the wicked trade that we had been both carrying on.

Our affair was in a very good posture; we purchased of the proprietors of the colony as much land for #35, paid in ready money, as would make a sufficient plantation to employ between fifty and sixty servants, and which, being well improved, would be sufficient to us as long as we could either of us live; and as for children, I was past the prospect of anything of that kind.

But out good fortune did not end here. I went, as I have said, over the bay, to the place where my brother, once a husband, lived; but I did not go to the same village where I was before, but went up another great river, on the east side of the river Potomac, called Rappahannock River, and by this means came on the back of his plantation, which was large, and by the help of a navigable creek, or little river, that ran into the Rappahannock, I came very near it.

I was now fully resolved to go up point-blank to my brother (husband), and to tell him who I was; but not knowing what temper I might find him in, or how much out of temper rather, I might make him by such a rash visit, I resolved to write a letter to him first, to let him know who I was, and that I was come not to give him any trouble upon the old relation, which I hoped was entirely forgot, but that I applied to him as a sister to a brother, desiring his assistance in the case of that provision which our mother, at her decease, had left for my support, and which I did not doubt but he would do me justice in, especially considering that I was come thus far to look after it.

I said some very tender, kind things in the letter about his son, which I told him he knew to be my own child, and that as I was guilty of nothing in marrying him, any more than he was in marrying me, neither of us having then known our being at all related to one another, so I hoped he would allow me the most passionate desire of once seeing my one and only child, and of showing something of the infirmities of a mother in preserving a violent affect for him, who had never been able to retain any thought of me one way or other.

I did believe that, having received this letter, he would immediately give it to his son to read, I having understood his eyes being so dim, that he could not see to read it; but it fell out better than so, for as his sight was dim, so he had allowed his son to open all letters that came to his hand for him, and the old gentleman being from home, or out of the way when my messenger came, my letter came directly to my son's hand, and he opened and read it.

He called the messenger in, after some little stay, and asked him where the person was who gave him the letter. The messenger told him the place, which was about seven miles off, so he bid him stay, and ordering a horse to be got ready, and two servants, away he came to me with the messenger. Let any one judge the consternation I was in when my messenger came back, and told me the old gentleman was not at home, but his son was come along with him, and was just coming up to me. I was perfectly confounded, for I knew not whether it was peace or war, nor could I tell how to behave; however, I had but a very few moments to think, for my son was at the heels of the messenger, and coming up into my lodgings, asked the fellow at the door something. I suppose it was, for I did not hear it so as to understand it, which was the gentlewoman that sent him; for the messenger said, 'There she is, sir'; at which he comes directly up to me, kisses me, took me in his arms, and embraced me with so much passion that he could not speak, but I could feel his breast heave and throb like a child, that cries, but sobs, and cannot cry it out.

I can neither express nor describe the joy that touched my very soul when I found, for it was easy to discover that part, that he came not as a stranger, but as a son to a mother, and indeed as a son who had never before known what a mother of his own was; in short, we cried over one another a considerable while, when at last he broke out first. 'My dear mother,' says he, 'are you still alive? I never expected to have seen your face.' As for me, I could say nothing a great while.

After we had both recovered ourselves a little, and were able to talk, he told me how things stood. As to what I had written to his father, he told me he had not showed my letter to his father, or told him anything about it; that what his grandmother left me was in his hands, and that he would do me justice to my full satisfaction; that as to his father, he was old and infirm both in body and mind; that he was very fretful and passionate, almost blind, and capable of nothing; and he questioned whether he would know how to act in an affair which was of so nice a nature as this; and that therefore he had come himself, as well to satisfy himself in seeing me, which he could not restrain himself from, as also to put it into my power to make a judgment, after I had seen how things were, whether I would discover myself to his father or no.

This was really so prudently and wisely managed, that I found my son was a man of sense, and needed no direction from me. I told him I did not wonder that his father was as he had described him, for that his head was a little touched before I went away; and principally his disturbance was because I could not be persuaded to conceal our relation and to live with him as my husband, after I knew that he was my brother; that as he knew better than I what his father's present condition was, I should readily join with him in such measure as he would direct; that I was indifferent as to seeing his father, since I had seen him first, and he could not have told me better news than to tell me that what his grandmother had left me was entrusted in his hands, who, I doubted not, now he knew who I was, would, as he said, do me justice. I inquired then how long my mother had been dead, and where she died, and told so many particulars of the family, that I left him no room to doubt the truth of my being really and truly his mother.

My son then inquired where I was, and how I had disposed myself. I told him I was on the Maryland side of the bay, at the plantation of a particular friend who came from England in the same ship with me; that as for that side of the bay where he was, I had no habitation. He told me I should go home with him, and live with him, if I pleased, as long as I lived; that as to his father, he knew nobody, and would never so much as guess at me. I considered of that a little, and told him, that though it was really no concern to me to live at a distance from him, yet I could not say it would be the most comfortable thing in the world to me to live in the house with him, and to have that unhappy object always before me, which had been such a blow to my peace before; that though I should be glad to have his company (my son), or to be as near him as possible while I stayed, yet I could not think of being in the house where I should be also under constant restraint for fear of betraying myself in my discourse, nor should I be able to refrain some expressions in my conversing with him as my son, that might discover the whole affair, which would by no means be convenient.

He acknowledged that I was right in all this. 'But then, dear mother,' says he, 'you shall be as near me as you can.' So he took me with him on horseback to a plantation next to his own, and where I was as well entertained as I could have been in his own. Having left me there he went away home, telling me we would talk of the main business the next day; and having first called me his aunt, and given a charge to the people, who it seems were his tenants, to treat me with all possible respect. About two hours after he was gone, he sent me a maid-servant and a Negro boy to wait on me, and provisions ready dressed for my supper; and thus I was as if I had been in a new world, and began secretly now to wish that I had not brought my Lancashire husband from England at all.

However, that wish was not hearty neither, for I loved my Lancashire husband entirely, as indeed I had ever done from the beginning; and he merited from me as much as it was possible for a man to do; but that by the way.

The next morning my son came to visit me again almost as soon as I was up. After a little discourse, he first of all pulled out a deerskin bag, and gave it me, with five-and-fifty Spanish pistoles in it, and told me that was to supply my expenses from England, for though it was not his business to inquire, yet he ought to think I did not bring a great deal of money out with me, it not being usual to bring much money into that country. Then he pulled out his grandmother's will, and read it over to me, whereby it appeared that she had left a small plantation, as he called it, on York River, that is, where my mother lived, to me, with the stock of servants and cattle upon it, and given it in trust to this son of mine for my use, whenever he should hear of my being alive, and to my heirs, if I had any children, and in default of heirs, to whomsoever I should by will dispose of it; but gave the income of it, till I should be heard of, or found, to my said son; and if I should not be living, then it was to him, and his heirs.

This plantation, though remote from him, he said he did not let out, but managed it by a head-clerk (steward), as he did another that was his father's, that lay hard by it, and went over himself three or four times a year to look after it. I asked him what he thought the plantation might be worth. He said, if I would let it out, he would give me about #60 a year for it; but if I would live on it, then it would be worth much more, and, he believed, would bring me in about #150 a year. But seeing I was likely either to settle on the other side of the bay, or might perhaps have a mind to go back to England again, if I would let him be my steward he would manage it for me, as he had done for himself, and that he believed he should be able to send me as much tobacco to England from it as would yield me about #100 a year, sometimes more.

This was all strange news to me, and things I had not been used to; and really my heart began to look up more seriously than I think it ever did before, and to look with great thankfulness to the hand of Providence, which had done such wonders for me, who had been myself the greatest wonder of wickedness perhaps that had been suffered to live in the world. And I must again observe, that not on this occasion only, but even on all other occasions of thankfulness, my past wicked and abominable life never looked so monstrous to me, and I never so completely abhorred it, and reproached myself with it, as when I had a sense upon me of Providence doing good to me, while I had been making those vile returns on my part.

But I leave the reader to improve these thoughts, as no doubt they will see cause, and I go on to the fact. My son's tender carriage and kind offers fetched tears from me, almost all the while he talked with me. Indeed, I could scarce discourse with him but in the intervals of my passion; however, at length I began, and expressing myself with wonder at my being so happy to have the trust of what I had left, put into the hands of my own child, I told him, that as to the inheritance of it, I had no child but him in the world, and was now past having any if I should marry, and therefore would desire him to get a writing drawn, which I was ready to execute, by which I would, after me, give it wholly to him and to his heirs. And in the meantime, smiling, I asked him what made him continue a bachelor so long. His answer was kind and ready, that Virginia did not yield any great plenty of wives, and that since I talked of going back to England, I should send him a wife from London.

This was the substance of our first day's conversation, the pleasantest day that ever passed over my head in my life, and which gave me the truest satisfaction. He came every day after this, and spent a great part of his time with me, and carried me about to several of his friends' houses, where I was entertained with great respect. Also I dined several times at his own house, when he took care always to see his half-dead father so out of the way that I never saw him, or he me. I made him one present, and it was all I had of value, and that was one of the gold watches, of which I mentioned above, that I had two in my chest, and this I happened to have with me, and I gave it him at his third visit. I told him I had nothing of any value to bestow but that, and I desired he would now and then kiss it for my sake. I did not indeed tell him that I had stole it from a gentlewoman's side, at a meeting-house in London. That's by the way.

He stood a little while hesitating, as if doubtful whether to take it or no; but I pressed it on him, and made him accept it, and it was not much less worth than his leather pouch full of Spanish gold; no, though it were to be reckoned as if at London, whereas it was worth twice as much there, where I gave it him. At length he took it, kissed it, told me the watch should be a debt upon him that he would be paying as long as I lived.

A few days after he brought the writings of gift, and the scrivener with them, and I signed them very freely, and delivered them to him with a hundred kisses; for sure nothing ever passed between a mother and a tender, dutiful child with more affection. The next day he brings me an obligation under his hand and seal, whereby he engaged himself to manage and improve the plantation for my account, and with his utmost skill, and to remit the produce to my order wherever I should be; and withal, to be obliged himself to make up the produce #100 a year to me. When he had done so, he told me that as I came to demand it before the crop was off, I had a right to produce of the current year, and so he paid me #100 in Spanish pieces of eight, and desired me to give him a receipt for it as in full for that year, ending at Christmas following; this being about the latter end of August.

I stayed here about five weeks, and indeed had much ado to get away then. Nay, he would have come over the bay with me, but I would by no means allow him to it. However, he would send me over in a sloop of his own, which was built like a yacht, and served him as well for pleasure as business. This I accepted of, and so, after the utmost expressions both of duty and affection, he let me come away, and I arrived safe in two days at my friend's the Quaker's.

I brought over with me for the use of our plantation, three horses, with harness and saddles, some hogs, two cows, and a thousand other things, the gift of the kindest and tenderest child that ever woman had. I related to my husband all the particulars of this voyage, except that I called my son my cousin; and first I told him that I had lost my watch, which he seemed to take as a misfortune; but then I told him how kind my cousin had been, that my mother had left me such a plantation, and that he had preserved it for me, in hopes some time or other he should hear from me; then I told him that I had left it to his management, that he would render me a faithful account of its produce; and then I pulled him out the #100 in silver, as the first year's produce; and then pulling out the deerskin purse with the pistoles, 'And here, my dear,' says I, 'is the gold watch.' My husband—so is Heaven's goodness sure to work the same effects in all sensible minds where mercies touch the heart—lifted up both hands, and with an ecstacy of joy, 'What is God a-doing,' says he, 'for such an ungrateful dog as I am!' Then I let him know what I had brought over in the sloop, besides all this; I mean the horses, hogs, and cows, and other stores for our plantation; all which added to his surprise, and filled his heart with thankfulness; and from this time forward I believe he was as sincere a penitent, and as thoroughly a reformed man, as ever God's goodness brought back from a profligate, a highwayman, and a robber. I could fill a larger history than this with the evidence of this truth, and but that I doubt that part of the story will not be equally diverting as the wicked part, I have had thoughts of making a volume of it by itself.

As for myself, as this is to be my own story, not my husband's, I return to that part which related to myself. We went on with our plantation, and managed it with the help and diversion of such friends as we got there by our obliging behaviour, and especially the honest Quaker, who proved a faithful, generous, and steady friend to us; and we had very good success, for having a flourishing stock to begin with, as I have said, and this being now increased by the addition of #150 sterling in money, we enlarged our number of servants, built us a very good house, and cured every year a great deal of land. The second year I wrote to my old governess, giving her part with us of the joy of our success, and order her how to lay out the money I had left with her, which was #250 as above, and to send it to us in goods, which she performed with her usual kindness and fidelity, and this arrived safe to us.

Here we had a supply of all sorts of clothes, as well for my husband as for myself; and I took especial care to buy for him all those things that I knew he delighted to have; as two good long wigs, two silver-hilted swords, three or four fine fowling-pieces, a find saddle with holsters and pistols very handsome, with a scarlet cloak; and, in a word, everything I could think of to oblige him, and to make him appear, as he really was, a very fine gentleman. I ordered a good quantity of such household stuff as we yet wanted, with linen of all sorts for us both. As for myself, I wanted very little of clothes or linen, being very well furnished before. The rest of my cargo consisted in iron-work of all sorts, harness for horses, tools, clothes for servants, and woollen cloth, stuffs, serges, stockings, shoes, hats, and the like, such as servants wear; and whole pieces also to make up for servants, all by direction of the Quaker; and all this cargo arrived safe, and in good condition, with three woman-servants, lusty wenches, which my old governess had picked for me, suitable enough to the place, and to the work we had for them to do; one of which happened to come double, having been got with child by one of the seamen in the ship, as she owned afterwards, before the ship got so far as Gravesend; so she brought us a stout boy, about seven months after her landing.

My husband, you may suppose, was a little surprised at the arriving of all this cargo from England; and talking with me after he saw the account of this particular, 'My dear,' says he, 'what is the meaning of all this? I fear you will run us too deep in debt: when shall we be able to make return for it all?' I smiled, and told him that is was all paid for; and then I told him, that what our circumstances might expose us to, I had not taken my whole stock with me, that I had reserved so much in my friend's hands, which now we were come over safe, and was settled in a way to live, I had sent for, as he might see.

He was amazed, and stood a while telling upon his fingers, but said nothing. At last he began thus: 'Hold, let's see,' says he, telling upon his fingers still, and first on his thumb; 'there's #246 in money at first, then two gold watches, diamond rings, and plate,' says he, upon the forefinger. Then upon the next finger, 'Here's a plantation on York River, #100 a year, then #150 in money, then a sloop load of horses, cows, hogs, and stores'; and so on to the thumb again. 'And now,' says he, 'a cargo cost #250 in England, and worth here twice the money.' 'Well,' says I, 'what do you make of all that?' 'Make of it?' says he; 'why, who says I was deceived when I married a wife in Lancashire? I think I have married a fortune, and a very good fortune too,' says he.

In a word, we were now in very considerable circumstances, and every year increasing; for our new plantation grew upon our hands insensibly, and in eight years which we lived upon it, we brought it to such pitch, that the produce was at least #300 sterling a year; I mean, worth so much in England.

After I had been a year at home again, I went over the bay to see my son, and to receive another year's income of my plantation; and I was surprised to hear, just at my landing there, that my old husband was dead, and had not been buried above a fortnight. This, I confess, was not disagreeable news, because now I could appear as I was, in a married condition; so I told my son before I came from him, that I believed I should marry a gentleman who had a plantation near mine; and though I was legally free to marry, as to any obligation that was on me before, yet that I was shy of it, lest the blot should some time or other be revived, and it might make a husband uneasy. My son, the same kind, dutiful, and obliging creature as ever, treated me now at his own house, paid me my hundred pounds, and sent me home again loaded with presents.

Some time after this, I let my son know I was married, and invited him over to see us, and my husband wrote a very obliging letter to him also, inviting him to come and see him; and he came accordingly some months after, and happened to be there just when my cargo from England came in, which I let him believe belonged all to my husband's estate, not to me.

It must be observed that when the old wretch my brother (husband) was dead, I then freely gave my husband an account of all that affair, and of this cousin, as I had called him before, being my own son by that mistaken unhappy match. He was perfectly easy in the account, and told me he should have been as easy if the old man, as we called him, had been alive. 'For,' said he, 'it was no fault of yours, nor of his; it was a mistake impossible to be prevented.' He only reproached him with desiring me to conceal it, and to live with him as a wife, after I knew that he was my brother; that, he said, was a vile part. Thus all these difficulties were made easy, and we lived together with the greatest kindness and comfort imaginable.

We are grown old; I am come back to England, being almost seventy years of age, husband sixty-eight, having performed much more than the limited terms of my transportation; and now, notwithstanding all the fatigues and all the miseries we have both gone through, we are both of us in good heart and health. My husband remained there some time after me to settle our affairs, and at first I had intended to go back to him, but at his desire I altered that resolution, and he is come over to England also, where we resolve to spend the remainder of our years in sincere penitence for the wicked lives we have lived.

WRITTEN IN THE YEAR 1683